LIST OF TABLES

To my wife Florence, for her support
and encouragement.

PREFACE

Much of the literature on crime and punishment has been written by social scientists in the fields of sociology, criminology, and psychology. Their works rely heavily on theoretical and political perspectives, statistical analysis, and for the most part concentrate on the contemporary, a characteristic sometimes referred to as "presentism." While a number of historians have ventured into the field, they have concentrated mainly on area or topical studies. To some extent, then, students have been disadvantaged by a shortage of works that offer a narrative view of the problem over time. As with most social phenomena, a better understanding of the past can be a substantial aid in dealing with problems of the present. James Inciardi and his collaborators, in *Historical Approaches to Crime*, explained the value of the historical perspective: "The longitudinal view offered by the observation and documentation of phenomena through time can provide for a more complete analysis and understanding of the emergence, scope, and persistence or change of given social organization and behavior, and as such, history becomes the very framework of detached inquiry."

A *History of Crime and Punishment in Canada* has been written with the intent of providing students and others with a longitudinal account of the evolution of crime and treatment strategies from the earliest days of settlement to the present. Part One constructs a profile of crime, its nature, and its growth, while Part Two offers an account of the variety of approaches that have been advocated and tried in dealing with the problem of crime and criminals. The topic of criminal justice is formidable and in its wider dimensions includes the law, policing, penal institutions, and the evolution of the courts. This book concentrates exclusively on crime and punishment. These issues have been the main focus of societal concern over the years and as well are at the heart of the criminal justice system. Defining crime can be arbitrary. Acts that are against the law at one point in time may subsequently be dropped from the Criminal Code. Behaviour that is legal in one period can later be criminalized. Changing values may challenge the designation of certain acts as crimes even though they remain in the statute books. To avoid a subjective criterion, in this work an act is treated as a crime if it violates the law of its day.

A work of this nature can only be carried out with the assistance of a considerable number of people and the use of many libraries and archives. While it is not practical to list all there are a number of people to whom I owe a particular note of thanks. First and foremost I wish to acknowledge my debt to the many scholars whose books, articles, and reports have been used to inform this study. Among the librarians who assisted, Heather Moore, chief librarian, and the staff at the Library of the Solicitor General of Canada were especially helpful and generous with their time. I also wish to acknowledge the assistance of the librarians at Saint Mary's University, in particular the very valuable help of Douglas Vaisey, head of information services. Among friends and acquaintances who were helpful and encouraging, I wish to acknowledge the contribution of John P. LeBlanc, former director general of Manpower and Immigration, province of Nova Scotia, and Vincent MacDonald, district director of Correctional Service of Canada – Nova Scotia District.

The major job of typing and retyping was done with skill and patience by the departmental secretary, Marjorie Warren. Considerable valuable assistance, with a variety of research tasks, was provided by my student assistant, Linda Andry. My wife, Florence, provided constructive criticism and put in many hours proofreading the manuscript. Last, but not least, I wish to thank the Senate Research Committee of Saint Mary's University and the Secretary of State of Canada for grants that helped to offset the expenses incurred in doing the research.

A Note on Statistics

Methods and procedures for gathering crime statistics over the years have been neither comprehensive nor uniform. While they are more reliable now than in the past, interviews with offenders and victim surveys tell us that the data provided still do not offer an accurate record of crime. In view of this the statistics in this book are used to indicate trends rather than to present definitive counts of the incidence of crime.

PART ONE

Crime in Canada
from Pioneer Days
to the Present

CHAPTER 1

Crime in Pioneer Canada

There is one thing which can hardly fail to strike an emigrant from the Old Country, on his arrival in Canada. It is this – the feelings of complete security which he enjoys whether in his own dwelling or in his journeys abroad through the land. He sees no fear – he need see none. This is a country where the inhabitants are essentially honest – Here you may sleep with your door unbarred for years. Your confidence is rarely, if ever, abused; your hospitality never violated – It is delightful, this conscious-ness of perfect security; your hand is against no man, and no man's hand is against you.[1]

This rather idyllic picture painted by Catharine Parr Traill's *The Canadian Settler's Guide* in 1857 is indicative of a long-standing perception of Canada as a relatively crime-free society. The Canadian character, our British tradi-tion of law and order, and the early presence of forces like the North West Mounted Police were all credited with contributing to the lack of serious crime. We took great pride in the belief that in comparison with our rowdy neighbour to the south we have been a well-behaved society. Doubtless there were rural communities, villages, and small towns across the country that were relatively free of crime. There were areas where, as the description claimed, "you may sleep with your door unbarred." However, another side to the picture was much less idyllic. Robbery, assault, and murder were not uncommon occurrences and there were times in a few communities when walking in the street was risky. In fact, rather than being a crime-free society, Canada has had its fair share of lawbreaking, which can be traced to the very earliest days of exploration and settlement.

The latter part of the fifteenth century saw the European nations concentrate on expansion and enhancing their wealth. Their attention naturally turned eastward, to the fabled Indies, a storehouse of gold and precious metals waiting to be taken. Searching for a shorter and safer route than sailing around Africa, they sent their seafaring explorers westward and discovered the New World. The French were relative late-comers to exploration but when they did join the quest for new possessions they came with a considerable appetite and great expectations. In 1534 Jacques Cartier set sail from the French port of St. Malo with a royal patent authorizing him to take possession of new lands on behalf of the King of France. It was the first step in what would ultimately give France possession of a major portion of North America. New France was to become an important colony as well as the battleground between England and France for control of a continent.

CRIME IN NEW FRANCE

Cartier was followed by explorers such as the Sieur de Roberval, another Breton nobleman, the Marquis de La Roche, and Samuel de Champlain. They came to explore and to establish settlements that would give France a permanent presence in the new land. They recruited wherever they could find volunteers, including the jails and slums. Criminals joined up in return for being released from jail or having their sentences cancelled. Roberval's expedition to the St. Lawrence in 1542 was made up of some 200 men and women, a mixture of military and civilians. In September, 1542, he and his party landed at Cap Rouge and proceeded to establish a settlement. The colony was short on rations and there was a good deal of sickness through the winter, mostly from scurvy. Yet in the midst of such trying circumstances a number of the party reverted to their old habits. One man was hanged for theft while others were put in irons or whipped. Roberval's attempt at settlement was a failure but the expedition earned the distinction of witnessing some of the first crimes and official punishments in pioneer Canada.[2]

The Marquis de La Roche came over in 1598 with a party of about 200 men and fifty women recruited from among beggars, vagabonds, and ex-convicts. They landed on Sable Island, a barren, inhospitable sand dune off the coast of Nova Scotia. La Roche returned to France in October. His fledgling settlement struggled for survival but by 1603 only eleven colonists remained. When they were removed it was determined that one source of trouble was a mutiny carried out by some of the ex-convicts that resulted in the murder of the island's commander, Querbonyer, the storekeeper, and several others.[3]

In 1608 Samuel de Champlain established the first permanent settlement in New France at Quebec. Before long he had to deal with a plot against his own life. A number of Champlain's company conspired to murder him and hand the fort over to the Basques in return for money. They had an outpost at Tadoussac and Champlain's men calculated that they would be willing to pay to prevent the French from establishing a settlement. One of the conspirators had second thoughts and revealed the plot to Champlain, who immediately arrested the five would-be murderers. He pardoned the informer, acquitted another, sent two back to France for punishment, and put the ringleader to death. The man was hanged and his remains put on public display on the end of a pike.[4]

The early history of New France was closely associated with the Company of New France or the Company of One Hundred Associates, as it came to be known. Formed in 1627 the French monarchy gave it control over the entire St. Lawrence Valley, together with a fifteen-year monopoly on trade. In return the Company agreed to take 200-300 settlers a year to the colony. The Company controlled New France until 1663. Impatient with the pace of settlement, the French crown assumed governing responsibility itself. By the early seventeenth century the primary interest in French North America was to exploit the fur trade. There was a ready market for furs in Europe, and as exploration and colonization progressed the trade in furs became the mainstay of the economy. The early trade began on the St. Lawrence River; by the end of the century it had expanded westward to the headwaters of the Mississippi.

Much of the credit for establishing this far-flung trading network went to a group of hardy, adventuresome, and courageous individuals collectively known as *coureurs de bois*. While men of all ages engaged in the fur trade, the *coureurs de bois* were usually younger men who hoped to improve their status faster by trading in animal pelts than by working on the farms. They were also attracted by the freedom of the wild and grew wise in the ways of the native Indian. One governor, obviously not enamoured with these unruly men of the forest, explained why the life was attractive: "It consists in doing nothing, caring nothing, following every inclination, and getting out of the way of all restraint."[5] Another observer succinctly summed up the lure of the wilderness as "Idleness, independence and debauchery."[6] In 1680 the Intendant Duchesneau estimated that over 800 men were off in the woods. The colonial population was less than 10,000 at the time.

The *coureurs de bois* made fortunes for many of the merchants and traders of New France but in the process some also cheated, stole, murdered, debauched the Indians, and turned many native women into prostitutes. The traders early discovered that the Indian had little tolerance for liquor. The natives were not used to alcohol and it had a particularly volatile effect on them. They called it *eau-de-feu*, or firewater. When traders realized this, French brandy became an important adjunct to doing business. An intoxicated Indian could be separated from his furs for little or no consideration. Some would part with the very furs on their backs for a drink. The Abbé de Latour described in vivid terms the effect of brandy on the natives. "The savage, for a glass of brandy, will give even his clothes, his cabin, his wife, his children. A squaw...will abandon herself to the first comer."[7] He denounced those responsible, observing that it was "difficult to understand the extent of the greed, the hypocrisy and the rascality of those who supply them with these drinks."[8] Thus, while there was fair and legitimate trading, considerable cheating and theft also occurred.

Because the fur trade was such a lucrative business, it became the focal point of widespread lawbreaking. The Church, a very powerful influence in New France, consistently denounced the use of liquor in the fur trade. Church leaders, time and time again, sought to have the liquor trade prohibited.[9] Mother Mary of the Incarnation, the first superior of the Ursulines at Quebec, complained that liquor was given to the natives "in order to get their furs for nothing when they are drunk. Immorality, theft and murder ensue. . . . "[10] Government officials shared the Church's concern and early on prohibited the sale of intoxicating liquor to the Indians. The King's State Council in 1657 renewed the prohibition, prescribing corporal punishment for those who broke the law. Officials, however, were caught in a difficult situation. If the French stopped supplying liquor to the Indians, then the natives would redirect their trade to the hated English, who laboured under no such restrictions. Consequently, the issue caused constant tension between Church and government and between both of these and the fur traders. In 1660 Bishop Laval decreed that those who broke the liquor restriction would be excommunicated; in 1663 the Sovereign Council of New France set fines of 1,500 to 2,000 livres for a first offence, whipping or banishment for a second. Governor Frontenac prescribed the death penalty for a third offence and at least one man was hanged for violating the prohibition. However, the threat of spiritual or temporal punishment failed to deter the traders.[11]

The English fur traders already had certain advantages over the French. They could offer the Indian two to three times as much for furs as the French because transportation of goods from England was cheaper, as was the cost of the array of items, such as blankets and muskets, used in the fur trade. The West Indies rum the English used in trade cost less than the brandy the French used.[12] Thus the French had to tread carefully with the Indians. Prohibition of liquor could jeopardize trading relationships, so when the authorities sought to stop the use of liquor, traders ignored the restriction and broke the law. The economic disadvantage that made the use of liquor so important to the French is illustrated by the comparative prices at Albany, New York, and at Montreal in 1689, listed in Table 1.

The English superiority in payment for furs also generated considerable illegal activity among French-Canadian merchants and *coureurs de bois*, and the general population. The French were forbidden to trade with the English and the Dutch yet many merchants, traders, ordinary citizens, and even government officials carried on a clandestine trade in order to benefit from the higher prices. In 1670 the Intendant Jean Talon estimated that over 1,200,000 livres worth of beaver had been sold to the English and Dutch. The

Table 1
Trade Prices at Albany and Montreal, 1689

The Indian pays for	at Albany	at Montreal
1 musket	2 beavers	5 beavers
8 pounds of powder	1 beaver	4 beavers
40 pounds of lead	1 beaver	3 beavers
1 blanket	1 beaver	2 beavers
4 shirts	1 beaver	2 beavers
6 pairs stockings	1 beaver	2 beavers

SOURCE: William Bennett Munro, *Crusaders of New France* (New Haven: Yale University Press, 1918), p. 161.

coureurs de bois were getting the furs from the Indians in the forest and taking them to the English and Dutch merchants. Governor Frontenac compared them to the banditti in Naples or the buccaneers of San Domingo. Officials attempted to stop the illegal trade in a variety of ways. For a time they tried requiring licences to go into Indian territory to trade and issued a restricted number of them. In 1673 a decree prohibited people from leaving their homes and wandering in the woods for periods longer than twenty-four hours. By 1676, however, the practice of issuing licences had to be discontinued and ones already issued cancelled because every move on the part of government was frustrated and led to more lawbreaking. In an untamed, unpoliced wilderness, greed took precedence over law. The problem was compounded by the fact that once the prohibitions were broken the violators became fugitives and outlaws and were then virtually forced to turn to the English and Dutch to trade. Their numbers became so large that finally the government declared a general amnesty in an effort to curb the outside trade.[13]

Yet another device used by officials in an attempt to put some order in the fur business was the trade fair. Rather than carry on transactions in the wilderness, traders were encouraged to bring their furs to the settlements. In the spring huge flotillas would form and work their way through the rivers to the colony. One such gathering in 1693 was made up of over 400 canoes, 1,200 Indians, and 200 *coureurs de bois* and took furs to Montreal worth over 800,000 livres. Even this marketing strategy backfired on the government as bootleggers came out in full force and set up their illegal shops along the banks of the St. Lawrence. They would entice the Indians with liquor and relieve them of their furs before they reached Montreal or other trade fairs.[14]

Violence was another dimension of the criminal activity that characterized the fur trade. Certain of the *coureurs de bois* were unruly individuals who would stop at nothing in their pursuit of furs. Some preferred to steal the pelts rather than buy them, and in the process they sometimes committed atrocities. One recorded incident described how four traders attacked and massacred a party of six Indian hunters and then made off with their furs, worth about 3,000 livres. As long as the fur trade was a source of wealth it also continued to be a focal point for theft, violence, and murder.[15]

While the explorers and *coureurs de bois* were pushing westward, land was being cleared in the east, settlers were arriving, and communities were springing up. About three-quarters of the population lived on farms with the remainder being town dwellers, a ratio that remained relatively constant throughout the French colonial period. *Habitants* had large families, so it is not surprising that a high percentage of the population was children. In 1706, for example, over 47 per cent of the population of 16,417 were under fifteen.[16]

The government of France kept the colony under strict control, but the administration was benign and paternalistic. The King himself set the tone for his officials by continually instructing his representatives to treat the populace "with gentleness and humanity."[17] To encourage settlement the immigrant was offered enticements ranging from assisted passage to free land. The state offered subsidies to newly married couples that included farm animals, salt meat, and cash. Baby bonuses were given to encourage fecundity, and pensions were offered to fathers of families that numbered ten or more children.[18] In 1700 a year's pay was still being offered to soldiers willing to settle in the colony upon the expiration of their tour of duty. Of the more than 10,000 people who settled in Canada during the French regime about 3,500 were former soldiers.[19]

A fairly extensive system of social services was in place to serve the populace. The Roman Catholic Church, through its religious orders of men and women, operated hospitals, asylums, and took care of the poor. The Church also maintained schools throughout the colony that offered education to males, females, rich and poor, and to native Indians. The state subsidized all of these endeavours while encouraging private benevolence as well.

Life in New France was regulated with myriad laws that covered a range of infractions from murder to swearing. Crimes against the state included counterfeiting, resisting a legal officer in the exercise of his office, desertion from the army, smuggling, sedition, and embezzlement of public funds. Another category that was much broader in pioneer days than today, and that was considered to have more import, was moral crimes. Such offences included adultery, bigamy, debauchery, rape, incest, indecent behaviour, sodomy, bestiality, prostitution, pandering, and concubinage. A third category was crimes against property, which consisted of theft, arson, concealment of stolen goods, and desertion of servants. The fourth major category covered by a variety of laws was crimes against the person, such as murder, manslaughter, rape, poisoning, abortion, infanticide, suicide, assault, slander, and defamation. There were also many regulations that might be termed municipal by-laws. Edicts were regularly issued by the intendants, ranging from providing fines for men who did not marry to rules governing children playing in the street. In 1706 the Intendant Raudot issued an edict prohibiting people from leaving church during the sermon. Butchers, bakers, millers, and innkeepers were regulated while weights, measures, and garbage disposal were covered by police regulations. The citizens of New France took all this in stride. They obeyed when it was convenient and ignored the law when they felt like it.

New France was in large measure an egalitarian society without the gulf between classes that existed in Europe. Most rural families owned their own homes, which they usually built themselves. For the most part they enjoyed a better standard of living than their counterparts back in France. All of this, together with the levelling tendencies of a pioneer society, developed a democratic spirit, and observers continually remarked on the independence and insubordinate manner of the *habitant*.[20] The citizens of New France jealously guarded their rights and nowhere was this more evident than when it came to property. Frequent turnovers of land and poor surveying methods led to many property disputes. In some cases neighbours cheated each other in transactions involving cattle, land, and other possessions. The average French Canadian, however, was quick to seek redress whenever rights were violated. For example, in the judicial district of Quebec between September, 1663, and August, 1664, 424 cases were dealt with. The population of the district numbered about 1,500.[21] Little wonder that the *habitant* established a reputation for being litigious.

Although generally law-abiding, the citizenry of New France did not leave crime solely to the *coureurs de bois*. There were ample incidents of lawbreaking in the settlements along the St. Lawrence, with the crimes ranging from petty theft to murder. During the period of French rule approximately forty-four offences against property were recorded at Quebec. Some of the crimes involved more than one person, so that fifty-five people were convicted for this category of crime. Of that number, forty-nine were male. Thirty-eight charges were for theft, three for housebreaking, three for desertion of domestic servants, and one for arson. Over the same period in Quebec there were twenty-three offences against the person for which thirty-two people were convicted, twenty-five of whom were male. There were four murders, four duels, four cases of defamation, three quarrels, two abortions, one suicide, one attempted suicide, one case of manslaughter, one poisoning, one infanticide, and one rape. Ten convictions were recorded for morals offences involving eleven people. These included four charges of drunkenness, two of blasphemy, two cases of violation, one of seduction, one of adultery and one of being profligate. Finally, in the category of offences against the state the criminal records for the capital at Quebec list ten offences for which all twelve convicted were males. Of that number, nine were charged with counterfeiting, one was prosecuted for desertion, one for being a *coureur de bois* (presumably being illegally in the woods), and one for trading brandy. Of the crimes prosecuted at Quebec during the French regime, forty-three took place during the seventeenth century and forty-four during the eighteenth century up to the Conquest. This represented a crime rate of one per 139 of the population in the early period and one per 150 for the latter.[22] The population of New France went from 21,000 in 1712 to 55,000 by 1759, and during that period there were about 925 people indicted by royal courts. The most common crimes were assault and theft, about 303 cases of the former and 143 cases of the latter. Other charges before the courts included sixty cases of counterfeiting, fifty-two homicides, fifty-six verbal offences, and sixteen cases of receiving stolen goods. Overall, males accounted for approximately 80 per cent of those charged with lawbreaking during the period. About 93.8 per cent of counterfeiting charges, 91.2 per cent of homicides, and 85.4 per cent of assault charges were filed against men. Males also accounted for 74.1 per cent of theft charges and 64 per cent of accusations of receiving stolen goods. The majority of convicted males during the period ranged in age from twenty to twenty-nine years old. Since some criminals were never caught and certain cases were settled out of court, the statistics tell only a part of the story. As one authority on crime in New France has pointed out, "Under the French regime in Canada, many crimes and criminals escaped prosecution because of geographic factors or because of the extremely limited size of the police force."[23]

While the incidence of crime in New France, especially major offences, appears small in comparison with modern statistics, crime was nevertheless seen as a problem by colonial officials. One writer has stated that some "denounced the immorality and lawlessness of the habitants almost as frequently as they attacked the coureurs de bois."[24] In 1725 the Bishop of Quebec publicly expressed alarm over the rash of thefts, highway robberies, and poisonings.[25] In 1730 Governor de Beauharnois complained that "as the population of the colony is growing every day, crimes are multiplying."[26] The officials were so agitated they asked the French government to stop sending "libertines" to the colony.[27]

Since there was always a military garrison in New France it is not surprising that soldiers also contributed to the crime problem. Most were young and untutored, and they preferred to be back in France. On occasion they vented their frustrations with acts of violence. Not untypical was an incident in the summer of 1669. Three soldiers got six Indian hunters drunk and then murdered them and stole their furs.[28] Others engaged in a variety of lawbreaking, such as the soldier who in 1686 deserted his company and in quick succession committed an act of rape and another of theft. The offences cost him his life. Theft, drunkenness, and assaults were common among the military. Another more swashbuckling crime, especially among officers, was duelling. High-ranking civilians were also given to duelling to settle a dispute or avenge an insult; up to 1706 there were nine recorded duels in New France and doubtless more that went unrecorded.[29] Thus, although crime never reached proportionately high levels, lawbreaking was common in New France throughout the colonial period. Companies of explorers, fur traders, soldiers, and ordinary citizens stole, raped, broke service contracts, committed assaults, and murdered. Crime was not the preserve of any particular social or economic group, nor was it the product of any special set of circumstances.

CRIME IN THE MARITIMES

English Canada also had its fair share of criminal activity. In 1713, by the terms of the Treaty of Utrecht, France ceded its colony of Acadia to England. The seat of government was Annapolis Royal and in April, 1720, Richard Philipps arrived to take up his duties as Governor of Nova Scotia and appointed a governing council. The minutes of that body periodically report trials that took place covering a variety of crimes such as spreading false reports, theft, arson, horse stealing, and illicit trade.[30] In 1734, incidences of theft and robbery were sufficiently frequent that the council issued an order authorizing a night watch and gave permission to the inhabitants to arrest any suspicious person.[31]

Halifax was founded in 1749 and the settlers were hardly off the boats when the thievery began. Pickpockets, prostitutes, thieves, and con artists plied their trades as the new settlement struggled for survival. The first murder took place on the very ship, the *Beaufort*, that was being used to house the governing officials of the fledgling colony. A seaman by the name of Peter Carteel killed one of his shipmates with a knife and wounded two others. The criminal element in Halifax became such a nuisance that as early as 1752 the justices of the peace petitioned the Governor and the Executive Council to build a jail. Early records show that a wide variety of crimes were regularly committed in Halifax, ranging from theft and fortune-telling to assault and murder.[32]

From the outset Halifax was a major seaport, a garrison town, a port of call for the British Navy, and a transit point for troops. When war broke out with France in 1755 Halifax was soon inundated with 3,000 soldiers, supplemented by more service personnel whenever the fleet came into port. The town was the rendezvous and port of embarkment for the forces that attacked Louisburg in 1758, and that summer Admiral Holborne's fleet, with 4,000 seamen, was anchored in the harbour. Two regiments of English soldiers and two American battalions spent the winter of 1758-59 in Halifax prior to joining Wolfe's forces in the attack on Quebec in 1759.

Thousands of soldiers and sailors passed through Halifax during the American Revolutionary War. In the spring of 1776 General Howe and his defeated army, along with hundreds of United Empire Loyalists, arrived. Again during the Napoleonic Wars and the War of 1812 soldiers and sailors piled into Halifax. In peacetime the garrison, trading vessels from all over the world, and regular visits by the British Navy kept things lively.

All this had a considerable impact on what was a relatively small population. In 1752 the town counted 4,249 inhabitants, increasing slightly to 4,897 by 1791 and to 11,156 by 1817. Reflecting the needs of a major seaport Halifax abounded with taverns, houses of prostitution, and a host of criminal types. The business of crime prospered with assaults, robberies, gambling, bootlegging, and murder. At times drunken military personnel literally controlled the streets and nightly the gutters of the more seedy sections and the waterfront were littered with bodies, either passed out or dead. One writer described the town in those days as "a ceaseless donnybrook."[33]

Military-civilian brawls were common in a port city like Halifax. Typical was an incident that took place on January 25, 1813, when five soldiers got into a dispute with a number of scallop men on the city wharf. They broke off the argument but returned sometime later to resume the confrontation, this time armed with bayonets. Four of the civilians were badly wounded and one subsequently died.[34] Ordinary citizens also faced the danger of impressment by the military. This was the forcible abduction of men right off the street who were then pressed into naval service. For example, on January 6, 1781, an armed party of sailors and marines, assisted by soldiers, seized a number of people, together with the crew members of a boat from Lunenburg. The captives were tied up, taken to the military guard house, and then forced on board ships of war anchored in the harbour. The incident was denounced by the Governor as "an outrageous breach of the civil law." However, the navy did not give up its captives, nor was anyone punished for the illegality.[35]

Crews were constantly deserting from visiting ships so the military simply replaced them by pressing civilians, or sailors from other ships, into service. Desertion was a crime, and between 1782 and 1814 approximately 101 men were tried for the offence in Halifax courts.[36] Press-gang activities sometimes generated considerable violence. One group sent into the streets to forage by Vice Admiral Sir Andrew Mitchell in October of 1805 encountered stiff resistance. Their intended recruits put up a fight and ran from their pursuers. The press gang followed, broke into stores where their victims were hiding, and in the course of the mêlée that followed one man was killed and several others were injured. This time the civil authorities were so outraged that the press-gang members were prosecuted and Admiral Mitchell was also penalized.[37]

At times crime in Halifax escalated to the point that magistrates punished even minor offenders very severely in an effort to stem the lawbreaking. In 1782, for example, a rash of street robberies resulted in one offender receiving the death penalty. The man was executed even though the grand jury recommended mercy. One of the most reprehensible and feared crimes in early times was arson, since fire could endanger an entire town. Yet, in spite of the consequences, arson was a common occurrence. One of the most flagrant cases in Halifax in pioneer days took place in August of 1799 when attempts were made on the same day to set fire to the dockyard, government house, and the fire station.[38]

Much of the day-to-day crime in port cities like Halifax was committed by an underclass of habitual offenders. Drunks, idlers, and an assortment of unsavory characters who chose to live by their wits constantly hovered around the wharves, the streets, and the taverns, looking for illegal opportunities. Descriptions of the people who settled pioneer communities were sometimes far from flattering. Governor Cornwallis estimated that out of a settlement of some 1,400 people in Halifax only about 300 were of good quality. "The rest are poor, idle, worthless vagabonds that embraced the opportunity to get provisions for one year without labour...."[39]

The so-called upper classes also had their share of those who marched to the beat of a different drummer. Life was hard, and even members of the social elite could be rough, ill-mannered, and disdainful of the law, or of social and religious conventions. Some engaged in violence and lawbreaking. Heavy drinking was not unusual and some prominent citizens frequented the whorehouses of the town, assaulted each other, and fought duels. Prince William, the future King William IV of England, visited Halifax in 1786. He was twenty years old and commander of the frigate *Pegasus*, through the favour of his father, George III. William was as raunchy as any seasoned salt on his ship and little concerned with status or convention. He gathered about him a group of revellers during his stay in Halifax and he and his friends spent their time drinking, hunting, fishing, duelling, cockfighting, and whoring. At one dinner party for twenty guests, sixty-three bottles of wine were consumed. The Prince did not restrict his nighttime revelries to the prostitutes and promiscuous young women of Halifax. He also established a sexual liaison with Frances Wentworth, the comely forty-two-year-old wife of John Wentworth, Surveyor-General of the King's Woods. Her favours paid great dividends for her husband, who, through William's intercession, was made Lieutenant-Governor of Nova Scotia in 1792.[40]

One of the most publicized duels in the early history of Halifax took place in the summer of 1819 and serves as another illustration of the temper of the gentry. The confrontation involved two of the town's leading citizens, Richard John Uniacke, Jr., a thirty-year-old lawyer and son of the Attorney-General of Nova Scotia, and William Bowie, a prominent merchant. During the course of a trial before the Supreme Court, Uniacke made comments that offended Bowie and the latter challenged Uniacke to a duel. The antagonists chose pistols. Both missed on the first shot, but they reloaded and this time Uniacke mortally wounded Bowie. The *Acadian Recorder* commented that "It is generally lamented that...two such worthy and respected members of the community should have allowed their passions so far to get the better of their reason...."[41]

Seaports like Halifax, and the larger towns, were not the only places where crime was committed. Along the coastal villages marauding ships stole fish where it had been laid out to dry on the shores. Crews hijacked their masters' vessels and sold off ship and cargo. Ships that were beached in storms but undamaged were burned by local inhabitants so they could get the iron fittings from the hulks.[42] Highway robberies were common, as were thefts of cattle and property. At Annapolis in 1785 a plot of major proportions was uncovered involving some fifty people. On the night of the Queen's birthday while most of the town's leading people would be at the anniversary ball, the gang schemed to murder Justice Bunhill and then rob the town. The conspirators planned to put their booty on a boat and escape to Boston.[43]

A crime peculiar to a seafaring province was piracy. By the late eighteenth and early nineteenth centuries the old-style pirates who preyed on other ships were gone from the Atlantic coast. However, there were still the occasional incidents of piracy that involved the taking over of a boat by the people on board. In October of 1809 the schooner *Three Sisters* was bound for Halifax from Gaspé with a cargo of fish. On board was the captain, John Stairs, a crew of three, and six passengers – Edward Jordan, his wife, and four children. Jordan enticed the schooner's mate to join him in a scheme to seize the schooner. They stole arms from the captain's quarters and at an opportune time, when Stairs and a crewman were below deck, put their plan in motion. They shot the crewman who was on deck and then proceeded to shoot the captain and the other seaman through the skylight. The wounded captain struggled on deck to find Jordan with a pistol in one hand and an axe in the other. A mêlée ensued during which the first wounded crewman was finished off, the captain and Jordan struggled, and the second wounded crewman was dispatched with an axe when he attempted to assist the captain. Stairs was finally able to disengage from Jordan, grab a hatch, and jump overboard, where he was left to drown. The hatch enabled the captain to stay afloat and within a few hours he was picked up by another boat and subsequently reported the events to authorities in Halifax. *Three Sisters* was captured and taken to Halifax, where Jordan was put on trial. He was convicted of piracy and hung, and his body gibbeted and put on public display.[44]

The most sensational case of piracy and mutiny to be tried in a Halifax court took place in July, 1844. On May 21 of that year the inhabitants of Country Harbour awoke to find a large barque had been blown on shore, and upon investigation it was learned that the ship was *Saladin* from Valparaiso. It had set sail from that port on February 8, 1844, with fourteen people on board and a cargo of guano, seventy tons of copper, thirteen bars of silver, and a large quantity of spice. Also on board was a chest full of money and bills of exchange. The ringleader in the piracy was a sea captain by the name of Fielding who, with his son, had taken passage on *Saladin*. The man had grown up in Gaspé and spent most of his life as a seafarer. He had built a reputation as a hard taskmaster who constantly had trouble with his various crews, and also as a shady character who got into trouble with authorities in a number of ports. Tempted by the valuable cargo, Fielding persuaded six of the crew to throw in with him and take over the ship. They either murdered or threw overboard the captain and crew and then changed course for the Atlantic coast. They planned to conceal the ship in some secluded cove, buy a smaller vessel, and remove the cargo for sale in the United States.

Fielding's co-conspirators discovered that the wiley captain planned to do them in as well and ultimately take the booty himself. He made the mistake of approaching each crew member with a proposition to get rid of the others and when they realized what Fielding was doing they seized him and his son and threw them overboard. The six remaining mutineers started a bout of steady drinking and eventually ran their ship aground on the Nova Scotia coast. At first they tried to claim that the captain and crew had died from sickness and accidents but finally two of the number confessed. Four were convicted and hung while the two who confessed were tried and acquitted.[45]

Aside from high-profile incidents such as piracy, duels, and murder, the bulk of crime in the Maritimes continued to be minor in nature. As in Halifax, there were people throughout the region who were idle, given to drink, and with little regard for authority. An official complained in 1766 that the province was being inundated with useless and bothersome persons. Among the pioneers who settled in Nova Scotia after it came under English rule were many New Englanders. Travellers through the province in 1774 claimed that they were "lazy, indolent people." In the same year inhabitants of Cape Breton were described as a "lawless Rabble" who were so unruly that the justice of the peace could not carry on his duties out of fear of being attacked.[46]

The patterns of crime that emerged in the early days of settlement continued throughout the pre-Confederation period. For example, a court session in Saint John, New Brunswick, on January 17, 1829, tried two cases of keeping a disorderly house, one case of forgery, two people for assaulting a magistrate, and one person for grand larceny.[47] Between October 1, 1857, and October 1, 1858, the police court in Halifax dealt with 1,288 cases. Of that number, 458 were for drunkenness, 108 for larceny, and 236 for assaults.[48] Repeat offenders were common among the jail populations of many communities. During the period October 1, 1861, to October 25, 1862, a total of 533 admissions were recorded at the city prison in Halifax, and of that number forty-two were incarcerated on two separate occasions, twenty-six: three times, eleven: four times, four: five times, one: seven times, and one: eight times. Approximately 71 per cent of those incarcerated during the year were male.[49]

Table 2 illustrates the crimes, ages, and numbers of male jail commitments typical for a one-month period in Halifax in the immediate pre-Confederation period. The statistics are for June 1-30, 1864. As the table shows the bulk of street crime continued to be minor in nature, with the majority of convictions being for drunkenness and theft. Sixty-one per cent of those incarcerted were twenty-five years old or under.

Table 2
Male Jail Commitments, Halifax, June 1-30, 1864

Crime	Age
Drunk	55
Drunk	42
Drunk	22
Assault	22
Assault	17
Assault	36
Drunk	35
Larceny	21
Drunk	28
Drunk	23
Assault	25
Drunk	67
Drunk and disorderly	22
Larceny	22
Drunk	18
Drunk	18
Drunk	54
Refused to board ship	43
Larceny	10
Common drunkard	19
Petty trespassing	15
Assault	30
Obstructing the street	45
Larceny	13
Larceny	10
Larceny	10
Larceny	13
Fighting	47
Assault	21
Drunk	24
Larceny	27

SOURCE: City Prison Registry, RG 35-102, Series 18B, VB2, Public Archives of Nova Scotia.

CRIME IN UPPER CANADA AND THE WEST

The types of crimes found in New France and on the east coast were pretty much duplicated as settlement pushed into central Canada. Present-day Ontario was separated from the territory of Quebec in 1791 as the new colony of Upper Canada. In 1841 it joined with Lower Canada to form the province of Canada and the two were divided again at Confederation in 1867 to form the provinces of Quebec and Ontario. From the latter part of the eighteenth century Upper Canada experienced a relatively rapid increase in population. The trend started with the influx of Loyalists after the American Revolution and by 1810 the population numbered about 75,000 people, rising to approximately 150,000 by 1825. Over the next sixteen years the pace of settlement quickened significantly, with the population increasing to about 450,000. By Confederation there were about 1.5 million people living in the province. Until 1825 free grants of land were available to newcomers, which was a considerable inducement to settlement. In 1834 the town of York, the seat of government, was incorporated as the City of Toronto. In 1835 it had a population of 9,252.

Many of the settlers were indigent and illiterate, since in the first half of the nineteenth century there was a large pauper immigration from England and Ireland. Authorities in England encouraged the destitute to migrate as a means of relieving the burden of social distress in the mother country. The main port of entry for immigrants was Quebec City. Between 1829 and 1836 approximately 235,693 people from England, Wales, Ireland, and Scotland entered Canada through the port of Quebec. They accounted for 98.67 per cent of all arrivals during the period. The bulk of those new immigrants settled in what is present-day Ontario. The Irish made up well over half the number.[50] The rough nature of some immigrants created an early society in which incivility, violence, and lawbreaking were no strangers to community life. One writer described it as a "heavy-drinking, brawling, pioneer environment."[51] There were many manifestations of the temper of the times and the crimes that resulted. On the extreme edge was one of the worst cases of child abuse in all of Canadian history. It came to public attention in February, 1819, when a farmhand, who lived in a log cabin with his thirteen-year-old stepson, threw the boy out in the cold winter night. He eventually took the half-frozen child back in but then tied him up in front of the fireplace. He put more wood on the fire and proceeded gradually to roast his son. Finally, when the boy's legs were burned black and could no longer support him, his stepfather forced him toward the flames until his hair caught on fire. The man stood and watched as his stepson burned to death.[52]

More representative of the criminal activity of the times were the offences listed in the court records of communities such as London. One study that examined the Court of Quarter Sessions reports for the years 1800-09 suggested that the bulk of crime was minor in nature and that the incidence, at least judged by convictions, was low. During the entire decade there were only fifty-one convictions. Of that number, twenty were for either assault or assault and battery, eleven for defaulting on jury duty, eight for swearing, three for breaking the Sabbath, two for contempt of court, one for bootlegging, one for a violation of the act regulating Miller's tolls, one for destroying the district stocks, one for petty larceny, and three for other offences.[53]

The Court of the Quarter Session of the Peace for the Home District recorded forty-eight convictions for assault and battery and three for theft and other crimes for the years 1800-10. Once again, the conviction rates suggest a low level of crime, although such statistics do not necessarily give an accurate picture. For example, during the period 1792-1802 there were 114 charges laid in the Upper Canada Assize Courts for crimes ranging from murder to blasphemy, but out of that number there were only thirty-six convictions. Punishments for even minor crimes were severe, so juries were reluctant to convict, jurors and judges were sometimes friends of the accused, witnesses failed to testify, proof was difficult to establish. For these and other reasons offenders escaped punishment for their crimes and thus did not show up in the conviction statistics. Even the record of charges was misleading. In a day when police forces were non-existent, investigation methods were primitive, and crimes went unreported, many offenders must have escaped detection. Thus, crime statistics can only tell us something about the nature of the crimes and the general level of the problem. The figures for 1827 illustrate the point. Jail admissions for that year totalled approximately 264 while the population numbered 167,229, so there were about 158 jailings per 100,000 of population. However, not all persons arrested and held in jail were convicted, and there were undoubtedly many offences for which the perpetrators were not caught. Thus the records offer only a very general picture.[54]

Nevertheless, crime in Ontario was considered to be sufficiently serious to warrant the opening of a full-scale prison in 1835. Kingston prison started operations with fifty-five inmates. The yearly intake of prisoners increased steadily: by 1848 the annual admissions had risen to 103 and the total prison population reached 454. Following the union of Upper and Lower Canada in 1840 Kingston was used to house criminals from both areas, so that by 1859 there were 723 male and female inmates in the institution.

There were 256 committals to the penitentiary in 1859. Among that group, eighteen were seventeen years old and under; 107 were between eighteen and twenty-five; forty-six were twenty-six to thirty years old; forty-five were between thirty-one and forty; twenty-eight were in the forty-one to fifty age group; eleven were aged fifty-one to sixty; and one was over sixty years old. Almost half of the number, 48.8 per cent, were twenty-five and under. Thirty came from Canada East and 226 from Canada West. The urban areas produced the largest number of offenders, with twenty-six of the thirty from Canada East coming from Montreal, and in Canada West thirty-four were from the counties of York and Peel and the City of Toronto, and thirty-five came from the County of Wentworth and the City of Hamilton.[55]

The prisoners admitted to Kingston during its early years were usually sentenced to terms ranging from one to six years for crimes such as grand and petty larceny, horse stealing, forgery, returning from banishment, and assault. As the prison population increased so did the range of crimes. The following excerpt from the Annual Report of the Warden for 1864 offers an overview:

GENERAL RETURN OF CRIMES OF CONVICTS REMAINING IN THE PROVINCIAL PENITENTIARY ON 31ST DECEMBER, 1864

Accessory to Felony, 1; Aggravated Assault, 3; Aggravated and Common Assault, 1; Arson, 25; Arson and Jail Breach, 1; Arson and Burglary, 1; Arson and Larceny, 1; Assault with intent to Rape, 10; Assault with intent to do grievous bodily harm, 5; Assault with intent to rob with violence, 2; Assault with intent to kill, 1; Assault with intent to rob, 2; Assault and Robbery, 1; Attempt to commit Buggery (Sodomy), 1; Attempt to procure Abortion, 1; Attempt to fire a building and Prison Breach, 2; Bigamy, 1; Breaking into and stealing in a Shop, 2; Breaking into a Shop and stealing therefrom, 1; Breaking into a Warehouse, 1; Burglary, 18; Burglary and Larceny, 11; Burglary, Horse Stealing and Larceny, 2; Burglary and Horse Stealing, 1; Burglary and Assault, 1; Burglary and attempt at Murder, 1; Carnally knowing a girl under 12 years, 1; Cattle Stealing, 8; Cattle Wounding, 1; Cutting and wounding with intent to do grievous bodily harm, 2; Feloniously receiving stolen money, 1; Feloniously receiving stolen goods, 3; Feloniously breaking and entering a house and stealing therein, 4; Feloniously wounding, 1; Felony, 34; Felony and assault with intent to kill, 1; Felony and Burglary, 1; Forgery, 27; Found by night with implements of House breaking, 1; Highway Robbery, 3; Horse Stealing, 44; Horse and Cattle Stealing, 1; Horse Stealing and Larceny, 5; Horse saddle and bridle Stealing, 1; House breaking, 1; House breaking, 1; House breaking and Larceny, 1; Inflicting grievous bodily harm, 1; Intent to Rape, 1; Killing a Ewe with intent to steal the carcass, 1; Larceny, 248; Larceny from a dwelling, 1; Larceny and Felony, 1; Larceny from his master, 1; Larceny in a shop, 2; Larceny after conviction for Felony, 1; Larceny from the person, 1; Larceny and Receiving, 5; Larceny and Stabbing, 1; Mail Robbery, 1; Manslaughter, 23; Misdemeanour, 4; Misdemeanor (Perjury), 1; Murder, 39; Obtaining Post Office Letter under false pretences, 1; Obtaining money falsely, 3; Offering, altering, disposing of and putting off Forged Promissory Note, knowing it to have been Forged, 1; Possessing and altering Forged Notes, 1; Pretended Marriage, 1; Rape, 15; Receiving stolen goods, knowing them to be stolen, 3; Receiving stolen property and Larceny, 2; Receiving stolen goods, 3; Receiving stolen goods and money, 1; Receiving stolen money, 1; Riotously beginning to demolish a house, 4; Robbery, 31; Robbery with violence, 3; Robbery and Stabbing, 1; Sacrilege, 1; Sheep killing, 2; Sheep Stealing, 10; Sheep Stealing and Burglary, 1; Sheep Stealing and House Breaking, 1; Shooting with intent, 2; Shooting with intent to kill, 1; Shooting with intent to do grievous bodily harm, 2; Shop breaking, 2; Shop breaking and Larceny, 3; Sodomy, 4; Stabbing, 2; Stabbing with intent to do grievous bodily harm, 5; Stabbing with intent to murder, 2; Stealing from the person, 14; Stealing two promissory notes, 1; Stealing money, 6; Stealing in a dwelling house, 1; Stealing in a warehouse and shop, 2; Stealing and house breaking, 1; Stealing from a shop and Counting House, 1; Stealing from a shop, 1; Substantive Felony, on being accessory before the fact to wounding with intent to commit murder, 1; Unlawfully wounding, 2; Unlawfully attempting to steal money, 1; Unnatural crime, 1; Uttering altered promissory note, 1; Uttering false coin, 3; Uttering counterfeit notes, 1; Uttering forged notes, 3; Uttering Promissory Note, forged endorser, 1; Wounding and Robbing from the person, 1; Wounding with intent to do grievous bodily harm, 2. – Total 729. [56]

The majority of crimes in Upper Canada were minor in nature and did not result in prison terms. Many, however, were punished with short periods of confinement in the local jail. Table 3 offers an overview of crime in Toronto in the year 1840. The highest number of charges were against males for assault, many of which were liquor-related. Males accounted for 72.8 per cent of all charges. The population at the time was 13,092 so the rate of charges per 1,000 of population was about 83.9.

The crimes for the mid-century period continued to consist of a high percentage of assault and liquor or liquor-related offences. For example, records for the United Counties of York and Peel for the period 1844-53 list 4,193 offences in the misdemeanour category, out of which some 2,600 were related to being drunk. The next largest number of offences were 1,189 for vagrancy and 313 for assault.[57]

While much of the crime for which people were arrested and charged was committed by the lower classes, they were not alone. Many prominent persons were involved in the kind of violence that reflected the times, people such as John Small, who on January 3, 1800, killed John White, the Attorney-General, in a duel. In 1810 George and Thomas Ridout, sons of the Clerk of the Peace, were charged and found guilty of assault. In 1817 S.P. Jarvis killed Thomas Ridout in a duel. The gentry of the town of York were well represented among those charged with violence – in 1820 even one of the presiding magistrates, D'Arcy Boulton, Jr., was convicted of assault. Boulton must have been a pugnacious character since some years later, in 1827, he was convicted of a similar offence. In 1836 another magistrate, William Augustus Baldwin, was also convicted of assault. Some among the social elite in the Canadas indulged their lower appetites and, as was the case in Halifax, were heavy drinkers and frequent patrons of houses of prostitution.[58]

Throughout the pre-Confederation period the majority of offences continued to be minor in nature and offenders were disproportionately inhabitants of the larger urban areas. In 1864, for example, approximately 3,566 people appeared in the Toronto Police Court, but some of the offences were minor

Table 3
Charges against Males and Females,
Toronto, 1840

Nature of Offence	Charges at Police Office	
	Male	*Female*
Assault	193	20
with fire arms or deadly weapons	2	–
with intent to commit buggery	1	–
upon constables in the execution of their duty	5	–
Burglary	5	–
Breach of provincial statutes and city laws, for which penalties under twenty shillings were inflicted	112	6
Contempt, refusing to give evidence	3	–
Disorderly conduct (whores, rogues, and vagabonds)	142	175
Disorderly houses (for keeping)	3	4
Drunk in public streets, unable to take care of themselves	120	37
Enticing soldiers to desert	2	–
Buying soldiers' necessaries	1	1
Distilling without licence	1	–
Keeping billiard tables without licence	4	–
Peddling without licence	2	–
Selling spirits without licence	31	1
Larceny	82	44
Receiving stolen goods	2	2
Frauds	2	–
Rape	1	–
Riot	9	–
Threatening personal violence	54	7
Trespassing upon private property	15	2
Selling poison contrary to statute	1	–
Uttering forged money	5	4
Practising medicine contrary to statute	1	–
Total	799	299

SOURCE: *Journals of the Legislative Assembly of Canada*, Appendix no. 1, vol. 1, 1841, appendix 5.

infractions of by-laws, including such things as failing to clear snow. Slightly over half of the charges, 1,876, were for drunk and disorderly conduct.[59]

Crime in Montreal during the first half of the nineteenth century ranged from murder to larceny. The following table offers an overview of the incidences of the more serious crimes. As was the case elsewhere, liquor violations accounted for the majority of lawbreaking. For example, the Recorder's

Table 4
Serious Crime, Montreal, 1812-40

Crime	Total Convictions
Murder	11
Burglary	51
Robbery	16
Shoplifting	4
Larceny	25
Horse, cattle, and sheep stealing	59
Forgery	10
Sacrilege	4
Arson	4
High treason	105
Rape	4

SOURCE: J. Douglas Borthwick, *A History of the Montreal Prison From A.D. 1784 to A.D. 1886* (Montreal: A. Periard, 1886), p. 269.

Court in Montreal in 1866 listed 6,897 arrests under the heading "Drunk and Vagrant" and another 4,375 in the category "Drunk."[60]

Further west, crime continued to be associated to a large degree with the fur trade. Settlements were few so the wilderness was the locale for lawbreaking, although the Canadian West never acquired the reputation for lawlessness that characterized its American neighbour. Yet for most of the nineteenth century there was considerable violence associated with competition in the fur trade between whites and whites, Indians and Indians, whites and Indians, and the fur-trading companies and their employees. There is no way of documenting the level of crime since so much of it went undetected, but many incidents illustrate the nature of crime in the West.

The unsettled regions of the country always attracted a breed of adventurers who paid little heed to convention and rules. Many of these were capable of committing any form of atrocity in pursuance of their own interests. David Ramsay was a prime example. A native of Scotland, Ramsay fought at Louisbourg in 1758 and at Quebec in 1759. He arrived in the Lake Ontario region in the mid-1760s and became a fur trader. He used watered down whisky to cheat the Indians of their furs and demonstrated a thoroughgoing dislike for natives. In two separate incidents over a three-week period in 1772 he killed two women and a man, and later three women, four men, and a child. On both occasions the adult Indians were drunk, and after the killings he scalped them all, including the child.[61]

The fur traders' use of liquor to befriend the Indians frequently generated acts of violence among them. A case in the fur-trading country of Saskatchewan in 1802 illustrates what could result from over-indulgence in alcohol.

During a drinking bout an Indian hunter accused his wife of being attracted to one of his companions and in a fit of jealous rage killed the man. Shortly afterwards the victim's young brother took revenge and in turn killed his brother's murderer with two shots from a rifle, then fled into the woods. When the dead man's friends could not find the boy they went to the tent of his mother and repeatedly stabbed her until she was dead.[62]

The violence that marred the fur trade in the West knew no boundaries, and victims were not only killed but often their bodies were also mutilated. This was a common practice when groups of warring natives fought each other. During the course of one such encounter heads and limbs were severed from the bodies after the battle and a number of the dead were scalped. One victim's skull was taken away to be used as a water dish after his limbs were severed, his stomach and chest ripped open, and his private parts cut off and stuffed into his dead wife's mouth. The woman was also dismembered, as were her children.[63] The violence generated by liquor, the unpoliced wilderness, and certain undisciplined types who were attracted by the unrestricted lifestyle of the fur trade continued through the period. With settlement, many western communities experienced the same kinds of crime familiar in the East. Even in the face of new opportunities and land for the taking, old habits were hard to break.

POLITICAL AND SECTARIAN VIOLENCE

While much of the lawbreaking in pioneer Canada was repetitive and might be described as run of the mill, there was sporadic crime that came out of particular situations or circumstances. One crime that was much more prevalent in earlier days than has been the case since Confederation is treason. English-French rivalries, split loyalties during the American Revolution, and personal ambition, among other factors, generated much treasonable activity. One of the earliest recorded incidents took place in Nova Scotia during the French regime. In 1628 an English adventurer, David Kirke, and his four brothers, set out to wrest the fur trade from the French. Britain and France were at war and King Charles I authorized the expedition. Kirke landed first in Nova Scotia, where he destroyed a number of trading posts. Among the prisoners he took with him was one Claude La Tour, a prominent settler at Port Royal.

Instead of accepting repatriation to France, La Tour was persuaded by Kirke to enter the service of the King of England and joined Sir William Alexander's colonizing company. He was a valuable asset to a group hoping to gain control of French possessions in the New World, so to cement his loyalty La Tour was given a large grant of land in Nova Scotia and made a knight-baronet. In 1629 he accompanied Kirke's second expedition back to Canada. It was hoped that he would be able to persuade his son, who controlled a number of trading posts in Acadia, to also defect to the English.[64] From Nova Scotia Kirke's fleet sailed for Tadoussac in the St. Lawrence River, where they encountered the famous Canadian explorer, Etienne Brûlé. Brûlé was an adventurer and a renegade who knew the country well and could speak the Indian language. He and three companions were persuaded to throw in with the English and they helped them pilot their ships upriver, where they laid siege to Quebec. Champlain, the Governor of New France, surrendered. Kirke and his men reaped a considerable income from the fur trade until England eventually restored New France to the French in 1632.[65]

The English also engaged in their fair share of treachery in colonial days. During the American Revolution a group of rebels in the Cumberland region of Nova Scotia decided to side with the Americans and revolted in the autumn of 1776. They were joined by the French Acadians living in the area.[66] The rebellion was eventually crushed by a special force dispatched from Halifax, which captured a number of the ringleaders and took them back to be tried. Among their number was one Richard John Uniacke. Much of the sentiment in Halifax and elsewhere in the colony was ambivalent if not hostile to the British, so Uniacke and his friends escaped punishment. He later became Solicitor-General of Nova Scotia. During the revolutionary period a number of people were charged with sedition in Halifax, including leading merchants and clergymen.[67] In 1765 Isaiah Thomas, a journeyman printer, was deported for the crime. He was publishing articles that claimed Nova Scotians were unhappy with the Stamp Act and, to add insult to injury, was circulating them in a government publication.[68]

The War of 1812 was another occasion for an outbreak of treason, especially in Upper Canada. Many Americans came north as pioneer settlers in Ontario as that part of Canada opened to immigration, but unlike the United Empire Loyalists they were not motivated by considerations of patriotism. They came seeking better economic opportunities and in many cases retained their old loyalties. Thus, when war broke out they were naturally inclined to favour the United States. During the conflict boatloads of traitors fled across the border, many of whom had engaged in illegal practices before leaving Canada. Some were eventually brought back for trial and convicted of sedition and treason.[69]

The major cases of treason prior to Confederation came in the form of rebellions in Upper and Lower Canada in the late 1830s. In Lower Canada the outbreak was preceded by a long-standing campaign on the part of a French-Canadian reform group to wrest control of affairs from the Legislative Council dominated by an English oligarchy. The reformers were led by Louis-Joseph Papineau. A lawyer by training, he came from a well-to-do family and was elected to the Legislative Assembly in 1808 at the age of twenty-six. He served as its Speaker almost continuously from 1815 to 1837.

The reform movement eventually came under the control of rabid nationalists and took a radical direction. By 1837 Papineau and his followers despaired of bringing about reform through constitutional means and began to talk of revolution. The contest had deteriorated into a clash between two extremist racial groups, with the English trying to maintain their control over Lower Canada while French-Canadian nationalists wanted to break their hegemony. On November 23, 1837, the two forces clashed at St. Denis and a number of other skirmishes followed. Papineau, after the St. Denis incident, fled to the United States and the rebellion was quickly put down with the arrest of 161 of the rebels. Eventually all but twenty-three were granted amnesty. Papineau and fourteen co-conspirators were sentenced to banishment and eight others were exiled to Bermuda, but in the face of a popular uproar the British government ultimately revoked the order. The leniency displayed by the authorities left many of the conspirators free to continue their agitation and unrest again broke out in 1838, led by some of the same people that were let off the previous year. When the second uprising was put down a military court tried 110 people.[70]

Meanwhile, a similar tension existed in Upper Canada. There, a group of reformers also wanted to break the hold of an entrenched ruling oligarchy. They, too, despaired of bringing about change democratically and on December 7, 1837, started an armed rebellion. Under the leadership of William Lyon Mackenzie, a group of rebels attempted to capture city hall, take the arms stored there, and overthrow the government. Mackenzie was a five foot tall fiery Scotsman who had come to Canada in 1820. He used the pages of his newspaper, started in 1824, to attack those who controlled politics in the region, a group referred to as the Family Compact. In 1828 he was elected to the Legislative Assembly and soon emerged as the reformist leader. The rebellion was quickly suppressed with many of the rebels arrested and two hanged. Mackenzie escaped to the United States, where he continued his challenge by setting up a government in exile.[71]

Besides treason, the American Revolution and the 1830s rebellions were occasions for a variety of other crimes. For example, the district of Niagara experienced considerable lawlessness during the Revolutionary War. Its proximity to the American border created a stressful situation because it was under constant threat of rebel attack. The unsettled conditions were made worse by the presence of the military, and robberies and assaults were everyday occurrences. There was a threatened mutiny by Butler's Rangers and constant brawls occurred between soldiers and civilians and between whites and Indians.[72] The rebellion in Quebec brought out armed night riders who attempted to intimidate others to join in overthrowing English rule or who took the opportunity to seek revenge on old enemies. They burned barns and outbuildings, maimed cattle, and pilfered property.[73]

Racial and religious disputes and political and economic disagreements were other sources of lawbreaking throughout Canada in pioneer days. Clashes and demonstrations frequently resulted in destruction of property, assaults, and loss of life, and incidents were plentiful. In Lower Canada there was a riot in Montreal between the French and English in 1833. In Upper

Canada there were riots over political and economic issues in Perth in 1823, in Nepean in 1826, on the Rideau Canal and in Kingston in 1827, in Humberston in 1832, in St. Catharines and Brockville in 1833, in Bytown in 1837, in Brockville and Kingston in 1838, and in Percy in 1839.

People of Irish extraction were at the centre of a number of incidents of sectarian violence during the period, often on the occasion of St. Patrick's Day celebrations. During the festivities on March 17, 1858, for example, the day was marred by clashes with Protestants. There were encounters during the parade and after a speech that night by the famous politician, Thomas D'Arcy McGee, a mêlée broke out that ended with one person dead. Later, a hotel where an Irish party was in progress was also attacked by a mob.[74]

The Irish seemed to have more than their share of trouble in pioneer days and their problems were not always with other ethnic or religious groups, as events in the Lucan district north of London illustrate. Many Irish immigrants settled in the region, with the first arrivals – a group of Protestants – coming in 1818. A second wave, mostly Roman Catholics, immigrated in the mid-1830s. The first group and the majority of the second came from Tipperary, a section of Ireland with a reputation for violence, sectarian strife, and feuding, even among co-religionists. The Roman Catholic population was poor and oppressed by the English. Consequently, they resented authority, were suspicious and mistrustful, and came down hard on anyone who challenged the code of silence and non-co-operation with officials.

Unfortunately, the impact of this conditioning was not left behind when they departed their native land. By the 1840s an explosive mix of settlers occupied the Biddulph region. The old religious and personal grudges and the group animosity were still very much alive. Heavy drinking and brawling were a part of life in the district and it was not long before an ongoing series of criminal incidents erupted. The turmoil lasted from the 1840s through the next two decades.

One of the early confrontations with tragic results began at a work bee in January, 1846. The liquor was plentiful and before the day was out an argument broke out. One side pursued the issue and, armed with an assortment of weapons, attacked their opponents in the woods when they were on their way home. They administered severe beatings, killed one, and wounded two others. Incidents like this became common over the years, and along the way property was destroyed by arsonists, cattle were killed, people were intimidated, and fighting and assaults continued. In 1857 an English Protestant cattleman on his way to market was murdered; later the same year a Tipperary Irishman was killed. In June of 1857 a fight broke out at a barn raising and once again two well-liquored antagonists decided to settle an old feud. James Donnelly struck Pat Farrell a sharp blow on the head with an iron handspike and three days later Farrell was dead. The murder triggered a series of events that culminated twenty-three years later in one of the most notorious events in Canadian criminal history – the brutal murders on the night of February 3, 1880, of James Donnelly, his wife, and their three children.[75]

The feuding in the area also spilled over into the political arena. There were open battles during the election of 1858 and many post-election confrontations. On one occasion a fight broke out at a well-patronized watering spot, known as Keeffe's Tavern, and among other injuries a man by the name of Calligham had his skull fractured. In 1859 a nineteen-year-old boy got into an argument with one William Calahan, a married man with eight children. The dispute ended with Calahan dead, having been hit on the head with a heavy metal balance. This was the fourth murder in the region in four years. One of the more grisly occurrences took place some years later, in September, 1865, when a man was murdered, decapitated, and his body mutilated. Arson, highway robbery, theft, assault, and drunkenness continued to plague the area well into the Confederation period. It was yet another example of how the feuds, animosity, and habits of the old world continued to cause trouble in the new.[76]

Ethnic rivalries and religious animosity frequently combined with politics to provide an explosive mix. Elections were often the occasion for public violence. Prominent party leaders and public figures were usually behind the scenes urging their partisans on and sometimes making the very arrangements that provoked physical confrontations. They were also responsible for a good deal of chicanery, ranging from vote buying to supporters casting their ballots more than once. Incidents connected with elections are legion in Canadian history. In 1830 during a campaign in Nova Scotia a riot was started by a group of stick-wielding partisans during which a man was killed. In the election campaign of 1832 a mob became so unruly in Montreal that troops fired into the crowd, killing three people. Two years later a French Canadian in Sorel was shot dead by a fanatic supporter of the English party. The election of 1836 in Upper Canada was marked by intimidation and rowdyism.

During the campaign of 1834 the streets of the newly proclaimed City of Toronto were virtually taken over by mobs supporting the different candidates. Tempers were fuelled by both political and religious differences and brawls between rival factions were common. During one riotous demonstration the marchers, armed with sticks, clashed with a contingent of constables, and a man by the name of Patrick Burns was killed. The Toronto papers fed the ill feeling by offering biased versions of what happened. The violence reached such a level that finally two companies of infantry were called out to restore peace. As was the custom, liquor had been freely dispensed by the parties. Patrick Burns, it was claimed, had been drinking heavily all day and was looking for trouble when he led the demonstrators through the streets of Toronto.[77]

One of the more violent episodes that again illustrates the mixture of partisan politics and religion took place in Toronto in 1841. The secret ballot was not yet in use and it was a common practice for candidates from all camps to have groups of toughs wandering about intimidating voters. Francis Hincks, the Inspector-General, estimated that during the course of the electioneering that year in Canada East and West, about ten to twenty people had been killed and hundreds more injured. In Toronto two Tory candidates, Henry Sherwood and J. Munro, who had the backing of the Orange Order, were defeated by the Reform Party standard bearers, J.H. Dunn and Isaac Buchanan, who had strong support among Roman Catholics. It was customary for the victors to hold a parade and a mile-long procession crowded the city's streets on March 22, the Monday following the election. There were rumours that trouble was in store for the celebrants and as the parade moved along there were sightings of people armed with clubs along the route. The anticipated trouble started when a house displaying an Orange flag was menaced by a group of Reform supporters. Shots were fired from the house into the crowd, killing one bystander and wounding a number of others. Buchanan and Dunn restrained their angry supporters until a contingent of troops appeared and arrested the people in the house.[78]

Even small communities did not escape the carnage that often accompanied elections. The events in Grand Lake, Nova Scotia, a small village fifteen miles from Halifax, during the provincial election of 1859 offer a typical example. The opposing Liberal and Conservative parties were well represented on election day, both occupying rooms at a community hotel and offering free liquor to their supporters. All day people drank, exchanged insults and threats, and engaged in minor scuffles. The political rivalry was intensified by religious animosity. Catholics overwhelmingly supported the Tories and frequent catcalls of "damn Catholics" were heard from Liberal Protestants. Tempers quickened and a major scuffle erupted when a group of Tories attacked and beat a Liberal supporter and then turned on his friend, who attempted to come to the man's aid. Earlier in the day, in anticipation of trouble, a gang of Liberals had stored a number of rifles and shotguns at a nearby farmhouse. In response to the Tory attack they retrieved the arms and headed back to the hotel. The Liberal gang of about twelve men was met by a much larger contingent of Tories, estimated at about 100 people. Verbal warnings were made by the small group and a shot was fired, but bolstered by drink and their larger numbers the Tories were not intimidated by the armed gang of despised Liberals. They waded into the group of Liberals, grabbed the firearms, broke some, and proceeded to beat their opponents with the stocks of their own guns. The mêlée continued until a Liberal under attack raised his gun to his shoulder and fired. He hit his opponent in the neck and the man bled to death within a few minutes. The gunman fled the scene but the Tories savagely beat the remaining Liberals.

The governing party itself made a significant contribution to the problem by arranging for a considerable number of Irish Catholic railway workers to be given the day off with pay and free transportation to Grand Lake. Every type of bribe was used to win votes, such as money, articles of clothing, and rum. Parties manipulated the process so that certain of their supporters could cast their ballots more than once. According to a Halifax newspaper one voter exercised his franchise so often that when asked if he intended to vote, he replied: "Och, by jappers, and isn't it tired of voting I am?"[79]

While religion mixed with politics often contributed to the volatility of election campaigns, religion by itself was also frequently a catalyst for public violence. The classic battles took place between the Irish Roman Catholics and the Protestant Orangemen. The Orange Society was formed in Ireland in 1795 after a violent conflict between Protestants and Roman Catholics known as the Battle of the Diamond. It was named for William of Orange, who on July 1, 1690, defeated the Catholic forces of King James II. The purpose of the Orange Society was to maintain the laws of the country and the Protestant constitution. The hatred engendered in Ireland between Orangemen and Roman Catholics was transported to the new world when both Orangemen and Irish Catholics came to Canada in large numbers in the nineteenth century. While there were sporadic fights and constant tension between the two groups, the main clashes usually came on March 17, when the Irish celebrated St. Patrick's Day with parades and liquor, and on July 12, when the Orangemen paraded. On occasion the confrontations escalated into major battles, sometimes with dire consequences. For example, a series of Orange-Catholic riots occurred in New Brunswick in 1847 and again in 1849, with numerous injuries and deaths.[80]

Public violence could be provoked by almost any event that served to arouse the anger of large numbers of people. In 1849 a Rebellion Losses Bill was passed to compensate those in Lower Canada for losses incurred during the 1837 rebellion. The prospect of compensating rebels raised the ire of the Conservatives. Demonstrations and riots ensued, during which the Governor was stoned in the streets of Montreal and the parliament buildings were burned to the ground.[81] In January of 1850 government agents appeared at the village of St. Grégoire, on the south shore of the St. Lawrence, to carry out an assessment for school taxes. They were soon confronted by a large mob and warned to leave. This was the beginning of a series of incidents over schools and taxes that went on for some time. During these disputes government agents were harassed and intimidated, property was destroyed, and schools were burned.[82]

On July 6, 1853, a former Roman Catholic priest by the name of Allessandro Gavazzi came to Quebec City for another in a series of anti-Catholic speeches that he had been making in a number of American and Canadian cities. His presence aroused the anger of the heavily Roman Catholic population and Gavazzi was attacked during his lecture. A few days later he appeared in Montreal and sparked a mêlée between Catholics and Protestants. The riot act was read and troops fired on the demonstrators. About forty people were wounded or killed, not all by police bullets. The violence resumed later, when authorities refused to make the results of an investigation into the affair public. Certain persons vented their anger by beating up members of the regiment that had fired on the crowd.[83]

PUBLIC ENTERPRISE AND CRIME

Throughout the early years of Canadian history, when some happening or project brought large numbers of people together, there was often an outbreak of crime. The discovery of gold was just such an event. In the 1850s and 1860s thousands poured into the west coast gold fields in search of wealth. In one four-month period in 1858 an estimated 25,000 people arrived from all over the world. Many were experienced miners from such places as California, but many were rank amateurs. While most came to dig for gold, others were more inclined to make their fortunes by their wits.[84]

The atmosphere in the gold fields made for high expectations, self-indulgence, impatience, and a disregard for rules and authority. The rough, independent spirit of the miners, the heavy consumption of liquor, the constant occasion for conflict over claims and in the gambling halls and saloons, and the practice of carrying guns and knives created a volatile situation. It was made worse by the seasonal nature of the work. During the winter months miners and hangers-on flocked to the more settled communities, bent on making up for the hard work and isolation that characterized their occupation. Assault, murder, robbery, claim jumping, and various other crimes marked the gold rush days. One edition of a Victoria newspaper listed a murder, two attempted murders, one stabbing, three burglaries, four cases of theft, and a number of petty crimes. As one observer noted, "It is a sad state of affairs when men, for the slightest offense, draw knives and pistols on each other. Nevertheless, it is a matter of daily occurrence. . . ."[85]

Bootleg liquor was plentiful. It was used not only to quench the thirst of the miners but also to bribe the Indians. The large number of single men, and men without wives, created a lucrative market for prostitution, and white brothel operators used liquor to entice Indians to sell native women to work as prostitutes. Many Indian women were sold into sexual slavery. Authorities made great efforts to suppress the illegal liquor traffic, including giving one-half of fines resulting from convictions to the arresting officer to encourage diligence. The whisky traders in turn took elaborate precautions to evade police.[86]

While tales of gold rush days are usually associated with the West, gold fever also hit the east coast in the 1860s, and once again the mining activity became a focal point for an outbreak of crime. Rough, hardy men gravitated to work the mines in Nova Scotia's first gold rush. As in the West, drunkenness, brawls, theft, and murder marked the mining areas, with religious and ethnic animosity adding to the problem. The theft of gold reached serious levels in the Waverly mines. The 1865 report of the Nova Scotia Department of Public Works and Mines, for example, estimated that "At least $50,000 to $60,000, or 2,500 to 3,000 ounces, if not more, were stolen by the miners the same year."[87] On March 17, 1865, Alexander MacKenzie, a Scots Protestant boardinghouse keeper, went to Windsor Junction to collect some money owed to him. While standing on the railway station platform he was attacked by a group of Irishmen. A piece of wood thrown at MacKenzie missed and hit Patrick Kady, one of his attackers. The next day Kady died from his injury. On Christmas night, 1865, a group of Scots miners went to an Irish boarding-house to get some liquor and a brawl broke out when one of the Scotsmen called for an "Irish son of a bitch" to come out of the house. During the battle John McPherson was shot; he died of his wounds two weeks later. The crime and violence in the area were so pervasive that the law-abiding among the residents petitioned the provincial government to step in and maintain order. They also requested that a jail be built.[88]

Labour-intensive economic enterprises and large-scale public works pro-jects also served as venues for heightened lawbreaking. These worksites attracted migrants in large numbers and created the conditions that spawned criminal activity. Two such developments combined, from the late 1820s to the 1840s, to set up Bytown, later Ottawa, and its environs for one of the most extended and worst bouts of public lawlessness in our history.

The Napoleonic Wars, which cut off the Baltic timber reserves from British trade, created a new market for lumber and for masts for the British Royal Navy and merchant fleet. In response, enterprising Canadi-ans opened up the vast timber resources of the Ottawa Valley. It was ideal for lumbering because log rafts could be assembled and floated down the Ottawa River to the St. Lawrence and on to market. People from all over migrated to find work in the lumber industry. The work was demanding because trees were cut and dressed by hand and lumbermen had to spend long winters in isolated bush camps. In the spring, after the log drives, they had a lot of pent-up energy to expend, as well as their accumulated wages. Many loggers went to Bytown to indulge their appetites and to live during the off season. Some lumbermen were hard drinkers, rowdy, and undisciplined, and their presence in Bytown attracted an assortment of drifters ready to take whatever advantage they could of the opportunity for some easy money.

The construction of the Rideau Canal in the late 1820s attracted to the Bytown region another group that, when mixed with the loggers, made for a volatile situation. Since work in the woods used up most of the available labour the canal builders went elsewhere for workers, recruiting many from the state of New York where they had just finished building the Erie Canal. Included in their ranks were hundreds of Irishmen who were disproportion-ately poorly educated, brash, and resentful of authority. All too often they were relegated to the most menial tasks and were discriminated against because of their Roman Catholic faith. In Bytown they soon established an

Irish ghetto in the east end of town, for the most part a squalid slum with some living in caves dug out of mounds of earth.

After the canal was completed in 1832 there was mass unemployment among the Irish labourers. The French-Canadian woodsmen treated them as an economic threat, while the townspeople held them in contempt and ostracized them socially because of their poverty and boisterous lifestyle. Some of the Irish responded by attempting to out-drink and out-fight everyone in sight, including their fellow countrymen. The result was that Bytown streets were frequently unsafe because of the heavy drinking and brawling of both the lumbermen and canal workers. Kept out of any meaningful citizenship, the more cantankerous element asserted their importance through fear and intimidation. Their large numbers and the obvious reluctance of the authorities to challenge them encouraged their abrasiveness, and soon roaming gangs of toughs, referred to as "Shiners," virtually controlled the streets. Beatings, property damage, and even arson became everyday occurrences. On January 5, 1835, a man was murdered in broad daylight on a street in Lower Town. A farmer who got into an argument with some Shiners had his house blown up.

Through the mid-1830s a veritable reign of terror existed in Bytown. The situation was made worse by the machinations of Peter Aylen, a major force in the lumber industry. The competition among the timber merchants was lively and the struggle for social position and power in the Bytown community just as bad. A number of the lumber barons sought to ingratiate themselves with the Shiners and use them to advance their own interests, and none was more successful than Aylen. He gave them jobs, provided them with direction, prostitutes, and booze, and soon had a band of loyal followers ready to do his bidding.[89] The *Brockville Recorder* offered a vivid description of the situation:

> in Bytown there is a band of about 150 desperados, who entirely swarm that place, a Canadian (French Canadian) is not allowed to live there, if he is caught on the bridge he is thrown into what is called the kettle (a whirlpool) and that terminates his miseries, but if caught in the woods or towns, these 150 Shiners (Irish immigrants who worked in lumber camps and river drives in the Ottawa Valley) as they are denominated, beat and injure him so that few recover. If any of this band enter a shop and demand any particular goods or ware, the shop keeper dare not refuse for should, he, his life is instantly sought, and failing to get which, his property is sure to be destroyed by fire.[90]

The local authorities could not control the Shiners. In July of 1835 a constable attempted to arrest a Shiner on a charge of rape but the Irishman and his companions administered a vicious beating to the officer. Other officials were threatened, shot at, and beaten. It seemed that no outrage was beyond the Shiners. On one occasion three of them raped an elderly Indian woman and on another a group of drunken Shiners attacked the pregnant wife and daughters of a well-known Orangeman by the name of Hobbs. They beat on the woman with sticks, and Mrs. Hobbs was dragged some distance when her clothing got caught up in her sleigh. All the while the men kept beating her. The victims eventually escaped but left behind their team of horses. When Hobbs came to town to retrieve them the animals' ears and tails had been cut off and one had been slashed with a knife. The attack on the defenceless women caused a wave of revulsion and the entire community, including the more respectable Irish, resolved to put an end to the Shiners' lawlessness. They persuaded the army to come to their aid and also beefed up their police force. With regular street patrols the situation improved considerably, but Bytown continued to be an unruly, boisterous community well into the 1840s.[91]

LIQUOR AND LAWBREAKING

Liquor was an ever-present adjunct to the crime and violence in Bytown and, as well, played a prominent role in other occasions of lawlessness, from the fur trade to election campaigns. Also, much of the day-to-day street crime in Canadian communities consisted of liquor or liquor-related offences. Crimes from theft to assault to murder were frequently committed when the perpetrator was under the influence of alcohol. The liquor trade was so pervasive that it might almost be characterized as endemic to the society of pioneer Canada; indeed, it was so inextricably connected to crime in all parts of the country that no treatment of the subject would be complete without examining the phenomenon of liquor in early Canadian history.

Intoxicating liquor and wines were a staple item in European diets and continued to be so among the immigrants who settled Canada, where every community had an ample number of liquor outlets. The long winters and the isolation also made liquor an important part of social and recreation activities. The Governor of New France, Denonville, in 1685 complained about the number of taverns, "which makes it impossible to prevent the disorder such places occasion."[92] He estimated that out of twenty-five houses in the small settlement of Three Rivers, as many as twenty sold liquor.[93] In October of 1725 the Bishop of Quebec complained about immigrants "who are intemperate and guilty of almost every crime."[94] In the 1840s travellers counted over 100 licensed houses in Quebec City and it was estimated that throughout the community there were probably as many illegal liquor outlets as there were licensed ones.[95]

As we have seen, liquor in New France became a mainstay of the fur trade. It was the means used to cheat the Indian and its abuse occasioned violence and bloodshed. Some measure of the impact that liquor had on the behaviour of the natives is evident from the description of one eighteenth-century observer who wrote: "Even in the very streets of Montreal, are seen the most shocking spectacles . . . husbands, wives, fathers, mothers, children, brothers and sisters, seizing of one another by the throat, tearing of one another by the ears, and worrying one another with their teeth like so many enraged wolves. The air resounding during the night with their cries and howlings. . . ."[96]

Many of the massacres and atrocities in the forests of Canada took place after drinking bouts. Parties of Indian hunters were kept well supplied with liquor by white fur traders who used alcohol as a control mechanism. The exploitation knew no bounds and even the tavern keepers who served native customers cheated them. Some kept what was known as the "Indian barrel" into which was poured the leavings of beer, wine, and brandy from customers' glasses. When a native ordered a drink he was served from the Indian barrel.[97] As we have seen the widespread detrimental effects of the liquor trade made it a constant bone of contention among clergy and officials in New France.

Liquor was also the focal point of much criminal activity in English Canada since rum and other spirits flowed freely. Cornwallis had difficulty getting his settlement built because he could not keep his people sober once liquor peddlers arrived from Louisbourg with ample supplies and set up makeshift grog shops on the beach at Halifax. One of the first industries started in the new colony was a rum distillery opened by Joshua Mauger, who was also involved in the West Indian slave trade. In the mid-1770s two distilleries were operating in the town, turning out over 90,000 gallons of rum a year. Drinking places were to be found at every turn. By the second decade of its founding there were around 100 licensed establishments operating in Halifax and it was estimated that there were at least as many illegal ones. Many people convicted of crime were drinking or drunk when the offence was committed. Assaults, murder, gambling, prostitution, and thievery were crimes closely associated with the consumption of liquor.[98]

The taste for alcohol, frequently in excess, knew no class boundaries and the rowdiness, immorality, and brawls engaged in by the gentry were frequently liquor-related. The consumption that was characteristic at social gatherings is illustrated by a dinner hosted by General Wolfe, who gathered his English troops in Halifax prior to the attack on Louisbourg. On May 24, 1758, Wolfe put on a dinner at the Great Pontac, Halifax's main hotel. The forty-seven guests consumed seventy bottles of Madeira, fifty bottles of claret, and twenty-five bottles of brandy.[99]

The flow of liquor in Halifax was only another manifestation of a problem that plagued earlier coastal settlements in the region and that was to be found as well in small and large communities throughout the period. A French official in 1716 protested that "All the inhabitants of Plaisance and other foreigners are accustomed to selling wine and brandy which causes disorder and debauchery continually as much among the soldiers as among the fishing crews."[100] The passage of time brought no changes. A half-century later, in

1767, a citizen of Liverpool, Nova Scotia, complained about the penchant of fishermen "to killing one another. The fatal effects of rum."[101] The demon rum contributed to a variety of crime among the fisherfolk. Crews of fishing vessels on occasion would sell their catch, which belonged to their employers, to New England Schooners for rum. They would then go on a drinking binge until the liquor was gone, sometimes losing out on the entire fishing season.[102]

Liquor also lubricated the settlement and development of Upper Canada. Work bees were a common device for getting help with clearing land, building houses and barns, and other large-scale projects. They were also social occasions when the liberal dispensing of liquor made the work seem easier and contributed to the conviviality. Some attended primarily to partake of the free booze. At least one host complained that "Many of the people came for the sole purpose of drinking and never once assisted in lifting a log."[103] Overindulgence at these work bees frequently resulted in brawls, serious injury, and loss of life.[104] Since liquor was easy to make it was an ever-present staple in many homesteads and farmers who sold their grain to distillers sometimes took payment in whisky.

Liquor was readily available in small and large communities and by the roadside on well-travelled routes. In 1833 on the forty-mile stretch between York and Hamilton there were twenty taverns. As one observer described it, "In travelling through the country you will see every inn, tavern and beer shop filled at all hours with drunken, brawling fellows, and the quantity of ardent spirits consumed by them will truly astonish you."[105] The flow of liquor is again well illustrated by the District of Bathurst. In 1836, a population of approximately 30,000 was served by thirty-five shops and sixty-five inns that sold liquor. These outlets were kept supplied by six distilleries. Some of the distilleries that dotted the landscape of Upper Canada were capable of producing as much as sixty to eighty gallons a day, all of which was readily marketed. In 1835 there were 407 licensed shopkeepers and 947 licensed inns, and in the same year eighty-eight distilleries in Upper Canada turned out approximately 6,834 gallons of hard liquor per day.[106] By 1842 the number had increased to about 147 distilleries with an additional ninety-six breweries and countless private stills and bootleggers.[107]

With alcohol in such abundance and considering the drinking habits of many of the adult populace, it is not surprising that a high percentage of crime consisted of either liquor or liquor-related offences. In 1836 the grand jurors of the Niagara District noted that "the greater portion of crime which has come under our cognizance has been occasioned by the intemperate use of ardent spirits."[108] Grand jurors in Toronto in the same year blamed an increase in crime on "the large number of taverns in the city."[109] In 1841 there were 119 licences issued for taverns in Toronto to serve an adult population (over sixteen years of age) of 7,315. Some years later, in 1848, the grand jury, in commenting on crime in the city, claimed "that the greater part of the offenses have occurred when the parties were in a state of intoxication."[110] The jury went on to observe that "Almost every case of murder, larceny, and assault have been traced and found connected with the numerous small taverns and grog shops with which the city of Toronto is infested."[111] Even the police broke the law by overindulgence. In Toronto, for example, at mid-century it was common for upwards of 25 per cent of the entire force to be disciplined during the average year for liquor-related offences. In 1865 the chief constable was suspended for being drunk on duty.[112]

Further west we have already seen the chaos created by the abundance of liquor in the fur trade. In addition, whisky traders came into western Canada, especially from the United States, in ever-increasing numbers until the appearance of the North West Mounted Police in 1873. Much of the crime in the forests, in mining camps, and in early settlements was liquor-related. Thus, in all parts of the country liquor was integral to lawbreaking; in addition, it was itself the focus of much criminal activity in the form of illegal production, bootlegging, and trade. More especially it was a common factor in every conceivable form of crime, including theft, assault, wife beating, arson, prostitution, murder, and massacres.

Whether liquor-related or not, as we have seen, incidences of crime were common throughout the pioneer period. Because of inadequate enforcement and a rather loose judicial system in the early days of settlement, much crime went unreported and unpunished. Therefore, there was probably much more than the records suggest. However, the level of documented lawbreaking was well below modern trends, and much of it could be classified as minor. It was nonetheless a cause of concern in many developing communities and for authorities throughout the pre-Confederation period. Although much crime was minor in nature there were many examples of violent and serious lawbreaking. The fur trade was the focal point for crimes against the person, but assaults, mayhem, and murder were to be found in all parts of the country. Crime in Canada respected no boundaries, either in its diversity or in its geographical distribution. Yet Canadians have long nurtured, with some degree of pride, an image of the country as a crime-free society in an earlier day. The record suggests that the image is more myth than reality.

SUMMARY

Crime in Canada started with expeditions of the earliest explorers and in seasonal fishing stations in inlets on the Atlantic seaboard. As permanent settlements were established and the colony of New France developed, many of the types of crime familiar in the old world were replicated in the new. Theft, arson, poisonings, counterfeiting, duels, assault, and murder were among the more serious offences that perplexed early settlers, churchmen, and officials. New France also set the stage for the lawlessness that characterized the fur trade and that continued long after the colony passed into English hands.

Similar patterns of lawbreaking appeared in every other part of the country as settlement progressed. The immigrants were hardly off the boats in Halifax when the thieves and cutthroats from the slums of Great Britain resumed the practice of their trades. The pioneer communities in Upper Canada experienced their fair share of lawlessness, which increased as the population grew. Often the offences were infractions of liquor laws or were committed by those under the influence of alcohol. A great deal of crime throughout the entire period was facilitated by a remarkable abundance of liquor.

The larger communities throughout the country frequently had an underclass of drunks, idlers, and petty thieves who accounted for much of the crime recorded in the police records. They were in and out of the jails, mostly on vagrancy, drunk, and assault charges and were chronic recidivists whose lives sometimes consisted of a regular pattern of drink, disorder, and jail. They inflated the arrest records and accounted for at least a part of the difference between rural and urban crime rates.

Pioneer Canada was populated by a hardy people, most of whom had little if any education or refined manners. The so-called "gentry" in this respect were often as rough and untutored as those they considered their inferiors. Many respected neither law nor convention. Given the free, egalitarian spirit of pioneer society and the presence of many who were heavy drinkers and who did not shirk from violence, what is surprising is not the incidents of murder, assault, and other crimes but that there was rather less than more.

While most of the criminal activity was generated by personal circumstances, it was also occasioned by events such as wars, election campaigns, gold discoveries, and large-scale undertakings such as lumbering and canal building. Almost anything that generated unstable conditions or brought large numbers of people together resulted in an outbreak of lawlessness. Wars brought troops and the navy to many districts and port towns, thus creating opportunities for a range of illicit activities from theft to prostitution. The American Revolution generated treason, smuggling, and a variety of other crimes. Gold mining, lumbering, and canal building attracted large numbers of hard-bitten men who too frequently sought respite from their work and lonely lives in a bottle of liquor. The heavy drinking sometimes led to brawls, destruction of property, and loss of life.

Crime, even in its pioneer phase in Canada, was a complex phenomenon. People from a variety of backgrounds and in a broad range of circumstances broke the laws of the times. Greed, lust, ambition, pride, opportunity, need, patriotism, religion, politics, intelligence, stupidity, personality, poverty, and alcohol are only some of the factors that were clearly associated with crime in pioneer Canada. Refugees from the jails of the old world picked up their trade in their new surroundings. Farm boys from the settlements of New France broke the laws of their society in pursuance of wealth in the fur trade. Religious and political loyalties provoked sectarian violence with great regularity. Passions brought to fever pitch often resulted in armed clashes, destruction of property, assaults, and murder. Even work bees that brought together friends and neighbours were occasions for brawls and murder, and leading citizens engaged in duels, treason, and other crimes.

The opinion on the extent of pioneer crime varies among historians. John K. Elliott concluded that "on the whole, our pioneer settlers set an example as law-abiding citizens."[113] On the other hand, M.T. Campbell claimed that "Murder, arson, burglary, and assault flourished, with the lesser crimes of larceny, horse stealing, jail break, and widespread wanton vandalism."[114] Official records of convictions tend to support Elliott's conclusion. However, the absence of effective policing, the sometimes ineffective and frequently inefficient jury and court system, and the reluctance of people to report their neighbours all meant that considerable crime went undetected. Pioneer Canada was by no means a crime-free society. The incidence of crime, however, was at a level with which the society of the day could cope, and of a nature that enabled most communities, for much of the time, to exist in peace and security.

CHAPTER 2

▼

Crime Since Confederation

In 1867 Nova Scotia, New Brunswick, and the provinces of Canada (Quebec and Ontario) united to form the Dominion of Canada. This did not signify the end of the pioneer period because there were still vast tracts of unsettled land, especially in the West. It did, however, set the stage for a national development that had an impact on British North America from coast to coast. This development, in part generated by government policies, in part assisted by world-wide technological advances, also influenced crime. With the formation of the provinces of Alberta and Saskatchewan and their admission to the federal union in 1905 the process of political formation was completed. Manitoba had joined in 1870, British Columbia in 1871, and Prince Edward Island in 1873. Newfoundland, until then a British colony, joined Canada in 1949.

Between 1867 and the outbreak of World War One the new country experienced a dramatic growth. By the beginning of the war the foundation of those influences that were to shape Canada in modern times was well established. The most significant development was the growth in population, from 3,689,257 in 1871 to 7,206,643 by 1911. All parts of Canada shared in the growth, with Quebec and Ontario experiencing the largest numerical increases. Ontario's population went up during the period by 906,441, Quebec's by 814,260. The decade between 1901 and 1911 witnessed an especially significant gain with the population rising by 34.17 per cent. Over 48 per cent of that increase was due to immigration. Throughout the entire period immigration contributed substantially to the rise in population. In 1913-14 alone over 400,000 immigrants entered Canada.

While the West was being opened up and many remote areas were being settled, a population shift was taking place that changed Canada from a predominantly rural to a predominantly urban society. In 1911 there were well over 100 communities across Canada with populations of 5,000 or more. By 1921 there were approximately 4,435,827 people classified as rural dwellers and 3,977,064 living in communities of 1,000 or more. By 1931 the urban population of Canada outnumbered the rural population, with 53.7 per cent of Canadians living in urban communities.

The population increase helped to fuel a dynamic economic expansion that in turn contributed to the growth in population. The first transcontinental railway in Canada was completed in 1885 and electric lighting, electric street railways, and the telephone were in common use before the end of the nineteenth century. Business was expanding at a rapid clip. In 1899 the Canadian Manufacturing Association listed 132 members; by 1910 its ranks had increased to over 2,500. The development touched all sectors of the economy, from forestry and fishing to mining. The Yukon gold rush, which started in 1898, encouraged exploration and development in other parts of the country as well. The manufacturing sector produced everything from steel products to textiles and shoes, with gross value of manufactured products rising from $481,053,375 in 1901 to $1,165,975,639 by 1911. Government spending also worked to encourage expansion. Generous subsidies were provided, roads were built, goods and services were purchased. Between 1896 and 1913 provincial and federal expenditures quadrupled. Banks also played a significant role and helped to fuel the growth. In 1886 there were approximately forty-one banks. By 1914 the number was reduced to twenty-two but they had over 3,000 branches throughout the country.

From railroads to mining, from shoe factories to distilleries, the economic expansion was built on a ready supply of labour. The labour sector experienced some dramatic changes during the period, the most significant being growth of the union movement. In 1872 unions were legalized in Canada. In 1886 the Trades and Labour Congress of Canada was organized, and in 1902 the Canadian Federation of Labour made its appearance. In 1901 over 344,000 men, women, and children were employed in the industrial sector of the Canadian economy.

CRIME TO THE END OF THE NINETEENTH CENTURY

The types of crime common at the Confederation period were the same ones that had dominated police records for some time. For example, the Montreal sheriff's report of February, 1868, listed a total of 3,985 offences for the previous year. Of that number, 2,958 were in the category of disorderly conduct, debauchery, idleness, and similar offences. The next largest number, 355, was for larceny, followed by 217 assaults. Recidivism had been a long-standing problem in urban areas and there were no signs of a change.

Incarcerations in Montreal included 300 people who were jailed twice, 159 three times, ninety-eight four times, and 138 five times or more. One person was confined sixteen times.[1] Also, crime continued to be a largely urban phenomenon. The Quebec sheriff's reports for 1875 listed a total of 5,350 prisoners, of which 3,406 were jailed in Montreal, 704 in Quebec, and 382 in Sherbrooke.[2]

Although the crime pattern was familiar, the dramatic development taking place in Canada created more scope for criminals. Changes in society, especially technological advances, would promote new forms of crimes, and the overall growth would dramatically increase long-standing types of offences. The dual impact on crime of population increase and development was especially evident in the West. A case in point was the construction of the Canadian Pacific Railway, which opened the region and substantially contributed to the increase in settlement.

The building of the CPR was the biggest commercial undertaking up to that point in Canadian history. The contract, approved by Parliament in 1880, provided that the company that built it would also own and operate the railroad. The promoters were initially granted $25 million in cash, plus 25 million acres of western land. In addition, the new company was handed over approximately 700 miles of existing rail lines that had cost the government about $35 million. During the course of construction a number of requests for more money resulted in a further outpouring of public funds.

Over 14,000 people were employed at times during the construction of the CPR. That number of transients provided a huge market for liquor as well as the occasion for considerable crime. The workers were strung out along hundreds of miles of worksites and the work was hard and often dangerous. Large numbers of labourers came from the United States and thousands were brought over from China because construction firms could not find enough people to meet their manpower requirements. One of the few refuges from the hard work, the isolation, and the loneliness was liquor. Recognizing the threat to productivity, the company placed a total ban on the sale of liquor along the worksites, thus creating a ready market for the illicit whisky traders who roamed the West.

The profits to be made from the sale of liquor were so high that no prohibitions, enforcement agents, or fines could deter the bootleggers. A gallon of liquor could be bought in the east for about fifty cents, diluted, and sold in the West for as much as a $45 profit. Illegal outlets were set up all along the work lines. The drinking, in turn, contributed to other forms of lawbreaking. Certain of the construction workers were rough characters. One observer described some of them as "the scum and off-scourings of the filthiest slums of Chicago and other Western cities."[3] They were bad enough sober but even more dangerous when they were drinking. Brawls, assaults, robberies, and stabbings were common. Razors could not only be used for shaving but also served as ready weapons with which to slash someone's throat.

The makeshift communities that sprang up as construction sites shifted were frequently hotbeds of lawlessness. The settlement of Rat Portage on Lake of the Woods in 1880 was a not untypical example. For a time it was home to a motley collection of gamblers, whisky traders, and prostitutes, and it supported a floating population of some 3,000. Arrests and convictions for crime generated over $6,000 in fines in one eight-month period. The offences included highway robbery, assault, liquor violations, prostitution, larceny, and burglary.[4]

While agents were obviously kept busy enforcing the law, on occasion they were not above breaking it themselves. Some were especially prone to pocketing the fines they collected while others were in the pay of the bootleggers. Illustrative was an incident in the summer of 1880. A warrant for the arrest of two whisky traders had been issued the previous winter but when the constable tried to serve it he was severely beaten. The traders then fled to Rat Portage. There they surrendered to the stipendiary magistrate, who, coincidentally, was in their pay. Their friend levied a small fine of $50 and provided them with a written discharge. Emboldened by their judicial connections the two men loaded up fifty gallons of whisky and headed for the work camps. A contractor spotted them plying their illegal trade and immediately reported them to a constable, who obtained an arrest warrant. When the constable and the contractor confronted the two outside a bawdy tent, one fled into the woods but the other stood his ground. His gun was wrestled from him and he was placed under arrest. On the pretext of needing to wash up, his captors allowed him to go into the tent, but once inside a friend handed him a loaded revolver. He then stepped back out with the gun pointed at the constable. The policeman happened to be a fast draw and before the trader could fire he was shot dead. The final act in this small drama came with the dismissal of the crooked magistrate who had released the traders in the first place. Appropriately enough, he took up the whisky trade.[5]

The building of the CPR brought with it an unprecedented land boom in the West. The location and progress of the railroad substantially affected the value of adjacent land and town sites, thus generating a virtual orgy of speculation with the boom reaching fever pitch in 1881 and 1882. In the community of Portage, for example, out of 148 businesses some fifty-eight of them were involved in real estate. People poured into the region hoping to get in on the action. The influx included the usual array of underworld characters. Land swindles were the order of the day, involving the lowest con artists and the highest government officials. Homesteaders were cheated out of their properties or intimidated into selling by crooked lawyers and agents, who then flipped the holdings for much higher prices. Speculators bought up huge parcels hoping to profit from a decision such as where the railroad station would be located or public buildings constructed. Often they benefited from inside information. Fortunes were made and spent, and established centres like Winnipeg for a time witnessed all the manifestations of greed run rampant.[6]

The railroad opened the West to settlement and immigrants came into the Prairies in ever-increasing numbers. The expansion substantially altered life in the already established settlements such as Calgary. The development attracted a variety of professional criminals, especially from the United States, hoping to find new opportunities. Soon the range of crimes common in eastern cities was to be found in the emerging communities in the West. Brawling, assault, theft, drunkenness, and gambling by the mid-1880s were typical of the crime scene in Calgary.[7]

Elsewhere in the territories one did not have to look far for examples of criminal activity. In the early 1870s a number of American whisky traders came into Canada and opened up posts with names like Fort Whoop-Up and Standoff. Many were renegades and fugitives from U.S. justice who traded liquor with the Indians in return for furs and buffalo hides. They were soon followed by wolf hunters. Together, the wolfers and whisky traders demoralized the Indians and interfered with their hunting. The liquor created a dependency in the Indian and diminished his ability to make a living. The wolfers gathered wolf skins by killing buffalo, cutting them open, and lacing the innards with strychnine. The remains attracted wolf packs and the poison killed them, but it also killed Indian dogs, and the buffalo slaughter reduced the herds, which were a main source of Indian livelihood. Naturally there was bad blood between the natives and the wolf hunters, which sometimes resulted in atrocities. On one occasion a gang of the Americans was pursuing Indians who had stolen horses from them. They came across an Assiniboine camp and slaughtered thirty men, women, and children.[8]

Horse stealing was a chronic problem in the West. Roving bands of Canadian and American Indians, as well as gangs of whites, were continually stealing horses. Indians also preyed on settlers and traders, robbing them of their possessions and goods. A typical incident was one that took place in April of 1882. A party of thirty-two Cree Indians set upon three traders returning from a trip across the border with a load of supplies. The Crees held the trio captive overnight and threatened to kill them. The next day they looted their victims' wagons, making off with blankets, rifles, and other supplies, but left them alive.[9]

The annual reports to Parliament by the Commissioner of the North West Mounted Police afford an overview of the nature and incidence of reported crime throughout the West. Table 5 presents a summary for the year 1882. The statistics do not include a large number of civil cases and actions for debt.

The most famous criminal event in the West in the 1880s was the Sas-

Table 5
Cases Tried throughout the Territories, 1882

Murder	3
Rape	3
Horse Stealing	16
Cattle Stealing	1
Perjury	1
Larceny	42
Killing Cattle	1
Injury to Property	18
Breaking Gaol	2
Illicit Liquor Traffic	39
Illegally in Possession of Intoxicating Liquors	52
Gambling	31
Assault	28
Buying Government Farm Produce from Indians	1
Contempt of Court	1
Lunacy	2
Miscellaneous Cases	36
Concealing Child-birth	1
	278

SOURCE: *Settlers and Rebels. Reports to Parliament of the Activities of the N.W.M.P. 1882-1885* (Toronto: Coles, reprint, 1973), p. 12.

katchewan rebellion. A group of settlers along the banks of the Saskatchewan River, mostly Métis, became alarmed at the prospect of encroachment on their lands by eastern speculators and white settlers so they wanted the government to grant them clear and official titles to protect their holdings. There were other grievances as well, including concern over crop failures, grain prices, and the high cost of transportation. Both the Métis and white settlers were angered when the government failed to respond satisfactorily to their demands. Some of the Métis had migrated from Manitoba, where they had earlier been involved in the Red River insurrection. That confrontation, led by Louis Riel, was concluded by the formation of the province of Manitoba in 1870. Riel was still a revered name among the Métis and the possibility was raised that he might be able to lead another successful campaign against the federal government so a delegation was sent to enlist his aid.

Louis Riel was a Métis born in St. Boniface. He was intelligent, spoke French and English fluently, and was well educated, having studied for the priesthood in Montreal. During the confrontation in Manitoba he had set up a provisional government but his leadership was challenged from the outset by a group calling itself the Canadian Party, led by Dr. John Schultz.

Riel threw Schultz and some of his followers into jail. Schultz escaped and organized a party to free the other prisoners. He was joined by a band of sixty men from the settlement of Portage la Prairie. The sortie failed and Riel proceeded to demonstrate the authority of the provincial government by arresting the men from Portage la Prairie along with their leader, Thomas Scott. Riel executed Scott on March 4, 1870.[10]

French Canada hailed Riel as a hero for his leadership in Manitoba but English Canada, especially Orange Ontario, condemned him as a murderer for the execution of Scott. Following the Red River episode Riel was eventually given a partial amnesty but banished from Canada for five years. The trauma of the entire affair brought on a nervous breakdown and Riel spent two years in a Quebec asylum. He was living in Montana teaching school when the call came to help his kinsmen in Saskatchewan. The Métis did not realize that the Riel of 1884 was a far cry from the Riel who led Manitoba into Confederation.[11]

In March of 1885 Riel set up a provisional government at Batoche and soon the whole countryside was in an uproar. The Métis and Indians went on a rampage. As Assistant Commissioner Crozier of the North West Mounted Police described it:

> Between the 19th and 26th March Riel and his followers had robbed, plundered, pillaged and terrorized the settlers and country; they had sacked stores, seized and held as prisoners officers of the Government, merchants, settlers and others; they had risen in armed rebellion or insurrection, they patrolled the country with armed parties, who seized, with the muzzles of rifles at their heads, loyal subjects, or any one else they chose, declaring that they had the choice of submitting to be made prisoners or of being shot; their orders were to massacre all those who would not allow themselves to be made prisoners; they had incited the Indians to take up arms and rebel against authority, a condition of affairs which must lead to murders, massacres and the most frightful atrocities; they had cut the telegraph wires and cut down the telegraph poles, and stopped all mail and other communication and traffic; had committed highway robbery, seized and plundered freighters and freight, and had fired upon and driven into the fort I was commanding, my patrols; they had denounced and repudiated the authority of the Queen, and plunged the country into a state of war, terror and anarchy; they had paralyzed all trade and business, and the legitimate and peaceful occupations and callings of the people.[12]

Before the territory returned to normal a battle took place between the NWMP and a band of Métis, during which ten police were killed. Fort Carlton and Fort Pitt were destroyed, and a number of whites were massacred by Indians at the settlement of Frog Lake on April 2, 1885. A contingent of troops was sent in to put down the rebellion. Riel was captured and he and seventy-three of his followers were put on trial. Riel was hanged in Regina on November 16, 1885, for high treason.[13]

In the meantime the railroad continued to bring people to the West, including prostitutes, thieves, gamblers, and confidence men. It facilitated their travel throughout the region and their escape when the law was closing in. In addition, the lawlessness associated with railroad building continued in the West through the turn of the century and followed a pattern similar to the one established with the building of the CPR line. Typical was a settlement that emerged at Crow's Nest Lake in British Columbia in 1898 and thrived during the winter months. The people who gathered were described as being mainly "illicit whiskey vendors, gamblers, thieves, and prostitutes, . . . all bent upon fleecing the poor railway man of his hard earned gains."[14] While the bulk of crime was bootlegging there were also cases of more serious crime, such as horse stealing and murder.

The Yukon gold rush also helped to keep the pot of crime boiling in the Northwest at the end of the century. The extent of lawlessness varied from place to place and from time to time throughout the territory. The population was estimated at about 20,000 in 1899, most of which was male, so circumstances continued to be conducive to criminal activity. Towns like Dawson attracted numerous lawless types, especially from the United States. Superintendent Steele of the NWMP noted in his 1899 report that "a very large number of desperate characters" were in the Yukon and especially in Dawson. "Many of them have committed murders, 'held up' trains, stage coaches and committed burglary and theft in the United States."[15]

Houses of prostitution operated openly, there was a great deal of drunkenness, and crime ranged from petty theft to murder. One of the most pervasive crimes was gambling. The very nature of prospecting focused on risk. Miners from all over the world took a chance on reaching the gold fields, they gambled their savings on prospecting, and when they struck gold many gambled their earnings. The story is told of two old sourdoughs who wagered $10,000 on a spitting contest, the target being a crack in the wall. While much gaming was either legal or tolerated by authorities some of it was illegal, and there was a great deal of crookedness associated with the business. Saloons catered to the miners' penchant for gambling with poker, blackjack, roulette tables, and fargo banks. The games were frequently rigged so that the players would be cheated out of their bets. When things got out of hand the authorities would periodically close down the gambling halls but immediately illegal games appeared.[16]

Given the potential for lawbreaking, the authorities were able to exercise a remarkable control so that things never really got out of hand. Detectives were used to gather background information on potential troublemakers and police responded quickly to incidents. Not only in the Yukon but throughout the entire West the early presence of the police substantially reduced crime. Nevertheless, the Canadian West was never as tranquil or crime-free as legend would have it. On the other hand, lawlessness never reached the levels that it did in the American West, where there were often thousands on the wanted lists. Much of the credit for restricting the rate of crime goes to the type of people who settled the Canadian West and to the work of the North West Mounted Police. The latter, established in 1873, built a reputation for effective law enforcement and were present at a very early stage of western development.

Although much of western lawlessness centred on the fur trade, railroad building, the gold rush, and conflicts between Indians and whites, a high percentage of crime involved transients who plied their trade as long as the opportunity was there. But the transients moved on to greener fields when conditions changed. The majority of permanent settlers came to establish homes and communities. They were not looking for criminal opportunities but rather sought to create a better life for themselves by honest work. One writer described them as "frugal, hard-working, and honest to an unbelievable extreme."[17] The prairie settlements established by such people were relatively crime-free.

Back East, the population continued to increase, large centres like Toronto and Montreal were becoming more influential, and crime was keeping pace with development. In 1890, Ontario appointed a royal commission to examine the prison and reformatory system and its report, released in 1891, offers a comprehensive profile of the types of crime and levels of arrests throughout the province at that time. Statistics quoted for Toronto for 1889 listed the number of offenders at 9,898 males and 1,689 females. Of that total, 4,570 men and 871 women were charged with being drunk and disorderly, 767 males and 111 females were accused of burglary, seventy-nine were charged with housebreaking, forty-three with highway robbery, sixty-five with fraud, twenty-three with forgery, 252 with trespassing, 650 with assault, and 177 with other property offences. Eleven were charged with murder and six with manslaughter. There were 153 people charged with other offences against the person, 333 with vagrancy, and 2,621 with breaches of by-laws and other offences. Almost 47 per cent of all charges were for being drunk and disorderly and by far the largest percentage of those arrested were males, who accounted for 85.4 per cent of the total.[18]

Crime rates were much higher in the larger urban centres and it appears that the larger the centre the higher the level of crime. In contrast to Toronto, the number of charges made by police in London, Ontario, in 1889 totalled 1,767, of which 1,045, or 59 per cent, were for being drunk. Kingston, with a population of approximately 19,000, recorded 552 charges. Of those, 379 or 68.6 per cent were for drunkenness, five for disorderly conduct, fifty-six for larceny, seventeen for other property offences, thirty-five for vagrancy, and sixty-three for other offences.[19] The rough comparative ratios for the three cities were 64 charges per 1,000 of population for Toronto, 55 per 1,000 for London, and 29 per 1,000 for Kingston. The pattern was consistent across the country. For example, in 1879 there were 4,072 people incarcerated in the jails of Quebec, and of that number approximately 56.3 per cent came from the judicial district of Montreal.

Among offenders such as drunks that inflated criminal statistics in Ontario a class of people known as vagrants also contributed. There was a large population of unemployed, needy, and idle by choice, who frequented the jails of the province. The commissioners in their 1891 report noted that vagrants accounted for 17.2 per cent of all committals in 1889. They observed that "Toronto is the chief winter quarters of the army of tramps that infest this province." Many of these people committed petty crimes for the express purpose of obtaining temporary lodging in jail. In some communities without welfare institutions, the needy, infirm, and aged were put in jail primarily to be cared for. They were simply arrested on vagrancy charges.[20] Table 6 affords a profile of the types of crime and the number of charges recorded for the province of Ontario over the first two decades after Confederation.

The statistics show that the numbers of committals for various crimes fluctuated although the trend for total offences was steadily upward. However, the actual conviction figures were much lower. For example, out of 12,979 persons committed on charges in 1889 a much smaller number, 7,692, were convicted and sentenced. Also, many people escaped being charged because either they were not apprehended or lenient law officers decided to let them off. Consequently, neither charges nor conviction figures offer an accurate account of the incidence of crime, although they do establish a profile of the types of crime common to the period, ones most frequently committed, and the overall trend in the level of crime.

While most offences were of a minor nature there was still much serious lawbreaking, and there was also considerable violence, some of which went unreported. Possibly the most serious in the latter category was wife abuse. Given the high rate of liquor consumption and the fights, assaults, and mayhem frequently associated with drinking, it is very probable that wife abuse was common. Relatively few cases came before the courts but the ones that did were particularly brutal. For example, on the night of September 21, 1877, Annie Williams was beaten to death by her drunken husband. She was the mother of fifteen children, fourteen of whom were alive at the time of her death. The husband was a steady worker but a frequent drinker who became violent when he consumed liquor and during his drinking bouts his wife was the usual victim of his brutality. The final beating was so vicious that the woman's features were beyond recognition.[21]

Drunkenness and crimes related to liquor continued to account for a high

Table 6
Crime in Ontario, 1869-89

	No. of Prisoners Committed				
	1869	*1875*	*1880*	*1885*	*1889*
1. Crimes against the person					
Assault, common	485	666	623	672	534
Assault, felonious	46	68	85	169	197
Cutting and wounding, stabbing, and shooting with intent	31	73	63	46	138
Rape, and assault with intent	27	57	44	68	39
Murder	38	37	42	25	31
Manslaughter	16	12	7	12	18
Attempt at suicide	–	5	9	5	9
Miscellaneous	42	50	31	46	2
	685	968	904	1,043	968
2. Crimes against Property					
Arson and incendiarism	34	65	31	35	51
Burglary	26	54	93	51	76
Counterfeiting and passing counterfeit money	16	6	15	10	4
Destroying and injuring property	29	96	130	112	86
Embezzlement	10	14	23	32	17
Forgery	22	33	50	60	49
Fraud, and obtaining money or goods under false pretences	52	99	101	149	125
Horse, cattle, and sheep stealing	44	85	70	73	81
Housebreaking and robbery	68	26	103	146	164
Larceny	1,019	1,602	1,669	1,589	1,606
Receiving stolen goods	19	33	42	38	48
Trespass	25	72	123	222	329
Miscellaneous	43	58	73	97	–
	1,407	2,243	2,523	2,614	2,636

3. Crimes against Public Morals and Decency

Bigamy	9	9	5	13	16
Inmates and frequenters of houses of ill-fame	29	123	236	172	136
Keeping houses of ill-fame	56	49	134	85	103
Perjury	6	19	27	19	25
Seduction	11	2	–	2	19
Indecent assault and exposure	8	36	40	40	76
Miscellaneous	3	77	50	45	59
	122	315	492	376	434

4. Offences against Public Order and Peace

Abusive and obscene language	34	76	95	44	70
Breaches of peace, breaches of by-laws, escapes from and obstructing constables	79	99	109	117	163
Carrying unlawful weapons	4	8	34	29	29
Deserting employment	74	82	27	3	6
Drunk and disorderly	1,793	3,663	3,795	3,996	4,777
Selling liquor without licence, and selling or giving it to Indians	24	33	115	60	157
Threatening and solicitous language	75	35	48	47	40
Vagrancy	783	1,641	2,210	2,455	2,611
Miscellaneous	20	239	207	220	316
	2,886	5,876	6,640	6,971	8,169

5. Other Causes for Which Persons Were Detained as Prisoners

Contempt of court	50	77	180	120	134
Debtors	78	66	86	63	107
Detained as witnesses	22	17	18	18	49
Lunatics and persons dangerous to be at large	271	323	346	433	437
Non-payment of fines and costs	30	41	–	–	–
Want of sureties to keep the peace	104	137	111	88	45
	555	661	741	722	772
Total number of persons committed for the respective years	5,655	10,063	11,300	11,726	12,979

SOURCE: Report of the Commissioners Appointed to Enquire into the Prison and Reformatory System of the Province of Ontario, 1891, pp. 19-20.
Note: Totals here and in subsequent tables are as they appear in original source.

percentage of charges, as they had throughout the century. The Ontario Royal Commission Report of 1891 claimed that "Drunkenness does more than any other cause to fill the gaols, and it unquestionably does much to recruit the ranks of the criminal classes," and noted that nearly one-third of all convictions in the province in 1889 were for drunkenness.[22] The situation was similar across the country. In 1882 over 2,000 people were jailed in Winnipeg on drunk charges, with countless more simply left alone or helped home since the police policy was to arrest only those causing trouble. Taking the nation as a whole, out of 348,460 convictions reported during the period 1882-91 approximately 121,956 were for drunkenness. The problem continued unabated into the twentieth century.[23]

While the crime profiles established earlier continued in the post-Confederation period, certain of the modern developments that were changing Canadian life were also broadening the face of crime. The building of the railroads is a case in point. They occasioned a wide variety of criminal activity, including train robbery. Probably the first train robbery in Canada took place on November 13, 1874, when a five-member gang disguised in Ku Klux Klan robes robbed the express car of the Great Western Railway between Toronto and Port Credit. They made off with $45,000.[24]

Train robbery also gave Canada one of its most famous criminals. Bill Miner was an American who had already carved out a reputation in the States as a notorious bandit. He had made a career out of robbing stagecoaches and as a reward had spent nearly thirty-four years in jail. Miner was a colourful character with a gentle manner and since he was always polite and courteous to his victims, he became known as "the gentleman bandit." He drifted into Canada sometime in 1904 and took up residence in the Nicola Valley of British Columbia under the name of George Edwards. He was a moustachioed old man with the demeanour of a kindly grandfather. No one suspected that beneath that benign exterior was a spirited, cunning desperado right out of the pages of a Wild West novel.

Bill Miner did not take long to return to the trade he knew best. In September of 1904 he and two companions held up the Canadian Pacific Railway's Transcontinental Express. They commandeered the engine, stopped the train, uncoupled the passenger cars, and forced the crew into the express and baggage sections. Further on they stopped again and looted the cars of about $7,000 in cash and gold dust. They then had the remaining cars dropped from the engine, proceeded further down the line, and eventually jumped from the engine and disappeared into the woods. The trio were never caught.

Two years later on May 8, 1906, Miner and two accomplices again robbed the Transcontinental Express on the line a short distance from Kamloops, British Columbia. They repeated the same procedure used earlier. This time, however, they made a costly blunder by leaving one of the express cars with the passenger section. Their main target was a safe holding $35,000 in gold, which was in the express car they left behind. Afraid that the police might already have been alerted, they could not chance returning to the passenger cars. They settled for what they could find in the mail bags, which wasn't much. At that they missed a bag containing $40,000 in cash.

The second robbery sparked a major manhunt, encouraged by the CPR's offer of a reward of $5,000 for the capture of the robbers, dead or alive. A combined force of North West Mounted Police, railroad police, cowboys, Indian trackers, and bloodhounds went after the trio and eventually found them in the deep bush posing as prospectors. Miner was sentenced to prison for life but he chose not to serve his time. On August 8, 1907, he escaped from the New Westminster penitentiary by digging under a fence. This time Miner fled across the border, where he continued to indulge in his old habits. In 1912 he was arrested for robbing a train in Georgia, escaped custody, was recaptured, and eventually escaped again. But he was not up to the rigours of tramping through the wild Georgia swamp. He was exhausted and critically ill when captured. He died in the prison hospital in September, 1913.[25]

Aside from crimes associated with railroads and a number of others that will be dealt with in later chapters, the bulk of crime in the last quarter of the nineteenth century continued as in the past. Table 7 offers an overview of the more serious offences and general conviction levels that characterized the last decade of the century. The Act providing for the collection of criminal statistics on a national basis became operative in 1876. The statistics were divided into two categories, indictable offences, made up of the more serious crimes as listed in Table 7, and summary convictions, which include all minor offences.

As Table 7 shows, the levels of convictions varied for most indictable offences during the decade. All crimes taken together, however, showed an increasing conviction level, from a total of 3,733 in 1888 to 5,705 in 1899. In 1891 the rate of convictions for indictable offences per 100,000 of population was 82.2; at the end of the century the rate was 107.2. The upward numerical trend therefore appears to be an actual one even when the increase in population is taken into account. However, the rise in the number of convictions could be due to larger police forces and better detection methods. Summary convictions also fluctuated over the same period, going from 34,041 in 1888 to a low of 30,907 in 1894 and rising steadily to 32,997 by 1899.

Table 8 offers a breakdown of statistics by provinces while Table 9 outlines the background of the people convicted for indictable offences. The two provinces with the largest population, Ontario and Quebec, also recorded the highest number of both indictable and summary convictions. However, when the statistics are compared on the basis of the rate per

Table 7
Convictions for Indictable Offences, 1888-99

Offences	1888	1889	1890	1891	1892	1893	1894	1895	1896	1897	1898	1899
Abduction	4	–	4	3	2	7	4	3	5	7	5	2
Abortion and attempt	1	1	1	1	1	–	3	1	4	5	6	7
Arson	24	17	13	18	18	30	23	31	32	36	32	30
Assaults, aggravated	186	262	212	187	190	215	158	170	174	211	238	197
Assault and battery	160	165	159	160	138	152	199	175	158	217	214	282
Assault on peace officer	200	251	152	244	343	425	453	444	415	377	364	347
Assaults, indecent	36	35	41	39	49	43	46	48	52	44	55	50
Assault on females	30	30	33	44	46	38	43	54	54	73	38	52
Bigamy	11	8	12	11	11	14	20	11	8	15	11	11
Bringing stolen property into Canada	19	12	12	4	7	3	10	3	8	6	4	2
Burglary	51	85	77	70	44	67	80	86	85	135	93	63
Carnal knowledge (a girl of tender years or an imbecile)	4	9	10	6	6	8	10	16	11	17	8	7
Concealing birth	1	–	2	3	–	3	1	3	1	5	4	3
Conspiracy	15	–	2	–	1	11	3	4	3	5	4	3
Deserting child	7	4	1	4	2	3	1	2	4	2	7	2
Election Act, breaches of	–	–	–	3	1	–	6	8	4	6	3	–
Embezzlement	30	41	38	39	30	43	16	7	7	10	4	9
Endangering safety of passengers on railways	9	6	8	5	12	9	11	18	25	36	14	15
False pretences and fraud	82	93	121	90	114	110	180	207	54	196	181	142
Feloniously receiving	59	51	29	70	44	58	78	77	58	116	88	127
Forcible entry	–	–	4	–	3	–	3	3	3	5	10	5
Forgery, etc.	45	41	46	36	42	46	37	61	87	82	85	108
Gambling acts, breaches of	5	6	27	–	7	3	19	44	29	76	42	49

Table 7 (continued)

Horse, etc. stealing	36	41	33	47	48	52	37	66	79	47	64	45
House, shop, warehouse breaking	127	147	157	159	173	232	310	323	248	287	398	331
Incest, rape, and attempt at	8	13	16	18	10	17	14	15	17	17	17	19
Indecent exposure	1	5	1	12	27	20	26	33	39	39	33	32
Larceny	2,017	2,328	2,139	2,214	2,184	2,499	2,898	3,040	2,934	3,115	3,259	3,294
from dwelling	9	24	8	9	8	4	14	18	8	9	5	7
from person	24	46	44	25	28	33	37	53	58	52	43	43
Libel	10	1	1	1	2	5	5	-	2	1	-	1
Malicious injury to horses, etc.	49	24	47	33	32	38	33	26	44	38	58	47
Manslaughter	12	19	20	10	7	16	19	6	7	11	18	13
Murder	9	8	8	7	5	6	11	5	6	11	13	13
Attempted murder	3	5	-	2	2	4	3	2	-	3	6	2
Perjury	8	4	10	4	10	10	11	19	16	17	24	20
Prison, breach, escape, etc.	18	35	14	17	26	44	33	67	54	53	55	33
Refusing to support family	27	36	70	53	62	67	39	28	29	24	31	40
Revenue laws, breaches of	4	8	2	1	9	14	7	4	11	15	31	22
Robbery	47	51	42	54	34	63	60	53	75	53	49	50
Seduction	-	-	5	5	4	7	4	6	3	12	5	3
Shooting, wounding	68	110	94	78	98	69	89	60	86	92	76	92
Sodomy and bestiality	5	5	5	3	5	4	5	10	7	1	9	10
Stealing, letters, etc.	6	10	7	4	9	3	14	7	7	7	11	4
Suicide, attempt at	10	31	5	6	4	8	15	7	10	26	14	23
Various offences against the person	31	29	40	24	37	31	25	41	47	31	23	23
Various other misdemeanours	203	92	162	131	104	101	126	105	19	55	17	22
Various offences against property without violence	22	9	14	8	1	-	-	-	-	-	-	26
Totals	3,733	4,198	3,948	3,962	4,040	4,630	5,239	5,470	5,087	5,691	5,769	5,705

SOURCE: *Statistical Yearbook of Canada*, 1899.

Table 8

Indictable and Summary Offence Convictions by Province, 1888-99

Provinces	1888	1889	1890	1891	1892	1893	1894	1895	1896	1897	1898	1899
Ontario	2,144	2,318	2,123	2,046	2,064	2,315	2,682	2,829	2,783	2,855	2,900	2,693
Quebec	1,201	1,361	1,220	1,356	1,338	1,374	1,653	1,615	1,420	1,737	1,603	1,779
N.S.	80	131	126	124	150	199	182	239	279	255	240	250
N.B.	71	80	79	96	93	121	109	119	116	95	104	125
Manitoba	67	93	91	93	82	168	186	160	181	245	200	224
B.C.	122	146	183	145	187	294	236	317	247	322	513	370
P.E.I.	13	22	20	29	31	24	39	39	34	42	37	16
Territories	49	57	92	75	85	135	171	156	144	170	156	173
Yukon	–	–	–	–	–	–	–	–	–	–	34	83
Total	3,747	4,208	3,934	3,964	4,030	4,630	5,258	5,474	5,204	5,721	5,787	5,713

Summary Convictions

Provinces	1888	1889	1890	1891	1892	1893	1894	1895	1896	1897	1898	1899
Ontario	20,873	20,209	19,178	17,343	15,017	15,047	14,033	13,852	14,109	14,151	13,911	14,091
Quebec	7,989	8,160	9,081	9,387	9,155	8,388	9,194	9,734	9,317	8,871	8,423	8,496
N.S.	1,123	1,242	1,353	1,354	1,469	1,755	2,266	2,938	3,042	2,421	2,440	2,009
N.B.	2,001	2,166	2,518	2,444	2,174	2,302	2,096	2,111	2,181	2,179	2,250	2,136
Manitoba	681	1,022	902	904	1,146	1,132	990	1,025	1,148	1,232	1,128	1,265
B.C.	667	736	898	1,215	1,134	1,450	1,201	1,244	1,115	1,477	1,960	1,992
P.E.I.	456	513	457	526	545	335	422	335	271	519	423	436
Territories	102	175	219	278	327	614	705	872	891	1407	1,428	1,060
Yukon	–	–	–	–	–	–	–	–	–	–	1,456	1,512
Total	33,892	34,223	34,606	33,451	30,967	31,023	30,907	32,111	32,074	32,257	32,419	32,997
Grand Total	37,639	38,431	38,540	37,415	34,997	35,653	36,165	37,585	37,278	37,978	38,206	38,710

SOURCE: *Statistical Yearbook of Canada, 1899*.

100,000 of population a different picture emerges. In 1899, for example, the rate for British Columbia, at approximately 207, was the highest for all the provinces. The rate for the Northwest Territories was even higher, at about 859. The rate per 100,000 of population for summary convictions was, again, highest in British Columbia, at approximately 1,114, with New Brunswick next at 641. In this category of offence both the Yukon, at 5,554, and the Northwest Territories, with a rate of 5,266, were well ahead of the rest of the country.

Table 9 shows that males were convicted for indictable offences in numbers far exceeding convictions of females, and of all offenders single males were the major perpetrators of crime. The bulk of people convicted fell into the 21-40 age category. As had been the case for so long, liquor continued to be a significant factor. A high percentage of those convicted each year were identified as immoderate drinkers. Another continuing trend was that the great majority of offenders came from cities and towns. In 1888 only 17.8 per cent were identified as coming from rural areas. The percentage shifted little over the next few years, with about 19.2 per cent coming from rural districts in 1899.

PUBLIC VIOLENCE

As has already been noted, statistics offer a very incomplete picture of crime. Certain kinds of offences, such as public violence, do not show up in crime statistics although related individual offences sometimes do. The nature of demonstrations, riots, and strikes is such that a good deal of lawbreaking is frequently generated, but authorities cannot always apprehend all or any of those responsible. The most common occasions for such activities in an earlier day were election campaigns. In 1874 a new Election Act provided for the secret ballot and voting on a designated day for the entire country. The Act substantially reduced the more violent aspects of the democratic process. However, there were still many incidents of brawling and intimidation – other forms of public violence continued and new ones appeared.

Railroad building, along with being the focal point of much individual lawlessness, also on occasion witnessed outbreaks of group violence. Illustrative was an incident in Manitoba in 1887. Construction crews of two rival railways, the CPR and a provincial government line linking Winnipeg and St. Paul, Minnesota, clashed over a disputed right-of-way. The confrontation sparked a general mêlée during which the two work crews proceeded to rip up each others' tracks.[26]

Labour unrest was yet another occasion for group violence. Between 1876 and 1914 troops were called more than thirty times to intervene in strikes. Between 1918 and 1928 there were approximately 3,126 strikes and lockouts. Industrialization brought with it a dramatic increase in the ranks

Table 9

Background of Persons Convicted of Indictable Offences, 1888-99

	1888	1889	1890	1891	1892	1893	1894	1895	1896	1897	1898	1899
Number of charges	5,871	6,319	5,831	5,993	5,930	6,766	7,601	7,730	7,395	8,027	8,153	8,170
Acquittals	2,081	2,067	1,847	1,952	1,838	2,053	2,282	2,154	2,065	2,172	2,247	2,355
Persons detained for lunacy	12	9	10	10	9	9	14	20	13	13	29	11
Convictions	3,751	4,213	3,946	3,974	4,040	4,630	5,258	5,474	5,204	5,721	5,787	5,713
Males	3,366	3,883	3,626	3,692	3,751	4,287	4,881	5,074	4,855	5,356	5,441	5,384
Females	335	330	320	282	289	343	377	400	349	365	346	329
Convicted 1st	3,270	3,678	3,543	3,532	3,606	3,828	4,517	4,412	4,192	4,528	4,568	4,529
Convicted 2nd	304	363	205	235	233	465	365	615	537	648	679	590
Reiterated	177	171	198	207	201	337	376	447	475	545	540	594
Occupations												
Agricultural	154	198	163	202	197	203	224	247	221	241	322	215
Commercial	341	420	367	412	389	455	593	585	532	611	654	707
Domestic	283	221	212	160	177	227	241	186	180	191	197	208
Industrial	462	553	610	634	644	674	791	672	684	793	756	686
Professional	72	85	72	52	37	53	48	49	31	60	47	46
Labourers	1,451	1,625	1,501	1,538	1,529	1,702	1,901	2,165	2,111	2,217	2,189	2,213

Table 9 (continued)

Civil Conditions												
Married	940	1,023	1,009	1,083	1,080	1,177	1,269	1,337	1,214	1,385	1,360	1,250
Widowed	77	62	91	111	115	115	141	120	127	112	110	160
Single	2,560	2,923	2,645	2,639	2,722	2,934	3,404	3,308	3,360	3,655	3,780	3,800
Educational Status												
Unable to read or write	555	628	627	919	820	873	793	769	729	839	827	711
Elementary	2,884	3,192	3,028	2,752	2,996	3,295	3,925	3,891	3,817	4,180	4,316	4,348
Superior	37	34	25	77	91	90	110	90	81	102	103	132
Ages												
Under 16	602	687	594	615	714	668	687	790	660	723	836	936
16-20	695	775	729	699	656	768	1,002	906	889	936	1,022	981
21-39	1,732	2,028	1,854	1,888	1,925	2,169	2,361	2,276	2,364	2,661	2,549	2,544
40 and over	513	498	520	545	530	658	670	724	663	715	744	716
Not given	209	225	249	227	215	367	538	778	628	686	636	536
Use of liquor												
Moderate	1,728	1,832	1,595	2,008	2,158	2,521	2,857	2,926	2,783	3,084	3,309	3,196
Immoderate	1,444	1,723	1,691	1,706	1,740	1,738	1,994	1,820	1,847	2,032	1,918	1,914

Table 9 (continued)

Birthplaces												
England and Wales	364	345	394	335	292	373	447	401	412	382	393	354
Ireland	294	276	263	249	240	265	259	226	201	233	246	169
Scotland	86	86	73	73	92	82	107	113	77	91	88	92
Canada	2,553	2,969	2,681	2,837	2,963	3,153	3,514	3,576	3,580	3,949	3,990	4,142
United States	211	240	230	202	195	238	269	263	254	246	272	222
Other foreign countries	114	116	128	126	118	163	206	172	151	223	200	232
Other British possessions	8	6	8	11	11	12	9	18	8	10	22	17
Religions												
Baptists	110	94	100	87	104	129	151	170	151	129	163	174
R. Catholics	1,807	2,062	1,896	1,952	1,969	2,044	2,282	2,172	2,174	2,374	2,405	2,428
Ch. of England	637	700	638	651	739	808	917	905	909	980	931	984
Methodists	377	434	419	417	393	467	468	550	497	528	569	566
Presbyterians	291	280	270	269	289	324	376	466	398	366	434	429
Protestants	209	292	235	292	267	287	328	296	321	395	607	533
Other denominations	156	117	98	146	149	213	261	194	163	316	114	121
Residence												
Cities and towns	3,087	3,444	3,175	3,081	3,199	3,499	3,986	3,902	3,769	4,090	4,067	4,238
Rural districts	589	747	717	807	736	846	864	1,009	974	1,138	1,216	1,010

Not including the "Not given"
SOURCE: *Statistical Yearbook of Canada*, 1899.

of wage labourers. There was a good deal of exploitation on the part of factory operators and the owners of businesses. To win decent wages, humane hours, and safer working conditions, many labourers turned to the emerging unions. Employers vehemently opposed the unions, so when strikes occurred considerable bitterness and animosity arose on both sides. Labour unrest and strikes were often accompanied by vandalism, destruction of property, beatings, and even murder.[27]

During a strike by sawmill workers in Buckingham, Quebec, in 1906 the strikers clashed violently with a group of strikebreakers accompanied by police and company guards. There were serious injuries on both sides and two strikers and a detective were killed. In 1918 police and firemen in Montreal went out on strike over wages and other issues. With the police restraint gone, extensive looting ensued and many incidents of violence were reported.[28] During a 1925 strike by Cape Breton coal miners a picketer was killed in a conflict with company guards, company stores were looted, buildings were destroyed, and two mines were flooded. The looted goods were valued at about $300,000 and the value of the destroyed buildings estimated at $200,000.[29]

The basis for so much industrial bitterness and so many confrontations is readily evident from the situation that existed at the Dominion Iron and Steel plant in Sydney, Nova Scotia. The plant employed a work force of about 3,800 people and operated on two shifts. The day shift worked eleven hours a day, seven days a week. The night shift worked thirteen hours, seven days a week. Once every fortnight, when the shifts changed over, the employees worked twenty-four hours in a row. The pay averaged forty-one cents per hour. Starting in 1917 attempts were made to unionize but the company put up strong resistance. Ongoing unrest continued over working hours, pay, and union recognition, which resulted in a four-day strike in February of 1923. Another strike was called on June 28, by which time about one-quarter of the work force had joined the union. The strike was marked by assaults, intimidation, destruction of property, and a riot. Police and militia were called out, 246 soldiers were sent from Halifax, and the provincial police sent a detachment. Six rioters were ultimately sentenced to two years in the penitentiary and five others were jailed. The strike finally ended on August 2.[30]

One of the most publicized labour-management conflicts in the first quarter of the twentieth century was the Winnipeg General Strike of 1919. A legacy of pre-war industrial strife, trade union growth and militancy, stiff management opposition to unionization and labour's demands, the work of foreign agitators, fear of Bolshevism, and uncertainty over post-war employment all combined to create a volatile situation. On May 15 a general strike went into effect for higher wages and union recognition in the building and metals trade. Some 35,000 labourers joined the building and metals trade unions already on strike. There were widespread sympathy walkouts across the country and on May 17 an estimated 10,000 returned soldiers paraded in Winnipeg in support of the strike. Even the city police publicly sided with the strikers and all but fifteen were fired, including the chief. In their place the city hired about 2,000 specials to patrol the streets. On June 10 they clashed with a group of protesters but the crowd dispersed. The arrest of twelve strike leaders on June 17 further heightened tensions but a few days later, on Saturday June 21, they were released on bail. Crowds milled around city hall and a riot erupted. A streetcar was overturned and the police clashed with the crowd, shooting one person dead and injuring some thirty others. On Monday soldiers and special contingents from the Royal North West Mounted Police were brought in and another demonstrator lost his life. On June 25 the strike was declared at an end.[31]

Many other incidents of violence were associated with ongoing religious and racial animosities and other circumstances, such as World War One. During the war a number of incidents in the province of Quebec were related to recruiting and, late in the war, to conscription. One of the more serious outbreaks occurred in August of 1917 when a protest rally of some 7,000 people in Montreal resulted in injuries to four policemen and one man being shot. About the same time a plot to dynamite the home of a pro-conscription newspaper publisher and to assassinate Prime Minister Borden was uncovered. At Easter of 1918 another anti-conscription riot, this time at Quebec City, resulted in the death of four protesters and an estimated seventy injured.[32]

The Orange Protestant-Catholic Irish conflicts so common in pre-Confederation days continued well after the union. In one fifteen-year period between 1867 and 1882 there were about twenty-two incidents between the two groups in the city of Toronto alone. Between 1876 and 1914 there were at least five occasions when troops had to be called out to quell riots involving Irish Catholics and Orange Protestants. While the so-called Orange-Green prejudice was based mainly on religious considerations, there was also growing prejudice and discrimination across the country based on colour, race, and nationality. The influx of immigrants generated strong anti-alien sentiments among many native Canadians, with much of the animosity directed against non-whites and non-Anglo-Saxons. Many, including government leaders, openly proclaimed that this was a white man's country and that they intended to keep it so. In the process there were many confrontations that resulted in immigrants being beaten and their property destroyed.[33] One of the most serious incidents took place in British Columbia in 1907.

The first significant numbers of Chinese to come to Canada arrived in the 1850s. By 1860 about 2,000 were working in the gold fields of British Columbia. Between 1881 and 1884 over 9,000 came to help build the CPR. In 1901 there were about 16,792 Chinese in Canada with over 14,000 of them living in British Columbia. Meanwhile, significant numbers of Japanese began migrating to Canada in the mid-1890s and by the turn of the century they numbered about 12,000. Between 1906 and 1908 over 11,000 Japanese entered Canada. Like the Chinese, most of them settled in British Columbia. Many worked in the canneries and as fishermen.

The influx of Asians in a relatively short period, their concentration in one province, and their distinctness raised fears on the part of native whites that B.C. would lose its British cultural identity. Both the Chinese and Japanese accepted work at wages below Canadian standards, thus raising the ire of organized labour and fears that they would take jobs from native Canadians. Their religion, their dress, their language, and their lifestyle provoked accusations that they were unassimilable, a matter of great concern before the days of multiculturalism. Using one excuse or another, many Canadians subjected Asians to the most degrading and humiliating treatment. Gangs sometimes physically attacked them and destroyed their property. Sentiment was so strong that a number of organizations appeared whose sole purpose was to close the door to Asian immigration and force those who were here to return to their homelands.

Serious anti-Chinese agitation began in British Columbia as early as the 1870s. The intensity of the opposition fluctuated with economic conditions and the pace of immigration over the next two decades but never completely subsided. The continued immigration of Chinese and Japanese fuelled the fires of prejudice and sparked sporadic outbreaks of violence. In early August of 1892 a mob of about 300 ransacked a number of Chinese laundries in Calgary. In the summer of 1907 the Asiatic Exclusion League was formed in Vancouver at a meeting attended by about 400 people. It immediately assumed the leadership in the anti-Asian campaign. On September 8 the League organized a parade and rally. A large crowd turned out, including community leaders and labour agitators from the United States. Inflammatory speeches aroused the crowd to fever pitch, turning it into an unruly mob. They invaded the Chinese quarters and after considerable destruction of property and beatings they then proceeded to the Japanese sector. Again, beatings and property damage ensued until the Japanese turned on their tormentors with sticks, bottles, and knives and forced them to retreat. The incident attracted international attention and British Columbians were generally denounced for their prejudiced attitudes and violence.[34]

CHANGING SOCIETAL VALUES

While such things as racial and religious attitudes and political convictions were the focal point for certain crimes, other less tangible attitudes can also contribute to lawlessness. For example, the atmosphere created in a country by the state of its general ethics and values can have an influence on crime. This was a belief widely held in Canada in an earlier day, when the level of crime was considered to be a measure of the state of the community's morality. Belief in a relationship between values and crime was sidelined for much of the century for environmental explanations. In recent years, however, many people are once again suggesting that the level of crime in our society is due, at least in part, to a crisis in ethics and values. Since a distinct change in values took place in the first three decades of this century, it is appropriate to examine the nature of that evolution along with the levels and type of crime that characterized the period.

The new century witnessed a liberalizing trend that was destined to culminate in a full-scale cultural revolution in the 1960s and 1970s. One of the first signs was the changing ideas on sex. During much of the nineteenth century it was widely held that repressed sexuality was the key to creating high moral values and, as a consequence, social stability. Moralists and purity crusaders, through an outpouring of literature, taught that sex was detrimental to health and that women were naturally frigid. Sex was portrayed as a primitive human tendency suited more to the lower species of animals than to an enlightened, advanced society. Young people were warned to avoid dangerous pastimes such as dancing and the theatre.[35]

By the beginning of the twentieth century the repression of human sexuality was being undermined by a theory of sex for pleasure. The notion was spreading that sex for reasons other than procreation was quite proper and that it could be pleasurable for both parties. Sex was being discussed more openly and novels were treating the subject with increased frankness. Another sign of changing ideas on sexual morality was the declining birth rate. More and more couples were practising birth control. The annual number of births per 1,000 women aged fifteen to forty-nine dropped from 160 in 1881 to 145 in 1901, and to 120 by 1921.

The challenge to conservative values picked up momentum with the outbreak of World War One. Young men and women were uprooted from all parts of the country. They were exposed to service life and many served overseas. In the process they also had the opportunity to escape the vigilance of parents, spouses, relatives, and neighbours. Freedom from such restraints, travel, and exposure to a more liberal and sometimes decadent old world all had their influence. As a popular song of the time expressed it – "How Ya Gonna Keep Them Down on the Farm After They've Seen Paree?" The war had a liberalizing effect on morals and values. Critics complained that the war contributed to a lessening of respect for law, order, and property. The relatively high wages made in the war industries both raised aspirations and contributed to a more extravagant lifestyle. Stories of huge profits being made by unscrupulous contractors contributed to a less sympathetic acceptance of existing codes of propriety. When the system allowed some to make exorbitant gains out of a national war effort it tended to reduce respect for all standards.

Another strong liberalizing influence was the influx of women into the work force. The industrial development of the late nineteenth century opened opportunities in textile mills, business, factories, and domestic service. By 1896 women accounted for 20 per cent of the paid work force and their rate of participation continued to rise, reaching 25 per cent by 1931. The war gave a significant impetus to this trend. Women, especially the young and single, flocked to the large towns and cities. By 1921 there were approximately 58,000 more women than men in Canadian cities. A large number were in the fifteen to twenty-nine age group. Many had come from farms, small towns, and villages, and not a few were immigrants. Life in the workplace and in the city was quite different from the restrictions of the small community and the protection of the family circle. It was a faster pace, with more independence, freedom, and anonymity. The very nature of city life encouraged less restrictive standards of conduct.[36]

If the first two decades of the twentieth century offered a challenge to conventional standards, the 1920s constituted an all-out assault. A number of factors merged to unloose a radical new spirit that defied tradition. Old manners, morals, and customs were challenged as the forces of modernism attacked on all sides. The aftermath of the war left a more liberal spirit abroad. The wartime ethic of "eat, drink, and be merry for tomorrow we may die" carried into the 1920s. As well, the uprooting and restlessness of the war years continued to influence life in the twenties. Also, the decade witnessed a prolonged period of economic prosperity that promoted a certain materialism and preoccupation with the good life that was not conducive to puritanical standards.

A major permissive influence also came from the United States. Movies, jazz music, prohibition, and the automobile all combined to create the "roaring twenties." The associated lifestyle was libertine by the standards of those days, and that lifestyle and its values had a significant influence on this country as well. The two chief conduits of American values were the movies and popular magazines. The movie craze hit Canada in much the same way as it did south of the border. The movies shown in the nation's theatres were imported almost exclusively from the United States. American magazines similarly dominated the Canadian market. Statistics for 1926 show a circulation of 152,011 for *The Ladies' Home Journal*, 128,574 for *Saturday Evening Post*, 128,320 for *The Political Review*, and 103,209 for *McCall's*. By comparison, *Maclean's* had a circulation by the end of 1925 of 82,103, *Canadian Home Journal*, 68,013, *Saturday Night*, 30,858, and *Canadian Magazine*, 12,604.[37]

Consequently, it was not surprising to find Canadians emulating their American cousins. Anyone not quite sure of what to do could turn to the movies and popular magazines for guidance. Jazz, with wailing saxophones, provided the background for racy new dances. Movies glamorized the liberated lifestyle, afforded a look at the new fashions, and their themes flouted conventional morality. A new generation of publications in the form of romance magazines flooded the newsstands with risqué stories of illicit love.

Life generally became more relaxed. The automobile afforded the opportunity for greater travel and more interesting vacations. By 1925 there were 639,695 automobiles registered in Canada, or one automobile for every 9.3 adults aged sixteen and over. Sports came into their own, becoming the pastime of hundreds of thousands of people who watched, participated, or followed the fortunes of their favourite hockey and baseball teams. Laboursaving devices such as electric irons, sewing machines, toasters, and automatic washing machines gave women more leisure time. Fast food outlets and bakeries added to the trend. People were becoming more preoccupied with the "good life" in a materialistic sense and much less in a spiritual sense.

While traditional values and morals were substantially challenged in the 1920s, this challenge represented only the first battle in a long war. Conservatives mounted a massive counterattack – the new dances, styles of dress, and liberated behaviour were condemned from the pulpits, by womens' organizations, and by certain magazines and newspapers. The modernist trends were checked but not halted, however. Nevertheless, for most people the conventional standards still guided their behaviour.[38]

The liberalization that did take place was manifested in a variety of ways, and one of the spin-offs was in the area of criminal activity. The breakdown of values in certain quarters seemed to create a more tolerant attitude toward what was previously considered anti-social or illegal behaviour. There was less respect for authority, and consequently for the law, and there was more of a tendency to experiment, to challenge restraints on human behaviour. The new materialism and the relaxed standards created a value system that, for many, made the means of obtaining wealth or experiencing pleasure less important. For some, instant gratification took precedence over moral scruples and laws. There were many signs of these tendencies, not the least of which was the growth in drug abuse in the 1920s. Although drug convictions actually dropped during the decade, from a high of 800 in 1922 to a low of 161 in 1928, the statistics do not reflect the reality. Other indices, such as interception of drug shipments, drug-related deaths, drug-related crime, and official and public perceptions, indicate that people violated the drug laws in much larger numbers than conviction statistics suggest.

Concern over drug usage grew in the latter decades of the nineteenth century, especially on the west coast, because of widespread opium use among the Chinese. Opium dens were common in Chinese communities, and by the early part of the twentieth century a number of Chinese merchants had grown rich on the drug trade. The use of opium was one of the many factors that generated the anti-Chinese sentiment in British Columbia. The magnitude of the drug trade was revealed as a result of the inquiry that followed the anti-Asian riots of 1907. Ottawa sent the deputy minister of labour, William Lyon Mackenzie King, to investigate the claims for compensation for damages resulting from the riots. His attention was drawn to the drug traffic because of claims made by a number of opium merchants for compensation. King's investigation revealed that at least seven opium manufacturing plants were operating in B.C. They were supplying markets in Canada, the United States, and China. Gross receipts for the year 1907 were estimated at $600,000 to $650,000. He also discovered that there was substantial opposition to the traffic. The Chinese in British Columbia were forming anti-opium leagues and one group petitioned King for help from the Canadian government with their efforts to suppress the use of the drug. Tung Cheng-Ling, the attaché of the Chinese legation in London, England, came to Canada to observe King's inquiry. He, too, told King that he would like to see the government take measures to suppress the opium traffic.[39]

In response to these petitions King recommended in his report that the government take immediate action. He also documented the fact that there was a world-wide movement under way to stamp out the opium trade and that Canada should do its part. King's report resulted in Parliament passing the Opium Act in 1908, which prohibited the importation, manufacture, and sale of the drug except for medical use. As the world-wide momentum of the campaign picked up, Canada progressively strengthened its legislation. A more stringent Opium and Drug Act was passed in 1911 and further amended in 1920.

The prohibitory legislation had little impact on the drug trade and the problem became increasingly serious throughout the 1920s. Vancouver and Montreal were the chief distribution centres, with organized gangs of drug dealers operating in both cities. Drugs were being smuggled into Canada in a variety of ways. In some cases they were dropped overboard in rubber bags from ships coming into Canadian ports, to be fished out of the water later by the dealers. They were also coming across the border concealed in various places in automobiles, including inside the spare tires. Customs officials and police were being bribed to turn a blind eye to the illicit traffic. The trade was said to be controlled by rings in New York, Chicago, and San Francisco with international connections and distributors all across Canada. In 1920 Lt. Col. G.C. Sanders, magistrate of the Men's Police Court in Calgary, claimed that drug use was "increasing to an alarming extent and today, it is a menace to the country."[40]

In 1921 there were 858 drug convictions in Vancouver, up from 293 in 1918. In January, 1923, a large opium shipment valued at $65,000 was discovered on a freighter docked in Vancouver; later that same year a ship on its way to Canada was seized with an estimated $500,000 worth of narcotics on board. Police claimed that drug use contributed significantly to crime in British Columbia and in 1921 city officials in Vancouver petitioned 100 cities and towns across the country to join them in requesting the federal government to provide stiffer penalties for drug infractions.

People in all walks of life were caught up in the drug trade. In one twelve-month period ending in March, 1922, a total of twenty-three doctors, eleven druggists, and four veterinarians were prosecuted for violations of the Drug Act. The coroner's office in Montreal revealed that in one year twenty-nine people in that city died from narcotic poisoning. Dr. H.S. Beland, Minister of Health, estimated that in 1923 there were 9,500 known addicts across Canada. About 2,250 of them lived in British Columbia and about 3,800 in Quebec. In January of 1923 the Anti-Narcotic Educational League of Canada was formed in Montreal. Its objects were drug education, co-operation with the police, establishment of a legal department, and care for addicts. The deputy minister of health described the drug situation as one of the most serious problems facing his department.[41]

Drug use, while a crime in itself, was also a contributing factor to other crimes. Many users turned to theft, prostitution, and other offences to make money to feed their habit. A significant number of criminals sentenced to jail and prison were discovered to be on drugs, although that was not the offence for which they were convicted. In a brief submitted to the Royal Commission to Investigate the Penal System of Canada, the Attorney-General of Manitoba claimed that the usual charge for which drug users were incarcerated was vagrancy.

At every turn during the 1920s, crime of one kind or another seemed to be on the increase. Even hitherto quiet western communities were hit by what local citizens described as a "crime wave." At one level were revelations of wholesale wrongdoing by brokers on the Grain Exchange and at another level was a spate of robberies. On January 17, 1922, the Provincial Savings Bank in Winnipeg was robbed of $5,200 and on August 29, the Union Bank at Lethbridge was hit by a gang of six men who made their getaway in an automobile with a haul of $82,000. Banks in Moosomin and Saskatoon were also robbed in 1922. In Vancouver on September 28 three men accosted the city paymaster on the steps of city hall and robbed him of $76,304. On October 26 a man, armed with a gun, stole $3,000 from a store in Galilee, Saskatchewan.[42]

On occasion there were some comical and blundered aspects to crime on the Prairies. In August of 1921 five men from Winnipeg decided to rob a bank in Elie, Manitoba. They set out in a taxi and proceeded to discuss their project in front of the driver, whom they eventually tied up and left in a ditch. They finally arrived in Elie after losing their way and taking several wrong roads. In the meantime the taxi driver had freed himself and hopped a train to the next town where, instead of calling the bank in Elie, he contacted the police in Winnipeg. While the gang was robbing the bank of $1,000 the police in Winnipeg were organizing a posse to go after them. The police and the bank robbers finally met up a short distance outside Winnipeg where the criminals were sitting in the stolen taxi, which had broken down.[43]

Eastern communities were also alarmed by dramatic increases in certain types of crime. Car thefts in Toronto were averaging over 1,000 per year and in Montreal about 500. Gambling was another crime that seemed to take off during the 1920s and continued to rise well into the next decade. According to criminal statistics, 458 charges were recorded for offences against the Gambling and Lottery Acts in 1922. The number rose steadily to 1,524 in 1928, to 2,200 in 1931, and to 2,308 in 1932. Since gambling is a type of activity that is easily hidden from the police, it is probable that the statistics tell only part of the story. Indeed, gambling was seen as so pervasive that calls were heard to legalize such forms as lotteries in order to enable the government to exercise a better measure of control. The Union of Municipalities of British Columbia, for example, asked for a provincial plebiscite on the issue. One senator claimed that gambling laws were openly broken by a majority of citizens.[44]

Another illegal activity that blossomed during the 1920s was bootlegging. Victories won by temperance and prohibition advocates created the opportunity for the expansion of the illegal liquor trade. As we have seen, the heavy consumption of liquor was a long-standing problem in Canadian society and alcohol abuse was a contributing factor to a range of social problems, including unemployment, work injuries, and crime. Mr. Justice T.G. Mather of Manitoba, for example, claimed in 1918 that "a very large proportion of the criminal cases that came before the courts were for the affliction of personal injury, such as wounding, stabbing and murder, committed during a drunken brawl or while under the influence of intoxicating liquor."[45] Many social reformers called for legal restrictions and the support for temperance organizations grew steadily. A major victory was won in 1878 when the federal government was persuaded to pass the Canada Temperance Act. It provided for local option by a simple majority vote in any city or county. The results were spotty and it wasn't until the First World War period that restrictions were put in place on a national level. Using grain for liquor and encouraging alcohol consumption during wartime appeared unseemly. Temperance advocates pressed the point and during 1916 and 1917 all provinces, except Quebec, banned the sale of alcoholic beverages, except for medicinal and scientific uses. In 1919 Quebec joined the other provinces in prohibiting the liquor trade.

Prohibition opened up a vast market for bootleggers. Although there was strong support for temperance all over the country, when the crunch came even activists were unwilling to obey the law. The restrictions did not last long in some provinces, but when they were lifted the sale of liquor was placed under government control. In 1921 Quebec, British Columbia, and the Yukon Territory ended prohibition and the governments entered the liquor business. Manitoba followed in 1923, Alberta in 1924, Saskatchewan in 1925, Ontario and New Brunswick in 1927, Nova Scotia in 1930, and Prince Edward Island not until 1948. Meanwhile, hardly a town in Canada did not have an ample supply of bootleggers and even when prohibition ended from place to place illegal sales continued. The hours of government stores were restricted so many illicit outlets thrived after hours. Also, many sold homemade or smuggled liquor and were able to sell at prices below what the government charged. In some cases the booze joints catered to a variety of needs and provided prostitutes and gambling for their customers.

Table 10 offers an overview of charges and convictions for indictable offences during the 1920s. It also illustrates the trend and the types of crimes common during the decade. The statistics start with 1922 because in that year juvenile offences were listed in a separate category. Most classes of offences show a steady rise in numerical terms although as a percentage of all charges and convictions there was little change in individual offences. Gambling rose from .024 per cent of all convictions in 1922 to .049 per cent by 1930, to some extent confirming the many observations that gambling was a growing problem. Theft continued to constitute the largest number of crimes throughout the decade. In 1922 theft accounted for 37.7 per cent of all convictions for indictable crimes and in 1930 for 37 per cent. Two categories of offences that saw a substantial rise in the number of convictions were offences against property with violence and offences against property without violence. The number of convictions for the former rose by 86.94 per cent between 1922 and 1930. The rate of convictions per 100,000 of population rose from 22.16 to 36.20. For property crimes without violence the conviction rate went up by 94.30 per cent, while the rate per 100,000 went from 85.18 to 144.65.

THE GREAT DEPRESSION AND CRIME

The stock market crash of 1929 ushered in a world-wide depression. In Canada as elsewhere, businesses collapsed and there was large-scale unemployment and social distress throughout the 1930s. Between 1929 and 1933 Canada's foreign trade dropped 67 per cent. The employment index, taking 1926 as the base year at 100, dropped from 119 in 1929 to 83.4 in 1933, the worst point of the depression. An estimated 750,000 people were out of work that year, amounting to almost 20 per cent of the labour force, and 65.8 per cent of workers in the construction industry were unemployed. While the situation gradually improved, recovery was spotty and sporadic. For example, in March, 1937, Manitoba, with a population of 711,216, had 115,155 individuals on the relief lists.

Widespread discontent and suffering led to an increase in crime and periodic clashes between unemployed demonstrators and the authorities. One of the worst incidents was the Regina riot on Dominion Day in 1935. In May a strike by workers in the relief camps in British Columbia took place.

Table 10
Indictable Offences by Class, 1922-30

	1922		1926		1930	
	Charges	Convictions	Charges	Convictions	Charges	Convictions
Class I – Offences against the Person						
Murder	56	19	51	15	54	17
Murder, attempt to commit	41	20	13	7	28	12
Manslaughter	88	45	78	45	130	51
Abortion and concealing birth of infants	39	25	23	19	42	29
Rape and other crimes against decency	650	350	613	370	741	458
Procuration	50	25	29	20	51	38
Bigamy	92	74	44	31	55	50
Shooting, stabbing, and wounding	215	119	267	168	266	182
Assault on females and wife	96	64	134	111	256	232
Aggravated assault	671	464	753	482	1,340	910
Assault on police officer	427	367	533	475	589	534
Assault and battery	1,270	987	1,487	1,261	1,780	1,358
Refusal to support family	274	154	307	218	396	264
Wife desertion	14	11	27	23	9	7
Various other offences against the person	141	80	134	106	167	116
Causing injury by fast driving	–	–	28	17	114	76
Total	4,124	2,804	4,521	3,368	6,018	4,314
Class II – Offences against Property with Violence						
Burglary, house, warehouse, and shopbreaking	2,111	1,754	1,711	1,417	3,575	3,268
Robbery and demanding with menace	323	212	273	207	569	428
Highway robbery	32	11	2	1	–	–
Total	2,466	1,977	1,986	1,625	4,144	3,696

Table 10 (continued)

Class III – Offences against Property without Violence

Bringing stolen goods into Canada	2	2	2	2	2	2
Embezzlement	35	19	10	6	11	6
False pretences	987	684	1,116	882	2,481	2,065
Feloniously receiving stolen goods	628	418	604	400	745	520
Fraud and conspiracy to defraud	773	466	882	593	880	688
Horse, cattle, and sheep stealing	82	50	53	37	123	95
Theft	7,848	5,938	8,139	6,651	12,405	10,540
Theft of mail	25	21	24	21	32	28
Theft of automobile	–	–	417	366	919	822
Total	10,380	7,598	11,247	8,958	17,598	14,766

Class IV – Malicious Offences against Property

Arson	69	31	76	38	86	51
Malicious injury to horses, cattle, and other wilful damage to property	246	187	269	201	501	381
Total	315	218	345	239	587	432

Class V – Forgery and Other Offences against the Currency

Offences against the currency	18	12	6	2	16	8
Forgery and uttering forged documents	532	453	451	383	1,092	1,001
Total	550	465	451	385	1,108	1,009

Table 10 (continued)

Class VI – Other offences not included in the foregoing classes

Breach of Trade Marks Act	–	–	49	48	37	36
Attempt to commit suicide	52	41	82	71	203	153
Carrying unlawful weapons	151	127	140	125	163	147
Criminal negligence	75	44	116	55	200	90
Conspiracy	62	33	135	53	99	65
Driving automobile while drunk	234	202	*	*	*	*
Indecent exposure and other offences against public morals	141	121	221	191	111	96
Intimidation	31	21	42	29	54	25
Keeping bawdy houses and inmates thereof	682	599	831	739	1,281	923
Offences against gambling and lottery acts	458	389	590	550	1,560	1,403
Offences against revenue laws	76	70	233	193	234	186
Illicit stills	686	643	400	376	361	345
Perjury and subornation of perjury	144	62	107	60	148	75
Prison breach and escape from prison	140	128	162	152	174	153
Riot and affray	67	49	145	113	201	169
Sodomy and bestiality	84	64	77	55	117	101
Various other misdemeanours	111	62	90	63	85	56
Offences against Opium and Narcotic Drug Act	–	–	–	–	268	217
Total	3,197	2,658	3,420	2,873	5,296	4,240
Grand Total	21,032	15,720	21,976	17,448	34,751	28,457

* Category dropped from Class VI.

SOURCE: *Canada Year Book*, 1925, 1927–28, 1932.

The camps had been set up across the country to provide temporary work for the unemployed, but conditions were far from satisfactory and there was a great deal of discontent, especially with the wage rate of 20 cents a day. Prior to the May strike there were rumours that a massive demonstration was being planned that included the destruction of the camps. The strike in B.C. was followed by a march eastward to Ottawa of some 1,500 unemployed. As the marchers progressed both the CPR and the CNR requested help from the Royal Canadian Mounted Police, thus heightening the animosity. By late June the army of unemployed reached Regina.

The government met with strike leaders in Ottawa on June 22. The spokesperson for the marchers, Arthur Evans, was a volatile individual with a criminal record for gambling, forgery, and fraud. He had served terms in the penitentiary and in jail. During the meeting he verbally attacked Prime Minister Bennett, at one point calling him a liar, and the meeting ended with nothing being accomplished. By late June tensions in Regina reached the breaking point. A Dominion Day protest involving some 400-500 strikers turned into a full-scale riot when the demonstrators clashed with the police. One man was killed, twelve people shot, both civilians and police were severely injured. Automobiles were damaged, store windows were smashed, and goods were looted.[46]

Crime in general continued to increase during the depression decade. Table 11 illustrates the trends in convictions for indictable crimes in the 1920s and 1930s. Both the number of convictions and the rate per 100,000 of population rose significantly during the period. Between 1922 and 1929 convictions rose by 34.7 per cent while the population rose by 13.6 per cent. Over the years 1930-39 convictions rose by 40.8 per cent while the population increased by 14.1 per cent. Overall, the pace of the increase accelerated slightly during the 1920s in comparison with the pace of change in the previous two decades. In spite of the widespread misery, poverty, and discontent during the depression years the pace of the acceleration in convictions remained just about static with the previous decade.

Within the various crime categories there were some slight shifts. In 1929 offences against the person accounted for 16.6 per cent of all convictions for indictable crimes whereas in 1939 they made up 11.3 per cent. Offences against property with violence were 10.5 per cent of the total in 1929 and 12.7 in 1939. Offences against property without violence dropped as a percentage of all crimes from 50.3 per cent in 1929 to 44.3 per cent in 1939. Forgery rose from 3 per cent of convictions in 1929 to 4.4 per cent in 1939. The category "other" was the one that experienced the biggest change, increasing from 17.78 per cent of all indictable convictions in 1929 to 25.4 per cent in 1939. This class included offences such as attempt to commit suicide, carrying unlawful weapons, keeping or being inmates of bawdy houses, breaches of the gambling and lottery acts, driving offences, and breaking revenue laws. In 1939 the most numerous crimes in this category

Table 11
Convictions for Indictable Offences, Sixteen Years and Over, 1922-39

Year	Convictions	Rate*
1922	15,720	276.24
1923	15,188	263.36
1924	16,258	276.90
1925	17,219	287.44
1926	17,448	285.52
1927	18,836	300.65
1928	21,720	337.81
1929	24,097	365.72
1930	28,457	422.51
1931	31,542	458.28
1932	31,383	448.26
1933	32,942	462.88
1934	31,684	438.03
1935	33,531	456.42
1936	36,059	482.51
1937	37,148	489.30
1938	43,599	564.82
1939	48,107	613.49

*Per 100,000 of population, sixteen and over.
SOURCE: Compiled from M.C. Urquhart, ed., *Historical Statistics of Canada* (Toronto: Macmillan of Canada, 1965).

were those related to bawdy houses, gambling, and driving. Out of a total of 12,243 convictions, 2,916 were for keeping or being inmates of bawdy houses, 2,832 were for offences against the gambling and lottery acts, 1,736 were for driving a car while drunk, and 1,536 were for dangerous or reckless driving. Driving offences were not classified as indictable crimes in 1930. These, together with increases in gambling and bawdy house convictions, accounted for 6,503 of the increase in the number of convictions for indictable crimes between 1929 and 1939.

Convictions for summary offences went from 136,322 in 1922 to 240,043 in 1929, an increase of 76 per cent. By 1939, summary convictions rose to 428,608, an increase since 1929 of 78.5 per cent. Thus, summary convictions outran indictable convictions by a significant margin of increase during both the 1920s and 1930s. Much of the increase over the period was accounted for by breaches of municipal acts and by-laws, and traffic regulations. In 1922 traffic violations were included under the former category. Combined, they numbered 68,657. By 1939 breaches of traffic regulations were listed separately and numbered 292,904 and breaches of by-laws numbered 25,852. Combined, they accounted for 74.3 per cent of summary convictions in 1939.

Overall conviction statistics offer the lowest indices of crime and are more useful for illustrating trends than for constructing a true picture. There were always many more charges than convictions. For example, in 1939 there were 56,352 charges recorded for indictable crimes but 48,107 convictions. While some of those charged were undoubtedly innocent, there were also many who had actually committed crimes but who escaped conviction on such grounds as legal technicalities or because of inefficient prosecution. In addition, many crimes went unreported or undetected. Since victim surveys were not done there is no way of even estimating the level of crime that actually took place.

WORLD WAR TWO

The next milestone on the "progressive" road of crime in the twentieth century came with World War Two. Statistically indictable offences dropped during the war years and did not again reach 1939 levels until 1957. Although serious crime diminished, chiefly because of the number of people in the services and overseas, certain types of offences increased and new ones appeared. Wartime rationing of meat, butter, sugar, coffee, and gasoline, introduced in 1942, opened opportunities for a black market. Many people engaged in the illegal sale of goods and in counterfeiting and selling ration coupons. Wherever military bases were located there was considerable activity in such crime as bootlegging, prostitution, and gambling. In addition, drunken soldiers were easy marks for thieves, who stole their money and sometimes articles of clothing. Ports shipping goods overseas became targets for black market thieves. The docks in Halifax, for example, had a major problem with theft. The RCMP uncovered one operation that focused on the theft of drugs from medical shipments, which were then sent to Montreal and other cities for distribution.[47]

Public violence also picked up during wartime. Brawls between military personnel and civilians were common in service towns and ports, as were street fights among the military. Sometimes a shopkeeper or place of amusement would cheat a serviceman and he and his friends would retaliate by wrecking the place. Ironically, the worst incidents of public lawbreaking came during the celebrations of the war's end; the most publicized was the V-E Day riot in Halifax.

Throughout the war Halifax served as a port of embarkation for troops going overseas, as a gathering point for convoys, and as a major naval base. The city was overcrowded and many took advantage of the situation to price gouge and cheat. Conditions generated a good deal of discontent among service people and merchant seamen. By the end of the war there was a considerable reservoir of resentment and ill will built up toward the city and its inhabitants. When the announcement of the German surrender came on May 7, 1945, thousands came into the streets to celebrate. As a precaution the government closed the liquor stores. At first the celebrations were orderly, but in the evening a group of naval personnel set fire to a streetcar. They then proceeded down Barrington Street, the city's main thoroughfare, with their numbers growing as they progressed. When they reached the downtown core the crowd broke into two liquor stores and looted them. The next day official celebration ceremonies attracted a large crowd to the central city and once again destruction of property and looting ensued. This time a full-scale riot erupted. Shop windows were smashed and the stores looted, two were set on fire, cars were destroyed, and liquor stores and a brewery were ransacked. Soon the entire city was in a shambles, with drunken men and women all over. A curfew was imposed and by nighttime order was once again restored. A subsequent official investigation blamed naval personnel as the main instigators.[48]

As was the case with World War One, the Second World War considerably disrupted Canadian society. More men and women served overseas and for a longer period of time than in any previous war. Young men and women left the farms and small villages and towns to join the service or to work in wartime industries in the larger cities. Women came out of their homes by the thousands to take jobs in industry, heretofore considered men's work. The effect was to create a more liberal society and, for a time, to accelerate the pace of change that had started in the early decades of the century.

Once the war ended, however, the primary aim was to restore the country to normalcy. Service personnel returned to civilian life and women went back to working at home. Many service people took advantage of special programs instituted by the government to improve their education and technical qualifications. They thereby equipped themselves to take advantage of better job opportunities that opened up with post-war expansion. The result was the building of a society far different from that of pre-war Canada.

THE CULTURAL REVOLUTION AND MODERN CRIME TRENDS

The generation that put their stamp on the country in the 1950s was hardworking and ambitious. They grew up during the depression in the midst of deprivation, austerity, and economic insecurity. They spent their early adult years fighting a war. When they came home, when they finished their education and training courses, they wanted to make up for lost time. They sought material success for themselves and, by extension, a decent life and economic security for their wives and children. They especially sought to give their offspring a quality of life that many of them had never experienced. A virtual renaissance of family life occurred in the 1950s. Families moved to the suburbs to enjoy the benefits of single-family homes, lawns, and backyards. Marriage was the preferred status for the majority of women. It was common for couples to have three, four, and five children.

The children growing up in the late 1940s and 1950s were indulged and surrounded with material possessions like no other generation in Canadian history. Mothers stayed home and catered to their nurturing. Parents taxied them to skating and music lessons and to hockey and baseball games. Consequently, when they came of age many were used to having their needs and desires met with instant gratification. When frustrated, they often became petulant and rebellious. Nowhere was the frustration level higher than in the universities, where students entered in unprecedented numbers in the 1960s and 1970s. Higher education was an extension of the better life that parents coveted for their children. They encouraged them to continue their educations and better equip themselves for success in the working world. Parental incomes and ample job opportunities enabled high school graduates to continue on to university. In 1950 there were 68,595 students enrolled in Canadian universities. By 1960 there were 113,729. Enrolment continued to rise, reaching 204,245 in 1965 and 371,062 in 1975.

The universities these young adults entered in such large numbers were by and large staid conservative institutions with fixed rules, regulations, and conventions. They were not ready for the indulged, liberal, idealistic, and impatient crop of students that hit the campuses in the 1960s. The rapid expansion turned institutions that were formerly small, personal, and characterized by high academic standards, into impersonalized places where students traded their individuality for a number. Classes became too large, with some courses catering to hundreds of students in large lecture halls. Certain professors despaired of trying to maintain human contact, taped their lectures, and played them in class on a tape recorder. The students responded in kind by leaving their recorders in class to tape the lectures.

The impersonalization was added to institutions that were paternalistic, authoritarian, and stuffy. Soon students began to vent their frustrations by demanding changes in governance, resident rules, degree requirements, and the quality of food served in the cafeterias. When administrations and faculty resisted the demands, students little used to compromising resorted to intimidation. Demonstrations, sit-ins, occupations of buildings, food riots, and class boycotts ensued. For a time university campuses across the country were in a state of upheaval.

The rebellion was intensified by similar developments elsewhere, especially in the United States. In that country the civil rights movement and the Vietnam War further fuelled the fires of discontent. Many Americans became disenchanted with their society and a mixture of draft dodgers, moral protesters, black power advocates, university professors, and drifters crossed the border. They had been active in the protest movement at home and they carried their anger to Canada, where they simply continued the battle. At the same time, many contributed to the disruptive tendencies in this country.

The revolt of the young soon broadened to include not only a protest against campus conditions but against a range of interests including social injustice. Many came to question the materialism that dominated Canadian society and they began to blame the older generation for everything from irrelevant degree requirements to poverty. Discontent with college campuses expanded into a full-fledged condemnation of society. Consequently, many young people concluded that they must distance themselves from the values and traditions of their elders and create a new society of peace, harmony, and love. They sought to remove restraints that they felt limited personal development, whether they be residence regulations or community laws and conventions. They protested by challenging authority and abandoning long-cherished standards of morality and deportment. In the process they created a counter-culture and ushered in the permissive society.[49]

Beginning on university campuses, there was a great deal of lawbreaking associated with the cultural revolution of the 1960s and 1970s. University property was destroyed and vandalized with damage running into the hundreds of thousands of dollars. New residences were hardly opened before furniture was broken up, windows smashed, and walls spray-painted. At Sir George Williams University in Montreal protesting students occupied a new computer facility, set it on fire, and did over $2 million worth of damage. The spirit of rebellion spread and soon it became a game to simply defy authority and convention whether there was a purpose to it or not.

Eventually the revolt of youth spread to society at large. Young adults, disproportionately from privileged backgrounds, adopted the slogan that you can't trust anyone over thirty. It became fashionable to challenge all authority and restraint and to signify one's disgust with the older generation by throwing off standards of dress, manners, and behaviour. The invention of the birth control pill encouraged the abandonment of moral restraints. Language took on a vulgarity that signified one's contempt for the old conventions of social interaction. Even the work ethic became a casualty of the cultural revolution. The rejection of materialism was signified by the adoption of blue jeans, denim jackets, and T-shirts as a standard dress for all occasions. Formerly the clothing of the poor, it was now the uniform of the cultural revolution.

Many decided to abandon completely what they described as a rat race for career advancement and material success. They dropped out of education or jobs and drifted across the country. Some became hippies and joined communes. Ironically, the carefree lifestyle adopted by so many was only possible because the very society they rejected supported them materially while they were rebelling. Alden Nowlan described it in *Double Exposure*:

In conversations with the young one should never ask questions such as: "Where's the money coming from?" They despise money, many of them, as few of their parents ever could, because they've never known what it can mean to be without it. The best of them are willing to be poor, but theirs is voluntary poverty, almost in the religious sense. It consists not in doing without the necessities but in refusing to possess things one doesn't really want; it's a poverty of security and self-assurance, rather than a poverty of despair and humiliation.[50]

The challenge to convention and values in the 1920s was limited by a strong counterattack by forces of conservatism. The 1960s revolution was so widespread that its impact was overpowering. Before it ran its course people in all walks of life – the young, the middle-aged, even the elderly – joined in. Certainly everyone did not discard the old standards, but enough did to strike a devastating blow to traditional morals, manners, and values. Hardly anything, from dress to sexual conventions, escaped the challenge of the counter-culture. The permissive society was a fact of life.

While certain aspects of the revolution, such as its idealism, greater freedom for the individual, a heightened social conscience, and a more tolerant society, were seen as positive elements there was also a negative side to the transition that took place. The cultural revolution in many ways stripped a layer of civility from society. The gross language, indifference to dress, and rough manners set the stage for a noticeable retrogression in the way people treated each other. The so-called "me" generation that emerged placed a great emphasis on personal indulgence and satisfaction, sometimes at the expense of other people. The erosion of values contributed to an ethical malaise that manifested itself at every level. The challenge to authority extended to a defiance of any and all restraints. The cultural revolution not only ushered in the permissive society but also seemed to be the catalyst for a dramatic increase in social problems. In no area was the impact more evident than in the world of crime. The liberalization taking place in society was accompanied by a dramatic increase in the level of lawbreaking, to the point where the 1960s and 1970s seemed to constitute a watershed for crime. In fact, certain types of offences seemed to be an integral part of the cultural revolution as well as a reflection of eroded values. Among them, drug abuse was the most serious.

Many people expressed their discontent with the society by looking inward and concentrating on personal growth and understanding. To help with the process they turned to so-called mind-expanding or hallucinogenic drugs. Others expressed their contempt for straight society by smoking up. Some turned to drug use simply to get high as a trendy leisure-time activity. Whatever the reason, the use of illegal drugs reached epidemic proportions. Sellers and users abounded on college campuses and in student residences. Joints of marijuana were passed around with the hors d'oeuvres at cocktail parties and social gatherings. A fiction developed that none of this was harmful. Soft drugs, it was argued, were non-addictive and not as harmful as alcohol. In the meantime, drug abuse grew by leaps and bounds. Conviction statistics, while once again telling a small part of the story, nevertheless offer some indication of the level of the problem. Convictions for drug-related offences were minimal for decades. As late as 1966 there were only 447. An upward spiral began in 1967, and by 1974 there were 30,485 convictions, a number that without question represented a small part of actual offences. The soft drug epidemic of the 1960s and 1970s laid the foundation for the growing increase in hard drug abuse that reached alarming levels in the 1980s and continues as a major problem in the 1990s.

The abuse of hard drugs such as heroin predates its criminalization in 1908. During the 1920s illegal use and traffic in heroin was a major problem. It continued to be a popular drug among users, with a significant escalation in the 1960s. By the early 1970s more and more young people were using the drug and abuse was no longer confined to the large cities. Drug laws were being violated in small and large communities in all sections of the country. Some indication of the growth in heroin trafficking is evident from the fact that between 1970-71 and 1971-72 bulk seizures increased from fifty-eight pounds to 195 pounds, or by 237 per cent. By 1981 it was estimated that there were 20,000 heroin users in Canada. Between 1976 and 1980 the crime rate per 100,000 for addictive drug offences went from 10.7 to 19.1, an increase of 78.5 per cent. In the same period the rate for restricted drugs rose from 8.2 to 15.8, an increase of 92.7 per cent.

Cocaine became increasingly popular through the 1970s and by 1981 police estimated that as many as 250,000 Canadians used cocaine during the year. Cocaine was a very expensive drug and was used primarily by the well-to-do. For much of the 1980s the typical cocaine user was a young male, under thirty, earning a professional income. By the end of the decade, however, prices had dropped and its use spread significantly to all income groups. A new, cheaper, and very potent form known as "crack" came on the market. It resembles a small pebble and 0.1 gram of the substance sold in 1987 for between $10 and $20, the low price substantially increasing its use. Between 1982 and 1988 recorded cocaine offences as a percentage of all drug offences rose from 4.2 per cent to 18.5 per cent.[51]

The introduction of crack brought with it a new form of marketing through "crack houses." Dealers buy or rent a property in a residential area, fortify it, and sell their crack to customers as a retail store would sell its merchandise. The difference is that the crack houses are usually protected by armed guards and are so set up that the dealers would have ample time to escape or flush the cocaine down the toilet if the police raided the premises. The latest development in the cocaine saga is yet another product, known as "ice," so called because it resembles a small ice crystal. Ice is more potent again than crack and probably will become the most popular form of the drug in the early 1990s.

For some time almost any form of drug that produces a temporary high has been bought and sold on the illicit drug market. Along with heroin and cocaine, a wide variety of pills and prescription drugs are available. Also, marijuana and its derivatives continue to be popular and account for the largest volume of drug sales. While much of the drug trade itself is controlled by organized crime, large numbers of street dealers have no direct connection with the higher-ups. One bust in Halifax in March of 1990 resulted in the arrest of thirty-three people and the confiscation of $1.5 million worth of cocaine.[52]

The drug trade is also the focal point for a range of other crimes. For example, many people are involved in the smuggling of drugs. Some do it only once or a few times as a means of making some quick money. Others do it on a regular basis, in some cases to support their own habits. They not only break the law by smuggling, but many endanger their lives in the process. A common technique used by smugglers to avoid detection is to put a certain amount of the drug into condoms and swallow them. If a condom happens to break before the person passes it, the carrier can die from an overdose as the drug enters the system.[53]

At the retail end there are many street dealers who are addicts and sell drugs in order to support their own habits. Their customers, many of whom are also addicts, engage in a variety of crimes to earn money for the purchase of drugs. Break-and-enter and common theft are the crimes most often committed by drug users. Police across the country estimate that over 50 per cent of such crimes in urban centres are committed by drug users. Some steal or otherwise obtain other types of drugs and then trade them to dealers for heroin or cocaine. One common method is known as double doctoring. A patient will go to a doctor and ask for a painkiller such as dilaudid. The person will then visit another doctor and get the same prescription. They then become a medium of exchange and since some people are dependent on prescription drugs, dealers have a ready market for almost anything that comes their way. This type of subterfuge has also created a market for counterfeit prescription pads and the services of people who can fill them in with authentic-looking prescriptions.

An indication of the volume of crime that some street dealers are involved in comes from a case in Nova Scotia in March, 1990. A man pleaded guilty to the charge of conspiracy to sell cocaine and while awaiting sentencing he was also facing a trial on thirty-one other charges. In a two-month period, between January 5 and March 2, he allegedly committed thirteen counts of false pretences, thirteen counts of fraud, one count each of possession of a weapon, possession of stolen goods, forgery, using a forged document, and failing to show up in court.[54] Many criminals, like the drug dealer, are guilty of multiple offences although they may get caught for very few.

Other spin-offs from the drug trade include sexual slavery, beatings, and murder. Sometimes pimps will get women addicted and then force them into prostitution in return for keeping them supplied with drugs. In other cases street dealers fail to pay their suppliers on time and are beaten to force payment or sometimes murdered as a warning to others. There has been nothing in our history that has generated the level of offences, both in its own right and in the form of related crimes, as has been occasioned by the illegal drug trade. Along with drug usage the age-old abuse of alcohol continues to be a major problem. In 1988 there were 238,830 offences against the Liquor Act recorded. Liquor is a factor in a wide variety of crimes ranging from assault to drunk driving to murder. Substance abuse of drugs and alcohol play a major role in lawbreaking in all parts of Canada.

The 1960s and 1970s witnessed a variety of crimes that might be described as a product of the times. Some were associated with the material prosperity that generated an interest in collecting and created a market for fake art, antiques, and other such items. Coin collecting provides one example of how the criminal element moved to take advantage of new opportunity. The hobby sparked a growing demand and some entrepreneurs obliged by turning out counterfeit rare coins. Two of the more skilled at the trade were apprehended by the RCMP in 1964. Among others, they were turning out 1936 dots, 1921 half-dollars, and five-cent silver coins, all items prized by collectors. Their forgeries were so good that they even fooled the experts.[55]

Like the drug trade, another type of crime that appears to have increased dramatically since the cultural revolution of the sixties and seventies is child abuse. There is no way of documenting child abuse in an earlier day because the detection mechanisms were not in place. Therefore, it is possible that there was always just as much abuse. On the other hand, many more circumstances in today's society create a climate conducive to abuse and consequently it is possible that the problem is in fact more serious than it was previously.

One of the most dramatic changes has come about in family relationships. Reflecting liberalized attitudes in the 1960s, the federal government passed the Divorce Act of 1967-68, which substantially broadened the grounds for divorce and made the process much easier. In 1961 there were 6,563 divorces granted in Canada. The numbers increased through the decade, rising to 11,165 in 1967. In 1969, the first full year after passage of the Act, the number of divorces rose to 26,093, then continued a steady incline, peaking at 70,436 in 1982. The rate rose from 54.8 per 100,000 of population in 1967 to 285.9 in 1982. Through the early eighties the number of divorces has fluctuated in the 60,000-70,000 range. A change in the divorce law in 1985 resulted in another jump to 78,160 in 1986, a rate of 308.8, and a further increase in 1987 to 86,985.

Common-law relationships were another phenomenon that increased dramatically in the 1960s. Earlier there were strong social and religious pressures against unmarried couples co-habiting. The changed morality and sexual habits that were a mark of the sixties revolution resulted in many more single couples living together. One estimate given in the House of Commons suggested that in 1967 nearly a half-million Canadians were co-habiting. Census figures in 1986 put the number at 486,940 common-law couples.

Two additional developments that have changed family life are the increased numbers of families in which both parents work and the large number of out-of-wedlock births. In 1981 there were 5,486,895 families in which both parents worked. Between 1931 and 1960 births to single mothers averaged about 4 per cent of all births; by 1983 they had risen to 16 per cent. High rates of divorce, single parents, common-law relationships, and working couples have created much more tension and stress. In addition, large numbers of children are being brought up in families where either the mother or father is not the birth parent. In single-parent families it is not uncommon to have boyfriends or girlfriends coming and going. The relationship, if any, between all of these changes and the increased incidence of family-related violence is difficult to determine. Nevertheless, there is a high correlation between the changes in family life that have taken place since the 1960s and reported rates of child abuse.

When it comes to assessing actual levels of abuse the situation is confused. The nature and circumstances of such offences make them easy to conceal. Many that are reported or uncovered do not result in criminal charges and therefore do not get counted in judicial statistics. There seems to be a consensus, however, that child abuse is a problem of considerable proportions. Child battering, emotional deprivation, and sexual abuse are to be found in all parts of Canada and among all socio-economic groups. Generally, the problem seems to be more pronounced in the larger cities but that could be due to better detection and reporting methods. The statistics that have been compiled suggest that the majority of the perpetrators are the natural parents. One Ontario government report covering the years 1966-70 estimated that of 1,603 cases of abuse reported to the Central Register, about three-quarters of the offenders were the natural parents, with common-law partners and step-parents accounting for the next largest number.[56] Nova Scotia Child Abuse Register statistics for the years 1984-87 show that out of 757 cases where the identity of the abuser was known, over 45 per cent were the natural parents. Approximately 23.5 per cent of the abusers were common-law spouses or the single parents' boyfriends or girlfriends.[57]

Among the offences committed against children, sexual abuse is especially serious. The 1984 Report of the Committee on Sexual Offences Against Children and Youths (Badgely Report) revealed that sexual abuse was much more common than was generally believed. The results of one

Table 12
Age Distribution of
Convicted Male Child Sexual Offenders

Age of Convicted Offender	Male Victims (n = 129)	Female Victims (n = 545)	Multiple Victims (n = 21)
Under age 21	10.1%	16.4%	4.8%
21-30 years	18.6	27.5	33.3
31-40 years	23.2	21.1	19.0
41-50 years	12.4	10.2	9.5
51-60 years	6.2	3.6	14.3
61 and older	4.7	1.6	4.8
Not reported	24.8	19.5	14.3

SOURCE: *National Corrections Survey, Badgely Report,* 1984.

survey carried out by the Committee suggested that over half of Canadian females and 30 per cent of males were subjected to unwanted sexual acts before they were twenty-one years old. The large majority of offenders are males. Table 12 gives the results of a survey discussed in the report. It affords an overview of the age distribution of one group of male offenders convicted of child sexual abuse. Other surveys referred to in the report gave age breakdowns slightly at variance with those in the table.

Reports of sexual assaults on children rose dramatically through the 1980s. In one year alone, 1984, they rose by 45 per cent in Alberta. Between 1984 and 1986 reports of sexual abuse of children rose by 21 per cent in Manitoba. Since 1983 reported cases in Toronto tripled.[58] One form of child sexual abuse that seems to have increased in recent years is the use of children in pornographic magazines, videos, and photographs. Since mainstream heterosexual content has become so widespread, more jaded tastes have created a market for offbeat fare such as sexual torture and kiddy porn. Practically every pornographic publication caters to the market with pictorial stories or layouts. Magazines like *Hustler, Penthouse,* and *Oui* have recognized the demand. In reality, the people such publications use may be of age but they are made up to look like young children, thus stimulating a certain type of reader. On the other hand, some pornographic publications do use child models. Most of the kiddy porn in Canada, however, is private. Pedophiles lure children with presents or take advantage of a trusted relationship and photograph them naked and engaging in sexual activities with other children or adults. According to a United States Federal Bureau of Investigation agent, Ken Lanning, a world-wide underground network exists through which pedophiliacs exchange child pornography.[59]

It appears that the problem of the sexual abuse of children can appear at any time in any place. In March, 1990, the small town of Prescott, Ontario, with a population of 5,200, was shocked by revelations that forty-two children, aged one to fifteen, had been the victims of abuse, mostly sexual, by a number of adults and teenage residents in the town. The abuse had allegedly been going on since October, 1987. When the situation came to light four adults and two youths were charged with thirty counts of abuse, including incest, sexual assault causing bodily harm, and sexual assault involving a weapon.[60] When pedophiles are caught it may only be for one offence, yet many have committed multiple offences by the time they are discovered. Studies suggest that the majority of pedophiles are multiple offenders.

Abuse of children is only one dimension of family violence that finds its way into modern crime statistics. Another area of serious proportion is wife abuse. There has always been domestic violence and the historical records document many cases of brutal assaults on women by their spouses. For much of our history, however, this type of assault went largely unreported so it is only in recent years that the actual extent of the problem has come to public attention. Some measure of the level of family violence can be garnered from police records across the country. In one six-month period in 1975 Vancouver police reported that over one-third of public requests for assistance were calls to domestic disturbances. A 1979 study of London, Ontario, police records revealed that over 47 per cent of domestic disturbance calls were incidents of wife beating.[61] In 1986 police in Metropolitan Toronto laid 2,067 charges against husbands or common-law companions for assaults on their partners.[62] During the first eight months of 1990 there were 3,600 domestic disputes reported to police in Montreal.[63]

Domestic violence is not limited to assaults but also includes a significant number of murders. One researcher who did a study of Toronto police records calculated that between 1921 and 1988 approximately 261 women were killed in that city by their married or unmarried partners. Ninety women were killed by their husbands in Canada in 1979. The figure for total partner murders was probably higher but Statscan figures identify only husband-wife relationships and not common-law unions. In 1989, seventy-six wives were killed by their husbands and twenty-two husbands killed by their wives. By October of 1990 an average of two women a week were being killed in Canada, most as a result of domestic disputes. Of forty-three killings in Toronto, nine of the victims were women whose suspected murderers were their partners or ex-partners. Between mid-August and early October of 1990, thirteen women were killed in greater Montreal, in most cases by their partners. In a number of incidents the men murdered their wives, their children, and then committed suicide.[64]

Family violence is only one segment of the mayhem that is so pervasive in today's society. Since the 1960s there has been an unrelenting increase in crimes of all kinds. Especially disturbing has been the large increase in the more serious offences and in crimes of violence. Table 13 illustrates the trend in Criminal Code offences for the years 1962 through 1988. The rates are calculated on the basis of the number of offences per 100,000 of the population.

As Table 13 shows the trend in Criminal Code offences has been steadily upward. These offences fluctuated in the early sixties but by the latter part of the decade began a climb that has not yet abated. Between 1962 and 1972 the rate increased by 97.1 per cent and over the next ten-year period, 1972-82, the rate went up by 63.7 per cent. The pace of increase has slowed in recent years but the overall trend continues. Criminal Code offences as a percentage of total crimes have also gone up. In 1977 they accounted for 74.3 per cent of all offence categories, which included federal and provincial statutes and municipal by-laws. In 1988 Criminal Code offences made up 80.9 per cent of the total.

As has been the case throughout Canadian history, males continue to be responsible for the bulk of crime. In 1963 males accounted for 91.8 per cent of those charged with Criminal Code offences; in the same year, males were charged with 92.1 per cent of non-Criminal Code offences. Since then, and possibly reflecting the changes that have taken place in Canadian society, the percentage of females charged with criminal offences has moved gradually upward. In 1971 87.9 per cent of adult persons charged with Criminal Code violations were male and 12 per cent were female. By 1988 males had dropped to 82.7 per cent of persons charged and females charged had risen to 17.2 per cent of the total. A slightly smaller change took place in the other crime categories. In 1971 males made up 92.4 per cent of persons charged and females 7.6 per cent, while by 1988 males had dropped to 88.7 per cent and females went up to 11.2 per cent.

The rebellion of the 1960s and 1970s was accompanied by a significant increase in violence in Canadian society. At the extreme end of the spectrum is murder. The number of yearly homicides more than tripled between 1961 and 1977, going from 233 to 711. In the next ten-year period the increase levelled off, with homicides fluctuating: 661 in 1978; 593 in 1980; 642 in 1987; 575 in 1988. Between 1961 and 1987 the rate per 100,000 nearly doubled, from 1.28 to 2.51. In addition, there has been a substantial number of attempted murders. Between 1977 and 1986 there was an average of 836 attempted murders per year.

Over the period 1961-87 males were the victims in an average of 62.4 per cent of homicides. Males also accounted for the largest number of offenders. For example, in 1987 males were the suspects in slightly over 85 per cent of the cases. A high percentage of murders involved family members and people who were friends or acquaintances. Between 1977 and 1986 approximately 38.2 per cent of solved homicides involved people related to one another through marriage, common-law union, or kinship. During the same period an average of 38.5 per cent involved acquaintances. Between 1977 and 1986 an average of 35.2 per cent of solved homicides involved

Table 13
Trends in Criminal Code Offences, 1962-88

	Total Criminal Code		Crimes of Violence		Property Crimes		Other Crimes	
	Actual Number	Rate per 100,000	Actual Number	Rate per 100,000	Actual Number	Rate per 100,000	Actual Number	Rate per 100,000
1962	514,986	2,771.2	41,026	220.8	351,483	1,891.4	122,477	659
1963	572,105	3,022.0	47,229	249.5	387,517	2,046.0	137,359	725.6
1964	626,038	3,245.2	54,769	283.9	414,048	2,146.3	157,221	815
1965	628,418	3,199.0	58,780	299.2	410,688	2,090.6	158,950	809.1
1966	702,809	3,919.9	69,386	346.6	451,980	2,258.2	181,443	906.5
1967	784,568	3,850.0	77,614	380.8	506,151	2,483.8	200,803	985.4
1968	895,983	4,328.2	87,544	422.9	584,996	2,825.9	223,443	1,079.3
1969	992,661	4,726.7	95,084	452.7	655,304	3,120.3	242,273	1,153.6
1970	107,452	5,200.0	102,358	480.6	748,522	3,514.7	256,572	1,204.7
1971	1,163,705	5,395.4	108,095	501.1	801,379	3,715.5	254,231	1,178.7
1972	1,192,891	5,464.3	110,468	506.0	807,468	3,698.8	274,955	1,283.8
1973	1,302,938	5,897.1	117,764	533.0	833,329	3,771.6	351,845	1,592.4

Table 13 (continued)

Year								
1974	1,456,885	6,490.5	126,053	561.6	946,793	4,218.0	384,039	1,710.9
1975	1,585,805	6,955.3	135,424	594.0	1,041,036	4,565.9	409,345	1,795.4
1976	1,585,805	6,955.3	136,935	592.5	1,062,952	4,599.5	437,817	1,894.5
1977	1,654,020	7,101.5	135,745	582.8	1,059,688	4,549.7	458,587	1,968.9
1978	1,714,297	7,300.7	138,972	591.8	1,097,242	4,672.8	478,083	2,036.0
1979	1,855,271	7,837.5	147,528	623.2	1,186,697	5,013.1	521,046	2,201.1
1980	2,045,399	8,553.0	155,864	651.7	1,334,619	5,580.8	554,916	2,320.4
1981	2,168,201	8,963.4	162,228	670.6	1,429,520	5,909.6	576,453	2,382.9
1982	2,203,668	8,945.6	168,646	684.6	1,466,923	5,954.8	568,099	2,306.1
1983	2,148,633	8,668	172,315	695	1,422,703	5,740	553,615	2,233
1984	2,147,697	8,598	172,395	718	1,408,663	5,640	559,637	2,240
1985	2,174,175	8,640	189,822	754	1,408,717	5,598	575,636	2,287
1986	2,277,749	8,984	204,917	808	1,448,550	5,714	624,282	2,462
1987	2,363,558	9,224	219,381	856	1,468,591	5,731	675,586	2,636
1988	2,392,419	9,233	232,699	898	1,458,821	5,630	700,899	2,705

SOURCE: Statistics Canada, Crime and Traffic Enforcement Statistics 1962 to 1988, Catalogues 85-201, 85-205.

drugs or alcohol. In 1987 approximately 49.1 per cent of all suspects were between eighteen and twenty-nine years old.[65]

Included in the murders and attempted murders in recent times have been a number of vicious attacks on groups of people. On October 27, 1975, an eighteen-year-old man who had been training with the militia handcuffed a girl to a bed in a youth home and set the place on fire. He then went to a school in Ottawa and shot and wounded six people, after which he killed himself. On March 12, 1977, a man entered a bar in Montreal armed with an M-1 semi-automatic rifle. He shot the manager, the barmaid, and three customers. On September 16, 1982, the charred remains of six people (a man, his wife, their eleven- and thirteen-year old daughters, and the wife's parents) were found in a burned-out car in a provincial park in British Columbia. The killer was eventually caught and admitted to the shooting. On May 8, 1984, a Canadian Forces corporal entered the Quebec National Assembly and opened fire with a machine gun, killing three people. On July 29, 1988, during the course of a drinking party, a Calgary man shot and stabbed to death two men, a woman, and her fourteen-year-old son.[66]

The two worst incidents of multiple killings in modern Canada were the serial murders committed by Clifford Olson and a massacre in Montreal carried out by Marc Lepine. In 1981 Olson killed eleven young people in B.C. – eight females and three males. He buried the bodies but eventually revealed their locations in return for an RCMP payment to his wife in the amount of $100,000. Olson was sentenced to life imprisonment and has been kept in protective custody in an isolation cell. He professes remorse for his deeds and has persuaded himself that the whole affair is behind him. He believes that God has forgiven him, stating, "I've asked for forgiveness; I've been forgiven, and that's the end of it."[67]

On December 6, 1989, twenty-five-year-old Marc Lepine entered the École Polytechnique, an engineering school on the campus of the University of Montreal. He was armed with a .223-calibre Sturm Ruger, a high-powered semi-automatic rifle, two boxes of bullets, and a thirty-bullet clip. He randomly murdered fourteen female students, wounded twelve other people, and then took his own life. Lepine was a war movie buff and an unemployed loner with a history of difficult relations with women. He blamed women for many of his failures and left a three-page suicide letter in which he stated, "feminists have always ruined my life." He also mentioned Denis Lortie, the soldier who killed three people in the Quebec National Assembly in 1984. In addition, the letter contained a hit list of fifteen other women. Lepine's parents separated when he was seven, he had difficulty holding down jobs, and he had been refused admission into the engineering program at the university.[68]

A number of the multiple and more vicious murders have been committed by people with serious emotional and psychological problems. A man abducted a twelve-year-old Brampton, Ontario, girl on December 11, 1987, murdered her, and then dismembered the body. Five months later her severed head was discovered in the car of the thirty-eight-year-old man, who had a prison record and a history of mental problems. In April of 1987 he was serving a nine-year prison term but was paroled, although in the opinion of prison officials he should have been put in a psychiatric facility. Doctors who had examined him believed him to be a dangerous sadist. In spite of the diagnosis he was neither confined in a mental hospital nor denied parole.[69]

The level of violence now so evident in Canadian society coincided with social changes in the 1960s and 1970s. For example, the percentage of new admissions to penitentiaries for violent crime went up from 28.6 per cent in 1960 to 52.6 per cent by 1978.[70] Between 1983 and 1988 the number of crimes of violence went from 172,315 to 232,699, while the rate per 100,000 of population rose from 695 to 898, an increase of 29.2 per cent. Over the same period there was an average of 16,688 weapons offences per year.

Crimes of violence are often random and can arise from the circumstances of the moment. As in the past, assaults continue to account for a significant number of serious offences. In 1984 non-sexual assaults accounted for 6.3 per cent of all Criminal Code offences and in 1988 for 7.4 per cent. Both sexual and non-sexual assaults are frequently liquor- or drug-related. This category of crime is an example of an offence that has wider repercussions than the deed itself. Assault frequently causes pain, injury, psychological damage, loss of work, and loss of income. Family-centred violence has repercussions for children, for the emotional well-being of all members, and has a wide range of effects, from the productivity of parents at work to the academic achievement of children in school.

While much of the growing violence in Canadian society is personal in nature, other forms also account for many incidents. Labour disputes, such as the one on the Hamilton, Ontario, waterfront in 1988-89, continue to be the focal point for a variety of disorders. Involved in that conflict were Local 1654 of the International Longshoremen's Association, the Hamilton Harbour Commissioners, the Maritime Employers' Association, and a group of twenty-four non-union longshoremen. The fight was over hiring practices and was marred by a series of incidents. In August, 1988, a union member's workshops were set on fire, and the following April the union president's truck was fire-bombed. In July, 1989, a twenty-five-year-old dock worker was found beaten to death shortly after being given a union card. In mid-September a worker was threatened at gunpoint and two days later another had Molotov cocktails thrown on his front porch.[71]

In mid-December, 1989, a bitter labour dispute that had run on for four years at the Manoir Richelieu resort in Quebec ended when the last seventy-five pickets decided to give up the fight. The resort had been taken over by a new owner who refused to recognize the union. When the 306 union members decided to fight for their jobs a stand-off ensued. The dispute was marred by vandalism, bombings, and one death. A large number of labour disputes and strikes are the occasions for vandalism, property destruction, and sometimes personal injury.[72]

Another form of violence that is a relatively new phenomenon in Canada is terrorism. One of the worst examples was associated with the FLQ crisis in Quebec. In 1960 a new Liberal government was elected in the province under the leadership of Jean Lesage. The Liberals set out to change the social and economic order in Quebec in a way that would clearly establish Francophones as the dominant social, political, and economic element in the province. Hitherto the English business community had exercised an influence out of all proportion to the numbers of Anglophones in Quebec. Lesage's efforts were referred to as "the Quiet Revolution" and his initiative both mirrored and encouraged a new spirit of self-assurance and self-reliance, and heightened Quebec nationalism.

The stirrings in Quebec gave rise to a number of strongly nationalistic groups whose members soon became impatient with the pace of change. The more extreme element demanded total independence from the Canadian federation. Among the latter was a small organization known as the Front de Libération du Québec. Made up of extremists who also espoused leftist political views, they decided to resort to terroristic activities to pursue their goals. Between 1963 and 1970 the FLQ was responsible for about 200 dynamite explosions, the theft of $50,000 through a succession of bank robberies, and the deaths of seven people. Their activities culminated in October, 1970, with the kidnapping of James Cross, the British trade commissioner, and Pierre Laporte, a Quebec cabinet minister. The federal government invoked the War Measures Act on October 16, 1970, and sent in troops. One FLQ cell released Cross but another cell murdered Laporte.[73]

Some terroristic activity has been sparked by ethnic groups resident in Canada carrying on disputes associated with their homelands. In August, 1982, Armenian terrorists shot the Turkish embassy military attaché in the garage of his home in Ottawa. A few months earlier, in April, a group of Armenians attempted to kill a commercial counsellor from the embassy, shooting him ten times while he was stopped for a red light on an Ottawa parkway. On March 12, 1985, Armenian terrorists armed with shotguns, revolvers, and explosives stormed the Turkish embassy in Ottawa. They killed a thirty-one-year-old Canadian security guard, blew down the front door of the embassy, and held twelve hostages for half an hour. Police quickly surrounded the embassy and captured the three gunmen without injury to the hostages. The terrorists were protesting the slaughter of Armenians by the Turks in incidents that took place in 1895 and 1896 when they were under Turkish rule.[74]

Another terrorist incident stemming from a foreign dispute was the bombing of an Air-India jetliner in June, 1985. A bomb was put on board the plane in a suitcase at Toronto's Pearson International airport. The registered owner of the suitcase was not a passenger on the plane. The bomb exploded when the plane was over the North Atlantic, killing all 329 people on board. Most were Canadians of Indian descent. The suspects in the bombing were Sikh extremists, presumably striking out against the government of India over the treatment of their co-religionists in that country.

In December of 1986 two Sikhs were convicted in Montreal of conspiring to blow up an airplane. Police uncovered a plot by the men to put a bomb on board an unspecified plane that would be flying out of a United States airport. Reports of the trial suggested that the men were hard-core terrorists who were prepared to sacrifice hundreds of innocent lives in the pursuit of their cause and apparently showed no signs of remorse. Both were members of a fundamentalist religious group dedicated to establishing a Sikh homeland out of the Indian province of Punjab.[75]

Acts of terrorism have victimized widely disparate groups and individuals in Canada in recent years. In May of 1989 the home of a tax inspector in Winnipeg was bombed. The device was thrown into the living room and did about $25,000 damage. The family was upstairs asleep at the time and no one was injured. Police suspected the bomber was someone the tax inspector had been involved with and the victim claimed he knew three or four people who were capable of committing such an act.[76] In January of 1990 a fire destroyed the office of the Toronto Urban Indian Society doing over $300,000 in damage. Police believed that gasoline was used by an arsonist to fire the building.[77]

Another form of violence that seems to have increased in recent years is something referred to as "gay bashing." Toughs who oppose homosexuality seek out gays to attack as a way of venting their hostility. In many parts of Canada there have been serious incidents that have resulted in injury and loss of life. The situation has become so serious that in some places spokespersons for the gay community have had to request special meetings with police in an attempt to limit the danger. A series of attacks in Ottawa-Hull that included beatings, torture, and attempted murder motivated the formation of the Ottawa-Hull Lesbian, Gay, and Bisexual Task Force on Violence. In September, 1989, a joint statement was issued by members of the task force and Ottawa city police, expressing concern "about anti-gay violence in Ottawa." It also announced the appointment of special police personnel to deal with the problem.[78] In another example of violence against gays a Halifax man was beaten to death in November, 1988, by three men who were looking for money to buy cocaine. They were using drugs earlier in the evening and when they ran out they decided to rob a homosexual because they felt a gay would be an "easier mark." They headed for an area of the city where homosexuals were known to frequent and in the process of a robbery two of the men attacked the victim. One continued the beating until the man was dead.[79]

In terms of its impact on the general society the most alarming forms of

Figure 1
Property Crime Clock, 1981

One Property Crime every 18 Seconds	Average Time Interval between Selected Actual Property Offences	
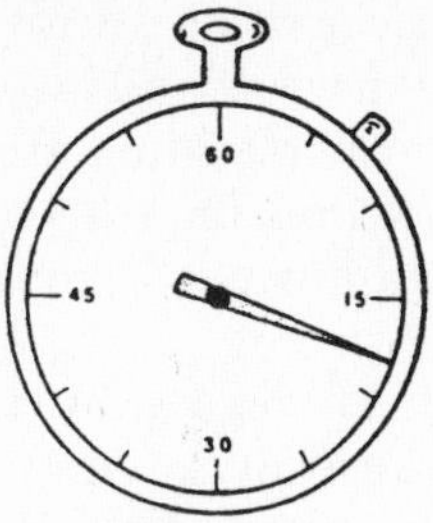	Robbery	20 minutes
	Breaking and Entering	86 seconds
	Theft – Motor Vehicle	5 minutes
	Theft	38 seconds
	Arson	55 minutes
	Wilful Damage	2 minutes

SOURCE: Statistics Canada, *Juristat*, v. 2, n. 5 (August, 1982), p. 9. Catalogue 85-002.

crime are the ones classified as property offences. While often seen as offences against things rather than people, this is far from the case. When someone's house is invaded the victim feels a sense of personal violation. Theft often involves the loss of prized possessions, family heirlooms, and other irreplaceable belongings. Frequently, burglars come armed, and an increasing number are under the influence of drugs. They thus pose a danger to the person as well as to the property.

As Table 13 shows, property crimes have consistently accounted for well over half of all recorded Criminal Code offences. Within this category the pace of the increase in break-and-enter offences seems to have steadily quickened. While statistics tell only a small part of the story, indicative of the trend is the fact that these offences went from 270,659 in 1977 to 367,250 in 1981, an increase of 35.7 per cent. Especially disturbing was the increase in residence break-ins: from 144,612 in 1977 to 216,222 in 1981, an increase of 49.5 per cent in the five-year period. Another indication of how serious the problem had become by the 1980s is afforded by the property crime clock for 1981, reproduced in Figure 1.

In the past few years property crime has increased to the point where police can no longer cope with the problem, and statistics do not come close to documenting actual levels. Especially in large cities a high percentage of people in all walks of life and from all geographical sectors can bear witness to the high incidence of crime. Across Canada homeowners and apartment dwellers are becoming more security-conscious. They live with special locking devices, burglar alarms, guard dogs, security personnel, and a variety of other protective devices. Restaurants and other public places have signs warning patrons to guard their belongings. Even university libraries post notices cautioning people against the "rash of thefts."

Certain categories of crime, such as property offences, have been with us since the first settlers arrived. Another form of lawbreaking that has deep historical roots is smuggling, a classic example of a crime of opportunity. In recent years governments have been loading taxes on cigarettes and liquor, thus substantially raising prices. Canadians living in close proximity to the United States border can buy alcohol and tobacco much cheaper across the line and some have seized the opportunity to become involved in large-scale smuggling operations. Individual entrepreneurs solicit orders from friends and neighbours and bring back truck loads of liquor from the U.S. Others simply load up with cigarettes or alcohol and have no difficulty selling their goods once they get them across the border.

Some Newfoundlanders have entered the business in a big way by taking advantage of the close proximity of the French islands of St. Pierre and Miquelon. Boats go over nightly, load up with cigarettes and liquor, and return to the many small coves that dot the coast. In early December of 1989 over 100 RCMP officers raided a number of small villages on the Burin Peninsula and arrested forty-nine people on smuggling charges. They also seized five boats, ten vehicles, approximately 1,400 bottles of liquor, 354 tins of tobacco, and fifty-two cartons of cigarettes. Police claimed that on the average night as many as twelve to fifteen boats were carrying back forty to sixty cases of liquor from the French possessions. A case of liquor costing $110 in St. Pierre could be sold in Newfoundland for $220.[80]

Since the 1960s the level of crime in Canadian society has escalated dramatically. There have been slight fluctuations but the trend has been inexorably upwards. The statistics are disturbing by themselves but even they tell only a part of the story. A Canadian Urban Victimization Survey, sponsored by the Solicitor General of Canada, concluded that almost a million crimes a year go unreported. The report was based on a survey done in January and February of 1982 of more than 61,000 householders in seven Canadian cities – Toronto, Vancouver, Edmonton, Winnipeg, Montreal, Halifax-Dartmouth, and St. John's. Respondents were asked to report on incidents that occurred between January 1 and December 31, 1981. The results estimated that as high as 84.1 per cent of robberies, 88.9 per cent of assaults, 58.9 per cent of burglaries of homes, and 77.1 per cent of thefts in various cities are not reported. The average figure for failure to report crimes in the seven cities surveyed was 62 per cent for sexual assault, 55 per cent for robberies, 66 per cent for assault, 56 per cent for household theft, and 71 per cent for personal theft.[81] Table 14 offers a comparison of police statistics with survey estimates indicating the level of unreporting and the low number of people charged in comparison with the actual and estimated number of offences.

The survey estimated that in the seven cities in 1981 there were 702,000 personal incidents, 352,000 of which were violent, plus 17,300 sexual assaults, 49,200 robberies, 285,700 assaults, and 349,800 incidents of per-

Table 14

Police Statistics, Survey Estimates, People Charged, January-February, 1982

Offence Categories	Toronto				Montreal				Halifax / Dartmouth			
	Police Stats	Survey Estimate	Not Known to Police	People Charged	Police Stats	Survey Estimate	Not Known to Police	People Charged	Police Stats	Survey Estimate	Not Known to Police	People Charged
Crimes of Violence Sexual Assaults	1,242	4,479	3,239 (72.3%)	507	1,030	(261,277) 5,754	4,724 (82%)	358	110	208	98 (47.1%)	42
Robbery	2,041	12,912	10,871 (84.1%)	739	8,754	15,731	6,977 (44.3%)	1,622	324	1,788	1,464 (81.8%)	115
Assault	11,439	90,006	78,567 (87.2%)	6,665	7,089	60,132	55,043 (88.2%)	2,853	1,069	8,136	7,067 (86.8%)	316
Burglary (Residential)	22,630	55,185	32,555 (58.9%)	3,938	43,036	80,951	37,915 (46.8%)	4,166	3,347	5,223	1,876 (35.9%)	575
Personal Theft and Household Theft	73,170	103,223 + 105,153 208,376	135,206 (64.8%)	13,529	65,610	90,226 + 102,470 192,696	127,086 (65.9%)	9,223	9,148	11,022 + 12,678 23,700	14,452 (60.9%)	1,471
Motor Vehicle Theft	5,871	6,712	841 (12.5%)	1,170	13,335	15,454	2,119 (13.7%)	1,456	833	999	166 (16.6%)	148

Table 14 *(continued)*

Offence Categories	Vancouver				Edmonton				Winnipeg			
	Police Stats	Survey Estimate	Not Known to Police	People Charged	Police Stats	Survey Estimate	Not Known to Police	People Charged	Police Stats	Survey Estimate	Not Known to Police	People Charged
Crimes of Violence Sexual Assaults	771	3,494	2,723 (77.9%)	161	517	1,670	1,153 (69%)	156	415	1,512	1,097 (72.5%)	189
Robbery	2,118	10,951	8,833 (80.6%)	480	1,176	3,769	2,593 (68.7%)	402	924	3,796	2,872 (75.6%)	414
Assault	8,563	77,214	68,651 (88.9%)	2,064	4,423	23,177	18,754 (80.9%)	1,107	1,906	23,432	21,526 (91.8%)	704
Burglary (Residential)	20,875	46,351	25,476 (54.9%)	2,002	12,341	17,032	4,691 (27.5%)	1,582	11,247	21,099	9,852 (46.6%)	1,943
Personal Theft and Household Theft	41,526	83,394 + 97,955 181,349	139,823 (77.1%)	6,127	29,192	29,121 + 40,601 69,722	40,530 (58.1%)	5,030	30,328	27,878 + 51,605 79,483	49,155 (61.8%)	4,043
Motor Vehicle Theft	5,259	9,974	4,715 (47.2%)	445	4,088	3,406		477	2,924	3,661	737 (20.1%)	455

Notes: (1) Survey did not include commercial vehicle thefts; police did.

(2) Actual unreported could be higher because survey figures do not include commercial thefts, burglaries, victims under sixteen. Police figures do.

(3) In addition to charging people, police may conclude offence for other reasons, e.g., not solvable.

SOURCE: *Globe and Mail*, 14 February 1985, p. 4.

sonal theft. During the same period there were an estimated 898,100 household incidents, consisting of 227,300 break and enter, 40,600 motor vehicle thefts, 417,200 household thefts, and 213,000 incidents of vandalism. The rate of personal incidents per 1,000 of population sixteen and over for the cities surveyed was 351.5. The rate of household offences per 1,000 households was 369.[82]

The study also revealed that males were the victims of violence more often than females by a margin of almost two to one. However, women were the victims in about 90 per cent of sexual assaults. In addition, the injury rate among female victims was high. About 61 per cent of the female victims of sexual assault were injured, about 28 per cent non-sexual assault victims were injured, and about 35 per cent of female robbery victims were injured. About 41 per cent of sexual assault victims were known to each other, and about half of actual rapes took place in the victims' homes. The government analysts pointed out that in addition to actual loss or injury, many victims of crime suffered psychological or emotional damage and that, especially among women, there was a considerable fear of becoming a victim of crime. Fifty-six per cent of women said they felt unsafe walking alone in their neighbourhoods at night.[83]

In the intervening years since this survey was taken Criminal Code offences have continued to increase so it is more than likely that unreported and undetected crime has as well. Between 1983 and 1988 the rate of Criminal Code offences per 100,000 has increased by about 6.5 per cent. Over the same period the rate of violent crimes increased by about 29.2 per cent.

Yet another consideration in evaluating the seriousness of crime in Canada is a comparison of our rates with those of other nations. One such study that compared Canadian Criminal Code offence rates per 100,000 with equivalent rates for similar offences in other countries concluded that Canadian rates were higher. The study compared Canadian rates over the years 1960-80 with Australia, England, France, Japan, the Netherlands, and the United States. The rates for all countries were not computed for each year but in every year that was, Canadian rates for serious crime were higher than those in every other country in the study. For example, the 1980 comparisons were Canada: 8,553.1; Australia: 2,113.2; England and Wales: 4,833.5; France: 4,903.1; Japan: 1,110.3; Netherlands: 3,806.2; U.S.: 5,899.9. It is very difficult to make accurate cross-national comparisons but, even allowing for the problems, the study suggests that rates for serious crimes in Canada were high for the period in comparison with those of many countries.[84]

While the vast majority of Canadians have not been victims of serious crime, that diminishes neither the risk nor the alarm. Contemporary crime is random and pervasive and therefore generates justifiable concern. The statistical chances of having your child kidnapped from a shopping mall, for example, are small. However, it is a frequent enough occurrence that people must exercise caution. We live in a society today where many people with psychological disorders and substance addictions are on the streets, thus increasing the dangers of personal injury or loss. There are neighbour-hoods in cities across Canada where most houses on the street have been burglarized. It is not safe to leave a purse or a jacket unattended in a public place. Anywhere, at any time, an average Canadian citizen can be victim-ized by crime. Many criminals commit hundreds of offences before they slip up and get charged with that one mistake. The issue, then, is not the statistical incidence of crime but rather whether or not the problem is at a tolerable or manageable level. The alarm that has gripped the country in recent years suggests that the level of crime has gone well past the point where it is perceived to be either tolerable or under control.

SUMMARY

Any study that focuses on a specific phenomenon can easily magnify the subject to an artificial level of prominence, and the study of crime is no exception. Pages of depressing statistics and examples can give an impres-sion that the problem is much more serious than it actually is. However, the reality to some extent depends on how much of anything a society is willing to tolerate. Among any group of people perceptions will vary. Drug users probably don't see the level of the drug traffic as serious, a perception obviously not shared by the community at large. And so it is with crime in general. Many see it as a major problem in society, others give it much less importance. Regardless of the impression, however, crime has been a stead-ily growing phenomenon throughout the years since Confederation.

The nature and increasing tendency of crime that emerged in the pioneer period continued with the establishment of the new nation. The passage of time witnessed a drop in some crimes, an increase in others, and the emer-gence of new ones. Technological development, population growth, and general expansion all influenced crime. With the appearance of the rail-roads and automobiles, criminals found opportunities for new forms of crime and the facilitation of old ones. The telephone, improvements in printing, and many other advances also aided criminals.

Attitudinal changes in Canadian society have had an effect on criminal activity. World War One and the liberalization of the 1920s created a climate seemingly more tolerant to the challenge of law and convention. The period witnessed, for instance, an increase in property crimes, violent crimes, gambling, and drug usage. Yet a strong counter-reaction by conser-vative forces kept the liberal tendencies in check and possibly limited the extent of lawlessness.

The depression ushered in a prolonged period of social and economic distress for Canadians that did not end until World War Two. While certain types of crime increased during the decade, overall growth trends were moderate. The war introduced new opportunities for crime and new types of offences such as black-marketing, and counterfeiting and selling ration coupons. Crime in general, however, levelled off – partly because of the large number of people serving overseas.

The post-war period witnessed the virtual disappearance of at least one long-standing type of crime, the public violence formerly associated with political campaigns and sectarian values. Elections were much more civilized affairs. There were still bribery, voting irregularities, and a variety of chicanery, but the beatings, intimidation, and riots had long since disappeared. Also, Canada was becoming more tolerant of religious and ethnic differences. As a consequence, the sectarian clashes that were so much a part of our history were no longer tolerated or fashionable. The Orange versus the Green and similar rivalries faded into the background. No longer did rival religious groups fight pitched battles in the streets of Canada's towns and cities.

The renaissance in family life and the baby boom that characterized the 1950s were accompanied by relatively stable crime rates. Society was lulled into a false sense of security that made people totally unprepared for the revolution that lay ahead in the 1960s and 1970s. The rebellion and the cultural revolution that took place ushered in a society that was termed "permissive." An integral part of the liberalization that took place was a widespread disregard for rules, regulations, standards, morals, values, and law. Along with the massive rejection of old conventions Canadian society also experienced an increase in certain social problems, including an unprecedented rise in crime.

The last three decades have seen the highest levels and fastest rates of increase in crime in Canadian history. Among the many offences that have dramatically increased, drug use seems to have the worst implications. Not only does it account for a large measure of lawbreaking by itself, it is also responsible for numerous other crimes, such as theft, burglary, and assault. Crime in contemporary society has reached the point where it is beyond the ability of the police to control. Notwithstanding its more widespread nature, crime continues overwhelmingly to be a male activity, although female crime rates have been going up.

Of particular concern to many Canadians has been the increase in crimes of violence, including family-centred abuse. As well, thefts and burglaries leave many with the fear that no thing or place is beyond the reach of criminals. Although some argue that crime actually touches a small number of the population, the vast majority seem to feel that they are at risk. The security industry has thrived with an ever-growing market for locks, alarms, guard dogs, and security services. The industry itself is testimony to the alarm that modern crime levels have generated. Daily newspapers in towns and cities all over the country feature regular reports on crime in their communities. They seem to document the widely held perception that lawbreaking has gone well beyond the level of tolerance.

The nature of crime in the post-Confederation period has been such that it would be foolhardy to try to relate it to any one cause. People in all walks of life break the law in significant numbers. Crime is far from the preserve of the unwashed, uneducated, and underprivileged, as the next chapter, on white-collar crime, will show. Even the institutions of higher learning and many representatives of wealth and privilege have a problem with crime. Theft, vandalism, rape, drug and alcohol abuse are no strangers to college and university campuses across the country.

The serious drug problem is yet another indicator of the broad background of today's lawbreakers. Drug abuse and trafficking cast a wide net and people from all socio-economic backgrounds are caught up in the problem. The street addict may turn to theft and burglary while others steal from their employers or violate trusts to obtain the money they need to support their habits. People who are involved with drugs are also sometimes caught up in a variety of other crimes, ranging from theft to family abuse.

Since Confederation, Canada has witnessed an inexorable growth in crime. The pace of growth has varied and for much of the period the level and nature of crime were such that it did not seem to pose a major problem. All that has changed since the 1960s and 1970s, when the pace of growth in crime quickened dramatically, coincidental with a cultural revolution that challenged conventional values and ushered in a much more permissive life style. Since then most types of crime have increased with some significant changes taking place in the level of more serious offences and crimes of violence. As the last decade of the century unfolds Canadian society faces a serious crime problem that shows no signs of abating.

CHAPTER 3

▼

White-Collar Crime

White-collar crime has much in common with other categories of lawbreaking in that many offences are committed by individuals and are similar to other forms of crime. Therefore, any definition is at best arbitrary. For purposes of this chapter white-collar crime is defined as lawbreaking committed by corporations, businesses, professionals, management personnel, and employees who enjoy professional status by virtue of their positions. Professionals include lawyers, doctors, and accountants. Managers are those with decision-making authority and supervisory responsibility. Employees enjoying professional status would be ones holding positions of responsibility and trust who might exercise some lower-level management tasks. This definition of white-collar crime focuses on the perpetrator rather than on the type of crime actually committed.

WHITE-COLLAR CRIME IN COLONIAL CANADA

As is the case with other categories of lawbreakers, white-collar criminals have been active since early pioneer days. The highest officials in New France used their positions for illegal gain. Governor Frontenac, during his first term of office from 1672 to 1682, joined forces with François Perrot, the subordinate governor at Montreal, to pursue illicit activities in the fur trade. All obligations to King and country were ignored in their pursuit of profit. They could get double the price for furs from the English so while they enforced the prohibition against trading with the British, they themselves reaped the benefit of higher prices.[1]

Frontenac and Perrot also used their positions to interfere with the trading activities of their rivals. They sought to control as much of the fur trade as they could and therefore used people under their command to beat and intimidate merchants in an effort to keep them away from the Indian traders. Both men earned considerable profits from their lawbreaking. In 1680, for example, Perrot realized an estimated 40,000 livres from his illegal trading.[2]

Corruption among officials in New France was widespread. Antoine Laumet, the commander of the trading post at Michilimackinac, located at the juncture of Lake Huron and Lake Michigan, became notorious for his high-handed trading practices. One writer described him as "one of the most scoundrelly, self-seeking adventurers in the history of New France."[3] Laumet was so ambitious that at one point he contemplated establishing a post at Detroit that would be outside French control. He would thus be able to carry on a large-scale trade with the English. Even Church officials in New France could not resist the temptation for illicit gain. Frontenac, in 1672, complained to Colbert, the French Minister of Finance, about the commercial activities of the Jesuits. He claimed that "they think as much about the conversion of Beaver as of souls." In view of Frontenac's own interests, it is possible he was more worried about the competition than the inappropriate dealings of the clergy.[4]

Duchesneau, Intendant of Police, Justice and Finance in New France, brought complaints against a number of prominent people, including Frontenac, Perrot, and the Abbé Dollier de Casson, the Superior of the Montreal Sulpicians. Duchesneau reported he was doing his best to prevent illegal trading activities but that some of the most prominent families in the colony were involved. He charged that Frontenac was protecting them and was sharing in their profits. Frontenac was recalled in 1682. His replacement, Le Febvre de la Barre, however, picked up where his predecessor had left off. He was accused of engaging in similar activities by both Duchesneau and his successor, de Meulles.[5]

Not only the fur trade in New France benefited from the attention of corrupt officials. The old European practices of defrauding the government were alive and well in the New World. In 1686 the Intendant de Meulles was dismissed for selling stores, arms, and powder belonging to the government. Merchants sometimes conspired with officials to sell supplies to the government at inflated prices and they also engaged in currency manipulation.[6]

Merchants joined with government officials, but also frequently carried on illegal activities on their own. In addition, many were involved in the fur trade and joined in the lawbreaking that was endemic to that industry. They cheated the Indians, stole from their rivals, and sold to the English. New Englanders frequently visited Montreal to arrange for illicit trading ventures with the French. Merchants cheated their customers by selling short-weighted goods and by charging prices at illegal levels of profit. For a time in New France markups on goods imported from France were fixed at 65 per cent, a fairly generous profit margin. Yet there were constant complaints about merchants charging much higher margins.[7]

Throughout France's North American colonies merchants flouted the laws of the mother country. An edict prohibited foreign vessels from entering or coming within a league of colonial ports, and the penalty was confiscation and a fine of 1,000 livres. The only exceptions were for goods that were badly needed by French-Canadian settlements. In such cases vessels from the British colonies were allowed to carry specified cargo but nothing else; however, merchants at Louisbourg used the exception to buy and sell other goods with the English. Merchant ships from New England would carry prohibited cargo along with their legitimate goods, then would leave port laden with merchandise sold to them by their French counterparts who were not supposed to sell to the English. In many instances the two groups did not even bother to use the ships carrying permitted cargo but simply carried on illegal trading and took their chances. The ledgers of the famous Boston merchant, Peter Faneuil, contain many entries of transactions with the merchants of Louisbourg.

As elsewhere, officials and military officers also defied the laws that they were supposed to uphold. Merchants complained that they were in competition with the colony's administrators in carrying on their trade with the New Englanders. They bemoaned the fact that they were put at a disadvantage because the knowledge of the military and officials about the coming and going of vessels placed them in a superior position to exploit trading opportunities. Louisbourg officials passed up few opportunities to turn a dishonest profit. Along with their illegal trading activities they also devised a profiteering scheme that used the government as an unwitting accomplice. They would take provisions from the King's stores in the autumn when they could sell them at a high price and would replace them the following year with goods that cost them much less.[8]

Many government officials and merchants viewed the colonies as places to exploit for their personal gain. It was almost a convention among the French upper classes that colonial service was an opportunity to enhance one's personal wealth, legitimately or illegitimately. Merchants, who sometimes came from well-to-do families in France, shared this ethic. Their offices and positions of status in the community were assets that enabled them to carry on illegal activities with impunity, or without detection. When their equals did expose them they still benefited from their connections and a high degree of tolerance. Perrot, for example, although imprisoned for his misdeeds, was subsequently appointed as Governor of Acadia, while Frontenac was sent back to New France for a second term.[9]

The white-collar crime that flourished through the French colonial period persisted and extended after the English Conquest. During the latter part of the eighteenth century the fur trade continued to be the focal point of much lawbreaking and some of the worst incidents came out of the rivalry between the Hudson's Bay Company and the North West Company. The battle began with the founding of the North West Company in 1783 as the new company soon challenged the venerable Hudson's Bay Company for primacy in the fur trade. Murder, theft, destruction of property, arson, intimidation, and assault marked the commercial rivalry. Raids on each other's posts were common. During one such foray near the Hudson's Bay Company's Red River colony twenty-one people, including the post's governor, were killed by employees of the North West Company. The carnage continued until the younger company finally gave in. In 1821 the two antagonists amalgamated under the name of the Hudson's Bay Company. An inventory of weapons revealed that the traders of the North West Company in the Pacific region had been equipped with an arsenal of rifles, small arms, and thirty-two cannons.[10]

In spite of the size and prestige of the Hudson's Bay Company it engaged in many of the same shady practices for which individual fur traders were guilty. Cheating the Indians was a case in point. The company bartered such things as blankets, food, and munitions in return for furs, and on occasion company employees were instructed to short-weight goods given to the Indians by an ounce or two. Another practice was to demand more furs than what the bartered item was worth. Since the native was totally dependent on the company for certain supplies there was little choice but to accept what was offered.[11]

While the fur-trading companies were setting precedents for corporate crime in the West, English settlements continued to spring up in the East. Like their earlier French counterparts, many experienced white-collar crime. Beginning with the first English enclaves on the east coast there were numerous high-placed criminals. One of the most notorious was the Halifax merchant and distiller, Joshua Mauger. He had been doing business at Louisbourg when Halifax was founded in 1749 and immediately transferred his activities to the new English settlement, obviously convinced that there were greener pastures in Halifax. His assumptions proved correct. Mauger was ambitious, shrewd, manipulative, and dishonest. In 1751 he succeeded in being appointed victualler to the navy, a post offering considerable opportunity. In the meantime Mauger maintained his connections with the French at Louisbourg. Governor Cornwallis accused him of smuggling goods from Louisbourg into Halifax but could never catch him in the act. Mauger accumulated considerable wealth, both legally and illegally, and eventually moved to England.[12]

The social elite that emerged in Halifax consisted of merchants, governing officials, members of the judiciary, and military officers. They formed a tight clique that, among other things, shielded wrongdoers of their class. Military officers who committed crimes were not charged, merchants were let off by the courts, and prominent citizens escaped justice. While most people of status were not criminals and did condemn those who were, they were afraid to expose them lest the image and prestige of the town's inner circle be diminished. In some cases, of course, white-collar offenders were in positions to shield themselves against detection or prosecution; in other cases they benefited from their friendship with the magistrates. The latter had the privilege of keeping their investigations secret and therefore could forgo any legal action if they so chose.[13]

Magistrates who covered up wrongdoing not only did an injustice to their office but also set a standard of ethics that made for a corrupt judicial system. With the passage of time the corruption touched all levels, from the common jailor to the prisons, to the judges on the bench. Jail officials in many instances committed a variety of offences. One of the most common in the early days was selling liquor to prisoners. Keepers were poorly paid so there was a temptation to augment their incomes by exploiting those under their care. They took bribes for special privileges, payoffs for lenient treatment, provided prostitutes on occasion, and even assisted with escapes.

Examples of lawbreaking by correctional officials are plentiful throughout our history and nowhere has the problem been more blatant than within the prison system. Canada's first major prison, Kingston, not only became the prototype for penitentiaries in this country but also set the precedent for official corruption. Within a few years of its opening in 1835 there were problems with the administration, and rumours about the institution became progressively more disturbing until finally the government in 1848 appointed a commission to investigate. The secretary was George Brown, editor of the *Globe*. Among the many revelations contained in the Brown Commission report of 1849 were stories of widespread graft and corruption among prison officials at all levels.

Guards supplied liquor to prisoners and undoubtedly made tidy profits in the process. They purchased goods made by the inmates and supplies from penitentiary stores at prices fixed by their fellow keepers. They also conspired with outside contractors to defraud the institution. Kingston was a market for prison needs – food for the prisoners and staff, hay for prison animals, supplies for the workshops. The Commission noted that there was no central office in charge of receiving and that some twenty people were responsible for accepting deliveries and handing out receipts, yet there was no system in place for overall supervision. Contractors and delivery people took full advantage of this, sometimes in collusion with institution officials. They received payment for more goods than they delivered and supplied goods of inferior quality, including spoiled meats and stale bread. Officials in charge of the kitchens served the inferior food to the inmates and also failed to provide the quantity of food called for by the regulations. In addition, contractors and keepers conspired in having work done outside the prison that could and should have been done by inmates.

The Commission's investigation also uncovered a substantial loss of tools and supplies at the prison. While the inmates were responsible for much of the pilfering, the guards were also to blame. The prisoners used the stolen property to trade with delivery people for tobacco; in some cases the guards would turn a blind eye to the thieving but then demand bribes from the prisoners in return. In other instances the guards themselves stole tools and other prison property for their own use. The whole situation offered almost unlimited opportunities for dishonest keepers to engage in criminal activity with little risk of being caught.

The malaise at Kingston went all the way to the warden. He hired his son, who got in on the action by misappropriating supplies and selling prison provisions. It is almost certain that the father knew of his son's activities. Among the warden's many failings was his practice of building facilities and providing amenities such as horses and carriages at institutional expense but for the private use of himself and his family. Much of the graft and corruption at Kingston were made possible by the warden's failure to keep proper records, to enforce regulations, and to carry out his responsibilities. The Commission found him guilty of "scandalous mismanagement" and "gross neglect of duties." He was dismissed but the practices uncovered by the Brown Commission by no means ended. They were examples of criminal activity that continued to plague the penitentiary system in future years.[14]

The wrongdoing of correctional officials at Kingston was replicated in many other jurisdictions. For example, sheriffs in the various judicial districts in Upper Canada were often political or patronage appointments who were not required to meet any standards of competency or honesty. Indeed, some sought government appointments because of the illicit money-making opportunities they offered. An abuse common to this type of official was the misappropriation of public funds. They were in charge of collections made by the judicial system and sometimes kept or misused the funds.

Two typical examples of bureaucratic dishonesty were documented by an investigation of a special Lower Canada legislative committee in 1835. Lewis Gugy was appointed sheriff of the district of Montreal in 1827. He was also a member of the Legislative Council. The sheriff's income consisted of an annual salary plus fees charged for his various services, such as the issuance of writs. Gugy was overcharging and reporting far less income than he was actually making. During the investigation he lied to the committee, but with the help of the chief clerk the members determined that between 1830 and 1834 he collected over £5,264 more than he reported as income. The committee found him guilty of charging unwarranted rates and recommended his dismissal.[15]

The same committee also investigated charges of irregularities in the Montreal prothonotary's office. The members discovered that appointments to that position were being made on condition that the appointees, out of their earnings, pay pensions to their predecessors, an arrangement that was illegal. In one case a prothonotary was obliged to pay the widow of his predecessor an annual pension of £75. The committee denounced the Executive, which was responsible for appointments and had imposed the obligation, stating that "Your Committee cannot too much regret that a system of favoritism so fraught with abuse, and so contrary to the public good, should have been practised in this country."[16]

The problem of dishonest officials, who were scattered throughout the judicial system, also struck other organizations in pioneer days, including the churches. On occasion, men of the cloth proved that they, too, were prone to sin. One such individual was the Reverend Patrick Horan, an Irishman, who was the first Roman Catholic priest to be posted to Bytown. Like many of his parishioners he had a drinking problem, and perhaps his need for liquor motivated his turn to crime. His superiors discovered that he was selling off church land and keeping the money. He was removed in 1829. A few years later church officials again encountered a problem when it was revealed that the man who had functioned as the parish priest from 1832 to 1835 was an impostor. He had been neither trained as a priest nor ordained. Bishop Macdonell, the head of the diocese, complained that "The Irish clergymen who were employed in this province have indeed done much injury to the cause of religion."[17]

As the population increased and settlement spread, so did the diversity of white-collar crime. Business expansion in particular afforded new opportunities for criminal activity, and all too often the illegalities were carried out by the uppermost level of management. The Montreal Mining Company affords an example of a number of shady business practices common at the time. At its annual meeting in 1855 shareholders complained that the company had painted a false picture of the value of its stock and its future earning potential. On the basis of the rosy picture presented by management, investors had been duped into buying the stock only to discover that its performance fell far short of the publicized expectations.

At the same meeting stockholders also uncovered a classic example of bribery and political corruption. The financial statement showed a transaction whereby the company bought stock back from one of its shareholders at a price well above the market value. The explanation was that the company wanted to have a jail and courthouse constructed at one of its communities, called Bruce Mines. In order to obtain a favourable decision from the government the company bought back 200 shares of stock from the Attorney-General of Canada West, who just happened to be the person who would have to make the decision on the jail and courthouse. The man not only made a very good profit on the sale but got rid of stock that had little value. The practice of bestowing favours on politicians in return for their support was common among corporations. It started early and became an integral part of doing business in this country.[18]

Before the government enacted appropriate legislation to stop abuses by corporations and their owners, there were certain practices which eventually were declared illegal but which for some time were technically within the law. Some of them might have violated breach-of-trust legislation, but activities such as price-fixing, combinations in restraint of trade, and what is today called conflict of interest were not covered by prohibitory laws until some time after Confederation. For example, one of the main pieces of legislation dealing with business practices, the Combines Investigation Act, was not passed until 1889. Nevertheless, the corporate, professional, and political corruption so common in the nineteenth century needs to be examined because it was a watershed for the business practices that eventually were prohibited by legislation and that are still with us today. Nowhere was the corruption so blatant and pervasive as in the building of Canada's railroads.

RAILROAD BUILDING AND POLITICAL CORRUPTION

The industrial development that was a prerequisite for nation-building in Canada called for large investment beyond the means or level of risk-taking of most private entrepreneurs. At a very early stage it was obvious that government support and involvement would be necessary. Consequently, the interaction of politicians and banking, insurance, railroad, and other business executives and promoters became common from the outset. The relationships opened up many opportunities for personal gain, both legitimate and illegitimate. Some people were drawn into politics not because of their interest in public service but because they saw it as a vehicle to advance their business interests. Certain of the highest-ranking officials of government during the Union period (1841-67) were also actively involved in business enterprise while they held political office. Politicians held stocks and offices in the very companies that sought favours from the governments of which they were members. John Ross, the Solicitor-General, was president of the Grand Trunk Railway. George-Étienne Cartier, the French-Canadian political leader, was the company's solicitor. Sir Francis Hincks, Inspector-General and future leader of the Union government, was also involved with the Grand Trunk, along with other ventures.

Possibly no Canadian politician devoted as much of his time to business ventures as Alexander Tilloch Galt, who actually entered politics in 1849 primarily to further his commercial interests. He was an active railroad promoter and contractor while functioning as a successful politician. In 1858 he became Finance Minister of Canada while still maintaining his business activities. One of Galt's ventures involved a major role in the St. Lawrence and Atlantic Railway Company, and when the latter faced the threat of losing route rights to a competing company, the Grand Trunk, Galt used his influence to arrange an amalgamation. Although the stock of the St. Lawrence and Atlantic had greatly depreciated, the takeover was arranged in such a manner that the stock was bought at par. By 1867 over $25 million in public money had been given to the Grand Trunk, augmented by an additional $10 million from the municipalities.

Because of the huge sums of money involved in railroad building and the importance placed on transportation, railroad ventures were a magnet for the unscrupulous. Promoters saw money-making opportunities in stock manipulation, land speculation, and appropriation of government funds. Contractors could take advantage of the anxiety to get the roads built and the sometimes loose accounting practices to inflate prices and cheat the promoters. Politicians could benefit from bribes, gifts of stock, and their dual roles of handing out money as members of government and receiving it as company directors. Sir Allan Napier MacNab, for example, was president of the Great Western Railway at the same time that he was chairman of the Committee on Railways and Telegraphs of the legislature of the Canadas. Greed on the part of promoters and contractors led to overbuilding and to promotional schemes devoted more to milking investors and the public purse than to actual building and operation.

The Grand Trunk Railway was a prime example of the graft and corruption associated with railroad construction in the nineteenth century. The promoters and the construction firm that built the road were English and the railroad had both an English and a Canadian board of directors. The latter included some prominent cabinet ministers, such as Sir Frances Hincks. By 1859 the Grand Trunk accounted for approximately 1,112 miles of railroad out of about 2,093 miles that had been constructed in Canada up to that time. It was originally chartered to run from Toronto through Kingston to Montreal.

The raids on the public purse started at the outset. The English bankers and contractors, when the stock was first issued, held back a sizable portion hoping to push up the price. Instead, the market value dropped and the promoters refused to buy the shares. The politicians then stepped in with a series of grants and bail-outs that kept an uneconomical business afloat. The entire venture was characterized by graft, fraudulent bookkeeping, and shoddy construction. Although the railroad was in debt, accounts were kept to show an operating profit, thus enabling the shareholders to be paid a dividend. The money, of course, was coming from the public purse and being voted by the very people who stood to collect a large share of the so-called profits. To facilitate the financial sleight-of-hand the government reduced its creditor position to that of a second mortgagee and allowed the company to pay dividends although it could not meet its debt payments. As each financial crisis developed the government responded with more grants while the Canadian directors collected dividends, sold personal property to the Grand Trunk at grossly inflated prices, and reaped a variety of other benefits.[19]

One of the more publicized cases of political corruption in Canadian history was the so-called Pacific Scandal of 1872-73. It developed out of a vigorous competition over rights to build the Canadian Pacific Railway. A Montreal company, led by Sir Hugh Allan and supported by American investors, attempted to improve their competitive position by heavily supporting the 1872 election campaign of Sir John A. Macdonald and his Conservative Party. Allan poured some $350,000 into campaign coffers. During the 1873 session of Parliament a Liberal member, L.S. Huntingdon, charged that Allan was given the contract because of his contributions to the Conservatives and a major political brouhaha ensued. A royal commission investigation revealed that Macdonald's right-hand man, George-Étienne Cartier, had requested contributions of $110,000, of which $35,000 was earmarked for Macdonald. It was also determined that additional donations were made in the amount of $20,000 for Cartier and $10,000 for Macdonald.[20] A motion of censure was moved in Parliament but before it came to a vote Macdonald and his government resigned. The Liberals came to power and then went to the country in the 1874 election campaign, which was extremely bitter and antagonistic. The Liberals won a resounding victory, capturing 133 seats to seventy-three for the Conservatives. Macdonald won a narrow victory of thirty-eight votes in his home riding of Kingston.

The Macdonald government was not the only one to become the victim of corrupt dealings with railroad promoters. Some years later, in 1891, the Quebec Liberal government of Honoré Mercier was forced from office over financial irregularities involving the Baie des Chaleurs Railway. Part of the subsidy given the railway by the government was rechanneled into the pockets of some cabinet members to pay election expenses and personal debts. In addition, the Mercier government was forcing contractors to give kickbacks by inflating the cost of government contracts. The money was being put in the party's election fund. In 1891 the Lieutenant-Governor of Quebec dismissed Mercier from office and his party was defeated in the elections that followed.[21] Mercier was charged and tried for corruption but was acquitted amid accusations that the jury was bribed.

Notwithstanding the backlash from the Pacific Scandal, politicians were still not deterred from involvement with the railroads. In return for promoting their interests in Parliament they were given bribes, land grants, shares of stock, and other consideration. The interaction of railroads and politicians, together with the corruption, was widespread. Some measure of the extent of involvement by members of Parliament can be garnered from a debate that took place in the House of Commons in May, 1886. Opposition was raised to giving yet another land grant to a Saskatchewan railway company. Dr. George Landerkin, Member of Parliament for the constituency of South Grey, Ontario, was among those who took strong exception to the proposal. He denounced the long-standing involvement of politicians with the railroads, citing the number of the sitting House members who had vested interests in railroads and the amount of money their companies had received in government grants. Among the revelations was the fact that one road had received land grants of 6,400 acres per mile, when, according to Landerkin, the subsidy should have been no more that 640 acres per mile. At least five members of Parliament were principals in the company, one of whom was the president. Even cabinet members were directors of roads that received substantial sums from the public purse. The Minister of the Interior was a director of the Pontiac and Pacific Junction Railway, which received a subsidy of $272,000. The Secretary of State was a railroad company director as was the Minister of Railways himself, and his company received grants totalling $2,550,000.

The corruption did not stop with railroads. Landerkin pointed out that one member of the House was a principal in a printing firm that did work for the House of Commons. He claimed that the firm was paid for work it did not do and for work actually done was paid as much as fourteen times more than the going rate. While the companies received the subsidies, grants, and overpayments, the members of Parliament were rewarded personally for their intervention on behalf of their companies. The magnitude that those rewards could reach was illustrated by the fact that one member had been given $386,000 worth of stock in a certain company in return for his influence. The debate, led by Landerkin, catalogued example after example of graft and corruption involving a broad range of government activities, including handing out printing contracts, land grants, and timber rights. Landerkin summed up the problem with his claim that "the members elected come here to serve their own special interests, and neglect the general interests."[22]

The political machinations of some members of Parliament cast a surprisingly wide net, as a case that came to public attention in 1890 illustrates. John C. Rykert had used his influence as a well-connected parliamentarian to persuade the Department of the Interior to make a grant of timber land in the Northwest Territories to John C. Adams for the paltry sum of $500. Part of the deal between Rykert and Adams was that Rykert's wife would be given half of any proceeds realized from the sale of the property – both hoped to make a sizable profit. Within a year Adams sold the land and paid Rykert $74,200 – $35,000 in cash and the remainder in notes worth $39,200. Subsequently, the sale was jeopardized when the Canadian Pacific Railway Company claimed that the land in question was encompassed within its holdings. A legal contest followed in which Adams, by some fortuitous coincidence, was represented by Hugh J. Macdonald, son of Prime Minister Sir John A. Macdonald, and J. Stewart Tupper, son of Sir Charles Tupper, Minister of Railways. Eventually the matter was settled when the CPR sold its claim for a low price per acre to the same American who had originally bought the land from Adams. When the matter became public a motion was introduced in the House of Commons condemning Rykert's conduct as "discreditable, corrupt and scandalous." In the face of public exposure both lawyers, Macdonald and Tupper, denied that they had ever represented Adams or that they were involved in the affair. The matter finally ended when on May 2, 1890, John Rykert resigned his seat in Parliament.[23]

THE GROWTH OF WHITE-COLLAR CRIME

Other forms of corporate abuse were also thriving in the last quarter of the nineteenth century. In 1883, for example, price-fixing agreements involving fire insurance companies, cotton manufacturers, and wholesale grocers were uncovered. The corporate conspiracies against the public interest became so flagrant that the government was finally forced to appoint a Select Committee of the House of Commons to examine the situation. The Committee's 1888 report revealed that combinations in restraint of trade were widespread and included wholesale jewellers, biscuit and confectionary manufacturers, coal sellers, oatmeal millers, cordage and barbed wire manufacturers, undertakers, stove manufacturers, and even egg buyers.[24]

Businesses across the country resorted to every conceivable form of subterfuge to increase their profits. In some cases they devised elaborate schemes to cheat the public or the government. Industries in every form of endeavour were caught up in illegal activities. Even gold-mining companies, which literally mined wealth, engaged in stock manipulation, the avoidance of royalty payments, and smuggling. One enterprising company in Nova Scotia, at the turn of the century, worked out a scheme to avoid royalty payments by forging duplicate gold bricks. One would be deposited in the local bank as the official product for royalty purposes and the other would be smuggled out of the country.[25]

As always, corporate crime was well augmented by crooked professionals and individual business people, many involved in high-stakes ventures. In March, 1887, two Montreal detectives were convicted of burglary. The pair had carried on an extended spree of robberies that had netted them thousands of dollars. Some of their burglaries were committed at the Bonaventure station belonging to the Grand Trunk Railway and when the police were not successful in catching the thieves, railway officials called in the Pinkerton detective agency. The Pinkertons did a great deal of work for the railroads in North America and had a reputation for the unrelenting and frequently successful pursuit of criminals. In this instance Robert A. Pinkerton himself directed the efforts that led to the capture of the Montreal detectives.[26]

Besides the police, many other public officials took advantage of their positions for illegal gain. A large number of civil servants held patronage appointments and some lacked the skill and dedication for their positions. Since they were well versed in the practice of trading political favours some were quite open to accepting bribes in return for their own interventions. Such was the case during the Klondike gold rush in the late 1890s. The Gold Commissioner's Office was in charge of registering claims and was staffed with patronage appointees who ran a thriving business selling information on unrecorded claims and accepting bribes to give precedence in recording claims. Sometimes there would be lines of miners waiting to register their claims and the clerks would accept bribes in return for allowing some to jump the queue to file their claims ahead of others, who might have been waiting in line for days.[27]

The many small business people who broke the law usually did so on a modest scale through such practices as overpricing, short-weighting, or selling inferior goods. On occasion, however, some, such as Frederick J. Whitaker, a prominent Saint John, New Brunswick, businessman, aspired to bigger things. In August, 1900, he pleaded guilty to a charge of uttering forged papers and was sentenced to five years in prison. His forgery amounted to $51,000, a substantial amount of money for the time.[28]

Like other segments of the criminal world, white-collar offenders have always been quick to recognize an opportunity for illegal gain. The changing morals and the increased curiosity about sexual matters that developed during the first decades of this century created a market for more titillating fare. The society was still conservative and puritan so strict controls were in place to keep such material from circulating or coming into the country. However, since there was money to be made in the distribution of prohibited books and magazines there were always those willing to take a risk. The pornography trade offers another illustration of the broad spectrum of illegal activities carried on by white-collar criminals.

One case in particular illustrates the ambiguous nature of such offences. For a number of years United States postal authorities had been complaining to Ottawa about material a certain Ontario company had been sending through the mail. Finally, in late 1909, police seized the company's inventory and the two owners pleaded guilty to a charge of selling and distributing obscene literature. On January 3, 1910, they were sentenced to a year in jail. The sentencing judge had no reservations about the nature of the books the men were selling. He declared prior to sentencing that the content was so bad that the court would "not be justified in allowing them to be read before any twelve jurymen."[29] That seemed to settle the matter, but just two months later an order was issued by the Minister of Justice for the release of the two prisoners.

A storm of criticism ensued but the minister defended his action on the grounds that while the books might have offensive passages they were nonetheless classics. He went on to state that "in my humble judgement, speaking as a lawyer, they were not guilty of the offence with which they were charged."[30] He also supported his decision by pointing out that a number of prominent people had petitioned for their release. *The Globe* took the lead in denouncing the release and in an editorial stated, "In the name of everything decent and clean in Canadian life *The Globe* makes deliberate and emphatic public protest against the clemency of the Crown being extended to men convicted of traffic in obscene pictures and vilely immoral books." The editorial also stated that *"The Globe* protests even more emphatically against the defence offered for their release."[31] Many other publications and interest groups made similar protests. The dispute was an early example of the differing opinions and attitudes that surrounded censorship issues and that continue to do so to this day.

Although white-collar criminals most often victimized the general public, there were many instances where they took advantage of their own employers. Both large and small businesses have always been easy targets for dishonest managers and trusted employees. Among the most vulnerable have been the banking institutions since the large sums of money accessible to people working in banks are a natural temptation. Even modern banks do not have foolproof security; in an earlier day they were especially at risk. Large sums of money were sometimes embezzled over long periods of time. The guilty parties were able to cover up their activities because of inadequate auditing procedures, the trust they enjoyed, and the positions they held. One of the most notorious incidents in the early days of the banking industry took place at the head office of the Bank of Nova Scotia in Halifax. The bank was founded in 1832 and from its opening James Forman was the chief cashier. In 1871 it was discovered that Forman had embezzled more than $300,000, a sum equivalent to about 15 per cent of the bank's total assets.[32]

On occasion the misappropriation of funds by bank employees contributed to, or was the cause of, a bank closing. La Banque du Peuple, founded in 1835 in Quebec, collapsed in 1895 partly because of poor business practices but also due to dishonesty on the part of its general manager. The man was charged with fraud but escaped punishment by fleeing to the United States. Another Quebec financial institution, La Banque Jacques Cartier, temporarily suspended operations in 1876 because of financial difficulties. It, too, was the victim of poor and dishonest management. Faced with problems, the general manager had tried to hide the bank's difficulties by falsifying the books. He also contributed to the adversity by embezzling funds, which he was using for his personal stock market investments.[33]

Another case involved not only high-placed management personnel but the owner as well. La Banque de St. Jean was controlled by Philippe Roy, Speaker of the Quebec legislature. In 1908 the bank failed due to the dishonest dealings of Roy, his general manager, and the manager's assistant. Total losses of creditors amounted to approximately $400,000, including all of the deposits kept in the bank by some 900 customers. Roy had forged his brother's name on notes, the bank's assets were claimed to be much higher than they actually were, and large loans had been made from customers' deposits to businesses either owned or controlled by Roy. During the trial the jury had to be kept under close surveillance to prevent intimidation or bribery. In a rather theatrical attempt at suicide Roy shot himself in the foot. He finally ended up in St. Vincent de Paul Penitentiary – but not for long. His connections enabled him to obtain a release from prison by 1911, after which he resumed his public persona, subsequently being appointed to the Senate and as Canadian trade commissioner to France.[34]

While examples of crime can be given for many and various businesses, one that spans many enterprises is stock fraud. The pace of business development quickened significantly from the mid-nineteenth century on. This led to increased activity in the buying and selling of securities and commodities. The middlemen, called brokers, facilitated these transactions and the increase in business activity created new opportunities for them. Previously, such dealings were carried on in rather informal surroundings. With the rise in volume, however, the brokers founded the Toronto Stock Exchange in 1861. For a number of years it had an up-and-down existence, but its fortunes revived in the 1870s and it was formally incorporated in 1878. Four years earlier brokers in Montreal had organized the Montreal Stock Exchange. For many years trading activity and the exchanges were unregulated. Consequently the business was ripe for dishonest operators. The shortcomings were evidenced in 1888 when the federal government proposed to ban stock sales that were merely for speculation and that did not require the actual delivery of the stock. The proposal was criticized on the grounds that the action would eliminate about nine-tenths of transactions.

The early brokers developed a number of devices to cheat their customers that have continued to cause trouble to the present day. One practice was for promoters to buy stock themselves to increase prices by making it seem that demand was heavy. When prices reached a certain level they would sell, thus making a nice profit before others realized that the real value of the stock was far less than the artificially inflated price. In some cases the stock was completely phony, that is, it did not represent an operating business of any kind. Manipulators would issue shares on a company that had gone out of business but was still listed on the exchange.

Making poor or phony stock appear to be an attractive investment was a common practice. Promoters would give shares to prominent people and then market it on the basis that this bank president or that company director was a stockholder. This helped to raise investor interest and confidence in the stock. Sometimes false claims would be made about the prospects of the stock for gain or about the capital of the companies whose stock was being sold. The bolder promoters even advertised false price quotations to induce sales. Mining companies received government certificates verifying that there was ore in the claim. Some brokers used these certificates to trick foreign investors into thinking that the mine had government backing.

A favourite scam among dishonest brokers was to manipulate the market to cheat their customers. They would take "buy" orders at a certain price but not immediately process them. A variety of shady schemes would be used to depress values. They would then purchase the stock ordered by their customers at the lower price but bill the higher price that prevailed when the order was placed. The difference between their own buying price and the price charged the customer was pocketed as profit. A twist on this ruse involved brokers selling large amounts of stock they did not actually own. The volume of "sell" orders would cause the price of the stock to go down, at which point the brokers would buy the stock. They would then fill the orders they had taken at the higher prices, thus making a personal profit without having put up a cent.

The unsavoury practices so common in the market itself gave rise to a number of other devious activities, such as cheque kiting. Trading activity required large sums of cash, sometimes for very short periods of time. To facilitate their activities some traders resorted to handing out cheques for amounts that were not actually in their accounts. They also conspired with other traders to delay the cashing of the cheque. They would complete the trade, then get their money and deposit it before the cheque was cashed. In the meantime, however, they had carried out a financial transaction with money that they did not have at the time of sale.

Many of the illegal practices and their practitioners were difficult to prosecute. The laws were inadequate and enforcement agencies lacked the skill and knowledge to make a case against the perpetrators that would stand up in court. In some instances the traders simply moved on when they suspected that they were about to be apprehended. In other cases the status of the people involved worked in their favour and they benefited from lenient treatment in the courts. For example, in 1897 fifteen Toronto brokers were arrested on charges of advertising false claims about the capital of companies whose stocks they were promoting. Those charged represented some of the most prestigious brokerage firms in the city. All charges were dismissed.[35]

As well as the reputable brokers who on occasion indulged in illegal practices, many full-time con artists set up fly-by-night operations known as "bucket shops." Their owners were high-pressure salespeople who would open a brokerage business long enough to carry out a dishonest scheme. As soon as it was executed they would close shop and run with the money bilked from trusting investors. One such business, which closed out in Montreal in early September of 1899, had operated in the same building as the Montreal Stock Exchange. Under the name Investors Guarantee Company, its location undoubtedly lent it an air of legitimacy. The company attracted money by advertising high rates of return on deposits made for investments. The business closed owing the investors and rent on the premises, and with an arrest warrant having been issued for the owner, who turned out to be a manufacturer of cloth caps and ladies' underwear.[36]

Bucket shop operators fleeced sizable sums of money out of unsuspecting customers. The case of J.J. Herbert illustrates just how much money could change hands and also shows the ongoing problem that banks had with embezzlement. Herbert was a teller at the Banque Ville Marie in Montreal. With the co-operation of Ferdinand Lemieux, the bank's accountant, approximately $173,000 of bank money was embezzled. Herbert's salary was $600 per year yet he sported a coon coat, a diamond ring, and a fur-lined overcoat. Most of the stolen money, however, went into stock specula-tion. Herbert set up a trading account under a false name and covered all transactions with the bank's money. By the time Herbert came to trial in January, 1900, his broker had gone out of business.[37]

The illegal stock market practices persisted into the twentieth century. Though detection skills improved and the authorities became much less tolerant of business crime, nevertheless the shady practices continued, and even greater opportunities came with the dynamic growth in the stock market through the 1920s. The decade witnessed a veritable frenzy of investing activity that opened the door for many slick swindles. Prosperity and steadily rising stock prices generated unprecedented speculation, which led many to be unconcerned with the nature or condition of the companies they invested in. They were primarily interested in the perform-ance of the stock itself. The higher the prices went the more the gambling spirit grew and the more gullible the investors became. By this time, how-ever, the risk was slightly greater for the swindler than it was in an earlier day.

Illustrative of some of the ambitious schemes concocted to bilk the unwary was one carried on in the prairie provinces by Joseph Xavier Hearst. He set up a musical publishing company to sell sheet music across Canada and the United States. The popularity of music in the 1920s no doubt gave the scheme some credibility. Hearst had a very persuasive sales pitch and he attracted some prominent investors, which gave an appearance of legitimacy to his venture and helped to attract more money. Greedy for big profits and fast results, he forged letters from the Chase Manhattan Bank and orders from the T. Eaton Company. Over a two-year period he built up a complex scheme that fooled both big and small investors, whom he managed to bilk of over $500,000. Hearst took off with the money and his company was placed in bankruptcy, but for reasons unknown he returned to Winnipeg and gave himself up to the police on July 28, 1925. Hearst was convicted of embezzlement and sentenced to seven years in prison. The money was never recovered. He was released after serving four years of his sentence and returned to the United States.[38]

By the 1920s there were more stock and commodities exchanges across the country and all were the victims of crime. In April, 1922, a Regina broker operating on the Grain Exchange was tried and convicted for illegal trading. During his trial it was revealed that it was a common practice on the exchange for brokers to use their customers' securities to cover their own liabilities when carrying on personal transactions.[39]

By the end of the decade a large number of brokers who had played fast and loose on the market were in the courts. In June, 1930, the president and vice-president of the Calgary firm of Solloway, Mills & Company were found guilty of "bucketing" and of "attempting to affect the market value of stocks." Isaac W.C. Solloway, the president, was sentenced to four months in jail and fined $225,000. His vice-president, Harvey Mills, was sentenced to one month in jail and fined $25,000. The two were similarly charged in Toronto and pleaded guilty to "gaming in stocks." Solloway was fined $200,000 and Mills $50,000.[40]

In trials that took place in Toronto in October and November of 1930 eight mining brokers were found guilty of illegal transactions. They were given sentences ranging from two and a half to three years. In Quebec City, René Dupont, the former president of the Corporation d'Obligations Municipales, was convicted of "conspiracy to defraud the public" and sentenced to five years' imprisonment. In Ottawa the heads of a number of brokerage houses specializing in mining stocks were convicted of bucketing and other fraudulent practices. In Toronto in 1931 the president, vice-president, and secretary-treasurer of Stimson Company, one of the most prestigious bond houses in the city, were convicted of a number of illegal activities, including falsifying mortgages. They were respectively sentenced to three years, two and a half years, and two years less a day.[41]

The machinations in the stock market in the 1920s continued such practices as short selling and bucketing that had been developed earlier. They were aided and abetted, however, by the use of the telegraph and telephone and by the advances in advertising techniques. High-pressure salesmanship, especially telephone marketing, was used by brokers to carry on their illegal scams with people not too knowledgeable about the market. The mystique of the gamble and the confidence in get-rich schemes made many people, both the rich and the less well-to-do, easy targets for the white-collar con artists of the day.

The dramatic growth in business activity that created more opportunities for crime among the traders, brokers, and promoters also opened up other sources for illegal gain. In 1878, for example, approximately 467 factories in central Canada employed 27,869 people. In just a few years, by 1884, the number had increased to 725 factories and about 55,533 employees. The industrial growth attracted many people from rural to urban areas. At the turn of the century the pace of immigration picked up. All this meant a ready supply of cheap labour to populate the growing businesses. Once again, while many employers operated by the rules, others sought to profit by exploiting men, women, and children.

For a time the lack of labour legislation created a great deal of uncertainty about just which practices were illegal. Nevertheless, there was seldom any problem in identifying abuse, and the success of many businesses in Canada was due to the exploitation of their employees. Long hours of work, low wages, and unsanitary and dangerous working conditions were all too common. Toward the latter part of the nineteenth century and into the twentieth century the provinces passed protective labour legislation, especially covering women and children. However, many of the exploitive practices continued. The 1889 Report of the Royal Commission on the Relations of Labor and Capital revealed a wide range of lawbreaking. One common practice was that of employers cheating workers out of their wages or holding back their pay long after it was due.[42] Among the worst illegalities was the employment of young children who were working in violation of the factory and education legislation in various provinces. They worked long hours for very low wages and in unhealthy and sometimes dangerous working conditions. Boys and girls as young as ten were found working in tobacco factories.[43] The Commission reported that while the factory Acts were being violated in some provinces, in Quebec the Act was not even being enforced. One Ontario factory inspector told the Commission that in his district in 1887 he had found six nine-year-old boys, forty girls under fourteen, and many ten- and eleven-year-olds working full time. The Ontario Act provided that girls under fourteen and boys under twelve could not be employed in factories.

The exploitation of working people took place in virtually every kind of business. Large-scale construction projects such as canals and railroads were rife with shady practices. At one end the promoters were bilking the government and investors; at the other end the contractors were falsifying work and material records, overcharging, and cheating their employees out of their wages. Illegal business practices were sometimes aided by corrupt municipal administrators. As towns developed and cities grew, many municipalities spent large sums on the purchase of goods and services. Contracts were let for the construction of public buildings and utilities, the building of streets, and the provision of equipment and materials. All this business presented municipal politicians and employees with illicit money-making opportunities. Graft, fraud, embezzlement, and corruption flourished. Land speculation, bribery, and kickbacks were sources of large incomes for many municipal officials across the country.

There are many examples of municipal corruption but the following two will serve to illustrate the practices that caused concern in local government. In the early 1880s corruption among municipal politicians in Winnipeg was so widespread that a Reform Party was organized to clean house. The city had been bankrupted by a number of inefficient, irregular, and illegal practices. The most blatant lawbreaking was committed by the chairman of the Finance Committee, George M. Wilson, who was illegally borrowing money for himself and certain friends from the city's Sinking Fund. Even his wife got in on the gravy train. She was given a loan from the fund and backed it with fraudulent collateral. The city solicitor was also a party to the financial scandals. The Reform Party succeeded in turfing out many of the offenders in the election of 1884.[44]

Some years later, in 1894, a number of aldermen in Toronto were caught up in revelations of wrongdoing. An official inquiry showed that certain of them were demanding money from companies who wanted to bid on contracts and franchises. Another favourite practice of some municipal politicians in Toronto, and elsewhere, was patronage. They promised jobs and contracts to people who supported their election campaigns with votes and money. Patronage was so widespread across the country that it was an integral part of the Canadian political system.[45]

While politicians were sometimes a nuisance to the business community, more often than not they were very protective of business interests. On occasion this meant a reluctance to pass legislation that would prevent companies from engaging in activities against the public interest. A prime example is the background to the Combines Act. Naturally, big business was opposed to combines legislation and it wasn't until 1889 that the first and rather mild combines bill was passed. Clarke Wallace, a Conservative Member of Parliament and consumer advocate, introduced a private member's bill in early 1888 calling for legislation that would make combinations illegal and proposing that a committee be struck to investigate the matter. A committee was formed and Wallace was made the chairperson. Among its findings was that combinations were already injuring the public interest and that the situation would probably get worse. In spite of the evidence a majority of the committee still concluded that legislation was not necessary. Nevertheless, supporters pressed on and succeeded in getting a bill introduced. At first it received lukewarm government support but was ultimately passed in watered-down form. Some measure of the government's sincerity in stemming illegal corporate practices can be garnered from the fact that no agency was set up to enforce the legislation. It was left to the provinces, whose politicians were equally, if not more, intimidated by big business.

As a result many corrupt practices continued, although they were now officially illegal. Corporate lawbreakers were shielded by an almost total lack of enforcement and over the next few decades many questionable practices took place, including large-scale business consolidation. Between 1909 and 1913, for example, there were approximately fifty-six mergers or amalgamations that involved a total of some 248 companies. Because of the inadequacy of detection and enforcement agencies there was no way of knowing how many of these contravened the anti-combines legislation.

Collusion between business and government for illegal purposes took place on a variety of playing fields, and sometimes entire government departments were entangled in the web of lawbreaking. For example, at one point the Department of Lands, Forests, and Mines in Ontario was directly involved in a scheme that allowed the exploitation of provincial forest lands for private gain. Between 1911 and 1920 Crown forests in the northwestern part of the province were literally under the control of a Conservative patronage committee that became known as the "Tory Timber Ring." Influential party supporters were granted timber rights in return for political contributions. The patronage committee controlled appointments to jobs in the Department of Lands, Forests, and Mines in the region. Members of the ring either stole or bought timber from the government at artificially low prices, then sold it in the United States for huge profits. All of this was done with the full knowledge of the minister, Howard Ferguson, his staff, and the department workers. Ferguson's connivance was so blatant that his private secretary was on the payroll of one of the pulp and paper companies.

In the months prior to the election of 1919 the minister violated the Crown Timber Act by selling off 962 square miles of timber rights without advertising for bids, and this was not an isolated incident. Earlier, in 1917, he sold timber rights to a lumber company whose president was a fellow Conservative member of the legislature. The rights were sold for $6.26 per thousand board feet, which was about ten dollars under the appropriate price. On another occasion he granted rights to a political friend for less than half of what they were worth. Both parties later justified the deal on the grounds that the company was going to perform some valuable forestry research for the government, but in fact no such work was ever carried out. In this case the company involved paid a heavy penalty for its dishonest dealings when the court levied a fine of $1.5 million for fraudulent business transactions.[46]

Business was ever watchful of its interests and did not hesitate to resort to illegal actions if necessary. For example, a public battle took place in Toronto in early 1908 over the question of private or public ownership of utilities, a volatile issue at the time. If municipal governments came down on the side of private ownership, business would be handed tremendous money-making opportunities. In the Toronto case, one paper, *The World,* was offered a $350,000 bribe to change its editorial policy in favour of private enterprise.[47]

The business community lobbied government incessantly for special legislation and for protection of its interests. While such advocacy was to an extent proper and quite legal, in some cases it was blatantly against the public welfare. When politicians sided with special interests against the general good it naturally raised suspicions. Too often the political support was purchased with money and favours, and campaign contributors were rewarded with patronage and contracts at the expense of the public purse. The problem was serious at all levels of government.

THE LIQUOR AND DRUG TRADE

Money-making opportunities have always attracted a certain element willing to break the law if necessary. The higher the stakes the bigger the risks they are prepared to take. Along with the chance to cheat investors in the stock market and to rob the public purse as development progressed at the municipal, provincial, and federal levels, one of the greatest money-making opportunities of the 1920s came with prohibition in the U.S. In January, 1920, the 18th Amendment to the Constitution of the United States came into effect. It prohibited the manufacture, sale, transportation, importation, and exportation of liquor for beverage purposes. The law was very unpopular with a large segment of the U.S. population, who had no intention of changing their drinking habits. Consequently, a vast market for illegal liquor was opened up and United States gangsters moved quickly to organize a distribution system. They sought supplies from whatever sources they could find and naturally looked to Canada.

Business people across the country were more than willing to take advantage of the opportunity. Many new corporations suddenly appeared to carry on the importation and exportation of liquor. On the surface the activity could be legal as long as the enterprise adhered to Canadian customs and excise regulations. However, the real money was to be earned by circumventing the law, which many did. An incident involving Manitoba Refineries, a British Columbia-based export liquor company, offers an interesting example of how certain corporations carried on their illegal business. The company purchased a large quantity of liquor from Great Britain and had it shipped to Victoria and Vancouver. The liquor was landed at the Canadian ports on a through bill of lading for forwarding to customers in the town of San Blas, Mexico. Manitoba Refineries hired a shipping company, Eastern Freighters, to deliver the liquor. However, there were a number of anomalies in all these arrangements. First of all, at the time the liquor was delivered in Canada, and although it was registered for forwarding, the company had no purchaser. In fact, the liquor remained warehoused for four months before transportation arrangements were made.

Eastern Freighters, at the time of its inception, consisted of one man and the company had no ships or other means of transportation. Coincidental with receipt by Manitoba Refineries of large sums of money from banks in Los Angeles and San Francisco, Eastern Freighters chartered a ship to deliver the liquor to San Blas. Although the money had come from American banks the company claimed that its customer in Mexico had sent it. Yet the liquor from England had already passed by San Blas on its way through the Panama Canal and on to British Columbia. Equally suspicious was the fact that, although the liquor was supposedly being shipped to San Blas by boat, the village did not have a port, nor was it near one.

After investigating this case the Royal Commission on Customs and Excise in 1926 reported that:

> The evidence thus far adduced indicates that the attempted shipment of this cargo of liquors is in disregard of the expressed provisions of the Customs Act and the regulations made thereunder – that the entry papers outwards are false and fraudulent, that the alleged consignee is fictitious, and that it is not intended that the liquors should be delivered at San Blas, the port of destination, but rather that the same should be made available elsewhere to rum runners or bootleggers for consumption in the western States.[48]

The Royal Commission uncovered a significant number of similar illegal activities on the part of Canadian corporations. Its investigation revealed that a number of companies were falsely labelling compounded alcohol as Scotch whisky, registering false shipping destinations while actually selling liquor to American customers, cheating on sales and income taxes, and offering bribes to customs officials. The Bronfman family, founders of the Canadian liquor dynasty, was involved with at least eight companies accused of irregularities by the commission. One of the inspectors with the Excise Department accused Harry Bronfman of offering him bribes to turn a blind eye to the illegal activities in which his companies were engaged.[49]

Large sums of money were at stake in the bootlegging business. One lone Detroit importer bought about $5 million worth of liquor a year from Canadian suppliers. A liquor export syndicate, operating out of Windsor, Ontario, did over $9 million of business in a nine-month period. The profit margins were high because the dealers were selling a low-quality product as premium liquor at high prices. They didn't pay excise duties because they were involved in illegal transactions and they didn't pay taxes because they didn't report their income.[50]

The huge amounts of money involved in the illicit liquor trade were also used to corrupt customs officials. At many Canadian border crossings customs officers turned a blind eye to the illegal shipments of liquor going through. They conspired with Canadian businessmen, organized crime figures, and others to carry on a level of customs violations possibly unsurpassed in Canadian history – officials, charged with enforcing the law, helped people break it. The bootlegging and corruption of customs officials continued well after prohibition ended in the United States in 1933. For example, one customs officer who worked on the Detroit-Windsor border estimated that between 1935 and 1936 he allowed close to 200 carloads of liquor across the border. He claimed that many other officials were doing the same, including the senior bridge officer.[51]

White-collar crime attracted a wide variety of practitioners in the 1920s. As we have seen, it was a decade of considerable social and economic change in Canadian society. Many new opportunities opened up for criminal activity and business, and professional people succumbed to temptation in seemingly unprecedented numbers. Along with such ventures as the illicit liquor trade and stock market frauds, drug trafficking added to the scope of white-collar crime. Vancouver and Montreal were the chief centres of the illegal drug trade. For the most part the trafficking was controlled by elements of organized crime, as we shall see in more detail in another chapter. However, businessmen, lawyers, physicians, and druggists, among others, were involved in drug trafficking in the 1920s. Some invested in the trade as a way to make fast profits but never became directly active in buying and selling. Others, such as doctors and druggists, became actual traffickers. The extent of professional involvement is illustrated by the fact that in one twelve-month period ending in March, 1922, twenty-three doctors, eleven druggists, and four veterinarians were prosecuted for violations of the Drug Act.[52]

WORLD WAR TWO

The next great white-collar crime opportunity in Canada came with World War Two. The entire nation threw its resources into the prosecution of the war and new industries sprang up to produce armaments and military needs. By the end of the war manufacturing production in Canada had more than doubled. In 1939 the country's gross national product was $5.7 billion; by 1946 it had risen to $12 billion. During the war Canada became a virtual arsenal and supply depot for the allied war effort. To maximize productivity the government established a number of regulatory bodies, such as the Wartime Prices and Trade Board to oversee prices and the supply of goods and the Department of Munitions and Supply to supervise production of war materials. Rationing of key commodities, such as oil, sugar, leather, steel, wool, and lumber, was also introduced.

The full employment brought on by the war, together with rising incomes, created a high demand at a time when the availability of consumer goods was being restricted. This created an opportunity to make money in the illegal supply of goods known as the "black market." Throughout the war there was a thriving industry in the illicit sale of rationed goods, in theft and bribery in the acquisition of goods for the black market, and in the sale of rationing coupons. Big and small businesses were caught up in wartime racketeering. Government officials contributed to the lawbreaking in some instances by accepting bribes and working with black marketeers to give them access to goods through favouritism or through bypassing government regulations. Techniques ran the gamut, from the falsification of records and invoices to outright theft.

The pressure for the production of armaments and other military supplies enabled some unscrupulous manufacturers to reap illegal profits. Overpricing, fraudulent claims for goods, and cheating on quality were some of the practices used to bilk the government. To expedite output the government quite often let out "cost-plus" contracts, an arrangement whereby the contractor would be paid the costs of production plus a fixed percentage for profit. While it served as an incentive it also offered ample opportunity to pad costs. Since production was such a priority much more emphasis was placed on encouraging work than on the prevention of illegal practices. And so while most Canadians, including business people, were busily engaged in making an honest effort to win a war, some were just as occupied in dishonest ventures to line their own pockets.

A number of employers, seeking to milk as much as possible out of wartime markets, violated many of the work and safety regulations put in place over the years to prevent the exploitation of labour. One owner of a radio parts manufacturing plant in Montreal was so greedy for profit that he did not allow his employees time off the job for lunch or smoking breaks or even to go to the toilet. Finally, two of the workers complained to the government and inspectors were sent to investigate. The subsequent report listed 132 infractions of everything from workplace codes to fire regulations. In spite of the large number of violations no action was taken. Of the two women who had filed the complaint, one quit shortly afterwards and the other was fired when the owner found the first excuse to let her go.[53]

Children were also the victims of greedy employers during the war. A number of businesses compensated for the shortage of adult workers by breaking the labour laws and employing children. They also enhanced their profits by sometimes paying less than the going wage to their young employees. The problem reached sufficient proportions that a number of concerned people called for public action. Miss M.S. Pettigrew, secretary of the Toronto Board of Education, in January of 1943 claimed that "We are rapidly reverting to the bad old days when child exploitation was on an unbelievable scale...."[54] Miss Janet Parker, secretary of the Big Sister Association, said it was a tremendous problem and that the children, their parents, and employers were all conspiring to break the law. Among the many examples of such exploitation was an eleven-year-old girl who after school every day worked in a factory until 8:30 in the evening pasting labels on bottles. When questioned by a field worker from the Big Sister Association the little girl refused to tell where she worked or to give the name of her employer. Since both parents and children were anxious to keep the revenue coming in, many employers were able to hire children throughout the war with impunity.[55]

The wartime expansion continued into the post-World War Two era. Gross national product rose from $12 billion in 1946 to over $30 billion in 1957. In the next decade it doubled, reaching almost $60 billion by 1966. In 1946 there were 1,622,4463 motor vehicles registered in Canada; by 1966 the number had grown to 7,035,261. In the same period retail trade grew from an estimated $5,787,377 to $22,107,709. New businesses opened, old ones expanded. The economic explosion was helped considerably by a dramatic growth in population. After the war immigrants poured into Canada from war-ravaged Europe; as well, a baby boom added to the population. In 1951 the population was 14,009,429; by 1961 it had risen to 18,238,247 and by 1971 to 21,568,315.

WHITE-COLLAR CRIME IN THE MODERN ERA

The impressive development that Canada experienced on practically all fronts in the post-war decades opened up unprecedented opportunities for white-collar crime. The dishonest professional found plenty of temptation in the prosperity of the times. The growing spirit of materialism, plus the changing values and morality, meant that an ever-increasing number of people in Canadian society felt less restrained about turning a dishonest dollar.

Many new forms of white-collar crime have appeared in the last few decades but much continues to replicate patterns established in earlier times. Political corruption is a case in point. Such things as the growth in social welfare programs, involvement in commerce through Crown corporations, subsidies, public works projects, and regulation of business have been accompanied by a substantial increase in the size of the government enterprise. It is a major contractor for, and regulator of, the supply of goods and services. As in the past, individual politicians and political parties continue to use their positions of influence for private gain.

Examples of political corruption at all levels of government are readily available. Nowhere was it more blatant than in Montreal under the administration of Camillien Houde. During Houde's tenure Montreal earned the reputation of being a wide open city. Brothels, gambling, and gangsters thrived. Patronage was openly dispensed and the corruption touched all levels of administration, from city council to the police. Even judges and newspaper reporters got caught up in bribery and the general corruption. Some measure of how hospitable the city fathers were to lawbreaking comes from the fact that when the Kefauver investigations in the United States, which will be examined in another chapter, made things too hot for organized gambling in that country, the bookies moved their business en masse to Montreal.

Post-war government action in such areas as mining, lumber, transportation, electric power, and manufacturing frequently reflected business interests. Much of the time the dealings were above board and were perceived by governments as being in the public interest. However, in many cases bribery, patronage, and fraud were the glue that cemented the business-government relationship. Sometimes, even if there was no visible corruption, the interaction was of such a nature as to provoke suspicion and to be clearly against the public interest. If any politician epitomized the total disregard for appearances it was Clarence Decatur Howe.

C.D. Howe served as Minister of Munitions and Supply in Mackenzie King's cabinet during the war. He promoted the use of "cost-plus" contracts, which opened the door to some remarkable price-gouging by certain wartime industries. Later he served as Minister of Trade and Commerce in the government of Louis St. Laurent. He again encountered considerable criticism over what appeared to be undue favouritism toward business. Howe expected recipients of government contracts to show their appreciation by donating to the coffers of the Liberal Party. On occasion, he actually served as a bagman and handled large sums of money himself. Among his many business friends he had a close personal relationship with Sir James Dunn, the head of Algoma Steel. He invested heavily in Algoma stock, and when Sir James died in 1956 Howe acted as executor of the estate. The prospect of Canada's Minister of Trade and Commerce hawking his own shares of Algoma Steel and negotiating the sale of Dunn's holdings provoked a storm of criticism from the opposition in the House of Commons. Howe's reply to charges of conflict of interest was "nuts."[56]

Many business people simply assume that their connections with politicians will guarantee them favourable treatment. When on occasion government decisions go against them they look to their political friends for redress. The Sky Shops incident offers a good example. Sky Shops was a Montreal company owned by Clarence Campbell, Gordon Brown, and Louis Lapointe. In 1976 the federal Ministry of Transport refused to renew the company's lease on duty-free shops at Dorval airport in Montreal. The owners approached a prominent Liberal, Senator Louis Giguere, to use his influence to get the decision reversed. Subsequently, Transport officials received letters from two Liberal cabinet members, one asking for information, the other requesting a reconsideration, and one of the ministers later admitted that Giguere had put pressure on him. In late 1976 the Ministry of Transport reversed its decision and renewed the lease through to 1981. In 1978 Senator Giguere and the three Sky Shops owners were charged with influence peddling and conspiracy to offer and accept a bribe. During the trial it was alleged that Campbell, Brown, and Lapointe had offered Giguere an option on Sky Shops stocks well below their market value in return for his help in obtaining an extension of their lease. Giguere insisted on his trial being conducted in French, so he was tried separately from the others. Lapointe died before the trial. Senator Giguere was acquitted on all charges except influence peddling and that one was dropped by order of the judge. In February of 1980 Campbell and Brown were found guilty on bribery charges. They were fined $25,000 each and sentenced to serve one day in jail.[57]

Along with governments the political parties themselves have always been co-conspirators in much of the corruption that afflicts politics. The political organizations are the vehicles that propel the politicians and it has been a very costly matter to keep them functioning. The heavy reliance on media and professional managers that has come to characterize campaigning in modern times has escalated costs dramatically. In response to the need for huge sums of money political parties have elevated fund-raising to a science. Yet many of the old money-raising mechanisms linger on, including the illegal ones. Among the oldest practices that continued well into recent years – and may not be dead yet – is the awarding of government contracts in return for kickbacks. Firms would be given government contracts and then submit inflated bills for their services. The extra money would be given to the party in the form of political donations. The scheme operated in many parts of the country.[58] In some cases favoured contractors were awarded work without competitive bidding on the understanding that they would make donations to party coffers. On occasion the exact amount was specified.

At the provincial level liquor companies were especially vulnerable to kickback schemes. In return for handling their products through provincial liquor stores, a corkage fee was levied. The liquor company would have to pay so much per bottle of its product sold to the fund-raiser of the party in power. In this manner the party war chest would be built up to help finance party expenditures and the next election campaign.[59] As more and more public exposure has taken place it has become more difficult for political parties and governments to get away with such practices. Nevertheless, bribery and other illegalities continue to flourish across the country. Unfortunately, the corruption touches individual politicians as well as their parties. In December of 1989 as many as fifteen MPs and senators were under investigation by the RCMP for alleged Criminal Code and election law violations.

The government of Brian Mulroney has had a particularly difficult time. Cabinet members have been forced out and members of Parliament have had to vacate their seats for a variety of corrupt activities. A number of MPs have been involved in the age-old game of bribery and kickbacks. They use their influence to obtain contracts or other favours in return for money or benefits. One MP pleaded guilty to receiving $97,500 in cash and other benefits in return for helping contractors get work on a government project. He was convicted on fifteen counts of bribery and influence peddling, sentenced to one year in jail, and fined $50,000.[60] Another pleaded guilty to eleven counts of fraud and breach of trust. He was also accepting kickbacks from contractors.[61] The record of the Mulroney government may give it the distinction of being one of the most scandal-scarred administrations in Canadian history.

In recent years some serious forms of political corruption, associated with land development, have been found at the municipal level. The urban growth, especially in cities like Toronto, Vancouver, and Calgary, has created problems related to municipal by-laws, licences, and construction codes. In some cases developers have sought to circumvent various restrictions and regulations by bribing municipal officials and politicians, and the public interest has been compromised by municipal councils changing by-laws and by officials turning a blind eye to code and other infractions.

Developers who court municipal politicians are not usually doing so for illegal purposes. However, sometimes the relationship can become so close as to raise suspicions of a conflict of interest. An example of the close ties that can form between a developer and a municipal politician was illustrated by the Toronto *Globe and Mail* in April, 1990. Over a six-year period a Toronto councillor had aggressively assisted a real estate developer in his dealings with the city. He helped win approval for two large residential projects, one of which involved a land exchange with the Toronto Transit Commission. The deal with the TTC had been pursued since 1985, with the councillor apparently taking much of the initiative. The first round started when the councillor submitted a proposal, on behalf of the developer, to swap a piece of land owned by the latter for a better-situated one owned by the TTC. A report by TTC staff pointed out that the proponent's land was worth about $1.5 million less than the parcel he hoped to acquire, and at that point the possibility of a deal ended. A year later the TTC called for development proposals for the site and one of those submitted came from a company in which the real estate developer in question was a partner. By this time the councillor had been appointed as a TTC commissioner. He brought pressure to bear on behalf of his friend's company and, in the words of one senior TTC staff member, "really bullied us."

The TTC commissioners approved the proposal supported by the councillor even though, as some claimed, the Commission could have made a better deal with another developer. The original proposal was for a sixty-six unit apartment building, but shortly after the purchase from the TTC was completed city council approved a rezoning that allowed the developer to increase the size of the project to 116 units, thus making the parcel of land much more valuable. Since then the councillor has again appeared before a city committee, in support of another real estate development proposed by his friend.

Final approval for the building project on the former TTC land was given on May 16, 1989. The following July the Toronto councillor started renovations on the $1.4 million home he purchased the previous May. Some of the renovations were done by tradesmen employed by the real estate developer on his apartment house project. Two of the workmen were quoted as saying, "We were told it was a hush-hush job." Some years earlier, in 1985, after the councillor had helped his friend with another real estate project, his parents purchased one of the homes built in the new subdivision. The developer very kindly arranged for his lawyer to give a second mortgage to the parents in the amount of $26,000. The lawyer said he was asked by the developer if he "had any mortgage funds available, and although I'm not in the mortgage financing business I looked around and found the money."[62]

The modern-day growth that fuelled real estate development has also given impetus to the country's stock and commodities markets. As with real estate, much of the activity is honest and above board, but some is not. The growth in Canadian enterprise has offered ongoing opportunity for illegal activities on the part of stock promoters and brokers. Along with a host of long-standing illegal practices, the fraudulent promotion of mining stocks has been a particular problem. Canada's vast mineral deposits have always sparked a great deal of mining activity and generated substantial investment interest both here and abroad. This in turn has spawned a steady stream of criminal ventures. Many mining stocks, because of the highly speculative and volatile nature of the business, are first issued at low prices to attract investors. They are referred to as "penny stocks." The low initial price makes them very attractive because a large amount of stock can be purchased for a modest investment and if the stock happens to take off a fortune can be made. But the low price makes them particularly vulnerable to manipulation.

A case in 1974-75 illustrates the nature of the fraud. Following an agreement to underwrite a share issue by a mining company, the promoter then proceeded to manipulate the stock from a floor of twenty cents to a high of $1.75 by arranging for friends and relatives to buy and sell the stock among themselves. They artificially raised the price and gave the appearance to the public of considerable trading action. The idea of a scheme like this is to sell the shares to unwary investors as soon as the shares have reached a certain price. The promoters make a considerable profit on their original outlay and the outside buyer is left with nearly worthless stock.[63]

In 1973 the RCMP estimated there were as many as 100 promoters across Canada carrying on commercial frauds. They specialized in bankruptcies and stock fraud and in some cases were aided by the very officials who were supposed to be protecting the public interest.[64] Brokers bribe officials by letting them in on their manipulations and allowing them to profit from the illegal activity. Thus, manipulations in the stock market cast a wide net. Increasingly, swindlers have been operating on an international basis, with a significant number working out of Canada. In other instances dishonest Canadian brokers co-operate with foreign criminals to fleece investors on the Canadian market. A case in 1987 involved the famous American actor Mr. T. In July of that year a video was shown on the Financial News network featuring Mr. T. encouraging investment in a company called OEX

Electromagnetic Inc. Decked out in his gold chains and commanding people to invest, he was presented in the video as a major shareholder and an important member of the OEX team. In actuality the actor owned no shares and was not active in the company.

OEX was an American company based in Fort Smith, Arkansas. In 1986 it negotiated the rights to manufacture and market a super-thin speaker, but its efforts to raise funding in the United States were thwarted by stock exchange regulators. Company officials then turned to the Canadian financial market. They contacted a brokerage firm called Four-Star Management Ltd., which operated on the Vancouver Stock Exchange, and worked out a fund-raising deal. OEX took over a shell company connected with the VSE called Amark Explorations and renamed it OEX Electromagnetic. (A shell company is a business still listed on the exchange but no longer active.) Four-Star mounted a high-pressure campaign to flog OEX stock. In 1987 its employees averaged 2,100 phone calls a month to potential investors and in addition the firm sent out over 1,000 packages of promotional material and featured Mr. T.'s video on television. The frenzy of activity met with some success – the stock went up to $7.75 by March, 1987, from a starting point of twenty cents.

To meet the requirements of the VSE the accounting firm of Coopers & Lybrand was hired to independently assess the company's potential. The consultant assigned the task, according to his own testimony, relied heavily on information supplied to him by the company rather than doing a thorough independent investigation. As it turned out he was given a completely false picture of the health of the OEX operation. When he visited the plant in Fort Smith employees were put to work loading empty boxes to make it look like business was booming. The consultant's report painted a strong but obviously false picture. It stated that there was a backlog of orders worth $1.7 million when in fact orders were minimal. Forty dealers were reported to have been signed up when actually there was only one confirmed agreement. The report claimed that sixty-five U.S. Army and Air Force stores had agreed to sell the speakers – this also turned out to be false.

The positive independent report further strengthened the company's image and made OEX look like an attractive investment. A stock offering was approved by the VSE and the Canadian OEX eventually advanced $2.4 million to its U.S. parent. In March of 1988 an accountant reviewing the company's books discovered that the Arkansas operation had spent all of the money that had been raised from stock sales. It was also revealed that between October, 1986, and January, 1988, the company had sold only $144,000 worth of its product. Consequently the stock, which had peaked at $8.25 on the basis of a fraudulent promotion, had little real value. The VSE suspended trading of the company's stock in April, 1988.[65]

Vancouver Stock Exchange officials held a hearing on the whole affair and handed out some stiff penalties. Two of the American principals were banned from trading on the VSE and from holding office in any British Columbia company, one for a twenty-five-year period, the other for twenty years. Four of the promoters connected with Four-Star Management Ltd. were suspended for twelve years and a fifth for two years. In the meantime some Americans and Canadians pocketed a considerable sum of money while a large number of investors were victimized by a classic scam.[66]

Stock market fraud often involves a large cast of characters including company officials, brokerage houses, floor traders, promoters, and people buying and selling stock. In some cases reputable companies can be unwittingly pulled into a fraud by their own dishonest employees. The extent of the web is illustrated by the case of United Services Funds, a Texas-based mutual fund. A group of Vancouver promoters bribed the fund's portfolio manager, with $1.2 million, to invest in fourteen of their companies listed on the Vancouver Stock Exchange. Investment by a reputable mutual fund like United Services quickly pumped up the worthless stock. In a twenty-six-day period in 1985 the price of one stock rose from forty-one cents to $3.35. One of the promoters was an employee of the firm of Richardson Greenshields of Canada Ltd., which handled many of United Services' stock purchases. The American company was fleeced out of an estimated $22 million. It took its case to court and was awarded a settlement of about $27 million, part of which was an out-of-court settlement from Richardson Greenshields of approximately $10 million. The company was also fined $250,000 for failing to properly supervise an employee.[67]

There are many variations on stock market fraud and Canadian brokers have mastered all of them. They dupe people from all over the world with their illegal practices. One such international scheme cost some 200 West Germans $1.5 million. Two brokers trading on the Vancouver Exchange persuaded a German investment dealer to sell shares of a company called Beauford Resources Ltd. The two promoters said that they eventually wanted to get control of the company themselves and had an option to repurchase the shares at a higher price. Instead of using the money that was sent by German investors to purchase stock for them, the Canadians bought shares in their own name, purchased stock for friends, and spent money on luxury items. On the strength of the sales the value of Beauford Resources rose from $3.80 to $12 in a six-month period. The scheme collapsed, however, when the Germans stopped sending money. Brokers still holding stock tried to sell but found no takers. When the price dropped the original investors were out their money, brokers lost some $1.3 million, and the fraud triggered a general collapse of prices on the Vancouver Exchange in October, 1984, that amounted to some $40 million. The two promoters who devised the scheme were each sentenced to seven years in penitentiary.[68]

Much of the illegal activity, especially in mining stocks, has centred on the Vancouver Stock Exchange. Anxious to establish a presence among

Canadian and world exchanges, it has courted the more exotic and volatile end of the business and has been less vigilant of shady practices with the result that the level of fraud committed through the exchange has sullied its reputation. For example, the *Report on Organized Crime in British Columbia* estimated that in 1974 between 20 and 30 per cent of mining and junior industrial stocks were manipulated on the Vancouver Stock Exchange.[69] In spite of attempts by officials to prevent dishonest promoters from using the exchange and to improve their image, the problem was still not solved. In May, 1989, an issue of *Forbes*, a leading business magazine, described Vancouver as the "scam capital of the world" and the VSE as "the longest standing joke in North America." It claimed that the exchange was "infested with crooked promoters, sons of crooked promoters and sons of friends of crooked promoters," and further claimed that brokers were arranging wash sales through the exchange for purposes of laundering money.[70]

The Vancouver Stock Exchange has not been the only exchange to be victimized by a long run of fraudulent activity. The Winnipeg Commodity Exchange has also had its fair share of dishonest members. Inadequate surveillance practices enabled a group of crooked brokers to carry on illegal activities over a five-year period in the 1980s that netted them earnings of up to $6 million. One scam started in 1981 when two traders conspired to buy and sell with each other in a manner that cheated one of the broker's clients. The floor trader for Cargill, a major grain company, arranged to sell his co-conspirator large quantities of canola at the lowest quoted price of the day and then buy the commodity back at the highest price. Cargill was out the difference and the two traders would split the profits. Over a four-year period the pair bilked the company of an average of $10,000 per month and in one particularly good month in 1983 they made $70,000.

Because of the inadequate regulation of the exchange the Cargill trader was able to cover up his dealings. Finally in February, 1985, someone who realized what was going on tipped off the company and the fraud was uncovered. During the investigation into the Cargill dealings the RCMP discovered that other brokers on the exchange were accepting kickbacks, falsifying documents, and breaking margin rules. Some of the most respected people in the business were guilty of illegal practices, including the former head of XCon Grain Ltd., who in 1988 was charged with fraud and accepting secret commissions. Between 1980 and 1983 he had made approximately $135,000 U.S. through his illicit activities.[71]

Over the years many business people have been every bit as innovative and devious in executing criminal schemes as the traders on the exchanges. Dishonest executives have taken advantage of every conceivable device to profit illegally. Some of the largest sums are reaped from insurance claims for arson, fraudulent bankruptcies, and rigged shipping losses. Troubled businesses hire a "torch" to set fire to their premises in order to collect the insurance, and sometimes certain goods are removed before the fire is set. In other cases owners milk everything they can from an enterprise, run up bills, and then file for bankruptcy. The money taken from the operation is channelled into their private accounts while creditors are left holding the debts. Shipping frauds commonly involve claims for short shipments of orders. Paperwork is falsified so that a shipment appears to be short on the quantity of goods shipped. The customer then puts in a claim and is reimbursed by the insurance company.[72]

These types of crimes are frequently difficult to detect or prove. A skilled professional can make arson look like any ordinary fire that started by accident. Many business crimes are elaborate, complex schemes that involve people like accountants and a long stream of doctored records. Fraudulent bankruptcies can be made to look like unfortunate business failures with no reason for authorities to be suspicious or to launch an investigation. Insurance fraud can appear like any legitimate loss and sometimes the scheme even includes crooked adjusters. The latter simply confirm the loss so the company does not hesitate to pay. All of this tips the odds against detection and encourages unethical people to engage in profitable lawbreaking.

Less complex but sometimes just as financially rewarding are other types of commercial crime, ranging from false advertising to the fencing of stolen goods, to the rigging of bids on contracts. Some of the largest and most trusted companies are among the offenders. Between 1962 and 1972 a total of 282 convictions were won by Canadian courts against companies for misleading price advertising. Among those found guilty were Simpson-Sears Limited, the T. Eaton Company, and George Weston Limited. In 1983 the Dominion Stores pleaded guilty in a Nova Scotia court to 400 counts of improper pricing.[73] In the year ending March 31, 1980, the courts examined 244 misleading advertising and deceptive marketing cases, concluded 134 proceedings, and handed down 100 convictions for which fines totalling $378,380 were imposed.[74]

Even children are not spared the manipulations of dishonest corporations. In 1980 Lowney Inc., one of Canada's largest candy bar manufacturers, mounted a major promotional campaign aimed at children. The company did not announce the value of prizes or the chances of winning. After the first three months of the campaign the company reduced the odds of winning free chocolate bars and tokens but did not publicize the change. In May of 1984 Lowney Inc. was fined $70,000 for contravening the Combines Investigation Act.[75]

One of the most flagrant cases of bid-rigging to be exposed in recent decades took place during the 1970s. Nine corporations and eleven executives were charged with conspiring to rig bids on federal contracts for harbour dredging. The conspiracy, sometimes referred to as Harbourgate, involved some of the biggest companies in the business headquartered in

Toronto, Montreal, and British Columbia. The companies were inflating government dredging costs by agreeing in advance what each one would bid on certain contracts and the winner would then pay the others a specified portion of the profit. The trial lasted fourteen months and the jury took another month to deliberate before rendering a verdict. In the spring of 1979 five of the executives were convicted and sentenced to prison terms ranging from two to five years; eight of the dredging companies were fined a combined total of $6.5 million. Three of the five later appealed and had their convictions set aside. The case also involved kickbacks to a former Ontario harbour commissioner, accusations against others, and suspicion of involvement of a federal and a provincial cabinet minister.[76]

The Harbourgate verdict was followed in 1980 by one of the biggest financial scams in Canadian history. Argosy Financial Group of Canada Ltd. collapsed after duping some 1,600 people out of approximately $24 million. The principals of the company had lured investors with promises of a higher interest rate than they could get elsewhere and assurances that their money was safe. They told customers that the company invested in sound mortgages on properties in Ontario and Alberta, but in reality the money was spent on low-value real estate belonging to officials of the company. Funds were also diverted for personal expenditures on race horses and gambling. After Argosy went under it was revealed that its founder had been convicted of theft by conversion in 1971 and in 1973 had been barred from dealing in mortgages through a subsidiary of the parent company. In addition, another Argosy official had been threatened with the cancellation of his mortgage broker registration for charging interest rates between 20 and 26 per cent when the prevailing rate was under 10 per cent. In 1978 the director of the Ontario Securities Commission turned down Argosy's registration as an issuer of securities because of its founder's criminal record. However, his decision was overruled by the Commission and the door was thus opened for the fraud. The money lost represented the evaporation of the life savings of many ordinary people and illustrates once again the price paid by victims of white-collar crime. John David Carnie, one of the principals, was sentenced to six and one-half years in the penitentiary, two other executives to three years, and another to three and one-half years.[77]

The more frequent apprehension of corporate criminals and stiffer penalties were still not sufficient to deter major companies from illegal practices. Among the crimes that continue to be committed by some very large corporations is bid-rigging on government contracts. In early December, 1990, three of Canada's biggest flour-milling companies were levied fines of $1 million each, and a smaller member of the scheme was fined $500,000 for rigging prices. All pleaded guilty to fixing bids on flour to be sold to the federal government destined for aid to Third World countries. The companies carried on the scheme between 1975 and 1987 on contracts worth an estimated $500 million. The conspiracy operated through the Canadian

Millers Association, which designated the company that would be the successful bidder and then told the executives what bids to submit. One company would bid just below the pre-determined ceiling while the rest would bid above it. The contracts with the Canadian International Development Agency included flour destined for famine-stricken countries such as Ethiopia.[78]

The age-old collusion between business and government officials is another form of crime that continues to thrive in contemporary society. In an earlier day the common payoff to corrupt civil servants was a monetary reward; some modern bribes are much more diverse. A not untypical case involved two quality control inspectors working for the Department of National Defence. They were assigned to work in a Toronto auto parts company to assure that goods sold to the Canadian or U.S. military met government specifications. The company had a contract with the U.S. Defense Department to supply certain new or unused parts for tanks. The Canadian business was buying surplus parts the U.S. Army was selling as scrap, reconditioning them, and then selling them back as unused or new equipment. In return for the inspectors allowing the corporation to carry on the deception they were rewarded with benefits that included the provisions of prostitutes, meals, liquor, baseball tickets, partially paid holidays, interest-free loans, and cash. Between April, 1979, and October, 1983, when the company was exposed, the inspectors had been provided with prostitutes on eighty separate occasions. The total bill for that benefit alone came to some $11,500. In all, the two inspectors had accepted bribes from the company worth approximately $20,000.[79]

Along with older forms of crime, businesses have also kept pace with new developments. The scope is evident by examining crimes in such diverse areas as art, computers, videos, government tax credit programs, and armaments. The interest in art, along with the market, has grown appreciably since World War Two. Today the works of the masters sell in the multimillion-dollar range while there are modern and contemporary artists whose works command six-figure prices and more. In November, 1989, for example, an oil painting by Montreal artist Clarence Gagnon sold for $495,000. The lure of big money has tempted some gallery operators into illegal practices, the most common being the selling of counterfeit works of art. The cheating started even before prices in the art world escalated so dramatically, and Canada holds the distinction of trying the first art fraud case in North America. Undoubtedly there were incidences before this but they were not officially detected and prosecuted. The first trial took place in Toronto in 1963-64 involving a number of dealers who were selling fake art at their galleries and at auctions. The police rounded up about 100 paintings as evidence for the trial. The fake art was attributed to such painters as A.Y. Jackson, Emily Carr, and Cornelius Krieghoff, among others.[80]

The computer has had an impact on contemporary society in a manner somewhat equivalent to the telephone, when it first came on stream. Just as criminals found many uses for the telephone the modern computer has opened up new opportunities for white-collar crime, such as illegal duplication of software, unauthorized access to information, and use of the computer for theft. Many companies are reluctant to report computer crimes, partly because they are embarrassed to admit that they have been victimized. Others are afraid that revelations of their problems will destroy customer confidence. Consequently, police estimate that as little as 5 per cent of computer crime is reported.

One crime to which computers have made corporations more susceptible is employee blackmail. Many businesses have transferred all their records to computers, so their daily activities depend heavily on the proper functioning of the machines and on their reliability in retrieving data. In one incident an employee changed the password that accessed the data bank, and before he would reveal the new password that he had programmed into the system he demanded $50,000 from his employer. The firm had little choice but to pay. Because of the embarrassment the company was reluctant to prosecute and so let the employee get away with the extortion.[81]

Another type of computer crime was discovered by a branch of one of Canada's major banks. On the occasion of the branch's tenth anniversary, as part of its celebrations, the bank decided to honour the customer with the most active account. Much to everyone's surprise it turned out to be one of the bank's employees. The man used the computer regularly to transfer a few cents out of customers' accounts into his own. The amount was so small that the customer would not notice but collectively the employee had accumulated about $70,000. If the bank hadn't decided on that particular anniversary project the employee might have stolen much more and possibly avoided detection. As it was he did escape punishment. When his scheme was uncovered he defiantly told his employer, "Go ahead and charge me. I will tell the public you have been doing this for years." By rounding off customers' accounts the bank had also been taking money that belonged to its depositors.[82]

Employees have devised many variations on computer crimes, ranging from the theft of computer time for their personal use to costly frauds. In one such incident an employee deliberately neglected to remove the names of four terminated co-workers from the company's computerized payroll records. The individual then opened four accounts in different banks in the names of the terminated employees and arranged to have paycheques deposited in the new accounts. The fraud was ultimately detected when it was noticed that one of the company's accounts was being overspent.

Computers have also created an opportunity for the illegal duplication and sale of software. Copying breaches the user's licence agreement and is also a violation of copyright law. Programs are expensive so a small-scale industry has developed supplying pirated software. The copies can be sold at much lower prices so naturally there is a ready market for pirated material. The companies that produce software claim that the clandestine trade costs them millions of dollars a year in lost business. The Software Publishers Association estimates that three to seven pirated copies are circulating for every one sold legitimately, and also claims that corporate employees are the worst offenders. They duplicate programs at work for friends or for home use.[83]

The whole problem of computer crime is still marked with many uncertainties. Companies are reluctant to lay charges, computer audits are complex and expensive, crimes are easy to cover up, and when someone is caught he or she frequently gets off with a light penalty. Judges tend to be lenient because they see the crime as victimless and because quite often the offender has no criminal record and is well educated. Many computer users are highly skilled. If someone wants to turn his or her talents to lawbreaking there are few checks in place to prevent this, and to many the offence is more of a game than a crime.

The record and cassette industry has always been plagued with counterfeiters and businesses willing to buy from them. A variation came with the introduction of videos. Criminals saw the same money-making opportunities in illegally copying videos that they did with records and cassettes. The video pirates are able to undercut substantially the prices of the legitimate producers because their only costs are for duplicating. The original producer has to absorb outlays for the performers, production, business overhead, and a number of other expenses. Consequently, the price the retailer pays for a video reflects all the costs of production plus the distributor's markup. Since the video pirate bypasses most of those costs the retailer is able to buy bootleg supplies at a lower cost and therefore make a much bigger profit on sales. The profit is so good that some of the largest outlets in the country have dealt in illegally produced videos.

The widespread market among otherwise legitimate businesses is evident from the fact that in 1987 police across Canada seized over 22,000 pirated videocassettes. Since the traffic in such a product is hard to detect and requires constant searches, the figure probably accounts for a small percentage of what actually circulates. Counterfeiting is an international business and frequently videos are copied in other countries and then sold to Canadian importers, eventually working their way through to distributors, retailers, and video-rental outlets. The more popular the product the more likely it is to be copied. For example, one of the biggest sellers in recent years has been video games, and in the late 1980s and 1990s one of the most successful producers has been the Nintendo company. In April of 1990 Nintendo of America Inc. filed lawsuits against twelve Canadian businesses in an effort to stop the sale of bootleg video games.[84] The video industry estimates that over 12 per cent of home video sales is made up of counterfeit cassettes, representing an annual loss to distributors in excess of $20 million.[85]

Nowhere has the ingenuity of business in criminal activity been better demonstrated than in relation to the Scientific Research Tax Credit program. The federal government operated the program in 1984-85 as an incentive to investment in scientific research. It allowed companies to receive a fifty-cent tax credit for every dollar invested in research. Almost immediately certain businesses worked out schemes to defraud the government. Before it was in place a year it was frozen and then was discontinued in 1985 because of widespread abuse. Investigators estimated that out of approximately $3 billion handed out in credits as much as $1 billion was misappropriated. Much of the money was spirited out of the country into foreign bank accounts. Prosecutions are difficult and it is doubtful if much of the money will ever be recovered.

The first case of defrauding the Scientific Research Tax Credit program to go to trial involved PBD Research Inc. The company sold a tax credit in the amount of $430,000 to Tandy Corporation. After paying a finder's fee of $50,000 to Burns Fry Ltd., PBD was left with a net profit of $380,000. While the company went through the motions of hiring staff to mount the research program they were all let go as soon as the tax credit was sold. The company and its owner were convicted of tax evasion. During the course of the investigation that led to charges being laid, Revenue Canada discovered that $230,000 went into the personal bank account of the head of the corporation and out of that, $12,000 was paid to another company he controlled for the lease of a Mercedes. He also paid himself $45,000 as a management fee.[86]

Another fraud on the Scientific Research Tax Credit program resulted in a prominent businessman ending up on the police wanted list. Howard White fled the country in late 1986 after he was charged with evading $14 million in income taxes. He also faced charges involving $23.6 million in claims made to the tax credit program for research supposedly done by four of his companies. A Revenue Canada audit revealed that although the businesses reported expenditures over $40 million, only $588,000 was spent on legitimate research. The government claims that much of the money was sent out of Canada to a number of foreign tax havens. White was living in southern California when he was arrested by U.S. Federal Bureau of Investigation agents in November, 1989.[87]

The numerous local and regional conflicts around the world have spawned a huge traffic in arms in recent decades. While national governments such as the U.S.S.R. and the United States carry on the bulk of the sales, many individual dealers also do a thriving business. Some specialize in the illegal side of the arms business by buying and selling in an underground market and violating national and international laws. In 1980 Space Research Corporation, a Quebec-based company, was convicted on seven counts of violating the United Nations embargo on shipments of arms to South Africa. Over a two-year period, between 1976 and 1978, the company shipped arms under falsified export certificates. It showed cargoes going to destinations such as Spain, Antigua, and Barbados that were actually being shipped to South Africa. Space Research Corporation was fined a total of $55,000.[88]

Another impact of population and economic growth in recent decades has been a dramatic expansion of the real estate industry. That expansion has been accompanied by considerable crime at all levels. Real estate agents cheat both sellers and buyers; builders shortchange home purchasers with shoddy construction and contract violations; mortgage lenders conspire with both at the expense of borrowers. The real big-league schemes, however, have usually been carried out by the developers. One common device is to turn over properties in a way that artificially increases their book value. A real estate owner will arrange for a piece of land or apartment complex to be sold to a friend or a dummy company at a price higher than its current market value and it will then be repurchased at an even higher price. The fake sales create the impression that the property is worth the last purchase price, thus raising its evaluation for mortgage purposes. The owner is then able to borrow money on the property in an amount far exceeding its real value. In this case the lender is left holding very low collateral for the loan, and if the mortgagee defaults, the lender stands to lose the difference between the loan and the sale price of the real estate.

Property frauds can sometimes amount to very large sums of money, with investors losing millions. One recent case in Ontario left investors and creditors with losses of approximately $93 million. The developer raised large sums of money by advertising high rates of return, up to 25 per cent, over relatively short periods of time. The company did own property and did start construction on a shopping mall, but much of its activity was designed to create a false impression to lure investors. One of its projects was claimed to be worth $170 million when an independent appraisal estimated its value at about half that figure. A piece of land was sold three times between December, 1988, and March, 1989. The first sale was for $280,000; the second sale was made to a business associate of the company owner; the third sale was made to another of the developer's firms. The third sale was for $4.2 million. Thus, by a series of friendly flips the paper value of the real estate increased by almost $4 million. The developer ran about a dozen companies but all the money collected by them was ultimately pooled in a single bank account, and he drew heavily on investors' money for his personal use. He spent $612,000 on a racing boat, owned an expensive home in a Toronto suburb and a villa in Acapulco, had bought a string of expensive cars, and even played the public-spirited citizen by making donations to a hospital and a university. In January of 1990 the Supreme Court of Ontario appointed a receiver to take over, but at that point the developer's various companies had run out of money. Since the remaining assets were only a fraction of the liabilities, some 5,800 people faced little prospect of recovering their investments.[89]

Although business crime can involve large sums of money and is engaged in by some very large and reputable companies, numerous small firms contribute significantly to the problem. The fencing of stolen goods is a common activity among small business outlets. The 1979 study on organized crime in British Columbia, for example, pointed out that "the largest category of fences could be described as businessmen."[90] Service stations, auto repair shops, pawn shops, secondhand stores, and a variety of retail outlets, including restaurants, fence stolen goods. Some even steal the goods with which they stock their own stores. One team of three women and a man, who operated a retail clothing business, shoplifted from fashionable boutiques and then sold the clothes out of their own shop. Some criminals specialize in hijacking shipments of clothing and other goods and sell them in discount outlets they open in suburban shopping malls.[91]

Cheating the government on payroll remissions is another practice engaged in more by smaller businesses, although large businesses also have been guilty. Employers collect money from their employees for taxes, unemployment insurance, and the Canada Pension program. Retail outlets collect sales tax. Most of the time this is done efficiently and honestly with the revenue being remitted in full and on time. However, the large sums of money are a temptation for some employers, especially if they are in financial difficulty, and every year large amounts of payroll deductions are kept by the employers. Sometimes the government is successful in retrieving the money or in prosecuting the guilty parties, but if a company has gone under it is difficult to trace the funds. The practice has been a long-standing one and the total of unremitted funds can be quite large. In 1975, for example, when bank robbers were getting bigger hauls than they do today, the Canadian Bankers Association reported a net loss of $5.17 million from bank robberies. By comparison, in the same year businesses failed to remit some $7.9 million and Revenue Canada prosecuted about 2,000 employers. The practice remains a problem, especially with the high level of business failures in recent years.[92]

Violation of safety regulations is another offence that seems to be more common among small businesses than large ones. Perhaps because profits are slimmer in modest operations there is a greater tendency to ignore costly safety practices. The construction industry has a particularly high incidence of accidents. For example, in the mid-1970s it was reported that about forty-five construction workers died on the job each year in the province of Quebec alone and another 13,500 were injured. While many accidents were due to human error, some were the result of failing to heed safety regulations. Annually cases are reported from across Canada of deaths and injuries due to the violation of safety codes.[93]

On occasion owners of small businesses exhibit considerable callousness in dealing with their customers. Some of the worst examples have come out of the funeral industry. Some funeral parlor operators take advantage of bereavement and shock to push very costly caskets and funeral arrangements on people who cannot afford the expense. One operator worked out a variation on this by switching caskets on deceased who were cremated. Some of the expensive caskets that families bought contained material that was difficult to burn and so would not be accepted by the crematorium. They were not told this, however, and a wooden box was used to replace the casket, which was then resold. The funeral director was convicted of fraud in 1985. In an ironic sequel to the case, he subsequently took his legal firm to court on the grounds that the fee charged for his defence was too high.[94]

When censorship laws were more stringent many small businesses made big money in the pornographic trade. They dealt in smuggled materials along with items and subject matter that were illegal under Canadian laws. The distribution networks were extensive and included small newsstands and neighbourhood stores across the country. One enterprising British Columbia businessman, in the late 1960s and 1970s, became the major distributor of pornography in western Canada. He had a long criminal record for theft, immigration law violations, receiving stolen goods, gambling, and possession of obscene materials. He imported much of his pornographic material from the United States and had connections with Mafia figures in that country.[95]

While businesses, through their owners and principals, sometimes engage in criminal practices, they are also often the victims. Crime among employees has been an ever-growing problem and studies suggest that the bulk of theft and embezzlement is committed by long-serving, trusted employees, frequently with management responsibilities. There has always been a reluctance to prosecute employee crime. Businesses are afraid of tarnishing their reputations or risking customer confidence, and fraud is especially embarrassing. As one executive explained it, "No one likes to admit that a trusted employee has taken him for a ride."[96] Consequently they allow employees to pay the company back and/or quietly dismiss them. There is no way of accurately documenting this type of white-collar crime, but indicators suggest the problem is widespread.

In 1965 claims against bonding and insurance companies came to $3.3 million. Such companies provide insurance for the employer against losses from employee dishonesty. Since many employees in a position of trust are not bonded, the above figure would be far below the actual level of loss.[97] In 1970 one investigating firm estimated that employers were losing as much as $1 million a day in cash and merchandise stolen by their own people.[98] Employee theft ranges from dipping into cash receipts to some rather elaborate frauds. One group of insurance company employees organized a fictitious automobile repair business and left no detail unattended. The non-existent company had an office address, stationery, and even its own invoices. The employees checked their company files for expired automobile policies. They would pull the records and use the customers' names and addresses to file imaginary damage claims. An outside insurance adjuster was brought into the scheme and all claims were filed through him. Authorized repairs were promptly paid for by the insurance company to the imaginary body shop. The fraud went on for three years before it was uncovered, and in that time it cost the employer over $200,000.[99]

Among the businesses that lose the largest sums of money to dishonest employees are the banks. As we have seen, the problem goes back to the earliest days of banking in Canada. Officials always seem to think they have the problem under control but are constantly proven wrong. One senior banking executive in 1966 was quoted as claiming that internal controls were "so tight that there are few opportunities for anyone below a manager to be in a position to remove sizeable amounts of money undetected." Yet in one ten-month period ending in May, 1982, banks and trust companies in the city of Toronto alone lost over $13.2 million to fraud. One of them involved a twenty-eight-year-old clerk who made $13,500 per year. He absconded with eighty-eight pounds of gold worth $648,000. The employee who handed over the gold was told a bank had ordered it.[100]

In October of 1988 charges of fraud were made against four Edmonton businessmen involving loans from the Canadian Commercial and Northland banks worth $22 million. The loans were allegedly obtained by giving fake insurance-premium finance contracts as security.[101] In January, 1990, two former Canada Trust executives were sentenced to six years in prison for stealing $4.6 million from their employer. The men set up thirty-five mortgage accounts for fictitious clients. The money was transferred from the accounts to a dummy company set up in Toronto and then into a bank account in Switzerland. The executives fled the country but were arrested in England in 1988.[102]

The most publicized embezzlement in recent years was carried out by Brian Molony, an assistant manager at a Toronto branch of the Canadian Imperial Bank of Commerce. In April, 1982, it was discovered that over the previous nineteen months he had managed to defraud the bank of $10.2 million, the biggest embezzlement in Canadian banking history. Molony's scheme was relatively simple. He set up ten fictitious loan accounts, some in the names of customers, and since one of his responsibilities was to approve loans he was in an excellent position to carry out the fraud. He would approve an application, have the money credited to one of his accounts, and then withdraw the funds.

Molony was a compulsive gambler and was using the money to finance his junkets to Las Vegas and Atlantic City. On one occasion he arranged for the U.S. dollar account of one of the bank's customers to be debited $45,000. He then told the woman at the foreign exchange desk that the customer wanted a bank draft in the name of the Marina. The woman thought she was making it out in favour of a company with which the customer was doing business. However, the Marina happened to be the name of a Vegas casino. Molony took the draft and flew to Las Vegas on a Saturday morning. By Sunday afternoon he had lost $45,000 and settled his debt by signing the paper over to the casino. In 1983 Molony pleaded guilty to theft over $200 and was sentenced to six years in prison, but after serving two and one half years he was let out on parole. Including the money that he stole from the bank, together with his winnings, it is estimated that he gambled away approximately $17 million.[103]

Crimes committed by businesses and against businesses have escalated at a steady pace. In 1988 a financial crime expert with the RCMP said the force was so overwhelmed with cases that it had to pick and choose which ones it would investigate.[104] In 1989 the chief fraud investigator for the Ontario Provincial Police, Douglas Ormsby, complained that the anti-rackets branch, with a staff of sixty-six, could not cope with the workload. In 1988 the force had investigated 600 cases. In January of 1989 it had 350 cases under investigation and another 250 at the trial stage. Ormsby pointed out that many frauds were not reported. Among those that were, he noted that the size of the frauds had grown ever larger: ten years earlier the average case involved sums averaging between $10,000 and $15,000; by contrast, frauds in the $10 to $15 million range are now common.[105]

While businesses and their employees account for a significant portion of white-collar crime, professionals such as lawyers, police, and doctors contribute their fair share. With the passage of time, especially since the sixties, an ethical virus seems to have settled within professional ranks and it continues to grow. Over the past two decades professionals have been hauled before the courts with increasing frequency. Lawyers have been convicted of raping their clients, embezzling trust funds, forgery, fraud, and a variety of other illegal activities associated with their practice. The amounts of money involved when they resort to lawbreaking can be substantial. One Ottawa lawyer cheated twenty-five investors out of over $1 million in a phony mortgage scheme and a Caisse Populaire out of $163,000. His dishonest activity spanned more than a decade and when he was finally apprehended he pleaded guilty to a total of forty-four fraud and theft charges.[106] A Toronto lawyer was disbarred in 1988 for misappropriating $126,000 from a client's trust fund.[107] As with other categories of criminals, crooked lawyers keep up with the times and exploit new opportunities as they arise. The drug trade and immigration, for example, are two areas that in recent years have opened substantial scope for illegal gain by the legal fraternity.

The impending takeover of Hong Kong by the Chinese Communists in 1997 has created a desire on the part of many to emigrate. The Canadian government sought to take advantage of this by setting up an entrepreneur program. If a Hong Kong investor was willing to open a business in Canada that person could be granted immediate citizenship. One member of the prestigious Toronto law firm of Lang Michener was kicked out because he helped clients devise phony business proposals to circumvent the regulations. In July, 1989, the RCMP charged him with uttering forged documents, making false declarations, and conspiracy. In January of 1990 the Law Society of Upper Canada voted to disbar him. Another member of the same firm was charged by the RCMP in 1988 with five counts of illegalities associated with his immigration practice.[108]

The illegal drug trade has tempted many professionals, including lawyers. Drug dealers pay high prices for legal protection and sometimes their lawyers get caught up in illegal machinations to help them escape prosecution. In other cases lawyers become directly involved with the activities of their criminal clients. The story of one small-town lawyer illustrates how much some professionals are willing to risk for the sake of enhancing their incomes. The proprietor of a very successful law firm and a pillar of the local community, he accepted a proposal from organized crime figures to launder drug money. He set up a number of corporations, including a currency exchange firm and a mortgage company. He used the mortgage company to make phony loans to his criminal clients, then would later show the loan as having been paid off although no money had actually changed hands. One such transaction processed a paper loan for over $324,000. He also defrauded the bank of $1.2 million with his phony loans and mortgage schemes. While he avoided detection he processed large sums of drug money through his law office and personally carried deposits to the bank. In May, 1985, his empire collapsed when he pleaded guilty to laundering, over a three-year period between 1978 and 1980, some $12 million for organized crime.[109]

Lawyers are officers of the court, from their ranks come the country's magistrates and judges, and their practice is based on a relationship of trust and reliability. Yet, too often they break that trust and break the law. In 1982 in Ontario alone fifty lawyers were brought up on disciplinary charges; in 1984, thirty-six lawyers were either disbarred or asked to resign; in 1988, twenty were brought before the Law Society; by November, 1989, another ten were disciplined. The Law Society finally had to hire a former policeman to monitor the problem of crooked lawyers.[110] A malaise, a crisis in values, appears to be spreading across the profession. Too often law firms and disciplinary bodies give out the message that wrongdoing is not a serious matter. One of the worst examples came out of the so-called "Lang Michener Affair." It centred on the firm's reaction when one of the partners became involved in unethical and illegal practices. He was eventually exposed and taken before the Law Society of Upper Canada, which disbarred him. However, it turned out that other members of the firm knew about or suspected the illegalities for some months before anyone took action. Senior partners became aware of the wrongdoing in January of 1986 but it wasn't until June that they expelled the partner from the firm. Another three months went by before they reported the matter to the Law Society.

The inaction was investigated by the Law Society of Upper Canada and in January, 1990, five members of the firm were found guilty of professional misconduct. They were reprimanded behind closed doors. The whole affair, including the penalty meted out by the Law Society, is illustrative of the crisis in legal ethics. Reporting the wrongdoing was almost an afterthought and the punishment was no more than a wrist slap. In spite of the fact that the firm was convicted of professional misconduct the Law Society took great pains in its findings to make such statements as "There is no complaint of conduct unbecoming a barrister and solicitor. . . ."[111] The judgement was an embarrassment to many lawyers across the country and an affront to the public interest. The editor of the *Law Times* described the Law Society's handling of the case as a "crisis of credibility."[112] The entire affair illustrates the problem in ethics and values that faces lawyers, and other professionals as well.

Medical doctors also contribute to white-collar crime. One of the more common offences committed by dishonest doctors is billing the medical services insurance plan for services not actually rendered. Performing unnecessary surgery is another resort of some doctors wanting to earn extra money. Unless such practices get completely out of hand the wrongdoing is difficult to detect and hard to prove. Drug abuse is also a problem sometimes associated with the medical profession. Doctors and nurses have been involved in theft of drugs from hospital pharmacies to feed their dependencies, and doctors have used their access to drugs to obtain them for illegal purposes and have become involved in trafficking to addicts.[113]

Even the clergy, among the most respected and trusted of professionals, have been caught up in crime. There has always been the odd case of stealing church funds or other peccadillos, but as a profession the clergy in Canada have maintained a relatively untarnished image. That pristine position has deteriorated somewhat in recent years with more and more revelations of wrongdoing, the most serious being the sexual and physical abuse of children. While there have been a number of cases across the country the most shocking revelations have come out of Newfoundland. There, case after case has been uncovered of priests and religious sexually abusing young boys, sometimes over the space of many years. The worst incidents took place at the Mount Cashel orphanage in St. John's, run by a Roman Catholic lay order, the Christian Brothers. For years there were rumours and charges of abuse, but the prestige that the order enjoyed enabled its members to evade prosecution. In some cases, rather than lay charges, authorities allowed the order to transfer offenders out of the province.

The orphanage somehow attracted an unusual number of abusers almost as if the word was out that it was a safe haven for disciplinarians and pedophiles. Finally, revelations of abuse by other clergymen encouraged victims to come forward with accusations. A provincial Royal Commission was established in 1989 to investigate. Witness after witness told lurid tales of lust, corruption, physical abuse, and sexual exploitation. Children were punched, kicked, neglected, and forced to perform a variety of sexual acts with the men who were supposed to be guiding them. One of the most pathetic stories to come out of the hearing was how one of the brothers prevented the adoption by a young couple of one of his charges. Instead of helping the boy to be placed in a good home he interfered in order to keep him at the orphanage for his own pleasure. At the time of writing twenty Christian Brothers, priests, former priests, and others have either been charged or convicted of sex offences.[114]

Clergy and members of religious orders are not the only professionals who have taken advantage of their positions to abuse children. A number of school teachers and administrators have also been convicted of sexual abuse. Some of the most disturbing incidents, however, have involved child-care workers whose job it is to protect children. Recently the heads of a number of agencies across Canada have brought to light problems with their own employees. To make matters worse they also revealed that incidents were covered up and the offenders were allowed to leave quietly. In some cases they immediately transferred to other agencies supported with positive recommendations from their former employers. One agency director claimed that abuse by child-care workers was often covered up with "a golden abuse handshake." Having been bought off the worker left, thus enabling the agency to avoid either litigation or embarrassment.[115]

Among the professionals who have most consistently been involved in criminal activity over the years are the police. An unbroken pattern of police involved in illegal activity throughout our history continues to the present day. The daily papers catalogue a litany of offences that include theft, accepting bribes, bank robbery, brutality, rape, and other sexual offences. In June, 1988, a Dartmouth, Nova Scotia, policeman was convicted of two bank holdups.[116] In October of 1988 a Halifax constable with nineteen years of service pleaded guilty to possession of stolen plywood worth over $1,000. The lumber had been taken from a shipment sitting at a local pier.[117] In June of 1989 an RCMP officer working with the commercial crime squad in Montreal was charged with accepting a $500,000 benefit from a firm he was investigating.[118] In January of 1990 a Winnipeg police officer was charged with sexual offences involving teenage boys, with uttering threats, and with unlawful possession of a weapon.[119] For a long time poor pay resulting in economic need was blamed for money-related police crime. Today, however, police in most jurisdictions are paid respectable salaries, yet the problem of police corruption continues.

At the beginning of the last decade of this century one of the highest-profile white-collar crimes is the pollution of the environment. Large and small companies alike have polluted over the years through oil and gas spills, the dumping of chemical wastes, and the direct release into rivers and lakes of toxic materials. Heightened awareness of the threats to the environment has resulted in much stricter laws. However, many companies find that conforming to such regulations can be costly so some choose to break the law. Others, even when conformity would not add appreciably to their operating costs, find old habits hard to break. Consequently, the pollution continues but offenders face a much less tolerant public and stiffer penalties when they are caught. In a case concluded in December, 1990, Inco Ltd. was fined $50,000 for polluting a creek near Sudbury and was required to put up an additional $50,000 to help rehabilitate the region's fish habitats.[120] In January, 1991, FibreCo Pulp Inc. of Taylor, B.C., was fined $200,000 for leaking toxic material into the Peace River.[121]

In July of 1990 the British Columbia Environment Ministry released a list of forty-one companies and municipalities accused of not complying with environment protection legislation. Included on the list were some large and well-known companies, such as Imperial Oil Ltd. and CP Rail.[122] Polluters now face not only fines but jail sentences also as a result of a precedent set by an Ontario court. The head of Blackbird Holdings Ltd., a company involved in marine construction, was sentenced to six months in jail in June of 1990 for violations of the Ontario Water Resources Act and the Environmental Protection Act. Investigators discovered 180 drums of chemical waste stored on the company's property. Some of the containers had leaked and polluted wells in the area.[123]

Yet another crime closely associated with more contemporary developments is money laundering. The term is used to describe the process of taking the revenues from criminal activity, covering up its origins, and getting it back in circulation as if it had been legitimately earned. The huge sums of money generated by modern crime leave criminals vulnerable. Unless they can show that their large holdings have been earned legally they could be subject to police investigations, seizure of property, and prosecution. According to RCMP officials the illegal drug trade in Canada alone generates more money each year than the combined earnings of General Motors, Algoma Steel, and Bell Canada.[124] This gives some sense of the amount of criminal money that is floating around the country. Most of it is earned by the big-time criminals and they are constantly faced with having to launder millions of dollars.

Their need has provided an opportunity for individuals and corporations to get into the money-laundering business. Because of the amounts involved and the complexity of conversion techniques, much of the business is carried on by white-collar criminals such as lawyers, accountants, and corporate executives. Some businesses can become unwitting accomplices through crooked employees. In one case a bank manager arranged for the purchase of over $40 million in bank drafts for a group of drug traffickers.

The drafts were then deposited in a number of financial institutions in foreign countries.[125]

Other types of businesses that deal with cash, such as vending machine companies, retail stores, and arcades, are also popular fronts for the laundering of money. Their owners accept pools of cash from drug dealers and then falsify their sales reports to make it look as if the money came from customers. They have to pay more income tax on their inflated earnings but their commissions more than offset the extra tax. The money, after allowing for taxes and fees, is handed back to the drug dealers as earnings from involvement in a legitimate business.

One of the most elaborate schemes for laundering money is the establishment of dummy companies. A series of corporations are set up in Canada and in foreign countries and the various firms interact and do business with each other. They make loans and buy businesses. The transactions are carried out with drug money but are so complex that they are difficult for auditors to trace. At any point in the chain it can be made to look like the transactions and the money involved are legal. The only way that police would be able to expose the scheme would be if they could trace all dealings to their ultimate source and to the people supplying the money. One such consortium was made up of a network of ninety Canadian and foreign companies. The difficulties in tracing money and people through such a labyrinth are obvious.

Other money-laundering schemes are carried out by numerous methods, including the use of foreign currency exchanges and brokerage houses. Foreign currency exchanges are sometimes set up as fronts. Since they deal in cash and transfer money all over the world they make good conduits for funds earned illegally. The brokerage houses can be used for buying and selling securities. An order can be placed from an overseas bank or customer, the securities are transferred and then held for sale at a later date when the holder needs the cash again.[126]

White-collar crime in contemporary Canada is probably more prevalent and diversified than at any time in our past. Although much still escapes detection, the record of exposure seems to be improving. As well, courts appear to be handing out stiffer penalties, especially to large corporations. The following list, taken at random, offers some examples of a cross-section of white-collar criminals who have been convicted within the past seven years, the offences they committed, and the penalties levied against them.

Stone Consolidated Inc.: spilling PCB-laced transformer oil; fined $35,000.
A Toronto developer: false advertising; fined $75,000.
Two former Canada Trust executives: swindling; six years in prison.
Coca-Cola Ltd. of Toronto: price fixing in Winnipeg; fined $65,000.

Blackwoods Beverages Ltd., the bottlers of Pepsi-Cola in Winnipeg: co-conspirator with Coke; fined $65,000.

Shell Canada: price fixing; fined $100,000.

Commodore Business Machines Ltd., Toronto: violating the Competition Act; fined $95,000.

Two Vancouver stock promoters: theft, fraud, and manipulating the stock market; seven years each in prison.

Another Vancouver stock promoter: fraud; $300,000 fine and 3 years in prison.

Amway: tax customs evasion; settled lawsuit for $45 million.

Hoffman, LaRoche Ltd., Toronto drug company: breaking Competition Law; fined $50,000.

Richardson Greenshields of Canada Ltd.: stock manipulation by an employee; company fined $250,000.

Quebec businessman: tax evasion; fined $100,825 plus taxes owing.

BBM Lakeview Wholesale Lumber Ltd. of Vancouver: falsely labelling inferior wood; fined $100,000.

Carburation Econex Canada Inc.: false advertising; fined $200,000.

Motorcycle and Moped Industry Council and five member companies, including Honda and Yamaha: price fixing; fined $250,000.

Zellers Inc., Dartmouth, Nova Scotia: sales prices above advertised levels; fined $35,000.

The Commodore Business Machines case is a good example of the extent of lawbreaking that major companies are engaged in and the lack of ethics on the part of some of the people who run them. The Toronto computer firm sought to reap maximum profits at a time when computer sales were brisk. In 1982 and 1983 the company offered volume rebates to two large retailers, Sears Canada and Zellers, but did not make them available to their major competitors. The rebates came to nearly $30,000. In a separate incident Atlantic Video and Sound Centre in Montreal was given a special advertising allowance of $30,000, together with nineteen display stands, but the company did not bestow similar incentives on Atlantic's competitors. Commodore executives also put pressure on a number of their distributors to raise their selling prices in an effort to maintain an artificially high price level. The offences took place when James Copland controlled Commodore's marketing policy. Copland was particularly aggressive and obviously willing to use underhanded methods. He was dismissed when the company discovered what he was doing. Commodore's lawyer described Copland as having "left a trail of destruction" in the computer industry.[127]

One of the largest settlements ever negotiated by the government was with Amway Corporation, an American-based company with its Canadian head office in London, Ontario. The company specializes in the manufacture and sales of household products and personal-use items. Its name stands for the American way and the company preaches the virtues of free enterprise and patriotism to its army of representatives. It concentrates on recruiting husband-wife teams and stresses the virtues of ambition, hard work, and family togetherness. In 1983 Amway pleaded guilty to evading customs duties and was fined $20 million while its Canadian subsidiary was fined $5 million. The government also launched a civil suit, claiming that between 1965 and 1980 the company falsified invoices and price lists of goods shipped to Canada. An audit estimated that the government had been cheated out of some $113 million in unpaid customs duties and taxes and the suit sought $148 million as a settlement. After nine years of arguments Amway finally agreed to a settlement of $45 million before a formal trial got under way.[128]

Although more offenders are being caught and harsher punishments seem to be handed down by the courts, all signs point to an ongoing increase in white-collar crime. Businesses cheat their customers, engage in price-fixing, false advertising, bribery, kickbacks, fraud, income tax evasion, arson, phony bankruptcy, and a variety of other illegal activities. They are joined by a host of professionals, including doctors, lawyers, educators, politicians, clergy, nurses, police, accountants, management personnel, and trusted employees. By and large they represent society's privileged, enjoying good jobs, better education and salaries, and respectable positions in the community. Yet, in common with the lowest level of street criminal, they choose to enhance their lifestyle by breaking the law.

SUMMARY

White-collar crime started in pioneer Canada with the early officials, merchants, and traders. The fur trade, a money-making business, was made even more lucrative by cheating and lawbreaking. Officials, merchants, and even the clergy took advantage of their positions of power and status to carry on illegal activities. Some officials set up elaborate schemes to defraud their own governments in the process of contracting for goods and services. Their merchant friends joined with them while also cheating the public by such means as overcharging and short-weighting.

As the country expanded official corruption extended into the democratic political process. Governments and politicians engaged in vote buying, patronage, bribery, and kickbacks. All levels of officialdom were stained with criminal activity, including the judicial establishments that were supposed to uphold the law. Even the local jailkeepers took advantage of their prisoners for illegal gain. Canada's first full-scale penitentiary, Kingston, was staffed with people who did not hesitate to pillage the public purse.

Crime committed by big business started with the giant fur-trading companies and continued with other large-scale enterprises. Canal and railroad building – indeed, every form of public works – attracted unscrupulous contractors and promoters. An unholy alliance developed between businessmen and politicians and both fleeced the public for personal gain. At times the corrupt politician and the dishonest business person were one and the same. No office was immune – often, cabinet ministers, premiers, and prime ministers led the way.

By the Confederation period white-collar criminals cast a wide shadow across the nation. Stock fraud, embezzlement, political corruption, swindles, and a host of other crimes were common fare among the country's more privileged citizens. A well-established pattern was further refined and expanded as the country grew. Industrial development brought with it the exploitation of men, women, and children. Certain technological advances, such as the telegraph and the telephone, not only advanced civilization but were also put to good use for criminal purposes.

As crime in general increased throughout the twentieth century, so did the white-collar variety. Every major event was viewed as yet another opportunity for illicit gain. War, prohibition, business prosperity all spawned more elaborate schemes for illegal money-making. Yet in comparison with what came after World War Two, the earlier period looked like a dress rehearsal.

The prosperity and materialism of post-war Canada and the cultural revolution of the sixties and seventies were accompanied by increased revelations of white-collar crime, spiced by some refinements and additions. More individual professionals turned to crime to enhance their lifestyle and keep up with the Joneses. The long-standing respect and prestige accorded to such professionals as lawyers, doctors, police, accountants, clergymen, and corporate executives were substantially diminished by revelation after revelation of wrongdoing.

For most of our history white-collar crime went largely unpublished and unpunished. The privileged elite of earlier days used their positions and contacts to cover up their wrongdoings and to shield themselves and their friends from prosecution. White-collar criminals have also long benefited from a lack of investigative facilities and difficulties with prosecution. Police forces across the country did not have personnel specially trained to deal with commercial crime. To some extent the lack of detection lured many into the false belief that white-collar crime was not a problem. It wasn't until 1967 that the RCMP organized commercial fraud units in each province. As their expertise improved and their numbers increased, more business crime was uncovered. For the first time the public began to realize the pervasiveness of white-collar crime.

Detection capabilities have vastly improved, but less progress has been made with prosecutions. Investigation of white-collar crime is often difficult and time-consuming, and gathering sufficient evidence to lay charges can sometimes take years. Consequently, trials are often long and complex.

Prosecutors are reluctant to pursue intricate cases with vigour because the process can tie them up for such long periods of time. Poorly prepared cases give an advantage to the accused and their lawyers in court. Another problem has to do with the juries. Evidence is sometimes so technical that jurors have difficulty understanding the issues and give the defendant the benefit of the doubt. Even if the accused is convicted sentences can be very lenient. No previous record and prominence in the community still go a long way toward mitigating punishments. Since white-collar criminals, when they get caught, sometimes suffer public humiliation or loss of high-paying jobs or businesses, some judges tend to take the view that they have already suffered enough for their crimes.

Although criminal justice records can easily leave the impression that white-collar crime is not as serious as other categories of lawbreaking, it is obvious from other indices that it is a problem of major proportions. The broad variety of crimes and criminals examined in this chapter offers some indication, and yet the incidents described represent only a small part of the picture. White-collar criminals are often economically successful and better educated. Their illegal activities say more about the role of greed and a lack of ethics and values than about other causes of crime.

CHAPTER 4

▼

Organized Crime

Organized crime contrasts with individual criminal enterprise in that the offenders are organized groups of people sometimes referred to as gangs or mobs. For such groups, crime is an ongoing enterprise characterized by leadership, organization, discipline, and planning. The gangs can consist of a few people who carry on specific crimes, such as burglary or bank robberies, or they can include hundreds of members who engage in a variety of illegal activities. In Canada we usually think of the Mafia in connection with organized crime and consequently see the problem as a phenomenon of modern times. In fact, organized crime can be traced back to the earliest days of our history and today includes many diverse groups in addition to the Mafia.

THE COLONIAL PERIOD

Among the first gangs of organized criminals were the pirates who frequented various ports on the east coast. The myriad inlets and fishing villages served as safe havens and storehouses for pirate booty, as well as sources of supplies, ship repairs, and manpower. The sea lanes were safe for the pirate fleets. They could operate with impunity between forays to the south to prey on Spanish treasure galleons. Pirate leaders frequently came from middle- or upper-class backgrounds. Their crews, however, were the flotsam and jetsam of the New World. Pirate crews were usually made up of young men but included a range of recruits from young boys to salty old sea dogs. Some joined of their own free will, others, especially skilled seafarers, were pressed into service from captured ships. Pirates operated in lone ships or in fleets that could number over a dozen ships. The vessels were well armed, carried large crews of up to 150 men, and functioned under a strict code of discipline.

The pirates would pull alongside a victim ship, board her, and subdue the crew. Sometimes they would first engage in a classic sea battle if their prey was well armed and chose to fight. While Spanish treasure was the preferred booty, French ships laden with wine or furs and English ships carrying cargoes of dried fish were attractive catches for the pirates. Even small vessels carrying supplies or usable items of any kind were fair game for the outlaw seafarers. Pirate ships operated in the Atlantic from the later part of the seventeenth century until well into the nineteenth century. The last hanging for piracy in Canada took place in Halifax in 1809. While most of the pirate leaders were foreign-born and operated in Canadian waters sporadically and for short periods of time, there were home-grown seafaring terrorists who achieved a degree of notoriety.

One such individual was Samuel Nelson. Born in Prince Edward Island, the son of a well-to-do landowner, Samuel started a merchant trade between Prince Edward Island and Halifax but soon discovered that more money could be made illegally than legally. He and a partner outfitted a ten-gun ship and recruited a crew of ninety. They preyed on trading vessels from Europe and would sell the captured ships and their cargoes in American ports. Nelson and his crew established a reputation for cruelty and viciousness. It was claimed that they sometimes tortured and murdered the victims of their predatory activities.[1]

With the advent of settlement, as we have seen, certain colonial administrators took advantage of their positions to engage in illegal activity. Most simply interacted with their equally corrupt colleagues to line their pockets. The odd one, however, put together a gang of people who conspired under his direction. François Bigot, intendant of New France from 1748 to 1760, set up an elaborate scheme to cheat the government on supplies for the army. In 1756 he arranged for a friend, Joseph Cadet, to be appointed commissary general and recruited a number of others in key posts to work with him. Over a two-year period Bigot and his companions sold provisions at highly inflated prices and cheated the governments of both New France and the mother country. Cadet bribed military officers at a number of forts to verify his false accounts and he, Bigot, and their friends shared profits estimated at 12 million francs.[2]

As settlements evolved across the country, organized gangs of criminals took advantage of the lack of effective law enforcement in pioneer society. Colonial seaports were especially attractive, with a constant traffic in goods, sailors coming and going, and well-stocked shops and warehouses. Most criminal gangs were made up of the shiftless element and specialized in low-level thievery, hanging around the wharfs and taverns of ports like Halifax, Quebec City, and Montreal. They were sometimes vicious and did not hesitate to beat or even murder their victims. They preyed on drunken sailors, on goods sitting at dockside, and on the small stores of the town. Their numbers and makeup varied because individually they were in and out of jail and sometimes were the victims of other characters like themselves.

By and large, organized criminal activity, until the twentieth century, was sporadic and local in nature. Gangs came together in certain places at various times, functioned for a while, and then either broke up or were apprehended. Quebec City and the surrounding parishes were terrorized by such a gang in 1834-35. A series of thefts and armed robberies, culminating with the looting of a church of sacred vessels and furnishings, filled the inhabitants with fear and indignation. The authorities posted a reward for information, but it wasn't until six months later that the culprits were finally apprehended. The gang was made up of five members led by a wood dealer, who was considered by his neighbours to be an honest man. The remaining members were educated, according to the standards of the day, and were all from good families. During their criminal rampage, they committed numerous break-ins and holdups and murdered five people. Convictions came as a result of one of the gang being persuaded to testify against his companions in return for a lighter sentence. He was allowed to disappear after the trial while the rest were all deported.[3]

A decade later a similar gang was found operating in the countryside outside of Toronto. The so-called "Markham Gang" consisted of five or so members who carried on a series of crimes over a period of several years. They engaged in burglary, robbery sometimes accompanied by violence, horse stealing, and petty theft. The authorities were able to round up gang members when one of them gave himself up in 1846 and agreed to give evidence against his companions. The one to be tried was convicted in November of 1846 and sentenced to four years in prison. Although not all were convicted, the arrests and trials, together with the guilty verdicts that were obtained, were sufficient to disperse the group and rid the region of what one paper described as "this iniquitous gang."[4]

Ordinary householders and roadside wayfarers were frequently the victims of these small local gangs and they had good reason to fear them. On the night of October 18, 1854, a band of five men forced their way into the home of a storekeeper in the small village of Nelles Corners in Haldimand County, in what is now Ontario. When the homeowner resisted their demands for money, he was shot twice and left to die. Later the same evening, the gang robbed two farmers they encountered while making their way to the railroad station. The men had been working together for some time but as a result of the murder at Nelles Corners they fled across the border to the United Sates and then split up. Shortly afterwards, three of the group were traced down and tried for murder. Two were hanged and the third was sent to prison for life. A few years later, in 1857, a fourth member of the gang was apprehended. According to the others, he was the one who actually did the killing. However, the jury could not agree on a verdict.[5]

In the late 1850s a gang working the streets of Toronto gained a degree of notoriety. They were known as the Brooks Bush gang because of the vicinity of the city in which they hung out. The group was made up of men and women who were described as being idle and disreputable. They engaged in petty theft, robbery, and break-ins.[6]

There are also examples in Canadian history of gangs led by men who aspired to status and power in a manner somewhat similar to certain cattle barons of the American West. They gathered about them groups of ruffians they used to intimidate and beat into submission those who stood in the way of their ambition. Such men were to be found competing with each other for hegemony in the lumber trade in the Ottawa Valley in the 1830s and none was more ruthless in the pursuit of power than Peter Aylen.

A typical self-made man of pioneer days, Aylen came to Canada from Ireland in the early 1830s. He arrived in Quebec as a sailor, jumped ship, and disappeared. He eventually became an influential businessman in the lumber trade in the Ottawa Valley and a very wealthy man. Not content with his success, he wanted to drive out the competition and monopolize the business. The large number of Irish labourers in the area, drawn to Bytown to build the canal, offered a fertile recruiting ground for Aylen's army. In 1835 he attracted a group of followers with the lure of jobs, entertainment, and visions of status and power. He even supplied prostitutes to win their loyalty. Aylen's mob was soon busy assaulting, murdering, destroying property, and intimidating everyone in sight. He wanted to force out the French-Canadian lumberjacks and clear the way for his fellow Irishmen. In the process, he hoped also to take over the lumber trade himself and become the dominant power in the region. Aylen's gang was the focal point of widespread violence and civil disobedience that wracked the area for a number of years. It wasn't until the military stepped in to restore order that Aylen gave up the campaign of lawlessness and intimidation. He subsequently moved to Aylmer and assumed the role of a law-abiding, public-spirited citizen.[7]

THE CONFEDERATION ERA

In sharp contrast to Peter Aylen was the McLean gang of British Columbia. If Peter Aylen was the Canadian equivalent of the American cattle baron, the McLeans were Canada's version of the lawless gangs that roamed the wild west, a group of outlaws who in some respects were the precursors of modern gangsters. The gang consisted of three brothers and a friend. The McLean brothers were the offspring of a brutal Scottish father and an Indian mother. The father was shot to death in 1864, and the boys grew up in poverty – neglected, abused, and uneducated. They became drifters, taking odd jobs and living by their wits, and resorted to petty theft to augment their meagre incomes. Soon they turned to full-time crime.

They were wild, undisciplined, tough, disdainful of authority, and cruel. During the late 1870s they terrorized the ranchers in the countryside surrounding Kamloops, B.C., stealing cattle, breaking into homes, robbing, intimidating, and on occasions beating and murdering their victims. The authorities were less than diligent in their pursuit, partly out of fear and partly because of lack of manpower. The gang's activities so outraged people in the region that private citizens finally joined the effort to arrest the McLeans. The gang was well armed with stolen guns and rifles and eluded their pursuers for some time, but finally they were captured in December, 1879, and locked up in the New Westminster jail. They were given a jury trial, found guilty, and all four were hanged on January 31, 1881.[8]

The ranks of organized crime in Canada were sometimes augmented by wandering gangs of U.S. criminals. For a time there was no extradition treaty, and in the 1870s especially an unusually large number of American criminals seemed to be in Canada, fleeing from U.S. justice and practising their trade in this country. One such group was suspected of robbing the Bank of Nova Scotia in Halifax on August 1, 1876. P.T. Barnum's great circus came to the city and, as was the custom in those days, put on a parade to advertise the show. As the parade passed the bank, every employee came into the street to watch. When they returned ten to fifteen minutes later, they discovered that $22,000 was missing from the tills. The subsequent investigation centred on two Americans who had been in the city for a few days. Their actions and comings and goings had aroused suspicion and both had criminal records. An initial trial resulted in a hung jury. One of the suspects skipped bail before the second trial but the other was acquitted. Although considerable evidence pointed to the original suspects and there was suspicion that others were involved with them, the crime was never solved.[9]

Like so many other categories of criminals, gangs are frequently generated and nurtured by the appearance of large-scale money-making opportunities. One of the greatest criminal opportunities was created by the work of moral reformers trying to suppress the traffic in liquor. Whenever the sale of alcohol was prohibited, a market was created for illegal booze. The illicit sale of liquor, or bootlegging, by its very nature lends itself to large-scale enterprise and is a natural venture for organized crime.

An example of the interrelationship can be found with the building of the Canadian Pacific Railway. Conditions were harsh for the builders of the CPR in the 1880s, they worked in remote areas for long hours and in difficult conditions, and many sought solace in drink. Afraid that abuse of liquor would slow the progress of track laying, the company prohibited the sale and possession of liquor within a ten-mile radius of the railway. Suddenly a golden opportunity was opened up to the bootlegging fraternity and they flooded into the north country. Sudbury became a main transit point and soon certain small settlements were transformed into little more than liquor emporiums complete with con artists, gamblers, and prostitutes.

One such community, Michipicoten, was literally taken over by a gang of bootleggers. Charles Wallace, an Englishman, saw an opportunity to make money with the pronouncement of CPR prohibition. He gathered a gang of toughs and set about to monopolize the liquor trade in Michipicoten and under his leadership the community became an outlaw town. He sold his liquor freely and intimidated, beat up, or murdered anybody who got in his way. Regional authorities and CPR officials were powerless in the face of the large gang of thugs that Wallace controlled. Finally, an appeal was sent to Toronto for help. The gang was eventually dispersed but Wallace himself was never convicted for more than a minor offence and was released in a matter of weeks from Toronto's Central Prison.[10] While gangs like Wallace's were broken up, society would not be as fortunate with the next generation of criminals spawned by prohibition. Once again a law generated by moral and social considerations created an opportunity for widespread lawbreaking. Gangs coalesced to carry on large-scale trafficking in illegal liquor. The trade spawned a number of criminal organizations whose offspring are still with us today.

PROHIBITION AND THE RISE OF MAJOR GANGS

The nineteenth century witnessed a religious and social crusade in the United States and Canada to ban the sale and consumption of liquor. Reformers had long blamed much of the poverty and social distress in North America on the "demon rum." In addition, religious people condemned alcohol on the grounds that it contributed to licentious behaviour and sin. Also, many argued that abuse of alcohol had detrimental effects on the economy because it interfered with industrial production. Temperance and prohibition advocates were active throughout the nineteenth century and their organizations grew in strength and influence. By the latter part of the century the battle was being led in the U.S. mainly by the Woman's Christian Temperance Union, founded in 1874, and the Anti-Saloon League, founded in 1893.

Temperance societies appeared in Canada as early as 1827. A Canadian branch of the Woman's Christian Temperance Union was founded in 1875 under the leadership of Letitia Youmans. In the same year, temperance and prohibition groups from across the Dominion united to form the Dominion Prohibitory Council. The following year it was renamed the Dominion Alliance for the Total Suppression of Liquor Traffic. The growing pressure in Canada from these groups forced the government into passing the Canada Temperance Act in 1878. It did not prohibit the sale of liquor but vested the power of local option in the provincial governments. From then on the liquor traffic was stopped in any area where temperance forces could muster the necessary votes.

The First World War gave the prohibition movement a strong impetus in both Canada and the United States. Advocates argued that to allow liquor trade in wartime was unseemly and unpatriotic and also that the grain used for alcohol production would be better utilized for food. By 1916, all provinces but Quebec prohibited the sale of liquor. In the U.S., the 18th Amendment to the Constitution banned the manufacture, importation, or sale of liquor. The legislation was passed by Congress in December, 1917, ratified by the States by January, 1919, and took effect in January, 1920.[11]

In both countries, the restrictions on liquor opened up a vast market for bootleg booze. The biggest profits were to be made through large-scale manufacture or procurement, efficient distribution networks, and monopoly of the market. Old gangs expanded and new ones organized in a rush to stake out their territory. The prohibition era thus gave birth to the large gangs of criminals that ultimately formed the organized crime cartels that we know today as the Mafia. Most of the big-time gangs were ethnic in makeup and included many immigrants among their members.

The most prominent and powerful of the prohibition-era gangs were made up of Italians. Some were born in the U.S. but many were immigrants. Certain of the Italian gangs that moved into bootlegging were already involved in criminal activities of various kinds. They came disproportionately from southern Italy and were the inheritors of a long legacy of defying the law. Southern Italy, especially the island of Sicily, had for many years suffered the vicissitudes of ineffective government and disorder. In an effort to protect themselves and their property in troubled times, wealthy landowners recruited their own security. Soon the protectors became a law unto themselves and established almost complete control in many communities. Leaders emerged who organized armed gangs of loyal followers and, like families, these gangs established close ties of kinship, loyalty, and a hierarchical structure. A strict code was observed that involved pledges of fidelity, vows of silence, and strict obedience. Operating outside the law and taking advantage of ineffective authority, the gangs established fiefdoms in which they controlled trade, extorted tribute, and when opposed, maimed and murdered. They became identified by the name Mafia, a word of unknown origin but used to designate criminality. The Mafia prospered in southern Italy throughout the nineteenth and twentieth centuries.[12]

Because of the poor economic conditions, many Italians joined the mass migration of people from all over the world to the United States in the late nineteenth century. In the decade 1871-80 alone, over 55,000 Italians left home to go to America. Their numbers continued to increase and over the next forty years more than four million Italian immigrants entered the United States. They settled chiefly in the cities and formed close-knit communities wherein they maintained their language, religion, traditions, and fear of the Mafia.

Large movements of population to the New World have always included a considerable representation of the criminal element. In the Italian communities, gangsters found the same opportunities as they had enjoyed at home. A population already inbred with the fear of the Mafia was an easy target for the age-old intimidation and extortion rackets. Moreover, these ghettos were also convenient refuges for Mafia leaders forced out of Italy by the periodic crackdown of authorities. By the early decades of the twentieth century, the offspring of the Italian Mafia were well entrenched in many immigrant communities in the United States. [13]

Italians came to Canada in much more modest numbers. According to the 1871 census, only 1,035 people of Italian origin were living in this country. By 1921, there was still a relatively small Italian population of 66,769. They came disproportionately from the poor villages of southern Italy and included in their numbers were Mafia members and others well acquainted with the criminal gangs and their practices. In areas with any concentration of Italians the criminal activities common in the homeland were sometimes to be found.

The first of the Italian gangs to operate in Canada appeared in Italian neighbourhoods in Hamilton and Toronto in the first decade of this century. They were sometimes referred to as the "Black Hand," another name for Mafia-style gangsters. Some of the criminals in the old country used an imprint of a black hand as a sign of their presence and as an intimidating symbol with which to warn peasants who might be inclined to resist their extortions. In their ethnic neighbourhoods some quickly discovered they could run the same rackets that they had at home. Their fellow immigrants were already conditioned to fear the Mafia and Black Hand because of their power and vicious tactics. The gangsters exploited this legacy of fear to extort money, at the same time being confident their victims would not go to the police. They would send their demands on notepaper imprinted with a black hand. If the intended victim refused to pay, the gang resorted to intimidation, beatings, bombings, and sometimes murder. Prohibition opened additional opportunities for the existing gangs and served as a catalyst for the formation of new ones. [14]

Among the earliest Italian-Canadian gangsters to build a formidable criminal organization was Rocco Perri. He was only thirteen years old when he arrived in Canada in 1903 from the village of Reggio in the Calabria district of southern Italy. He drifted from job to job and place to place and in 1912 arrived in Toronto. For a time he boarded with the Starkman family. The wife, Bessie, was an attractive thirty-year-old immigrant from Poland with two children. Rocco fell in love with Bessie and persuaded her to leave her family and go with him. The couple settled in Hamilton in 1915 and opened a small grocery store catering to the needs of an Italian neighbourhood. With the ban on the sale of liquor as part of the war effort, Rocco saw a chance to augment his income and began to sell liquor from the back of his store. He then decided to branch out. With a group of hirelings, he forced out the competition in the bootleg liquor business. When prohibition in the U.S. opened up another vast market, Perri had the organization and the experience to take quick advantage of the opportunity. He was also ruthless enough to tramp on anyone who attempted to give him competition. Before long, Perri was a major supplier to gangsters like Al Capone, who were using prohibition in the United States to expand their criminal organizations.

People like Perri could buy supplies from Canadian distillers but government regulations prevented shipments to countries with prohibition legislation. Perri bought liquor from distillers and from operators of illegal stills and established an elaborate network to deliver the booze to the United States. He avoided legal complications by never handling shipments himself but took care of any of his employees who got caught: providing bail money, paying legal expenses, and on occasion bribing the police to forgo charges. Perri used the Windsor-Detroit border crossing for many of his shipments. He bribed customs officials who turned a blind eye to Perri vehicles carrying booze. In the course of his criminal activities, Perri and his gang stopped at nothing to advance their interests. He soon became the self-styled "King of the Bootleggers." When prohibition ended in the U.S. in 1933, the flow of alcohol changed course. It was now a source of good-quality cheap liquor and since there were still certain restrictions on sales in Ontario, there continued to be a good market for bootleg booze. Perri smuggled liquor from the States and also expanded into other areas of criminal activity.[15]

Rocco Perri is one example of a number of gangs spawned by prohibition. They had close connections with U.S. gangsters, and like them, sometimes fought with each other for control of certain territory. Along with bootlegging, many of the gangs were involved in gambling, prostitution, and extortion rackets. With the passage of time, these activities assumed more importance, especially as the bootleg liquor business waned. When World War Two broke out, some of the gangs expanded into wartime profiteering and got into black market activities. Even before the war ended the criminal element began preparing for post-war opportunities and started to manoeuvre for position. Rocco Perri became an early victim of the competition when he disappeared in Hamilton on April 23, 1944. Canadian gangs moved into the drug business in a big way after the war. It wasn't long before the profits to be made from criminal activities in Canada attracted the attention of the American Mafia.

More than in Canada, prohibition in the U.S. led to a dramatic expansion of criminal gangs and gangster activity. The U.S. had a much larger population and there were many more gangs already operating when the nation went dry. The existing ones expanded and new ones emerged to compete for control of the illicit liquor trade. The more established were Irish, Jewish, and Italian gangs, but other ethnic groups were also well represented in the ranks of organized crime. Many of the gangs had hundreds of members and they sometimes fought open wars for control of the liquor business. It was not uncommon for gun battles to take place in the streets of major American cities.[16]

In an effort to halt the bloodbath and reduce public pressure for more stringent law enforcement, the mobsters, led by Salvatore (Lucky) Luciano, eventually organized a national crime syndicate. The cartel divided the country up into territories over which a particular gang or "family" was given exclusive control. A national commission was established to enforce discipline and maintain order among the various families. By the time the syndicate was organized, the Italian gangs had established a dominant position in criminal circles in the United States. After prohibition ended the gangs had the money, the power, and the influence to expand their activities substantially. Gambling, extortion, prostitution, loan-sharking, labour racketeering, and the drug trade all came under the control of Mafia crime families.

THE MAFIA IN CANADA

The nature and extent of Mafia operations were largely unknown to the American public until a Senate investigation into organized crime was launched. A committee, chaired by Senator Estes Kefauver of Tennessee, held public hearings and submitted a report to Congress in 1951. The committee hearings shocked and disturbed the American public because they revealed just how entrenched and powerful organized crime had become. The resulting public outcry led to a crackdown on Mafia activities across the U.S. Ironically, that pressure sparked the first large-scale move of American gangsters into Canada. There were widespread contacts between the Canadian and American gangs during prohibition and ongoing interaction since, but up to the 1950s there had been no major American gangster activity in Canada.[17]

As a result of the pressure brought about by the revelations of the Kefauver Committee, the U.S. Mafia moved its gambling headquarters to Montreal. The city was already a big gambling centre with a gross turnover estimated at about $50 million a year. Much of the gaming and other forms of crime in Montreal were controlled by people who had contacts with both the American and Italian Mafia. The Canadian gangsters had also formed good connections with certain Quebec politicians and the police. The municipal government and law enforcement agencies were known to be very co-operative with the city's organized crime bosses and tolerant of illegal activities.[18] The tolerance for corruption went all the way to the provincial government and, according to one researcher, even included Premier Duplessis, who was alleged to have told the provincial police that "any policemen [sic] that cannot earn his keep on his own is not worth having on the force."[19] Even the general public seemed to be blasé toward the corruption.

Big-time crime had been thriving in Montreal for some time. Throughout the 1920s a substantial drug trade operated in the city. During the 1930s Montreal drug dealers did business with some of the most notorious gangsters in the United States, people like Hyman Holtz, Charles Groh, and Louis Buchalter. The latter was one of the most powerful of the Jewish gang leaders and ran a major drug distribution network. Gambling, prostitution, drug trafficking, and numerous rackets had prospered in Montreal for some time. As Canada's largest city and a major port, it had a natural attraction for the criminal element. Its reputation as a hospitable host to gamblers, bookies, prostitutes, and criminals made the city an attractive choice for the temporary relocation of the U.S. Mafia's gambling operations.

Much of the gambling in Montreal was controlled by Harry Ship and his associates. Therefore, he was the one given the task of preparing for the American invasion. He set up a front of dummy companies, arranged for the rental of accommodations, and ordered the telephones that were such an integral part of the bookie industry. When everything was prepared, a group of about 100 American mobsters moved into Montreal and for two years made the city the bookmaking capital of North America.[20]

The Americans came to a city that had a fair number of its own crime figures. One of the most prominent was Lucien Rivard, who during the 1950s was a drug trafficker and an organized crime kingpin. Rivard was part of an international narcotics ring and controlled a network that distributed drugs across Canada.[21] He was one of the most influential people in the Montreal underworld. Another of the city's organized crime bosses was Frank Petrula. The son of Ukrainian immigrants, Petrula had worked his way up in organized crime circles in Montreal. A sometime automobile thief and bankrobber, Petrula eventually linked up with Rivard and others in the drug trade. He had connections with the exiled Lucky Luciano in Italy and also with drug dealers in the United States.[22]

Frank Petrula offers a good example of the corrupt relations between the Montreal criminal world and the city's administration. During a 1954 RCMP investigation into Petrula's suspected drug activities, they searched his expensive home in Beaconsfield. His wife showed the Mounties where her husband's wall safe was located and in it they discovered $18,000 in cash and a record of money spent to bribe journalists and pay politicians. During the municipal elections, which had taken place a few days before, organized crime in Montreal had spent over $100,000 in an effort to defeat the reformist Civic Action League and its mayoralty candidate, Jean Drapeau. The crime bosses had also turned their goons loose at a number of polling stations in an effort to deter people from supporting the reform candidates. Petrula's notes listed names and amounts paid in organized crime's effort to keep a friendly administration in power. The money was spent in vain because Drapeau won and for the next few years carried on a campaign to clean up Montreal.[23]

The most powerful of the crime bosses in Montreal at the time of the American invasion was Vincenzo (Vic) Cotroni. Born in 1911 in Calabria, Italy's southernmost province, he came to Montreal with his family in 1924. He worked for a while with his father as a carpenter and then became a professional wrestler using the name Vic Vincent. In the world of professional wrestling, he became acquainted with an assortment of shady characters and the associated underworld of gambling dens, bootlegging joints, and houses of prostitution. He saw in all of this money-making opportunities and was soon investing his earnings in a number of illegal business ventures.[24]

Vincenzo Cotroni gradually spread his interest over a wide variety of illegal endeavours that included extortion, gambling, prostitution, loansharking, and drug trafficking, gathering about him a coterie of gangsters and thugs who advanced his fortunes by strong-arm tactics. While people of various ethnic backgrounds worked for Cotroni, his inner circle was composed almost exclusively of Italians. Like so many of his countrymen, he modelled his organization after the Mafia families of southern Italy.

At the top was Cotroni himself, the Don, commanding respect and absolute loyalty from his "family." In charge of various aspects of the criminal business and presiding over certain gang members were a number of lieutenants. In addition, others with specific responsibilities took orders directly from the Don. At the bottom were the rank and file of loyal servants known as "picciotti." The family structure was held together by a code of loyalty, respect, and silence. The Don must constantly be shown signs of deference and respect, not only by members of his crime family but by others as well. His importance and power must be recognized and acknowledged. The loyalty came out of the strict discipline and order enforced over the entire organization. Orders must be obeyed and instructions had to be carried out to the letter. If a mistake was made and a gang member was caught, he must willingly take the blame and never involve any other gang member. Similarly, he must keep within himself everything he knows about the family's activities. The penalty for breaches of the code could be severe, including beatings and death. The combination of fear and a code of intense loyalty maintained obedience and gave the gang coherence and strength.

Outside of this structure was an assortment of individuals and groups doing business under the protective umbrella of the Cotroni family. Bookies, drug dealers, pimps, loan sharks, con artists, and thieves all paid a percentage of their take to the Cotroni mob for the privilege of practising their criminal trades. Anyone causing trouble or refusing to pay up was ruthlessly dealt with by Cotroni's thugs. In addition to the Cotroni organization, a number of other gangs operated in various parts of the city.[25]

Thus, when the U.S. bookies moved into Montreal in force they found a favourable climate for their illegal activities. Once settled in, their criminal overlords were not far behind. In late 1953, the New York Mafia sent Carmine Galente, an under-boss of the Bonanno family, to Montreal to oversee the bookies and to make sure they paid their dues. Galente immediately recognized the potential for criminal earnings and, with the co-operation of Cotroni and others, moved to establish American Mafia control throughout the city. Galente and his Canadian Mafiosi systematically took control of nightclubs, blind pigs, gambling dens, bookmakers, and prostitutes. They attempted to buy protection by bribing police and politicians. Unfortunately for Galente, his protection did not extend beyond the province of Quebec and he was expelled from Canada in the spring of 1955.[26]

In the meantime, Jean Drapeau had mounted a campaign of harassment that forced the American bookmakers out of Montreal. The local crime lords also temporarily adopted a low profile but by that time they were too well organized and entrenched to be put out of business. The connections with their American counterparts were also solid, so the Mafia presence in Montreal was destined to hold firm for many years. Through their grip on the drug trade they also exercised some influence in organized crime circles in other parts of Canada.

Small gangs of criminals continued to appear and disappear in various communities. Some came together to get in on the drug trade that was fast developing after the war, others saw opportunities to exploit the growth and development the country was experiencing. The drug gangs that appeared were usually associated with the Montreal and American Mafia. One such group was organized by two brothers, John and George Mallock from Winnipeg, and their rise in organized crime circles was typical of the experience of many such gangs. The brothers started as street toughs and small-time criminals. In 1947, John Mallock started dealing in heroin while his brother was serving a jail term for assault. He made money selling drugs and began to build an organization with which he moved into other rackets, the main one being counterfeiting. He used his musclemen to force out the competition in Winnipeg and then turned his strong-arm tactics on competitors throughout the prairie region. By the time his brother got out of jail in 1949, the Mallock mob was moving into Vancouver. John Mallock had tapped into Lucien Rivard's drug network and had also established contacts in the U.S. His ventures were so successful in the West that in 1950 he expanded into the state of Washington. The police eventually closed in on the Mallock operation and on March 1, 1954, George Mallock was sentenced to twenty-one years in prison and fined $17,000. His brother, John, was seriously injured in an automobile accident in Mexico and died on April 22, 1954.[27]

During the short interval in which the Mallock brothers rose and fell, they had become part of an international drug network with connections in France, Mexico, the U.S., and Canada. Lucien Rivard continued to be a key figure in that web until he got caught up in a continent-wide crackdown on drug traffickers. In January of 1964, on the basis of testimony from two of Rivard's couriers, he was indicted in Texas for international trafficking in heroin. In June, at the request of the U.S. government, extradition proceedings were started in Montreal. Rivard was arrested and denied bail.

In November, 1964, a national political storm erupted with Rivard at the centre. The whole affair once again illustrated the unhealthy connection between organized crime figures and some politicians. Tommy Douglas, leader of the New Democratic Party, and Erik Nielsen, Progressive Conservative Member of Parliament for the Yukon, brought documented accusations in the House that two former assistants to cabinet ministers had tried to bribe the lawyer acting for the U.S. government in an effort to get Rivard released on bail. The accusations caused such an uproar that the government was forced to establish a commission of inquiry headed by Frederic Dorian, chief judge of the Quebec Superior Court. Dorian submitted his report in June, 1965, and confirmed that Rivard's friends had tried to use their connections within the Liberal Party and had offered bribes to obtain his release. The cast of characters included party workers and officials, the two former assistants to the cabinet ministers, and at least one Member of Parliament. In the end, the Minister of Justice, Guy Favreau, resigned along with the MP, Guy Rouleau, and André Letendre, a ministerial assistant.

The Rivard saga took another twist, while the commission investigation was still on, when on March 2, 1965, he escaped from Bordeaux jail. An extensive manhunt ensued but it wasn't until the following July that Rivard was recaptured. He was extradited to the U.S. where in September, 1965, a Texas judge fined him $20,000 and sentenced him to twenty years in the penitentiary.[28]

Although certain criminal organizations across the country moved into the drug business after the war, many concentrated on more traditional crime. Some had a long history, others, like the Mallock gang, enjoyed a brief period of prosperity and then broke up. Among the latter, few attracted as much attention as the infamous Boyd gang.

Edwin Alonzo Boyd grew up with two brothers and a sister in a Toronto policeman's family. His mother died when he was fifteen and the family was dispersed to foster homes. He soon quit school and drifted around the country, working sporadically at a number of jobs. He also augmented his income with a series of petty thefts and burglaries. Eventually, he returned to Toronto and went to live with his father. During World War Two, he served overseas, married an English girl, and returned to Canada with a wife and three children.

Boyd drifted in and out of a number of jobs and because he was usually short of money, he once again turned to crime. On September 9, 1949, he robbed a branch of the Bank of Montreal in Toronto. He followed with a series of robberies, sometimes alone and sometimes with a companion. In 1951, Boyd read about the exploits of a gang of armed robbers who had been hitting a number of banks in nearby communities over the spring and summer. He conceived the idea of forming a similar organization and immediately recruited two acquaintances. On September 1, 1951, the new Boyd gang robbed a branch of the Dominion Bank in Toronto. Their first venture turned out poorly – within a few weeks Boyd and one of his accomplices were captured and taken to the Don Jail.

Coincidentally, members of the group that had initially given Boyd his inspiration to expand were also incarcerated in the Don Jail. Boyd struck up an acquaintance and on November 4 joined them in an escape. Over the next few months, the escapees, their colleagues, and a number of women carried out a series of robberies that put a great deal of public pressure on the police to apprehend them. A formidable manhunt was launched, during which two of the gang critically wounded a policeman in a shootout. Efforts to capture the gang were again stepped up and Boyd was finally apprehended on March 15, 1952. Police found an arsenal of guns, ammunition, knives, and an electric cattle prod. They also found about $26,000 in cash from what was at the time the biggest bank robbery in Canadian history. On September 8, 1952, Boyd and three of his companions again broke out of the Don Jail but were recaptured a week later. Two of the gang were put to death for the shooting of the policeman and Edwin Boyd was sentenced to life imprisonment.[29]

While small gangs were to be found in many provinces, the big-leaguers of organized crime continued to be the Mafia. Following the expulsion of Carmine Galente a replacement was sent to Montreal, but soon the Cotroni family emerged as the representatives and main link to the New York Mafia. Mob activities in Montreal covered the full range of underworld crime. In 1958, an American gangster was convicted of selling bonds stolen from Montreal banks by Mafia mobsters. In the mid-seventies, police estimated that loan-sharking alone was a $700 million business in Montreal. The drug trade was part of an international network that involved Mafia in various parts of the world, and Montreal was a major port of entry. On November 10, 1975, thirty-one pounds of pure heroin, with a street value of more than $15 million, were seized on a French ship in Montreal harbour. The Mafia organization in the city was also a conduit for recruits going to the United States. Italian gangsters would come to Canada, receive forged papers, and then enter the States to work for the Mafia families there.[30]

Concern over the activities and growing power of the Mafia in Quebec finally led to an official inquiry into organized crime. The first complete report was submitted in October, 1975. Between October, 1975, and June, 1976, the commission continued its investigations, concentrating on the Mafia and a French-Canadian group known as the Dubois gang. The Commission's report revealed a pattern of constant interaction among the Quebec, American, and Italian Mafia leaders. The relationship was so close that Italian and American gangsters fleeing from the law found a safe haven with the Montreal Mafia.

The work of the Quebec Crime Commission and an investigation into organized crime undertaken by the government of British Columbia in the late seventies, as well as a number of other reports, offered the Canadian public a detailed account of the range of activities and the magnitude of the earnings associated with organized crime. The most money was made in drug trafficking. Everybody associated with the business made substantial incomes. One courier who worked for a Toronto heroin ring claimed that he made $1 million a year transporting drugs. Some idea of the money to be made at the other end can be garnered by the value of drug seizures made by police in various parts of the country. In 1978, Toronto police confiscated more than $2.2 million worth of cocaine. In the winter of 1980, Montreal police in one raid found $700,000 in cash and a quantity of hashish worth an estimated $9 million. Just two months later in a raid on a clandestine drug factory, police confiscated ten pounds of phencyclidine, which they claimed had a street value of $3.2 million.[31]

Loan-sharking – or lending money at usurious rates of interest – is another lucrative racket run or controlled by the criminal organizations. They lend money to other criminals or to people who can't borrow from legitimate lenders. One of the standard loans at the time was known as a "six-for-five." For every $5 loaned, the borrower would have to pay back $6 within a week. Large sums at compound interest could put the borrower in a position of making regular interest payments without ever paying off the principal. The Quebec Crime Commission estimated that between 1962 and 1975, William Obront, a member of the Cotroni gang, handled $84 million, most of which was generated through lending to small and big-time criminals to finance their varied illegal activities.

As we have already seen, gambling is a major component of organized crime. Police in Toronto estimated that in the late seventies there were about 600 bookmakers, each taking in anywhere from $1,000 to $40,000 per week. A police investigation in Vancouver revealed that one group of seventeen bookies was collectively handling over $120,000 per week. In some cases, the organized gangs run the operations themselves, in other cases they collect a percentage of the bookies' profits. One syndicate in British Columbia that ran its own operation was grossing between $2 million and $5 million per year. The head of the organization was paid over $4,000 a week as his share of the take.[32]

Yet another type of crime favoured by criminal organizations is counterfeiting. During 1979, authorities across Canada seized counterfeit currency with a face value of $1,201,473. In addition, about 2,754 counterfeit notes were circulated. Police claimed much of the counterfeiting done in Canada was the work of syndicates in Quebec, and particularly in Montreal. Fake American federal reserve notes comprised the largest percentage of what was being circulated.[33]

By the 1970s organized crime was also moving into the construction industry, especially in Ontario. A number of gangsters became involved with certain construction unions, lined their pockets with union dues, and in return for payoffs negotiated contracts favourable to the construction companies or guaranteed union peace. The rivalries sometimes became violent and there were threats and beatings administered as various factions competed for control. The Ontario government, in reaction to a series of incidents in the summer of 1972, appointed Harry Waisberg, a county court judge, to undertake an inquiry into the activities of certain unions. Waisberg also probed the violence that had scarred the industry in recent years as well as the activities of certain people with criminal records who had become associated with various unions.[34]

Through the 1970s organized criminal groups were becoming involved in an ever-widening range of activities, including the operation of legitimate businesses. One British Columbia report estimated that criminals in the greater Vancouver area were involved in 134 legitimate businesses. The Quebec Crime Commission calculated that the Montreal gangster William Obront had an interest in at least thirty-eight companies. For the most part, however, the business of organized crime was crime and few were more successful than the Cotroni organization in Montreal.

The Cotroni operation had continued to strengthen over the years to become the most influential crime family in the country. Through frequent resort to violence, Vincenzo Cotroni had established control over a major portion of criminal activities in the city and a dominant position in the drug trade. He built a powerful structure of about twenty full-time members cemented together by family ties, friendship, common ethnic origins, and a strict code of loyalty and silence. The Quebec Crime Commission provided a chart to illustrate the structure and the relative positions of the people who made up the Cotroni organization. The chart is reproduced in Figure 2.

At the time the Quebec hearings were completed several members of the Cotroni Mafia were already in difficulties. The variety of their problems offers some insight into their activities and methods of operation. Vincent Cotroni, the Don, was awaiting trial in Toronto on a fraud charge involving

Figure 2

Organizational Chart   Leadership and Chain of Command

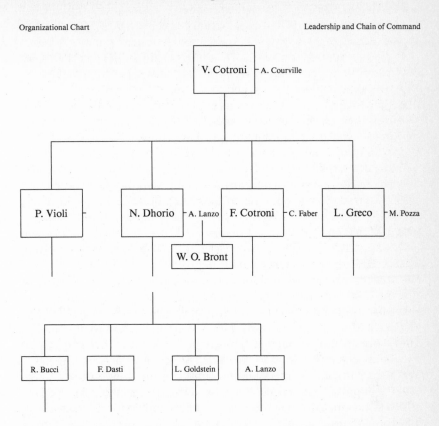

SOURCE: Report of the Quebec Commission of Inquiry on Organized Crime, 1976.

$250,000 worth of stocks and bonds and a close associate, Paolo Violi, was also awaiting trial in connection with the same case. In addition, Cotroni and Violi had been principals in a meat marketing firm that had been closed down for selling meat unfit for human consumption. The manager of the firm was Armand Courville, an old friend from Cotroni's wrestling days. Angelo Lanzo, another member of the inner circle, was found dead while hiding out to avoid testifying before the Commission. William Obront was awaiting trial on a charge of fraud and forgery amounting to $515,000. Frank Cotroni, Vincenzo's brother, was serving a fifteen-year prison sentence for cocaine trafficking between Montreal, the United States, and Mexico. As yet another illustration of the violence that was the trademark of organized crime, Luigi Greco, an under-boss of Vic Cotroni's, died in an explosion that blew up his business premises.[35]

As a result of failing health and the attention focused on him by the

Quebec Crime Commission, Vincenzo Cotroni passed the reigns of control to Paolo Violi. However, he remained a powerful influence in Mafia circles. Violi was murdered in 1978 in his ice cream and coffee bar and Cotroni died a natural death in 1984. By 1980, the Cotroni mobsters' grip on Montreal had been substantially weakened. Their internal difficulties and challenges from competing organizations reduced their power, but they were still a force to contend with. They continued their criminal activities and attempted to fight off encroachments by rival gangs. A murder committed by two of their hit men in 1983 underlined the fact that they were still a dangerous element. On November 29, 1983, Robert Clément and Réal Simard entered a room in the Seaway Hotel in Toronto and gunned down two drug dealers, killing one and severely wounding the other. Simard was arrested the next day but Clément escaped and eventually fled the country. During his trial, Simard admitted to five murders carried out on the orders of Frank Cotroni and was sentenced to life imprisonment. He also broke the code of silence and turned police informer. Clément returned to Canada in 1987, was tried for murder, and convicted with the help of testimony from Simard. He, too, was sentenced to life imprisonment.[36]

The Mafia also established a commanding presence in the province of Ontario. Local ethnic Italian gangs had been operating for some time in places like Hamilton, Guelph, Toronto, and Windsor. Between 1958 and 1962, U.S. Mafia members enlisted their assistance in a move to establish control over criminal activities throughout the province. Ontario was an important conduit for drugs to the United States, and the American gangsters were particularly interested in controlling the drug business. Also, with the population and economic growth that was taking place the U.S. mobsters anticipated expanding opportunities for their illegal enterprises.

Vincent Mauro, an under-boss of the New York-based Genovese family, was in charge of Mafia drug operations in Ontario. When he decided to consolidate and branch out, he recruited a number of gangsters, chief among them "Johnny Pops" Papalia from Hamilton. Like others of his kind, Papalia had served a formidable criminal apprenticeship. In 1949 he was arrested for selling drugs in Toronto and served two years less a day in a reformatory. Sometime after his release he moved to Montreal and went to work in Carmine Galente's organization. He eventually returned to Toronto and by the mid-fifties was involved in a variety of activities with a group of local criminals. Papalia and many of his friends had connections with the New York, Buffalo, and Detroit Mafia families.[37]

The Ontario takeover was achieved with large doses of intimidations and beatings. One of the many victims was Max Bluestein, operator of a large gaming enterprise and a fairly influential figure in criminal circles in Toronto. Bluestein wanted to maintain his independence and was disdainful of Mafia attempts to take control of his operations. On March 21, 1961, he agreed to a meeting with syndicate representatives in the Town Tavern in

Toronto, but he again repulsed their overtures to join up. On his way out, Bluestein was hit from behind with a blackjack and as he fell was attacked with iron bars and brass knuckles. A broken bottle was pushed in his mouth and the brutal beating finished off with a kick in the face. When the police arrived, they could not find one person who would admit to having witnessed the carnage.[38]

Through such tactics, the Mafia established their hegemony in Ontario and both diversified and prospered. The dynamic growth in the province of both population and industry has created steadily improving opportunities for organized crime. It has also given an impetus to the expansion of Canadian-based Mafia gangs. They operate as part of a complex syndicate that spans the Canada-U.S. border. Mafia mobsters in both countries work with each other, share international connections, and on occasion fall out and fight over their turf. Their tentacles reach into all parts of Canada and the United States. They are involved in drug trafficking, smuggling illegal immigrants, stock market frauds, fencing of stolen goods, gambling, loansharking, labour racketeering, extortion, and other illegal activities. They have elaborate money laundering operations and are major investors in legitimate business.

Some Ontario Mafiosi got their start by operating extortion rackets. Usually they would begin by threatening people in the growing post-war immigrant communities. Many of these new arrivals were suspicious of authority or afraid to go to the police. If they were in business and they resisted, their shops would be smashed up and their property destroyed. Sometimes their wives and children would be threatened. Typical was a case that came to police attention in 1969. A beauty parlor operator in Burlington, Ontario, was being intimidated by a small gang led by a boyhood friend with whom he had grown up in Italy. Faced with threats of bodily harm to him, his wife, and his children, over a two-year period he paid out $29,000.[39]

The extortion rackets were a favourite of the gangs even when they were involved in other activities. On occasion people from varied backgrounds found themselves being victimized. In 1965 Richard Angle, a Toronto businessman, was threatened with bodily harm unless he paid out $17,500. The principals in the extortion were three brothers from Toronto, Paul, Albert, and Eugene Volpe, and a mysterious third party known initially as Mr. Palmer. The Volpes were well connected in international crime circles and for a time ran a Mafia-owned gambling casino in Port-au-Prince, Haiti. Palmer was the heavy in the scheme and threatened Angle that he would take control of his business and harm him physically. At one point he told him to pay up "or blood will run in the streets of Toronto. I've got an army behind me."[40] Fearing for his life Angle went to the police, who arrested the gangsters on charges of extortion. Palmer was ultimately identified as Pasquale Natarelli, a lieutenant of the Buffalo-based Stefano Magaddino Cosa Nostra family.

What followed offers a good illustration of the difficulties police had and continue to have in dealing with organized crime. The first trial was halted and declared a mistrial when part way into the proceedings a juror stood up and announced that his comprehension of English wasn't good enough to follow the evidence. The second trial ended in a hung jury when one lone member, for some mysterious reason, insisted on an acquittal. The third trial was stopped when a juror revealed that a friend of the Volpes had offered him a bribe. The fourth trial ended with a not guilty verdict but the Crown was granted an appeal on the grounds that the judge had misdirected the jury. Before the fifth and final trial Pasquale Natarelli was arrested for a series of crimes in the United States. Albert Volpe fled the country and went to Greece. The two remaining brothers pleaded guilty to a lesser charge of conspiring to obtain money or stocks by threat. Paul Volpe was sentenced to two years and Eugene Volpe to three months.[41]

The Mafia's tentacles ultimately spread across Canada. In some cases gang members established a permanent presence, in others they maintained contact with local criminals. A B.C. investigation in the 1970s revealed that the Mafia was also well established on the west coast. Members were involved in the usual range of endeavours, including drug trafficking, organized theft, commercial crimes, gambling, and prostitution. They were headquartered in Vancouver and had connections in Toronto, New York, Boston, and various other cities.[42]

For a long time, the leading Mafia figures in Canada were people who came from the Calabrian district of Italy. Since at least the mid-1980s, however, the Sicilian Mafia has grown in strength and assumed a dominant position. On occasion the rival groups have come into open conflict with each other. Intimidation, beatings, and murder are their stock in trade. Between 1976 and 1980, Cecil Kirby, a Satan's Choice motorcycle club member, worked as a mob enforcer. His record illustrates the violence that maintains the power of organized crime. He carried out over 100 contracts that included arson, assault, bombings, and attempted murder. In 1977 he blew up a Toronto restaurant. The explosion killed one person and injured four others.[43]

Anthony Musitano is a typical example of the people who run organized crime in Canada. He used a bakery business in Hamilton as a cover for his criminal ventures. In the 1970s he ran an extortion racket and hired motorcycle gang members to intimidate his victims. In pursuit of his criminal activities he carried out a series of arsons and bombings for which he was convicted in 1983 and sentenced to life imprisonment. The sentence was subsequently reduced on appeal to fifteen years. Three members of his gang were also jailed. In prison, Musitano shared the company of members of the Commisso mob from Toronto.[44]

By the late 1970s the Commisso crime family was one of the most powerful and brutal gangs in Ontario. The Commisso brothers were born in the southern Italian town of Marina di Gioiosa in a region controlled by the Calabrian Mafia. Their father was killed in a Mafia shootout in 1949. Cosimo, the dominating figure in the family, was sixteen when they moved to Canada in 1961. He and his brothers, Remo and Michele, eventually put together a ruthless organization of gangsters that worked out of Toronto and had connections across Canada, in the the United States, and in Italy. They were involved in the drug trade, counterfeiting, fencing stolen goods, fraud, extortion, and contract killing. Finally in 1981, the crime spree was ended. The Commisso brothers were convicted of conspiracy to commit murder and sentenced to eight years in the penitentiary. In 1984, they were convicted of more crimes and another eight years were added to their original sentences.[45]

Even when incarcerated, organized crime bosses can still be dangerous. The long arm of the Mafia is illustrated by a conspiracy that ensued when the Commissos and Anthony Musitano met in prison. From inside the walls, Musitano arranged the execution of a Toronto mobster by the name of Dominic Racco. He was the son of Michele Racco, a former Mafia Don. It is alleged that the Commissos let out a contract to Musitano to kill Racco for non-payment of a drug debt. Musitano was charged with plotting the murder and pleaded guilty in February, 1985. Three other members of his gang were also charged. Musitano was given a twelve-year sentence to run concurrently with his original fifteen-year term.[46]

The violence and the killings are consistent with the long-standing macho ethics of the Mafia. In 1986, Rocco Zito, another powerful organized crime figure, killed sixty-year-old Rosario Sciarrino in Toronto. Sciarrino, a freelance photographer, borrowed $20,000 from Zito and couldn't pay off the loan. The interest, as much as $9,000 a month, was crippling and the photographer fell further and further into arrears. Zito pressured Sciarrino for payment and threatened his family. Terrified, they moved their place of residence, but through a chance meeting with Zito's son, Sciarrino's whereabouts was uncovered and again pressure was put on him to pay the loan. In January of 1986, Zito arranged a meeting with Sciarrino and when the two came together an argument broke out. Sciarrino insulted Zito and the latter shot him dead. The body was put in garbage bags and left in the trunk of his car near Toronto's Pearson International airport. Sciarrino was shot in the head and chest, and had more than a dozen fractures on his face and head. Zito went into hiding but eventually gave himself up. He pleaded guilty to manslaughter and in October, 1986, was sentenced to four and a half years in prison. In 1987 he was given an additional two years for an unrelated crime. At Zito's original trial a drug trafficker, obviously interested in the outcome, was interviewed by a reporter. In reference to Zito's actions, the man commented that in Italy "a man is a man . . . you are your own law." He said that if someone bothered him or his family, "I take a shotgun and blow their head off." He added that he had known Rocco Zito since coming to Canada and said, "He's a man."[47]

The Canadian Mafia has been, and continues to be, an intricate web of complex relationships. Members of Mafia families come from the same parts of Italy, sometimes are blood relatives, intermarry with family of other mobsters, and maintain contacts in Italy, the U.S., and elsewhere. Mafia mobs compete with outsiders and with other Mafia gangs. Although they are the largest criminal cartel in the nation, and their activities are well known, for much of the time they have been very successful in avoiding prosecution. They bribe police, politicians, and newspapermen, intimidate witnesses to their crimes, and murder informers. They cover their tracks well and are difficult to prosecute. The police investigation of Anthony Musitano's activities in Hamilton cost in excess of $1 million. When he was finally brought to trial after years of violent criminal activity, his only prior convictions were for possession of a weapon and obstructing police.

When Mafia members are arrested, they come to court with the best legal talent that money can buy. They win reduced sentences by plea bargaining and buy privileges in prison that make life relatively easy. Generally, they are model prisoners and so are usually paroled in the minimum amount of time. Better policing, breaks from informers, successful prosecutions, intermittent rivalry, competition from other gangs, old age, and new laws have all combined to weaken the Mafia grip on organized crime in Canada. Nevertheless, the Mafia gangs remain a potent force in criminal activities across the country.

THE DUBOIS GANG

While the Mafia members have long been the main players on the criminal stage in Canada, they have not been alone. In every major city there are criminal organizations, some simply collections of small-time gangsters, others involved in fairly big-league crime. For many years the largest, most feared, and most ruthless gang outside of the Mafia families was the Dubois gang in Montreal. The controlling element was nine French-Canadian brothers. At the height of their power they ran an organization of about 200 people.

The brothers grew up in a poor family in the working-class district of Saint-Henri in southwest Montreal and very early cultivated a reputation for toughness. They started their criminal activities with burglary and armed robbery and graduated to protection rackets, loan-sharking, and drugs. Collectively and individually they were violent and cruel. On one occasion, in a Greek restaurant, a number of them attempted to renege on paying their bill. When the owner pressed the issue, they informed him of who they were, proceeded to beat him severely, and carved a cross on the man's body with a knife. The Dubois brothers established complete control over criminal activities in their neighbour-hood. They forced others to work for them, used terror tactics to intimidate the inhabitants, and made it clear that revenge would be swift for anyone who informed on them. In the early 1960s they branched out into protection rackets for owners and employees of nightclubs, taverns, and businesses, and also moved into loan-sharking and drugs.

They would approach the owner of a club or tavern and demand protec-tion payments. If the owner refused, they would arrange a fight on the premises, causing considerable damage, or intimidate the person until he gave in. The Dubois gang did not stop at payments alone. They frequently insisted on staffing the business with their own people. In this way the club could be used to carry on a wide range of activities, including selling drugs, loan-sharking, selling stolen goods, and gambling. In one case they literally took the business over by insulting, harassing, and beating employees until they all quit. Even the head of the union was forced out. They then replaced them with their own people. In other cases, they forced employees to pay a weekly fee in order to hold their jobs.

Owners who resisted their racket were given a rough time. On February 5, 1971, an enterprising businessman bought a tavern in downtown Montreal. Attracted by its success, the Dubois brothers paid a visit on June 19, 1971, and offered him protection. When the owner refused to go along, he was systematically harassed, his staff beaten up, he was shot at, hit with a billiard ball, and finally two attempts were made on his life. In October, 1973, he sold the tavern.

In the early 1970s the Montreal Mafia was weakened by a series of police raids. The Dubois gang took advantage of the situation to further extend their territory. They also expanded their activities to include a major book-ing agency for striptease dancers. As well, they extended their drug business by muscling a motorcycle gang out of prime territory. They took on anyone who got in the way of their ambition. In 1974 they started an open war with the McSween gang, a smaller group of mobsters who had staked out the territory east of Atwater Street.

Before the battle was over, the Dubois brothers staged their own St. Valentine's Day massacre. On February 14, 1975, a group of hired hit men burst into a bar frequented by members of the McSween gang and started shooting. Four people were killed and several wounded. With the McSweens out of the way, the Dubois gang controlled crime in major segments of Montreal. They established a drug distribution network throughout the province, ran a major loan-sharking business, and were so vicious and powerful that the Mafia had to co-exist with them. Although only one of the brothers actually held down a job, they drove expensive cars, owned townhouses and country homes, and indulged in an ostentatious display of wealth. Like the Mafia, their fortunes have varied since the publicity generated by the Quebec Crime Commission and as a result of stepped-up police action. However, they remain a dangerous element in organized crime circles in Quebec.[48]

MOTORCYCLE GANGS

Motorcycle gangs are one of the more recent arrivals on the organized crime scene in Canada. Motorcycle clubs began to appear after World War Two. They were begun by ex-service personnel and at first were merely recreational organizations. The nature of the activity, the open road, the power of the cycle, and the feeling of freedom soon attracted a different element. By the 1960s clubs of toughs began to appear dressed in leather and fancying themselves as free spirits, even outlaws of the road. They extended the outlaw concept by becoming criminals in the real sense of the term. At first they indulged in low-level crime, but soon they had graduated to more sinister activities.

A typical case history was the evolution of a club called the 13th Tribe, started in Halifax, Nova Scotia, in 1968. Originally made up of Navy and ex-Navy personnel, it soon attracted a large number of undisciplined and unruly characters. By 1971, the club had over 100 members and associates, and a criminal element had taken over. Many had records for possession of dangerous weapons, assaults, and resisting arrest. Club members took a defiant and hostile attitude toward police and authority in general. In an attempt to intimidate the police, they made it generally known that an officer caught alone would be in for trouble.[49]

In addition to their violence and street crimes, the gang became involved in the trafficking of speed. Partly in pursuance of their drug business, they developed connections with motorcycle gangs in other parts of the country. There were now part of a loose association that had put many clubs in contact with each other and enabled them to co-operate in joint ventures. The 13th Tribe, for example, carried on its drug trade in association with the Popeye Motorcycle Club in Montreal and the Grim Reapers from Alberta. Meanwhile, they continued to enhance their reputation for violence and lawlessness in Halifax.[50]

In the early 1970s the 13th Tribe launched a virtual reign of terror in metropolitan Halifax. They gang-raped a teenage girl, viciously beat a policeman working with the city drug squad, assaulted a Dartmouth man, and shot at another police officer patrolling a busy downtown street in his squad car. The carnage resulted in a number of arrests and key members of the organization were jailed for periods of three to twelve years. Other club members, following the crackdown, became relatively unobtrusive and concentrated on their drug business.[51]

By the late 1970s, with many of their jailed leaders out on the street again, they once more took the limelight. In 1980 they appeared en masse at the Atlantic Folk Festival held in the rural village of Stewiacke. Motorcycle clubs from Ontario, New Brunswick, Newfoundland, and the U.S. joined them in an orgy of booze, drugs, sex, and violence.[52] The broad representation of the motorcycle gangs again illustrates the vast network that the clubs had established. Across Canada there were gangs involved in the same activities as the 13th Tribe. Drug manufacturing laboratories, trafficking, prostitution, automobile theft, and contract violence, from arson to beatings and murder, were part of their ongoing business. Because of the large incomes from their criminal activities, many club members across the country were becoming conspicuously wealthy.[53] For example, one member of the Grim Reapers motorcycle club in Calgary had twenty-three prostitutes working for him. His gross income from the women was estimated at between $50,000 and $60,000 a month. He invested in businesses, owned property worth over $600,000, and when he was arrested had $207,000 in cash in his possession.[54]

As more and more clubs came on the scene and earnings from such activities as the drug trade escalated, a fierce competition developed among the outlaw gangs. In a manner somewhat similar to the Mafia families they began to challenge each other for territorial control. The rivalry was widespread and included the nation's capital. The two most powerful competitors were the Hell's Angels and the Outlaws. Police expressed concern that Ottawa could become "a blood-spattered battleground" as the rivals fought each other for control of the drug trade. The superintendent of Ottawa police, in September, 1981, observed that "Motorcycle gangs overall have become a major part of organized crime. They are a much bigger problem than the Mafia in this part of the country."[55]

Gang warfare broke out across the country as clubs fought pitched battles with each other, bombed and burned clubhouses, destroyed prized motorcycles, and murdered their rivals. Over one two-year period in 1979-80, about fifteen motorcycle club members lost their lives in the course of gang battles. Between 1981 and 1983, Quebec police claimed that forty-two murders in the province were linked directly to bikers fighting for control of the drug trade. Many clubs began to consolidate and join forces to strengthen their chances of survival. One of the largest entities to emerge from the process was the group known as the Hell's Angels, who either ran rivals out of business or absorbed them. Some reluctantly joined their ranks, others willingly entered the marriage. Among the latter was Halifax's 13th Tribe, who became full-fledged Hell's Angels in 1985.[56]

By the end of the 1980s the Hell's Angels had established themselves as one of the premier organized crime cartels in Canada and were a part of an international organization with branches in at least thirteen countries.[57] Other clubs, some large, some small, continue to operate in various provinces and sometimes function as part of an international bikers' network. Collectively, led by clubs like the Hell's Angels, the motorcycle gangs constitute one of the major organized crime problems faced by the nation. They are tightly run organizations with strict membership requirements and elaborate codes of conduct. Before being admitted, prospective members must prove themselves during an apprenticeship period by carrying out various tasks, including the commission of crimes.

Full members must adhere to a code of conformity and loyalty. Among other things, they are forbidden to use drugs and are required to be honest in their dealings with each other. In their criminal transactions and drug dealings with other chapters, they are expected to be completely upright. Serious infractions of club rules are severely dealt with. In 1986, members of the Laval, Quebec, chapter of the Hell's Angels were caught cheating the Halifax members in drug deals. As a result, the Laval club was put out of business and a number of their members murdered in the process. The motorcycle gangs are involved in the manufacture of certain drugs such as speed, in trafficking, in organized theft and fencing, in prostitution, and in agencies for striptease dancers. They commit arson, fraud, and act as enforcers and contract killers. Some have become millionaires as a result of their illegal activities, have adopted the lifestyle of successful business people, and invest in a variety of legitimate enterprises.

They have also used their money to establish a formidable buffer to the police. They have sophisticated electronic equipment to monitor police movements, bribe staff working in the criminal justice system, hire the best lawyers, intimidate witnesses, and buy off jurors. They also maintain an impressive arsenal of weapons. One raid, carried out by Calgary police, netted over 100 assorted weapons, including hand guns, rifles, and a cross-bow. Many clubhouses are veritable fortresses, with steel doors and warning devices.[58]

ETHNIC GANGS

While not as formidable as the Mafia and motorcycle gangs a number of ethnic organizations are also well established in the ranks of organized crime. For many years, Chinese gangs have operated within Asian communities in Vancouver and Toronto. They run extortion rackets, gambling, and prostitution, smuggle aliens, and traffic in drugs. Like their counterparts, they resort to violence and murder to achieve their goals and rely on fear and superstition within their communities to escape arrest. They have contacts across Canada and international connections, especially with Hong Kong. As more Chinese come to Canada, fleeing the planned Communist takeover of Hong Kong in 1997, the ranks of the Chinese gangs are expanding. The wealth of many new immigrants, making them targets for extortion, and the continued growth in drug usage in Canada are powerful incentives to stepped-up activity on the part of Chinese gangs.[59]

There is also evidence that some of the most powerful of the Hong Kong gangs are systematically moving their headquarters to Canada to avoid the

Communist takeover. Among them are secret societies, known as triads, which operate internationally and are involved in gambling, extortion, prostitution, robbery, fraud, and drug smuggling. Police have determined that since the mid-eighties they have been investing money in Toronto businesses and real estate. At least three gangs have been identified: the Luen Kung Lock, with an estimated fifty members, the 14K, with thirty-five members, and the Ghost Shadow, a gang of about twenty-five. They have also made Canada a main link in their international drug-smuggling network, using Vancouver and Toronto as trans-shipment points for drugs destined for the U.S.[60] The intricacy of the network is illustrated by one shipment police were able to follow as it moved along to its final destination. The heroin originated in the Golden Triangle of Southeast Asia, passed through China, and was shipped from Hong Kong to Vancouver, concealed in boxes of umbrellas. From Vancouver, it was sent by rail to Toronto, then taken to Ajax, Ontario, and finally flown to New York. The ease with which foreigners can enter and remain in Canada makes the country very attractive to gangs like the triads seeking a new base from which to run their criminal empires.[61]

Less organized but equally dangerous is a collection of criminals known to police as the Big Circle Boys. Many are from Guangzhow, a Chinese city near Hong Kong. Attracted by better economic opportunities and ease of entry, they started coming to Canada around 1983-84. Once in this country they began to prey on the Chinese community, executing armed robberies and home invasions. The structure of the Big Circle Boys gangs is fluid and promotion through the ranks can be fast. Members rely on their common origins and acquaintances in organizing for criminal endeavours. They usually operate in small groups of four or five and interchange membership. Some also plied their criminal trade in Hong Kong before coming to Canada. Collectively, they are involved in robbery, alien smuggling, and the drug trade. They have international connections, a storehouse of recruits to come to Canada, and a willingness to be as ruthless as necessary to carry on their illegal activities.[62]

Among the ethnic gangs assuming a more prominent presence in the ranks of organized crime are the Vietnamese. They prey on their own communities with robbery and extortion rackets, taking advantage of immigrants who are unfamiliar with Canadian ways, who are afraid to go to the police, and who sometimes have little capacity in the English language. Police find the Vietnamese gangs particularly violent and suspect that some members are experienced criminals who fled their homeland for the safer haven of Canada. Their background makes them difficult to deal with since they have little fear of the Canadian police or justice system. As a member of Toronto's Asian Organized Crime Squad explained it, "They laugh at jail, saying it's better than a refugee camp."[63] Their pattern of operation is similar across the country. They stay mostly within their own communities and take advantage of the reluctance of their countrymen to complain. One Vietnam-born police officer in Montreal estimated that up to 75 per cent of the crime committed in the Asian community is not reported.[64]

A number of the new arrivals taking advantage of Canada's open door are turning to drug trafficking as a way of making quick and easy money. Ethnic groups organize gangs that take advantage of connections in their homelands to obtain drugs. Montreal police claim that in recent years immigrants from Iran, Sri Lanka, and Turkey have set up organizations that control as much as 50 per cent of the heroin traffic in the city. Even Middle East terrorists have exploited the market by setting up drug dealers in Canada who send the profits home to finance their violence.[65]

The CTV television program *W5* in early January, 1989, examined the participation of Iranians in the drug trade in Montreal. Reporters estimated that as many as 300 are involved. In some cases they operate openly in houses heavily barred, the dealers well armed with an assortment of weapons. Fear and intimidation are their stock in trade and anyone who informs risks being knifed. They even threaten the police. The report estimated that as much as a billion dollars of drugs a year are being brought in by this group.[66]

The desire of so many people to come to Canada has itself created a new industry in smuggling aliens and selling phony passports. Many people do not want to take the time involved in going through regular immigration procedures and so are willing to pay for help in bypassing the queue. International gangs with branches in Canada have developed a thriving market in stolen or forged passports and smuggling services. One ring that was broken up in Vancouver in April of 1989 was smuggling into the U.S. aliens who had come to Canada.[67] Another gang with members in Toronto and Hong Kong was broken up in August, 1990. Over a three-year period they smuggled thousands of Asians into Canada, some of them known criminals from China and Hong Kong, by providing forged documents and charging up to $19,000 for their services.[68] Immigration officials estimate that thousands of people who have come here in recent years were assisted with illegal entry by organized immigration rings in this country working with counterparts in various parts of the world.

Yet another dimension of organized crime is the travelling gangs that work in various parts of Canada from time to time. In 1980, for example, the Canada Gang, a mob of over thirty-seven members, worked out of Vancouver. They operated nationally and internationally, specializing in such things as hotel burglary, shoplifting, credit card fraud, narcotics, and smuggling. Gangs like this rendezvous in various cities, systematically work their trade, disperse, and then reconvene in another city.[69]

TACTICS AND ACTIVITIES OF ORGANIZED CRIME

While criminal gangs vary in size, ethnic origin, and specialization, most have in common a membership of ruthless thugs. Violence is the stock in trade of organized crime. Gangs use brute force to establish territorial control, in the commission of crime, in competition with each other, to discipline their own members, and to intimidate the public. They attract to their ranks people who thrive on aberrant behaviour and use the gang image to enhance their own power and status. Cecil Kirby is a typical example. A member of Satan's Choice motorcycle club, he broadened his horizons by going to work in 1976 as an enforcer for the Commisso Mafia. He had already established a reputation for brutality and ruthlessness and did not hesitate to carry out any contract, even if it called for murder.[70] Kirby, however, acquired so much information about Mafia activities that he finally feared for his own life. He became afraid that he would be eliminated because he knew too much, a common gangland happening. Thus, in November, 1980, he turned to the police with an offer to become an informer. Because police have so much difficulty getting evidence on organized crime, they welcome informers with open arms. In return, officials usually have to grant immunity from prosecution and ongoing protection. As distasteful as the arrangement is, the justice system goes along because it is a very effective means of combatting crime.[71]

Kirby gave information and testimony that was instrumental in bringing a number of mob figures to justice. His antics, however, even while under protective custody, continued to expose his character. He allegedly administered a savage beating to a girlfriend in a hotel room while his police bodyguards stood outside, but the woman did not press charges. In a subsequent incident, he eluded his escorts and was later picked up on a weapons charge. He was out of jail the next day. While he was carrying on these escapades, his immunity arrangement provided him with free hotel accommodation, $525 per month, bodyguards, a leased car, and $150 per month for alimony payments to his ex-wife. When his witness appearances were completed he was to receive $200,000 for relocation and help to assume a new identity. When the Kirby story was exposed in the press, a public outrage ensued that brought a storm of criticism about the practice of granting immunity from prosecution and paying money to criminal informers.[72]

Kirby was not the only ex-biker to reveal the tactics employed by organized crime. In 1984, Yves (Apache) Trudeau, a founder of the Quebec chapter of the Hell's Angels, turned to the police for protection when a number of his friends were murdered and he suspected that he was next. He confessed to having killed forty-three people over the years. Trudeau specialized in explosives, which he planted under cars or wired to motorcycle ignitions. On one occasion, a video machine he had packed with explosives killed four people when it blew up.[73]

Other contract killers told similar stories to the police as they sought protection from their former employers. Michel Blass, while he was working as an advance man for rock bands, carried out an estimated twelve contracts for organized crime. Donald Lavoie worked for the infamous Dubois gang until he learned that he was about to be eliminated. In the twelve years that he worked for the Dubois, he killed fifteen, helped plan another thirty-four murders, and had knowledge of at least seventy-six others. The confessions gave further confirmation to the magnitude of violence associated with many of the criminal gangs.[74]

Besides generating considerable carnage, organized crime also produces huge sums of money. The biggest earner, the drug trade, police estimate to be worth over $10 billion and growing.[75] Every socio-economic group provides a market for drugs. In 1988, there were an estimated 10,000 regular users of heroin and cocaine in Toronto and up to 2,200 in Vancouver.[76] Profits are so huge that most organized crime groups engage in the trade. Earnings finance everything from legitimate business enterprises to terrorist activities. In August of 1989, six people were arrested in Toronto who were planning an armed attack on Collins Bay Penitentiary to break out five colleagues. They intended to attack with a helicopter and machine guns. They were involved in an international heroin smuggling ring, and when arrested were in possession of over $7 million worth of high-grade heroin. They intended to finance the aborted jail break with proceeds from the drug sale.[77]

Drug trade links are intricate and difficult for the police to penetrate. At the top of the chain are international syndicates that buy the raw product and arrange for processing and transportation. Supplies are delivered to gangs across the country, which in turn have a network of street vendors. The latter sometimes get caught, but it has proven extremely difficult to reach the management level of the chain and to intercept the flow of drugs. In 1988, customs officials on the west coast alone seized forty-one kilograms of heroin, with a street value of about $250 million. Between 1985 and 1988, Canada Customs, a team of over 3,000 people, confiscated drugs with a street value of about $1.3 billion. Yet officials estimate that they intercept no more than 10 per cent of the quantity that comes into the country.[78]

Stolen securities are another big-ticket item for organized crime. In 1975, police estimated that the float of stolen stocks and bonds was worth well over $27 million. While some of this amount represented white-collar crime, much of it was in the hands of organized syndicates who worked in an international market. In the mid-seventies Canadians were losing an estimated billion dollars or more a year to frauds of one kind or another, many perpetrated by organized crime.[79]

Society is sometimes deluded by a belief that organized crime touches only the esoteric world of big business or the tortured existence of the drug addict. However, ordinary citizens are the direct victims of the crime cartels every day. They engage in auto theft rings, fencing of stolen goods, and credit card fraud. When someone's car disappears or his wallet is stolen, there is a good chance that both will end up in the hands of an organized gang of criminals, usually far removed from the place of the theft. Also, the huge sums of money taken in by organized crime are frequently invested in legitimate businesses. These firms are in competition with honest operators who do not have the financial resources held by the gangsters. They also use businesses for money-laundering purposes and ordinary people who patronize them are unwittingly helping with their illegal activities.

In modern times, the profits earned by criminal gangs are so large that they face the problem of hiding the source of their money. They face as much danger of being caught by Revenue Canada as they do of being apprehended by the police. The possession of large sums of money naturally interests the tax people. Therefore, mobsters have to devise ways of making it look like their holdings are the product of legitimate business. Elaborate schemes are worked out, frequently involving overseas interests, domestic banks, real estate companies, and so on. The financial proceeds of crime are passed through a number of accounts or dummy corporations until the money returns to its owners as if it were earned in a legitimate investment or business venture. It has been "laundered" and now the owner can claim it as income, pay taxes on it, invest it, and above all, enjoy it without worrying about Revenue Canada or the police. Thus, money laundering has become yet another activity of organized crime.[80]

Some progress has been made in recent years in the fight against organized crime, but it continues to be a growth industry. It is difficult to comprehend that major Canadian cities have been divided up among criminal groups and that the lawbreaking that goes on in the various districts is either controlled or licensed by the gangs. Montreal is a case in point. The Mafia, the Dubois or West Island gang, the Cotronis, Iranians, Haitians, Chileans, Hell's Angels, and others have established criminal supremacy over certain sections of the city. Some control the heroin trade, some cocaine, others specialize in different criminal activities. Many bars, restaurants, strip joints, and a host of other businesses are either owned or controlled by organized crime. The gangsters are so entrenched that it is virtually impossible to break their stranglehold on the city.

As fast as one gang chieftain is put away, another steps in to take his place. If one group is broken up, another emerges or a rival takes over the territory. The immigrant groups have further complicated the picture so that the police must carry on the battle on a wide variety of fronts. The gangs become ever more powerful and sophisticated while the police are hampered by a lack of money, inadequate manpower, and the restrictions of laws that inhibit investigations and make prosecutions difficult. Unfortunately, the prospects for any real improvement within the near future are not very bright.

SUMMARY

Crime statistics have never documented the nature or extent of organized crime in Canada. In more recent years, we are aware of individuals who get arrested from time to time and are identified as gangland figures. On an individual basis, however, the charges brought against them differ little from those for which hundreds of other criminals are taken before the courts. They are convicted for fraud, tax evasion, murder, and a variety of other offences that by themselves say little about the complexities of the crime syndicates. Therefore, anecdotal and other evidence must be used to construct a comprehensive picture of the nature of organized crime and how gangs function. That evidence leaves little doubt that, throughout our history, organized groups of criminals have contributed significantly to crime. Gangs are responsible, either directly or indirectly, for a major share of criminal activity. They have spread like a cancer and firmly entrenched themselves in all parts of the country.

Organized crime in Canada started with pirates, local gangs of cut-throats and thieves, and the odd group of government officials. Gangs were to be found in colonial seaports, carrying on the whisky trade out west during the building of the CPR, and intimidating settlers in rural and urban areas. Whenever money-making opportunities that lent themselves to organized gang activities appeared, some group or other coalesced to exploit them.

Ironically, the moral crusade against the demon rum created the circumstances for development of big-league, ongoing, organized crime. Out of prohibition in the United States and Canada emerged the large, powerful, well-financed gangs of criminals that dominated the scene until recent decades. From a base of bootlegging they expanded into everything from prostitution to loan-sharking, to labour racketeering. When the market for illegal liquor waned, they turned to drugs. Not only did they move in on an existing demand, but over time they contributed substantially to the growth of the market. By the 1970s the most powerful and ruthless of the gangs, the Mafia, had established a dominance across the country. They subverted police, politicians, and tramped over anyone who got in their way. They were a virtual state within a state in certain cities and were able to hold the forces of justice at bay.

The Mafia hegemony was challenged from at least the early seventies by a number of local gangs, then by the motorcycle clubs, and finally by a number of ethnic organizations. Today, many elements of organized crime co-exist, share the market for their illegal activities, compete against, and assault and murder each other. The key element in the rise of so many rival gangs has been the drug trade. The stakes are so high that new players are willing to enter the game and compete with the older established organizations. They put together instant gangs that are too powerful to be easily put out of business. The start-up financing they have available and the huge profits they make enable them to gather together a large group of well-paid and well-armed people. In the case of the ethnic gangs, many members are experienced criminals with international connections. Some ethnic gangs are simply so vicious that they fear neither other gangs nor the police. Even the small dealer survives in the drug trade. It is so amorphous and undisciplined that there are too many people involved for the big cartels to control.

Gangs of organized criminals throughout our history have exhibited many common characteristics. They are commanded by strong, usually ruthless leaders who have organizational skills and personal qualities that instil loyalty and fear in their followers. Most gangs maintain discipline through some informal or defined code of conduct. Family ties, national origins, friendships, common interests, status, fear, and severe punishments are some of the factors that bring and keep the gangs together. They are a microcosm of the criminal world, drawn from all strata of society and from all backgrounds.

The common denominator of organized crime is brutality. Practically every gang in our history has used violence – threats, intimidation, harassment, beatings, bombings, and murder are the tools of organized crime. They seek to create an invincible image and a climate of fear, and their violent nature is itself an attraction for many of the thugs who form gangland associations.

The violence, combined with their money and power, also protects gangs against the civil authority. In an earlier day, sheriffs, police, and politicians were sometimes afraid to take on the gangs because of the danger involved. There were cases where citizens' groups, soldiers, or other reinforcements had to be called in before a certain gang's activities could be closed down. In this century, the Mafia gangs have used money to corrupt officials, police, and politicians. In recent times, the combined resources of the larger gangs and the intricate nature of their activities help them to avoid the law. Their criminal networks are so complex that only the lower echelons are exposed. They also have formidable counter-surveillance programs to monitor the authorities – from electronic bugs to women in bars frequented by the police.

The prestige and status that many organized crime figures enjoy in their communities also act to shield them from the law. From the early days of the big-time gangsters the North American public has shown a strange deference to such people who are in reality thieves and murderers. When Big Jim Colosimo, the vice lord of Chicago, was killed in a gangland slaying in 1920, an estimated 5,000 people paid their respects at his wake. Among his honorary pallbearers were two congressmen, eight aldermen, three judges, and an assistant state attorney. Today in Canada, crime bosses are the friends of politicians and government officials, are admitted to membership in exclusive clubs, and are given the VIP treatment wherever they go. They maintain their veneer of respectability by posing as business people who give to charity and support their communities. Consequently, if they do get into trouble, they have very influential people ready to come to their aid and unlimited resources with which to fight prosecution, and their community status sometimes gets them a light sentence even if they are convicted.

Because of the clandestine way that organized crime operates, the general public is not as aware of their activities as they should be. As late as the 1960s police and officials in some jurisdictions were still claiming that organized crime was not a problem in Canada. A 1963 Ontario Royal Commission report found very little evidence of organized crime except in gambling. It also stated there was no evidence "that any of the activities of those engaged in organized crime were in any way associated with the Mafia." The Attorney-General at the time the commission was established went even further. He confidently stated that any suggestion that the Mafia was operating in Ontario was "ignorance and loose talk." He went on to claim that, even in Italy, the Mafia had been pretty well eliminated by Mussolini. Subsequent revelations have shown that such statements were rather uninformed and naive. Today organized gangs of criminals operate in all parts of Canada and are so entrenched and powerful that many are beyond the ability of law enforcement agencies to control.

CHAPTER 5

▼

Juvenile Delinquency

Crime knows no time, social, or economic boundaries, and such is also the case with delinquency among the young. As far back as the days of ancient Greece the philosopher Socrates and the poet Hesiod complained·about boys and girls of their day being destructive and undisciplined. Therefore, the juvenile delinquents found in Canada since the early days of settlement are the successors to a long historical line of problem children. Much in the spirit of their adult counterparts, some children got into trouble shortly after landing in the New World.

JUVENILE DELINQUENCY IN PIONEER CANADA

One of the first recorded examples of a juvenile delinquent in New France was a girl of fifteen or sixteen who was an inhabitant of the settlement founded by Samuel de Champlain. As we have already seen, many among the companies that came over with the early explorers were well practised in crime. This particular young girl was probably among those recruited from the slums and jails of the mother country. In any event she was convicted of theft and hung for her crime. She thus became the victim of what was probably the first official hanging of a juvenile delinquent in Canada.[1]

The famous explorer Étienne Brûlé was another of Canada's early juvenile delinquents. He was a youth of sixteen when he arrived with Samuel de Champlain in 1608. Although normally Champlain's servant, Brûlé was sent to live with the Indians and to learn their customs. The boy spent his first winter with the Indians and learned their language and much about their way of life. Brûlé readily adapted to native ways and before long was even fighting in tribal wars. Champlain encouraged him to take up residence with the Hurons and it was while living with that tribe that he began the explorations that earned him a place in the history books. The young Brûlé not only learned the language and customs of the natives soon after his arrival in New France, but he also developed a taste for their sexual habits, which in the eyes of the Europeans were permissive and violated the French laws of religion and morality. The libertine lifestyle would prove to be an irresistible attraction for many juveniles destined to follow in Brûlé's footsteps.[2]

Conditions in pioneer Canada were conducive to young people enjoying a great deal more freedom and indulgence than their counterparts in Europe. With the growth of settlement, families with ten to fifteen children were common. A birth was an occasion for celebration. Children were loved for themselves but they were also prized for the contribution they made to family survival. There was a great deal of work to do, so the more hands available to do it the better. Partly because of the primitive and harsh conditions mortality was high – the average survival rate was about six children per couple. This made young people even more appreciated.

Because children were so important and numerous in pioneer society they enjoyed a certain status and were given a considerable degree of freedom, especially as they grew older. Visitors from Europe continually remarked on how much more indulged and undisciplined the children of New France were in comparison to those of the mother country. Local clergy and officials frequently complained about the laziness of children and that they were given too much freedom. In one of his reports in 1685 Governor Denonville claimed that "from the time children are able to carry a gun, fathers are not able to restrain them and dare not anger them."[3]

The independent and egalitarian spirit engendered by pioneer conditions and the natural precociousness of youth were expressed in various ways. In the larger communities children became such a general nuisance that officials tried to keep them in check with a series of regulations covering a range of youthful annoyances such as throwing stones and snowballs, sliding in the streets in the winter, and interfering with adult pedestrians. For some, their provocations took on a more serious nature and included vandalism and petty theft.

In spite of the high percentage of young people and their apparently boisterous nature, the level of delinquency was low. The population was small, with approximately 6,705 people scattered over the colony in 1673 and only about 16,000 residents by the turn of the century. Until 1660 the Jesuit religious order exercised considerable control over settlement. They tried to keep undesirable elements out by encouraging the immigration of families. Even when the state took over, Church influence remained strong, and the proliferation of ordinances, the work requirements of pioneer life, and the closeness of people in small settlements all mitigated against serious juvenile lawbreaking.

Nevertheless, as more immigrants continued to arrive and the native-born population grew, an increasing number of young people were both available and inclined to test the laws of the new land. Typical of the juveniles being sent over from France were two groups that arrived in 1684. One consisted of sixty indentured servants, all of whom were under seventeen, with the majority ranging in age from twelve to fifteen. Authorities could not place all of them so many were left to survive as best they could. Another group consisted of six young girls who were sent for the express purpose of teaching domestic skills to Indian girls in a school operated by one of the religious orders. It turned out that the girls had been picked up from the streets and the sisters did not consider them to be of good character. They would not risk letting them mingle with the native children so they released them from their contracts. They, too, were left to fend for themselves. On occasion the ranks of problem children were also augmented by the sons of well-to-do French. They arrived in the colony from time to time, ostensibly on visits, but in reality sent so their parents could be rid of them.[4]

The presence of many young people with questionable backgrounds increased the potential for juvenile delinquency. However, there is no way of knowing how many actually became involved in lawbreaking. The documented delinquency consisted primarily of vandalism, petty theft, acts of immorality, the breaking of local ordinances, the abandonment of indentured service contracts, brawling, and swearing. In addition, there were isolated incidents of serious offences committed by juveniles and doubtless others that escaped detection. For example, in 1672 a thirteen-year-old girl helped her parents do away with her husband, who had become a source of annoyance. She married the man against her will when she was twelve, and when he turned out to be a heavy drinker and wife beater she persuaded her parents to get rid of him. Because of her age she was spared the death penalty but was required to attend the execution of her parents. She was fined, released from custody, and a year later had remarried.[5]

The records refer to cases of other young people being involved in murder and serious crimes, but since their ages are not given there is no way of determining whether they were juveniles or young adults. Doubtless there were juveniles guilty of abortion and infanticide. Many indentured servants were juvenile girls who were subject to the sexual exploitation that sometimes marked such a work arrangement. A servant who became pregnant was under a great deal of pressure to conceal her condition. Also, the chances for any young girl to find a desirable husband were substantially diminished if it became known that she had had sexual relations. Consequently, young girls probably resorted to abortion and infanticide on occasion, as did their older sisters. To whatever extent they did, they were breaking the law of their day.

The most widespread juvenile delinquency in the eighteenth and early nineteenth centuries was to be found among the teenage boys engaged in the fur trade. A number of factors encouraged young people to seek their fortunes in the fur industry. In New France it was customary for parents to leave their farm to the eldest son so many younger members of the family looked elsewhere for a livelihood. The seigneurial families were another source of recruits. Sometimes poor but proud, they did not want to see their sons working as hired farmhands so they often encouraged them to get into the fur trade. Military officers and merchants also saw opportunity for their sons in the trade. By apprenticing boys to experienced voyageurs they would learn the business from the bottom up and possibly build a career in what was one of the most lucrative businesses of the times. Many young people simply succumbed to the lure of the wilds. The freedom of the forests and the adventure were powerful attractions and clergy and officials were constantly complaining about young people abandoning the farms and their parents to go wandering among the natives in the country's wilderness.

From the early days of settlement to well into the nineteenth century the *coureurs de bois* and the voyageurs included in their ranks successive generations of younger men, many of whom were juvenile boys. One authority has pointed out that "The canoemen were typically illiterate young farm boys."[6] As we have seen, the fur trade was rife with fraud, immorality, theft, assault, and murder. Liquor and violence were endemic, and while there is no way of knowing the extent to which teenagers participated, they probably contributed their fair share to the lawlessness.

Sometimes even very young children were caught up in the violence that permeated the fur trade. One example comes out of a quarrel among a group of western hunters in March, 1802. During the course of a drinking bout one member of the party stabbed and killed another. In retaliation for the murder the man's young brother, a boy of about ten, took his brother's gun, loaded it with two balls, went to the killer's tent, and shot the man dead. The incident illustrates how even the very young were skilled in the use of firearms and did not shy from violent deeds when faced with provocation.[7]

The undisciplined and sometimes criminal lifestyle that characterized the fur trade left its mark on the *coureur de bois* and voyageur, and many continued their unruly ways when they returned to their homes. As one observer noted, they contracted "an habitual libertinism" in their profession.[8] The immorality among the young was a particular problem and was not limited to those initiated in the fur trade. Officials sometimes complained about the immoral habits of children, especially those who came from the homes of "gentlemen." They accused them of "debauchery" and of abusing the daughters and wives of the natives.[9]

Elsewhere the pattern of lawbreaking established in the early days of New

France was duplicated with petty crime and vandalism interspersed with the occasional serious offence. For example, on April 19, 1737, a ten- or eleven-year-old indentured servant by the name of Isaac Provender set fire to his master's house at Annapolis, Nova Scotia. The house burned to the ground along with the owner's furniture, clothing, and personal possessions.[10] In contrast, after the town of Halifax was well established an irate citizen in 1818 complained in the pages of the *Acadian Recorder* about young vandals breaking off door knockers, pulling down signs and downspouts, and smashing windows. Since he did not list any more serious crimes, presumably these were the typical juvenile offences in the community at the time.[11]

The relatively minor nature of juvenile delinquency was again confirmed by convictions in the province of New Brunswick. Between 1846 and 1857 approximately 305 young people between the ages of twelve and fifteen were incarcerated in the New Brunswick provincial prison. Most were in for minor crimes and many were put in jail on drunkenness, theft, and vagrancy charges.[12] Juvenile offences followed suit in central Canada. The High Bailiff's report for Toronto for the period February 1 to December 31, 1847, listed thirty-nine convictions under the heading "boys." Of those, seventeen were for larceny, eleven for assault, nine for trespass, and two for disorderly conduct. While some of the assaults might have been serious, the majority of the offences were minor in nature.[13]

The preponderant petty nature of juvenile crime made it easy to escape the detection of authorities, so there was likely more delinquency than statistics suggest. Also, an unusually large number of children throughout much of the eighteenth and nineteenth centuries might be described as "at risk." Especially in the larger communities and in seaports there were always numbers of orphaned, abandoned, and neglected children. One of the contributing factors was the long voyage faced by immigrants coming to Canada. Before the days of steamships the sailing vessels could take up to three months to make the crossing from European ports. Many people could not withstand the rigours of the voyage and died at sea or shortly after arriving. As a result a considerable number of children landed in Canada as orphans or with one parent.

Canadian authorities actively promoted immigration and sometimes painted an overly rosy picture in their zeal to entice settlers. Some who came failed to find the prosperous life they had hoped for and simply went from being paupers in the Old World to being paupers in the New. Unemployment, destitution, sickness, and misery took a toll and resulted in some parents simply abandoning their children because they found them too much of a burden. Others allowed their offspring to run loose in the streets and survive as best they could.

A vivid picture of the plight of many children is afforded by the experience of the port of Halifax in the early years of its settlement. From its founding it has been a port of arrival for immigrants coming from Europe. Between 1752 and 1760 the Orphan House in Halifax admitted a total of 275 children. Of that number 114 were orphans while the remainder were either neglected or abandoned. Of the children who were taken into care during that period of time, 173 were listed as being physically unfit. One ship that arrived in Halifax in 1752 landed eight orphans whose parents had died during the voyage. More deaths shortly afterwards increased the number of parentless children to fourteen.[14]

The problem continued across the country as settlement spread. In a two-year period between 1832 and 1834 one relief agency in York cared for 535 orphans. That was only one sign of the widespread social and economic distress in Upper Canada. The population of the region rose from 186,488 in 1828 to 374,099 by 1836. This large influx of people over a short period of time put great stress on the meagre resources of the region, especially since many of the newcomers were destitute. Available sources of relief quickly dried up and the older settlers tried to stem the tide by discouraging further immigration into the area. Many children became the victims of both poverty and abandonment.[15] Archdeacon John Strachan, a Church of England minister and pioneer in Canadian education, reported in 1831 that York was "overwhelmed with Widows or Orphans." He further noted that some fathers "in despair of bettering their situation" had deserted their families.[16]

The Irish famine immigration of the mid-1840s was another example of how large numbers of orphans were left to the care of Canadian authorities. Canada could not place restrictions on immigrants from the mother country, so settlers had to be admitted regardless of their economic or physical condition, or the numbers at any given time. The dirty and overcrowded ships, the long voyage, and the lack of proper food were the breeding grounds of typhus. As large numbers of Irish began to arrive in 1846 and subsequent years, many of them had already contracted fever. In 1847 an estimated 20,000 immigrants died from sickness. Some 5,000 died at Grose Isle, the quarantine station in Quebec, the rest in places like Quebec City, Montreal, Kingston, and Toronto. One estimate suggested that 500-600 orphans were left in Montreal from this epidemic.[17]

The poor frequently congregated in shanty towns in the larger communities and these pauper ghettos sometimes became the locus for immorality and crime. One official described the shanty town that grew up in York as a receptacle "for drunkenness and vice."[18] Children in such environments learned delinquent ways early in life because many were completely unsupervised, undisciplined, and neglected. Observers complained about children who were vagrants, who were begging in the streets, and who were involved in petty crime and vandalism. The Duncombe Report of 1836 noted "the ragged and uncleanly appearance, the vile language, and the idle and miserable habits of numbers of children" to be observed in the streets of York.[19]

Partly because of the concentration of neglected children in the larger centres juvenile crime throughout the Victorian period was disproportionately an urban problem. There were few indications of juvenile delinquency in rural areas but many in the larger towns and cities. For example, the mayor of Halifax, in his report for 1861-62, complained about the number of young troublemakers in the Nova Scotia capital. He noted that juveniles of both sexes were "constantly brought before the Police Court, charged with thefts and similar offenses." He also claimed that the number of young offenders was "far greater than would be imagined."

The urban environment was not the only contributor to juvenile delinquency. A wide range of events, circumstances, influences, and developments affected the problem, not the least of which was the continual arrival of delinquents from Britain. One group of seventy women who landed in Quebec in May, 1865, were sent over from Ireland by the Poor Law guardians. They came from deprived backgrounds and many had been in trouble with the law. As soon as they arrived in Canada they caused a stir with immigration officials as some sold their few possessions to buy liquor. They were seen intoxicated and in the company of soldiers. Twenty-one of the group were nineteen or younger and authorities used the episode as evidence that women from such backgrounds should not be encouraged to come to Canada.[20]

Liquor contributed to crime throughout our history, and adults were not the only ones who imbibed. Alcohol was easy to come by for both young and old. In Newfoundland, for example, it was common for boys to take up commercial fishing at a young age. Part of their provisions was a rum jug from which it was the practice to drink three times a day. Further evidence of juvenile access to liquor came from the fact that drunkenness and related offences were common among the charges for which young people were brought to court. Alcohol remained a factor in juvenile delinquency throughout the period. For example, in 1859, officials at the reformatory for Lower Canada at Isle aux Noix claimed that many of the parents of young inmates were drunkards and that at least half of the detainees themselves were heavy drinkers before admission.[21]

The military presence in many communities in colonial days also contributed to juvenile delinquency, especially among girls. In every garrison town and port, soldiers and sailors sought out the company of women. The military attracted to their ranks men who were given to drinking, brawling, petty thievery, and other forms of criminal and anti-social behaviour, and on occasion the women and girls they consorted with became involved in their lawbreaking, especially theft. Another way in which the military influenced juvenile delinquency was by increasing the demand for prostitutes. Brothel operators were continually on the lookout for young girls to staff their establishments. Especially vulnerable were those on their own or whose parents were uncaring and neglectful.

Halifax, which was not only a major seaport but from 1749 to 1906 also a British army base, affords a premier example of young girls working as prostitutes. Prostitution thrived from the very early days of settlement and was a major industry throughout the pre-Confederation period. One writer, describing the scene in an earlier day, wrote that "old, young, black, white, mothers, sisters, and daughters, engaged in a horrid commerce." There were thirteen- and fourteen-year-old prostitutes working the streets of Halifax in the late 1850s.[22] A not untypical example of the young girls who got caught up in the trade was Mary Ford. She was first arrested in 1864 at the age of sixteen in the company of her mother, and both were charged with drunkenness and disorderly conduct. Mary also worked as a prostitute and at one point in her career both she and her father were charged with operating a house of prostitution. Eliza Munro, a black orphan girl, was another who earned her living as a prostitute. She was first arrested at the age of fifteen and spent most of the next ten years in and out of jail or the poorhouse. There were always young girls who fled refuges, foster homes, or domestic service and turned to prostitution to earn a living.[23]

The ongoing transportation of orphans, paupers, and delinquent children from Great Britain, according to many observers, continued to add to the ranks of juvenile delinquents in Canada. Between 1873 and 1903 over 95,000 children came to Canada under the sponsorship of child immigration agencies. The children were gathered from the slums and orphanages, screened and prepared at agency homes, and then sent off to Canada in hopes of giving them a better life. Counterpart branches of their sponsors met them upon arrival in this country and arranged for their placement in indentured service. Many of the girls were placed as domestic servants. There was a big demand for these children so the agencies had no difficulty in finding placements. They were supposed to follow the progress of their charges to see that they were properly treated and that their work contracts were honoured. In fact, few did, and for the most part the children were at the mercy of their new Canadian families. Many found good homes; others were simply exploited until they were old enough to strike out on their own.[24]

Because of their backgrounds many were suspicious of these immigrant children and claimed that they were a pool of potential delinquents. Labour leaders claimed that they gave unfair competition and took jobs from native Canadians. To gain support for their opposition they also charged that the child immigrants were prone to delinquent behaviour. The flames of suspicion were further fanned by claims from other quarters. In the 1891 Ontario Prison Report the commissioners concluded that the importation of these children was "fraught with much danger." They expressed concern that they would "swell the ranks of the criminal classes."[25] J.G. Moylan, Inspector of Penitentiaries, argued that the immigrant children added to the criminal ranks and that their immigration should be stopped.[26]

Some of these children undoubtedly did pick up where they left off in England and continued with their delinquency. For example, in 1889 the jailer in Brampton, Ontario, reported that one of the immigrant boys was among the worst he had ever had in his jail.[27] On the other hand, there is little evidence to suggest that they added significantly to the ranks of young offenders. One Toronto detective, Inspector William Stark, attempted to refute the charges by offering statistics to prove his point. He described one six-month period during which an unusually large number of crimes took place. Out of 213 convictions, 195 of the offenders were under twenty. Although twenty-seven of that group had come from Britain, not one had come from the homes involved in the child immigrant movement.[28]

The vast majority of the children who came over were sent out to farm homes. They worked hard, were closely supervised, and, like their rural peers, were relatively isolated. This went a long way in keeping them out of trouble even if they were so inclined. Indeed, rather than being sources of trouble, they were sometimes the victims of cruelty, abuse, and exploitation. For example, one young boy, less than ten years old, was sent to work on a farm whose owner discovered that the child was afraid of pigs. The man took great delight in tormenting the boy by forcing him into the pigpen and whipping him if he attempted to get out.[29] There were other cases of guardians failing to live up to the terms of the service contract by not seeing to the education of the children or by cheating them out of wages that they were entitled to upon the expiration of their indenture.

In view of the large population of orphaned, abandoned, or neglected children at risk, the level of delinquency was not that great. However, as was the case with adult crime, there were doubtless many undetected offences. Of the juveniles apprehended during the Victorian period, the typical offender was a white male, poorly nurtured, with little or no schooling, born in Canada, and an urban dweller. Some were orphaned or abandoned and most were unsupervised and allowed to roam about at will. These urchins or "street arabs," as they were called at the time, could be found in run-down neighbourhoods in many of the larger towns and cities across the country.

Trends in the nature of juvenile crime and criminals are illustrated by incarceration statistics from various institutions that housed young offenders. For example, before juvenile reformatories were opened many young people convicted of more serious offences were sent to Kingston prison. In 1849-50, thirty-six inmates were released whose ages at the time of committal ranged from ten to seventeen. One boy had been convicted of murder at age fifteen, another of manslaughter at age ten. Of the remainder, five had been convicted of horse theft, one of stealing a cow, one of burglary, one for robbery, one for committing a felony, and one for a misdemeanour. Well over half of the group – twenty-four – had been convicted of larceny. Thus, while the offences ranged from misdemeanour to murder, two-thirds of the boys were in prison for larceny and only two of the offenders had committed crimes of violence.[30]

Table 15 lists the number of juveniles of both sexes who passed through the jails of Upper and Lower Canada in the year 1860. The statistics afford a good overview of the trends in juvenile arrests in the Canadas and the relative distribution by region. As the table shows, few young offenders passed through the majority of community jails in Upper and Lower Canada. Many jails had no juvenile female inmates during the entire year. The majority of incarcerations were in the more populated areas, with Toronto and Hamilton accounting for slightly over 60 per cent of all juvenile inmates in the jails of Upper Canada. In Lower Canada, Montreal and Quebec accounted for 93.5 per cent of all the juveniles who passed through the jails in 1860. Overall, juveniles made up a small percentage of the jail population of both Canadas. Of 11,268 incarcerations, 682 or 6 per cent were young offenders under sixteen years of age. Of those 682, only 23.2 per cent were female.

POST-CONFEDERATION DELINQUENCY

As a comparison with the previous statistics, Table 16 illustrates the trend in juvenile incarcerations in Ontario for a twenty-one-year period following Confederation. In 1869 approximately 6.6 per cent of all people put in Ontario jails were juveniles. The percentage dropped to 4.2 in 1879 and to 3.9 in 1889. The percentage fluctuated over the years but there was never any significant increase. The trend was consistently down in comparison with the statistics for 1860. In 1869 girls accounted for 21.8 per cent of juvenile incarcerations, dropping to 11.3 per cent in 1879 and to 9.2 per cent in 1889.

When the number of juveniles put in Ontario jails during this period is compared to the population, the statistics show considerable fluctuations. In 1869 the rate of juvenile incarcerations was 23.2 per 100,000 of the population. Over the next two decades it rose to 25.9 in 1875, then to 31.6 in 1880, dropped to 23.8 per 100,000 of population in 1885, and took another slight drop to 22.3 by 1889. Even at the highest points the level of juvenile incarcerations for the period remained consistently low.

The pattern of minor crime also continued to characterize juvenile lawbreaking. The Brantford jailer, for example, reported that for the sixteen boys who came under his supervision in 1889 the charges consisted of trespass, petty larceny, and stealing candy. At Brockville the jailer reported that most of his juvenile inmates were in for petty larceny. At Lindsay the seven boys and one girl who passed through the jail were convicted of stealing such things as sugar and fruit. The jailer at Saint Thomas expressed the opinion that none of his young offenders were very bad and that they should not have been jailed in the first place.[31]

Table 15
Juveniles in Jail, Upper and Lower Canada, 1860

Upper Canada Jails	Under 16 Years of Age	
	Boys	Girls
Brantford	17	4
Outaouais	6	2
Saint Thomas	1	1
Sandwich	5	–
Kingston	1	1
Owen Sound	2	–
Cayuga	3	–
Milton	3	–
Belleville	7	–
Goderich	2	–
Chatham	2	–
Sarnia	4	–
Perth	–	–
Brockville	4	2
Niagara	6	1
London	20	8
Simcoe	6	8
Cobourg	2	–
Whitby	1	–
Woodstock	7	–
Stratford	7	–
Peterborough	5	–
L'Original	1	–
Picton	3	–
Barrie	4	–
Cornwall	–	–
Berlin	3	–
Welland	4	–
Guelph	–	–
Hamilton	48	31
Toronto	114	41
Totals for Upper Canada	288	99
Lower Canada Jails		
New Carlisle	1	–
Percé	–	–
Kamouraska	–	–
Montreal	127	31
Aylmer	–	–
Quebec	96	22
Sherbrooke	7	5
Three Rivers	5	–
Totals for Lower Canada	236	59
Totals for Canada	524	158

SOURCE: Adapted from First Annual Report of the Board of Inspectors of Asylums, Prisons, etc., 1860.

Table 16
Number of Prisoners Who Passed Through the Common Jails of Ontario,
1869-89

Year	Total	Total Juveniles	Boys Under 16 Years	Girls Under 16 Years	Population of Province
1869	5,655	376	294	82	1,618,400 est.
1870	6,379	427	319	108	1,620,851
1871	6,615	387	329	58	
1872	6,958	337	281	56	
1873	7,877	397	323	74	
1874	9,488	444	377	67	
1875	10,073	459	389	70	1,770,000 est.
1876	11,236	504	434	70	
1877	13,481	604	542	62	
1878	12,030	534	480	54	
1879	11,220	469	416	53	
1880	11,300	608	549	59	1,923,228
1881	9,229	541	468	73	
1882	9,620	584	522	62	
1883	9,880	471	423	48	
1884	12,081	504	458	46	
1885	11,426	500	450	50	2,100,000 est.
1886	10,645	390	352	38	
1887	11,017	447	409	38	
1888	12,454	616	551	65	
1889	12,531	497	451	46	2,230,000 est.

SOURCE: Report of the Commissioners. . . Province of Ontario, 1891.

A high percentage of juveniles arrested through the nineteenth century were young children. The 1889 report for the juvenile reformatory at Penetanguishene stated that many of the inmates were so young "that it would be wrong to require them to do much work." Of eighty-five boys admitted in 1889, forty-seven were thirteen years of age or under. One boy was seven, five were nine, six were ten, six were eleven, seventeen were twelve, and twelve were thirteen.[32] As usual, the largest number of youths arrested were in the urban centres, and there, too, a high percentage were young. In 1889 some 527 boys and 34 girls arrested in the city of Toronto were between ten and fifteen years of age.[33] Part of the explanation for the high number of urban delinquents was that the more populated centres attracted a significant number of problem families. As social welfare studies have shown, the unemployed, the unemployable, and the destitute gravitated to the larger communities because job opportunities or social assistance were more readily available. They also attracted a hard-drinking, hard-working, undisciplined element. The towns and cities produced the large number of children most at risk of becoming delinquent.

Many children were poorly nurtured and given little or no schooling. Neglected, they were left to their own devices and became street urchins. They were frequently shuffled from orphanages to poor houses, jails, and refuges. Along the way they often became schooled in vice and crime. Complaints were to be found in many newspapers throughout the nineteenth century and earlier about the "guttersnipes" hanging around the streets. They were considered to be prone to theft and amenable to seduction. In 1889 the reformer J.J. Kelso estimated that there were as many as 800 young people roaming the streets of Toronto "begging and pilfering."[34]

In some cases all the children in a family became embroiled in criminality at an early age. One case, which was not necessarily typical, illustrates the degrading and harsh existence that was the lot for some. Between 1879 and 1882 the oldest boy in the family was in and out of jail for a variety of petty offences. At the age of fifteen he had taken up with a prostitute and at one point was living with two women in a shed outside of a hovel occupied by his sick mother. The arrangement must have held some fascination, for the locale attracted about a dozen other youths who came by regularly to hang out. Before his sixteenth birthday the young teenager was sent to the penitentiary for a three-year term, after which his criminal career continued into adulthood. A younger brother in the same family started his long journey at the age of ten. He, too, was in and out of jail and when he was twelve years old he was sent to Penetanguishene. Like his older brother, his delinquency was a dress rehearsal for a career as an adult offender. The boys had a sister who became a prostitute before she was eleven. Between 1879 and 1890 the family spent a combined time of twenty-two years in jail.[35]

A long-standing correlation of juvenile delinquency was the lack of school attendance on the part of many young people. School attendance was not compulsory in most parts of Canada until late in the nineteenth century. Ontario did not have a school requirement until 1871 and then it only applied to children between seven and twelve years of age for an annual period of four months. Compulsory attendance was not enforced until 1891. In the meantime large numbers of young people did not attend school even when free education was available. Consequently, many spent their time in idleness and some fell into delinquent behaviour. Egerton Ryerson, Ontario's first Superintendent of Schools, estimated that in 1860 as many as 2,500 children of school age did not attend any classes. That represented about 25 per cent of the eligible school population in Toronto.[36]

The problem continued in many jurisdictions for some time. As late as 1895, for example, school officials in Nova Scotia were complaining about the large number of children not in school even when they lived near a schoolhouse. They claimed that from the ranks of those non-attenders came the young people who hung around the streets or outside the saloons at night and ended up getting into trouble.[37]

The large number of unsupervised children to be found running about many communities was one manifestation of broad parental neglect that contributed significantly to juvenile arrest statistics of poor children. The lack of a proper diet, malnutrition, unsanitary living conditions, drunken and desolute parents, and inadequate or no medical care contributed to such things as truancy, lack of interest in schooling, and to mental and emotional problems. Many children were picked up by the authorities more for humane reasons than because they had committed an offence. In some communities the courts and jails were the welfare agencies. Children were taken into custody to protect them and even sent to detention centres as a means of removing them from a bad environment. Custodians often considered disadvantaged children who committed a petty offence to be more unfortunate than guilty. This would partially explain why so many children were incarcerated for such minor infractions. Children from stable home environments who were picked up for minor offences were frequently turned over to their parents to be dealt with. This option was not open for the children from problem homes, who had to be dealt with by the police and magistrates. They were also the ones who were noted in arrest and conviction records and became part of the statistics.

Young people from more stable families were less likely to get into serious trouble because they were better disciplined and supervised. However, such children did break the law on occasion. The jailer in Milton, Ontario, reported in 1889 that the three boys sent to him that year for housebreaking and larceny "were children of respectable parents."[38] A school official preparing a report on delinquency in 1895 was surprised to find that a large number of problem children came "from the homes of respectable, intelligent and well-to-do parents."[39] His discovery was based on his own study of young people rather than on arrest statistics. His findings once again suggest that delinquents from advantaged backgrounds were better able to cover up their offences.

Rural youth were in a similar position. Doubtless they were not as much at risk to break the law as their slum-dwelling peers. The nature of their work and living conditions kept them under closer supervision. Also, the opportunities for such crimes as vandalism and theft, the most common among urban offenders, were not as plentiful in the country. When they did engage in crime, however, they were also less likely to be caught. The isolation made it much easier to escape detection for offences such as theft or destruction of property. In addition, the police forces that patrolled the urban streets were not present in rural areas so the chances of apprehension were low. Nevertheless, there were always rural youth involved in lawbreaking and periodically there were incidents of serious crime, such as the murder of a five-year-old girl in Upper Canada in 1849. Margaret

O'Connor and eleven-year-old George Green were adopted children living with a farm family in the County of Peterborough. The foster parents took good care of their children and showed affection to both, but the boy became jealous and resentful of his adopted sister. One day when the two children were working alone in a potato field George attacked the little girl and hacked her to death with a sharp hoe. He buried the body in a shallow grave and then told his parents that Margaret had been carried away by a bear. A search party uncovered the girl's body and George was put on trial for murder. He was found guilty and sentenced to be hanged but his punishment was subsequently commuted to life imprisonment. Shortly after his admission to Kingston prison he became sick and died.[40]

Besides the urban-rural dichotomy in juvenile crime, there was another noteworthy anomaly between the numbers of male and female offenders. For example, in 1859 girls under the age of sixteen made up 29 per cent of young offenders detained in the jails of Upper and Lower Canada. The ratio declined even further over the next few decades. Many jail reports for Ontario in 1889 listed no juvenile female detainees. In that year girls accounted for only 10.2 per cent of all juvenile incarcerations.

More so than boys, young girls were frequently taken into custody for their own protection. This continued to be the case even when social welfare agencies began to appear. For example, most of the nineteen girls admitted to the Ontario Industrial Refuge for Girls in 1889 were very young. One was four years old, two were eight, two were nine, three were ten, two were eleven, three were twelve, and two were thirteen. Twelve of the nineteen were committed simply because they were uncared for and homeless. Of the remainder, four were convicted of larceny, one of arson, one of frequenting, and one as incorrigible. The level of neglect suffered by many of the children was underscored by the high level of illiteracy among girls sent to the refuges. The Ontario Industrial Refuge reported in 1893 that nearly 72 per cent of detainees were illiterate.[41]

The girls sent to detention centres for specific offences, as opposed to welfare considerations, were largely convicted of minor infractions. Perhaps the epitome was the case of a young Ontario girl who in 1880 was convicted of stealing gooseberries from a garden. She spent fourteen days in jail and after her trial was sent to a reformatory for six months.[42] There were always a number of young girls apprehended for more serious reasons, such as immoral or disorderly conduct and prostitution. One enterprising ten-year-old was arrested in Toronto in 1845 for keeping a bawdy house.[43] The charge of vagrancy for which many were arrested was often a euphemism for a morals offence.

While reported levels of juvenile offences were low and crimes were predominantly minor in nature, evidence suggested that young people committed many more offences than were recorded. One survey among eighty inmates at the juvenile detention centre in Isle aux Noix in 1859 revealed that at least twenty-six of their accomplices in the crimes for which they were convicted escaped apprehension.[44] In some cases the judicial system itself covered up juvenile lawbreaking. For example, a Quebec government regulation in 1892 required municipalities to pay half the costs of board for incarcerated delinquents. To avoid such costs, pressure was sometimes put on justice officials to let young offenders off rather than send them to reformatories.[45]

Another dimension of juvenile crime that sometimes escaped notice was gang activity. Young people have always had an affinity for congregating in groups and over the years organized gangs of juveniles were to be found in most large centres. Many were primarily social in nature but others became involved in lawbreaking of one kind or another. On occasion gangs of children showed that they were capable of some rather sophisticated criminal activity. In Vancouver during April and May of 1897 one gang of six boys broke into a total of nine businesses. They stole a variety of items, including shoes, a camera, and a watch, which they in turn sold to a fence they had located. The fourteen-year-old gang leader used his share of the take to purchase a revolver. Apparently he had bigger ventures in mind. However, before they could get into more trouble the gang members were caught by the police.[46]

The patterns of juvenile crime established in early pioneer days remained relatively constant to the end of the nineteenth century. Table 17 illustrates the trends in juvenile crime and the number of convictions for indictable offences that prevailed during the years 1885-99. The number of convictions of young people for indictable offences was low and females accounted for a small percentage of the total. In 1899 females under sixteen made up approximately 4 per cent of all convictions in that age group and over the period 1885-99 they contributed 4.8 per cent of convictions. To obtain a more accurate indication of trends it would be helpful to have figures that would include sixteen- and seventeen-year-olds. However, even when the convictions for sixteen- to twenty-year-olds are included, as in Table 17, the total annual number of convictions for young people was still very small, although the female percentage was slightly higher than for the younger age group. In 1899 females constituted 7.5 per cent of convictions and 7.9 per cent over the period 1885-99 in the older age category. In the younger age group offences against property without violence predominate while there is a tendency toward more offences against the person and against property with violence in the older age group.

Table 18 offers a statistical breakdown of convictions for indictable offences by provinces. As would be expected, the two most populous provinces provided the largest numbers of convictions. Ontario also accounted for a higher percentage of the total convictions than its percentage of the

Table 17
Juvenile Convictions for Indictable Offences, 1885-99

Offences in 1899	Under 16 Years		16-20 Years	
	Males	Females	Males	Females
Offences against the person	42	–	123	4
Offences against property with violence	87	–	124	1
Offences against property without violence	740	37	602	64
Malicious offences against property	19	–	18	1
Forgery and offences against the currency	8	–	16	2
Other offences not included in the above classes	3	–	24	2
Totals	899	37	907	74
Offences, 1885-99				
Offences against the person	371	16	1,593	62
Offences against property with violence	805	4	1,456	3
Offences against property without violence	7,750	398	7,328	704
Malicious offences against property	161	10	144	5
Forgery and offences against the currency	24	1	106	5
Other offences not included in the above classes	125	40	336	169
Totals	9,236	469	10,963	948
Average	616	31	731	63

SOURCE: Adapted from *Statistical Yearbook of Canada*, 1899.

total population. In 1899 approximately 55.2 per cent of convictions of young people under sixteen years of age were made in Ontario, although the province's population was about 40 per cent of the Canadian total. Quebec, on the other hand, contributed about 30 per cent of convictions in the same category and made up approximately 30 per cent of the total population. Overall, juveniles under sixteen years of age made up 11 per cent of all convictions for indictable offences in 1886 and 16.4 per cent in 1899. Expressed in percentages there would appear to be a significant upward trend, but actual numbers of convictions, as Table 18 shows, remained minimal.

Specific examples of the crimes for which juveniles were being put in detention in the last decade of the century are afforded by statistics for the reformatory at Penetanguishene in Ontario. The annual report for 1893 listed the following offences committed by the sixty-two boys incarcerated that year: assault – one, housebreaking and larceny – eight, indecent assault – two, incorrigible – four, horse stealing – one, larceny – thirty-five, obstructing the railway – one, obtaining goods under false pretences – one, shopbreaking and larceny – five, vagrancy – four.[47]

Table 18
Juvenile Convictions for Indictable Offences by Province, 1885-99

Provinces in 1899	Under 16 Years		16-20 Years	
	Males	Females	Males	Females
Ontario	492	25	473	35
Quebec	276	8	307	30
Nova Scotia	39	1	39	3
New Brunswick	22	–	30	1
Manitoba	36	3	30	1
British Columbia	29	–	25	3
Prince Edward Island	2	–	–	–
Northwest Territories	3	–	3	1
Totals	899	37	907	74
Provinces, 1885-99				
Ontario	5,687	242	6,550	580
Quebec	2,516	200	3,095	256
Nova Scotia	367	14	446	42
New Brunswick	181	4	218	16
Manitoba	209	7	311	22
British Columbia	174	1	192	19
Prince Edward Island	81	1	57	9
Northwest Territories	21	–	94	4
Totals	9,236	469	10,963	948

SOURCE: Adapted from *Statistical Yearbook of Canada*, 1899.

THE GROWTH OF JUVENILE DELINQUENCY

The expansion that took place in Canada in the first quarter of the twentieth century and the increase in population were accompanied by a concomitant growth in many communities. As towns became cities many developed the same social problems that had plagued the larger centres in earlier years. Even prairie communities took on many features that were more characteristic of eastern industrial cities. For example, the slum areas of Winnipeg expanded with the dynamic growth in the region. Regina had a congested area of dwellings little better than shacks, the majority of which lacked amenities such as indoor plumbing. However, the neighbourhood was well supplied with bars, dance halls, and poolrooms. As was the case in the East, the children who lived in such slums were frequently the victims of parental neglect and were the ones most likely to be picked up by police for nuisance offences. Thus, with national expansion many of the old patterns of delinquency continued.

On the other hand, the twentieth century also saw the emergence of new trends. The incidence of juvenile crime began to increase, as did crimes of a more serious nature. Also, changing times created more criminal opportunities, as well as a new array of offences. The extension of railroads brought more breaches of the Railway Act. The growing popularity of the automobile was accompanied by the appearance of juvenile car thieves, while the growth of the banking industry attracted teenage bank robbers and safe crackers. On all fronts juvenile crime appeared to be taking on new dimensions.

Newspaper editorials, expressions of concern from public sources, and observations of criminal justice officials were all manifestations of a perception that juvenile crime was on the increase. Criminal justice statistics bore out the suppositions. In the 1911-21 period, convictions of children under sixteen for major offences went up by over 124 per cent. During the same period the population of ten- to fifteen-year-olds increased by about 28 per cent. The increase continued through the 1920s, with convictions rising between 1921 and 1931 by over 67 per cent while the population in the same age groups rose by about 19 per cent.[48]

Part of the increase might be accounted for by the fact that police forces across the country were expanding and police were being better trained and organized. However, the high rate of increase, together with the other indicators, suggests that a good part of the rise was due to more juveniles committing more offences. If anything, it is possible that official statistics told only a small part of the story. For example, in 1928 there were 5,063 juveniles reported convicted for major offences and 2,636 convicted for minor offences – a total of 7,699 convictions. Yet in the same year police across Canada reported that 8,057 bicycles were stolen. Bicycle theft is a predominantly juvenile crime; thus, the fact that there were more bicycle thefts reported in one year than the total number of juvenile convictions indicates that the statistics offer a far from accurate picture of trends in juvenile delinquency rates. This is further supported by the fact that police sometimes complained about the difficulties in getting victims to press charges against young offenders.

Within the overall upward trend in juvenile crime there was also a significant rise in more serious offences. In 1911 the rate of convictions of young people between ten and fifteen years old for major offences was 172 per 100,000 of the population in that age group. In 1921 the rate rose to approximately 300 per 100,000 and by 1931 it was up to 423 per 100,000. However, while the rate rose by over 59 per cent during that time period the actual number of major offences committed by ten- to fifteen-year-olds remained small.[49]

Another dimension of juvenile crime was the appearance of more gangs in certain cities. While many continued to be little more than mischievous, some engaged in crime of a more serious nature. Typical of the latter was a Montreal gang known as the Maple Leafs, which was active in the city in 1932. The group's activities included disrupting public meetings with stink bombs, stealing personal belongings in school, and breaking into freight cars, tobacco stores, and candy shops. The gang had about twelve members and at least some had a potential for violence. Police found a revolver in the possession of one gang member when he was arrested for burglary. Another Montreal juvenile organization, known as the Alerts, had both male and female members, which facilitated the sexual activities in which the gang was known to indulge. They were a mixed-language group of French and English and committed some major crimes such as stealing automobiles.

The growth of immigrant neighbourhoods in cities like Toronto also contributed to the rise of gangs. Children in these areas grew up subject to racial and religious slurs, to discrimination from native Canadians, and to intimidation from each other. Consequently, they sometimes formed gangs among their own ethnic groups, partly for social reasons and partly as a means of self-protection. There were Jewish gangs, Irish gangs, Italian gangs, and others. These street gangs fought each other, got into various kinds of mischief, and, like generations of their predecessors, were seen as a social problem by city authorities. In Toronto in the 1930s a number of these gangs were involved in break-and-enter and minor theft. They also had a penchant for gambling, thereby emulating their elders who through the twenties and thirties raised gambling activities to new heights. The youngsters specialized in crap games and euchre in back alleys and on street corners. Some of the gangs were the training grounds for people like the Volpe brothers, who grew up to become key figures in organized crime in Toronto.[50]

Although young girls seemed to be getting more adventuresome in their lawbreaking, the vast majority of female delinquents stuck to familiar territory. Many continued to be arrested on morals charges, sometimes masked as vagrancy. Promiscuity was a particular problem with neglected girls who were allowed to hang around the streets. Authorities automatically suspected that they were sexually active and there was considerable evidence to support their assumptions. In 1918 the newly appointed superintendent of an Industrial School for Girls in British Columbia had all the residents examined by a doctor. Half of the forty girls had venereal disease. Between its opening in 1914 and 1918 the school had admitted a total of eighty-three girls, thirty-five of whom were committed for vagrancy and twenty-eight for stealing. Thirty-nine of the detainees were listed as coming from "bad home conditions," eighteen as having "no home," and twenty-six as "associating with bad companions."[51]

The profile was common in refuges across the country. The Maritime Home for Girls in Truro, Nova Scotia, opened in 1914 to serve the provinces of New Brunswick, Prince Edward Island, and Nova Scotia. By 1918 the institution had received eighty-three girls. According to the matron most of them had come from a home which "was a den of vice in which the children were schooled." Thirty-five of the residents had been sentenced for vagrancy, twenty-eight for stealing, one for truancy, two for incendiarism, and seventeen simply because they were neglected children.[52]

Young female vagrants and their male counterparts were automatically at risk when any new form of street crime appeared. Consequently, it was not surprising that juveniles got drawn into the drug traffic that became trendy in the 1920s. Investigators, criminal justice officials, and even the federal Health Department claimed that drugs were being sold to children in the streets of many cities. One magistrate told the story of how a distraught father came to her for help because his fifteen-year-old daughter had developed an unusual attachment for an older woman. It turned out that the woman had been supplying drugs to the daughter with the intention of developing a dependency. She had planned to take the girl to the United States, probably for the purposes of prostitution.[53]

Authorities in Vancouver claimed that drugs were in common use among boys and girls fifteen to eighteen years of age, and children were brought before the courts on drug charges in a number of cities. Judicial officials also found evidence among some teenagers brought up on charges such as theft or vagrancy that they had been using drugs. By 1922 there was sufficient corroboration of the problem that the government distributed forms to Juvenile Court officers asking for a statement as to whether or not the child before the court had a drug addiction.[54] Newspapers carried stories claiming that young girls were being lured into prostitution through drugs and that young boys were selling in the streets. Dope dealers, it was claimed, were offering free drugs to young people to get them addicted. As is the case today, it is not possible to determine the actual level of juvenile involvement with drugs in the 1920s. However, there is little doubt that juveniles, to some degree, used and trafficked in drugs.[55]

Aside from new ventures like drug usage and trafficking, the bulk of juvenile crime in the 1920s continued to involve theft. Ethel MacLachlan, a Juvenile Court judge in Regina, stated in a speech in February, 1922, that during the previous four years approximately 1,045 boys and girls had come through the system in her jurisdiction. The offences included theft, which accounted for about two-thirds of the crimes, property damage, assault, indecent assault, obstructing the railways, shooting dogs and horses, forgery, arson, drinking, driving under-age, fishing and shooting out of season, and indecent behaviour. The judge was making the point that juvenile delinquency was taking on more serious dimensions because juveniles were committing "all the offences that adults were usually guilty of."[56]

The profile of the typical delinquent of the 1920s changed little from the previous century. Convicted offenders were still predominantly white, male, and native-born. They were urban dwellers, usually from troubled homes, who mixed with bad companions and had repeated run-ins with the law. One not untypical example was a Toronto boy who came from a family of seven. He grew up in poverty and an unkempt home with parents who quarrelled and were heavy drinkers. While still young his mother deserted the family and the boy started on a path of truancy and petty theft. By the time he was eleven he had graduated to shop-breaking and stealing automobiles. He was in and out of detention until he eventually reached adulthood. He ended his criminal career in Kingston Penitentiary on a fifteen-year sentence for armed robbery.[57]

The ranks of juvenile offenders were far from homogeneous, however. More and more young people from advantaged backgrounds were being apprehended. One study, begun in 1927, of fifty-six young men who had been sentenced to penitentiary prior to their twenty-second birthdays illustrates this. While the sample was not scientific the study was thorough. The participants were drawn from penitentiaries across the country and subjected to detailed examination. Many came from problem homes characterized by crime, drunkenness, and break-up. Seven of the fathers had criminal records and six were alcoholics. Fifteen of the group had lost their fathers through death and two through desertion.

On the other hand, many in the study came from comfortable, stable environments. One was described as coming from a wealthy family while thirty-four were described as having had "ample means." Many identified themselves as church members and had attended Sunday school on a regular basis. The one common thread was that most had become problem children early in life. Thirty-six of the group had histories of truancy beginning as early as the second grade. Some had belonged to street gangs or associated with companions who were poor influences. Most were in and out of trouble on a regular basis and continued the pattern into young adulthood. By the time they entered penitentiary the group had already served a combined total of 101 years in various forms of detention. At the time of the survey they were collectively serving sentences totalling 223 years.[58]

With a few exceptions the profile of juvenile crime changed little through the 1930s and into the 1940s. The next series of statistics, starting with Table 19, illustrates the trends in juvenile crime and offers a comparison for the years 1922 to 1945. The figures refer to young people under the age of sixteen and are based primarily on reports from juvenile courts. The rates listed in the tables are based on the entire population of the country for the specified years. Rates and percentages are not always comparable with earlier figures presented because they have been calculated on different bases.

As Table 19 shows, conviction rates of juveniles peaked in 1925, dropped slightly in subsequent years, and peaked again in 1930. Between 1931 and 1941 the rates fluctuated slightly, rose to 60 per 100,000 of population in 1942, and started a downward slide the next year. The highest number of juvenile crimes are against property without violence. This category consistently accounted for more than half of the total convictions, fluctuating

Table 19

Convictions of Juveniles for Major Offences, by Classes of Offence, Years Ended September 30, 1922-45

Year	Offences Against the Person		Offences Against Property with Violence		Offences Against Property without Violence		Malicious Offences Against Property		Forgery and Offences Against Currency		Other Offences		Total Convictions	
	No.	Per 100,00 Pop.	No.	Per 100,000 Pop.	No.	Per 100,000 Pop.	No.	Per 100,000 Pop.	No.	Per 100,000 Pop.	No.	Per 100,000 Pop.	No.	Per 100,00 Pop.
1922	172	2	806	9	2,560	29	441	5	13	*	73	1	4,065	46
1923	179	2	755	8	2,740	31	464	5	9	*	18	*	4,165	46
1924	221	2	818	9	2,724	30	786	9	10	*	96	1	4,655	51
1925	207	2	794	9	3,306	36	593	6	7	*	173	2	5,080	55
1926	220	2	659	7	3,470	37	583	6	14	*	144	2	5,090	54
1927	179	2	772	8	3,311	35	798	8	7	*	89	1	5,156	54
1928	184	2	824	8	3,265	34	637	6	13	*	140	1	5,063	51
1929	223	2	976	10	3,096	31	690	7	12	*	109	1	5,106	51
1930	199	2	951	9	3,686	36	733	7	17	*	67	1	5,653	55
1931	256	3	961	9	3,150	30	788	8	10	*	146	1	5,311	51
1932	232	2	927	9	3,104	30	695	7	11	*	127	1	5,096	49
1933	247	2	972	9	3,164	30	661	6	4	*	96	1	5,144	48
1934	227	2	1,072	10	3,114	29	804	7	11	*	125	1	5,353	49
1935	248	2	1,031	9	3,562	33	612	6	12	*	49	1	5,514	50
1936	203	2	1,019	9	3,106	28	554	5	11	*	77	1	4,970	45
1937	186	2	1,222	11	3,143	28	575	5	10	*	86	1	5,224	47
1938	184	2	1,122	10	3,062	27	612	5	9	*	66	1	5,055	45
1939	190	2	1,207	10	2,926	26	589	5	13	*	93	1	5,018	44
1940	208	2	1,261	11	3,058	27	662	6	8	*	101	1	5,298	47
1941	263	2	1,407	12	3,467	30	947	8	14	*	106	1	6,204	54
1942	206	2	1,536	13	4,039	35	1,015	9	11	*	113	1	6,920	60
1943	258	2	1,550	13	3,658	31	892	8	21	*	115	1	6,494	55
1944	215	2	1,739	15	3,393	28	1,022	9	22	*	138	1	6,529	55
1945	218	2	1,513	12	2,964	24	933	8	29	*	101	1	5,758	47

SOURCE: *Canada Year Book*, 1947.

* Too small to be shown.

from 68.2 per cent in 1926 to 51.5 per cent in 1945. An increase in offences against property with violence began in 1938 and continued upward to 1944, with a drop the following year. Offences in this category include robbery, burglary, and house- and shop-breaking.

Delinquency tends to increase as children get older. Generally, eight-year-olds commit twice as many offences as seven-year-olds and nine-year-olds twice as many as eight-year-olds. Boys aged thirteen-fifteen committed 58 per cent of the major offences, with fifteen-year-olds being responsible for 22 per cent. Girls between thirteen and fifteen years of age made up 64 per cent of female convictions, with fifteen-year-olds accounting for 27.6 per cent of the total. Also, the court records reveal a correlation between delinquents and school performance. Approximately 77 per cent of the children convicted in 1945 were one or more years behind their age group in school. The finding was consistent with earlier observations – many delinquents were poor school attenders and had difficulty with their studies. This does not necessarily mean that problems in school led to their delinquency but rather suggests that children who get into trouble sometimes develop a range of problems that might be interrelated.[59]

Table 20 shows the trend in convictions of juveniles for all offences by provinces. It affords a comparison of the trends across Canada for the period 1922 to 1945. The two most populous provinces accounted for a high percentage of all convictions over the 1922-45 period. In 1922 convictions in Quebec and Ontario made up 63.9 per cent of the total for Canada. In 1932 the two provinces accounted for 61.9 per cent and by 1942 the precentage had moved up significantly, to 71.8. The figures show a number of anomalies in conviction trends. For example, Manitoba's numbers began to drop at the beginning of the depression and took a significant fall in 1934, remaining low for the rest of the decade. Ontario's numbers were consistently much higher than Quebec's but in 1934, 1940, and 1941, the latter had a higher number of convictions than the former. The year 1942 witnessed a jump in convictions in most provinces but, with the exception of Nova Scotia and New Brunswick, an across-the-board decline occurred the following year.

Tables 21 and 22 offer an illustration of the trends in specific types of offences for which juveniles were convicted. Table 21 gives the profile for minor offences for the period 1922-45 while Table 22 provides the breakdown of major offences for the years 1941 to 1945. Convictions for minor offences peaked in 1924 at 3,104 and did not reach that number again until 1940, when there were 3,133 convictions. Total offences remained relatively static through the 1930s and overall the year-by-year convictions were not high. In the major offence category, theft and burglary accounted for the majority of convictions of male juveniles. The two leading categories of female crime were theft and immorality, but female convictions for major offences were consistently very small. There was a high percentage of repeat

Table 20
Convictions of Juveniles for Major Offences, by Province, Years Ended September 30, 1922-45

Year	P.E.I.	N.S.	N.B.	Que.	Ont.	Man.	Sask.	Alta.	B.C.	Canada
1922	5	167	45	655	1,852	627	196	240	278	4,065
1923	10	253	60	864	1,633	581	249	246	268	4,165[1]
1924	31	251	59	782	1,977	750	362	192	251	4,655
1925	18	263	77	971	2,064	915	280	215	277	5,080
1926	6	187	55	870	2,081	1,002	246	326	317	5,090
1927	21	174	169	888	2,033	989	253	267	362	5,156
1928	11	225	145	880	1,800	970	273	340	419	5,063
1929	7	158	130	882	1,962	976	318	349	374	5,106
1930	10	203	131	1,033	2,155	869	381	443	428	5,653
1931	14	155	166	1,260	1,758	885	297	430	346	5,311
1932	4	184	186	1,293	1,772	820	229	306	302	5,096
1933	9	209	262	1,426	1,686	786	149	261	356	5,144
1934	9	300	155	1,444	1,814	635	185	409	401	5,353[2]
1935	33	240	247	1,633	2,059	428	239	318	317	5,514
1936	20	321	204	1,324	2,021	275	228	315	262	4,970
1937	46	344	276	1,392	2,016	196	311	344	299	5,224
1938	21	283	224	1,357	2,162	222	225	298	263	5,055
1939	45	228	244	1,245	2,164	293	201	321	277	5,018
1940	41	195	251	1,461	2,229	286	208	364	262	5,298[2]
1941	58	244	344	1,637	2,588	315	263	378	377	6,204
1942	60	220	279	1,617	3,071	503	397	472	301	6,920
1943	53	373	337	1,455	2,804	363	359	349	401	6,494
1944	82	362	363	1,212	2,901	345	356	431	477	6,529
1945	55	390	221	1,239	2,394	277	282	384	516	5,758

[1]Includes one conviction in Yukon.
[2]Includes one conviction in the Northwest Territories.
SOURCE: Canada Year Book, 1947.

Table 21

Convictions of Juveniles for Minor Offences, by Classes of Offence, with Percentages to Total Minor Convictions, 1922–45

Year	Traffic Regulations		Disorderly Conduct and Disturbing the Peace		Incorrigibility		Truancy		Vagrancy and Wandering Away from Home		Other Minor Offences		Total Minor Offences
1922	149	6.7%	381	17.1%	146	6.5%	206	9.2%	281	12.6%	1,070	47.9%	2,233
1923	240	10.0	376	15.6	195	8.1	263	10.9	291	12.1	1,041	43.3	2,406
1924	283	9.1	517	16.7	247	7.9	345	11.1	309	10.0	1,403	45.2	3,104
1925	176	6.2	470	16.8	325	11.6	271	9.7	286	10.2	1,279	45.5	2,807
1926	276	10.1	447	16.3	364	13.3	244	8.9	273	9.9	1,137	41.5	2,741
1927	142	4.7	479	15.5	340	11.3	182	6.1	381	12.6	1,505	49.8	3,029
1928	170	6.5	420	15.9	298	11.3	320	12.1	265	10.1	1,163	44.1	2,636
1929	197	7.2	347	12.8	327	12.0	327	12.0	240	8.9	1,282	47.1	2,720
1930	261	9.4	403	14.5	311	11.2	448	16.2	264	9.5	1,085	39.2	2,772
1931	298	12.1	430	17.5	288	11.7	329	13.4	326	13.3	786	32.0	2,457
1932	111	4.9	300	13.2	304	13.4	339	15.0	361	15.9	852	37.6	2,267
1933	115	5.0	457	19.8	498	21.6	203	8.8	217	9.4	819	35.4	2,309
1934	174	7.1	567	23.1	574	23.4	268	10.9	225	9.2	645	26.3	2,453
1935	107	4.9	312	14.4	495	22.9	234	10.8	301	13.9	716	33.1	2,165
1936	159	7.0	476	21.5	530	23.6	277	12.3	203	9.1	595	26.5	2,240
1937	193	7.7	428	17.2	702	28.2	274	11.0	117	4.7	778	31.2	2,492
1938	201	10.2	312	15.7	677	34.2	264	13.3	77	3.9	449	22.7	1,980
1939	273	10.5	454	15.7	761	29.3	264	10.2	138	5.3	705	27.2	2,595
1940	399	12.7	604	19.3	951	30.4	289	9.2	125	4.0	765	24.4	3,133
1941	835	20.4	501	12.2	1,145	27.9	366	8.9	209	5.1	1,050	25.5	4,106
1942	994	20.6	418	8.6	1,275	26.4	348	7.2	360	7.4	1,443	29.8	4,838
1943	463	12.2	283	7.4	984	25.9	372	9.8	435	11.4	1,265	33.3	3,802
1944	637	18.8	199	5.8	873	25.8	498	14.7	267	7.9	914	27.0	3,388
1945	487	15.5	216	6.8	838	26.6	424	13.5	222	7.0	964	30.6	3,151

SOURCE: *Canada Year Book*, 1947.

Table 22

Convictions of Juveniles for Major Offences, by Type and Sex, Years Ended September 30, 1941-45

Offence	1941		1942		1943		1944		1945	
	Males	Females	Males	Females	Males	Females	Males	Females	Males	Females
Manslaughter and murder	–	–	1	–	1	–	3	–	–	–
Rape, carnal knowledge, and incest	6	3	5	–	1	–	5	–	13	1
Indecent assault	43	–	30	–	46	–	38	–	30	–
Aggravated assault and wounding	54	5	22	1	24	4	53	3	25	2
Common assault	80	13	94	13	95	23	71	9	103	12
Endangering life on railway	54	–	38	–	63	–	26	–	30	–
Other offences against the person	2	3	2	–	1	–	3	4	1	1
Burglary, breaking and entering	1,378	18	1,468	29	1,509	23	1,675	27	1,467	27
Robbery	11	–	39	–	18	–	37	–	15	4
Theft and receiving stolen goods	3,289	150	3,863	160	3,462	178	3,218	162	2,810	134
Embezzlement, false pretences, and fraud	20	8	16	–	17	1	11	2	15	5
Arson	32	2	20	1	23	–	35	2	19	–
Wilful damage to property	907	6	978	16	839	30	969	16	895	19
Forgery and offences against currency	13	1	8	3	20	1	18	4	23	6
Immorality	19	42	25	28	16	47	21	48	23	26
Various other offences	39	6	54	6	40	12	62	7	47	5
Totals	5,947	257	6,663	257	6,175	319	6,245	284	5,516	242

SOURCE: *Canada Year Book, 1947.*

offenders among juveniles convicted of major offences. Between 1922 and 1945 approximately 25 per cent of young people who came before the courts were not appearing for the first time.

The restriction of juvenile statistics to the fifteen-and-under age group for so long was perhaps too limited and did not portray an accurate profile of juvenile crime. Since the introduction of the Young Offenders Act in 1984 the age limit for identifying juvenile offenders was made uniform at eighteen years old and under. Given the incremental nature of crime with age among juveniles, the sixteen-to-eighteen-year-olds break the law in larger numbers than the younger age group. For example, in 1939 juveniles between seven and fifteen accounted for 5,018 convictions for major offences while their counterparts in the sixteen-to-eighteen age group had 6,030 convictions. In 1945 the comparative figures were 5,758 convictions for the younger age group and 6,958 for the older group. Thus, when the offences are combined for all seven-to-eighteen-year-olds the incidence of juvenile crime takes on a slightly more serious dimension.[60]

The period represented in the previous tables saw the introduction of juvenile courts and a generally more efficient system of responding to juvenile crime. Nevertheless, crime reports fell far short of accurately documenting juvenile offences. The delinquent sons and daughters of the middle and upper socio-economic groups still disproportionately escaped the juvenile justice system. Police delivered them home to be dealt with by their parents rather than the courts. In many communities children's courts were still non-existent and either there were no facilities for dealing with juveniles or they were inadequate. Consequently, offenders were simply given a dressing down, a stern warning, and sent on their way. Their offences never found their way into the records.

Then there was the age-old problem of offenders simply escaping justice. Children in rural areas had a particular advantage in this regard since police forces were often non-existent. In some cases juveniles were simply smart enough not to get caught. In other cases, certain categories of crime, by their very nature, went either unreported or undetected. Examples would be sexual attacks, morals offences, assaults on the person, and theft. While there is no way to document all this, personal experience will nevertheless attest to its accuracy. Most people examining their childhood memories can recall acquaintances who were involved in lawbreaking but who never got caught. Delinquent individuals were not always from lower-income groups or broken homes. Poor delinquents were sent by the state to reform school while wealthy delinquents were sometimes sent by their parents to boarding school.

MODERN TRENDS IN JUVENILE LAWBREAKING

The 1950s was the last decade for what might be described as old-fashioned delinquency. The 1960s ushered in a dramatic upheaval in Canadian society and with it a significant change in the pattern of youth crime. The experience would confirm something that had long been suspected, namely, that the sons and daughters of the rich had as much potential for delinquency as the sons and daughters of the poor. It would challenge the belief that economic and social distress was the main cause of crime rather than one of the accompanying circumstances.

The youth of the 1950s were brought up in relatively prosperous times. In contrast, their parents grew up deprived during the depression and then spent their young adult years fighting the world war. Consequently, the 1950s for them was a time to rebuild their lives and establish their careers. They sought material prosperity and stability to make up for their deprived youth. They built homes in the suburbs, surrounded themselves with material possessions, and in the process many indulged their children. Intent on giving them the advantages that they never had, they fed, clothed, educated, and catered to their children like no previous generation in our history.

For some, the material possessions and allowances they gave their children were status symbols for themselves. Others coddled the youth as a natural expression of a family-centred society. Marriage and family were important to Canadians and children were the focal point of family life. Fathers strove to move up the corporate ladder so as to better provide for their wives and children while the majority of mothers concentrated on homemaking. They looked after all the family needs, including chauffeuring Dick and Jane to a host of activities. Magazines and newspapers encouraged domesticity with a steady stream of articles, touching on all aspects of family living. The famous baby doctor, Benjamin Spock, sold millions of his books advising mothers to cater to baby's every demand.

A whole generation grew up relatively indulged, comfortable, and economically secure. They were accustomed to instant gratification and they developed high expectations. Consequently, when they became young adults they were not prepared for a world of rules, regulations, and stop signs. They reacted as they had been taught and demanded that society conform to them rather than the reverse. When they encountered resistance they rebelled and helped to spark a social and cultural revolution. That revolution was accompanied by a dramatic increase in crime on all fronts.

Among the young, drugs became an instrument of protest, a trendy form of indulgence, and the means of escape from an imperfect world. University campuses and the pampered baby boomers were the focal points for the first wave of widespread drug abuse. Soon people in all walks of life began to "turn on." It was not long before juveniles started to emulate the example of their college-age brothers and sisters. Doing drugs became both a sign of rebellion and a status symbol. They were sold or passed around in junior and senior high schools and even in some grade schools. One survey of 6,447 students in grades 7, 9, 11, and 13 in Toronto high schools in 1968 revealed that about 14 per cent used drugs. The researchers discovered that the highest incidence of use was among students at the grade nine level. No appreciable difference was found between users and non-users relative to parents' occupations. However, the study did find that more of the users came from broken homes.[61] In an earlier day drug charges against juveniles were minuscule, but by the mid-1970s usage had reached alarming levels. In 1976, 2,239 boys and 576 girls were charged with drug offences across Canada.

For many young people drugs were at the centre of a whole spectrum of lawlessness. Rape, assault, theft, vandalism, and promiscuous moral behaviour were all a part of the drug scene. The level of drug use by juveniles was unprecedented in Canadian society. It wasn't long before the other aspects of the rebellion – the erosion of values, the abandonment of traditions, the challenge to authority, the growing incivility – were accompanied by some disturbing trends in juvenile delinquency. Heretofore, juvenile crime rates had been very low and serious offences were a small percentage of the total. All that changed in the 1960s and 1970s as increasing crime rates and more violent behaviour among the young became another manifestation of the revolution.

In 1965 the Department of Justice Committee on Juvenile Delinquency Report was released. Already the Committee noticed the upward trend that had started. The report pointed out that between 1957 and 1961 convictions increased by 27 per cent, a rate nearly triple the rate of increase in the overall population. The Committee also noted that over 50 per cent were in the twelve-to-fifteen age category. The report observed that the "increases tend to become alarming," and concluded that "it would seem to be inevitable to expect a marked increase in juvenile delinquency in coming years."[62] In commenting on the accuracy of recorded crime rates the Committee stated that "only a relatively small percentage of youthful delinquent conduct is brought to the attention of authorities." The Committee also reiterated something that was known in judicial circles for a long time – that children from middle-class homes were less likely than children from lower socio-economic families to become delinquency statistics. The former were more likely to be "dealt with either in the home or by social agencies, apart altogether from formal legal proceedings."[63]

These predictions about marked increases in juvenile delinquency in coming years proved to be all too accurate. In 1962, 5,034 boys and 761 girls were convicted as juvenile delinquents. By 1967 convictions rose by 28 per cent and 34 per cent, respectively. In 1968 there were 23,644 reported convictions of juveniles between the ages of seven and sixteen. In 1973 the figure for the same age group was 44,151. The ratio of convictions in 1966 for the juvenile population between seven and fifteen was roughly 459 per 100,000. By 1983 the ratio had risen to roughly 2,568 per 100,000. Equally disturbing was the trend to more serious and violent crimes. In 1970 juveniles between seven and seventeen were charged with approximately 8,939 crimes of violence. By 1980 the figure had risen to 11,885. The ratio of violent crimes per 100,000 of the juvenile population was about 197 in 1970; by 1980 the ratio had risen to over 265. In 1970 approximately 169 juveniles were convicted of offensive weapons charges; in 1980, 1,601 were found guilty of the same offence.[64]

Although the young have always been involved in violent and callous acts, such incidents were relatively rare in an earlier day. By the 1980s they had become much more common. In addition, there was growing evidence that violent young offenders were indifferent to the immorality of their actions and insensitive to the pain and suffering they were causing. Contemporary society faces a new kind of delinquent, some of whom portray an image of being basically amoral, undisciplined, societal outlaws, and oftentimes rootless.

Examples can be found in all parts of the country. In Mission, British Columbia, in 1988, a seventeen-year-old boy, accompanied by a friend, used an axe to hack to death four members of his foster family. He was angry because he had been disciplined and denied television privileges. A psychiatric report described him as a "psychopathic deviate."[65] In 1985 two young hitchhikers were picked up in Quebec by a middle-aged couple on a vacation trip. During the course of an unprovoked attack the woman's throat was slit and her husband was stabbed and left in a ditch for dead. The youth responsible was not suffering from any mental problems and was judged as normal with a good chance for rehabilitation. His act of violence was random and totally callous.[66]

In April, 1985, a fifteen-year-old Scarborough, Ontario, boy shot a man, his wife, and their seven-year-old daughter. The killer was a devil worshipper and had the satanic symbol 666 carved on his chest.[67] In November of 1989 a thirteen-year-old Winnipeg boy was found guilty of murdering an eighty-six-year-old woman and her fifty-nine-year-old daughter. The boy was twelve years old at the time of the killings and apparently committed the crime in the course of robbing the women's residence. He showed little concern for what he had done and the next day was found playing in a gymnasium.[68] More and more young people are acquiring firearms, apparently with little difficulty. One Toronto teenager, interviewed in 1989, admitted to owning four guns. He had a firearms acquisition certificate he had apparently obtained with ease.[69] In February of 1990 a seventeen-year-old dressed in army fatigues and armed with a seven-millimetre semi-automatic pistol entered a high school in a Hamilton suburb and shot his former girlfriend, her new boyfriend, and another girl. The boy was upset over his broken romance.[70]

A particularly disturbing aspect of contemporary youth violence is that much of it is unprovoked, random, and unpredictable. Offences are committed anywhere. In October of 1989 a seventeen-year-old girl attending a birthday party at a friend's house in Toronto was forcibly restrained in a bedroom and gang raped by about fifteen teenagers who had crashed the party.[71] A thirteen-year-old boy borrowed a pair of scissors from his teacher, walked over to an eleven-year-old girl in his class and said, "You're dead." He then stabbed her in the chest with the scissors. The boy had a reputation as a bully and apparently was in the habit of threatening his schoolmates.[72] A sixteen-year-old babysitter, over a number of days, systematically tortured an eighteen-month-old child, leaving him bleeding inside the skull and paralysed on one side.[73]

One of the worst examples of cold, calculating violence in recent years took place in the small town of New Waterford, Nova Scotia, in May, 1989. Two fourteen-year-old junior high school students killed their school bus driver, fifty-nine-year-old Rupert Newman, while he was driving his all-terrain vehicle in a wooded recreation area. The boys had hidden a shotgun in the woods two days earlier. As Newman came riding by, one of the pair fired through the trees, hitting him in the leg and chest. When he cried out for help the boy handed the shotgun to his companion and ran. The provincial medical examiner later testified that Newman would have lived had he received medical attention. However, the other youth responded to his calls for help by shooting him through the head at close range.[74]

These incidents are only a small example of the amoral behaviour common among juvenile delinquents in today's society. Newspapers regularly carry stories of brutal acts committed by young people. In contrast, there was a paucity of such items in publications of an earlier day. In both small and large communities, in slums and wealthy suburbs, one need not look long for examples of serious juvenile crime. One of the most conspicuous contrasts with juvenile crime in the not-too-distant past is the nature of gang activity that plagues many parts of the country.

Young people have always had an affinity for hanging around in groups and city street gangs of juveniles involved in vandalism, petty theft, drinking, and gambling were common throughout our history. Never before, however, has juvenile gang activity reached the threatening level that it has since the 1970s. This is readily evident when the activities of contemporary delinquent youth groups are contrasted with those of the past. One comprehensive examination of juvenile gangs, undertaken in Toronto during the summer of 1944, illustrates the point. The survey made contact with twenty-six different gangs of boys. Members ranged in age from seven to eighteen, the majority between seven and fourteen years old. Not one of the gangs was involved in what we would describe today as major or violent crime. Petty theft, gambling, drinking, immorality, and vandalism were the main offences.[75] Yet, judged by the standards of the time, seven of these gangs were described as representing "a serious menace to society."[76]

In contrast, the juvenile gangs of Toronto today are involved in major theft, intimidation, drug dealing, and violence. One estimate suggested that in early 1989 there were as many as forty separate youth gangs in the city. They go by names such as Rude Boys, the Untouchables, Posse, and the Chinese Mafia. Some wear distinctive clothing and haircuts. The youth gangs of an earlier day frequented the streets and back alleys of poor neighbourhoods and committed their offences as clandestinely as possible. The modern gangs are open and brazen about their activities.

Upscale clothing stores are favourite targets. A group will enter a shop during business hours and while some of their number distract the sales clerks the remainder proceed to steal the merchandise. One store owner described how they openly flaunt their intentions: "they tell you right out that they are going to steal from you." Toronto police report that some roaming gangs take clothing and shoes from people walking down the street. If the victims resist they risk being beaten up or spray-painted, and sometimes they get assaulted even if they don't resist.

A number of schools in affluent areas of the city have also been targeted. In one incident four youths entered the school and started to grab clothes off students walking in the halls. A teacher who attempted to intervene was punched several times before the group fled. Similar attacks have taken place in the subways where juvenile gangs have stripped expensive jackets and even shoes from passengers. Violence, beatings, sexual assaults, and intimidation are the stock in trade of many of these gangs. It appears that no part of the city is safe from their depredations. In one incident a group of knife-wielding young toughs surrounded a family outside the Eaton Centre in downtown Toronto and proceeded to taunt and threaten them. In another incident at the Eaton Centre five teens attacked an eighty-year-old woman, grabbed her purse, and flung her to the ground, breaking her hip.[77]

Contemporary youth gangs span all classes, cultures, colours, and ethnic backgrounds. One group, known as the Socials, was made up exclusively of members from upper-income families. They modelled themselves on S.E. Hinton's book *The Outsiders*. The gang dissolved after several of their members were jailed for sex offences.[78] Many young people with gang affiliations are motivated not by need but by an acquisitive ethic that allows them to steal something just because they want it. One sixteen-year-old female member of the Untouchables explained it this way: "If I see something I want I take it ... It's a game, right? To see how far you can go without being caught. I've been doing it since I was twelve and I haven't been caught yet." A fifteen-year-old girl expressed a similar rationale in connection with a gold chain that she had ripped from the neck of another teenager: "I liked it. I wanted it. I took it. If she wanted to keep it she could have fought me for it."[79]

Juvenile gang members are sometimes considered to be shiftless youths with little ambition and no career goals. Yet many have a sense of purpose and aspirations similar to their law-abiding peers. A not untypical example was a grade eleven student interviewed in March, 1989. She planned to become a lawyer, yet she had developed a very lax conscience although she was only fifteen years old. "Who wants to spend $200 on a track suit?" she asked. Her close friend chimed in, "You want something, you have to go out and get it." The girl and her gang obviously put the precept to frequent use. She described how she had stolen the device that stores used to remove the security tags from clothing, which she and her friends used to steal about fifty leather jackets.[80]

A particularly disturbing aspect of juvenile gang activity is the increasing violence. A Toronto Board of Education trustee interviewed in May, 1990, said that violence had become such a problem that the Board might have to consider putting security guards in some schools. A police raid on a student's locker in one Toronto school uncovered two knives, a piece of heavy chain, two empty bottles assumed to be used as clubs, and a homemade wooden baton with a strap. The student was thought to be a member of a gang known as Posse. The cache was only one example of the weapons being carried by an increasing number of students, both gang members and non-members.[81]

Juvenile gangs are as much of a problem in Montreal as they are in Toronto. The Director of Intelligence for the metropolitan police force estimated that in early 1989 there were up to twenty-seven organized gangs in greater Montreal with a combined membership of over 300 young people. They go by names such as Skinny Boys, Fat Boys, Demolition, and Dynamite. Groups of delinquents seem to find the city's transit system particularly attractive for the commission of crime, possibly because public transportation offers a ready means of escape for thieves and pickpockets. Washington, the capital city of the United States, has a notoriously high incidence of crime in its buses and subways. The Montreal transit system has a comparable rate and juvenile gangs make a substantial contribution to the problem. In 1989 they were responsible for some particularly violent incidents. In March of that year one group attacked a homosexual, who happened to be dying with AIDS, on a bus outside of a subway station. They stabbed the man to death. That same night three other stabbings were committed by groups of youngsters on the Metro system.[82]

A week later a sixteen-year-old boy was stabbed on a bus by a youth of the same age. The attacker took offence because the boy had glanced his way so he drove a knife into his chest and killed him. The victim was dressed in the style of a type of youth known as skinheads, who wear close-cropped hair, black army-style boots, and affect a generally ratty appearance. The teenage killer was said to belong to a gang called the Fresh, whose trademark was neat attire and a clean-cut look.[83]

Montreal officials acknowledge that many delinquents carry weapons, especially gang members, and that there is an increase in violence among youth, much of which is unprovoked and gratuitous. The changing nature of juvenile crime was evident in Montreal for some time. For example, during the first nine months of 1979, 129 people were charged with 285 armed robberies of banks or other financial institutions. Of the 129 people charged, forty-one were juveniles under the age of eighteen.[84] In 1982 police estimated that 46 per cent of all armed robberies in the city were committed by teenagers. Many of them wanted money, either to support a drug habit or to finance their own trafficking business. Montreal juveniles are also involved in prostitution, yet another venue for gang violence. A few weeks before the mayhem on the transit system a sixteen-year-old girl was attacked with an axe when she refused to co-operate with a group of young pimps who were trying to persuade her to work as a prostitute.[85]

Juvenile gangs with violent tendencies are also appearing in smaller cities across the country, such as Halifax and Calgary. In October, 1990, Calgary police reported that charges against young gang members had increased "dramatically" and that more than twice as many criminal charges were laid in comparison to the previous year. The report also made reference to the gang fights and violence, and a police superintendent observed that "The kids are fighting to win and that means a fair amount of severity in these assaults."[86]

Another dimension of the juvenile gang problem in Canada is the increasing number of Asian gangs. Among the earliest to appear were Chinese organizations in British Columbia and elsewhere in the West. In 1974 Chinese restaurant owners reported that youth gangs from Vancouver and Edmonton were operating an extortion racket. Because of the hesitancy of Chinese citizens to go to the police, this type of crime was favoured by many of the gangs as they got under way. Over a half-dozen ethnic Chinese gangs of varying sizes have functioned in British Columbia since the 1970s. One of the largest was a Vancouver group known as the Hung Ying or Red Eagles, with a membership estimated at over 100. Besides extortion, these gangs have been involved in assault, theft, drug trafficking, loan-sharking, and attempted murder.[87]

In recent years the Chinese gangs have stepped up their drug trafficking and extortion activities. The influx of immigrants has provided fresh recruits as well as better contacts in the East for drug supplies. Also, the large number of students who come to Canada from Hong Kong to study has created an expanding market for extortion. The gangs contact the parents of some of these students and demand protection money. While the Chinese have been the dominant Asian gangs for some time they are now being challenged by other ethnic groups.[88]

The flood of immigrants has brought with it some violence-prone youth from Latin America and from Vietnam and other Pacific countries. A typical example is the Vancouver-based Los Diablos, made up mostly of young people from Latin America and the Philippines. They started out as musclemen or enforcers for the Chinese gangs but eventually struck out on their own and challenged their former employers for a share of the illegal business. Gang wars, brawls, and shootouts have resulted from the growing competition among these various ethnic gangs.[89] Police have estimated that there are between 250 and 300 gang members active in Asian, Hispanic, and multi-ethnic gangs.[90]

Ethnic gangs of teenagers have also appeared in other major cities. Many carry on as broad a range of criminal enterprise as their adult counterparts and with just as much brutality. They carry weapons and do not hesitate to assault, maim, and kill. Police find the immigrant youth gangs particularly difficult to deal with. They are accustomed to harsh and repressive conditions in their own countries and in comparison the Canadian criminal justice system and its sanctions appear tame. They fear neither the system nor the penalties and consider the risks minor in comparison to the rewards for their lawlessness.[91]

Along with delinquent gangs, teenage criminal involvement has escalated in other areas as well, one of the more notable being an increase in the number of sex-related offences. Studies suggest that up to one-quarter of all sexual offences in Canada are committed by adolescents under eighteen and that almost half of the group are fourteen years old. In Ontario in a one-year period between 1984 and 1985 the number of sexual offences rose by 25 per cent; in the same period convictions of sixteen- and seventeen-year-olds for crimes in this category more than doubled.[92] A high percentage of charges are for sexual assault, sometimes involving attacks by a group of teenagers. In November of 1989 six Brampton, Ontario, teenagers were sentenced for the gang rape of a fourteen-year-old girl. One of the gang was in turn raped himself by two other youths while he was being held in detention for a bail violation.[93] More teenagers are also becoming involved in the business of sex. Girls as young as eleven years old have been picked up by police for soliciting. One member of a national research group on adolescent prostitution estimated that in 1988 there were between 5,000 and 10,000 child prostitutes working the streets of Canadian cities. Frequently, teenage prostitutes are drug users, in many cases addicted by pimps so that they can get the girls to work for them. They then get drawn into other crimes, such as shoplifting, stealing credit cards from customers, and dealing drugs.[94]

The drug business is another area of illegal activity that continues to attract significant numbers of juveniles. In 1982 the head of the Montreal police drug squad reported that the drug trade had reached unprecedented levels in city high schools. He said that students were turning to crime to support their habits and in some cases were setting up their own distribution networks. Robbery was one of the crimes motivated by youth drug use and police statistics suggested that about 46 per cent of armed robberies in Montreal were carried out by teenagers. In some cases the money realized from the robberies was used to finance their own trafficking business.[95]

A report of a survey carried out in British Columbia in 1989 claimed that one in ten adolescents was a regular user of cocaine. The study was done in the greater Vancouver area and it also found that the average age for initial cocaine use was thirteen. A director of a youth detention centre in suburban Vancouver observed that many of the drug users were regular school attenders and came from stable two-parent homes. The mayor of the Vancouver suburb of White Rock, Gordon Hogg, was quoted as claiming that drug use was breeding "a new kind of youth that is unconcerned with sanctions or consequences."[96] One example of such a youth was a thirteen-year-old Cambridge, Ontario, girl who admitted to using alcohol, hashish, cocaine, and LSD. She had run away from home to live with a nineteen-year-old boyfriend who beat her, gave her drugs, and used her for sex. At a court hearing she pointed out that it would be useless to put her in open detention because she would just run away. When she left the hearing she returned to her mother's home long enough to put on her high heels and a miniskirt, and to tuck a knife into her waistband. "If we want to screw up our lives we should be able to," she said.[97]

The signs of a tendency toward more serious crimes and violence by young delinquents have been manifest since the 1960s. However, there is still no completely accurate documentation on the level of juvenile crime. Judicial records and reports are far from comprehensive and, as is obvious from interviews with delinquents, a very high percentage of offences goes undetected. Therefore, the following statistics offer only a partial picture of the juvenile crime problem. They present an overview in trends of juveniles dealt with by the police for selected crimes between 1963 and 1983.

Table 23
Juvenile Crime: Selected Offences, 1963-83

Offences	1963	1971	1976	1980	1983
Assaults	652	1,390	1,926	7,792	6,439
Robbery	345	790	1,339	2,641	1,354
Breaking and entering	8,052	14,989	23,212	42,175	34,524
Theft – motor vehicle	3,736	5,178	7,680	10,064	5,651
Theft, over $50	1,849	4,663	2,263*	6,120*	6,329*
Offensive weapons	202	340	700	1,601	2,104
Provincial statutes	3,974	8,860	12,062	21,666	20,116
Municipal by-laws	1,571	1,345	1,023	2,420	2,959

* Theft over $200.
SOURCE: Statistics Canada, Catalogues 85-201, 85-202, 85-205.

Consistent with other indices, Table 23 shows a significant increase in more serious offences over the period. Between 1963 and 1980 the number of charges for assault rose by 1,095 per cent, offensive weapons charges went up by 692 per cent, and breaking and entering increased by 423 per cent. In 1980, of the 42,175 charges for breaking and entering, 22,416, or 53 per cent, were for breaking into residences. During the early 1980s there were encouraging signs of a drop in juvenile crime, as the statistics for 1983 illustrate. Nevertheless, the numbers remained a cause for concern and in more recent years seem to be again on the rise. In 1972 juveniles made up about 7.2 per cent of offenders dealt with for crimes of violence. By 1980 the share rose to 18.4 per cent. In 1988 young offenders represented about 15.4 per cent of persons charged in this category and 16.9 per cent in 1989. The juvenile share of property offence charges went from 28 per cent in 1972 to 36.9 per cent in 1980. The young offenders accounted for about 35.7 per cent of persons charged in the category in 1988 and for 38 per cent in 1989.

Overall, juvenile crime as a percentage of all crime rose significantly. In 1972 juveniles made up approximately 19.5 per cent of all persons charged for Criminal Code offences but by 1980 the share had risen to 32.2 per cent. In 1989 young offenders accounted for 30 per cent of Criminal Code charges. Through the 1970s, and possibly since, female juvenile crime rates remained low. In 1972 girls made up 11.5 per cent of juvenile Criminal Code charges and in 1978, the last year in which male and female offenders were distinguished in the statistics, they constituted 13.5 per cent of the total.[98]

In 1984 the official designation of juvenile delinquent was changed to young offender with a uniform age specified between twelve and eighteen in all provinces. Table 24 offers an overview of the types of crimes committed by young offenders and the statistical trend in charges since the new legislation came into force. Between 1984 and 1989 an upward trend has again developed in a number of the more major crime categories. Charges for assaults, robbery, breaking and entering, theft of motor vehicles, and offensive weapons all went up between 1984 and 1989. The minor theft category in 1989, raised to $1,000 and under, continued to account for a high percentage of all property crimes at 55.4 per cent of the total.

A crime that attracts little attention and yet has some broad implications is the one that is unobtrusively listed in statistical tables as mischief, but usually is referred to as vandalism, the destruction or defacement of property. There were 16,197 young offenders charged with mischief (property damage under $1,000) in 1989 and another 2,432 for property damage over $1,000. While such offences are sometimes dismissed as inconsequential they are often committed by younger children and frequently represent their first foray into crime. Also, since many acts of vandalism involve destruction of property, there is an element of violence associated with this type of offence. Schools are frequently the victims of substantial damage. While many individual offences translate into small monetary losses, some seemingly minor incidents can cost hundreds of dollars to repair and the cumulative cost of this type of delinquency can amount to huge sums of money. For example, in 1974 the Alberta school system incurred damages amounting to over $770,000. When the damage from deliberately set fires was

Table 24
Crimes Committed by Young Offenders

Offence	1984	1988	1989
Homicide			
First degree murder	6	27	16
Second degree murder	19	18	21
Manslaughter	3	5	11
Infanticide	3	5	1
TOTAL	28	50	38
Attempted Murder	39	65	68
Assault			
Aggravated sexual assault	30	30	45
Sexual assault with weapon	28	50	51
Sexual assault	948	1,772	2,073
Assault level 1	5,110	9,215	11,297
Assault with weapon or causing bodily harm, level 2	1,271	2,698	3,102
Aggravated assault, level 3	136	199	256
Unlawfully causing bodily harm	178	285	373
Discharge firearm with intent	12	28	22
Other peace-public officers	110	289	334
Other assaults	18	57	48
Other assaults	259	268	324
TOTAL	8,100	14,891	17,932
Other sexual offences	151	180	185
Abduction			
Abduction of person under 14	3	6	10
Abduction of person under 16	1	3	1
Abduction contravening custody order	1	1	3
Abduction no custody order	1	5	1
TOTAL	6	15	15
Robbery			
Firearms	136	179	268
Other offensive weapons	313	562	652
Other robbery	655	975	1,311
TOTAL	1,104	1,716	2,231
Crimes of violence – TOTAL	9,428	16,917	20,480
Breaking and entering			
Business premises	8,386	10,032	9,657
Residence	13,020	15,450	13,736
Other break and enter	5,594	5,210	4,909
TOTAL	27,000	30,692	28,302
Theft – Motor Vehicles			
Automobiles	2,564	4,647	5,431
Trucks	809	1,421	1,649
Motorcycles	717	821	841
Other motor vehicles	784	963	1,000
TOTAL	4,874	7,852	8,921
Theft over $1,000			
Bicycles [1]	761	46	66
From motor vehicles	1,345	436	621
Shoplifting	568	155	184
Other thefts over $1,000	2,456	1,115	1,331
TOTAL	5,130	1,752	2,202
Theft – $1,000 & under [2]			
Bicycles	2,483	2,680	66
From motor vehicles	3,035	6,825	7,429
Shoplifting	33,729	31,986	36,489
Other thefts $1,000 & under	9,878	13,910	14,667
TOTAL	49,125	55,401	61,009
Have stolen goods	2,986	5,826	6,135
Fraud			
Cheques	628	1,215	1,174
Credit cards	206	662	716
Other frauds	948	1,440	1,586
TOTAL	1,782	3,317	3,476
Property crimes – TOTAL	90,897		110,045
Prostitution			
Bawdy house	3	27	22
Procuring	3	27	12
Other prostitution	5	539	984
TOTAL	11	579	2,231
Gaming and betting			
Betting house	–	–	–
Gaming house	1	2	4
Other gaming & betting offences	2	3	5
TOTAL	3	5	9

Table 24 *(continued)*

	1984	1988	1989
Offensive weapons			
Explosives	68	92	134
Prohibited weapons	554	522	662
Restricted weapons	64	77	140
Other offensive weapons	1,247	1,604	1,809
TOTAL	1,933	2,295	2,745
Other Criminal Code offences			
Arson	924	803	897
Bail violations	523	3,750	4,593
Counterfeiting currency	16	28	24
Disturbing the peace	2,994	3,035	6,530
Escape custody	584	1,748	1,509
Indecent acts	280	299	291
Kidnapping	18	52	38
Public morals	24	11	39
Obstruct public peace officer	138	509	668
Prisoner unlawfully at large	297	1,002	1,211
Trespass at night	756	804	1,037
Mischief (prop. damage) over $1,000	11,786[3]	2,188	2,432
Mischief (prop. damage) $1,000 & under	3,324[4]	15,265	16,197
Other Criminal Code offences	4,511	8,596	9,905
TOTAL	26,175	38,090	45,371
Other Crimes – TOTAL	28,122	40,969	49,143
Criminal Code – TOTAL	128,447	162,726	179,668
Heroin			
Possession	2	6	4
Trafficking	1	10	3
Importation	–	–	–
TOTAL	3	16	7
Cocaine			
Possession	28	105	139
Trafficking	8	81	141
Importation	1	1	7
TOTAL	37	187	287
Possession	71	97	287
Trafficking	24	25	54
Importation	1	2	2
TOTAL	96	124	282
Cannabis			
Possession	1,954	2,922	2,836
Trafficking	244	648	626
Importation	5	5	9
Cultivation	5	12	18
TOTAL	2,208	3,587	3,489
Controlled drugs – (trafficking)	14	10	13
Restricted Drugs			
Possession	38	87	75
Trafficking	39	101	100
TOTAL	77	188	175
Drugs – TOTAL	2,435	4,112	4,253
Other federal statutes			
Bankruptcy Act	0	4	1
Canada Shipping Act	8	83	113
Customs Act	1	3	19
Excise Act	0	3	2
Immigration Act	21	12	11
Other federal statute offences	1,048	2,028	2,563
TOTAL	1,078	2,133	2,709
Federal statutes – TOTAL	3,513	6,245	6,962
Provincial statutes			
Liquor Acts	7,515	23,886	24,711
Securities Act	4	8	14
Other provincial statutes	6,076	6,609	10,596
TOTAL	13,595	30,503	35,321
Municipal by-laws	3,021	3,742	3,815
All Offences – TOTAL	148,576	203,216	225,766

1. Theft over $200.
2. Theft under $200.
3. Wilful damage – private.
4. Wilful damage – public. The categories for notes 1–4 existed only in 1984.

SOURCE: Statistics Canada, Canadian Crime Statistics, 1984, 1988, 1989, Catalogue 85-205.

included the cost came to $1,981,885. Vandalism to school property in Montreal in 1975-76 amounted to $2.5 million. In 1976 the bill in British Columbia schools, including damage from fire, totalled $7 million. The serious level that destruction of property can reach is illustrated by a neighbourhood vandalized in 1978. The repair bill for six homes came to $120,000. It is difficult to estimate the overall dollar equivalent for this type of crime because so much goes unreported. However, the figure is usually put at over $100 million a year for damage to private property alone.[99] Some indication of the widespread nature of vandalism comes from a study carried out by the Ontario Task Force on Vandalism between 1979 and 1981. A survey of 1,222 students between nine and nineteen years of age revealed that 89 per cent of the high school students in the group had committed an act of vandalism in the previous twelve months.[100]

All indications are that levels of crime committed by young people are higher than at any time in our history. More and more juveniles appear to be engaging in serious forms of lawbreaking, while there is a proliferation of gangs with many pursuing a range of criminal activity on a par with their adult counterparts. An especially disturbing development is that adults are now instructing children to commit crimes on their behalf because those under twelve are outside the jurisdiction of the Young Offenders Act while older children face only the prospect of light punishment.[101] The increasing incidence of random, unprovoked violence continues, while major theft, drug law violations, prostitution, sexual assault, assault, and breaking and entering are commonplace crimes among the young. It also appears that an increasing number of the children who break the law are callous, lacking in values, sometimes unfeeling, and in too many cases unrepentant.

SUMMARY

Juvenile delinquents have been breaking one law or another since the earliest days of our history. Much of the crime was minor in nature but there were always sporadic incidents of serious offences. The forests and the fur trade, in particular, created conditions conducive to criminality on the part of young people. Throughout the pioneer period the ranks of children at risk of becoming delinquent were continually augmented by the immigration of problem youth and by the presence of large numbers of orphans and pauper children. Such young people were at risk because so many of them were uncared for, neglected, and left to run in the streets.

The children of the poor, the street urchins, were the ones most often picked up by the police and identified as delinquents. Most committed very minor offences by today's standards and many were taken in for their own protection and to get them off the streets. Overall, the level of crime was low, with young girls representing a small percentage of juveniles who were charged. However, it was also evident that much juvenile crime went undetected and that rural youth and those from more privileged backgrounds in urban communities were in a better position to hide their wrongdoing or to escape the judicial system if they were caught.

The patterns established during the early years of settlement became the model for juvenile crime well into the twentieth century. There were periods when crime increased, such as the 1920s, and there was an inexorable rise in the incidence of crime over the years. However, the level of crime remained relatively low and the nature of the offences mainly minor. Even the gang activity, with a few exceptions, was concentrated in the area of nuisance offences. Delinquents in all categories engaged disproportionately in theft.

The post-World War Two era witnessed some dramatic changes in juvenile delinquency. Offences increased significantly and the trend was toward more major crimes and more violence. Manifestations of the new direction were found in all parts of the country as young people turned to alcohol and drugs, and captured media attention by the commission of major and sometimes brutal crimes. The violent turn taken by many delinquents in the form of assaults, weapons offences, and destruction of property has continued; indeed, this trend seems to have worsened by the early 1990s. The most publicized examples are the gangs of teenagers who now terrorize many communities across the country. They have been responsible for every kind of crime – from theft to extortion and murder. The nature of these gangs, in contrast to those of an earlier day, offers a vivid illustration of the changed direction that modern delinquency has taken. In 1965 the Department of Justice Committee on Juvenile Delinquency reported that "gang delinquency is generally not a problem in the large urban areas of Canada." Obviously things have changed.

The change in patterns of juvenile delinquency was coincidental with major changes in society at large. The social and cultural revolution of the 1960s and 1970s saw the challenge to, and erosion of, traditional values, the elimination from school textbooks of values and moral content, the diminution of the influence of the church and the family, a high incidence of marriage breakdown, a dramatic increase in one-parent and reconstituted families, and a significant increase in the numbers of working couples. All of these trends have continued to expand and modify. This has had an impact on the way children are nurtured and guided and is an area that merits more examination in terms of the relationship to modern levels and patterns of delinquency.

In an earlier day the majority of young people who got caught up in the judicial system came from poor socio-economic backgrounds. This led to a widely accepted assumption that poverty was the main cause of juvenile delinquency. There are a number of explanations for the fact that children from impoverished backgrounds have dominated delinquency statistics. Apprehended delinquents have come disproportionately from urban centres, especially larger towns and cities. Coincidentally, the larger urban centres had organized police and enforcement agencies, and within these centres there was a natural suspicion of economically depressed areas. Unemployment, drunkenness, poverty, and distress characterized certain neighbourhoods. This is where the "dangerous classes lived" and where the police were most watchful. Criminals, especially juvenile delinquents running unattended in the streets, were much more likely to be apprehended than their more advantaged peers living in the "good" neighbourhoods.

Nevertheless, there were always children from advantaged circumstances and stable homes who got into trouble and broke the law. In recent times more evidence indicates that delinquency is not the preserve of any particular economic, social, or geographical group. For example, a study of 500 children who passed through the Vancouver Family and Children's Court mapped the location of their residences. They came from various sections of the city and from diverse income groups. A self-reporting study carried out in Montreal in 1979 discovered that 92.8 per cent of the twelve- to eighteen-year-olds surveyed had committed at least one delinquent act, defined as status or criminal offences, in the previous year. The study also revealed that a higher percentage of working-class youths, in comparison with their middle-class peers, had not been involved in any criminal activity.[102]

The emphasis on economic factors and delinquency has also overlooked the fact that much larger numbers of children from deprived circumstances did not become delinquency statistics. In many cases boys and girls growing up in the same family with a delinquent sibling did not get into trouble. There were innumerable poor but honest families in disadvantaged neighbourhoods whose sons and daughters were well brought up and who did not become young offenders.

One example that makes the point was a Toronto Jewish neighbourhood populated with poor immigrant families through the 1920s and 1930s. Such immigrant ghettos were the spawning grounds for juvenile gangs and delinquents, yet they also produced more young people who were not delinquents, some of whom went on to become prominent in Canadian life. Although poor, many immigrants nurtured their children well and pushed them to get a good education. Harbord Collegiate, a school that educated many children from the surrounding poverty-stricken neighbourhood in Toronto, produced a particularly impressive number of high achievers. Out of the immigrant neighbourhood and Harbord in the 1920s and 1930s came such people as Louis Rasminsky, governor of the Bank of Canada; the man who built the Shopsy hot dog chain, Sam Shopsowitz; the comedians Louis Weingarten (Johnny Wayne) and Frank Shuster; the CBS program host of *60 Minutes*, Morley Safer; New York City Ballet prima ballerina Melissa Hayden; and Toronto Mayor Phil Givens.[103] Other schools could provide just as impressive a list of graduates. The point is that the poverty-stricken neighbourhoods of Canada, while producing criminals, produced many more law-abiding citizens who earned an honest living through hard work and who fill the ranks of professions across the country.

Another tendency that merits rethinking is one that dismisses youth crime as being of little consequence. As we have seen, a significant number of serious offences are committed by the young. Even the minor infractions represent for many young people their first involvement with lawbreaking and, possibly, the first step toward further problems. If there is a level at which crime should be taken seriously, it is among the young. As experience has shown, too many juvenile delinquents grow up to become adult criminals. From a society in an earlier day that dealt with juvenile offences that might be described as mainly mischief, we have evolved to a society wherein juvenile crime is a serious problem. Indications are that the problem is not about to diminish but will continue to get worse.

CHAPTER 6

▼

The Female Offender

The overwhelming majority of women who helped to settle and develop Canada were honest and hard-working. Native women contributed to the growth of the fur trade by making it possible for Europeans to survive in the forests for long periods of time. They gathered the gum used to make the birchbark canoes, they made moccasins and snowshoes, they treated hides, and they made pemmican for food. Many married the fur traders, bore children, and provided a family life that enabled the Europeans to endure the isolation and the fur-trading companies to keep their employees. Marriage to a native woman also provided the husband with the protection of the tribe and the good will of Indian hunters in carrying on the fur trade.

Many European women came with their husbands and children and helped to carve a home out of the wilderness. Some were single women who came seeking a better life or perhaps more freedom and an opportunity for adventure. Others were born here and carried on the work started by their parents. Women helped to clear the forests, build log houses, till the soil, and harvest the crops. They also took care of a host of domestic tasks, from making soap and clothes to the preparation of daily meals. On occasion women ran the farms while their husbands and sons were roaming far and wide in the fur trade. In the coastal communities pioneer women frequently took charge of drying and salting fish on shore, a key part of the process of preparing the product for the European market. The Jesuit historian F.X. De Charlevoix, who visited New France in 1720-21, observed that the women were "quick witted, steadfast, resourceful, courageous."[1] Judging by the work carried out by pioneer women the description would apply across the country.

The hard work and frequent isolation that were the lot of so many women in pioneer days left them with little time or chance to dabble in lawbreaking. Also, there was ample opportunity for women in the New World to live honest lives if they so chose. Societal standards of those days defined homemaking and domestic service as the most respectable and rewarding occupation for women. Marriage was regarded as the natural state for both sexes, and women were expected to work either at home or in domestic service until they got married. Throughout most of our early history marriage proposals and work as domestic servants were readily available.

In New France especially, there were considerable pressure and inducements for young people to marry and have families. Newly wedded couples were given farm utensils, animals, money, and provisions by the government. Pensions were offered to the fathers of families with ten or more children. When a boatload of single women arrived from France, bachelors were expected to marry up within two weeks. If they refused they lost their hunting, fishing, and trading privileges and were forbidden to go into the woods. In 1670 approximately 165 single girls arrived in Canada. All but fifteen were married within a year. Soldiers who married were allowed to leave the service, given one year's pay, and permitted to keep their arms and equipment. In both New France and English Canada during pioneer days men outnumbered women, in some parts of the country by wide margins. Consequently, there were always plenty of marriage-minded males for women who were interested in careers as homemakers.

From the very early days of settlement there was a demand for domestic servants. Military officers garrisoned in such places as Quebec, Louisbourg, and Halifax, government officials, merchants, traders, and professionals all provided plenty of work. Large families were common among all income groups and the better-off hired servants to help with household chores. Domestic service was seen as an honourable profession for women waiting to be married or for indigent or widowed women trying to avoid abject poverty. A strong demand for domestic servants in all parts of Canada lasted well into the twentieth century.

Aside from homemaking and domestic service, employment opportunities for women were extremely limited during the pioneer period. Nevertheless, some enterprising females made a living in ventures normally reserved for men. There were women in New France, for example, who ran very successful industrial and commercial enterprises. The records show that a variety of businesses were run by women, including sawmills, brick factories, tile works, flour mills, tanneries, pottery works, and trading posts.[2] Across Canada women ran taverns, inns, boarding houses, and shops. Consequently, through marriage, domestic service, and to a lesser extent other forms of endeavour, there was ample opportunity for women to work and live within the law. Nevertheless, there were always those who engaged in criminal activity.

FEMALE CRIME IN NEW FRANCE

Female lawbreakers were among the earliest groups of settlers. As we have seen, many of the company who came over with such explorers as Sieur de Roberval, de la Roche, and Champlain were recruited from the slums and jails of France. Some of the women were petty thieves and prostitutes who, upon landing in the New World, resumed their Old World habits. Even in the midst of the most abject sickness and deprivation experienced by these earlier settlers, they practised their craft.

With the growth of permanent settlement in New France women became involved in a wide range of lawbreaking, though never to the extent of the male population. In 1662 a Quebec woman was arrested for breaking the prohibition against the sale of liquor to the Indians. At the time it was considered by authorities to be a serious offence and the woman was put in prison.[3] In 1667 the Attorney-General at Quebec brought charges of scandalous conduct against a number of women in the town.[4] In 1671 Françoise du Verger was tried and found guilty of multiple abortions, infanticide, and complicity in the murder of her first husband.[5] In 1672 Gilette Baune helped her husband murder their son-in-law with a spade and dump his body in the river. The man was a heavy drinker and had been abusing her daughter. When she told her parents they decided to murder the man as the easiest solution to the problem.[6] In 1675 Marie Pacault was convicted of theft and of being a madam.[7]

Even in the early days of the colony, women worked as prostitutes in Quebec and Montreal. The Marquis de Denonville, who served as Governor from 1685 to 1689, at one point became so incensed that he proposed sending the women back to France. The home government, however, refused permission, making it clear that New France would have to take care of its own problems.[8] Denonville also expressed concern about certain women who participated in the heavy drinking that was so common. He noted that "Numbers of women drink constantly and several become intoxicated."[9]

Although there are ample examples of female offenders, the level of female lawbreaking in New France in the seventeenth century was low. This pattern continued into the next century, through to and beyond the Conquest. One researcher, who studied the court records for the period 1712-59, calculated that while women constituted about 49 per cent of the population they accounted for only about 20 per cent of indictments. Of approximately 977 people accused of crimes during the period, 192 were women. Included in the total were fifty-two charges of assault, fifty of theft, twenty-six verbal offences, twenty-three accusations of resisting a legal officer, eleven of prostitution and public scandal, nine of receiving stolen goods, five of murder, four of infanticide, and four of counterfeiting. The unusual offence of resisting a legal officer is partly explained by the fact that it was frequently the woman who was at home when an official came to call. Men were working in the woods or fields, or were away in the fur trade. The *habitant* was an independent type and officers of the court were not popular. A number of women who had occasion to deal with them gave the officials a difficult time and ended up being charged with assault.[10]

It is impossible to determine the real extent of female crime in New France. The population was sparse and scattered, police were few in number, and many crimes went undetected. In some cases matters were settled informally by the seigneur or crimes were not prosecuted and therefore were not recorded. This was especially the case with domestic servants. They were frequently in short supply so employers were reluctant to press charges because they might not be able to replace them. In addition, certain crimes more commonly committed by women, such as prostitution, abortion, and infanticide, were sometimes easily hidden.

For example, recorded instances of abortion and infanticide were few during the French regime, yet the frequency with which the clergy preached on the subject suggests that these offences were more numerous than official records would indicate. The legal prohibition was officially known as the Ordinance of Henry II and it provided severe punishment for any woman who either concealed her pregnancy or killed her child. The ordinance was regularly publicized by parish priests throughout the colony. Periodically, women were brought up on charges, and some were severely punished as a deterrent to others. However, such cases likely represented a small percentage of the total offences.[11]

There was a great deal of pressure on unmarried women in New France to conceal and terminate pregnancy. In the eyes of the church pre-marital sex was a serious sin; therefore, out-of-wedlock pregnancies brought moral condemnation and social ostracism. The economic consequences for single women could also be severe. Servants who became pregnant were frequently dismissed and encountered difficulty finding re-employment. A single mother with a child faced the additional burden of child care. In the face of such pressures some women resorted to abortion and infanticide to escape their dilemma.

Although women were seldom before the courts in New France, and when they were their offences were most often minor in nature, on occasion females committed some serious and violent crimes. Marie-Joseph Ethier hacked her husband to death with an axe and shovel. Catherine Charland, a twenty-two-year-old servant girl, killed her mistress by repeated blows on the face and head with a pewter plate.[12] In 1734 a black servant by the name of Angélique set the home of her mistress on fire – the fire spread and burned down forty-six houses in Montreal.[13]

One of the most infamous murders at the end of the French reign in New France was committed by a woman, Marie Josephe Corriveau of St. Vallier.

Marie married in 1749 and lived with her husband until his death on April 27, 1760. Immediately, rumours spread that she had murdered him by pouring melted lead into his ear when he was asleep. Within three months of her husband's death Marie married Louis Dodier. Her second marriage was of much shorter duration – in January, 1763, she killed Dodier with a pitchfork while he was sleeping. She then dragged the body to the stable and placed it at the heels of a horse hoping to make it look like her husband had been kicked to death.

Both Marie Corriveau and her father were charged with murder. At first inclined to protect his daughter, the father claimed responsibility and subsequently was sentenced to hang. But faced with death the father recanted and revealed that Marie had killed her husband. A new trial was ordered and this time the daughter was sentenced to die.[14] French law was still being used so the woman was hanged. Had she been tried under English criminal law, which was introduced in October, 1763, she could have been burned at the stake, the English penalty for wives who murdered their husbands.

Another woman who earned a place in the early annals of crime was the pirate Maria Lindsey. She was not a resident of New France but she practised her trade along the waterways leading to the colony. The traffic in the North Atlantic and the St. Lawrence was easy prey for pirates and in the early eighteenth century Maria Lindsey and her male companion, Eric Cobham, raided the French supply ships as well as any other vessels that might have worthwhile booty. Maria was an Englishwoman who during her pirate days compiled a record unsurpassed for female cruelty. She tortured crewmen of captured ships, fed them poison, and sometimes had them tied in sacks and thrown overboard alive. She and Cobham killed entire crews and burned ships to cover up their crimes. The pair eventually retired to France with their ill-gotten booty.[15]

FEMALE LAWBREAKING IN ENGLISH CANADA

Female crime in pioneer English Canada followed a pattern similar to that of New France. The first settlers were hardly off the boats in Halifax in 1749 before the practised female criminals among them picked up their trade. One of the most persistent thieves was a woman by the name of Mary Ann Hollwell. She stole a looking glass, knives, handkerchiefs, a bottle of lavender water, and silk stockings from the traders Joshua Mauger and Isaac Deschamps. Over the first few years of the struggling colony she continued her thieving ways and became well known among the merchants of the settlement.[16]

Being a major port and garrison city, Halifax early developed a virtual industry that catered to the recreational needs of seamen and soldiers. Eventually, two entire streets in separate sections of the town consisted of taverns, dance halls, and houses of prostitution. At any given time large numbers of women were caught up in the life of these streets. They were involved in drunkenness, prostitution, bootlegging, theft, and assault. A formidable level of debauchery gripped the city for well over a century. As late as the 1850s police estimated there were over 600 prostitutes working in Halifax.[17]

Some of the female habitués of the town's seedier sections followed a regular pattern. They survived by prostitution and thievery in the warmer months and in the winter would commit a crime they knew would earn them a limited stay in jail. Others were in and out of jail sporadically because they were continually found in the streets drunk. Their ages varied but the majority were younger women. A not untypical example of this group of females was a streetwise thief and prostitute by the name of Sall Ross. In January of 1825 she was caught breaking into a store and arrested. It was her fourth time in court for theft in four years. Sall had long since learned how to handle the judicial system. On one of her appearances she borrowed two young children from a friend and proceeded to suckle them in court. She calculated that no judge would jail a breast-feeding mother and she was right. On another occasion she escaped from jail and took refuge in a nearby brothel, where she remained for sometime.[18]

The military garrison, the sea trade, naval visits, and wars created ongoing opportunities for the female prostitutes, thieves, and degenerate women in Halifax. One generation replaced another and sometimes mothers and daughters were both caught up in the street life at the same time. The lives of many were a constant round of alcohol, poverty, and abuse. On occasion they were joined by women who came from substantially different backgrounds. The aftermath of the American Revolution, for example, brought women to Halifax who engaged in criminal activity for the first time in their lives.

In 1783, when hostilities ceased, over 25,000 refugees came to Nova Scotia, more than half of them landing in Halifax. Those who could not move on were housed in makeshift accommodations and with the onset of winter suffered severe hardship. Faced with such destitute circumstances some women from respectable families turned to prostitution to survive. The town was inundated with discharged soldiers so it was not difficult even for inexperienced women to do business. For the initiated the sharp increase in population simply meant bigger and better opportunities for a whole range of illegal activities. The famous evangelist Henry Alline visited Halifax on a soul-saving mission in 1783. He left in disgust, observing that "the people in general are almost as dark and vile as Sodom."[19]

While most female offences in Halifax were minor in nature there were always sporadic incidents of serious crime. Many women grew up tough and hardened and if they weren't they soon changed after exposure to the Halifax underworld. Women were frequently involved in brawls and some would use a knife as quickly as a man. Consequently, both males and females who aroused their anger sometimes ended up with serious injuries. There were many unsolved crimes of violence, including murder, in the port's early history. Also, authorities paid little attention to the happenings in the town's rum rows unless things got too far out of hand. Therefore, there is no way of determining to what extent women were involved in the mayhem that was a nightly occurrence. Incidents that were detected, however, indicate that women were more than onlookers or victims. In 1853, for example, three prostitutes were involved with the murder of a sailor in a Halifax brothel.[20]

Given the conditions in Halifax it is not surprising that abortion and infanticide were common offences. The level of prostitution and promiscuity, combined with primitive birth control methods, resulted in unwanted pregnancies. Some servants were coerced into giving sexual favours to their employers. Young women kept company with soldiers stationed at the garrison and some became pregnant. These circumstances contributed to a significant level of abortions and infanticides, although there were few official prosecutions. The open ocean and the numerous outdoor privies made ready hiding places for aborted fetuses and dead babies. In addition, it was very difficult to prove if a newborn was killed or died of natural causes. But the remains that washed up on shore or were found when privies were cleaned out, together with the dead babies that were simply abandoned in the streets, left little doubt that this was a common crime of the times. Between 1850 and 1875, for example, about 124 dead infants were found in the streets of Halifax.[21]

On rare occasions females got caught up in crimes that were unusual for their sex and therefore attracted considerable public attention. For example, Mary McDaniel committed armed robbery in 1781, an infrequent crime for a woman at that time.[22] Many years later on October 13, 1809, Edward Jordan's wife helped him with an act of piracy off Cape Canso. Mrs. Jordan joined in the mêlée that ensued when her husband and the ship's mate moved to take over the schooner. Two crew members and the captain were shot. Jordan finished the seamen off with an axe and then went after the wounded captain. Mrs. Jordan joined in and attacked the man with a boat hook. The captain escaped overboard and was left to drown but was picked up by another boat and reported the incident to the authorities. Both Mrs. Jordan and her husband were charged with piracy.[23]

Outside of port cities like Halifax, incidents of female crime were infrequent. Opportunities were fewer, needs differed, and the watchful eyes of family and neighbours were powerful deterrents. The corruption so commonplace in a port simply didn't exist in the small towns and rural districts throughout the region. Even in Halifax, as we have seen, much of the criminal activity was carried on not by the general female population but rather by a specific underclass of women who had taken up a life of

Table 25
Female Incarceration, Halifax, June 1-30, 1864

Crime	Age	Sentence
Assault	21	60 days
Vagrancy	19	90 days
Drunk	38	30 days
Drunk	36	30 days
Drunk	42	90 days
Drunk	20	10 days or $1.00
Drunk	22	10 days or $1.00
Drunk	20	10 days or $1.00
Vagrancy	40	10 days or $1.00
Drunk and disorderly	18	90 days
Drunk and disorderly	60	90 days
Larceny	36	90 days
Drunk	51	90 days
Larceny	36	60 days
Larceny	27	60 days
Larceny*	32	60 days
Drunk	28	30 days
Drunk*	20	60 days
Vagrant	20	90 days
Vagrant	21	90 days

* Arrested twice for same offence.

SOURCE: City Prison Registry of Prisoners, RG 35-102, PANS.

dissipation and petty crime. Their offences were repetitive and largely minor in nature.

The report of the Halifax city prison for the period October 1, 1861, to October 25, 1862, is indicative of the types of crime committed by women. In that year a total of 159 females were incarcerated. Of that number, fifty-eight were sentenced for being drunk, thirty-four for vagrancy, sixteen for larceny, fourteen for keeping houses of ill fame, six for disorderly conduct, five for assault, three for lewd conduct, and two for picking pockets. Recidivism was significant, with forty-two being incarcerated twice, twenty-six – three times, eleven – four times, four – five times, one – seven times, and one – eight times. Females accounted for approximately 26 per cent of persons jailed in the city prison during the period.[24]

Table 25 affords a look at the crimes, ages, and sentences of women incarcerated in the Halifax city prison between June 1 and June 30, 1864. The table illustrates how consistent the nature of female crime was at the time, while the sentences confirm the minor nature of the offences. As the table shows, there was considerable variation in the ages of women who were put in jail, the youngest being eighteen and the oldest sixty. The majority, however, were younger women with nine of the twenty under twenty-five years of age. During the same month, thirty-one males were put in jail, so females accounted for over 39 per cent of the total incarcerations. It was not unusual for women to make up a high percentage of incarcerations in the city jail. A sampling of the records over the thirty-year period between 1854 and 1884 reveals that there were frequently almost as many females jailed as males. It wasn't until the city's vice neighbourhoods were toned down in the latter decades of the century that female convictions began to drop off. For example, in June, 1884, fourteen men and twelve women were sentenced to terms in the city jail. In contrast, for the same month in 1894, twenty-two men and nine women were jailed. The pattern of crime for women, however, remained constant through the entire period. Of the nine women sentenced in June of 1894, six were jailed for being drunk, one for loitering, one for larceny, and one for prostitution. The women ranged in age from nineteen to forty-one, with six under thirty years of age.[25]

As settlement in Canada moved through New France, then to the east coast, and ultimately into Upper Canada and westward, a remarkably similar pattern of female crime emerged. Women's offences across the country were predominantly minor in nature, consisting for the most part in breaches of the law for drunkenness, petty theft and prostitution. Frequently, all three were connected. The offenders were disproportionately younger women and mainly resident in the larger towns and cities. Many were caught up in a lifestyle of idleness, drink, and immorality. Some were frequently in and out of jail and formed a virtual underclass of females who gathered in the run-down and tavern-infested neighbourhoods that characterized many of the more populated centres. A citizen of the town of York complained in May of 1831 that "Houses of infamy are scattered thro' every corner of the town. . . ."[26]

The following table affords an overview of female crime in Toronto during the year 1840. It offers a profile of the types of crimes, a comparison with male offences and crime levels, and the ultimate disposition of those charged. During the year approximately 27 per cent of all charges were laid against females.

The overwhelming number of charges against women in Toronto in 1840 were for minor offences and were disposed of summarily. The most serious crimes listed were the twenty for simple assault and the seven for threatening personal violence. As was the case in Halifax, a large number of the arrested females were involved in morals offences and drunkenness, which accounted for approximately 70.9 per cent of all charges against women. Of the remainder, larceny made up the next largest number of charges, at forty-four or 14.7 per cent.

Some years later, in 1847, the report of the High Bailiff revealed a similar

Table 26

Males and Females Tried for Offences Committed within the City of Toronto, 1840

Nature of offence	Charges at Police Office		Committed to Assizes		Tried at Mayor's Court		Disposed of Summarily	
	Male	Female	Male	Female	Male	Female	Male	Female
Assault	193	20	–	–	4	–	189	20
with fire arms or deadly weapons	2	–	2	–	–	–	–	–
with intent to commit buggery	1	–	1	–	–	–	–	–
upon constables in the execution of their duty	5	–	5	–	–	–	–	–
Burglary	5	–	2	–	–	–	3	–
Breach of provincial statutes and city laws, for which penalties under twenty shillings were inflicted	112	6	–	–	–	–	112	6
Contempt, refusing to give evidence	3	–	–	–	–	–	3	–
Disorderly conduct (whores, rogues, and vagabonds)	142	175	–	–	–	–	142	175
Disorderly houses, for keeping	3	4	–	–	–	–	3	4
Drunk in public streets, unable to take care of themselves	120	37	–	–	–	–	120	37
Enticing soldiers to desert	2	–	2	–	–	–	–	–
Buying soldier's necessaries	1	1	–	–	–	–	1	1

Table 26 (continued)

Distilling without licence	1	–	–	–	–	–	1	–
Keeping billiard tables without licence	4	–	–	–	–	–	4	–
Peddling without licence	2	–	–	–	–	–	2	–
Selling spirits without licence	31	1	–	–	–	–	31	1
Larcency	82	44	30	20	21	12	31	12
Receiving stolen goods	2	2	–	–	1	–	1	2
Frauds	2	–	1	–	1	–	–	–
Rape	1	–	1	–	–	–	–	–
Riot	9	–	2	–	–	–	7	–
Threatening personal violence	54	7	–	–	–	–	54	7
Trespassing upon private property	15	2	4	–	–	–	15	2
Selling poison contrary to statute	1	–	–	–	–	–	1	–
Uttering forged money	5	4	–	–	–	–	1	1
Practising medicine contrary to statute	1	–	–	–	–	–	1	–
Total	799	299	50	20	27	12	722	267

SOURCE: *Journals of the Legislative Assembly of Canada*, Appendix 1, Vol, 1, 4-5 Victoria, Appendix S, A1841, Appendix C.

picture, suggesting that, as elsewhere, female offences tended to be highly consistent. The report covered the period from February 1 to December 31 and showed that the largest number of charges, 135, were made against women for being disorderly characters. In descending order, fifty-five were charged with being drunk in the streets, thirty for threatening, twenty-nine for being drunk and disorderly, twenty-eight for larceny, and twenty-seven for assault. Out of a total of 342 charges, 223, or approximately 65 per cent, were for being either disorderly, drunk, or both. Over half of the women were charged once during the period, but 143 women were charged two or more times. Obviously a fair number were in and out of jail with some frequency.[27]

Table 27 compares the pattern of incarcerations across both Upper and Lower Canada in the year 1860 and once again illustrates the consistencies with earlier periods. The statistics show that the vast majority of women arrested in both of the Canadas came from the larger urban centres. In Upper Canada 77.9 per cent came from the four regions of Toronto, Hamilton, Kingston, and Outaouais, with 49 per cent coming from the Toronto area alone. In Lower Canada over 60 per cent came from the Montreal area and another 30 per cent from the Quebec region. In 1860 women accounted for 33.4 per cent of reported adult incarcerations in Upper Canada and 37.6 per cent in Lower Canada.

Drinking and immorality continued to play a prominent role in female crime. The inspectors of prisons claimed that almost all of the female jail inmates were prostitutes. They used the jails almost as hostels, seemingly coming and going as they pleased. The inspectors observed that "The jail is for them a resource in distress, a refuge during the inclement season, and a sort of common rendezvous."[28] Many of the early jailbirds were immigrant women. For example, out of 347 female incarcerations in 1847 in Toronto, 328 were foreigners; of that number, 293 were Irish.[29] Many of these women arrived in the Canadas with higher expectations than they could quickly satisfy. They disdained servant work because of the low pay, yet without work they soon became destitute. In the face of necessity they would then commit petty larceny, get caught, and end up in jail. Even a short stay was sufficient to introduce them to a variety of unsavoury women and for some to be drawn into the corrupt lifestyle of their new friends.

As was the case in Halifax certain crimes, such as infanticide, were committed by more women than official statistics suggest. Through the 1860s in Toronto, approximately seven women were charged with infanticide, yet between fifty and sixty dead infants were brought to the attention of the coroner. It is quite possible that these were only a part of the number put to death, since there were many places where the bodies of dead babies could be disposed of without ever being found.[30]

Female incarcerations as a percentage of all persons passing through the jails of Upper Canada rose significantly throughout the middle decades of

Table 27
Male and Female Prisoners, Upper and Lower Canada, 1860

Name of Gaol	Upper Canada Over 16 Years of Age Men	Women
Brantford	151	49
Outaouais	251	110
Saint Thomas	32	3
Sandwich	118	23
Kingston	226	189
Owen Sound	50	2
Cayuga	74	15
Milton	43	2
Belleville	45	29
Goderich	111	7
Chatham	86	11
Sarnia	55	–
Perth	81	10
Brockville	198	62
Niagara	48	17
London	221	38
Simcoe	69	4
Cobourg	102	70
Whitby	74	42
Woodstock	76	15
Stratford	44	4
Peterborough	48	6
L'Orignal	14	3
Picton	68	2
Barrie	109	12
Cornwall	40	2
Berlin	23	1
Welland	51	5
Guelph	108	8
Hamilton	453	274
Toronto	915	984
Totals for Upper Canada	3,984	1,999
	Lower Canada	
New Carlisle	2	1
Percé	5	–
Kamouraska	30	4
Montreal	1,736	1,104
Aylmer	16	2
Quebec	867	606
Sherbrooke	89	5
Three Rivers	125	11
Totals for Lower Canada	2,870	1,733

SOURCE: Report of the Board of Inspectors of Asylums, Prisons, etc., 1860.

the century. The increase was especially notable in Toronto and coincided with the rapid increase in population that the city experienced, as well as the build-up of its pauper population. In 1833 approximately 2.8 per cent of people jailed in Toronto were females. The percentage rose to 8.3 per cent in 1835, 27.2 per cent in 1840, and 51.8 per cent in 1860. Since female offences were mostly minor in nature they received short sentences, so some were in more than twice in the same year. This would partially explain the high ratio of female incarcerations. For example, in 1847 approximately 42 per cent of the women were in jail two or more times during the year. In contrast, only about 17 per cent of male inmates were jailed more than once during the period.[31]

With the opening of Kingston prison in 1835 females convicted of more major crimes were sent there to serve their sentences. However, most of the women put in prison through much of the nineteenth century were not guilty of crimes that would merit prison sentences today. For example, the first three women sent to Kingston in 1835 were convicted for larceny. On December 31, 1859, sixty-eight females were incarcerated in Kingston in comparison to 753 males. Of the females incarcerated during that year, twenty-one were in for the first time and one was in for a third time. The majority of women in Kingston in the pre-Confederation period were sentenced for larceny.[32]

TRENDS IN THE POST-CONFEDERATION PERIOD

Through to the end of the nineteenth century the pattern of female offences remained consistent. However, as Table 28 shows, the number of women jailed in Ontario in the post-Confederation period dropped steadily as a percentage of the total jail population. As we saw earlier, women accounted for 33.4 per cent of adult incarcerations in Upper Canada in 1860. Ten years later, as Table 28 shows, that percentage had dropped to 29. Female incarcerations remained almost static over the next two decades, totalling 1,737 in 1870 and 1,685 in 1889. By comparison, male incarcerations fluctuated through those years but with an overall upward trend from 3,599 in 1869 to 10,349 in 1889. As a percentage of all prisoners in Ontario jails females made up 26.4 per cent in 1871, dropped to 17.4 per cent in 1880, and to 14 per cent in 1889. The rate of female incarcerations per 100,000 of population of the province also dropped significantly in the early Confederation period. In 1869 the rate was 103.8 per 100,000, dropping to 88.5 in 1875, rising slightly to 96.9 in 1880, and then dropping again to 71.8 by 1885. The rate remained low over the next few years and was 75.6 per 100,000 of population in 1889.

The superintendent of the Mercer Reformatory for Women in Toronto, testifying before the Commission to Enquire into the Prison and Reformatory System of Ontario in 1890, noted that a high percentage of female

Table 28
Prisoners over Sixteen Years Old in the Common Jails of Ontario, 1869-89

Year	Men	Women	Total Population
1869	3,599	1,680	1,618,400 estimated
1870	4,215	1,737	1,620,851 actual
1871	4,586	1,642	
1872	5,006	1,615	
1873	5,745	1,735	
1874	7,298	1,746	
1875	8,048	1,566	1,770,000 estimated
1876	9,005	1,727	
1877	11,053	1,824	
1878	9,537	1,959	
1879	8,995	1,756	
1880	8,829	1,863	1,923,228 actual
1881	7,007	1,681	
1882	7,286	1,750	
1883	7,858	1,551	
1884	9,858	1,719	
1885	9,419	1,507	2,100,000 estimated
1886	8,831	1,424	
1887	8,996	1,574	
1888	10,060	1,778	
1889	10,349	1,685	2,300,000 estimated

SOURCE: Report of the Commissioners Appointed to Enquire into the Prison and Reformatory System of the Province of Ontario, 1891.

offences continued to be liquor-related. She claimed that most of the women committed for vagrancy and larceny, the two largest categories of crime, were drunkards.[33] In most major population centres groups of women, dissolute and often destitute, accounted for the bulk of female crime. Many were alcoholics whose day-to-day existence depended on petty theft and prostitution. For some, life was a constant round of drink, immorality, terms in jails or poor houses, and an early death.

Throughout the nineteenth century, as the country expanded, there was a consistent pattern of female crime from region to region. Across Canada drinking offences, prostitution, and petty larceny accounted for most female lawbreaking. In many large communities a high percentage of female crime was committed by an underclass of women who populated the run-down neighbourhoods, staffed the brothels, and hung around the drinking places. The more respectable types continued to benefit from their social positions when and if they indulged in crime. They seldom showed up in the country's jails and prisons.

The only significant change in the profile of female crime came in the latter part of the century. The predominance of certain types of offences committed by women remained the same but there appeared to be a significant drop in the level of female crime. The data are not available with which to compile accurate statistics or to draw exact comparisons, but the crime reports issued for the period suggest a downward trend. In 1888 there were 386 female convictions for indictable offences reported from across the country. The number of convictions remained almost static through to the end of the century. In 1899, 329 were recorded. Between 1888 and 1899 the number of reported convictions of females for indictable offences averaged 343 per year. In 1888 females accounted for 10.2 per cent of all convictions in this category, and for 7.4 per cent in 1893 and 5.7 per cent in 1899. The rate of reported convictions of females dropped from 8.3 per 100,000 of total population in 1888 to 6 in 1899. Females also accounted for a small percentage of summary convictions. In 1899 women made up 10.5 per cent of all reported convictions for summary offences.[34] Table 29 compares female convictions for indictable offences for the years 1888, 1893, and 1899.

There are a number of possible explanations for the apparent drop in female convictions for indictable offences. The bulk of crime was always committed in the larger centres. As towns and cities became more sophisticated and civilized, many cleaned up the neighbourhoods prone to criminal activity. Stricter controls were put on drinking establishments, more houses of prostitution were closed down, and police became more effective and efficient at patrol. Purity crusaders and temperance advocates added to the pressure to reduce street crime and especially to rescue "downtrodden women." Educational and work opportunities had also improved for women, so various influences might help to account for the apparent drop in female crime.

While most female offences were consistently minor in nature, there continued to be sporadic incidents of serious crimes committed by women. In 1872 Phoebe Campbell, a twenty-four-year-old London, Ontario, housewife, killed her husband with an axe. She had fallen in love with a farmhand and wanted her husband out of the way. Instead of being able to pursue her affair she went to the gallows and became the first woman to be hanged after Confederation. Hilda Blake, a young lesbian servant girl from Manitoba, killed her female employer in late 1889 in a fit of jealousy. She subsequently worked her charms on a female jail guard who helped her escape custody. She was recaptured and executed on December 27, 1889. In 1899 Cordélia Viau was executed in Quebec City for helping her boyfriend murder her husband.[35] Minnie McGee, a Charlottetown mother of eight, wiped out her entire family at the turn of the century by feeding her children tea mixed with sulphur that she scraped off the end of matches.[36]

Women over the years committed arson, vicious assaults, and some

Table 29
Females Convicted for Indictable Offences, 1888-99

Offences	Convictions		
	1888	*1893*	*1899*
Abortion and attempt	–	–	2
Arson	4	3	–
Assaults, aggravated	11	9	7
Assault and battery	7	14	15
Assault on peace officer	10	18	25
Assault on females	1	1	–
Bigamy	2	2	2
Concealing birth	1	3	2
Conspiracy	1	–	–
Deserting child	4	3	2
False pretences and fraud	6	4	4
Feloniously receiving	7	4	10
Forgery, etc.	3	–	5
Horse, etc. stealing	–	1	3
House, shop, warehouse breaking	1	1	1
Incest, rape, and attempt at	–	–	1
Indecent exposure	1	2	2
Larceny	184	196	219
Larceny from person	1	2	1
Libel	1	–	–
Malicious injury to horses, etc.	3	–	3
Manslaughter	1	–	1
Murder	–	–	1
Perjury	–	–	1
Refusing to support family	–	1	–
Revenue laws, breaches of	–	–	1
Robbery	1	2	1
Shooting, wounding	3	5	3
Stealing letters, etc.	1	–	–
Suicide, attempt at	6	1	10
Various offences against the person	9	3	3
Various other misdemeanours	118	68	4
Totals	386	343	329

SOURCE: Adapted from *Statistical Yearbook of Canada*, 1899.

joined men in organized criminal activity such as smuggling and theft. The Brooks Bush gang that operated in Toronto in the late 1850s, for example, had female members.[37] Some of the women who ran houses of prostitution also engaged in a form of child abuse. They recruited very young girls to work for them, sometimes enticing them with extravagant promises and sometimes by coercion. Young girls were prize catches for brothels because they could charge more for their services.

Other forms of child abuse were also common throughout the period. There were always cases of women abandoning their children, exploiting them, and inflicting physical injury. On occasion an example of unusual female cruelty came to public attention. The victim of one such incident was a fifteen-year-old boy who lived on a farm in Keppel, Ontario. An English immigrant, he had been brought to Canada by one of the immigration agencies active in arranging for orphan and delinquent children to start anew in this country. The boy's sponsoring agency had placed him in the care of a forty-one-year-old spinster by the name of Helen Findlay who turned out to be a cruel taskmaster. He was blind in one eye and sickly, so he found farm work difficult. Findlay took great delight in punishing him for his lack of productivity and neighbours reported having seen her kick him, hit him with an axe handle, and stick him with a pitchfork.

In November, 1895, after being in Canada less than a year, the boy was found dead, lying on two bare boards in an upstairs room in the farmhouse. The room was dirty, caked with excrement, and the only furnishing was an old straw mattress. The boy was emaciated and covered with bruises, scabs, and flea bites. Doctors testified that his death was due to violence and starvation. Helen Findlay was charged with murder but tried on a reduced charge of manslaughter. Testimony at her trial suggested that because of his handicap, the woman considered him to be less than human and therefore impervious to her cruel treatment.[38]

Violent females like Phoebe Campbell, Minnie McGee, and Helen Findlay were relatively rare in Canadian history. However, their more mundane criminal sisters were not, and throughout the pioneer and early post-Confederation periods their ranks were continually augmented by British immigration policy. To relieve social distress at home the English early on adopted a strategy of encouraging destitute and criminal elements of their populace to remove to British North America. An example of the type of immigrant this policy sometimes produced arrived in Quebec in May, 1865. Some seventy young girls and women had been recruited from the slums, jails, and poorhouses of Ireland and sent to Canada by the Poor Law Guardians. They were hardly off the boat when some began to sell whatever they could of their meagre belongings to buy liquor. Soon they were picked up by soldiers and were seen hanging around the taverns. They quickly became a nuisance and embarrassment to immigration authorities and even the tavern keepers were kicking them out of their establishments. The affair caused an international scandal as newspapers and officials on both sides of the Atlantic picked up the story. The women were described by various sources as "incorrigible," "profane," and "thoroughly disgraced characters." Their behaviour and the resultant notoriety prompted both Canadian and English officials to mount investigations.[39]

The actions of that particular group of women were not unique. Immigration agents frequently complained about women getting intoxicated as soon as they arrived in port. They also noted with dismay the poor character of some of the sponsored female immigrants. For example, the Halifax agent in his 1887 report complained that he had had "a great deal of trouble with some of the girls sent out by societies."[40] He observed that their sponsors simply wanted to get rid of them. The problem persisted, for in 1902 another agent observed that troublesome women were being sent to Canada in hopes of improving their situation but claimed that the experiment had "met with very poor success."[41] Canadian authorities were willing to take a chance on such women because for much of the period jobs awaited female immigrants in cities like Montreal, Ottawa, Hamilton, and Toronto. While some of the immigrant women became problems in Canadian communities, many lived honest and rewarding lives. Indeed, judging by the records proportionately few women, immigrants and native-born, got into trouble with the law. The outstanding feature about female crime in pioneer Canada is not that there was so much of it but that there was actually very little.

FEMALE CRIME TO WORLD WAR TWO

Nineteenth-century female crime patterns continued into the twentieth century. About the only significant development that had an impact on female crime in the early years of the century was the pace of western growth. Settlers were coming into the West in great numbers and urban communities were growing. The population of Calgary went from 4,398 in 1901 to 43,704 by 1911. In the same period the population of Edmonton increased from 4,176 to 30,479. One of the notable features of this growth was the disparity between the numbers of males and females. In 1911 there were 200,000 more males than females in the prairie region. The difference was especially pronounced in the larger towns and cities. The abundance of young, single, immigrant males created a wealth of opportunity for prostitutes. While the older cities in the East were cleaning up their tenderloin districts the liquor trade, gambling, and prostitution were flourishing in many western communities.

Prostitution in the West dated back to the days of trading posts, the fur trade, and whisky runners. The profession prospered during gold rush and railroad-building days and the population growth over the early decades of this century acted as yet another impetus. Most of the prostitutes in earlier times were native women, many of whom were lured into the business through alcohol addiction or were forced into it by fathers, husbands, and others who bought and sold native women for prostitution. When the CPR was being built, tent cities of gamblers, prostitutes, and whisky vendors moved with the railroad builders as they strung the tracks across the West. By the turn of the century more women of various colours and nationalities were gravitating westward to ply their trade. As was the case in the East, houses of prostitution abounded in rundown districts of towns and cities surrounded by taverns and dance halls. Women of many races worked the streets, and brothels were run by black, Japanese, and white women. The tents of old were replaced by well-appointed establishments, but the basic business remained the same: sex, liquor, and gambling.[42]

Prairie prostitutes were both aggressive and progressive. They used the railways to sell their favours on a circuit that ran all the way to British Columbia. Some travelled from town to town with male companions who hustled in the local pool halls while the women worked the streets.[43] They also learned that it paid to advertise. The better-kept women would frequently dress up in their silk finery and drive around town in their horse-drawn carriages as a means of reminding the local gentlemen that they were in business. Later, when the automobile came into its own, at least one enterprising western madam also put it to good use to promote business. Every Saturday afternoon during the summer months she would dress her girls in their best clothes, put them in a taxi, and tour the shopping streets of the town waving to the farmers and ranchers.[44]

The women who worked the trade in the West seemed to conduct themselves in a more refined manner than their eastern sisters of an earlier day. Descriptions continually refer to their fashionable and expensive dress and to their well-decorated and carefully operated houses. Also, the women were on good terms with the police in many communities. This suggests that not only was prostitution tolerated, but women were not seen as public nuisances by the legal authorities. The periodic crackdowns that took place were more in response to moral indignation and outrage on the part of upright citizens than to any police concern about criminal activity on the part of the women. Once a few examples were made, the ladies were left to pursue their interests in peace until the next purity campaign.[45]

Prostitution in British Columbia also responded to population growth. As far back as the gold rush days single men and married men without their families had been coming to British Columbia at a steady pace. Especially prominent among the influx were Asians. By 1901 there were 16,792 Chinese in Canada. Over 14,000 of them lived in British Columbia. Between 1906 and 1908 over 11,000 Japanese entered Canada, the majority of whom settled in British Columbia. A high percentage of these immigrants came by themselves and lived in overwhelmingly male communities. They naturally became a huge potential market for the prostitution business. In response, prostitutes and brothels gathered in and near some of these settlements. The largest concentration of brothels in Vancouver, in the first decade of the century, could be found in Chinatown.

The First World War also gave a boost to prostitution, not only in the West but in all parts of Canada. Military training bases sprang up across the country and brought together concentrations of men on their own. Most were far removed from girl friends, wives, and families, and many were away from home for the first time. This lucrative market attracted a variety of entrepreneurs – nearby any military base could be found an ample supply of bootleggers and prostitutes.

Halifax, a major port of embarkation for troops going overseas and a strategic naval base, affords a good example. The Nova Scotia government instituted total prohibition on July 1, 1916. Immediately, so-called "blind pigs" opened up to meet the demand for bootleg alcohol. Some of the illegal liquor outlets were associated with the city's brothels. Prostitutes from across the country flocked to Halifax to take advantage of the wartime business. Soon they branched out from the traditional locales and ladies of the evening could be found in all parts of the city night and day. One of the favourite fronts for some of the more enterprising were cigarette and tobacco shops, which seemed to spring up all over. Each such shop had a few rooms in back for special customers.[46]

The uprooting that accompanied the war and the changes in Canadian society that came in the 1920s have been described elsewhere. Those changes had a major impact on the lives of many women. The industrial development of the late nineteenth century opened up new work opportunities for women, and by 1896 women accounted for 20 per cent of the work force in Canada. Their rate of participation continued to rise, reaching 25 per cent by 1931. Many more women were working outside the home and the young and single were gravitating to the larger towns and cities. By 1921 there were approximately 58,000 more women than men in Canadian cities. Many had come from small communities, and more than a few were immigrants. Life in the workplace and in the city, for many, was far removed from friends and the protection of the family circle. The very nature of this experience encouraged less restrictive standards of conduct.

Many other influences also challenged the moral values of women. Jazz music and the new sensuous dances, the liberated lifestyle glamorized in the movies, a new generation of sex-and-confession magazines, Freud's theories suggesting that sexual repression was unhealthy – all challenged women's conventional role. Even the automobile brought new pressures on women to part with their virtue. In response women shortened their skirts, put on make-up, bobbed their hair, and smoked and drank in public. The cherished conventions of their parents were often cast aside.

Women both demanded and exercised a new freedom. They had won the right to vote in 1917, and now the liberated female sought an end to the double standard of morality as well as equal social and economic opportunity with men. Further evidence of the change in attitude was the increasing divorce rate. Though minuscule by today's standard, the divorce rate was viewed with alarm at the time. In 1922 Parliament considered 192 petitions for divorce, compared with only thirty-six petitions ten years earlier.[47] Significantly, an even higher proportion of divorce proceedings were being initiated by women. Of 816 divorces granted in Canada in 1929 by Parliament and the courts, 440 were granted to wives.[48]

For some women the new opportunities and changed values found expression in ways that not only challenged long-standing conventions but also broke the law. So coincidental with the many changes that took place was a steady increase in the incidence of female crime. Table 30 illustrates the trend in convictions of women for indictable offences during the 1920s. From 1922 to 1930 the number of convictions rose by 65.3 per cent. Over the same period convictions of females sixteen and over for summary offences went up by 127 per cent and the rate per 100,000 of population sixteen and over went up by 91.8 per cent. Thus, during a period in our history when society was experiencing significant changes in lifestyle, attitudes, and values the trend in female crime also went up. It is important to note, however, that the numerical base was small so a modest increase in the number of offences could translate into seemingly high percentage increases.

Table 30
Convictions for Indictable Offences, Females Sixteen Years and Over, 1922-30

Year	Convictions	Rate per 100,000 Total Population
1922	1,609	28.3
1923	1,609	27.9
1924	1,826	31.1
1925	2,035	33.9
1926	2,055	33.6
1927	2,013	32.1
1928	2,200	34.2
1929	2,637	40.0
1930	2,660	39.5

SOURCE: Compiled from *Canada Year Book*, various years.

A category of crime that involved an increasing number of women through the 1920s and beyond was drug usage. Official statistics do not support this contention, but many other indicators do. Newspapers, magazines, moral reform organizations, and government and judicial officials all expressed alarm over the growing drug problem and left little doubt that

women were among the offenders. More and more women who were
arrested by police for various offences were discovered to be drug users. For
example, of fifteen women confined in Oakalla jail in British Columbia in
1919, nine were drug users.[49] They were also traffickers, and as well became
involved in other illegal activities such as theft and prostitution to earn
money to feed their addiction. The main centres for female drug users and
traffickers were Montreal, Toronto, and Vancouver.[50]

Another type of lawbreaking that witnessed an increase in the level of
female participation was bootlegging. Temperance legislation in parts of
Canada, the government takeover of retail liquor sales, and prohibition in
the United States, as we have seen, acted as catalysts for a tremendous
growth in the illicit liquor industry. Women have always been involved in
bootlegging, and with the greater activity in the twenties and thirties many
more women got in on the action. They ran illegal outlets and many became
involved in rum-running, using anything from flowing skirts to baby carriages to hide the liquor they delivered. A few women got into the business
in a big way, none more successfully than Bessie Starkman.

A thirty-year-old Polish immigrant, Bessie was married with two
children when she fell in love with Rocco Perri, a twenty-three-year-old
boarder. In 1913 Bessie abandoned her family to move away with Rocco.
From then on she was a close accomplice in the illegal activities that
eventually earned her common-law husband the title, "King of the
Bootleggers." Their criminal ventures enabled Bessie to live the life of a
wealthy socialite in a nineteen-room mansion in Hamilton. All went
well until Bessie got caught up in the hearings of the Royal Commission
on Customs Violations in 1927.[51] Rocco Perri had been called to testify
because of his reputation as a big-time bootlegger. During testimony,
Rocco claimed that Bessie was in charge of the couple's financial affairs
and looked after the books. Consequently, she was called before the
Commission. She claimed that they had a balance of $98.78 in their
bank account but their lifestyle obviously belied the claim and an investigation was launched. An account, containing one million dollars, was
discovered in a local bank in the name of Bessie Starkman. Warrants
were issued for Bessie and Rocco on eight counts of perjury. For a time
they evaded arrest but they were eventually found, convicted, and sentenced to six months in jail in 1928. On August 11, 1930, Bessie and
Rocco were returning late from a party when the couple was ambushed
by gunmen and Bessie was killed with two shotgun blasts. The fact that
Rocco was uninjured raised some suspicion, but the crime was never
solved.[52]

Some years later Bessie's place was taken by Mrs. Anne Newman,
another enterprising Polish immigrant but this time younger than Rocco.
Like her predecessor, she became deeply involved in Rocco's bootlegging
and other mob-related activities. Among other roles, she acted as a go-

between with American mobsters in Detroit and Chicago and handled payoffs to Canadian Customs officials. She showed a real flare for big-time crime and during the war, when Rocco was interned as an enemy alien, Anne ran an international gold-smuggling ring.[53]

While women like Bessie Starkman and Anne Newman were involved in bootlegging and organized crime, a few others were gaining notoriety for different reasons. As we have seen before, there were always women capable of violence and extreme cruelty. Two such females came to public attention in Windsor, Ontario, in 1933. They were matrons of a children's shelter and were discovered to be abusing the children under their care. The police charged them with acting in an inhumane manner, using harsh punishment, and maintaining a prison-like atmosphere in the home. The case caused such a public furore that the Ontario government appointed a commission of inquiry. The commission discovered that the matrons had made frequent use of corporal punishment and had kept the children in a state of fear. It was also discovered that the home kept an unusually large supply of bi-chloride of mercury tablets, which could be poisonous if administered in quantity.[54]

Incidents of headline-grabbing crimes committed by women continued to be minimal through the 1930s; on the other hand, female convictions for indictable crimes rose at a steady pace. Table 31 presents trends in convictions, by province, for the latter half of the decade. As the table shows, in absolute numerical terms, the increase in female convictions was not great and there were only slight fluctuations in female convictions as a percentage of all convictions. The increases in one province, Quebec, accounted for most of the overall rise.

A slightly different picture emerges, however, when other indices are used. For example, between 1931 and 1939 convictions of females for indictable offences rose by 85.1 per cent. That was a larger increase than was experienced in the previous nine-year period. Also, the rate of convictions per 100,000 aged sixteen and above went from 37.9 in 1931 to 61.5 in 1939. This was also a higher increase than in the previous nine years. On the other hand, the rate per 100,000 for convictions for summary offences went up by only 26.7 per cent between 1931 and 1939. Female crime continued to consist primarily of petty theft, prostitution, and alcohol-related offences, and also continued to be a predominantly urban phenomenon. Quebec affords a good illustration. As Table 31 shows, much of the increase in female convictions between 1935 and 1939 is accounted for by increases in that province, and much of that is due to increases in the city of Montreal. During most of this period Montreal was governed by an administration led by Mayor Camillien Houde. Corruption thrived and the city was considered to be wide open for crime, including gambling, prostitution, and bootlegging. While male criminals dominated the scene, many females became involved in the lawbreaking that characterized the city at that time. The

Table 31

Females Convicted of Indictable Offences, by Province, Years Ended September 30, 1935-39

Province	Convictions					Percentage of Females Convicted to Total Convicted				
	1935	1936	1937	1938	1939	1935	1936	1937	1938	1939
Prince Edward Island	2	1	5	15	16	3.4	1.3	5.1	6.7	6.0
Nova Scotia	67	67	78	71	73	6.7	5.8	7.2	5.6	4.5
New Brunswick	39	50	52	59	50	6.8	6.7	6.8	6.5	4.5
Quebec	1,533	1,466	1,652	1,880	2,589	16.4	15.4	21.2	18.3	23.9
Ontario	865	847	983	947	897	6.8	6.2	6.7	5.5	4.5
Manitoba	252	270	273	258	240	10.6	10.3	9.6	8.4	6.3
Saskatchewan	76	86	167	133	210	3.9	3.9	5.4	5.2	6.1
Alberta	140	229	246	246	317	5.8	7.3	6.8	6.8	7.7
British Columbia	362	354	325	567	427	11.7	11.7	9.7	12.8	11.5
Yukon and N.W.T.	-	-	2	-	6	-	-	11.1	-	19.3
Canada	3,336	3,370	3,783	4,176	4,825	9.9	9.4	10.2	9.6	10.0

SOURCE: *Canada Year Book*, 1941.

269

situation was also a comment on the relationship among the level of tolerance, standards of law enforcement, and the degree of crime.

World War Two brought with it dramatic changes in the lives of Canadian women. Anxious to mount an effective war effort and faced with an
acute labour shortage due to the number of people in the services, the
government called on the women of the nation for help. First single women,
then married women without children, and finally women in general were
actively recruited to work in war industries. The government mounted an
advertising campaign, offered income tax incentives, and set up a day-care
program in co-operation with the provinces. Soon women were building
ships, assembling airplanes, and making armaments. By 1943 over 255,000
women were working in war industries in Canada.[55]

Convictions of females for both indictable and non-indictable offences
dropped steadily through the war years, as Tables 32 and 33 illustrate. A
high percentage of convictions continued in Quebec but that province also
experienced the most significant reduction by 1945. Female convictions as a
percentage of all convictions reached a high point in 1942 and then fell off
substantially by 1945.

As Table 33 shows Ontario far surpassed Quebec when it came to convictions for non-indictable offences. Levels fluctuated from province to province between 1940 and 1945, with Quebec experiencing a steady rise from
1940 to 1943 and Manitoba a steady drop over the same period. By 1945
traffic violations and drunkenness made up the largest number of female
offences in the non-indictable category. Out of the total of 23,323 convictions, 9,001 were for breaches of traffic regulations, 3,451 for drunkenness,
2,801 for vagrancy, 1,829 for infractions of liquor laws, and 676 for operating a radio receiving set without a licence.

Although conviction statistics suggest that female crime diminished during the war years, certain types of offences probably increased. Military
bases always attracted a large number of hangers-on to nearby communities. Prostitutes and bootleggers usually did a thriving business in any area
where there were large numbers of service personnel. Halifax was a case in
point. One writer described it as a "courtesan's paradise" and said that
"there was nothing like it since 1815."[56]

MODERN TRENDS IN FEMALE CRIME

The Second World War destabilized Canadian society and many were
particularly concerned about the impact of hundreds of thousands of
women working outside the home or serving in the armed forces. Some saw
it as a manifestation of the decline of the old order and argued that traditional values were gone and that home and family were destroyed. The
pessimism and gloom proved to be unfounded because when the war ended
women left the workplace with almost the same enthusiasm as they had in

Table 32
Convictions of Females for Indictable Offences, by Province, Years Ended September 30, 1941-45

Province	Convictions					Percentage of Females Convicted to Total Convicted				
	1941	1942	1943	1944	1945	1941	1942	1943	1944	1945
Prince Edward Island	19	23	15	20	12	9.2	11.2	8.6	7.6	5.2
Nova Scotia	80	108	100	94	89	4.8	6.6	5.8	5.3	4.2
New Brunswick	72	82	83	126	75	6.1	7.7	6.9	9.6	6.0
Quebec	3,573	3,313	3,422	1,574	783	31.0	32.3	29.4	15.2	8.2
Ontario	1,303	1,183	1,463	1,251	1,296	8.2	7.9	8.7	7.1	7.5
Manitoba	288	312	246	241	199	10.2	12.9	11.9	10.2	7.9
Saskatchewan	299	305	188	166	168	9.6	11.6	8.5	8.0	7.6
Alberta	251	267	253	258	281	7.7	8.4	9.1	8.2	8.8
British Columbia	332	298	361	372	369	11.1	10.7	11.7	10.9	10.6
Yukon and N.W.T.	–	3	1	2	3	–	9.7	2.4	2.4	3.4
Canada	6,217	5,894	6,132	4,104	3,275	14.6	15.0	14.7	9.7	7.8

SOURCE: *Canada Year Book, 1947.*

Table 33

Convictions of Females for Non-Indictable Offences, by Province, 1940-45

Province	Convictions						Percentage of Females Convicted to Total Convicted					
	1940	1941	1942	1943	1944	1945	1940	1941	1942	1943	1944	1945
Prince Edward Island	56	96	75	75	69	82	4.5	5.8	4.9	7.3	5.7	5.9
Nova Scotia	456	530	554	466	562	645	5.0	5.2	5.3	5.3	6.8	6.6
New Brunswick	244	379	320	321	420	424	3.9	4.9	3.9	4.2	4.7	4.3
Quebec	4,541	6,907	8,893	9,139	5,299	7,066	4.8	4.5	4.5	5.0	3.7	4.5
Ontario	14,966	15,159	13,521	9,455	10,343	10,780	5.6	5.2	4.7	4.6	5.5	5.1
Manitoba	1,624	1,563	1,459	1,234	1,293	1,211	5.2	4.8	4.5	5.6	6.1	5.3
Saskatchewan	340	401	360	425	402	427	3.7	3.8	4.2	5.4	5.4	4.7
Alberta	779	460	678	711	634	754	5.3	3.0	4.7	6.1	5.6	6.5
British Columbia	1,708	1,810	1,453	1,227	1,391	1,907	7.4	6.4	5.8	6.0	6.8	8.3
Yukon and N.W.T.	22	8	9	25	19	27	10.8	3.6	5.1	10.0	4.9	7.8
Canada	24,736	27,313	27,322	23,078	20,442	23,323	5.4	5.0	4.7	5.0	5.0	5.1

SOURCE: *Canada Year Book, 1947.*

entering it. Service people returned home anxious to get on with their lives and the late 1940s and 1950s witnessed a virtual renaissance of family life.[57] The overriding issues of concern seemed to be the merits of natural childbirth and the reliability of Dr. Benjamin Spock's advice on bringing up children.

Female crime dropped to even lower levels during the late 1940s and 1950s. Table 34, showing the breakdown of indictable offences that women were convicted of in 1954 and 1955, illustrates the trend in female crime at the time and types of offences committed by females, and offers a comparison with males. In 1949 the base for compiling statistics for indictable offences changed from counting total convictions to counting people convicted, thus making it difficult to draw comparisons with earlier years. However, the table still affords an overview of the types of crimes women were committing in the 1950s and the numbers of women being convicted. Over 39 per cent of females convicted for an indictable offence in 1954 were found guilty of theft. The next largest number was for assault; next came the offenders found guilty of keeping or being inmates of houses of prostitution. Under the old system of counting, female offences as a percentage of all indictable convictions had reached a low of 6.8 per cent in 1946. Under the new system female offenders as a percentage of all persons convicted continued small, amounting to 5.9 per cent in 1954 and 6 per cent in 1955.

As Table 35 shows, convictions of females for summary offences also remained low as a percentage of all convictions. They accounted for 5 per cent of convictions in 1941 and 6.5 per cent in 1951. By 1955 they had dropped to 4.9 per cent of total convictions. The provinces of Ontario, Quebec, and British Columbia, in that order, were the ones with the largest numbers of convictions for summary offences. Over the five-year period Ontario alone accounted for an average of over 67 per cent of all summary convictions.

In the midst of the low levels of female crime there were, as always, incidents of serious offences. For example, Table 34 shows that in 1954, six women were convicted for manslaughter or murder, fifteen for attempted murder, shooting, and wounding, sixty-five for burglary and robbery, and five for arson. Among a number of women offenders who came to public attention for particularly sensational crimes during the early post-war period, none attracted more notoriety than Evelyn Dick. Evelyn grew up in Hamilton, Ontario, as a somewhat indulged only child with aspirations to acquire wealth and social position. Upon finishing school, and with the prospects of fulfilling her ambitions rather dim, she sought the company of well-to-do men. Soon she was living the life of a high-class prostitute, escorting dates to social functions in Toronto, going to dances, and attending the races. While she didn't achieve the social position for which she longed, she did for a time manage a life of luxury that included furs, jewellery, and a new Packard automobile.

Table 34
Adults Charged and Convicted of Indictable Offences by Class of Offence,
1954 and 1955

Class and Offence	1954			1955		
		Adults Convicted			Adults Convicted	
	Adults Charged	M.	F.	Adults Charged	M.	F.
Class I. Offences against the Person	7,066	5,274	277	6,323	4,676	221
Abduction	26	17	1	24	8	4
Assault, common, aggravated, and on police	4,802	3,539	226	4,486	3,330	153
Offences against females[1]	1,083	834	10	855	641	19
Manslaughter and murder	169	90	6	112	55	4
Attempted murder, shooting, and wounding	290	202	15	175	119	11
Non-support, desertion	162	134	4	92	70	4
Other offences against the person	534	458	15	579	453	26
Class II. Offences against Property with Violence	5,181	4,678	65	5,020	4,542	64
Burglary and robbery	5,181	4,678	65	5,020	4,542	64
Class III. Offences against Property without Violence	12,836	10,574	886	12,101	9,914	874
Fraud, embezzlement, and false pretences	2,017	1,646	136	1,935	1,542	139
Receiving stolen goods	1,109	899	34	1,071	823	55
Theft	9,710	8,030	716	9,095	7,549	680
Class IV. Malicious Offences against Property	381	312	15	603	464	30
Arson	74	55	5	107	63	14
Malicious damage to property	307	257	10	496	401	16
Class V. Forgery and Other Offences against the Currency	742	636	75	704	661	65
Offences against currency	5	4	–	14	10	–
Forgery and uttering forged documents	737	632	75	750	651	65

Table 34 (continued)

Class VI. Offences not included in the Foregoing Classes	9,072	7,561	495	7,556	6,311	451
Dangerous or reckless driving	847	656	6	307	245	3
Driving car while ability impaired	3,690	3,505	41	3,161	2,985	40
Driving car while drunk	1,100	897	6	751	641	10
Opium and Narcotic Drug Act, offences against	351	239	67	396	249	100
Gambling and lotteries	442	341	40	684	566	36
Keeping bawdy houses and inmates	287	51	196	265	65	137
Various	2,355	1,872	139	1,992	1,560	125
Totals	35,278	29,035	1,813	32,367	26,568	1,705

1. Includes abortion, assault against females or wife, indecent assault, carnal knowledge, incest, procuration, rape, attempted rape, and seduction.
SOURCE: *Canada Year Book*, 1957-58.

Evelyn's comfortable existence came to an abrupt halt when in quick succession she gave birth to two children. The first was a baby girl whose father she claimed was away in the navy. When the second child, a boy, was born Evelyn's father had had enough and refused to allow her to come home with the new baby. The boy suddenly disappeared and the mother explained that she had given him up to the Children's Aid Society. Evelyn's parents split up and in 1945 she moved into an apartment with her mother.

On October 4, 1945, Evelyn married John Dick, a street railway motorman. Much to her husband's surprise she refused to consummate the marriage and insisted that he continue to live at his boarding house. She later admitted that she celebrated her marriage by sleeping with another man on the night of her wedding. Dick soon began to suspect that he was being used. The relationship with Evelyn and her parents became strained and continued to deteriorate until Dick began receiving threats from his father-in-law, Donald Maclean, and from a male friend of his wife's by the name of Bill Bohozuk.

On March 6, 1946, John Dick disappeared. Ten days later his torso was found, minus the head, arms, and legs, on a hiking trail outside the city. Police launched an investigation and while searching Evelyn's home uncovered the body of an infant in a cement-filled suitcase. Evelyn, her parents, and Bill Bohozuk were all charged with murder. Evelyn Dick was convicted of murder and sentenced to death but on appeal she was acquitted at the second trial. Within three weeks of the verdict she was again in court, this

Table 35

Convictions of Females for Summary Conviction Offences, by Province, 1951-55

Province or Territory	Number of Convictions					Percentages of Convictions of Females to Total Convictions				
	1951	1952	1953	1954	1955	1951	1952	1953	1954	1955
Newfoundland	206	309	328	241	550	4.1	5.0	5.2	3.4	6.4
Prince Edward Island	40	57	47	46	46	1.8	2.2	1.9	1.6	1.3
Nova Scotia	471	685	602	469	438	3.2	4.6	3.5	2.6	2.3
New Brunswick	501	611	455	586	439	2.0	1.9	1.4	1.7	1.2
Quebec	9,056	7,156	9,168	9,024	8,590	3.4	2.3	2.6	2.0	1.9
Ontario	57,135	69,057	53,987	63,384	77,321	8.5	8.4	5.6	5.9	6.3
Manitoba	1,745	6,244	3,838	4,309	4,853	1.5	4.6	2.8	3.0	4.4
Saskatchewan	592	570	617	641	847	2.6	1.8	1.8	1.4	1.8
Alberta	1,208	1,568	1,812	1,628	1,604	3.0	3.1	3.2	2.9	2.7
British Columbia	13,596	15,109	13,714	13,864	11,149	9.8	9.5	8.5	8.6	5.8
Yukon and N.W.T.	51	136	148	186	9	4.1	7.4	7.3	10.2	19.6
Canada	84,601	101,502	84,716	94,378	105,846	6.5	6.5	4.8	4.8	4.9

SOURCE: *Canada Year Book*, 1957-58.

time facing charges of killing her infant son. She was convicted of manslaughter and sentenced to life imprisonment.[58]

Another sensational crime committed by a woman was the bombing of a passenger plane in Quebec on September 9, 1949. Marguérite Pitre, a mother of two, placed a package on board a Canadian Pacific Airlines DC-3 as a favour to a friend and as payment for a $600 debt. The plane, with twenty-three people on board, exploded in the air forty minutes out of Quebec City. On board the plane was the wife of Pitre's friend, Albert Guay. The man had been having an affair with a young co-worker of Pitre's and he wanted to get rid of his wife so he could marry the girl. Guay and the man who had actually made the bomb, Genereux Ruest, Marguérite Pitre's brother, were convicted of murder. Marguérite Pitre had bought the dynamite for the bomb and took the bomb to the airport and shipped it as cargo. It was sometime before police were able to establish Pitre's role in the bombing and bring her to trial. She was convicted, appealed, and was again found guilty at her second trial. She was executed on January 9, 1953.[59]

As Table 36 shows the convictions of females as a percentage of all persons convicted for indictable crimes began a steady increase in 1959. By 1968 females accounted for 12.4 per cent of all persons convicted, and the percentage was still climbing.

Table 36
Persons Convicted for Indictable Offences, 1958-68

Year	Total Convictions	Females	%
1958	34,546	2,034	5.9
1959	31,092	2,115	6.8
1960	35,443	2,552	7.2
1961	38,679	3,163	8.2
1962	38,663	3,148	8.1
1963	42,914	3,736	8.7
1964	42,097	4,170	9.9
1965	41,832	4,840	11.6
1966	45,670	5,729	12.5
1967	45,703	5,816	12.7
1968	49,963	6,187	12.4

SOURCE: Dominion Bureau of Statistics, Crime Statistics (Police), Catalogue 85-205.

There is no ready explanation for the upward movement in female crime trends suggested by the figures in Table 36. There was no great economic downturn; in fact, work opportunities for women were steadily expanding. Some have suggested that the feminist movement had an impact on female crime rates by encouraging women to be more aggressive and persuading more women to seek fulfilment outside the home, thus making them more at risk to criminal opportunities. However, the trend developed well before the women's liberation movement came on stream in Canada. One of the few obvious correlations to the increased levels of female offences was the changing values and attitudes sweeping Canadian society in the 1960s and 1970s.

The changes in society brought many new expectations, pressures, and stresses for women. The female labour force participation rate went from 26.7 per cent in 1959 to 40.9 per cent by 1975. Over the same period the percentage of married women in the work force increased from 17.9 per cent to 38.4 per cent. Between 1961 and 1982 the divorce rate went from thirty-six per 100,000 of population to 286 per 100,000. The high divorce rate in particular has brought dramatic changes to women's lives, leaving many of them on their own to bring up children as single parents and to provide economic support. In 1981, out of approximately 713,815 Canadians raising children on their own, 589,435 of them were women. The proportion of children being brought up in single-parent families went from one in eighteen in 1961 to one in nine in 1976. How much these stresses on women had to do with the increase in crime is difficult to say, however, it is a correlation that is worth noting. Table 37 affords a more detailed look at the trends in charges against adult females through the 1960s and 1970s.

As the table shows, recorded charges against adult females rose in practically every category of offence between 1963 and 1979, and for certain offences by significant numbers. One area suggesting that not only was the level of crime going up but that patterns were also changing is violent crime, including murder, attempted murder, rape, indecent assault, wounding, inflicting bodily harm, assaults against the police, other categories of assaults, and robbery. In 1963 women accounted for about 4.7 per cent of adults charged in this group. By 1979 females made up 9 per cent of the adults charged. Taking the offences listed in Table 37 for comparison, women were charged at the rate of about 483.9 per 100,000 population of females fifteen years of age and above in 1963 and 939.5 per 100,000 in 1979.

The progressive movement of women into work outside the home and the changing Canadian society were accompanied by increased levels of female crime as well as by sporadic examples of offences that were unusual for women. One of the highest-profile cases of stock manipulation to be prosecuted in Canada in the 1960s involved a female mining promoter by the name of Viola MacMillan. She used a number of accounts to trade on the Toronto Stock Exchange and in July of 1964 she instructed her broker to sell from one of her accounts 244,000 shares that she owned in a company called Golden Arrow. The problem was that the purchaser of the shares was also one of her companies. Such a practice was known as "wash trading" and was illegal because it gave a false impression of market demand and

Table 37
Trends in Charges against Adult Females, 1963-79

Offences	1963	1967	1971	1975	1979
Capital and non-capital murder	14	15	38	61	58
Attempted murder	4	6	33	53	80
Manslaughter	1	4	5	10	6
Rape	–	–	5	3	16
Other sexual offenses	28	37	31	41	45
Wounding	53	75	106	187	267
Assaults (not indecent)	763	1,001	1,779	2,702	3,519
Robbery	95	124	217	398	429
Breaking and entering	238	316	639	1,098	1,665
Theft – motor vehicle	93	127	231	458	610
Theft over $200	–	–	–	947	1,754
Theft over $50	605	940	1,523	–	–
Theft $200 and under	–	–	–	17,426	23,834
Theft $50 and under	2,848	5,091	10,166	–	–
Having stolen goods	247	335	658	1,056	1,519
Frauds	907	1,191	2,475	3,954	6,632
Prostitution	924	1,487	1,595	2,372	921
Gaming and betting	159	248	231	187	118
Offensive weapons	53	118	178	352	516
Other Criminal Code[1]	3,326	3,988	4,864	7,120	10,159
Federal statutes[2]	1,110	1,891	1,184	1,550	2,297
Narcotic Control Act	169	376	–	3,829	–
Food and Drug Act	8	5	–	463	–
Addicting opiate-like drugs	–	–	237	–	449
Cannabis	–	–	1,143	–	4,259
Controlled drugs	–	–	88	–	136
LSD	–	–	162	–	–
Provincial statutes	15,574	19,382	15,209	17,537	23,264
Municipal by-laws	3,594	5,833	5,286	2,960	4,307

1. Except traffic.
2. Except traffic, Narcotic Control Act, and Food and Drug Act.
SOURCE: Dominion Bureau of Statistics, Crime Statistics (Police),
Catalogue 85-205.

legitimate trading in the stock. The transfer was recorded on the exchange and the large sale generated considerable interest. Investor demand raised the price from twenty-five cents to fifty-eight cents per share. As the price rose Viola MacMillan sold off her holdings at a substantial profit. She was subsequently convicted and spent a few months in jail.[60]

A not untypical example of embezzlement by a trusted, long-standing employee netted the woman responsible the sum of $15,268. She was in charge of filling orders for her company, some of which were paid for by customers in cash. Over a number of years she pocketed some of the cash and did not record the sales. She used the money to finance her son through medical school.[61]

The trend for female crime continued upward through the 1970s and 1980s. By 1988 females accounted for slightly over 17 per cent of all charges against adults for Criminal Code violations. The largest single category continued to be theft, at about 39.2 per cent, followed by fraud at about 13.8 per cent, and then crimes of violence at 12.7 per cent. In 1987 adult females – those nineteen and older – accounted for approximately 839 charges per 100,000 females. The higher age base in 1987 reflects the changes that came with the Young Offenders Act in 1984, which raised the age of young offenders to the uniform limit of eighteen years of age in all provinces.

Criminal statistics are useful trend indicators but it is quite likely that women commit more crimes than ever get documented. The perpetrators of certain types of crime favoured by women, such as theft, fraud, and prostitution-related offences, are often not caught so there is no way of determining the real frequency of such crimes. Also, documentation of certain female crime can vary with the intensity and efficiency of law enforcement. Prostitution is an example of this phenomenon. In Montreal in 1944, police mounted a campaign against houses of prostitution and the resultant charges inflated female crime statistics for that year. The following year, without the same enthusiastic level of enforcement, arrest statistics dropped.[62] Prostitution has been shielded over the years by friendly police and politicians and in more recent times it has also masqueraded behind massage parlors, strip clubs, and escort agencies.

Theft is another crime committed by a high percentage of female offenders that frequently escapes notice. Certain businesses are reluctant to publicize theft or embezzlement on the part of their employees because public knowledge would reduce confidence among their customers and, consequently, business. Store managers confirm that shoplifting has reached epidemic proportions. Women in all economic strata shoplift, and an increasing number of incidents involve very bold theft. Employees report cases of women openly grabbing merchandise and physically forcing their way out of the store. Proprietors of carriage-trade clothing stores, jewellery stores, and antique shops recount theft by well-dressed and well-to-do people. In some instances women work in pairs or gangs to execute carefully planned thievery.

An additional category of crime that involves significant numbers of women is fraud. In 1976, 4,727 adult females were charged with fraud – 3,313 involving cheques, 254 involving credit cards, and 1,160 other types of fraud. In comparison, in 1988 a total of 9,988 adult females were charged with fraud – 5,886 involving cheques, 714 with credit cards, and 3,388 for other types of fraud. The nature of certain types of fraud makes the crime possible to hide so this is yet another category where the statistics give only a partial picture.

Among the many examples of female crimes that are underreported in statistics, drug offences rank high on the list. As we have seen, it was a problem of some proportion in the 1920s but appeared to have diminished in subsequent decades. The problem resurfaced at an unprecedented level in the 1960s and 1970s as women got caught up in the drug scene. Drug use was rampant on university and college campuses and it soon became widespread in all sectors of society, with women of all ages becoming users, abusers, and dealers. Before long, "soft" (e.g., cannabis) drug usage was followed by a growth in the market for hard drugs, and many women got caught up in the use of heroin and cocaine. Women using and selling drugs could be found in businesses, universities, and communes, on the streets of city slums, and in the homes of fashionable suburbs.

Women continue to commit drug offences in significant numbers. Statistics tend to minimize the problem but other evidence suggests that large numbers of women are involved with drugs. The watering spots of any city, social gatherings, the babies born addicted, and the number of female patients at drug rehabilitation centres all offer testimony to the extent of the problem.[63]

One of the biggest seizures of cocaine ever made in Nova Scotia was found in the possession of a woman in June, 1989. The police raided her apartment and discovered four pounds of the drug with an estimated value of $180,000.[64] A survey carried out in 1989 on 1,100 adults in Ontario by the Addiction Research Foundation of Toronto discovered that increasing numbers of women in the eighteen-to-twenty-nine age group were using alcohol and drugs. At the same time, use among men was either stabilizing or dropping in certain categories, such as cannabis use.[65] Drug usage has been shown to be present in a wide variety of crimes, such as theft, fraud, prostitution, and shoplifting. It is not uncommon that women arrested for other than drug offences are found be be substance users. A test done on 248 women in a Montreal medium-security prison in 1989 revealed that 130 of them had used drugs intravenously in the year before they were jailed. Also, 14.6 per cent of the drug users tested positive for the AIDS virus.[66]

Another dimension of recent female lawbreaking is the evidence that women are continuing to branch out into a wider variety of crimes in growing numbers. Any casual sampling of Canadian newspapers and magazines turns up numerous examples. In 1981 Yolanda Macmillan pleaded guilty to a charge of conspiracy to commit fraud by being involved in the drafting of a phony will to a $3 million estate.[67] In more recent years she gained notoriety for her involvement with the now deceased sports figure Harold Ballard and her disputes with Ballard's family.

Illegal stock manipulations are another type of fraud that has attracted more women in recent years. In March of 1989 a British Columbia woman pleaded guilty to being a party, with her husband, to one of the biggest stock frauds in the province's history. They helped to manipulate the stock of a New York-based insurance company on the Vancouver Stock Exchange. As a result of their deceit the price rose from 20 cents in January, 1985, to $77 in 1986. The stock was delisted when the irregularities were discovered and about $172 million in stock certificates became worthless. The woman and her husband made an estimated net profit of $866,000 on the venture. The husband was sentenced to three years in prison and fined $300,000, while his wife was fined $200,000 and sentenced to one year in jail.[68]

Frauds against insurance companies have become increasingly popular in recent years. Here again women are well represented. One recently uncovered scheme involved a mixed group of women and men. They were staging automobile accidents with each other and then filing for damages with their respective insurance companies. Frauds against insurance companies are so common in some communities that they have resulted in much higher policy rates in those particular areas.[69]

Smuggling rings set up to bring illegal immigrants into Canada have done a thriving business in recent years, and this is yet another enterprise that has attracted women. In April of 1989 an international gang based in Vancouver was uncovered and its four B.C. members, including one woman, were charged. The gang had been operating at least since mid-1987 and was arranging for the illegal immigrants to continue on into the United States.[70]

One of the few females apprehended for arms smuggling was arrested in May, 1989. A Vancouver woman, she and her husband were charged with conspiring to smuggle over $1 billion worth of military equipment to Iran. They were also charged with laundering money. Police alleged that the couple planned to transport the military hardware to Canada, shipped as spare parts, and then on to Europe and Iran. The woman was a full partner in the scheme, including inspecting the armaments being considered for purchase.[71]

Even prostitutes are expanding their criminal endeavours. In Vancouver organized groups have been preying on tourists. One director of a security firm said that the prostitutes operate in groups and move from hotel to hotel and from city to city. They are well organized and sophisticated, carrying two-way radios and knockout drops. In one case two male tourists were robbed of $4,000 by two prostitutes working a major Vancouver hotel. In another case a man was drugged by a prostitute and robbed of over $2,000 in cash and jewellery. A common method used by prostitutes involves one going to a man's hotel, leaving the door unlocked, and then suggesting that her customer take a shower with her. While they are occupied the woman's accomplice enters the room and steals the customer's money.[72]

In other areas of crime, women are becoming increasingly more involved.

Table 38

Abused Children, by Gender and Alleged Perpetrator, Nova Scotia, 1983-87

Alleged Perpetrator	1983 M	1983 F	1984 M	1984 F	1985 M	1985 F	1986 M	1986 F	1987 M	1987 F
Mother	14	14	12	9	9	13	14	20	13	11
Father	8	18	25	37	21	37	24	39	21	32
Both parents	–	–	–	–	4	2	3	–	–	–
Stepfather	1	3	3	15	11	22	4	28	6	20
Stepmother	–	–	–	1	–	–	–	1	1	1
Sibling	2	4	1	6	5	17	4	7	–	7
*Mother's common-law spouse/boy friend	–	–	7	9	1	10	10	6	7	14
*Father's common-law spouse/girl friend	–	–	–	–	–	1	–	–	–	–
*Relative	–	–	2	16	5	22	9	35	5	26
*Foster parent/adoptive parent	–	–	–	1	–	2	6	1	3	7
*Babysitter/caretaker	–	–	–	1	–	2	6	1	3	7
*Identity unknown	–	–	1	7	5	9	3	11	7	6
Other	12	19	16	17	11	24	10	23	8	13

*Data not sorted for 1983.

SOURCE: Nova Scotia Child Abuse Register, 1983-87.

Child abuse is a case in point. It is frequently assumed that males monopolize this category of offence, but as Table 38 illustrates, it is a crime also committed by significant numbers of women.

Of the incidents of abuse recorded in the Nova Scotia Child Abuse Register for the years 1983-87, women were the perpetrators in 133 cases. In addition, women were involved with their husbands in nine cases. Also, sixty-eight of the offences were committed by babysitters or caretakers, some of whom were undoubtedly women. In 202 of the incidents, no perpetrator was identified. It is also possible that some of them were women. The incidents for which the sex of the perpetrator was identified as a woman, either alone or with her husband, accounted for 13.6 per cent of the total. Over half of the children in the register had also been abused prior to the reported incident.

There is no way of knowing how much child abuse actually goes on or under what particular circumstances it takes place. Cases that have come to light involved both married and single women and women who are living in common-law arrangements. Abuse takes place both inside and outside the family and much of it is sexual, in some cases carried on by women. One example was that of a forty-eight-year-old elementary school teacher who was convicted of having sexual intercourse with a minor. At the trial the victim, a nine-year-old boy, claimed that the woman had performed sexual acts with him at least eleven times over an extended period.[73]

The federal *Report of the Committee on Sexual Offences Against Children and Youths*, released in 1984, offered examples of the broad range of sexual abuse to which children are subjected. One case documented how a young girl was victimized by both her father and her mother. The father sexually abused his daughter and the mother, who was a part-time prostitute, forced the child to work with her. On one occasion when the child was eleven years old the mother put her in the cabin of a ship and allowed nine or ten members of the crew to have sex with her. The child was paid for her services in liquor, which she in turn had to hand over to her father.[74]

One of the most disturbing incidents of child abuse by a female in recent Canadian history took place in Nova Scotia in 1982. The victim was four-year-old Teddy MacHielsen and the abuser was twenty-six year old Coleen Gottschall, a live-in babysitter and friend of the boy's father. Teddy's mother was killed in an automobile accident when he was nine months old, after which he was shunted around among three or four families until eventually being taken in by an aunt. After living with the woman for two years Teddy's father decided to take the boy, who moved in with his father on May 24, 1982. At that time he was healthy, weighed over fifty pounds, and was described as a normal, happy child. Three months later, on August 23, Teddy was taken to the hospital – bruised, battered, partially scalded, and unconscious. He was emaciated, and his weight was down to about thirty-five pounds. Teddy MacHielsen died shortly after being admitted and Coleen Gottschall was charged with second-degree murder.

Witnesses at the trial testified that soon after the child came under Gottschall's care they noticed cuts, bruises, and burn marks on the boy's body. The most vivid evidence was given by the woman's brother. He reported that on one occasion he saw his sister straddled over the boy, beating him on the head with her fists. Another time he saw the handle of a large plastic spoon shoved up the child's anus. He also testified having seen his sister cover her finger with a cloth and insert it into the boy's anus. On more than one occasion she placed him in a bath of scalding water and then punched him when he resisted.

The brother testified that the day before the boy's death his sister was giving Teddy a bath when he heard screaming in the bathroom. The brother rushed in and found his sister hitting the boy on the side of the head. She then left the child in the bathroom. A few minutes later he came into the kitchen and Gottschall kicked him in the eye, causing him to fall into the side of the cupboard and strike his head. The brother then put the boy to bed but a few minutes later discovered his sister straddled over the child on the floor, hitting him repeatedly with clenched fists. Teddy went unconscious and was put to bed. The next morning he was still out cold and an ambulance was called.

The pathologist who did the autopsy testified that the boy's body bore "strangulation marks on the neck, bruises and contusions on the scrotum, penis, face, legs, stomach, back and arms, and a dilated anus." He said he also found acute hemorrhaging in the head area and the brain pushed down in the skull. Another doctor testified that it was the worst case of child abuse that he had seen since he started medical practice. After five hours of deliberation the jury found Coleen Gottschall guilty as charged and the judge sentenced her to life imprisonment.[75]

Although women seem to be moving into less traditional crimes in larger numbers the majority of offences committed by females continue to fall into familiar categories, as Table 39 suggests. Females were charged with 9.9 per cent of assault charges, 9.9 per cent of charges for all crimes of violence, 12.9 per cent of property crime charges, 17.2 per cent of Criminal Code charges, and 14.6 per cent of charges for all offences. The relative distribution of charges in 1988 remained similar to the pattern for previous years. Criminal Code charges continued to outnumber other categories and shoplifting accounted for 33.6 per cent of those. Crimes of violence ranked next at 23.4 per cent of the total, followed by prostitution at 7.5 per cent of Criminal Code charges against females.

Over the longer period the most significant change has been in the number of women charged with theft. This category of crime experienced a steady increase in the percentage of charges laid against women. The rise started in the early 1960s and has continued to the present. In 1962 females accounted for 8.9 per cent of all reported charges against adults for theft. The female share of charges rose to 24.7 per cent in 1975, to 27 per cent in 1984, and to 29.8 per cent in 1988. The number of males charged with theft increased sharply over the same period but the rate of increase in charges against females was higher.

In recent years the only other significant change has been in the number of women charged with murder, attempted murder, and assault. In 1983 the rate per 100,000 of the female population aged nineteen and over reported charged with those offences was 60.9. In 1988 the rate had risen to 86.7, an increase of 42.4 per cent. In 1983 charges against females for those crimes accounted for 8.8 per cent of all Criminal Code charges against women and in 1988 they accounted for 11.8 per cent.

It appears, then, that both the incidence and the rate of female crime have risen over the past few decades. There have also been some small shifts in the nature of offences, with more women committing acts of violence in recent years and growing evidence of a greater involvement with drugs. The broad range of offences and the perpetration of some very serious crimes suggest that women are as adept at lawbreaking as are men – if they choose to break the law. Fortunately, when they do the majority of female offences continue to be non-violent, minor in nature, and at a level well below that for the male population.

Table 39
Police Reported Crime by Offence, Canada, 1988

Offences	Male	Female
Homicide		
First degree murder	207	17
Second degree murder	174	33
Manslaughter	28	7
Infanticide	–	3
TOTAL	409	60
Attempted murder	598	92
Assault		
Aggravated sexual assault	194	8
Sexual assault with weapon	435	17
Sexual assault	7,640	111
Assault, level 1	43,710	5,324
Assault with weapon or causing bodily harm, level 2	15,149	1,751
Aggravated assault, level 3	1,508	239
Unlawfully causing bodily harm	2,043	167
Discharge firearm with intent	74	3
Police	3,458	582
Other peace/public officers	416	36
Other assaults	1,294	134
TOTAL	75,921	8,372
Other sexual offences	943	27
Abduction		
Abduction of person under 14	58	25
Abduction of person under 16	20	–
Abduction contravening custody order	80	47
Abduction, no custody order	46	19
TOTAL	204	91
Robbery		
Firearms	1,502	92
Other offensive weapons	1,543	141
Other robbery	2,397	302
TOTAL	5,442	535
Crimes of violence: TOTAL	83,517	9,177
Breaking and Entering		
Business premises	12,988	469
Residence	18,767	1,094
Other break and enter	3,941	138
TOTAL	35,696	1,701
Theft – motor vehicles		
Automobiles	5,416	459
Trucks	2,187	109
Motorcycles	539	8
Other motor vehicles	768	20
TOTAL	8,910	596
Theft over $1,000		
Bicycles	51	3
From motor vehicles	820	25
Shoplifting	326	158

Table 39 (continued)

Other thefts over $1,000	4,308	838
TOTAL	5,505	1,024
Theft $1,000 and under		
Bicycles	903	74
From motor vehicles	7,294	297
Shoplifting	30,433	24,237
Other thefts $1,000 and under	17,465	3,685
TOTAL	56,095	28,293
Have stolen goods	12,100	1,635
Fraud		
Cheques	14,959	5,886
Credit cards	2,771	714
Other frauds	9,773	3,388
TOTAL	27,503	9,988
Property crimes: TOTAL	145,809	43,237
Prostitution		
Bawdy house	214	373
Procuring	130	162
Other prostitution	4,835	4,910
TOTAL	5,179	5,445
Gaming and betting		
Betting house	25	2
Gaming house	791	77
Other gaming and betting offences	397	105
TOTAL	1,213	184
Offensive weapons		
Explosives	65	8
Prohibited weapons	1,397	71
Restricted weapons	1,169	379
Other offensive weapons	4,479	379
TOTAL	7,110	542
Other Criminal Code Offences		
Arson	773	141
Bail violations	26,793	3,967
Counterfeiting currency	94	17
Disturbing the peace	8,082	1,122
Escape custody	1,424	117
Indecent acts	2,740	227
Kidnapping	299	22
Public morals	107	9
Obstruct public peace officer	4,932	845
Prisoner unlawfully at large	3,202	251
Trespass at night	988	20
Mischief (prop. damage) over $1,000	3,923	356
Mischief (prop. damage) $1,000 and under	16,191	1,680
Other Criminal Code offences	34,702	4,821
TOTAL	104,250	13,595
Other crimes: TOTAL	117,752	19,766
Criminal Code: TOTAL	347,078	72,180

Table 39 (continued)

Heroin		
Possession	185	82
Trafficking	237	46
Importation	30	12
TOTAL	452	140
Cocaine		
Possession	3,582	662
Trafficking	3,071	546
Importation	82	20
TOTAL	6,735	1,228
Other drugs		
Possession	793	270
Trafficking	377	108
Importation	4	–
TOTAL	1,174	378
Cannabis		
Possession	18,737	1,928
Trafficking	5,519	801
Importation	142	44
Cultivation	458	128
TOTAL	24,856	2,901
Controlled drugs (trafficking)	166	42
Restricted drugs		
Possession	424	58
Trafficking	649	73
TOTAL	1,073	131
Drugs: TOTAL	34,456	4,820
Other federal statutes		
Bankruptcy Act	129	15
Canada Shipping Act	2,432	109
Customs Acts	201	29
Excise Act	48	4
Immigration Act	612	112
Other federal statute offences	4,281	666
TOTAL	7,703	935
Federal statutes: TOTAL	42,159	5,755
Provincial statutes		
Liquor Acts	173,062	19,161
Securities Act	54	13
Other provincial statutes	46,293	6,277
TOTAL	219,409	25,451
Municipal by-laws	25,606	5,230
All offences: TOTAL	634,252	108,616

SOURCE: Statistics Canada, Canadian Crime Statistics 1988, Catalogue 85-205.

SUMMARY

Women have committed crime in Canada since the earliest days of settlement. Some were involved in serious crimes such as murder, violent assault, armed robbery, major thefts, fraud, arson, and the torture of children.

However, the bulk of female offences were minor in nature, consisting of theft, drunkenness, and prostitution. The pattern of female crime was established early and maintained a remarkable consistency for a long period of time as settlement expanded and the population grew.

While women from all walks of life committed crime under a great variety of economic and social conditions, in the pioneer period much of the recorded female crime was committed by an underclass of women who were alcoholic, poor, dissolute, and, in the language of the day, debauched. Many of them survived by petty thievery and prostitution. They accounted for a high percentage of the people who passed through the jails of seaports and the larger urban centres. Some broke the law as a means of getting food and shelter in the winter months. Others were put in jail to protect them from the dangers of the tavern-infested streets.

In addition to the ongoing street crime there were always women who were one-time offenders. They killed or committed some other criminal act out of a particular circumstance, and for most this was their only brush with the law. The majority of women lived in protected home environments and were neither attracted to crime nor had much opportunity for lawbreaking.

Although statistics suggest that crime rates were low, it is also possible that much female crime was unreported or undetected. Many of the offences commonly committed by women, such as abortion, infanticide, drunkenness, prostitution, and petty theft, were also by nature easily hidden. Therefore, it is probable that women broke the law in greater numbers than were ever apprehended by the police. However, the incidence of hidden crime would have had to be quite high to have appreciably changed the level of female offences. Also, if hidden crime was in the same relative proportions to known offences, it would still mean that most of it was minor in nature.

Female convictions as a percentage of all convictions dropped significantly toward the end of the nineteenth century and remained low through the first half of this century. Over the period, fluctuations and changes in the incidence of certain crimes accompanied societal upheavals, such as the two world wars and the liberalization of the 1920s, but for the most part the level of female crime remained low and offences predominantly were minor in nature.

The social and cultural revolution of the 1960s and 1970s was accompanied by a dramatic increase in female crime rates. The pace of the increase subsided but the general rise in crime levels continued through the 1980s. While the bulk of the increase came in traditional offence categories, violent crimes and especially drug offences rose significantly. Also, it appears that some women are branching out more into what might be described as traditional male territory, though not necessarily in large numbers.

Women continue to break the law in much smaller numbers than men and the bulk of female offences still fall into the minor crime category. Therefore on a comparative basis female crime is not seen to be nearly the problem that the male offender poses. Like many things, however, reality is in the eyes of the beholder. To the victim all crime is serious and it is probably little consolation to storekeepers that much female crime consists of shoplifting. For those who are the victims of violence and other serious crimes it is not much consolation that females are not major offenders in this category.

Contemporary female crime is a more complex phenomenon than in the past, as more and more women from diverse backgrounds try their hand at a wider variety of illegal acts. At the beginning of the last decade of this century one of the more critical aspects of female lawbreaking is drug offences, which quite often lead to spinoffs such as theft, armed robbery, break and enter, prostitution, and addicted babies. It now remains to be seen if after over three centuries of comparatively low levels of crime committed by women the drug epidemic that plagues contemporary society will be the catalyst that will significantly increase the number of female offenders.

PART TWO

The Treatment
of Criminals
in Canada

CHAPTER 7

▼

The European Legacy and Pioneer Punishments

Robert François Damiens, on January 5, 1757, made an attempt on the life of King Louis XV of France but he failed, managing to inflict only a slight knife wound on the monarch. For attempting to murder the King, Damiens was sentenced to be taken in a cart to the front of the Church of Paris to make the *amende honorable*. He was to wear

> nothing but a shirt, holding a torch of burning wax weighing two pounds, then, in the said cart, to the Place de Grève, where, on a scaffold that will be erected there, the flesh will be torn from his breasts, arms, thighs, and calves with red-hot pincers, his right hand, holding the knife with which he committed the said parricide, burnt with sulphur, and, on those places where the flesh will be torn away, poured molten lead, boiling oil, burning resin, wax and sulphur melted together and then his body drawn and quartered by four horses and his limbs and body consumed by fire, reduced to ashes and his ashes thrown to the winds.[1]

The unfortunate Damiens remained alive and conscious throughout his ordeal. When the final stage of punishment was reached the four horses used proved inadequate for the job of quartering and two more were added but even all six needed assistance. To enable the horses to pull the body apart it was necessary to sever the sinews and joints.

The punishments meted out by the French state reflected the twin considerations of revenge and deterrence. Rooted far back in history, the concept of revenge was summed up in the formula "an eye for an eye and a tooth for

293

a tooth." As civilization advanced the concept of deterrence gradually evolved and contributed to the introduction of a range of harsh punishments. When Christianity became dominant in Western Europe punishment for crime was also influenced by the theological teachings of the Church on sin, penance, and remorse. Consequently, punishment reflected cumulative influences and consisted of a number of elements, including a ritual, admission of guilt and remorse, and public chastisement as penance, revenge, and deterrence. Thus Damiens was made to apologize to God and man for his sin and this was done ritualistically before the church door and carrying a lighted candle. His punishment was administered in public so as to strike terror into the hearts of any potential lawbreakers. For the offender the ordeal was both revenge for the state and penance for the sinner.

The treatment of criminals in France in the seventeenth and eighteenth centuries included the use of torture, branding, galley service, the iron collar, the pillory, the whip, exile, hanging, and breaking on the wheel. The use of torture to extract a confession was based on another long-standing Christian practice of oracular confession. To prove his sorrow, the prisoner was expected to confess freely the details of his sin, with the admission being a prerequisite for forgiveness. Before criminals were punished, it was important to authorities that they confess to their crimes as a sign of repentance and, as well, a justification for the punishment. In cases meriting the death penalty, admission of the crime was considered almost mandatory. It was a small step from this belief to employing the means necessary to extract a confession and feeling justified in doing so. Thus torture was employed to make the guilty person admit to the crime.

Next to hanging the most dreaded punishment was sentence to galley service. Galleys were large fighting ships powered by a combination of sails and oars. The oars were manned by criminals sentenced to serve on the ships as punishment for their crimes. The average galley employed 300 to 500 rowers who were arranged on different levels, seated five to a bench, and chained in position. They were given little clothing, exposed to extremes of weather, and frequently whipped to make them produce more speed. In a sea battle they suffered the most. They were whipped raw, and often slaughtered in their seats or sunk with the ship. Galleys were eventually made obsolete by the sailing ships and went out of use in the French navy by 1748.

For crimes that did not merit the death sentence branding was one of the most widely used punishments. The guilty party was branded by a red-hot iron on the right shoulder or the fleshy part of the hand, with various letters used to denote the crime. Thus, the criminal was both punished for the offence and marked so that others would know that the person had broken the law. The brand also made it possible to identify a previous offender. The second conviction would bring a much severer penalty, usually death.

Penalties in seventeenth- and eighteenth-century France were usually carried out shortly after sentence, so little use was made of jails or prisons for detention. Judicial procedures were straightforward. The accused was tried by a judge without benefit of counsel, and since punishments were at the magistrates' discretion there was great lack of uniformity. The requirements of reasonable evidence, certain guilt, or sanctions appropriate to the crime were of little concern. As we will see later, penal reformers of the day considered the entire system to be characterized by caprice, injustice, and cruelty.

The English judicial system, in the context of the treatment of criminals, laboured under shortcomings as bad as those in France. In 1760 the famous jurist, Sir William Blackstone, listed 160 offences in English law punishable by death, and by the early years of the nineteenth century the number was over 200. A person could be put to death for very minor crimes such as stealing food. Alternatively, a variety of devices were used to punish, maim, humiliate, shackle, and mark criminals. They included the stocks, the pillory, whipping, branding, and public punishment. The pillory was made of two pieces of wood mounted on a post, with holes for head and hands, and could be found in the market areas of many communities throughout England. People would be placed in it for hours, during which time passersby could insult them and throw anything from rotten vegetables to sewage. The punishment was both painful and humiliating. The stocks were a similar device except that they locked the legs rather than the hands and head and the victim was in a seated position instead of standing.

The English used the whip for punishment more frequently than the French. Like the pillory, whipping posts were common sights in public places in villages and towns across England. Their presence was calculated to be a constant reminder to potential criminals of the penalty for breaking the law and thereby served as a deterrence to crime. Obviously the psychology didn't always work. Offenders punished in this manner would be tied to the post, stripped to the waist, and flogged until the back was bloody. The weapon of choice was known as the "cat-o'-nine tails" because it was made of nine knotted cords or thongs of rawhide attached to a handle.

Another punishment popular with the English was deportation. People convicted of even minor crimes were deported to the colonies as a means of permanently ridding the mother country of undesirables. Sometimes criminals were sent to the British colonies in America – until the American Revolution closed the door. The government then started a penal colony in New South Wales in 1787. Exiles were deprived of all their possessions, shipped out of the country, and put in penal servitude. If they returned before their sentence expired, or in some cases if they returned at all, they could be put to death.[2]

Unlike the French, English criminals had the benefit of the jury system as well as clearly defined legal procedures. However, there was a lack of uniformity in sentencing and some judges took delight in handing down particularly harsh punishments. One of the most notorious was Francis Jeffreys, appointed to the office of chief justice of Chester in 1680. Jeffreys tried those involved in the Duke of Monmouth's rebellion against King James II in 1685. On his orders at least 320 were put to death and hundreds more were exiled into servitude in Barbados. Many of those punished were only remotely connected with the rebellion. Jeffreys's sentences were so severe that the trials of the rebels became known in history as the "Bloody Assizes." Jeffreys was at his worst when sentencing women. The unfortunate Alice Lisle, a lady from a good family, took pity on two hungry rebels and gave them shelter, not knowing that she was harbouring fugitives. Jeffreys sentenced her to be burned at the stake but mercifully allowed her to be beheaded instead. On another occasion he sentenced a woman to be whipped, instructing the hangman to "scourge her till her blood runs down."[3]

PUNISHMENT FOR CRIME IN NEW FRANCE

This legacy of harsh and cruel punishments was carried to the New World by the immigrants from France and England. In New France the same laws that governed the district of Paris, known as the Coutume de Paris, prevailed. In English Canada the laws and judicial system of England were put in place, including the death penalty for very minor crimes. In both jurisdictions the extreme penalties of the respective mother countries were put to early use. As we have seen, shortly after the founding of the first permanent settlement by Samuel de Champlain, a teenage girl was put to death for theft. In English Canada in 1749 permanent living quarters hadn't even been constructed in Halifax when Governor Cornwallis hanged one of his crew members and put the corpse on display.[4]

Penalties in New France included hanging, galley servitude, exile, breaking on the wheel, branding, flogging, the iron collar, the pillory, mutilation, fines, confiscation of property, and incarceration.[5] As was the case in France, accused were subject to the whim and fancy of the magistrates since they appeared without the benefit of counsel. Their rights were entrusted to the judges, so the latter were in effect both prosecutors and defence, and if the accused was found guilty, the penalty was left to the sole discretion of the presiding official.[6] The ritual that accompanied punishment in France was also prescribed in the colony. When possible the practice was to administer the penalty at or near the place where the crime had been committed. This was done to serve as an example and deterrence to other inhabitants of the district. In most cases sentences were carried out immediately after the trial so there was little use made of detention facilities.[7]

The more elaborate rites were reserved for those sentenced to death. The convicted person would first be taken to the front of the local church to ask forgiveness of God and the King. The hanging would then take place, following which the remains would be put on public display. The deceased's property would be confiscated and a fine levied. Jacques Begeon, who killed his neighbour in 1668, was put through just such a ritual in the town of Quebec. He was sentenced to be tortured and then taken to the door of the parish church dressed only in a nightshirt, a rope around his neck, and carrying a torch. On his knees he was to ask forgiveness of God and the King and justice for the crimes that he had committed. He was then to be hung on the gallows in the marketplace of upper town, after which his right arm and head were to be cut off and placed on public display, mounted on a stake. In addition to this, he was given a heavy fine, part of which was to be used to have prayers said for the soul of his victim.[8]

On occasion even the trial process could be an ordeal for a person accused of crime. If a preliminary investigation turned up evidence against a particular individual, that person was arrested, charged, and held in jail incommunicado. The person would be put to the *question ordinaire*, that is, interrogated about the crime. Other people purporting to have knowledge about the affair would also be questioned and sometimes faced by the one on trial. This process could be repeated and could last for prolonged periods, during which the accused was kept in confinement. Finally, if the evidence warranted and the suspect refused to admit to the crime, the person could be put to the *question extraordinaire*, that is, tortured. The usual practice was to tie boards to the shins of the accused, insert wedges, and strike the boards with a hammer, thus crushing the bones. After each blow was delivered the question would be put until, at length, an admission of guilt was obtained or the interrogators decided to end the proceedings.[9]

Punishments were handed out for every type of infraction, including offences against religion. For swearing, a person could be fined or put in detention for a short time. Repeaters could be put in an iron collar for public ridicule while chronic offenders could have their lower lip cut.[10] People detained in jail complained of being given a diet of only bread and water and were subjected to unhealthy conditions such as poor ventilation, humidity, and cold. Sometimes prisoners were kept in ankle irons. Where jails did exist they were usually makeshift facilities and the conditions sometimes took a heavy toll on the health of the detainees. In the summer the quarters were humid and damp and in winter extremely cold since they were unheated. In 1686 Governor Denonville reported having to cut the feet off certain prisoners in Quebec because they had developed gangrene from the cold. In 1699 the prison in Montreal was virtually unusable because the wooden walls had rotted out.[11]

There was little uniformity to sentencing and severe punishments were handed out for both major and minor crimes. At least forty-seven *Canadiens* were sentenced to galley servitude in the navy during the French regime for crimes ranging from murder to counterfeiting and theft.[12] One man caught thieving at the Hôtel Dieu, when Jean Talon was intendant, was sentenced to be branded with the fleur-de-lis, exposed four hours in the pillory, and then to do three years' galley service. Another convicted of larceny was sentenced to be whipped and to serve for three years in the galleys. Both men escaped and were subsequently caught. One was hanged while the other was whipped, marked with the fleur-de-lis, and put in prison in irons. Among those condemned to serve in the galley was a man convicted of rape. He was sentenced to a nine-year term. In contrast, another man convicted of the same crime was sentenced to hang and executed two days later.[13]

The crime of theft incurred punishments ranging from incarceration to hanging. Sometimes if a thief escaped the noose on the first conviction a second offence brought the death penalty. One such criminal in 1665 was branded the first time with the fleur-de-lis and put in the yoke for public ridicule. Another conviction for theft the following year resulted in his right ear being cut off and again spending time in the yoke. The same year the man was again arrested, along with a companion, this time for a different crime. His luck ran out and his third conviction so exasperated authorities that he was sentenced to be hanged. His accomplice was forced to stand at the foot of the gallows with a rope around his neck while the sentence was carried out. He was then sent to prison and placed in ankle irons.[14]

Sometimes punishments for crime reflected the nature of the problem. For example, from time to time indentured servants took advantage of pioneer conditions to flee their domiciles and thus escape having to fulfil the terms of their contracts. To discourage this the authorities, in 1676, informed the public that the punishment for such an offence would be to put the offender in an iron collar. For a second offence the servant would be beaten with rods and branded with the fleur-de-lis.[15]

The treatment of crime and criminals in New France included some practices that were rather bizarre, judged by contemporary standards. For example, if a convicted offender managed to escape custody the penalty process would still be carried out at the designated time and in the prescribed manner as if the criminal were there. An early illustration of this practice happened in 1672 when a convicted murderer sentenced to be hanged escaped custody. The penalty was carried out in effigy. Many years later, in 1715, a young man of noble birth was accused of murder but fled to France before he could be tried. He was nevertheless declared guilty and, being a member of the aristocracy, had the right to have his head cut off instead of being hanged like an ordinary criminal. The decapitation ceremony was duly carried out just as if the guilty party were there to meet his fate. Meanwhile, back in France, the young man used his family connections to obtain a full pardon from King Louis XV.[16]

An equally unusual practice was set in motion when someone committed suicide. Taking one's life was considered to be a very grievous sin by the Church and condemned as a crime by the civil authority. When it happened the body of the deceased would be dragged through the streets and then hung by the feet on public display for twenty-four hours, after which it would be thrown in the river.[17] The punishments inflicted on representations of escaped criminals or on the corpses of suicides were symbolic of the state taking its revenge for the offence. Even though the guilty party was absent the macabre bit of theatre was calculated to achieve the other objective of the penal drama, which was to frighten the inhabitants away from crime.

While prescribed punishments for those who broke the law were cruel and harsh in the extreme, in practice they were often mitigated by the seigneurial courts, by the Sovereign Council, and on occasion by the intervention of the parish priests. In a manner somewhat similar to the great estates of the nobility in France, large land grants under seigneurial tenure were made during the settlement period in New France. The seigneurs were given certain feudal-style rights over the inhabitants on their land, which included judicial powers. In France such rights could be profitable, but not in the North American colony. In addition, settling legal matters was a nuisance so the judicial prerogative was not frequently exercised. When it was the process was very informal, with the seigneur hearing the case in his own home and working out a not too burdensome settlement. The parish priests had no official legal authority but that did not prevent them from intervening in a judicial capacity on occasion. Priests enjoyed considerable influence, and they did not hesitate to intervene when so inclined or called on to do so. Their judicial proceedings were quite informal and their settlements usually tempered justice with mercy.[18]

The Sovereign Council was first established by the King in 1647 after the government of France took over effective jurisdiction following the failed efforts of private companies to establish the colony on a firm footing. In 1663 the Council was stabilized within a more centralized system of government and henceforth was the ruling authority in the colony. The senior official was the governor, but the most important office for the day-to-day conduct of affairs was that of intendant. The first occupant of the office was Jean Talon, appointed in 1665. Among the administrative responsibilities of the intendant was the maintenance of law and order. These two chief officials were assisted by the Sovereign Council, which included the bishop, five councillors, an attorney-general, and a recording clerk, as well as the governor and intendant. Among the Council's prerogatives were passing legislation for governing the colony, acting as a court for civil and criminal cases, and also hearing appeals from the decisions of lower courts. All cases heard by a lower court for which death or severe corporal punishment was the sentence had to be reviewed by the Council.

When legal business came before the Council the attorney-general would submit his report and then withdraw. The matter would be opened for general discussion and each member given the opportunity to voice his opinion. The final decision was made by the intendant on the basis of the opinions expressed – no formal vote was taken. In the event that a council-lor was a friend or relative of an accused, or had any direct interest in the case, he was required to withdraw from the hearing. Also, an accused had the right to challenge a Council member who had any connection to the matter before him if he did not voluntarily withdraw. Consequently, it was sometimes difficult to muster the necessary numbers for a trial since five judges were required. To remedy the problem, in 1703 the membership of the Council was increased to twelve.[19]

The Sovereign Council frequently reduced the severity of penalties handed out by lower courts and sometimes set aside the verdict. For exam-ple, in 1690, Jean Haudecoeur was convicted in Montreal of murder. The judge ordered that his right hand be cut off in front of his victim's house, that he be beaten about the thighs, legs, and arms, and then broken on the wheel. The Council reduced his suffering prior to execution, allowing the man to be hanged before being put on the wheel.[20] In another case of a murder conviction by a Montreal court the Council undertook a thorough investigation and eventually set aside the verdict and ordered the man's name cleared. In 1754 Pierre Gouet was found guilty of theft and sentenced to the galleys for five years. On appeal, the Sovereign Council changed the sentence to six weeks in prison and service as an executioner. This was an unpopular job and Gouet asked for the post, knowing that it would help him get out of a very severe penalty.[21] Of twenty-nine cases of serious crime for which the person charged was subjected to the *question extraordinaire*, nineteen either had their original sentences reduced or were acquitted.[22]

A number of other considerations inherent in the administration of justice in New France also worked to make the system less severe. Debtors could not be imprisoned, nor could their property be confiscated. No legal fees could be charged for cases heard by the Sovereign Council. In 1717 a Council was set up at Louisbourg and no fees could be charged for its deliberations either. Minor civil cases could be dealt with by the intendant at Quebec without charge. Even in more serious cases, if both parties agreed they could be arbitrated by the intendant with the decision binding on both parties. Intendant Jacques Raudot claimed to have handled some 2,000 such cases in 1705. The Crown made a sincere effort to ensure that justice in New France was fair and equitable. In an effort to keep the costs of judicial procedures down so as not to disadvantage the poor, lawyers were not allowed to practise in the colony and strict controls were placed on fees. A schedule was established for the work of officials such as notaries, judges, and bailiffs, which kept the cost of court services very low.[23] As one observer of the society of New France described it, "Our Themis is prompt, and she does not bristle with fees, costs and charges."[24]

Even military justice, which was normally severe in the extreme, was mitigated by the realities of a pioneer country. This was especially true in Louisbourg. Between 1713 and 1758 the fortress played a key role in

France's North American defence system. Yet the garrison was always undermanned. Therefore, commanding officers were anxious to hold on to the troops they had. Partly for this reason they were inclined to treat military lawbreakers less harshly than was called for by the military code of discipline. This was a significant concession because the calibre of troops left something to be desired. For example, of those stationed at Louisbourg in 1752, approximately 26 per cent were guilty of desertion at some point in their careers. They were a motley collection, lacking in discipline, poorly trained, and given to drink. They frequently got into trouble for such infractions as brawling, drinking, swearing, and theft. The Code Militaire called for soldiers found guilty of theft to be put to death or sent to the galleys for life, while the punishment for fighting was left to the officers to determine. For showing up for duty drunk the Code Militaire prescribed a ride on the wooden horse. This was a narrow plank of wood to which legs were attached, giving it the semblance of a horse. The offender was forced to sit astride the contraption for long periods, sometimes with weights attached to his legs to increase the pain. When faced with infractions officers commonly handed out much lighter sentences than those prescribed. Short jail sentences, from a few days to a couple of months, were the usual penalties. Once in a while, for very serious crimes, a soldier would be shot, made to run the gauntlet, or ride the wooden horse.[25]

Notwithstanding the sometimes merciful application of the law in New France, there were many cases when authorities prescribed extremely cruel penalties and carried them out with full force. Sentences for capital crimes in particular could be carried out with an extra degree of cruelty, as Jean Baptiste Goyer found out when he was convicted of murder in 1752. Goyer broke into the house of a neighbour and when he was caught in the act wounded the man with a shot from his pistol and then finished him off with a knife. When the man's wife tried to come to his rescue Goyer stabbed her, too, and then beat her with a spade until she was dead. He then proceeded with the robbery. He was arrested and put to both the *questions ordinaire* and *extraordinaire*. He was sentenced to be put on a scaffold in the marketplace in Montreal and then to have his arms, legs, thighs, and kidneys broken. Afterwards he was to be placed on a wheel with his face turned upward to the sky and remain there until he died. When the sentence was fulfilled Goyer's body was buried and the grave marked with a red cross.[26]

JUSTICE IN ENGLISH CANADA

Criminal justice in English Canada was also based on the laws and judicial practices of the mother country. This included the arbitrary practices, such as an accused not being informed of the evidence, not being allowed to call witnesses, and not having the right to be represented by legal council, as well as the provision of harsh penalties for even minor offences. Hanging could be prescribed as the penalty for almost any crime, ranging from murder to petty theft and begging. Other penalties included flogging, branding, being placed in the stocks or the pillory, cutting off the ears, and fines. Sett Mathew Hurry of Annapolis Royal in Nova Scotia was convicted in August, 1734, of stealing a £3 note from James Thompson. Hurry was sentenced to be flogged fifty times on the bare back with the cat-o'-nine tails and to repay the money.[27] In early Halifax the tendency was to apply frequently the most extreme punishment – people were hanged for petty theft as well as murder, sometimes with little heed paid to the niceties of proof of guilt. On June 18, 1751, two men were hanged for the crime of house-breaking.[28] Hangings were always public spectacles, and the bodies usually were put on display as a grim reminder of the wages of sin. Hangings in those days were not carried out by a drop, which normally snaps the neck and brings on a quick death. Rather, the victim was simply strung up, and therefore the punishment did not always come to an instantaneous end.

Halifax, being a naval port and garrison town, naturally faced a considerable problem with unruly service personnel. The military in Halifax were not as lenient as their counterparts in Louisbourg. Some offenders were shot; others were flogged or sentenced to ride the wooden horse naked with weights attached to their feet. Seamen who were not hanged for their crimes were usually given a severe flogging. They would be conveyed from ship to ship in the harbour and whipped on the gangway of each vessel.[29]

Although the military dealt severely with their own for internal offences, they were much more lenient when it came to punishment for crimes committed against civilians, and civilians sometimes fared poorly before the courts after conflicts with the military. For example, one night in 1759 a number of officers, following a bout of drinking, went in search of female companionship but got the wrong house. Thinking they were being put off, they became aggressive and so frightened the householder that he fired his musket and killed one of the officers. The circumstances surrounding the affair were completely ignored and the man was summarily tried and hanged. In another incident of military-civilian confrontation, troops working on a road began using the stone fence from a nearby farm for fill. When the owner protested the soldiers killed him. The three accused were tried but all escaped punishment.[30]

Military officers were influential persons in a community like Halifax. The economic health of the town was strongly influenced by the presence of a garrison as well as by the comings and goings of troops and the British Navy. Consequently, if the officer corps intervened on behalf of an accused or if the accused was a member of the military, chances of acquittal or a light sentence were good. One such case involved an officer of Gorham's Rangers. The man was an immigrant Italian of noble birth known as Peter, Marquis of Contes and Gravina. In 1758 he was found guilty of attempted rape of a child under ten years of age. Rape was normally punishable by death but in this case the man was spared. Instead of hanging he was made to walk the Grand Parade with a paper outlining his crime hanging on his breast, jailed for three months, and fined £30. Even then the first part of his sentence was remitted by the Governor.[31]

Another example of the benefits of good connections involved Richard John Uniacke, whose grandfather was a cavalry commander for William of Orange at the Battle of the Boyne. Uniacke was accused of joining a group of rebels who supported the American Revolution and attempted to seize Fort Cumberland in 1776. When the uprising was quelled he was arrested and taken to Halifax for trial. Uniacke failed to appear for the hearing and disappeared. It was claimed that he was helped by some prominent Irish citizens of the town and by army officers who knew his family in Ireland. Uniacke never did come to trial. The matter was quietly dropped and the young man left for Ireland, where he studied law and was admitted to the bar. He subsequently returned to Nova Scotia and eventually became attorney-general of the province.[32]

As in New France, there were some novel practices associated with certain crimes, such as suicide. In one case the Governor ordered that a carpenter who hanged himself be denied the right to a Christian burial. As a further act of deterrence to other troubled individuals he also had a stake driven through the man's body.[33] Another departure from the norm involved the treatment of prisoners interned in Halifax during the Napoleonic Wars. In light of the times and the circumstances they were dealt with in a very generous and humane manner. Early in the century the British government purchased a small parcel of land in the Northwest Arm known as Melville Island as a site for a naval prison. Seamen captured on ships of war and merchant vessels were brought there during the war with France. Officers, instead of being incarcerated, were placed on parole and were allowed to live across the harbour in Dartmouth. Ordinary seamen were imprisoned, but some were allowed to hire out their services and went to work on farms or in other occupations, and some entered into domestic service. Even incarcerated prisoners benefited from benign treatment. They were given good accommodations, were well fed, and were allowed to work at crafts and to sell their products to the public. They made small items from bones and scrap materials and larger items, such as domino sets and ships' models. A section of the prison was set aside for the display of their work and townspeople were allowed to visit with them and buy their crafts. During visiting days the prisoners also put on entertainment and even ran games of chance. The inmates of the local jails probably wished they were treated half as well as the enemy prisoners.[34]

Unlike the policy applied to the wartime inmates, mitigation of punishment for Nova Scotia offenders was much more a matter of chance, especially in the early days of settlement. Many considerations influenced official judgements, which resulted in a great lack of uniformity in dealing with offenders. For example, in the spring of 1751 three men were sentenced to be hanged for felonies. Two of them were given a reprieve but the sentence was carried out for the third man. The level of crime at a given point in time affected the severity of penalties. During periods when there was an increase in crime officials tended to be stricter, especially in carrying out the death penalty. They believed that harsh punishment would reduce the level of crime.

On rare occasions a criminal survived by pleading "benefit of clergy." This was an ancient tradition that dated back to medieval times. In those days if one could show that he was a member of the clergy he could claim the right to trial in a Church court if accused of lawbreaking. Penalties were usually much lighter so there was an obvious advantage to being a clergyman. The privilege was also extended to clerks and eventually to anyone who could read and write. Since at one time few ordinary people, other than clergy, were educated, it was possible for anyone who could read and write to claim to be a cleric or in training for the religious life. Consequently, the test for claiming "benefit of clergy" was literacy.

Following the invention of the printing press, as more people learned to read and write, the privilege was extended generally as a means of mitigating the harsh punishments provided by the criminal code. People condemned to death for certain crimes could plea to have the sentence remitted by claiming benefit of clergy.[35] The practice became entrenched in custom and was put to use in the colonies for a time in both French and English Canada.

Although magistrates did not shrink from using the hangman, corporal punishment was the preferred sanction and was frequently prescribed for a variety of crimes. The common penalty for stealing fish from flakes was a fine amounting to fourfold the value of the fish, plus costs of prosecution, plus being whipped twenty times, put in the stocks for one hour, and fined treble damages plus the cost of prosecution. Anyone caught stealing in public places, such as the beach or the streets, could be required to make restitution in the amount of fourfold of the value of the stolen property, to be whipped in public, and to pay the costs of prosecution.[36] Detention was used chiefly for those awaiting trial or punishment but on rare occasions it was used as a sentence option or for those unable to pay fines. For example, Richard Mainwaring in January of 1751 was fined £100 in Halifax for pretending to be a clergyman and performing a marriage. He was put in jail until such time as he could pay the fine. Punishments were usually carried out immediately following the verdict. Branding was sometimes done in the courtroom at the time of conviction. A red-hot iron was used to impress the letter T on the fleshy part of the thumb of a thief's left hand. A second offence could bring the death penalty.

As settlement in the province of Nova Scotia increased and spread, the government attempted to provide better law and order by the appointment of magistrates and the provision of circuit courts. The experience of some of these early magistrates showed another side of criminal justice in pioneer days. While the populace undoubtedly feared their judgements, the magistrates on occasion encountered a defiant and hostile citizenry. A return, dated November, 1774, showed the population of Cape Breton Island as being approximately 1,500. Governor Legge reported that the justice of the peace was often interfered with in carrying out his duties. He complained that the citizens were "in general such a lawless rabble that he is in continual apprehension of danger whenever he puts the laws in execution."[37]

The nature of the people in early times had a significant impact on the treatment of criminals. As we have already seen, along with the hard-working and law-abiding settlers, the colonies attracted an unsavoury element who tended to gravitate to the larger centres. They were not inclined to seek a living by hacking down the forests and establishing farms. They were the flotsam and jetsam of their communities with no education, given to idleness and drink, and living by their wits: life was hard and consequently, for many of them, also cheap. Violence, assault, and even murder were of little significance to this underclass if the result was money or goods that could buy them some temporary pleasure. They were designated as the rabble, the mob, the misfits in colonial communities.

Given the nature of the times and the hardships of a pioneer society, the so-called better classes were not always models of refinement. They were often uncouth, untutored, and rough in manners and demeanour. Fear and suspicion, bred by ignorance, abounded. Inhumanity came easily in such surroundings where the struggle for survival was a reality for all classes. Gentlemen resorted to duels to avenge insults while people in all ranks used fists, knives, and any other handy weapon to settle disputes. Liquor flowed freely, lubricating everything from social gatherings to judicial trials. Even men of the cloth engaged in buying and selling human beings. People attended hangings as they would the theatre, only they enjoyed the performance more. In short, the populace was still far short of being civilized, so it is little wonder that cruelty was so common.

Human beings who did not earn their way in such a society or who threatened social stability were given short shift. They were considered either dangerous or a nuisance, or both. It was widely held that the best way to deal with such so-called riff-raff was to get them out of the way. This sentiment was very much the motivation for the building of the early jails. Halifax was still in its embryonic stages of getting established when the justices of the peace, in 1752, petitioned the Governor and Executive Council to build a Bridewell. This was a name commonly used to refer to early jails and workhouses. The name came from the former royal palace at Bridewell, which in 1553 was given to the City of London by Edward VI to be used as a workhouse for the poor. The name was eventually applied to all workhouses and every county in England was required by law to have one.

Ultimately, the Bridewells became catch-alls, housing the indigent, sick, insane, and petty criminals. With the passage of time the Bridewells were used more and more as jails.[38]

Concerned about the increasing number of petty criminals appearing before them, the Halifax justices asked for a Bridewell, "to which such offenders might be committed and there employed in hard labour, and also be subject to such punishment as your Excellency & Honours shall think reasonable."[39] The justices were not motivated by considerations of reform. Rather, they wanted a place to get these people out of the way as well as a place of incarceration that could be used to punish minor offenders. The long-awaited Bridewell finally opened in 1758. It was to house "all disorderly and idle persons," such as "drunkards, persons of lewd behavior, vagabonds, runaways, stubborn servants and children," and persons who failed to support their families. The inmates of the Bridewell were to be put to work. It was the intention that the work of the inmates would earn sufficient money to cover the costs of the institution. Those guilty of idleness or disobedience were subject to such punishments as whipping, being fettered and shackled, and deprivation of food. A special keeper was assigned to oversee idiots, lunatics, and invalids.[40]

The Bridewell was constructed of wood and was thirty feet wide by forty feet long. The motley array of inhabitants, combined with the lack of sanitation and proper ventilation, quickly made the jail unfit for human habitation. A nauseating stench from vomit and human waste permeated the building. It was too hot in summer and too cold in winter. Though punishment enough, jail conditions were not the only misery criminals had to endure. Thieves were usually given thirty-nine stripes before being incarcerated for up to one year. Prostitutes and drunks did a stint in stocks before being sent to jail, usually for three months. In addition, each inmate received ten lashes on admission to the jail. In keeping with this general attitude toward criminals, little concern was given to their health during incarceration. Their diet was sparse, consisting usually of bread and molasses tea. Sleeping on vermin-infested straw mattresses laid on damp floors, prisoners sometimes became ill. Seldom did they get the benefit of medical attention.

The criminal element in Halifax could also enjoy the amenities of the county jail, another facility that illustrated the treatment of criminals in pioneer days. The county jail housed debtors, convicted offenders, and the accused awaiting trial. Inmates were charged for their meals and upon release required to pay the keeper a fee for his services. Those not able to pay could be kept incarcerated until they came up with the money. By way of assistance, they were allowed to go into the streets to beg until they succeeded in raising the sum needed, a practice that continued until stopped by the Grand Jury in 1817. Another privilege available to county jail inmates was the opportunity to buy liquor from the keeper. In view of the conditions it was a merciful concession.

The state of the jail was so bad that an accused murderer who had been in for seven months awaiting trial petitioned for his case to be heard on the grounds that he was fearful his health would be destroyed and that he wouldn't last the winter. Another detainee, for the same reason, asked to be either brought to trial or let out on bail. To add to the misery, inmates' lives were sometimes made worse by cruel and sadistic keepers. One complaint received by the Executive Council accused the jailor of beating prisoners, extorting money for favours, and profiteering on the sale of food and liquor. In another incident in 1815 the Grand Jury recommended the dismissal of one of the staff for cruelty. A year later two more were charged with treating inmates inhumanely. They were being whipped and neglected, and their food was being confiscated.[41]

A distinction was drawn between the debtors and the criminal prisoners. Debtors were kept in a separate part of the building with better accommodations. They could send out for food and clothing, receive visitors, and were permitted to go outside for exercise. They were generally shown more consideration and were rarely abused. They enjoyed the additional comfort of having family and friends to attend to their needs.

The jails were only one part of widespread deficiencies that characterized the entire criminal justice system. There were no specific requirements for jail keepers other than that they be willing to work for low pay. Some were drunkards and others, in character, not a step above the criminals they were guarding. Policing was carried on by volunteer and usually reluctant citizens. Magistrates were appointed from the ranks of the general population, had little or no knowledge of the law or judicial procedures, and some could barely read or write. They were the subjects of constant complaints and ridicule. Richard Gibbons, a prominent Halifax resident who later became Solicitor-General, remarked that judicial proceedings differed in each county with the exception that they were all "equally absurd, defective, and confused."[42]

Trials were sometimes postponed or cancelled because of the failure of a magistrate to show. They were too busy looking after their own affairs to see to their judicial duties. Court proceedings were also hampered by problems with jurors. Many citizens were unwilling to do jury duty so instead of an accused being tried by his or her peers the proceedings were conducted solely by the magistrate. Because of a growing backlog of cases, emergency provisions implemented in 1785 permitted the magistrates to conduct trials without a jury. The irony of the temporary expedient was that while it allowed a trial it prohibited the imposition of a sentence unless an accused was convicted by a jury.[43]

The laxness of the judicial system apparently worked to the advantage of many because there was considerable opposition to improving it. In 1824 some members of the Nova Scotia Legislative Assembly introduced a bill to have "professional men" appointed to preside over the Inferior courts throughout the province. They were concerned that the existing practice – under which the courts were presided over by judges "ignorant of the laws" and "regulated by no fixed principles" – was causing problems.[44] There were too many expensive appeals to the Supreme Court because of the inexactitude of justice in the lower courts. The opposition to the proposal is indicative of public sentiment at the time and the monetary considerations that took precedent in dealing with criminals. Opponents argued that the decisions of the lower courts, as they presently functioned, were more acceptable to the people "than if too nice an observance were paid to legal terms and distinctions."[45] The appointment of lawyers, they argued, and the cost of the proposed changes "would forever burden the people of Nova Scotia with a tax, unnecessary, oppressive, and against their inclination."[46] In spite of strong opposition in the legislature, a bill was passed by a one-vote margin and public opposition immediately coalesced. A petition, signed by about 330 people, was submitted to the Lieutenant-Governor, asking him to delay approving the bill until the sentiments of the public could be determined. The petitioners raised the argument that the laws must "be comfortable to the habits and necessities of the inhabitants."[47] Earlier legislative opponents had also argued that "the country was too young for such expensive and material innovations."[48] In the end the lawyers, who formed an influential cabal in government, prevailed and the legislation was passed.

While the criminal justice system might have suffered from problems with magistrates and juries, the laws themselves left little to chance. Even the most minor infractions, such as swearing or lewd conduct, were covered by the statutes and suitable punishments prescribed. The problem was that while some laws were poorly enforced others were almost unenforceable. For example, laws covering such things as concealment of pregnancy, abortion, infanticide, support of bastard children, and child neglect or abandonment, because of the nature of the crimes, were difficult to monitor. Many children were cared for at government expense because their military fathers and camp-following mothers had abandoned them and moved on. In such cases it was almost impossible to track down and punish the parents. Therefore, the lack of detection capabilities served as yet another modifying influence on the punishment of crime in an earlier day.

Elsewhere in the Atlantic region English criminal law was applied with the same severity and sometimes the same unevenness as it was in Nova Scotia. For example, in 1778 a Prince Edward Island woman was sentenced to death for theft but a hangman could not be found who was willing to do the job so the woman was released. In 1786 Jupiter Wise, a black man, was convicted of stealing two gallons of rum. He pleaded benefit of clergy and instead of being hanged he was banished. In 1815, two other blacks were not as fortunate. They were convicted of break and enter and of stealing a loaf of bread. For such a heinous crime the two were hanged. The whip was also well used in Prince Edward Island and laid on for some very minor offences. In 1817, for example, a Charlottetown man accused of stealing an axe was flogged at three separate locations in the town and given thirty-nine stripes at each stop. The next day another offender was sentenced to be whipped, but his punishment was spaced over three days and he was lashed a total of 351 times.[49]

As was the case in Nova Scotia, judicial procedures were usually carried out in quick succession. For example, on March 29, 1826, Dan Cunningham shot a police constable at Westfield, New Brunswick. Cunningham was arrested the same day. On May 5 he was tried, convicted, and sentenced, and on May 8 he was hanged. While justice was swift it was not always as severe. Jail terms were commonly used to punish New Brunswick offenders and the sentences were sometimes combined with supplementary punishment, such as a flogging, branding, or time in the stocks.[50]

While the English judicial system, with its colonial embellishments, was becoming established on the east coast, British-style penal practices, after the Conquest, were also making inroads in France's former possessions. Civil and criminal courts were established, judges, justices of the peace, and other legal officers were appointed, and the justice dispensed became more reflective of English rather than French customs. The favourite weapon of punishment, the whip, came into more widespread use and the application seemed to take on a greater severity. For example, soldiers found drunk were expected to reveal the source of their liquor. If they refused they were given twenty lashes each morning until they gave up the information. The seller, when apprehended, was also whipped and then either fined or imprisoned. The punishment was administered to both male and female grog merchants. As in the past, whipping was carried out in public with the one to be punished tied to the tail of a cart and stripped to the waist. The prisoner was led along a specified route accompanied by another man who would lay on the lash at various intervals. For example, a Montreal resident found guilty of theft in 1764 was tied to the tail of a cart outside the jail and led through certain streets of the town. During the journey he was whipped twenty-five times on the bare back, and in addition he received another twenty-five stripes at the marketplace. In 1765 a black man admitted to stealing two pieces of silk ribbon, his second conviction for theft in fourteen months. He was stripped to the waist, tied to the tail of a cart, and led through the streets of the town. Six times at various stops along the prescribed route he was flogged ten times with the cat-o'-nine tails.[51]

The penalty of flogging was applied in a variety of ways and in different circumstances. In French Canada offenders were tied to a cart, but the English normally used a whipping post. After the Conquest it was common to tie the offender to a fixed object in a public place and administer the beating. The prescribed number of lashes was usually thirty-nine. The figure was based on a biblical reference from St. Paul's second epistle to the Corinthians, wherein he tells of being whipped forty stripes save one. For some reason that became the standard throughout the Christian world when the whip was used for punishment. The penalty of time in the pillory was sometimes also enhanced with the whip. The executioner, who apparently was a jack-of-all-penal-trades, would stand near the prisoner and if he or she turned to avoid the rotten eggs and other debris, the whip would be used to force him to face the full brunt of the abuse.

The English penchant for the whip was especially evident when it came to the military. Soldiers stationed at Quebec and Montreal in the years following the Conquest were subjected to extreme punishment. One soldier in 1759 was flogged 500 times; another was given 300 lashes on the mere suspicion of theft. In 1779 five soldiers were involved in a fracas, a not unusual happening among the military of the day. One received 300 stripes with the cat-o'-nine tails, another 500, and the remaining three were each flogged 1,000 times. Two soldiers who were caught selling liquor in the camp were each whipped 300 times and fined £5.[52] Such severe beatings must, on occasion, have resulted in the death of the soldiers.

Branding also continued to be a common form of punishment under the English. The penalty was administered in the courtroom where the trial took place, usually immediately following the verdict. The offender's hand was held down, palm up, and the hot iron was pressed on for as long as it took to repeat three times the phrase "Vive le Roi" or, if the offender was English, "God Save the King."[53]

Although the English seemed to favour corporal punishment, fines were actually much more common, being prescribed for a wide range of offences such as theft, running over a child with a horse and carriage, doing business on the Sabbath, and swearing. Jail sentences were rare but people were sometimes incarcerated while awaiting trial or occasionally sentenced to short terms when convicted. Those who were incarcerated suffered conditions as bad as those in the Halifax jails. The standard food allotment was bread and water. The poor diet, coupled with the foul atmosphere, took a heavy toll on the health of inmates. The situation in Montreal was so serious that in June, 1787, the justices authorized the hiring of a doctor. Many prisoners had been sick for some time and had had no medical attention. The lack of concern is evident from the fact that the facility remained in use for many years, and it wasn't until 1802 that the Grand Jury condemned it as "totally inadequate to the purposes of a gaol."[54]

On occasion sentences handed down by the courts still called forth the full wrath of the state, as David McLane discovered in 1797. A year earlier the American had come north to try to persuade the French to rebel and join the United States. The following year he made another visit, intent on sowing the seeds of sedition. This time he was arrested and convicted in Quebec City of high treason. He was sentenced to be hanged, but with the proviso that he be cut down alive "and your bowels taken out and burned before your face; then your head must be severed from your body, which must be divided into four parts."[55] The sentence, as carried out, departed slightly from the court's instructions. McLane was ritualistically put on a sled with iron runners, seated with his back to the horse, and a block and axe placed in front of him. He was hanged but mercifully left until he was dead and so was spared the drama that followed. His body was cut open and his heart and bowels removed and burned. The executioner then cut off his head and held it up to the crowd as a grim and bloody warning to any would-be rebels.[56]

Death sentences and corporal punishment were usually carried out with dispatch. For example, on March 7, 1803, Antoine Deslories was convicted of murder and condemned to death. Two days later he was hanged. It had become the practice of certain courts to donate the bodies of criminals put to death to local doctors to help them with research and to improve their medical skills. Deslories's corpse was given to a Montreal doctor "to be dissected and anatomized."[57]

As elsewhere, justice in Lower Canada was, at best, dispensed very unevenly and in a most inequitable manner. The personal temperament of judges, the level of crime in the community, public tolerance to sentences, and a number of other considerations coloured the penalties given out by the courts. The Montreal experience during the first quarter of the nineteenth century affords a vivid example of just how capricious a judicial system could be. Between 1802 and 1825 over forty-four men were hanged for crimes as varied as murder, horse-stealing, rape, burglary, larceny, shoplifting, and sacrilege. Over the same period the exact same crimes were punished with a variety of other sentences. In 1814 a man was hanged for stealing but the next year another man convicted of theft was given thirty-nine lashes and branded on the hand. In 1817 and 1818, four men were hanged for horse theft, yet in 1819, of two men convicted of the same crime, one was given thirty-nine lashes and three years in jail while the other was sentenced to hang, but his sentence was subsequently commuted and he was sent to jail for three years. In 1818 a man sentenced to be hanged for grand larceny claimed benefit of clergy and had his sentence reduced to two years in jail.

In 1822 a thief was put in the pillory and then sent to jail for three months while another offender, convicted of stealing a book, was flogged thirty-nine times and incarcerated for twelve months. In the same year two men, convicted of murder, were branded, yet the following year another murderer was sentenced to be hanged but had his sentence remitted and was banished to Quebec for five years. In contrast, another murderer was branded and jailed for six months. In the same year, 1823, a man convicted of drowning another was also branded and jailed for six months. The year 1823 seemed to be a particularly bad one for inconsistent penalties because four more criminals were executed for burglary and horse-stealing, while murderers were being put in jail. At Lachine that year, five men were found guilty of larceny. Three of them were hanged but the other two were put in jail for six months. In 1825 two horse thieves paid the supreme penalty for their crime. However, two others convicted of the identical offence were first sentenced to hang but their sentences were commuted and they were incarcerated instead. If in one year severe penalties brought a negative public reaction, sentences would be much more lenient at the next court session. Toward the end of the period more jail sentences were being handed out, either as the sole punishment or in conjunction with another, such as branding. In 1825 eight death sentences were commuted to serving time in jail.[58]

In view of the conditions that prevailed in the lockups a jail sentence could be severe punishment. An official investigation that followed the death of a prisoner in the Montreal jail in December, 1835, revealed a rather bleak picture. The jailer was described as "a man of a hasty and violent temper, addicted to profane swearing, and apt to get into a passion, for the most trivial cause, with those who visit the Gaol."[59] The man's two sons worked for him as turnkeys. They were depicted as "worthless characters, and given to drunkenness and debauchery."[60]

The cells in the jail were twelve feet square. They were arranged in apartment groupings around a central hall, which contained the only fireplace. The prisoners were locked up at eight o'clock in the evening, at which time the fire was extinguished until eight in the morning. Not only were they without heat overnight but they also went without adequate bedding. Even when the fire was on during the day, each apartment was allotted only an eighth of a cord of wood, an amount totally inadequate for cold weather.

The administration of the facility was arbitrary, inefficient, and cruel. Some prisoners were not even locked up at night, yet those accused of murder were chained to a wall and put in irons even though they had not been tried or convicted. At one time the issue of wood had been a quarter of a cord but the jailer arbitrarily decided to cut it back to an eighth. On November 27, 1835, James Millar was taken into custody for vagrancy. He was already sick when admitted, and although he complained to the keepers no doctor came to check on him until December 9. He died the next day.[61]

The whim and caprice that characterized the dispensing of sentences, the indifference to the treatment of criminals in jail, and the inhumane conditions that prevailed spread with settlement as if they were endemic to the criminal justice system. In 1791 the divisions of Upper and Lower Canada were created. The treatment of criminals in the new jurisdiction of Upper Canada followed the practices already in place further east. Soon the worst aspects of criminal justice in the older parts of the country were replicated in the new. As well, the main mechanisms of punishment continued to be hanging, banishment, public exposure in the pillory and stocks, branding, whipping, fines, and short jail terms.

The first legislature of Upper Canada decided in 1792 that the laws of England would regulate affairs in the new province. This was confirmed by a statute passed in 1800 establishing British criminal law as of September 17, 1792, as the basis of justice. At the local level the law was administered by a district sheriff and justices of the peace. These officials were appointed by the government. As elsewhere, they were appointed from among the local people and had no legal training. Chief Justice William Osgoode commented in 1795 that "seeing the Bench filled with unprofessional men has made every one that can read and write half wild."[62] The only qualification for the job, it seemed, was loyalty to the political party making the appointment. This procedure immediately lessened respect for the officials because they were seen to be patronage appointments, agents of the governing party. Justices of the peace presided over the Courts of Quarter Session, which met in the various districts four times a year. Their other duties involved matters of local government, ranging from tax-collecting to building jails and roads. By 1795 the Courts of Quarter Session had merged with the civil district courts, which became the main dispensers of justice at the local level until 1841.

A trial began with a preliminary hearing before a grand jury. If it was decided there was sufficient evidence, the case went immediately to trial by a judge and jury. If the verdict was guilty the judge passed sentence right away. The courts dealt with cases ranging from assault to petty larceny, swearing, and Sabbath-breaking. The usual penalty was a fine and sometimes a short jail sentence, depending on whether or not there was a suitable place of detention in the district. Since initially there were no courthouses, trials took place in churches, taverns, or any available space.

At another level the assize courts handled the more serious cases – murder, manslaughter, larceny, rape, horse theft, and forgery. A conviction for murder called for strangulation by hanging, followed by dissection of the body. Other serious crimes for which the death penalty was sometimes prescribed were forgery, burglary, and robbery. The assize court records for the period 1792-1802 list the following distribution of punishments: hanging – seven; branding – five; branding and jail – one; whipped and fined – one; whipped and jailed – two; put in the pillory and jailed – two; jailed and fined – two; fined – nine; bond – two; and banished – four.[63] A not untypical example of the justice of the day was the penalty assessed to Frederick Peper, who was convicted on April 14, 1790, of stealing a ploughshare, coulter, and bolt, valued at ten shillings. He was given thirty-nine lashes on the bare back at the public whipping post, put in jail for one month, and one day each week of that month put in the stocks wearing the sign "thief."[64]

Jails in Upper Canada, as elsewhere at the turn of the century and during the first decades of the nineteenth century, were used chiefly as holding places for people awaiting trial or imposition of sentence. Gradually, they also became one of the sentencing options. Among the first jails constructed in Upper Canada was one at York built about 1800. It was made of logs and measured thirty-four feet by twenty feet, and it provided accommodation for the keeper plus three rooms, each measuring twelve feet by ten feet, for prisoners. The building was heated by two fireplaces. The London district also had a wooden building, built in 1803 and consisting of two large rooms. The Johnstown and Gore districts both had log jails, built respectively in 1808 and 1816. In contrast, Windsor had a brick jail built in 1799 and the Niagara district had a stone jail built in 1817-18. The latter was described by a traveller as "the finest building in Canada." By 1841 there were sixteen district jails in Upper Canada.[65]

While these early jails varied in size and construction, they all quickly became run down with use. Some were poorly constructed and poorly maintained and many were inadequately heated and ventilated. Most lacked adequate sanitary facilities so they became permanently foul smelling, damp, and unsanitary. They were vermin-infested, cold in winter, and too hot and humid in the summer. Many provided little food and bedding, and prisoners had to make do with the clothes they came in with. They slept on decrepit straw mattresses on the floor. One prisoner in York jail complained in 1829 that his bedclothes had not been washed in over six months.[66]

Prisoners in the York jail continued to suffer from poor conditions for some time. The standard food allowance was a pound of bread per day and water. In January, 1836, by which time York had become Toronto, a quart of soup was added to the menu. No clothing was provided so inmates had to wear whatever they came in with. For those sentenced to hard labour, ten hours per day were spent breaking stone to be used for street construction. If the sentence did not specify labour, then the inmate could not be required to work and spent the time in idleness without recreation or exercise.[67]

The jailers were poorly paid so the job did not always attract the best people. Some were cruel and added to the misery of their charges. As noted, the jails were not initially meant to be places of punishment but rather temporary holding places. With the tendency to resort less to corporal punishment, however, incarceration became more common and the early jails quickly became inadequate, especially because debtors were being constantly put in them. They were held until their creditors were paid and constituted the largest number of prisoners in many communities. Some were detained for debts as small as one dollar and whole families could be jailed. As a result, debtors could lose their jobs and businesses.[68] One case in particular vividly illustrates the level of cruelty and indifference to human suffering common at the time. A debtor incarcerated in York jail in 1839 for a debt of one pound had had his obligation forgiven by his creditor, but he could not be released because his lawyer would not forgo his fees.

The small facilities effectively eliminated any possibility of segregation or classification – except for the separation of the sexes and debtors, offenders of all varieties and ages were thrown together. Treatment varied with the personality of the jailors, as did such things as the quality and quantity of food served. In some places debtors were allowed to purchase liquor and extra food, but selling liquor to other inmates was generally forbidden. The prohibition, however, did not prevent a number of keepers from augmenting their incomes by peddling booze. Inmates were allowed to have visitors but had to communicate through the bars. Recreational activities, such as card-playing or gaming, were forbidden and, since there was little or no work available, prisoners spent their time in idleness. Provisions were made for medical care and religious services, and inmates were allowed to receive letters, packages, and newspapers. Although there were no prescribed programs or activities, rules and regulations ordered the institutions. People who disobeyed or caused trouble could be put in solitary confinement or on a reduced diet. Whipping, as a punishment, was used very little in district jails. Unruly prisoners, if not isolated, were sometimes constrained in hand or leg irons.[69]

The mixture of people channelled to district jails helped to make a bad situation worse. Since the jails were usually the only public holding places they became the dumping ground for a variety of welfare needs – the aged, the insane, and the indigent. While a jail sentence was nominally lighter punishment than some of the options, conditions were so bad that many inmates found their time in confinement to be rather severe punishment. In contrast, the public saw them as getting free room and board at public expense and living better than some of them were normally used to.

The statute books provided some very severe penalties for most crimes, yet the results of judicial procedures were much more lenient. A number of factors contributed to this. The population was sparse and scattered so it was often difficult for witnesses to get to the place where the trial was being held. Consequently, many guilty parties escaped punishment altogether for lack of evidence. Offenders also benefited from the reluctance of their neighbours to serve on juries. Trials were sometimes cancelled for want of a jury, and many people were charged before the various district courts for defaulting on jury service. The very severity of the law itself was a problem. Juries were reluctant to convict when a guilty verdict could mean a sentence of death or harsh corporal punishment. Quite often jury members were dealing with friends, acquaintances, and relatives and so were not about to find them guilty. In 1795, John White, the Attorney-General of the province, complained that while there was hardly a district in which one or two people had not been tried for murder, they were all acquitted by the juries although the evidence against them was strong.[70]

The magistrates also made their contribution to offenders escaping punishment. Most were untutored in the law and so were unsure of how to conduct a trial or what punishments were appropriate for various crimes. Many did not hold the law in the same regard that a learned judge would and so dispensed minimal sentences. Some were friends of the accused and therefore not inclined to hand out severe penalties. The poor calibre of magistrates, their lack of training, and their personal biases resulted in some very uneven justice. For example, a case of murder and another of rape came before the London district court. The cases were summarily dismissed without even being brought to the grand jury.[71] In one of the first trials in York, six men were accused of stealing a variety of items from a local tavern, including a kettle, an axe, a hat, and two quarts of brandy. One was pardoned for agreeing to give evidence against his companions, three were acquitted, and two were found guilty. One of the convicted men was branded for his crime while his companion was flogged in the marketplace. Even common drunks could not count on the same treatment in various jurisdictions. In some places they were dumped in jail and left to sober up; in others they were put to work. In early York, for example, drunks were made to clear stumps from the village streets.[72]

Although many offenders escaped the full wrath of the law in early Upper Canada there were those who paid the prescribed penalty for their crimes. One such individual was Josiah Cutan, who, at a trial in Hesse district on September 7, 1792, was convicted on charges of burglary and theft. He had broken into the shop of a local trader and stole some smoked skins, pelts, and two kegs of rum. He was tried, convicted, sentenced to hang, and duly executed.[73] Another person who paid the full penalty was John McIntyre, a miner who in 1820 raped a friend's wife. Rape was viewed as a very serious crime punishable by death. McIntyre was tried, found guilty, and condemned to hang. The victim took pity on her attacker and both she and her husband petitioned the court to set aside the death penalty. The judge, however, refused on the grounds that women who were frequently alone in their houses had to be protected. The hanging of McIntyre would make the point and serve as a deterrent to others.[74]

Further west the treatment of criminals was even more haphazard than in the East. When the Hudson's Bay Company charter was granted in 1670, the Company was given the right to make laws and enforce them in the territory under its jurisdiction. This power was subject to all laws being compatible with English standards. The governor and his council were to exercise the legal authority while the chief factors were delegated the right to hold trials and punish wrongdoers at company trading posts. For much of the period fines were the most common form of punishment. There were no jails and if someone had to be restrained they were simply locked up in a room. Serious offences that would merit the death penalty were not tried by the factors; rather, the accused were sent either to England or to Lower or

Upper Canada. By 1803, because of the high costs of sending someone to England for trial, the English Parliament provided that all cases should henceforth be handled by the courts of Lower and Upper Canada.

In 1812 when a settlement was started at Red River more stringent regulations were set down for dealing with lawbreakers. They could be sentenced to prison and hard labour. Prisoners who caused trouble could be disciplined with solitary confinement. These provisions, however, were largely academic since as late as 1822 no jail had been built. The same situation prevailed elsewhere, so for the first quarter of the nineteenth century punishment for crime in the West continued to be mainly in the form of fines, with the perpetrators of capital crimes being sent East.

A dimension of punishment in pioneer days common to all regions was the participation of ordinary people. Punishment was frequently a public spectacle. While the authorities saw this as a deterrent, many people saw it as theatre and joined in the play. They abused people who were locked in the stocks and pillories; they attended trials and cheered on the participants, frequently agitated by generous consumption of liquor. A hanging was the occasion for a holiday. The entire family packed a lunch and in a festive mood went to watch justice take its course. The person to be hanged was expected to deliver a parting soliloquy and many complied.[75] The hangman was obliged to execute every detail of the proceeding and if he failed in any way he was jeered and abused by the crowd. Such a discriminating audience demanded nothing less than a professional performance. Thousands showed up to watch a man or woman hanging from a rope in convulsions until the last flicker of life was gone, therefore the scaffold always had to be placed in a location large enough to handle big crowds. At one double hanging in Toronto in 1828 an estimated crowd of 10,000 people came from miles around to witness the event.[76] Such occurrences were yet another manifestation of the temper of the times.

THE ENLIGHTENMENT AND PENAL REFORM

While pioneer Canadian courts were struggling with the legal niceties of France and England, a penal reform movement had begun that would ultimately bring about some major changes in the treatment of criminals in Canada. The roots of that reform movement were to be found in the period known as the Enlightenment. The eighteenth century witnessed a great intellectual ferment in science and philosophy as a new generation of thinkers challenged long-standing ways of looking at and explaining society. A system of thought emerged that amounted to an intellectual revolution. The natural was substituted for the supernatural, science challenged theology, natural law replaced divine law, human reason was exalted, a belief in progress and the ultimate perfectibility of the human race was posited, and a concept of individual rights and the advantages of humanitarianism were put forward. These ideas were developed, expanded, and championed by some of the most outstanding intellectuals of the day: men like Voltaire, Rousseau, Diderot, and Montesquieu in France; Bentham, Hume, and Adam Smith in Great Britain; Beccaria in Italy. They took a scientific, rational approach to their society that gave the name Enlightenment to their age.

Among the many changes that were influenced by the thinkers of the age was a fundamental shift in the evaluation of the nature, rights, and role of ordinary people in society. Whereas kings, queens, nobles, and princes of the Church were the main actors of an earlier day, the common man became important in the eighteenth century. Jean Jacques Rousseau advanced the concept of the natural man, or mankind in a state of nature, as a virtuous being, a "noble savage." In a natural state, according to Rousseau, all men were free and equal. In 1761 he published a pamphlet called *Social Contract* in which he argued that governments derive their power from a social contract. This was an agreement whereby people gave up certain rights and bestowed them on government so that everyone could live in peace and harmony. The idea that rulers derived their authority from the people and not from God was revolutionary. Rousseau's concepts of liberty, equality, and fraternity became the rallying cry of the French Revolution.

The concept of natural law, which was so fundamental to Enlightenment thought, was closely associated with the concept of natural rights. These prerogatives were seen to be so inextricably bound up with the human condition that they should not be denied the individual under any circumstances. Natural rights included such things as equality before the law, freedom of speech, freedom of the person, and freedom of religion. Thomas Jefferson summed them up in the American Declaration of Independence: "that all men are created equal; that they are endowed by their Creator with certain unalienable Rights, that among these are Life, Liberty and the pursuit of Happiness." The French Declaration of the Rights of Man of 1789 again summed up natural rights: "Men are born and remain free and equal."

Enlightenment thinkers were absorbed with an interest in humanity and a belief that society could be improved. They sought reform of economics, of ethics, of religion, of government, and of society. They believed that if the shackles of the past could be broken, society could progress. They shared an optimistic humanitarianism summed up by Alexander Pope, who wrote, "Know then thyself; presume not God to scan; The proper study of mankind is man." This faith in human nature, this humanitarianism, found expression in a variety of movements. Some called for the abolition of slavery; some demanded education for the masses; some campaigned for democratic government; some agitated for penal reform.

The repressive laws and severe punishments that characterized the judicial system in all countries were not compatible with the humanitarian view of mankind. People were masters of the state, not servants. Liberals who believed in individual worth and dignity recoiled at the sight of human beings being whipped, mutilated, or hung for minor transgressions. They called for a system that would help, improve, and reform rather than simply punish. Thus, out of the philosophy of the Enlightenment came a penal reform movement that would ultimately bring about some major changes in the way criminals were treated throughout the Western world.

One of the most articulate and influential spokespersons in the cause of penal reform was the Italian, Cesare Beccaria. A nobleman and professor of law and economics at Milan, Beccaria was an enthusiastic believer in the ideas of progress and reason. Through discussions with friends he was persuaded to turn his critical talents to an evaluation of the criminal law. Between March, 1763, and January, 1764, he worked on the project and published the results in his *Treatise on Crimes and Punishments*. The book was so well received that a second edition was printed, then a third edition in 1765.

Beccaria spotlighted "the cruelty of punishments, and the irregularities of criminal procedures." He argued that in keeping with the idea of the social contract a magistrate did not have the right to inflict punishment on a fellow citizen at his own discretion. Rather, that power belonged to the state and therefore punishments should be fixed by the legislator. He further argued that if it could be shown that punishment achieved nothing, then to continue to punish would be contrary to reason and justice. Beccaria made the point in his treatise that, to avoid any arbitrariness, laws should be clear and precise. He reasoned that fewer crimes would be committed when people clearly understood the law. He attacked the practice of detention before trial, condemned the use of torture, and denounced capital punishment, describing the latter as barbarous and illogical. He pointed out it was absurd that the same law that condemns one murder should sanction another. Beccaria called for a more just and ordered legal system, arguing that people had the right to be judged by their peers – and if they are found guilty, the punishment should fit the crime and be administered swiftly. He also recommended that more attention be given to crime prevention by improving education.[77]

Beccaria's work was translated into twenty European languages and had a major impact on penal thinking. It was one of the first systematic and concise expressions of a blueprint for reform. It was a humanitarian work that expressed a clear sympathy for ordinary people in society and recognized universal rights. The treatise was a call to action that reverberated throughout Europe. Beccaria's work influenced heads of state such as the Grand Duke of Tuscany and Catherine II, Empress of Russia, as well as other reformers, such as Jeremy Bentham and Sir Samuel Romilly in England.

Jeremy Bentham was another proponent of penal reform. He was born in

1748 into a well-to-do family of London lawyers. Bentham was a child prodigy who followed the family tradition by attending Oxford and then gaining admission to the bar. His interests were wide ranging and included philosophy, economics, religion, and philosophy. One of his most influential concepts, which he applied to penal reform, was "utilitarianism." Bentham maintained that the test of the value or usefulness of a given deed was its utility in promoting the happiness or welfare of the doer. He suggested that individuals should pursue their own self-interest and in so doing would promote the best interest of society. Enlightened self-interest, he argued, would promote the "greatest happiness of the greatest number." Bentham borrowed this idea from Beccaria, although it predates the Italian reformer's work.

Bentham, who had a strong interest in law and penal reform, applied the principle of utilitarianism to punishment. He held that all punishment was evil and therefore only that amount of punishment should be used sufficient to offset the degree of pleasure realized from the crime. He was also interested in the reform of criminals. He favoured classification, education, and adequate provision for discharge. He went so far as to design a model prison that would be conducive to moral reform, good health, and industry. For years Bentham pressed his idea of a Panopticon on the British government. It was a new type of prison that would enable all convicts housed in the institution to be monitored from a central point. Though he did not succeed with his proposal, he did exert a significant influence on reform of criminal law and procedures in England.[78]

Samuel Romilly, born in Westminster in 1757, was a friend of Bentham's and an influential reformer in his own right. Like his colleague, he had an inquiring mind and wide-ranging interests. He early embraced the ideas of Rousseau and read the works of Beccaria. Romilly was admitted to the bar in 1783 and was soon writing critical tracts on the criminal law. He had a very successful career, including a number of terms as a Member of Parliament. By 1807 he had turned his attention to law reform and was successful in subsequent years in getting passed a number of bills that lessened severe punishment for minor crimes. His career came to an abrupt halt on November 2, 1818, when, despondent over the death of his wife, he committed suicide.[79]

Among the most famous and influential of English penal reformers was John Howard. Born at Hackney in 1726 the son of a successful merchant, he inherited considerable property on the death of his father and thereafter enjoyed a life of leisure and travel. In 1773 he was appointed high sheriff of Bedford. His duties acquainted him with the jail conditions of his day and he was repelled by what he saw. The inhumane conditions and abuses motivated him to devote himself to prison reform. He travelled extensively in Scotland and Ireland and on the continent to acquaint himself with prison conditions and carefully recorded what he found. In 1777 he published *The State of the Prisons in England and Wales, with Preliminary Observations, and an Account of Some Foreign Prisons.* The book created a heightened awareness of the need for change and gave a strong impetus to the cause of penal reform.[80]

The work and ideas of European and English penal reformers had a significant impact on reform in North America. The humanitarian philosophy was the subject of discussion on both sides of the ocean and the concrete legal reforms introduced in England were extended to her colonies in the Canadas. After the American Revolution, Dr. Benjamin Rush and a group of humanitarian Quakers founded in 1787 the Philadelphia Society for Alleviating the Miseries of Public Prisons. Rush was a well-known physician with a strong interest in philosophy and reform. He was a member of the Continental Congress and a signer of the Declaration of Independence. Rush was an early advocate of the modern penitentiary system. He and his colleagues in the Philadelphia Society were influenced by the work of John Howard, among others.[81]

Rush and his group of reformers persuaded the Pennsylvania state legislature to modify the Walnut Street Jail in Philadelphia as an experiment in new penal methods. A building with separate cells was constructed in 1790 and a new regimen was introduced. Corporal punishment was abolished, classification of prisoners was introduced, and inmates were put to work at hard labour. An emphasis was placed on reforming the criminal through religious instruction. The experiment was the foundation for what became known as the Pennsylvania system. Prisoners were isolated from each other in a separate, silent system of incarceration. To some extent it borrowed from the model of the Christian monastery. The idea was to isolate the wrongdoer in his cell so he could reflect on the evil that he had done and do penance for his sins. Silent reflection, moral instruction, and repentance were the underlying principles of the system. While the Pennsylvania approach might have been a good spiritual exercise, appropriate for monks, it was psychologically debilitating and caused many mental and emotional problems among the inmates during the early years of its existence.[82]

Another experiment that got under way around 1821 at Auburn prison in New York offered an alternative approach to the Pennsylvania system. Prisoners were kept in separate cells and allowed to work together in groups, but they were not allowed to converse or communicate with each other in any way. Discipline was considered to be an integral part of repentance and reform, so rules and regulations were strictly enforced. This in turn led to the use of severe punishments for prisoners who disobeyed. The restrictive, punitive dimension of both systems quickly predominated over the reform objectives so that these new penal systems in some respects were as inhumane as what they were supposed to replace.[83]

The Pennsylvania and Auburn experiments were by no means the first to utilize the so-called modern penal methods. In 1703 Pope Clement XI established the Hospice of San Michele for boys. The emphasis in this reformatory was moral reform. Inmates were classified by age and the seriousness of their crime. Each prisoner had his own cell, was required to work during the day, and spent the night in solitary reflection. Religious instruction was considered to be the key to reformation and was the focal point of the program.[84] Another predecessor of the American prisons was the House of Correction, founded in Ghent, Flanders, in 1771 by Vicomte Jean Jacques Philippe Vilain XIV. There, men, women, and children were segregated in separate sections. Inmates were taught trades and the objective of the institution was to restore the individual to a useful, law-abiding life.[85] Neither the Rome nor Ghent models caught on in Europe. Rather, the new American penal systems attracted the interest of reformers. Europeans visited the United States to observe how the two prisons worked. The Pennsylvania model was preferred by Europeans; in the United States and Canada the Auburn prison became the favoured prototype.

PENAL REFORM IN CANADA

The humanitarian philosophy that came out of the Enlightenment and that so influenced penal reformers witnessed its first concrete expression in Canada in the form of less severe treatment of criminals. By the 1820s and 1830s the old-style punishments were falling into disuse. The harsh penalties prescribed by English law were always ameliorated in practice but now, instead of magistrates being more humane by whim or circumstance, they were beginning to reflect a conscious policy based on the new humanitarian philosophy. Floggings, mutilations, and branding were being replaced with fines, incarceration, and hard labour. Even some rudimentary attempts at reformation were being made. In Halifax a new Bridewell was opened in 1818 because the old one could no longer handle the increased jail population. The Halifax magistrates noted that the new facility had been built "to mitigate the old form of punishment."[86] By the 1820s Halifax was also experimenting with some of the new methods of treating prisoners. Inmates were put to work at tasks such as cutting granite and building roads. Tradesmen were permitted to practise their specialties in the jail yard while other prisoners were given the opportunity to work as apprentices so they could learn a trade before they were released. Another practice implemented in Halifax was the provision of religious services and instruction to prisoners.

A court in Saint John, New Brunswick, affords another example of changing penal practices. In 1829 the court levied a £10 fine for keeping a disorderly house; two months in jail for forgery; and six months at hard labour for grand larceny. Not too much earlier, crimes such as these would have earned harsher punishments.[87] In Montreal between 1826 and 1828, approximately sixteen death sentences were substituted with other punishments, including jail, branding, and transportation to Bermuda. In 1829 three men were convicted of stealing an ox and hanged for their crime. The incident caused such public outrage that it brought an end to capital punishment for cattle stealing. While branding and whipping continued in use through the 1830s the tendency was toward more frequent use of incarceration and very limited use of the death penalty.[88]

Punishments in Upper Canada tended to be less severe than in the East. The population was sparse and by the time urban centres began to develop, the more lenient judicial practices had become entrenched. Fines were the most common punishments for lawbreakers. Thus, when the reform ideas began to circulate, there was not much need to change existing practices in most jurisdictions. The jails in the 1830s and 1840s could not accommodate reformatory programs and there was little interest in introducing them. For the most part improvements were along the lines of medical attention, better food, and better accommodation. However, there was no consistent pattern and changes were sporadic. Since the jail population was small in those communities that had such a facility, the introduction of new programs or services was not a pressing concern. From time to time an advanced idea would be put forward but greeted with little enthusiasm. For example, in 1830 inmates in the Hamilton jail were given limited opportunity to practise their trades. A proposal was made to extend the concession by allowing prisoners to work outside during the day and return to jail at night. If implemented it might have helped many prisoners to get back on their feet, but the concept received no support.

Along with greater use of fines and jail sentences to punish criminals, there were other manifestations of the growing humanitarianism. In 1832 the death penalty was abolished for cattle stealing and larceny. By 1833 the number of capital crimes in Canada had been reduced to twelve, including murder, rape, treason, robbery, burglary, and arson. By 1841 only murder, rape, and treason carried the death penalty in Upper Canada. The use of the pillory was abolished by statute in 1841 and banishment as a punishment was officially discarded in 1842. By 1830 both public flogging and branding had been discontinued for civilian criminals but branding continued after this date as a military punishment. In 1835 the minimum debt for which a person could be sent to jail was raised to £10. Also abolished was a legal loophole that had allowed many a crafty criminal to escape punishment. The privilege of claiming "benefit of clergy" was dropped during the reign of George IV.

In the West, population remained sparse and there was little need for jails. The first real judicial facility was begun at Fort Garry in 1835, consisting of a courthouse and a two-room jail. Prisoners were expected to provide their own necessities, including food. In the event that this was not possible, the unfortunate individual was given a daily ration of one pound of pemmican at public expense. In 1841 officials decided to provide all inmates with a free daily ration of one pound of pemmican and water. Although the same severe penalties provided by law in the East governed the West, in practice neither laws nor punishments were strictly enforced.[89] Public attitudes were not receptive to harsh punishment. On April 28, 1836, a man was being whipped in public at Upper Fort Garry. The onlookers became so insensed that they started to stone the person administering the flogging. The police had to lock him up to protect him from the crowd.[90]

While practices varied across the country a fairly well-defined penal philosophy was shared by most reformers by the first quarter of the nineteenth century. There was still a strong belief in punishment both as the wages of sin and as a deterrent. However, there was also a belief that criminals could be reclaimed to a useful, law-abiding life. To achieve this, it was believed, prisoners should be placed in separate cells and classified according to their crimes and past records. They should be assigned to hard labour and strictly disciplined. During the course of their imprisonment they should be given religious instruction and provided with regular religious services. It was firmly held that the wayward could only be reclaimed through moral reformation.

Much of the attitude toward criminals was founded in the teachings of the Christian churches. Indeed, most offences that broke the state's laws were also violations of moral precepts. Drunkenness, theft, swearing, cheating, rape, prostitution, sexual licentiousness, assault, and murder were all transgressions of the moral law as well as the civil. In the eyes of the churches these activities were sins and offences against God. Therefore, the simple explanation for illegal behaviour was that offenders were lacking in moral education. The criminal was considered to be a sinner, a person lacking in character and moral fortitude. The Church offered the wayward a prescribed ritual through which they could regain a state of grace or spiritual worthiness. The punishment for sin was penance and the offender had to be willing to accept the penalty. The sinner must also show remorse and through religious exercises strive for spiritual reformation and resolve to transgress no more. Once punished, repentant, and reformed, the sinner was ready to return to the God-fearing Christian community. People who returned to their evil ways were obviously unrepentant and deserved little consideration.

In this theology the individual was completely responsible for his or her own actions since human beings were possessed of free will. One could choose to do or not to do a given act and therefore was solely accountable for the choice. If people lived good lives the credit was all theirs, and if they chose to sin the blame was all theirs. Thus when people committed crimes they were labelled as sinners and since they had freely chosen such conduct they alone were responsible. They deserved to be punished, they had to repent, and they needed religious instruction to help them – both to see the error of their ways and to return to a good life. From the perspective of contemporary society it is hard to understand how influential and pervasive religious beliefs were in an earlier day. Yet the proof was everywhere. In New France the Church was the focal point of every community. Criminals, as we have seen, started their punishment outside the church door, asking forgiveness of God. In English Canada the religious sects were prominent in every community, and frequently one of the first permanent buildings constructed was a church. In the early part of the nineteenth century the small village of Newcastle, in what is now the province of Ontario, with approximately 500 inhabitants, had seven churches.[91] Religious revival meetings in pioneer days attracted hundreds of people who came from miles around to attend the camp meetings.

It is understandable, then, that when people started to talk about the reformation of criminals they thought in terms of spiritual change and looked to the penitential rights and teachings of the Church as the reform model. Jails would become places in which offenders would be isolated from the outside world and be able to reflect in solitude on their wicked ways. Hard labour would be the penance that would cleanse the soul and strict discipline would help to break dissolute habits. Religious instruction and church services would see to the inmates' moral education and bring about a rebirth of the Christian spirit. Finally, the offender would be released to sin no more.

Unfortunately for reformers, the conditions prevailing in most jails were not conducive to penance, discipline, or reform. Few communities were either able or willing to spend the money necessary to build jail facilities that would allow the separation of inmates or in which any type of reform program – spiritual or otherwise – could properly function. In fact, some government authorities were even reluctant to spend money on such basic needs as food because of demands on the public purse. In the early years in Toronto, for example, magistrates were saddled with the responsibility of paying salaries to legislators and financing the costs of elections. In 1836 they gave this as an excuse for not making jail repairs and for not providing better food for prisoners. Because of cost, staff were kept to a bare minimum in most jails, usually one poorly paid keeper. Reform was not a high priority.

As we have seen there was a significant increase in population through the first half of the nineteenth century, much of it due to immigration. In many urban communities crime rates increased and law-abiding citizens became alarmed. They saw more people being sent to jail but seemingly with little improvement. Crime continued to increase, recidivism rates were high, and tales of jail conditions and inmate behaviour were shocking. The jails, rather than being places of reform, were condemned as being schools for crime. This led to an ambivalence in the minds of the general public. Some called for a return to harsher penalties, arguing that the more humane methods were not working and that prisoners were being maintained in idleness and sometimes debauchery. Although in many jurisdictions there was a desire to put prisoners to work, and in a few jails they actually were, in most places no work opportunities existed. Facilities were too small to accommodate work programs and governments too parsimonious to pay for tools and materials. Even outside work programs ran into trouble because free labour complained that prisoners robbed them of jobs. Idleness was seen as a major problem, so much so that the Nova Scotia provincial legislature in March, 1824, entertained a motion to introduce the tread mill. The supporters of the idea had even designed a building for the "stepping mill." The proposal failed to pass, by a margin of one vote. Besides its being a remedy for idleness, proponents had also argued that a tread mill would discourage would-be criminals more than the light punishments that were in vogue and that were failing to deter crime.[92]

On the other hand were those who argued that the problem was not lighter penalties but the conditions under which offenders served their sentences. They wanted more appropriate facilities, prisons in which proper programs could be introduced and discipline maintained. The less humane element also favoured the building of prisons but for a different reason. They believed that a better structured environment would facilitate the introduction of hard labour and stricter discipline. Consequently, this early movement for prison-building in Canada reflected the beliefs of both those who wanted harsher treatment and those who called for a better, more scientific approach to dealing with criminals. The two viewpoints were succinctly summed up by Charles Duncombe in his 1836 Report on Prisons and Penitentiaries. He pointed out that many of his contemporaries questioned whether or not the new jails, the greater leniency in the treatment of criminals, and the emphasis on reformation were not a mistake. Some believed the old style of punishment was more effective in controlling crime. He suggested that the prisons in England and the United States were established "as a remedy for the increase of crime under the milder administration of the criminal laws, and the vices of the system of detention in common jails...."[93]

Duncombe made it clear that he did not see prisons merely as more orderly and punitive devices. Rather, he emphasized that they should also be places of moral and intellectual improvement and reformation. He defined the ends of punishment as being threefold: "to deter others from crime; to prevent the aggressor from a repetition of his offences; and, if possible, to effect the moral reformation of all those who become amenable to the laws."[94] Reflecting the ideas of Beccaria and other European reformers, he called for classification of prisoners, speedy trials, and punishments "least likely to debase the human mind" and that are "just and consistent."[95] He condemned flogging in prisons and called for more humane treatment. He also reiterated the widely held belief of his day that criminals were responsible for their own misery, but that they could also become the authors of their own reformation if they so chose.[96]

With so much criticism and concern being expressed over lenient penalties, crowded jails, idle prisoners, recidivism, the lack of reform programs, unscientific approaches to crime, and the growing numbers of offenders, there was considerable pressure on government to take some action. The result was a decision to build a new institution and to model it on Auburn prison in the state of New York. Although Auburn was hailed by reformers as the epitome of the new penal philosophy in action, it is easy to see why it was also admired by those calling for stricter measures. The concept underlying Auburn was hardly permissive, as is evident from the following statement made by the board of directors of Auburn in 1821:

> The end and design of the law is the prevention of crimes, through fear of punishment, the reformation of offenders being of minor consideration.... Let the most obdurate and guilty felons be immured in solitary cells and dungeons; let them have pure air, wholesome food, comfortable clothing, and medical aid when necessary; cut them off from all intercourse with men; let not the voice or face of a friend ever cheer them; let them walk their gloomy abodes, and commune with their corrupt hearts and guilty consciences in silence, and brood over the horrors of their solitude, and the enormity of their crimes, without the hope of executive pardon.[97]

The use of total solitary confinement at Auburn resulted in prisoners going insane, attempting to commit suicide, and mutilating themselves. The situation became so bad that the state governor ordered the abandonment of the practice. By the end of 1823 most of the first group of prisoners subjected to solitary had been released or pardoned. As some measure of the efficacy of harsh punishment it is worth noting that one man committed a burglary on the very night he was released and twelve more were recommitted later on for more lawbreaking.[98] With the exception of keeping prisoners in solitary confinement, most of the system of silence, strict discipline, and punishment remained intact. This Auburn system served as the model for Canada's first experiment with the scientific treatment of criminals: Kingston Prison.

The new prison was designed to reflect the most up-to-date thinking in penology and to accommodate the new philosophy of reform. A prison would provide an environment of discipline, order, and authority for the reformation of criminals. It also reflected conditions in Upper Canada at the time. There was growing concern over costs of building and maintaining district jails, the conditions of the jails, and the lack of security and inadequate facilities. A new central prison would not only respond to many of these problems but held out the additional advantage of lowering the cost of keeping long-term prisoners. In a new, large facility prisoners could work and thus contribute to their upkeep. The committee formed to study the matter of a penitentiary assured the legislature that the prison would be self-sustaining. It also recommended that the new facility be constructed along the Auburn model. Hence, Colonel William Powers, deputy keeper at Auburn, was hired to supervise the construction.[99]

The first stage of the complex was opened in 1835. The cells numbered about 150. Each was eight feet, four inches long, seven feet, six inches high, and thirty inches wide. Every cell had a barred window thirty-six by twenty inches. The only furniture in a cell was a bed hinged to the wall, which, when it was down, took up practically all the cell space. The toilet facility consisted of buckets, which the prisoners emptied each morning as they came out in unison from their cells. The light regard with which many held criminals at the time is illustrated by the explanation given by one of the planners for the small cells: "The occupant has ample room to dress and undress, turn around, lie down, stand or sit, and a lengthened space for walking back and forth. And what more does he need?"[100]

The discipline at Kingston was harsh in the extreme and, like the building, was modelled on Auburn and the philosophy behind that system. In its everyday application, however, it also reflected the attitude and personalities of the officials at the prison, including the warden, deputy keeper, and the staff. As the Brown Report, which will be examined later, amply demonstrated, the warden was an inappropriate choice for the job. His stated belief that sentences were too short and that second offenders should be incarcerated for life was anathema to the reform impulse of the day. The staff were untrained and by and large fell in line with the spirit set by the administration.[101]

The regimen introduced at Kingston was simply a copy of the Auburn system. It was supposed to be a humane replacement for the inhuman system that prevailed for so long. The emphasis was on the reform of the criminal rather than punishment alone. Discipline was believed to be the key to this reformation, and the inmates at Kingston were well disciplined. They were not permitted to communicate with each other in any way. In the dining room they sat in rows with their backs to each other and even in the chapel they were arranged so that they could see the preacher but no one else.

Prison rules forbade inmates to "exchange looks, winks, laugh, nod, gesticulate to each other."[102] The staff were on notice to enforce the rules strictly. They were told that the success of the system depended "on the absolute prevention of intercourse among the Convicts."[103] If communication was necessary, in the workplace for example, it could only take place by signs or under the direct monitoring of guards. Infractions were punished most often by flogging with a whip made of bull's hide. The guards were allowed to administer six to twelve lashings for rule infractions.

Upon admission a convict was stripped, washed, shaved, and his hair cropped. His street clothes were taken and destroyed if in poor condition. If the clothes were in good condition they were laundered and given out to other prisoners upon release. The inmate was issued a full outfit of prison dress in the form of an allotment for the year. In the early years the prison day began with the sound of a bell at 5:15 a.m. when the prisoners were released from their cells. The first duty was to empty their toilet buckets, after which they proceeded to their workplace until about 6:15 a.m. In single file they marched into breakfast. They were allowed a short recess period after breakfast before going back to work. Lunch was served at noon, after which they again returned to work until around 5:00 p.m. They then washed up, picked up their toilet buckets, and returned to their cells. The evening meal was eaten in the solitude of their own cells, where they remained without human contact until the next morning.[104] The staples of the weekly food allowance were brown bread, beef, salt pork, and potatoes. The regulations required that each prisoner be provided "with a sufficient quantity of inferior but wholesome food."

The majority of prisoners sentenced to Kingston were sent for relatively short periods of time, usually ranging from one to three years. However, the harsh discipline, the hard work, and the silence made the experience much worse than serving time in the most decrepit district jail. Most inmates were a long distance from their homes and prisoners were not allowed to have visitors. Aside from officials and guests of the warden the only visitors were the curious, who paid an admission fee for the entertainment of being able to gawk at the convicts. This sport was open to the public six days a week between 10:00 a.m. and noon and 1:00 and 3:00 p.m. Upon the expiration of their terms they were released into the streets of Kingston clothed in an outfit that had, at one time, belonged to a fellow prisoner. Released criminals were given a sum not to exceed £1, which was supposed to return them to their place of residence. They were expected to go out reformed and to sin no more.[105]

The noble experiment in reform penology that was Kingston encountered difficulties from the outset. There were too many rules and regulations, which the prisoners themselves could not remember. Consequently, constant infractions necessitated frequent punishments. Rumours of problems and mismanagement at Kingston eventually attracted public attention. Led by George Brown's *Globe*, a campaign for an investigation culminated with the government establishing a commission of inquiry in 1848. George Brown was the commission secretary.

The Brown Commission, as it became known, delivered its report in 1849. It told a story of cruelty, graft, corruption, crooked politics, and mismanagement. The most sensational part of the report was the revelations on the frequency and severity of punishments. One man of low intellect was punished so frequently that he went insane. In an eight-year period he had been whipped thirty-five times and received a total of 1,182 lashes. Many other prisoners received similarly barbarous punishments. The warden's report for 1846 listed fourteen inmates who had been whipped twenty times or more during the year. One man was flogged forty-eight times and another sixty times. Some days there were as many as twenty to forty inmates flogged in one morning. The cat-o'-nine tails was laid on the bare back, drawing blood and making the whole back raw and black. Sometimes those being punished had to be given water to keep them from fainting, and some prisoners were punished in this manner for a repeat offence before their backs had healed from the previous whipping. The frequency of discipline escalated over the years leading up to the inquiry. In 1843 there were 770 punishments, 2,102 in 1845, 3,445 in 1846, and 6,063 in 1847. Even young girls and very young boys were punished with the whip at Kingston Prison.

Along with the cat-o'-nine tails and the rawhide whip, punishments at Kingston included being put on a diet of bread and water, and being placed in solitary confinement in a dark cell or in a box. The latter required a prisoner to hunch up so as to fit in a box shorter than the inmate's height. The device numbed and cramped the body and sometimes a person could not walk on his own for a time after a session in the box. The punishment was found to be so harsh that some inmates claimed they preferred to be whipped. The commissioners observed that the severity and frequency of the punishments had a hardening effect on the prisoners. They maintained that seeing large numbers of inmates regularly whipped in front of the entire prison population for frequently minor offences was demoralizing and concluded that the experience "must have obliterated from the minds of the unhappy men all perception of moral guilt, and thoroughly brutalized all their feelings."[106]

The inhumane discipline was only one of many shortcomings of the prison administration. The warden's son, Francis W. Smith, worked in the penitentiary as a keeper. He frequently amused himself at the expense and discomfort of the inmates. He stuck pins in them, shot arrows at them, threw objects, and hit them. One of his favourite sports was to require a prisoner to open his mouth on the pretext of searching for tobacco. Smith would then throw salt or some other offensive substance into the man's mouth. In addition, he sold penitentiary stores and took various supplies for his private use. The senior Smith was charged with running the prison merely as a place of detention, neglecting his duties, and mismanaging the institution. Henry Smith frequently quarrelled with his deputy warden, showed favouritism among the convicts, on occasion was not able to maintain prison discipline, allowed his son to mistreat prisoners and steal, and generally neglected his duties. While the prison lacked a chapel, proper schoolroom, and a decent library, lavish stone stables were built for the horses and a summer house for the warden.

The commissioners took strong exception to the system that prevailed at Kingston and made recommendations that touched on a wide number of the problems that plagued the operation. In respect to the treatment of prisoners they recommended: that the congregate system be maintained but that new prisoners be segregated for a period of up to six months, during which time they would be given instruction and work, as well as counselling by the warden and chaplain; that a better classification of prisoners be introduced; that harsh punishments be done away with and that punishments be resorted to less frequently; more moral, religious, and secular instruction; that school instruction be available at least one hour every second day; that training in job skills be improved; that the practice of allowing the public to come and gawk at the prisoners be stopped; that punishments be uniform for rule infractions and administered equitably; and that prisoners be given money on release. The commissioners also encouraged the organization of prisoners' aid societies, discouraged payment of convicts for their labour, and criticized the use of pardons and incentives to good behaviour.

The commissioners gave a strong imprimatur to the concept of the prison being a place of reform. They acknowledged its role in guaranteeing public safety and as an agent of deterrence but they took pains to emphasize the reformatory role of the prison. As the commissioners expressed it, "the permanent moral reform of the Convict is the chief aim."[107] Many of the Commission's recommendations were related to this objective – an institution that would treat its charges humanely, improve them through moral and secular education, teach them order and discipline, equip them with a trade, and turn them out better than when they came in. Their revelations helped to focus public attention on the treatment of criminals. Their recommendations gave encouragement to criminal justice officials and public-spirited citizens working for prison reform.

Many recognized the shortcomings in the treatment of prisoners that were highlighted in the Brown report. In fact, officials frequently made recommendations for improvements that are sometimes assumed to have originated in more recent times. For example, the inspectors of the provincial penitentiary in their annual report for 1839 noted the need for a system of probation that would provide some form of supervision after a prisoner's discharge. They expressed the belief that the current system accomplished little by way of reform and noted that "until a plan is devised and put in operation to place him in a state of probation, under some sort of surveillance after his discharge, little permanent reformation will be effected."[108] Penal reform ideas were well circulated among Europeans and North Americans of the time and the proposals were both enlightened and comprehensive. The problem in Canada and elsewhere was that the public was apathetic and governments at all levels were reluctant to spend money on criminals.

A decade after the Brown Commission the treatment of criminals seemed to have improved significantly at Kingston. The biggest change was in the discipline. The majority of rule breakers were now being punished with bread and water diets and deprivation of bed, with the next most common punishment being confinement in a dark cell. During the year 1859 twenty-seven convicts were punished with the cat-o'-nine tails and administered a total of 616 lashes, a far cry from the 1840s. More time was devoted to education and there was a wider range of trades training. Inmates worked at and received training in shoemaking, blacksmithing, agricultural implement making, cabinetmaking, tailoring, carpentry, masonry, and cooking. While much of this was an improvement over the days of Warden Smith, the primary object – reform – continued to be elusive. The very nature of the prison militated against reform. Authorities continued to pay lip service to the objective but admitted that for the average inmate a stay in prison had little impact.[109]

While the results of imprisonment in Kingston were at best questionable, there was no doubt about the consequence of a term in the jails of the land. In 1841 the Act of Union came into effect uniting Upper and Lower Canada under one legislature. Upper Canada was known as Canada West and Lower Canada as Canada East. In an attempt to standardize and improve institutional conditions throughout the Canadas the government established a Board of Inspectors of Asylums and Prisons in 1859. One of its first acts was to conduct a survey of jail conditions by sending a questionnaire to all keepers. In addition, members of the Board conducted a number of on-sight inspections.

Based on the survey returns and their own observations, the inspectors concluded "that our common Gaols are schools of vice."[110] They critically observed that defects in the system were pervasive. They found problems with the design, capacity, and maintenance of buildings, problems of inadequate staff, problems with discipline, administration, and sanitation. In effect, little had changed since the earlier days of the century. The result, according to the inspectors, was that none of the objectives of incarceration were being achieved and some of the worst aspects of earlier days still existed. Many jails were damp, improperly heated, and poorly ventilated. There was a total lack of uniformity, with discipline being severe in some jails, lax in others. Similarly, food was abundant in one jail but inadequate in another. And so it went. Under such conditions there was no hope of reform. Prisoners were given no opportunities that might help them. Indeed, the indiscriminate mixing that went on in many jails served to make the inmates more vicious than repentant. As the inspectors succinctly put it: "The present system of our Gaols (which is in fact an utter absence of all system), fails entirely in effecting the objects of penal institutions. We do not punish, or we punish improperly. We do not deter from crime, and we do not reform the criminal."[111]

Along with the jails the courts added to the chaos of the criminal justice system. Trials were still being held in makeshift facilities in some communities. Where formal courts did exist they, too, reflected the parsimonious nature of local government – many were small and cramped, and the condition of some of those on trial made the air in many a courtroom putrid. The police magistrate in Toronto, for example, complained to city council in April, 1854, that the police office was "fetid and oppressive."[112] Many magistrates were still untrained and some who were qualified conducted their courts in a very informal and highly personal manner. On occasion the same magistrate that bound a person over for trial also heard the case. The magistrate acted as prosecutor, defence, and judge.

A verdict did not always reflect the merits of the case and political interference was not unusual in the dispensation of justice. Aldermen and other politicians commonly interceded with magistrates on behalf of constituents. Indeed, in certain cities, such as Toronto between 1834 and 1851 and Halifax from 1841 to 1867, the mayor and aldermen actually presided over the police court.[113] Some politicians went so far as to instruct the judge as to whether or not the accused should be found guilty and, if so, what penalty should be levied.[114] Many judges depended on civic politicians for their salaries and so were amenable to their influence. In those communities where the politicians themselves supervised the lower courts they were naturally prone to deal lightly with their supporters. Consequently, justice in many courts was subject to a number of influences, some of which had little to do with the actual guilt or innocence of the accused.

While justice could at times be uneven, the atmosphere in which it was dispensed could be raucous. Trials were a great attraction for the general populace. In rural areas, especially when trials were conducted in a nearby tavern, many in the crowd, as well as those on trial and sometimes even the judge, were inebriated. In the larger urban areas the unemployed, the idle, and the vagrants were regular spectators at the courts. Some women even brought babies with them. Courts were a refuge in inclement or cold weather and good entertainment at any time of the year, so much so that spectators were known to bet on the outcome of trials. Proceedings were sometimes rowdy – the gallery booing or cheering as the circumstances warranted and counsel and magistrates trading insults.[115]

The treatment of criminals that characterized the Canadas was pretty much duplicated in the Atlantic region. Deficiencies were to be found in virtually every jail. Facilities were inadequate, a permanent stench from poor sanitation permeated the buildings, prisoners spent their time in idleness, and there were no reformatory influences and little attempt to provide any. The only serious efforts at introducing modern penal methods came in the form of two new prisons. A House of Correction was opened in Saint John, New Brunswick, in 1841, which ultimately changed its name to the Provincial Penitentiary. In 1844 a new Provincial Penitentiary also opened in Halifax, Nova Scotia. The supporters of both institutions were motivated by a desire to provide an alternative to the run-down jails and to implement a reformist penal program. The system in both penitentiaries was modelled on the Auburn and Kingston prisons.

The underlying penal philosophy was that order and discipline were the twin pillars of a successful institution. Staff were cautioned to maintain close supervision and to enforce strictly the rules; inmates were expected to maintain silence and obey the regulations. When prisoners moved they marched in single file and lock step, and some were shackled and chained. Every aspect of their lives – from the number of times they had to wash their face (once a week), to haircuts (monthly) – was regulated. The usual punishment for unruly inmates was a stint in solitary confinement on bread and water. Hard work was an integral part of the daily routine and considered necessary to develop character. Criminals were assumed to be shiftless and idle by nature, so hard work would break them of their lazy habits. In the eyes of authorities, however, an even more important aspect of prison work was the income it would generate to offset operating expenses.[116]

The Halifax prison soon demonstrated the difficulties in running a reformist institution with recalcitrant clients, a custodial environment, and an ineffective administration. Thomas Carpenter, the prison warden, had a drinking problem and during one of his frequent binges, in 1849, helped a number of prisoners escape. Discipline had completely broken down and on occasion guards showed up for work intoxicated. Things improved somewhat when Carpenter was replaced but the facility never succeeded in fulfilling the objectives of its promoters.

Even when genuine attempts were made to introduce new programs or reforms the experiments could be substantially affected by the attitudes and practices of management. For example, a mark system was introduced in the Nova Scotia Penitentiary in 1851. The idea was to reward prisoners for good behaviour by awarding marks, which could in turn earn special privileges. The concept was advanced for its day but was subject to the whim of prison officials. Also, any good it might have done was undercut by the tactics of the superintendent and by prison conditions. In the same year the mark system was introduced food rations were reduced as an economy measure. As late as 1863 the main diet consisted of hard biscuit, bread, and water. The good will earned by one measure was destroyed by another.[117]

A number of factors contributed to the problems with the treatment of criminals in the pre-Confederation period. There remained an ongoing ambivalence over the appropriate way to deal with lawbreakers. Many supported reforms, but many others firmly believed that criminals should be locked away and forgotten. Some very influential people, including churchmen, shared the latter sentiment. For example, the December, 1860, issue of the *Methodist Christian Guardian* left no doubt where it stood. It stated unequivocally: "We believe the principal end of punishment is to punish the offender as a warning to others, and as a means of maintaining the authority of the law." While some supported reforms and others called for stricter measures, most Canadians were little concerned with what was going on in the courts, jails, and prisons. Most were too occupied with the business of survival to give much attention to the treatment of criminals. Consequently, the governing authorities in most communities felt little pressure to take action. Even if they were inclined to institute reforms, spending money on the criminal justice system took a back seat to more pressing needs. Money was scarce and the first call on what could be raised came from other community needs such as roads, hospitals, and care of the indigent.

When and where new facilities were built, such as in Saint John and Halifax, much lip service was paid to reform philosophy but there was little by way of follow-up. For example, New Brunswick authorities described the purpose of the law as being "to benefit and reform the criminal."[118] Similarly, Nova Scotia officials saw their new prison as a means of forming habits of industry and bringing about moral and religious reformation. Yet to achieve these objectives they ran institutions administered by unqualified political appointees that were poorly funded, inadequately equipped, and lacking in programs.

One of the main roadblocks to reform, however, was the very essence of the system. Prisoners were expected to go through a born-again experience in which they would develop habits of discipline and hard work, reform their morals, and find religion. However, they were hardly in a receptive mood for all this since they were there against their wills. Prison conditions, the myriad rules, and strict discipline made them more embittered and resentful. They were expected to maintain silence and obey every command, and were deprived of natural human intercourse. All this was hardly conducive to reform. The prison staff were simply custodians who were there to maintain order, supervise the prisoners in their daily routines, and make sure that they did not escape. The job required no special training or qualifications. Thus, outside of their fellow convicts, the only people that prisoners interacted with on a daily basis were guardians who had no therapeutic role. They were not equipped, inclined, or obligated to assist with the rehabilitation of a criminal.

Few programs were offered to prisoners that might help with rehabilitation. In a day when reform was seen in moral and religious terms, very little of what went on in a prison might be construed as values or character development education. Usually religion was represented by a lone chaplain, visiting church people, and the distribution of Bibles. There was little actual religious or moral instruction. In the area of secular education, which could serve to broaden horizons or raise aspirations, little was done. Educational upgrading programs were limited to a few hours a week at most. Library holdings were meagre and vocational training was restricted to occupations that might earn money for the prison. Even when an inmate did learn a trade, little effort was made to make him want to earn an honest living with his trade skills when he completed his sentence.

Another roadblock to effecting positive change in inmates was the short time that most of them spent in the jails and prisons. Offenders were incarcerated for relatively short periods of time, usually ranging from ten to ninety days. These were the drunks, the vagrants, and the petty criminals. Many were frequently in and out of jail and thus most in need of a rehabilitation program. For many, as the jail records show, the root cause of their problem was alcohol. Yet there was no such thing as a treatment program of any kind in the jails of the land. Even if there had been, the time spent incarcerated was too short for any positive results. Indeed, the short duration of sentences itself served as a justification for the lack of interest in jail programs.

The same problem existed in the prisons. Kingston differed to a degree because inmates sent to that institution averaged sentences of one to three years. However, it, too, lacked alcohol abuse treatment, and, as elsewhere, the emphasis was more on custody than reform. The prisons in New Brunswick and Nova Scotia faced the same problems as the jails insofar as they housed short-term inmates, with a high percentage of sentences being under one year. For example, the average stay of prisoners in the Saint John penitentiary in 1857 was sixty-nine days. The institution provided work and instruction at brickmaking, tailoring, shoemaking, and carpentry. The Halifax penitentiary offered shoemaking, barrel-making, tailoring, and work in the blacksmith shop. However, the emphasis was not so much on learning trade skills but on earning money for the institution.[119]

Cruelty was another part of prison life that inhibited reform. It embittered inmates and caused them to become resentful and rebellious rather than amenable to rehabilitation. Some guards were brutal, abusing prisoners and goading them into breaking the rules so that they could be punished. Administrators were inefficient and arbitrary. One might lean to a less restrictive regimen while another might introduce harsher measures. In 1852 the superintendent of the Nova Scotia penitentiary was dismissed on charges of cruelty. A decade later another superintendent decided to tighten up on discipline and provoked a good deal of unrest. The institution was kept in a state of agitation until the man died in 1868.

In spite of a lack of progress and setbacks, the humane trends in the treatment of criminals that developed early in the century continued to grow throughout the period. The use of the pillory was abolished by statute in 1842. In 1851, as we saw, an incentive system of marks for good behaviour was introduced in the Nova Scotia penitentiary and in 1853 a new superintendent discontinued the use of chains and shackles. In 1857 an Act was passed by the legislature of the Canadas abolishing prison for debt. In 1865 crimes punishable by death were reduced to murder, treason, and rape.

Fines and jail sentences became the most frequent punishments. Inside the jails and prisons discipline was less severe, with corporal punishment used sparingly. Many supervisory personnel tried to inculcate a more enlightened attitude throughout their systems. The commissioners of the Nova Scotia penitentiary in Halifax, for example, pointed out "that fallen and degraded as the greatest criminals may be, they are still members of the human family . . . and having therefore a kindred claim to our sympathy."[120]

While there was progress at the philosophical level, and some specific improvements in the statutes, the judicial system continued to be plagued with problems. The jails were considered to be the weakest link in the chain and a cause of constant concern to governments, officials, and reformers. In addition to their other weaknesses many were at the point where they could not implement the sentences passed out by the courts. It was common practice for judges sending people to jail to stipulate that the time was to be served at hard labour. However, most jails did not have the wherewithal to put inmates to work at any kind of labour. The enforced idleness was blamed for the general malaise that characterized the jails in all parts of the country. As in the past, considerable ambivalence existed as to the direction to take to improve things. Some wanted changes because penal facilities were not reforming criminals or preparing them to make an honest living. Others were more concerned over recidivism rates and the general level of crime and called for more order, discipline, and harsher punishments in penal institutions. One group wanted new jails built to accommodate reform, others wanted them to facilitate a tougher policy.

In the Canadas the Board of Inspectors attempted to make the jail experience more of a deterrent influence by establishing a uniform and better-ordered regimen. Jail inmates were put in uniforms, a fixed diet was prescribed, stricter segregation was enforced, and an attempt was made to provide a more sanitary and healthful environment. A large number of new jails were built and old ones upgraded. These changes were not meant as reformist measures but rather were motivated to make incarceration more of a genuine punishment. For example, one inspector described the changes as "hard fare." He pointed out that the prison uniform was adopted as a sign of shame and degradation. The inspectors were not so concerned that jail conditions were harsh but rather that the lax discipline, idleness, and communication among inmates were not sufficiently punitive. One of the main shortcomings was the absence of work.

E.A. Meredith, a member of the Board of Inspectors of Prisons, addressed this problem in a speech delivered in Montreal in 1864. His observations and proposals illustrate the ambivalence toward criminals that prevailed up to Confederation. On the one hand many, including the inspectors, favoured humanitarian treatment of criminals. On the other hand they were frustrated by the failure of the judicial system to stem the tide of crime. Consequently, they espoused a number of changes in the jail procedures that in some respects were a throwback to the days of more inhumane punishment.

Meredith defined the main function of jails as being to deter crime. He maintained that they were failing in this because the incarceration experience was too easy. He attributed the main cause to idleness but acknowledged that most jails did not have the facilities to accommodate a work program, pointing out that the inspectors had already proposed the construction of central prisons to remedy this. These would be intermediate institutions, between local jails and penitentiaries. They could be built to remedy the shortcomings of jails but still house short-term prisoners. Since such institutions were still in the future Meredith called for the establishment of a program of solitary confinement in the jails.

Meredith proposed that prisoners be kept in separate cells completely cut off from all intercourse with each other. He recognized that this could be dangerous to the mental health of prisoners so he also recommended that jail sentences be shortened. He felt a period of confinement up to one month would not be psychologically damaging. The experience of total confinement would, however, "inspire evil-doers with a wholesome dread" of jails. Meredith believed that spending a jail term in idleness and ease had little deterrent impact on an offender; in contrast, the unpleasant experience of total confinement would instil an aversion for jail and a criminal would not want to repeat the experience. [121]

For Meredith and like-minded people of his day, toughening up the jail experience was a thin line between a humanitarian reformist approach and straight punishment as a deterrent to crime. Whatever the ideas for changes in the system, reformist or otherwise, the day-to-day reality of supervising criminals, some of whom were dangerous, indolent, belligerent, mentally or emotionally unstable, or of marginal intelligence, became the main concern of keepers. The custodial function thus took precedence over reform. Although authorities continued to emphasize the role of the prison in the conversion of the criminal, more emphasis was placed on administrative detail, security, discipline, and attempts to have prisoners earn their keep. As a result the treatment of criminals in the years prior to Confederation did not result in any significant improvements in the level of crime or in the recidivism rate of criminals.

SUMMARY

Pioneer Canada inherited from the mother countries of France and England a set of severe laws and extremely cruel punishments. Fortunately for the criminals of the day, their treatment was tempered by the conditions of a frontier society; criminal justice officials were frequently untrained; a high priority was placed on settlers in a land where population was sparse; Canadians had a democratic and egalitarian spirit; courts were inefficient;

jails were scarce; witnesses refused to testify; friends and neighbours were reluctant to convict; and officials frequently tempered justice with mercy. Consequently, instead of the harshest punishment provided by law, criminals frequently got off with lighter sentences and in some cases got off completely. Nevertheless, the punishments meted out were still cruel. Branding, banishment, mutilation, flogging, the stocks and pillory were all severe penalties. They reflected the prevailing penal philosophy of the day, which emphasized punishment and deterrence. They also reflected the still backward state of civility of the society.

While jail sentences and fines were in use to a limited extent, they were usually accompanied by a flogging. With the Enlightenment and reformers like Beccaria and Howard, the basic philosophy behind the treatment of criminals began to change. Humanitarian ideas circulated widely among the intellectuals and the educated in both Europe and North America. By the 1820s and 1830s the criminal justice system in Canada began to reflect those ideas. Jail sentences and fines were more often being substituted for the harsher punishments, and, to accommodate the trend, the pace of jail construction accelerated. The more humane procedures, however, proved themselves to be a problem. The jails were catch-alls for the first offender, the hardened criminal, the indigent, the aged, the sick, the infirm, and the insane. The facilities quickly deteriorated into vermin-infested, foul-smelling, unhealthy holes.

Reformers, officials, critics, and the general public became concerned about the sanitation. All agreed that the conditions had a detrimental effect on offenders. Some argued that they were inhumane, others that they coddled criminals by allowing them to spend their time in idleness in a level of comfort better than what they were used to. There was a consensus that the jails had no positive or reformative impact, that they were actually schools of crime. Also, public apathy, combined with a scarcity of money, resulted in widespread neglect and a reluctance to remedy the situation. In response, some seized on the concept of a prison as a potential cure – scientific methods based on order and discipline could be followed; inmates could be put to work, supervised, disciplined, and given moral instruction. All this, reformers were convinced, would generate a change in the criminal's morals, character, and attitude, and the criminal would return to the world outside as a good citizen.

The prison experiment quickly degenerated into a regimen far removed from the dreams and expectations of the reformers. Cruelty, mismanagement, neglect, inadequate programs and facilities became the outstanding characteristics of the early prisons. They were custodial facilities first and foremost. Reform was a secondary priority, if a consideration at all. Meanwhile, the jails across the country continued in their abject state. New, larger jails with better facilities were built, but practically all lacked work, education, or any type of reform or rehabilitative programs. Many of them quickly deteriorated to the same condition as the ones they replaced. Consequently, by Confederation the approach to dealing with criminals that had evolved could show little, if any, positive results. Crime rates continued to increase and recidivism rates remained high. When the statutes called for severe penalties people still risked getting caught and committed crimes. Even when they knew they risked the death penalty for a second offence they continued to break the law. Whether offenders were whipped, branded, humiliated in the stocks and pillories, or languished in vermin-infested, unhealthy, and uncomfortable jails, people were not deterred from breaking the law. The worst experiences at Kingston prison did not keep prisoners from offending again upon release. When the system moved to lighter penalties and a more humanitarian philosophy, it had little impact on the reformation of criminals. Over the entire period recidivism rates remained high and crime levels inexorably rose.

There were roadblocks to reform at every turn. Many crimes in pioneer society were liquor-related. Yet no programs addressed the problems of alcohol abuse. The penal environment was not conducive to reform of any kind. In the prisons the whole regimen was more likely to embitter an inmate than make him or her amenable to reform. The jails were in such chaos that it was not possible to introduce programs of any kind, and the vast majority of people were not incarcerated long enough for a reform program to have any impact, even if one were available. In the final analysis the attempts at moral reform were reduced to the distribution of Bibles, the sporadic administration of a cleric, and occasional church services. The entire system boiled down to a custodial function.

The failure was not due to any one factor. Governments did not have the funds needed to build the proper facilities or mount the proper programs. Public apathy and other priorities moved the governments in other directions. When and where they did respond to reformist agitation the result fell short of what was asked. A shortage of staff, a lack of training, and inadequate facilities resulted in the custodial function taking precedence over all other considerations. The lacunae that characterized the entire criminal justice system were not the result of any grand design on the part of officials – that would attribute to judicial authorities a sophistication and competence they simply did not possess. The reformers and correctional officials of the day did not conspire to build institutions that would grind down the criminal underclass. Rather, the system of punishment that evolved through the years prior to Confederation was at first a pragmatic but haphazard response to pioneer conditions. The changes introduced during the reform period were intended to reflect the liberal, humanitarian sentiments of the time, but the response was piecemeal and inadequate because the entire system, like topsy, just grew. The problem was that it didn't grow very well. It was a human product and, like its architects, it was less than perfect.

Another dimension of the problem was that the individuals whom reformers hoped to rehabilitate were also less than perfect. From the earliest days of settlement there were those who refused to share the burden of building a new society. From Cornwallis's "poor, idle, worthless vagabonds that embraced the opportunity to get provisions for one year without labor" to the wandering vagrants who strained the charity resources of pioneer Upper Canada, there were those who chose a life of idleness and crime. The thievery, the conniving to outwit the authorities, the drink, the whoring, the temptation to live an easier life than farming and hacking down forests were all part of the crime equation. In other words, just as there were those who chose hard work and probity, there were those who opted for idleness and lawbreaking. For many petty offenders and recidivists the jails of this country were not deterrents to crime. Rather, they were an integral part of the lifestyle. They were a place to sober up, a refuge in inclement weather, or a small price to pay for the privilege of marching to the beat of their own drummer.

Thus the failure of the judicial system to reduce crime or reform offenders was due to many factors. Just as there is no single, overriding explanation for crime, there is no all-embracing element underlying the chaos that permeated corrections in pioneer Canada. Officials firmly believed they knew the cause of crime and that they could devise a scientific plan to solve the problem. The fact that their aspirations were derailed by human failings at all levels is itself a comment on the difficulties inherent in trying to devise any kind of a monolithic solution to a human problem.

CHAPTER 8

▼

The Treatment of Criminals Since Confederation

The British North America Act, passed by the English Parliament in March, 1867, brought into existence on July 1, 1867, the first federal union in the British Empire. The new Dominion of Canada consisted of the provinces of Nova Scotia, New Brunswick, Quebec, and Ontario. In 1869 arrangements were completed with the Hudson's Bay Company to hand over Rupert's Land to the jurisdiction of the government in Ottawa. It was a vast territory that stretched to the Rocky Mountains. In 1870 Manitoba became a province of Canada, followed the next year by British Columbia, thus extending the country's boundaries to the Pacific Ocean. In 1873, Prince Edward Island joined the six other provinces.

Within a short time after Confederation the federal government assumed a major role in the administration of justice. The British North America Act granted the power to legislate in the field of criminal law to the central government. Sir John A. Macdonald had been a strong advocate of this during the negotiations that preceded Confederation. He believed it was important to have one uniform system of law governing the entire country, arguing that this lack of uniformity was a fatal weakness in the United States constitution and that Canada should not make the same mistake. He maintained that Canadians should be subject to the same laws and the same punishments in all parts of the country.

Along with establishing a uniform legal system the new government also decided that it would be based on the criminal law of England. While criminal law became the jurisdiction of the federal government, authority over correctional institutions was split between the government in Ottawa and the provinces. Offenders sentenced to two years or more would serve their time in federal penitentiaries; those sentenced to less than two years would be incarcerated in institutions under provincial control. In 1868 Parliament passed An Act Respecting Penitentiaries and the Directors Thereof. The legislation made provision for the management of the prisons under federal jurisdiction. The prisons at Halifax, Saint John, and Kingston were taken over and were uniformly referred to as penitentiaries.

Next, the government moved to consolidate the myriad laws that governed criminal justice in the various provinces. A series of consolidation acts were passed, the main ones being the Criminal Law and Amendment Acts of 1869. The Canadian legislation was based on the English law that Prime Minister Macdonald greatly admired. He believed that "It would be an incalculable advantage that every decision of the Imperial Courts should be law in the Dominion."[1] Partly to achieve a more systematic penalty structure, Sir John Thompson, the Minister of Justice in 1892, introduced a bill to codify Canadian law. The draft code was modelled on an English code that had been the work of Sir James Fitzjames Stephen but which had never been adopted by the English Parliament. It fared better in Canada and the new code became law on July 1, 1893.[2]

There were a number of other significant developments in the criminal justice system in the period following Confederation. The 1868 Act Respecting Penitentiaries and the Directors Thereof established a Board of Directors to supervise the institutions under Ottawa's control. Also, it introduced a system of earned remission for federal prisoners. The Act provided that up to five days per month of sentence remission could be earned for good behaviour and hard work. In 1869 public hanging was abolished in Canada and in 1875 the use of the ball and chain was discontinued. The new law code of 1892 introduced a provision that permitted an offender to appeal a conviction, thus extending the rights of the accused.

Besides codifying laws and introducing reforms, the federal government also found itself in the business of prison construction. With the growth in population and an accompanying increase in crime, existing buildings were inadequate. In response the federal government built a number of new penitentiaries. St. Vincent de Paul, near Montreal, was opened in 1873, Manitoba Penitentiary, later called Stoney Mountain, in 1877, British Columbia Penitentiary at New Westminster in 1878, and Dorchester Penitentiary in New Brunswick in 1880. The latter replaced the prisons in Halifax and Saint John.

Correctional developments in the nineteenth century were only one segment of a widespread reform movement that sought to eradicate a number of evils plaguing the society of the day. There was agitation for the abolition of slavery, for legislation to improve working conditions, for better health care, for hospitals for the insane, for societies for the prevention of cruelty to animals and children, and for less severe discipline in the armed forces. Reformers fighting for these causes were to be found in many countries.

They exchanged ideas, wrote tracts, and corresponded. Consequently, there was a certain homogeneity to the reform agendas from country to country. As we saw with the intellectuals of the Enlightenment, the ideas of some individuals had an international impact.

ALEXANDER MACONOCHIE AND THE CROFTON SYSTEM

In the field of penal reform one of the more influential activists in the nineteenth century was an Englishman, Captain Alexander Maconochie. He pioneered many of the ideas that later formed the cornerstone of penal reforms in the United States and Canada. Although Maconochie's experiments took place in the first half of the nineteenth century they so influenced reform and reformers in later years that it is appropriate to examine his work in the context of late nineteenth-century reform.

Alexander Maconochie was born in Edinburgh, Scotland, in 1787 into a family of lawyers. His father died in 1796 and he went to live with a kinsman who, at various stages of his career, was a lawyer, a professor of law, and a judge. Thus Maconochie came about his interest in judicial matters naturally. His guardian intended that he should become a lawyer but he was more interested in a naval career. During his service he spent two years as a French prisoner of war, an experience that doubtless had some impact on his later interest in penal reform. Maconochie was well educated and after leaving the navy he published works on a number of different subjects, including geography. He became the first secretary of the Geographical Society of London when it was formed in 1830 and was also the first professor of geography at University College, London. He held the position from 1833 to 1836. As a geographer Maconochie had developed an interest in the Pacific area so when he was invited by his friend, Sir John Franklin, to accompany him to Van Diemen's Land he accepted the offer. Franklin was appointed as Lieutenant-Governor and Maconochie went along as his private secretary.

After the American Revolution the former British colonies were closed as a dumping ground for English felons so the government opened a number of penal colonies in what is now Australia. Before Maconochie left England some acquaintances in the London Society for the Improvement of Prison Discipline asked him to send back a report on penal conditions and practices in Van Diemen's Land. In carrying out the request he learned first hand of the inhumane conditions that prevailed and was strongly critical in his report. Not inclined to be a mere reporter, he formulated some ideas as to how the entire system might be improved.

Maconochie sent his report to Franklin, who in turn distributed copies of it to other administrators in the colony. He also sent his report to England, where his ideas on penal reform eventually sparked some official interest. As a result Alexander Maconochie was put in charge of the prisoners in the penal colony of Norfolk Island in 1840. For the next four years, until he was replaced in February, 1844, he experimented with his advanced ideas for the treatment of prisoners. The system he introduced featured elements that were subsequently adopted as part of the emerging modern and enlightened penology. The central thrust in Maconochie's program was rehabilitation. To achieve this he introduced a better system of classification, more humane discipline, the indeterminate sentence, education and recreation programs, and measures to prepare prisoners to return to free society.

The core of his reform program was the mark system. As an incentive to good behaviour a prisoner could earn marks for co-operation, hard work, and good conduct. These marks could be used to buy such things as extra food or supplies or they could be accumulated and eventually earn prisoners time off their original sentences. The prospect of early release was seen as the driving force that would make prisoners co-operative. Meanwhile, the prison regimen would teach them good habits and also prepare them for ultimate freedom. The whole idea was to develop in the prisoners characteristics such as self-discipline, responsibility, and thrift. As Maconochie described it, "the object of the New System of Prison Discipline is, besides inflicting a suitable punishment on men for their past offenses, to train them to return to society honest, useful and trustworthy members of it."[3]

Among the many converts to Maconochie's approach to the treatment of criminals was Sir Walter Crofton. In 1854 he was appointed chairman of the Directors of Convict Prisons in Ireland. He borrowed many of Maconochie's ideas and with some modifications introduced what became known as the Crofton or Irish system, destined to influence reform ideas in both the United States and Canada.[4] In 1863 Gaylord B. Hubbell, warden of Sing Sing prison in the United States, visited Britain and studied the managerial methods then in use in the prisons of England and Ireland. He was greatly impressed with the Crofton system in the Irish prisons and returned home a staunch advocate of its implementation in the United States. A number of other Americans, partly through Hubbell's influence, also became converts to the Crofton system. Included among them were the Reverend Enoch Cobb Wines and Dr. Theodore W. Dwight.

Enoch Cobb Wines (1806-1879) was a Congregationalist minister. Wines, after involvement in a number of ventures, moved to New York and in 1862 became secretary of the Prison Association of New York. From that point on Wines gave himself completely to the work of prison reform. Dwight was the vice-president of the Prison Association and the first head of Columbia Law School. Concerned about the disgusting conditions that prevailed in the prisons and jails of the state, the Prison Association commissioned Wines and Dwight to make a thorough study. The result was a *Report on the Prisons and Reformatories of the United States and Canada*. The *Report* reviewed conditions in eighteen northern states and the province of Canada and was submitted to the New York state legislature in 1867.[5]

The work of Wines and Dwight gave considerable impetus to prison reformers. One tangible result of their efforts was the founding of the National Prison Association and the holding of its first meeting in Cincinnati on October 12, 1870. Wines was also instrumental in organizing the first International Penitentiary Congress, held in London, England, in 1872. An international network of reform-minded people was forged, which helped spread ideas for the improvement of the treatment of criminals in many countries. Program proposals reflected the ideas of a long list of people, from the thinkers of the Enlightenment to officials like Maconochie and Crofton.

Typical of the reform agenda that emerged was the Declaration of Principles adopted by the American Prison Association in Cincinnati in 1870. The reformation of criminals was defined as the primary aim of prisons. The Declaration called for a system of rewards for prisoners, special training for institutional officers, religious and educational instruction, the use of indeterminate sentences, industrial training, proper classification and grading of prisoners, work for discharged prisoners, improved prison facilities and sanitation, and a host of other improvements in the prison system and for its inmates.[6] The thirty-seven principles gathered together reforms that had been advocated or experimented with for some time. They became the focus of reform agitation for at least the next half-century.

CANADIAN REFORMERS AND REFORM PROGRESS

The ideas circulating on the international scene and in the United States were well known in Canada. As in other countries, they formed the framework in which debate, changes, and experimentation were taking place. Some of the changes already outlined, such as earned remission, were indicative of the confluence of thinking that characterized reformers of the period. Canadians were active in the National Prison Association, stayed abreast of developments in other countries, and maintained contacts with reformers, officials, and politicians.

Among the more prominent proponents of penal reform in Canada in the early post-Confederation period were J.M. Ferres, T.J. O'Neill, and T.Z. Tasse. All three were members of the first Board of Directors of Federal Penitentiaries. They took a public position against the practice of contracting out prison labour, advocated paying wages to inmates for their work, established a rudimentary system of classification based on rewards for good conduct, and in general placed greater emphasis on the reform of the prisoner.[7]

James Moir Ferres was warden of Kingston prison from 1859 until his death in 1870. Between 1867 and 1869 he was chairman of the Board of Directors of Federal Penitentiaries. One of his first acts at Kingston was to cancel all punishments. He ordered irons removed from a man who had been shackled for nine years; he had prison garb numbered so inmates would get back their own clothing from the laundry; he introduced church music to services and allowed the men to sing; he permitted the inmates to write their own letters, thus eliminating the requirement that they be written by the chaplain; and he cut back on the use of corporal punishment. His work placed him in the forefront of reform-minded officials of his day.[8]

People like Ferres were succeeded by others who were equally dedicated to improving the system. None was more persistent than James G. Moylan. In 1872 Sir John A. Macdonald appointed Moylan as one of the three Directors of Penitentiaries. In 1875 the Board was dissolved and Moylan was made Inspector of Penitentiaries for Canada, a position he held until his retirement in 1895. In his annual reports he consistently called for changes and reforms, predicated on his belief that "the cardinal object to be effected in our penal institutions is the reformation of the criminal. This is above and beyond every consideration."[9]

Notwithstanding some enlightened thinking in this country, there were many roadblocks to prison reform. Since people were involved with nation-building, concerns such as settlement, industrial development, railroads, and politics were naturally higher priorities than the treatment of criminals. Consequently, reformers and judicial officials encountered many frustrations in their efforts to bring about change.

As in the past, public opinion continued to be a problem. There was always a price tag on new institutions and programs, and governments were reluctant to spend money on criminals. Also, many still believed that severe discipline and hard labour were the most effective treatment strategies for criminals. Others were ambivalent but reluctant to see too many changes that might ease the life of inmates. Typical were the views of Macdonald. In a letter dated October 31, 1871, the Prime Minister wrote to his old friend, John Creighton, whom he had appointed warden of Kingston Penitentiary, offering some advice on the treatment of inmates. He told Creighton that his kind disposition might cause him to forget that the most important purpose of the penitentiary was punishment and that reformation was an "incidental concern."

> You say that you desire to feel you are the means of making five or six hundred of your fellow creatures more happy than they have previously been in the Penitentiary. I could quite sympathize with your desire if it were to make them less miserable than they have been previously rather than more happy – happiness and punishment cannot and ought not go together. There is such a thing as making a prison too comfortable and prisoners too happy.[10]

The intellectual climate in which changes in the treatment of criminals was evolving was itself in a state of flux. The dominant approach continued to be based on the assumptions of the Classical School, which explained crime as the product of individual character deficiencies. According to that system of thought, reform could be realized through moral regeneration and the inculcation of habits of industry, thrift, sobriety, and discipline. On the other hand, more mention was being made about the influence of the environment, biology, inheritance, and personality, reflecting the fact that science and the scientific method had replaced older systems of inquiry among many intellectuals.

The scientific model was adopted by progressively more people concerned with ameliorating nineteenth-century social problems. While penal reformers still stressed individual responsibility, many believed that reform should be attempted by the use of scientific methods. What they meant was that criminals should be exposed to a well-planned program offered within the confines of a structured, ordered, and disciplined environment. They compared moral weakness to a physical disease. Just as the sick went to a hospital to be cured, a criminal would go to a penitentiary for treatment.

This parallel was behind the advocacy for the indeterminate sentence, a concept popular with reformers and officials in the latter part of the century. Sick people did not enter a hospital for a fixed term; rather, they received treatment until they were well, and only then were they released. Proponents of the indeterminate sentence used the same rationale. They argued that if the main purpose of incarceration was reform, then criminals should be sentenced to terms sufficiently long to allow the treatment program to have some effect. They would be released when they showed signs of being ready to abandon their former ways, that is, when they were cured of their moral disease.

Unfortunately, the environment within which the cure was supposed to take place continued to be wracked with problems. Even the new penitentiaries fell far short of the reformers' expectations. They were characterized by untrained staff, inadequate programs, and poor classification of prisoners. The physical facilities were better but they were still primarily custodial institutions. There was always greater emphasis on discipline and security than on reform. The British Columbia Penitentiary at New Westminster, opened in 1878, was a good example of the improvements as well as the problems.

The penitentiary was a large three-storey edifice, 170 feet long, constructed of brick and stone. The building contained sixty-seven cells, each eight feet long by four feet wide. Five were designated as punishment cells "so constructed as to ensure the dreaded penance of solitary confinement – not a voice can be heard by the inmate or a human form seen."[11] The prison was embroiled in controversy from the outset. There were construction delays and after completion Inspector Moylan reported a number of deficiencies, which seemed to have been remedied quickly by the contractor. More serious was the criticism surrounding the first warden, Arthur

McBride, who was not the choice of some well-connected persons in the province. McBride had been the jailor at New Westminster and critics of his appointment argued that he was not qualified for the job as warden.[12]

McBride was a humane individual in many respects, but when a discipline problem arose he could respond with severity. The silent system was in place and if prisoners disobeyed the rules they were made to work in chains. The first prisoner who tried to escape after the new institution opened was lashed thirty-six times and placed in solitary confinement in chains on a diet of bread and water.[13] Guards were more concerned with discipline and security than anything else. Some measure of the temperament of those who were hired is evidenced by an incident that took place outside the prison. On November 4, 1884, a guard who shared a house with three of his colleagues took offence when he went to wash up and discovered that one of his housemates had left his dirty water in the wash basin. A verbal confrontation ensued, upon which the offending officer simply drew his revolver and killed the man for criticizing him.[14]

Facilities and programs were inadequate at the British Columbia Penitentiary. There was no proper hospital, so sick inmates had to be treated in their cells. If the doctor had to operate, this was done in a makeshift accommodation. The blacksmith and carpentry shops lacked adequate machinery, tools, and a water supply. There were no instructors for the tailor and shoemaker shops. The blacksmith and carpentry shops were also without instructors – inmates were recruited to fill in. The dining room was too small so some convicts ate in the corridors until the warden decided to feed them in their cells. By the early 1880s the prison was overcrowded and there were accusations of financial improprieties. Finally, the recurring problems prompted the government to mount an investigation. The Royal Commission Report found that the institution had been incompetently managed and Warden McBride was finally dismissed, in 1894.[15]

The general atmosphere, the lack of programs, and the untrained staff were all roadblocks to inmate rehabilitation at the British Columbia institution. In addition, the prison came under close scrutiny from the press and the public, sometimes to the detriment of attempts to improve life for the inmates. On one occasion, for example, a clergyman treated the prisoners to some entertainment. Immediately a local newspaper went on the attack, claiming that "the penitentiary is intended as a place of punishment, not entertainment."[16]

In contrast to the McBrides in the system, administrators continued to come along who not only made life easier for those under their direct supervision but tried to move the entire regimen in a more enlightened direction. Such a person was Samuel Lawrence Bedson, the first warden of the Manitoba Penitentiary. A British army colonel by training, he instituted a number of practices that were well ahead of their time: he removed the ball and chain from prisoners who had to work outside during winter weather; he developed an education program for inmates who could not read or write; he took a special interest in native Indian prisoners, encouraging them to take the literacy classes and recognizing the special burden that incarceration meant for them. Bedson did not believe in the use of corporal or severe punishment, arguing that it only generated fear, which in turn engendered cunning and a propensity to lie. He preferred to promote what he called "moral growth" through more humane measures. He maintained that "you must redeem the prisoner by sympathy," believing that deep down there was good in everyone and that if you tried hard enough you might eventually trigger the desired response and motivate a criminal to reform. He argued that one could "conquer violence by gentleness."[17]

Warden Bedson opened a zoo at the penitentiary and put the prisoners in charge of looking after it. He also had them construct a seven-hole golf course. They were allowed to play on the course as well as engage in a number of other sports. He started a therapy program for mentally disturbed inmates that included such activities as singing and dancing and he enlisted the help of his wife and prison inmates with the project. He also conceived a scheme to start a penal colony along the Athabasca River. His idea was to allow long-term married prisoners to settle in the area. They would be given free land and partial remission of their sentence if they lived up to the terms of the agreement. He saw the concept as a rehabilitation program and a way to encourage settlement. Along with his concern for inmates, he also was an advocate of better training for penitentiary guards.[18]

One of the worst aspects of the treatment of prisoners in federal penitentiaries in the latter part of the nineteenth century was the lack of uniformity. Although the regulations were the same for all institutions, their application was subjective and far from uniform. How the rules were enforced and how the philosophical objectives of the system were pursued were influenced by such things as the competence and personality of the warden, the character and temperament of the guards, and the nature of the inmates. An inquiry into affairs at St. Vincent de Paul Penitentiary in 1897 illustrates how far an institution could stray from the operational guidelines.

The commissioners discovered that the warden carried out a number of practices calculated to irritate the inmates and make life more unpleasant for them. One of the meanest was the holding back of mail. Hundreds of letters from and to prisoners were discovered in the warden's quarters. The inquiry also revealed that guards were negligent in their duties and that some were carrying on a very profitable sideline by selling food to the prisoners. The officer in charge of the stone shed was so inept that the prisoners controlled the shop and were selling the raw materials. Elsewhere in the institution prisoners who had access to food supplies were selling extra rations while others were using prison materials to make various articles they then sold for personal profit. Some convicts even managed to set up their own printing press and were contracting outside work. Throughout the prison discipline was lax, and there was a good deal of theft and intimidation.[19]

Facilities varied throughout the system. Some penitentiaries had reasonable-sized cells, others had very small ones; some were bright, others were dark and damp. At some places the food was adequate, at others, poor. Discipline was harsh at certain institutions and lax at others. Some had indoor plumbing, others still relied on a waste bucket. Not only did conditions differ from place to place, they also varied from time to time within the same institution as administrators came and went. It is little wonder that the federal system failed to make any significant headway toward the rehabilitation of criminals.

If conditions were less than ideal in the penitentiaries, they were much worse in the country's jails. Earlier there had been some hope of relieving the problem by building intermediate institutions to fill a niche between the jail and the penitentiary. However, with the exception of Ontario, they were never built. In that province the Central Prison was opened in Toronto in 1874 as an intermediate facility. The majority of inmates sent there were sentenced for terms of six months or more. The institution had 380 cells but on occasion housed many more prisoners. The emphasis of the administration was on hard work and strict but not inhumane discipline. One or the other, or perhaps both, apparently frightened many criminals because the institution quickly acquired a reputation as a place to be avoided. There were cases of offenders requesting judges to give them longer sentences so they could be put in Kingston rather than serve a shorter sentence in the Central Prison.[20]

The largest number of lawbreakers across the country continued to pass through the local jails. In 1890 Ontario appointed a commission to examine its prison and reformatory system. The subsequent report, submitted in 1891, offered a detailed look at the jails of the province. The commissioners noted that jail facilities generally were much improved from earlier years. "Now the gaols, with very few exceptions, are well built, well ventilated and well drained and the sunlight is admitted freely into corridor and cell."[21] Much of the improvement was due to the fact that all jails were subject to the government inspectors. They had the authority to make rules for the treatment of prisoners, to suggest improvements to the buildings, and to require the municipal governments to carry out their recommendations.

Although facilities were generally satisfactory, there were a number of exceptions. The jails in police stations in some urban areas were in poor shape. The commissioners observed that "they seem to have been designed in utter disregard of decency and all sanitary conditions."[22] The holding places in London consisted of a few small dark cells off two narrow hallways. The commissioners described the cells in the police station in

Kingston as "a disgrace to the civilization of the province."[23] Sanitation was still a problem in many jails, with the prisoners' quarters permanently smelling foul. The stench in some cases permeated the entire building.

Facilities generally were considered improved, but the conditions of incarceration were not. Classification and separation were still not possible in most jails because they were too small. Consequently, the old and the young, the first offender and the hardened criminal, the drunk and the sober were all herded together. Many communities still lacked facilities for the care of the aged, the infirm, and those with mental problems, so they, too, were housed in the local jails, although they had committed no crime. Idleness was another problem endemic to the jails. Short sentences and a lack of facilities made it impractical to sponsor work programs in most places. Prisoners were made to chop wood, clean the jail, and sometimes break stone. However, these were not full-time occupations and many were left with considerable free time to mingle and socialize with each other, the very thing that officials wanted to prevent.[24]

The jails in Ontario and elsewhere in Canada made no pretense to being reformatory institutions. They were simply short-term holding places. By their very nature they were not appropriate facilities in which to mount reform programs. Another stumbling block was the type of offender sent to the jails. A very high percentage were in for being intoxicated or for liquor-related crimes, and there were also many vagrants and poor people. The Ontario commissioners estimated that up to 50 per cent of the jail population fell into these categories.[25]

The commissioners made a number of enlightened recommendations to address this problem. They proposed the establishment of industrial reformatories for inebriates, which would basically be hospitals for the treatment of alcoholism. The courts would sentence problem drinkers for terms of not less than six months. A second commitment would automatically be for a term of not less than one year and a third for two years less a day. An inmate sentenced to more than six months and showing a positive response to the program could be released on parole. A fourth conviction would require the time to be served in the Central Prison. The commissioners also recommended that the poor, aged, and infirm be housed in special facilities that the government would require the municipalities to build. They reasoned that if their recommendations were followed then a large number of the standard jail population would be removed. This would reduce pressure on facilities and enable the jails at least to establish effective classification.[26]

The 1891 Ontario study served to heighten public awareness of the needs of the criminal justice system and to further encourage reformers. The fact that the government had seen fit to commission the inquiry was a positive step and another in a chain of happenings that, although sporadic, were signs of progress. For example, in 1874 the Prisoners' Aid Association was founded in Toronto and the following year the practice of putting prisoners in balls and chains was discontinued. One of the more significant advances in the treatment of criminals in the latter decades of the nineteenth century came with the passage of the Penitentiary Act in 1883. The practice of hiring out convicts to private contractors was abolished by the Act. As we have seen, there was a strong belief in the rehabilitative value of hard labour and by hiring out not only was the inmate provided with work but the institution earned money with which to offset operational costs. Nevertheless, the practice was controversial and had always generated considerable opposition. Labour opposed the contracting out of prisoners on the grounds that it was unfair competition, depressed wages, and robbed them of jobs. Reformers and many judicial authorities were opposed to it on the grounds that it was exploitative. The contractors were not interested in assisting with the reform process, rather, their concern was with making a profit on cheap and captive labour.

While the issue of outside contract labour was laid to rest, another side of the problem continued to spark debate. Penitentiary officials had long favoured useful and instructive work for inmates. James Massie, warden of the Central Prison in Toronto, maintained that, "as a factor in the preservation of good order, for the elevation and fitting of the prisoner for his place in the contest for an honourable living, labour in its several pursuits stands next to Christianity, first and indispensable; without it reformation of character may be said to be impossible."[27] To better equip them for the job market a succession of officials tried to put prisoners to work making products for the outside. Some recommended that the inmates be given part of the money earned to motivate production and good behaviour. They argued that if the outside market was closed it limited work to the internal needs of the institution. However, the labour movement was opposed to prison-made goods for the same reasons that they were against inmates working for private contractors, and workers' groups put considerable pressure on politicians to support them.

At the hearings of the Royal Commission on the Relations of Labor and Capital opponents argued that prison-made goods competed unfairly with the products of free labour. Because such goods could be put on the market at lower prices they put people out of work. One critic claimed that many jobs in the broom-making business were lost because of prisoners entering the trade. Among the solutions proposed was one suggesting that prison products be sold only on the export market and another that machinery not be allowed in prison shops, thus giving inmates experience at hand labour.[28] The general conclusion, however, was that "no solution has been found which gives universal or even general satisfaction."[29]

The ongoing debate illustrated the dilemma that faced prison officials. It was also a manifestation of political attitudes that reformers encountered in their campaign to establish rehabilitation programs. One of the most extreme examples came out of the discussion of the issue in the Ontario legislature in 1895. One MPP, George Ryerson, announced his opposition to any kind of commercial labour in prison. He argued that it undercut free labour. Instead, he suggested that it would be better to "keep the prisoners employed in carrying balls and chains or digging holes in the sand and filling them up again."[30] He apparently realized the Neanderthal nature of his proposal and subsequently suggested that prisoners could be put to work doing the printing for the legislature.

In the face of opposition to such prison programs as remunerative work, progress was piecemeal and gradual. Reform remained an elusive goal and the rate of crime continued to increase. Undaunted, reformers maintained their efforts, recruited new members to the cause, and refined and expanded their program. For example, a meeting in Toronto in 1892, sponsored by the Prisoners' Aid Association of Canada, attracted representatives from thirty-nine organizations. Included were delegates from the churches and the Trades and Labor Congress, as well as lawyers and judges. The thrust of the meeting was to step up the campaign for prison reform. In many communities across the country judicial officials, church and community organizations, and women's groups were active in the movement. Prominent citizens throughout Canada took a leading role in advocating improvements in the treatment of prisoners. In Ontario, for example, the ranks of activists included the Lieutenant-Governor, A. Campbell; W.H. Howland, Mayor of Toronto; G.W. Ross, Minister of Education; Goldwin Smith, historian, columnist, and publicist; A.S. Hardy, the Provincial Secretary; James Massie, warden of the Central Prison; E.A. Meredith, former federal penal inspector; S.H. Blake, president of the Prisoners' Aid Association; and Lizzie J. Harvie, Sunday school assistant superintendent and teacher at Mercer Reformatory.

NEW WINE IN OLD BOTTLES

By the turn of the century, reformers had developed a consensus on an agenda that would guide them for the next fifty years. They campaigned for the use of the indeterminate sentence, the introduction of probation and parole, a better system of classification, better educational and vocational programs, training for guards and officials, an end to political interference, more effective work programs, preparation for release, provisions for aftercare, and a genuine effort at rehabilitation. They sought to heighten public awareness and to win a more sympathetic hearing from government officials.

Many were also proceeding on a base of changed assumptions and had abandoned the old classical belief in individual responsibility. Environmental theories of crime causation were replacing the idea of moral weakness. Factors external to the individual, such as poverty, parental neglect, and the failure of government to respond to societal needs, were blamed for producing criminals. Thus, reform was no longer seen exclusively in terms of religious and values education and character development. Many argued that improving social conditions was the most effective way to combat crime. For those already caught up in the criminal justice system the best path to reform was thought to be education and job training. Some maintained that criminals should not be condemned as moral failures but rather viewed as victims of circumstances beyond their control. Therefore, society had an obligation to help them overcome the results of a deficient and sometimes cruel environment.

While individual responsibility for crime was being questioned, there was ample evidence of individual responsibility for many of the problems that beset the criminal justice system. As we have seen, the personal beliefs and the competence of wardens and other prison officials had a marked impact on the atmosphere that prevailed from time to time in the country's penitentiaries. The monetary concerns of members of provincial and municipal governments affected the conditions of local jails. Political patronage determined the calibre of prison and jail staff, and the quality of goods and services provided by contractors.

Even the judicial process itself was influenced by the nature of those appointed to the bench. For the most part judges across the country and at all levels were patronage appointments. While many were quite competent, others had neither the qualifications nor the aptitude for the position. If justice was blind, so, figuratively, were some who dispensed it. As was so often the case in the past, judges continued to prove that the law was not fixed in stone or evenhanded. Too often it was subject to the whim and fancy of the presiding magistrate. The results were unjust sentences, vindictive and biased judgements, and sometimes bizarre proceedings.

There are innumerable examples of incompetent, arbitrary, and eccentric magistrates. One of the most arbitrary was Colonel George T. Denison, police magistrate for Toronto from 1877 to 1920. Denison was opinionated and dictatorial, and he dealt out summary and subjective justice. On one occasion he tried 180 cases in the space of three hours, a feat he duplicated a number of other times. The police court magistrate had little time for criminals and little use for their defenders. Lawyers citing legal precedents particularly annoyed him. According to the learned magistrate they wasted his time. "Why read me another judge's opinion?" he asked. "If it agrees with my view, what is the object? If it takes a different view why should I follow another man's mistakes?"[31]

Newspapers frequently ridiculed court proceedings and criticized judges for the way they conducted the hearings. Obviously some merited the bad press.[32] Another example of subjective justice involved a former RCMP officer who, upon retirement, became the police magistrate at Peace River. He operated his court on the assumption that the RCMP never arrested an innocent man. Consequently, any lawyer's challenge or questioning of an officer's testimony was pretty much in vain. There were also problems with civilian judges in the North. The Commissioner of the North West Mounted Police complained in his 1884 report that local magistrates were reluctant to try liquor cases because their friends and customers were sometimes the ones on trial.[33]

In spite of the many problems, from time to time major advances were realized. One of the most significant before the turn of the century was the introduction of the so-called ticket-of-leave. Most penitentiary officials favoured early release as an inducement to co-operation and good behaviour, and as a powerful incentive to reform. In the past, prisoners could gain early release through executive pardon. However, the practice was limited and depended more on political intervention than on the discretion of institutional administrators. Officials wanted it removed from the political arena but were never successful. The introduction of remission was a step forward, but it was not designed to ease the prisoner back into the outside world or to assist him or her with the transition after release.

The ticket-of-leave or parole had been favoured by reformers and prison officials not only as an incentive but also as a means of assisting with the prisoner's reintegration into society. An Act to Provide for the Conditional Liberation of Penitentiary Convicts was assented to on August 11, 1899. It authorized the Governor General to issue to any convict sentenced to a penitentiary "a license to be at large in Canada." Every offender released on parole was required to register with the chief of police of the community in which the person chose to reside. The parolee was to report monthly to the chief police officer and also to notify him if, at any time, he left the district. The conditions of leave also stipulated that the person must not break the law, must not habitually associate with people known to be bad characters, and must not lead "an idle and dissolute life." The penalty for violating the conditions of parole was an additional three months added to the original sentence. If a parolee broke the law any penalty upon conviction was to be added to the initial term. Thus a leave violation meant the return of the convict to the penitentiary to serve out the remainder of the original term plus whatever additional sentence that was incurred. While the original Act applied only to inmates of federal penitentiaries it was extended the following year to cover provincial prisons.[34]

Parole in the eyes of many reformers was a key piece of the reform process. Incarceration would provide an opportunity for prison officials to modify the convicts' behaviour. Programs of work, moral instruction, discipline, and order would help the criminal to develop those personal habits that were prerequisites to a useful law-abiding life. Education and vocational training would equip the inmates to find useful employment upon release and to support themselves without turning to crime, and the possibility of parole would encourage prisoners to be diligent, co-operative, and well behaved. Parole itself would provide a period of gradual restoration to society during which the former prisoner would still be under the threat of re-incarceration. The hope was that by the time the parole period expired he or she would have completed a normal adjustment and be fully restored as a good member of society.

The fatal flaw in the original legislation was that it made no provision for supervision and assistance. Aside from the reporting requirement the parolee was left on his own. J.T. Gilmour, the warden of Central Prison, remarked that the "mode of enforcing it was so imperfect that we derive but little benefit from it."[35] The only post-release assistance came from private agencies. One of the most active and effective among such groups was the Prisoners' Aid Association. Founded in Toronto in 1874, it branched out and in 1878 the Prisoners' Aid Association of Canada came into being. By the turn of the century it was engaged in a broad range of activities. The Association helped ex-prisoners to find employment and provided them with other forms of assistance, ran a home for released inmates, carried out evangelical work in jails and prisons, sought reform in prison management and criminal law, and pursued crime prevention programs.[36]

The Salvation Army, through its Prison Gate Movement, also worked with criminals both inside prison and after release. Members visited jails and prisons and helped released inmates to find employment and adjust to life on the outside. Canadian branches of the Salvation Army, which had been started in England in 1865, opened in Toronto and London, Ontario, in 1882. In 1884 Canada was declared an independent territory with its own Commander and its headquarters in Toronto. By the 1890s branches of the Army were to be found in all parts of the country. It began its institutional welfare work in 1886 with the opening of a home for fallen girls in Toronto. In 1890 the Salvation Army opened its first prison-gate home, also in Toronto, and the following year similar refuges were started in Montreal, Kingston, Hamilton, Winnipeg, Victoria, and Vancouver.[37]

A moving force in the Salvation Army's work with criminals was W.P. Archibald. He was a leader in the Prison Gate Movement and established such a reputation for his work that in 1905 the federal government appointed him as the first Dominion Parole Officer. Archibald was an enthusiastic supporter of the parole program. Under his leadership a staff of parole officers was built up to supervise and assist criminals on early release. From its inception an increasing number of prisoners were given parole each year. During the first year of the program seventy-one convicts were granted parole and by the first year of Archibald's tenure five years later 181 were given early release.[38]

Archibald exemplified the ambivalence that continued to characterize the criminal justice system. Though a supporter of parole, he opposed other proposed reforms such as the indeterminate sentence and probation. He argued that the former would be a "cumbersome and automatic hindrance" to parole and the latter might encourage lawbreaking. He feared that if a person knew that a first offence would not bring a prison or jail sentence it might increase the temptation for certain people to commit crimes.[39] Although Archibald opposed the general use of the indeterminate sentence he did favour its introduction for repeat offenders. He described the recidivist as "the great plague of society," and believed that the indeterminate sentence should be used for everyone sentenced to jail or prison for a third time – this would be of considerable assistance to officials in trying to help relapsed criminals work out their problems.[40]

In spite of shortcomings the ticket-of-leave program worked well in many respects. A high percentage of parolees did manage to complete their sentences without any violations. In the first seven years of the program approximately 893 convicts were granted parole. Of those, eighty-three were returned to prison for parole violations and another thirty-two were convicted of new offences, so the success rate was slightly over 87 per cent.[41] Possibly the most disappointing part of progressive experiments such as the ticket-of-leave was that overall recidivism rates remained very high. W.P. Archibald estimated that about 63 per cent of the prison population was comprised of repeaters. Some, over the course of their criminal careers, were convicted as many as thirty and forty times and were effectively serving life sentences by instalments.[42]

Other than the ticket-of-leave and the abolition of banishment as a penalty in 1902, few significant changes in the treatment of adult criminals occurred during the early part of this century. Many of the conditions that prevailed in the criminal justice system remained static or deteriorated through to the Second World War. There were a great deal of pessimism and an increasing number of problems. The cynicism was summed up in an editorial in *Saturday Night* in December, 1906. The writer observed that convicts seldom reformed, and posed the question, "what is there in the system that could reform him?"[43]

The growing discontent with the penal system resulted in the formation of a Royal Commission on Penitentiaries, which reported in 1914. The Commission's examination of Kingston Penitentiary revealed that the primary agencies for reform continued to be religious instruction, solitary confinement, and a heavy dose of sometimes useless labour. The report observed that the regimen in place crushed the spirits of the inmates and debased their manhood. The following excerpt from the report offers a vivid illustration of why the system was so demoralizing:

A Convict's Experience

When he arrives at the prison, he is taken before the warden for an interview and then handed over to the chief keeper. That officer records his measurements and other physical characteristics in a book kept for the purpose. The personal belongings, jewelry, money, etc., of the prisoner are inventoried. Then he is put in charge of the chief keeper's officer for a bath, hair crop and shave. Finally he is dressed in the prison garb with his number on the back of his coat.

Assigned his cell, the convict takes his place in the routine of the prison. He rises at six-thirty in the morning, washes himself, makes his bed, and at seven marches out for breakfast. This he receives in a tin vessel as he moves with the line past the serving boards in the kitchen. Returning to the cell, he eats his meal with a spoon. Knives and forks are not allowed. As he goes out to work, he deposits his dish and spoon in the kitchen. At noon he takes up his dinner as he passes to his cell. There he pulls the meat apart with his fingers, eats it, and carries back the empty vessel to the kitchen as he goes to work. When he quits his labours at night, the performance is repeated. He snatches his supper on his way to the cell and there remains until the following morning. Silence is the rule throughout the day. He must not speak to an officer or fellow convict while at work "except from necessity or with respect to the work." He must not speak nor look around while in line and of course he has no one to speak to in his cell. Thus the man's life in prison is divided between the cell and work shop or stone pile, with not even a break in the monotony at meal time. In his cell he is not allowed pictures or photographs of his relatives; he is not allowed to have or read a newspaper, but he is furnished books from the prison library. If he is unable to read, he must put in fourteen hours of each day alone, sleeping or meditating. On Sunday, the whole day – with the exception of one hour for Divine service – is spent in the cell, and when a holiday falls on Monday, he celebrates it with an additional twenty-four hours of solitary confinement.

A convict whose conduct is satisfactory may receive visits from members of his family once in two months. He may "receive letters from relatives or friends, but such letters must be short and devoted exclusively to family or business matters." No enclosure such as newspaper clippings, pictures, cards, stamps, etc., are delivered. Christmas boxes, hampers or packages of fruit, food, or confectionery are not permitted to be sent to the prison.

Thus it will be seen the daily round of penitentiary offers little to stimulate or encourage the well-disposed convict. On the contrary, its silence and solitude must breed moroseness and resentfulness. One convict said to us: "If a man is battered down until he feels that he is nothing much more above the beast, how can you expect him to go out feeling better? It requires a very strong will to keep you from feeling that you are finished."[44]

The attitude and penal philosophy of officials at Kingston again illustrate how much the treatment of criminals depended on personalities.

Reformers and countless judicial authorities had stressed, for over a century, the importance of academic education in reform. Yet at Kingston, school instruction was provided only four days a week for about forty minutes a day for those interested. The convicts would be lined up after their lunch at 12:15, marched to class, and returned to their cells at one o'clock. The explanation for this is a revealing comment on the reform philosophy, or lack of it, that characterized Kingston. It was pointed out that the judges sentenced convicts to hard labour, not to go to school. The rationale was also used that it would be unfair to allow some inmates to attend school while their colleagues had to work. Finally, it was argued that it was not the obligation of the state to provide education for criminals. They must put in their regular hours of work.[45]

Further criticism was levelled at the treatment of those who were sick in body or mind, at the severe punishments used to discipline inmates, and at the regulations governing Kingston and other penitentiaries. One of the Inspectors of Prisons, testifying before the commissioners, explained that the rules and regulations were designed with the worst prisoners in mind. The problem was that everyone was guided by them, with no distinctions allowed for special circumstances. For example, one man sentenced to four years and twenty-five lashes for rape in 1906, was discharged in 1910 but recommitted within three months for a similar offence. This time he was sentenced to twenty years with lashes. In a period of just under three years the man was put on report sixty-seven times for rules violations. He was punished severely, including being hosed with cold water at sixty pounds of pressure, and spent considerable time in isolation and in punishment cells. The man was described as an imbecile, yet he was expected to conform to the regulations in the same way as other prisoners. Although the punishment was futile it was administered anyway and no attempt was made to treat his mental illness.[46]

Other areas of penitentiary operations were equally defective. The commissioners contended, for example, that "there is not a single well-equipped, well-managed, continuously busy shop in the whole circle of prisons."[47] This sorry state of affairs was the result of the agitation by labour against allowing prison-made goods to be sold on the open market. A universal problem was the calibre of the guards hired to supervise the prisoners. Staff were patronage appointees who were recommended by party officials, politicians, and members of Parliament. They were not trained for the work and some had little regard for the people under their supervision. Added to all this was the subculture of prison life. Homosexuality, intimidation, brutality, extortion, theft, and drug and alcohol use were everyday realities. Guards sold tobacco and drugs to prisoners, usually at exorbitant prices.

Other segments of the judicial system had just as many problems. At no level, from the police to the magistrates, were the authorities able to construct an effective set of practices. Worst of all was the continuation of many of the shortcomings that went well back into the previous century. Law enforcement was still entrusted to poorly paid and inadequately trained amateurs. Political patronage put many people on the bench who lacked the talent to do the job. The result was ineffective policing and rough justice. For example, a Montreal judge, in September, 1922, sentenced a forty-one-year-old drug trafficker to prison for twenty years. The man was convicted of selling opium and causing the death of a user. The judge announced that he had given the severe penalty as a warning to others, "and in future, I think I may give life sentences to those found guilty of a similar charge before me."[48] Within two months the same judge handed down a sentence of two years at hard labour to a man convicted of giving drugs to friends, causing the death of one of them. His standards changed dramatically in a short period of time.

Lower down the penal totem pole were the county and local jails. Little improvement was realized over the years and many jails in the 1930s would fit the description of their counterparts from the previous century. A detailed look at the situation was afforded by the 1933 *Report of the Royal Commission Concerning Jails* in Nova Scotia. The commissioners discovered that many jails were housed in old buildings in a bad state of repair. Some were badly overcrowded and lacking in many other respects. The Commission described conditions as "primitive" and blamed the situation on the parsimony of municipal governments.

Many jails had worn and dirty fixtures, torn bedding, and insufficient furnishings. Dirt, vermin, and a foul stench were common. Many lacked exercise and even bathing facilities. One jailor had to take the inmates to the beach when they needed a bath. Conditions were so bad in a few jails that inmates shared a common towel and drinking cup, and a lack of segregation meant that prisoners could easily mix and communicate. Most inmates spent their time in idleness, playing cards, and conversing.

The Commission arrived at the following conclusions:

(1) that the Province is faced with a growing prison population,
(2) that the jails are for the most part inadequate in accommodation and equipment and lacking in provision for the proper classification, isolation and employment of inmates,
(3) that there is frequent laxity of administration and that many of the regulations governing county jails are unobserved,
(4) that as a result of the present system of administering and constituting jails prisoners are maintained in idleness, the young learn evil from the sophisticated, the women often lack sufficient privacy and supervision by matrons, the innocent experience the privations of social outcasts and first offenders are deprived of that social treatment which might prevent permanent delinquency.[49]

As was the case with every previous study, the commissioners concluded that a term in jail had little positive impact. As elsewhere, the rate of recidivism was high. In 1932, out of 4,263 admissions, 1,297 were repeat offenders. In one jail in the province the same man had been admitted forty-two times. The commissioners concluded that frequent arrest and short jail sentences accomplished little.

The Commission heard submissions from a wide variety of citizens. Many were enlightened and the vast majority favoured reform. In contrast, practically every municipal official brought up the subject of finance and expressed more concern about costs than rehabilitating criminals. As one councillor put it, "The cost factor is the serious one. Municipal institutions have to be run as inexpensively as possible."[50] An interesting statement came from the summary of observations by the judges of the Supreme Court, which revealed that because of the state of the jails, judges were sentencing people to penitentiary terms.[51]

Jail conditions were not uniform across the country. The older and less well-maintained facilities were in the East, with the situation in Quebec characterized by similar problems. The western provinces, by contrast, were dotted with modern facilities. They were generally clean, well heated and ventilated, and had electric lights and flush toilets. Saskatchewan and Alberta joined Confederation in 1905. Prior to that time, and for some years after in the North, where law was administered by the North West Mounted Police, the guard rooms of the force served as the local jails. Unlike many of their southern counterparts, northern criminals did not lack work. They were kept busy chopping firewood for the stoves.[52]

Ontario had a mixture of old and new jails and conditions varied. However, the province was in the forefront of innovation. In 1911 an industrial farm was opened at Fort William and in 1913 a brick-and-tile plant was started near Toronto to provide prisoners with useful labour. The products from the plant were sold for use in government projects. In 1914 the industrial farm at Burwash was opened. In 1915 the old Central Prison in Toronto was closed and a new reformatory built in Guelph the following year. For a time it was taken over as a hospital for returned soldiers but then was reinstated as a reformatory in 1921.[53]

These institutions offered new environments, constructive work programs, and substantially different atmospheres. At Guelph, for example, prisoners carded their own wool in a mill and used the yarn to make blankets and socks. They also operated an abattoir, a canning factory, and a woodworking factory, built beds, and could attend school. Discipline was reasonable and inmates were given the opportunity to bring their problems or complaints directly to the superintendent. Dental, medical, and psychiatric services were provided on a regular basis. In addition, the province ran the Ontario Hospital for the Criminally Insane at Guelph.[54]

The parole system was also in use in Ontario. The province had a parole board and a staff of officers to supervise parolees. In 1913 an Act was passed by the federal government to allow the provinces' courts to experiment with indeterminate sentences for those sent to provincial institutions. Ontario also had the power to grant special permits, which would allow an inmate to work outside the institution – even completely removed from it if necessary. This accommodated hardship cases where a prisoner's family was in dire need. The convict was not paroled but simply allowed out to work. When the job was in another community the released person would be under the scrutiny of someone appointed for that purpose or might be housed at night in the local jail. The permit system was only used for those who were judged to be very minimal risks.[55]

While some progress was being made in places, there were few signs of positive results even in the better institutions. Recidivism rates remained high and the system in general was plagued with problems. Among them was the issue of aftercare. Prisoners were still being released with little money, sometimes inadequate clothing, and few sources of help to get readjusted. An offender incarcerated in the warm weather would be released in the winter with the same clothes he had worn on admission because the jails made no provisions for clothing. Some inmates did not have enough money to get home and would steal a train ride. Those who were caught ended up back in jail for violating the Railroad Act. Others found it impossible to find work, especially if released in the winter, and turned to crime to survive.

In response to such problems a number of aftercare agencies were formed by humanitarian-minded people, but these were staffed by volunteers, uniformly underfunded, short of personnel, and consequently not as effective as they could be. The Big Brother movement, which had been started in New York City in 1904, opened a Canadian chapter in Toronto in 1913. Some years later, in 1929, a variety of community organizations in Toronto banded together to form the Citizens' Service Association. It concentrated on aftercare and finding job placements for released prisoners. The Canadian Prisoners' Welfare Association, founded in Montreal, was another agency that worked to help offenders and their families with a variety of problems. The difficulty some of these agencies worked under is illustrated by the comments of John Kidman, secretary of the Canadian Prisoners' Welfare Association, made before the annual meeting of the American Prison Association in 1929. He stated "that the work has been cribbed, coffined and confined by lack of money, by indifference and even by active opposition on the part of those who are afraid of 'coddling the prisoner'."[56]

Although the work of prison reform and aftercare was frequently discouraging, many were willing to devote their time and energies to the cause. Among them were Kidman, Robert Bickerdike, and Agnes Macphail. Kidman developed his interest in criminals as a result of his experiences as a court reporter in Montreal. Along with his work on the *Montreal Gazette*, he devoted considerable time to helping convicts and their families.[57]

Bickerdike, after a career in the livestock export business, was elected Liberal Member of Parliament in 1900 for the constituency of St. Lawrence in Montreal and remained an MP until 1917. During his tenure in the House of Commons, Bickerdike was an outspoken supporter of prison reform and a leader in the campaign to abolish the death penalty. In numerous speeches in the House of Commons he denounced the death penalty as murder and a blot on Christianity. He argued that capital punishment was not an effective deterrent and attempted to get an abolition bill passed in 1914, 1915, 1916, and 1917. While he garnered some support there was no strong interest in his cause.[58] Nevertheless, he succeeded in enlisting assistance outside of Parliament and abolition agitation kept up until the mid-1920s. At no time, however, did it become a major public issue.

The most prominent penal reformer in the pre-World War Two period was Agnes Macphail, the first female Member of Parliament. Born on a farm in Ontario, she taught school in her home province and in Alberta. In 1921 she was elected to Parliament as a member of the United Farmers of Ontario for the constituency of Southeast Grey. She held a seat for the next nineteen years. Early in her political career she demonstrated a humanitarian and reformist bent that brought to her door a variety of people in need of help, including former prisoners or their families. She soon became a proponent of social welfare legislation and prison reform. In the House of Commons she frequently pushed government ministers for social legislation and in March, 1925, she introduced a resolution in support of providing productive work and remuneration for prisoners. The money earned would go to help support their families or be given to them on discharge. She persisted until she succeeded in getting her bill approved the following year. Since she was not a member of government, the passage was testimony to her influence and her political acumen.

In subsequent years she became even more closely identified with penal reform. Convicts with tales of hardship and ill treatment sought her out and found a sympathetic ear. The more she learned about conditions inside Canada's penitentiaries, the more concerned she became. She heard tales of severe discipline, brutal guards, and patronage appointments. She expressed her concerns in pointed questions and speeches in the Commons and her advocacy attracted national attention. In some quarters she was dismissed as a naive, emotional woman, duped by a group of manipulative convicts. The government, embarrassed by her constant harassment, also attempted to undermine her credibility. She persisted, however, and succeeded in winning many to her cause, including members of Parliament.[59]

Among the issues that reformers pursued in the late 1920s and into the next decade was the provision of public defenders. People like John Kidman and organizations such as the Canadian Prisoners' Welfare Association argued that the justice system had become so complicated that to guarantee a fair trial an accused needed to be represented by counsel. Since many could not afford legal help the government should fund a public defender. Kidman underscored the disadvantage suffered by someone without legal aid by pointing out "that frequently the verdict of 'guilty' or 'not guilty' depends upon the way in which the case is presented by the prosecution and refuted by equally expert methods on the part of the defence."[60] His remarks were not only an argument in favour of the proposal but an insightful comment on the way the justice system worked.

A TROUBLED SYSTEM

An accused who encountered problems in the court was only getting a small taste of what was ahead if a conviction resulted in a prison sentence. By the 1930s the situation in Canadian penitentiaries had reached a boiling point. The prison population chafed under a number of indignities that made them resentful and unco-operative. For some the problem started before they even entered. It was the practice to convey criminals by public transportation from the communities in which they were tried to the prisons. Thus, a convict would be taken to the train in handcuffs and in full view of other passengers; the cuffs would be removed and replaced with shackles to secure the prisoner during the trip. It was a humiliating experience, with more to follow in quick succession. Upon arrival the new inmates were stripped naked, their heads clipped bald and then rubbed with acetic acid. In Kingston prison they were put in cells five feet wide by eight feet long and ten feet high. The furnishings consisted of a bed that folded against the wall in the daytime, a table, a chair, a wash basin, and a seatless toilet. The cells had taps but the water was not drinkable because the prison sewage was discharged near the water intake pipe. Well water was provided for drinking but not always on a regular basis. On the shelf was a Bible and a catalogue of books in the library. No mirrors or pictures were allowed in the cells.[61]

Inmates were awakened at 6:30 a.m. and after washing and making their beds they were marched to breakfast at 7:00. Meals were picked up in a serving room and taken back to the cells. After supper inmates were allowed to read until 9:00 p.m., when the lights were turned out. The same fixed routine was maintained day after day, and any violations of the rules could bring harsh punishment. One of the sanctions used to punish rule-breakers was whipping. The offender would be blindfolded, bent over with his pants down, and secured to a table. The paddle was a leather strap about three feet long and two inches wide secured to a wooden handle. The leather was punctured with a series of holes so that when it hit it would draw blood and by the second or third lash pick up pieces of flesh. The standard punishment was ten stripes.[62]

The worst punishment of all was solitary confinement. Troublemakers were put in these isolation cells normally for a period of one week. They were shackled to the bars and sometimes secured in a manner that forced them to stand on their toes because their arms were tied so high. The decision to punish was arbitrary and made by the warden on the basis of an accusation by a guard. There was no investigation so it was the prisoner's word against the guard's. It was not uncommon for keepers to lie about rule infractions so a disliked inmate would be punished. Although many staff were humane and attempted to do their jobs properly, there were always those who were cruel and sadistic. One prisoner who wrote of his experiences estimated that 20 per cent fell into the latter category.[63]

The level of indifference to inmates was sometimes carried to extreme and cruel lengths. One prisoner, in for the theft of food stolen because his family of six children was hungry, was serving a three-year term. While he was in prison his wife died, but he was not allowed out to go to her funeral or to console his children. Approaching his third Christmas in prison he was awaiting word on parole. Unfortunately, his papers were delayed by a bureaucratic mixup and did not arrive at the penitentiary until Christmas Day. Since the institution was officially closed on December 25 no one would process his papers and arrange for his release, and so although paroled he spent another Christmas in his cell.[64]

The tensions and ill will that permeated the prisons were heightened by overcrowding. In 1920 approximately 1,800 people were in federal penitentiaries; by 1933 the number had risen to over 4,000. An already troubled system was made worse when the Conservative government of Richard B. Bennett appointed General D.M. Ormond as Superintendent of Penitentiaries on August 1, 1932. He was a war veteran, a member of the Manitoba bar, and a former divisional superintendent in the Royal Canadian Mounted Police. Ormond was an autocratic, opinionated individual, filled with a sense of self-importance. He insisted on being kept informed on very minute operational details and required prison officials to get his permission even for small expenditures. In early 1934, without consulting with his wardens, he increased the number of prison regulations from 194 to 724 with orders that they be enforced immediately. He continued with great regularity to elaborate on the regulations – issuing over 800 circulars. There were so many petty restrictions that prisoners could not possibly know all the rules or avoid breaking some of them.[65]

The penal philosophy of some wardens fell comfortably in line with functionaries such as Ormond. For example, Colonel C.E. Edgett, the warden at British Columbia Penitentiary, appointed in 1929, was a firm believer in the use of the lash as a punishment for criminals. He contended that it "changed the criminal's grin to a frown of despair."[66] On one occasion Edgett had twelve months added to the sentence of a man who tried to escape. The prisoner had only six weeks left to serve, was of low intelligence, and had been egged on by a fellow convict.[67] Among the many irritating practices that people like Ormond and Edgett permitted in the prison system was the one of issuing tobacco to inmates but no cigarette papers. This forced them to use toilet paper or smoke a pipe. The myriad regulations, the petty annoyances, the injustices, and the frustrations of prison life provoked a series of incidents. Between 1932 and 1937 there were sixteen riots in Canadian penitentiaries.

An investigation launched at Kingston Prison as a result of the riots in 1932 gave individual prisoners a chance to bring their grievances to the attention of authorities. Following is a summary of the main complaints:

1. Deprivation of cigarette papers.
2. Close cropping of hair.
3. Lack of recreation and amusement.
4. Insufficient open-air exercise.
5. Lack of newspapers and magazines.
6. Insufficient lighting in cells.
7. Harsh treatment by officers.
8. Compulsory church attendance.
9. Insufficient medical treatment.
10. Insufficient dental treatment.
11. Lack of toilet articles, combs, and mirrors.
12. Punishments improperly awarded for breach of rules.
13. More frequent letters to and from convicts.
14. Increased number of visits to convicts.
15. Lack of paroles.
16. Objection to steam-cooked food and monotony of prison diet.[68]

By 1936 the government was under so much pressure from people like Agnes Macphail and from growing public unease with prison disturbances that it finally appointed a Royal Commission to investigate the penal system of Canada.

The disorder in the criminal justice system belied the efforts of reformers. Changes that had been recommended as far back as the Brown Commission had still not been implemented. Meanwhile, the reform agenda had been expanded and fine-tuned. A detailed, humanitarian list of proposals had been worked out that would serve as a working guideline to the present day. Many were of long standing while some reflected new ideas about rehabilitation. The agenda pursued by reformers in the 1930s included the following proposals:

- Better classification of prisoners with individual assessments done by trained personnel.
- More diversity of facilities, including institutions for first offenders.

- The provision of rehabilitation programs tailored to meet individual needs.
- The use of indeterminate sentences so release would depend on personal progress with rehabilitation.
- Provision of more useful work and payment of wages to prisoners.
- Better educational and vocational training programs.
- Less regimentation of inmates' lives and more privileges.
- Trained administrators and guards appointed on merit rather than political influence.
- Special care for those with mental problems.
- Treatment for alcoholism or drug addiction.
- Use of the permit system for supervised work release.
- More use of parole and the appointment of a parole board for each institution and the hiring of more parole officers to supervise and assist parolees.
- The provision of aftercare to help released convicts to adjust.

Besides recommendations designed to help restore the criminal to a productive life, much consideration was also given to helping people caught up in any aspect of the criminal justice system. Reformers recognized that many people ended up in jail partly because they could not afford legal advice. They called for government provision of legal aid and the appointment of public defenders; for the use of probation officers to provide courts with background information on the accused; for the use of probation as a sentencing option; and for the allowance of the payment of fines by instalments. They also proposed that citizens' committees be established to monitor court proceedings and to inspect penal facilities. In cases where an accused was convicted and sent to jail they argued that provisions should be made to look after the prisoner's family.

The long list of proposed reforms ultimately served the general interest and so were supported by many in the criminal justice system, including jail and penitentiary officials. However, the proposals ran up against bureaucratic inertia, incompetent people, opposition, and public apathy. For example, as far back as 1892 the revised Criminal Code provided for the use of probation as a sentence option. Yet very limited use was made of this because no background reports on accused were provided to judges and neither the federal nor provincial governments made provision for probation officers. Even prison regulations in certain instances were much more liberal than actual practices. The prison inspectors prevented their implementation in some cases on the grounds that the changes required would be too expensive. An additional problem was that where improvements were made, the results were at best questionable. Recidivism rates did not come down and crime continued to increase. Nevertheless, reformers remained optimistic and persisted in their efforts to change the system.

The malignancy that permeated the penitentiaries was fully exposed by the Royal Commission, headed by Justice Joseph Archambault. The Commission completed its report in 1938. It revealed a system in which the main emphasis was not on reform but on custody and discipline. For example, the warden at St. Vincent de Paul at the time of the commissioners' visit was described as suffering "from a security and control complex and . . . [had] lost sight of the necessity for humanitarianism."[69] The guards were described as being apathetic and brutal. They were not only cruel but could be very dangerous, as is illustrated by a disturbance at Kingston on the night of October 20, 1932. During a mêlée the Communist leader Tim Buck was fired at in his cell. He was disliked by the guards and had a reputation as a troublemaker. Although the disturbance was in another cell block and Buck was locked in his cell, four gunshots were directed at him. Three hit the inside of his cell, one of which was a shotgun blast that sprayed pellets. No other shots were fired in the block. Buck complained to officials but no investigation was conducted until he had the chance to reveal the incident in a court hearing involving another inmate.[70]

Prisoners spent an average of sixteen hours a day alone in their cells and even their meals were taken in confinement. They were allowed a half-hour a day for recreation, and such things as writing and visiting privileges were severely restricted and wound up in petty bureaucracy. If a prisoner wished to write a business letter the warden had to secure permission from the Superintendent of Penitentiaries in Ottawa. Visitors were not allowed in the prisons on Saturdays, Sundays, and holidays. Yet these were the times when family and friends could most easily travel. When visitors were permitted, communication was carried on through a wire screen. The trivial annoyances continued even at the time of release. They were given very little money, only what they earned while in prison, and their clothes were usually ill-fitting and drab.

The atmosphere that characterized the institutions was soul-destroying. Inmates were not allowed to "sing, whistle, or make any unnecessary noise." They were not allowed to converse with their fellow prisoners or with the guards. Their cells were poorly lit and many prisoners developed eye trouble. To save money or because of inadequate electric systems certain prisons used 25-watt light bulbs in the cells. Some facilities experienced heating and ventilation problems, and inadequate sanitation was a frequent problem. For example, over 300 cells in St. Vincent de Paul Penitentiary used buckets for human waste.

Many prisons still lacked proper education and vocational programs. With a few exceptions library holdings were inadequate. Workshops were poorly equipped and there was a shortage of trained personnel, such as teachers and shop instructors. The same people who were supposed to teach the inmates were also expected to act as their custodians. Little counselling was available and there were still no treatment programs for alcoholics and drug abusers.

Although official philosophy in the 1930s unequivocally held that the primary purpose of the penal system was the reformation of the criminal, the system undermined its own objectives. The penitentiary experience was so bad that it had little, if any, positive impact. The commissioners concluded that inmates "became spiritually, as well as physically anaemic, lazy, and shiftless, physically and mentally torpid, and generally ineffective and unreliable."[71] The recidivism rate offered more evidence of failure to rehabilitate. The annual report of the Superintendent of Penitentiaries for 1936-37 indicated that 72 per cent of inmates during that year were recidivists.

The Archambault Commission made eighty-eight specific recommendations to remedy the problems it uncovered. As a starting point it called for the reorganization of the entire penal system on a national basis under the control of the federal government. The provinces would continue to run a few institutions for violators of provincial statutes, people on remand, and those sentenced to short terms. As a part of the remodelling the Commission also proposed the restructuring of prison administrations, better training for staff, the retirement of untrained personnel, and the dismissal of Superintendent Ormond. To assist with the recruitment of better-qualified people the report called for an end to political interference in appointments. Commissioners recommended a complete revision of the methods of classification of inmates and the segregation of the various categories of prisoners. The need for improved medical and psychiatric care was stressed, as was the need for new, improved prison facilities. The report called for an end to the host of petty restrictions, for better education and vocational training and work programs, and it recommended new approaches to probation and parole.[72]

The focus of the commissioners was on the more humane and enlightened treatment of prisoners. The report gave a strong endorsement to the principle of rehabilitation while reiterating the importance of prisons to protect society and deter crime. The commissioners stressed their belief that penal treatment "must be directed unceasingly to the advancement of the individual's personal and emotional rehabilitation."

The Royal Commission brought to light the many shortcomings in the federal prisons, but these shortcomings were by no means the only problem areas in the criminal justice system. Police throughout the country lacked proper training, jails were inadequate and for the most part were little more than holding tanks, and there were few treatment programs of any kind. Most judges were political appointees and many were incompetent and arbitrary. There were no uniform sentencing standards across the country so penalties for similar offences varied from court to court. Consequently, for the criminal there was no certainty of being caught, of being convicted, of getting a just sentence, or of receiving humane treatment if incarcerated. Worst of all, it was very unlikely that a term in penitentiary would have any rehabilitative result.

The revelations of the Royal Commission served to heighten public awareness of the problems within the criminal justice system. The recommendations were an endorsement of the long-standing proposals of reformers, as well as a source of encouragement. Unfortunately, before any meaningful action could be taken a problem of graver magnitude monopolized national attention. The Second World War replaced all other matters as the primary concern of government and the nation.

POST-WORLD WAR TWO REFORM

When the war was over government once again turned its attention to domestic affairs and the problems of post-war adjustment. Among its obvious concerns were crime and criminals. The interest in this area was so pronounced that one writer, upon examining the range of developments, claimed that "The year 1946 marks the real beginning of penal reform in Canada."[73] Since the Archambault Commission report a number of reforms had been implemented within the penitentiary system, mainly in the area of personal conveniences for prisoners. They were given more liberal visiting and writing privileges, got increased leisure and smoking time, were allowed to listen to daily radio broadcasts, and were provided with better library facilities and more books. As well, requirements for earned remission were liberalized.[74] This more benevolent trend was accelerated after the war and touched on almost all aspects of the criminal justice system.

In 1946 the federal government, under an order-in-council, appointed a Commissioner of Penitentiaries and instructed him to review the entire system, a signal that the government was prepared to take action. At the provincial level there were also signs of a new attitude. Ontario unified a number of services under a new Department of Reform Institutions. The government of Saskatchewan established a commission to report on its penal services. In 1948 British Columbia launched an examination of its jail system. In addition, there were stirrings in the private sector. J. Alex Edmison, a name well known in reform circles, took the initiative in organizing the John Howard Society of Ontario, a prisoners' welfare and aftercare agency, and also helped to found the Canadian Penal Association.[75]

The laws themselves also underwent change, as reformers and judicial officials pressed for revisions. One of the more controversial was legislation in 1947 that established a new category of criminal, the "habitual offender." Under the new law a person convicted of being a chronic recidivist could be put in prison for an indeterminate period. The criteria to be used in making the determination were that the person so designated must have been convicted at least three times prior to the most recent conviction, and after reaching the age of eighteen must have been convicted of an indictable offence punishable by at least five years' imprisonment. The authors of the legislation must have anticipated a goodly number of such sentences because the new law also provided for prisons "set apart for that purpose."[76] Less controversial was the establishment in 1949 of a Royal Commission to revise the penal code.

In the meantime, progress was manifest in other areas and continued into the next decade. In the penitentiaries, education and vocational training programs were modernized and expanded, more and better-qualified staff were hired, library collections were updated and enlarged, and new equipment was purchased. Some institutions permitted their inmates to enrol in correspondence courses and some offered them the Dale Carnegie course. The vocational programs included training in such trades as barbering, welding, plastering, drafting, electricity, sheet metal work, and upholstering, along with the more traditional ones of bricklaying, carpentry, and auto mechanics. Farm work programs were also expanded.[77]

The prison atmosphere improved dramatically. The guiding principle was that loss of freedom was punishment and it was not the role of the penitentiary to add further to it.[78] The purpose of the prison was to provide an appropriate environment for the work of rehabilitation. In 1946 the silent system of incarceration was discontinued and inmates enjoyed less restrictions and more privileges than was the case in an earlier day. They were allowed to carry on crafts in their cells, they were permitted to shave themselves and use safety razors, and they were provided with more entertainment. Competitive sports became a regular part of leisure activities. The old restriction on newspapers was abolished and prisoners were even allowed to produce their own publications. Inmates were paid more for their work and were able to spend some of their earnings to buy supplies and treats at prison canteens.

A number of long-sought-after programs of a reformative nature were introduced. In 1947 classification officers were hired in the penitentiaries to assist the classification boards. This signalled a greater emphasis on the classification of prisoners and more attention to individual backgrounds and needs. Alcoholics Anonymous was organized to work with alcoholics and treatment programs for drug addicts were started. The remission service was expanded and federal financial assistance was provided to private aftercare agencies. More use was made of probation and additional probation officers were hired.[79]

Considerable progress was also made in improving the qualifications of penitentiary personnel. Administrators were expected to be better trained and educated. In 1948 a new training program for officers was started. It lasted six weeks and covered subjects ranging from gun handling to sociology. In 1952 a Penitentiary Staff College was opened in Kingston, which offered basic training courses, teaching methods for instructional person-nel, in-service programs, and conferences for administrators. Guards' sala-ries were increased and by 1955 working hours were reduced to forty per week.[80]

At another level many improvements were being made in jails, prisons, and reformatory institutions in the provinces. New facilities were built, treatment centres opened, and some institutions experimented with reha-bilitation programs. Industrial farms and forest camps offered an alterna-tive to the traditional type of incarceration. Security and living conditions at these facilities were much less restrictive. More emphasis was placed on hiring appropriately trained staff, and counselling programs were intro-duced at a few institutions. Unfortunately, the reforms taking place at the local, provincial, and national levels were not having any appreciable impact on rehabilitation. Nearly 80 per cent of penitentiary inmates had been incarcerated at one level or another prior to their latest term of imprisonment.[81]

The road to modernization was not without its roadblocks. The lack of funding continued to be a deterrent to the construction of an adequate correctional system. Probation affords a good example of the problem. Greater use of probation as a sentencing option had been favoured by reformers and some correctional officials for many years. However, the lack of probation officers had always been a drawback. In 1953 only about fifty officers were serving the adult courts across Canada while an estimated 700 were needed. Six of the ten provinces had no probation facilities in their adult criminal courts.

Other long-standing problems in the criminal justice system, such as unequal sentencing, persisted into the 1950s and beyond. A comparison of sentencing statistics for theft in 1955 offers one example of the nature of discrepancies across the country. In that year 8,159 persons were convicted. At the national level 29 per cent were given suspended sentences; at the provincial level 23 per cent had their sentences suspended in Quebec, 36 per cent in Manitoba. Nation-wide, 19 per cent of persons convicted for theft were fined; in Quebec 22 per cent of those found guilty were fined while in Manitoba 26.5 per cent were fined. The national average for jail sentences under one year was 36 per cent, compared to 49 per cent in Quebec and 28.6 per cent in Manitoba. The most severe penalty, a prison sentence, was handed out in 5.4 per cent of cases at the national level, in 11.4 per cent of convictions in Quebec, and in 4 per cent in Manitoba.[82]

The drawbacks were simply seen by many reformers to be part of the challenge and among the deficiences that still needed to be remedied. The progress that was made proved to be a precursor of an ongoing series of reforms and Criminal Code revisions that have continued to the present day. Underlying the evolution has been a strong commitment to the idea of rehabilitation. Reform of the criminal as one of the objectives of incarceration was clearly defined as far back as the Brown Commission. A succession of officials, governments, and commissioners had reiterated it and over time gave it an increasingly stronger emphasis. However, it was not until the post-World War Two period that a concerted effort was made to develop meaningful programs and a truly rehabilitative system. The one that evolved reflected a number of influences, but three studies in particular helped to shape the nature of post-war reform.

The Archambault Report provided the broad outline for the correctional program; two later studies offered refinements. In 1953 a committee was appointed to examine the remission service of the Department of Justice. Mr. Justice Gerald Fauteux was elected chairman by the committee and its report was submitted in April, 1956. Although struck primarily to study the remission service, the committee considered and made recommendations covering many aspects of the criminal justice system.

The report was predicated on the belief that "the true purpose of punishment is the correction of the offender and not mere retribution by society." The term "corrections" was now in vogue. As the committee defined it the term was used "to describe the total process by which society attempts to correct the anti-social attitudes or behavior of the individual."[83] Among the many recommendations were ones calling for liberalizing the provisions for probation, parole, and the granting of pardons; construction of medium security institutions; specialization of facilities and treatment programs; greater use of pre-sentencing reports; automatic parole review; the establishment of a national parole board; and aftercare programs especially for alcohol and drug addicts, sex offenders, and psychopaths.[84]

Some years later, in 1965, another major study of the correctional system was launched. The Report of the Canadian Committee on Corrections, known as the Ouimet Report, was released in 1969. This committee, like its predecessors, strongly endorsed the rehabilitative function of the criminal justice system. It also struck out in new directions by seeking a narrow definition of criminal conduct and with recommendations regarding the rights of the accused and the convicted. With this report the policy foundation of Canada's modern justice and penal system was complete.[85]

In the late fifties and through the 1960s the pace of change in the treatment of criminals accelerated, especially in the areas under federal jurisdiction. In 1957 there were eight federal institutions. A major new building program got under way in 1961 and by the end of the decade thirty-four penitentiaries were in the federal system. Even more significant was the fact that these institutions were divided into minimum, medium, and maximum security facilities. This greatly aided classification and segregation as well as the introduction of more and varied rehabilitation programs. It also helped to relieve the overcrowding in the older penitentiaries, which was a prime consideration behind the construction. Many new therapy programs were experimented with during the 1960s. In part this was an attempt at new approaches to treatment and in part it reflected the growing fascination of the times with self-analysis, personal growth movements, and gestalt therapy. Encounter groups, psychologists, psychiatrists, and a variety of behaviour modification programs became a part of prison life.[86]

In 1959 the Parole Act introduced one of the major reforms recommended by the Fauteux Committee. The Act created a National Parole Board and replaced the ticket-of-leave and the remission service. Parole was considered to be an extension outside the prison of the rehabilitation efforts that went on inside. The Parole Board was invested with jurisdiction over all matters of parole and was empowered to release inmates in federal and provincial institutions if it was satisfied "that the reform and rehabilitation of the inmate will be aided by the grant of parole." The Act required the Board to "review the case of every inmate serving a sentence of imprisonment of two years or more, whether or not an application has been made by or on behalf of the inmate."[87] The original Board was made up of a chairperson and three members, but various changes and practices have been introduced. The Board now consists of 130 members, thirty-six of whom are full-time. It has jurisdiction in provinces other than British Columbia, Ontario, and Quebec, which have their own parole boards.

Parole, like its predecessor the ticket-of-leave, is a form of conditional release prior to the expiration of sentence. It is designed to help ease the transition of inmates from prison life back into free society. Initially, aftercare agencies were relied on to help the released prisoner reintegrate, but in 1970 mandatory supervision requiring all parolees to be under the supervision of a parole officer was introduced. Generally, inmates selected for parole are supposed to be ones who have shown signs of being reformed and who pose little risk of committing crime upon release.

There are four types of conditional release: temporary absence, day parole, full parole, and mandatory supervision. A temporary absence may be granted for up to forty-eight hours per month for inmates from medium and maximum security institutions and up to seventy-two hours per month for inmates from minimum security institutions. The leaves are granted for humanitarian, medical, or program reasons, and prisoners may be escorted or unescorted. Day parole usually requires an offender to return nightly to a supervised facility such as a halfway house and is granted for a variety of reasons, such as work or education. Day parole is normally granted for periods of four to six months to people on their way to full parole. A prisoner is eligible for consideration for full parole on completion of one-third or seven years of the sentence, whichever comes first. Parole is not automatic and comes only after thorough consideration by the Parole Board. Most categories of offenders are entitled to time off for good behaviour and may be released after the first two-thirds of their sentence. They are permitted to go out into the community under mandatory supervision.

Accompanying the changes within the criminal justice system through the 1950s was a steady growth in prisoners' aid associations. These volunteer citizens' groups worked in close co-operation with government departments and the importance of their work was recognized by the fact that some were receiving public funds. The various community agencies – the John Howard Society, the Elizabeth Fry Society, the Société d'Orientation et de Réhabilitation Sociale of Montreal – helped released prisoners to readjust. Their work started inside the prisons prior to release. They did an inventory of the inmates' talents and experience and an overall assessment of individual traits. They then helped released prisoners to find suitable employment, provided financial assistance, and in some cases worked with the remission service and provincial parole boards to supervise people on leave. They also helped those who were having legal problems, but that aspect of adjustment was progressively taken over by provincial bar associations that offered legal aid services.[88] The work of aftercare agencies was destined to become increasingly important as the numbers of offenders and, hence, former inmates increased.

The 1960s and 1970s were decades of turmoil accompanied by a challenge to authority grounded in a glorification of the individual. There was disenchantment with materialism and the socio-economic system that produced pollution, poverty, prejudice, and the threat of nuclear destruction. Many called for drastic surgery; the extreme left called for destruction of the system. The concept of "rights" came front and centre and any form of restriction on the individual was not acceptable. Some translated their philosophy into a campaign to place social issues in the context of rights. They argued for the right of the poor to state support, of women to equity, of racial minorities to equality, and of the downtrodden to protection.

The emphasis on rights extended to those accused of crime and to criminals serving prison sentences. People incarcerated for crime were disproportionately young adults, who took with them to prison the alienation and iconoclasm of their generation. Legal aid services expanded so that many who normally could not afford a lawyer now had access to counsel. Prisoners' rights advocates took up the cause of proper care and treatment of inmates and fuelled the spirit of defiance already developing inside the country's penitentiaries. Inmates got caught up in the spirit and rhetoric of the times. While concerned groups challenged penitentiary practices from outside, many prisoners demanded more rights from within.

The concept that a criminal conviction and incarceration meant the loss of all civil rights was no longer accepted. Prisoners insisted on more respect from guards and officials, amenities as rights not as privileges, and the same protection from arbitrary justice inside prison as outside. The new spirit that touched many inmates was abetted by therapy programs. Assertiveness training and criticism of offensive behaviour were as easily directed at prison staff as at fellow inmates. The atmosphere in many institutions became tense as a struggle for power developed between aggressive inmates and prison personnel. In some cases the contest turned violent. Between 1974 and 1984 protesting inmates killed thirteen penitentiary employees. In comparison, eleven were killed in the previous 104 years. In 1975-76, there were sixty-nine incidents categorized as "major" in Canadian penitentiaries, including thirty-five hostage-takings involving ninety-two victims and the murder of a corrections officer.[89]

The internal problems did not deter officials from proceeding with reformative changes. The guiding philosophy was that "The two basic objectives of the Canadian Penitentiary Service are to administer the sentence imposed by the court and in so doing, provide every reasonable, human and material resource to assist the offender in his rehabilitation in order that he may return to the community as a responsible, productive citizen."[90] In this spirit the correctional service pursued a series of progressive measures. The practice of granting temporary absences for work or study has been continually expanded and staff training has been upgraded. By 1970 two more staff colleges were operating and the initial training for guards lasted twelve weeks. In recent years more university-educated personnel have been taken into the system. Some institutions have introduced the "living unit" in which a small number of inmates, together with a living-unit officer, cohabit in a more home-like environment.

A further concession to making prison life more tolerable was the introduction of conjugal visits. Special accommodations have been set up at certain facilities permitting inmates to enjoy private visits with their wives or girl friends. The latest extension of this privilege came in November, 1989, when a homosexual prisoner won a court judgement granting him the right to conjugal penitentiary visits from his partner.[91] Among the more innovative developments has been the introduction of women as staff in male prisons. Women were hired as guards in the late seventies, and in 1980 the first woman to serve as warden of a male institution was appointed. In 1984 approximately half of the new personnel hired for the correctional service were female.[92]

Another significant advance in the rehabilitation program has been the more frequent use of halfway houses. The dearth of transition care was a long-standing problem with the old ticket-of-leave system. It continued for some years after the new Parole Act came into force. The growth in the number of community organizations involved with criminal justice went a long way to alleviating the difficulties. By 1977 there were some 650 such agencies functioning across the country. However, the establishment of halfway houses as an integral component of the aftercare system has been especially important.

The halfway house is a home-like facility in which an offender, on parole, can live for a period of time after release. The house provides accommodation and a stable environment at a crucial point in the transition process. The parolee is given assistance in finding work and aid, and encouragement in readjusting to life outside prison. The first real halfway house was established by the Anglican Church in Toronto in 1954. Some years later, in 1962, St. Leonard's House was opened in Windsor, Ontario, under the auspices of the Roman Catholic Church. It was the first of a series started in a number of communities. By 1968 the Correctional Service itself opened a halfway house in Montreal for men on day release. Since then both the Correctional Service and private agencies have gone into the business in a big way. In 1972 there were about 156 community-based residential centres and by the mid-eighties there were approximately 163 privately run halfway houses in Canada and another twenty-one operated by the Correctional Service.[93]

Today halfway houses include private homes that offer room and board, group homes, and hostels. Some offer minimal assistance while others provide a structured program that might include counselling, a variety of services, and life skills training. Certain group homes offer specialized help with such things as addiction problems and follow-up psychiatric treatment. The clientele for the majority of houses are people on day parole, full parole, and mandatory supervision. While many cater only to men or only to women, a number are open to both.[94] Although the regimen is fairly fixed, some staff have experimented with resident management, group purchasing of food, group meal preparation, and resident industries. The importance of halfway houses and aftercare agencies is obvious from the fact that by the mid-eighties the number of persons on day release, parole, and mandatory supervision from federal and provincial institutions averaged about 10,000 per day.

One of the latest developments in the area of parole and halfway houses is a plan by Correctional Service Canada to open a special office for the supervision of high-risk parolees. A series of violent incidents involving parolees has prompted the penitentiary service to experiment with a special office that would maintain very close supervision of high-risk offenders out on early release. The government, while acknowledging the risks, also hopes to persuade the public that the new program will not increase the potential danger of taking a chance on inmates with violent backgrounds. The intention is to deal with prisoners who are nearing the end of their terms and would soon be released in any event. Officials argue that it is better to let such people out a little early under close supervision rather than wait till the end of their terms when they would be out completely on their own. Specially trained staff will work at the unit and parolees will undergo psychological tests and periodic urine tests for drugs or alcohol, will be put in special treatment programs, and helped to find suitable employment.[95]

New approaches are also to be found at the entry level of the criminal justice system. Much greater use, for example, is made of probation as a sentencing option. While the practice goes well back in our history, it was legally sanctioned in 1889 with the passage of the Act to Permit the Conditional Release of First Offenders, which provided that convicted felons could be released on their own cognizance. In 1921 a refinement was introduced, which required the person on probation to report to a supervisor. Except in Ontario, probation was not widely used until the post-war period. The Archambault Commission encouraged more use of probation, observing that "there are many proper cases where adult probation is preferable to imprisonment." In 1956 the Fauteux Committee report recommended the "expansion of probation facilities in all provinces." The committee also recommended that the law be amended so a person could be placed on probation without having to be convicted. The use of probation as a sentencing option steadily increased; by 1984 a daily average of about 74,000 people were on probation.

Restitution to the victim and community service are additional sentencing options that have come into common use in recent years. After acknowledging guilt or upon conviction, an offender may be permitted to work out a restitution agreement with the victim. In this way the victim is compensated for the loss or damage and the perpetrator avoids a fine or stays out of jail. The arrangement helps to promote a reconciliation and brings home to the offender the personal nature of the crime. The community service option puts the offender to work at some task useful to the community. This is seen as being more productive than a fine or simply locking up the offender for a short time. Another option being tried is sentencing offenders to incarceration during weekends. This leaves them free to keep their jobs and earn a living.

Along with the correctional changes in the treatment of criminals there have been ongoing changes to the Criminal Code. One of the most controversial that has had a direct impact on the punishment of offenders was the abolition of the death penalty. Support for the abolition of capital punishment began to grow during the early post-war years. By the 1950s a number of churches, intellectuals, humanitarians, and penal reformers were publicly voicing their opposition. In response, the government appointed a Joint Committee of the House and Senate in 1953 to study the question. It reported in 1956 and recommended against abolition. Support, however, continued to grow, both inside and outside Parliament, and by the 1960s there was sufficient pro-abolition sentiment that the Conservative government of John Diefenbaker commuted 52 of 66 death sentences. When the Liberals returned to power in 1963 they continued to commute capital sentences.

For a change the government was leading public opinion. Throughout the 1960s the majority of Canadians favoured retention of capital punishment, but strong pressure for abolition sparked national debate. After several attempts to produce compromise legislation the Liberals in 1967 succeeded in getting a bill passed that abolished capital punishment, except for the murder of a peace officer, for a five-year trial period.[96] In 1973 the trial period was extended and in July of 1976, by a vote of 130 to 124, Parliament abolished the death penalty. At the same time the sentence for first-degree murder called for life imprisonment with no parole eligibility for twenty-five years.

The last executions in Canada took place at 12:02 a.m., December 11, 1962, at Toronto's Don Jail. Two murderers were put to death for separate crimes. Arthur Lucas, a Detroit gangster, was convicted of killing an FBI informant and his common-law wife in Toronto. Ronald Turpin was sentenced to death for killing a Toronto policeman after a robbery. The moratorium and subsequent abolition have never laid the issue to rest. It resurfaced with particular vigour in the early 1980s. A number of slayings, including those of three policemen in Toronto and two prison guards in Manitoba, as well as the Clifford Olson murders, caused a wave of public indignation. These incidents, coupled with the perception that violent crime was on the increase, provoked a call for the reinstatement of the death penalty. Public opinion polls showed that up to 70 per cent of Canadians favoured capital punishment for certain categories of murder. The police associations across the country have consistently supported use of the death penalty. The majority of churches, on the other hand, maintain a strong opposition to reinstatement. Within society at large many still argue that capital punishment is a deterrent. Others favour it simply as a retributive measure, which they feel is justified for such a serious crime as murder.[97]

An indirect result of the abolition of the death penalty in Canada was the addition to the Criminal Code of dangerous offender legislation. Introduced in 1977, the measure was designed to protect society against repeat offenders who were criminal psychopaths or particularly dangerous and who showed no signs of responding to rehabilitation programs. It replaced the 1947 Habitual Offenders Act discussed earlier. The 1977 Act came on the heels of concern over public perceptions of increased vulnerability due to the abolition of the death penalty. Being able to incarcerate dangerous offenders for indeterminate sentences gave the police and courts a powerful new weapon with which to fight crime. However, the whole concept has been mired in controversy and continually attacked by civil libertarians and others. In practice, little use has been made of the dangerous offender law.

The 1980s witnessed continued changes in the treatment of criminals as well as ongoing refinements to the guidelines. The prevailing philosophy was summed up in 1985 in the form of the following Standards for Adult Corrections in Canada, compiled by the Canadian Criminal Justice Association:

> Correctional services are an essential part of a coordinated and interdependent criminal justice system, and are provided by various levels of government as well as the voluntary sector in Canada.

The primary purposes of the correctional component of the Canadian criminal justice system are to contribute to the achievement of a safe and just society and to promote responsible citizenship by:

(a) providing the court with the widest possible choice of options in sentencing;

(b) carrying out the decisions of the court;

(c) providing appropriate measures of security, direction and control for the accused or the convicted offender;

(d) encouraging the offender's participation, whether in the community or in a correctional institution, in programs provided and designed to aid his/her successful integration into the community;

(e) cooperating with persons and agencies within and outside the criminal justice system to prevent crime and offer services to all persons involved in the criminal justice process.

In accordance with the primary purposes of the correctional component of the Canadian justice system, the following principles apply:

1. At all times the rights and dignity of all those involved in the correctional process must be respected and upheld.

2. The offender remains a member of society and forfeits only those rights and privileges which are expressly taken away by statute or as a necessary consequence of the custody and control imposed by the court.

3. The loss of liberty, restriction of mobility, or any other disposition of the court constitutes the sanction. Correctional services must not impose further punishment in relation to the offender's crime and must adopt the least restrictive course of action that is sufficient to meet the legal requirements of the dispositions.

4. In the essential exercise of discretion, correctional agencies must adhere to procedural safe-guards that are not only fair but are perceived to be fair.

5. Correctional policies and practices must not deny the offender the hope of regaining status as a free citizen.

6. Correctional agencies have the responsibility to assist the offender to develop or maintain positive and supportive personal and family relations.

7. The achievement of law abiding behavior is ultimately a matter of personal choice and individual responsibility. However, many offenders who would not otherwise seek change will respond positively to a favorable environment, encouragement and support by corrections personnel. Correctional services must provide such stimulation and support.

8. Correctional agencies have a responsibility to present and promote a wide range of programs and services developed to meet the legitimate

needs and interests of the offenders and to encourage and facilitate their participation.

9. Services available to the general public must be utilized in the correctional process whenever possible and practical.

10. Correctional objectives should be met through shared responsibility and cooperative action by the community, correctional workers, other segments of the criminal justice system and the offenders themselves.

11. Correctional agencies must be open. Specific procedures are needed to enhance public awareness and understanding of and participation in the correctional process in view of the social investment involved therein.

12. Staff are of paramount importance in accomplishing the goals of any correctional agency. They will make their optimum contribution if supported by effective personnel development opportunities and positive working conditions. Staff should have the opportunity to participate in the formulation of policies related to both programs and administration. Staff organizations should be involved in furthering this process.

13. Correctional agencies must be characterized by the effective use of resources. Efforts to achieve and maintain effectiveness require a responsiveness to a continuing program of data gathering, evaluation and review.

14. The advancement of knowledge is vital to progress in corrections and should be a primary objective. Correctional agencies should promote and support efforts to promote the state of correctional knowledge and to communicate such knowledge within the criminal justice system and to the public.

15. Correctional agencies must be accountable. They should be subject to regular, independent and public assessment.[98]

The principles enunciated in 1985 have completed a process that was begun with the opening of Kingston Prison in 1835. A reformatory objective was introduced to go along with punishment deterrence and the safety of the public. Although little progress was made in rehabilitation it continued to be a stated goal of the system. The Canadian Criminal Justice Association statement emphasizes the importance of rehabilitation almost to the exclusion of all other considerations. To some extent it picks up the nineteenth-century concept of a prison as a hospital. The socially maladjusted or sick citizen may be institutionalized if necessary and if so should be made as comfortable as possible and given the benefit of the best care and attention available.

This theme is continued with the latest mission statement from the Correctional Service of Canada. In 1988 the government appointed Ole

Ingstrup as the new Commissioner of Correctional Service Canada. Ingstrup worked in the correctional system in Denmark before coming to Canada and has been described as "reform-minded." One of his first undertakings was to compile a set of fifty-five goals and principles for the people under him, which he hoped would help to arrest the cynicism and lack of direction that he saw as plaguing the Correctional Service. The central thrust of the mission statement is for a more defined role for all staff in the rehabilitative process: "All staff are correctional staff and are responsible for being active, visible participants in the correctional process and in achieving the objectives of the Service."[99]

The intent is that virtually all employees of the system be directly involved in the therapy process of reforming criminals. They are to be well paid, well trained, dedicated, and enthusiastic. Above all, they must "spend as much time as possible in direct contact with offenders."[100] Ingstrup also wants to promote greater citizen involvement in the rehabilitation process and to make more use of community resources in dealing with offenders. Overall, the intent, once again, is to provide the prisoner with a humane, dignified, and just experience and to concentrate on treatment and rehabilitation. The hope is that offenders will respond positively, accept responsibility for their condition, and co-operate in the reform program.[101] As an additional device to promote all this the Correctional Service proposes to dress their staff in civilian clothes and discard the more intimidating uniforms.[102]

The current trend is to avoid incarcerating criminals if possible and to release more people already in prison. Existing institutions are overcrowded and all indications point to the situation getting worse. Court dockets are backlogged and the rapid increase in such things as drug-related offences portends to bring more pressure on prison facilities. In view of the rising population and tight budgets the Correctional Service is attempting to get non-violent offenders out as soon as possible and to step up the parole process for new admissions. Officials have put together a plan that would redirect the penitentiary system "from a custodial emphasis to a releasing emphasis"[103] with special programs that would concentrate on preparing inmates for early release. The new approach seems to have percolated through all levels of corrections. In May, 1990, Fred Gibson, head of the National Parole Board, made a public statement to the effect that more prisoners should be released on parole. He said that the Board has to take chances by releasing more prisoners instead of responding to public pressure to avoid risks.[104]

The judicial system is also experimenting, with the general trend being toward the use of sentence options that keep people out of jail. Probation, fines, community service, restitution, and part-time incarceration have become the preferred penalties for non-violent offenders. In addition, greater use is being made of community counselling programs with the courts requiring certain types of offenders to enrol for therapy or go to jail. Much of the de-emphasis on incarceration reflects a belief that institutionalization is not conducive to rehabilitation and that this objective can be better achieved by treating criminals in community settings.

Even the victim has been brought into the modern approach to the treatment of criminals. Since the 1970s more attention and research have been focused on the trauma experienced by victims, on their needs, and on their potential role in the criminal justice system. In 1981 a Federal-Provincial Task Force on Justice for Victims was set up to study the latter of these concerns. The result has been a growing tendency to bring the victim into the correctional process in the form of victim-offender confrontation programs and victim-offender reconciliation. The idea behind the former is to heighten the offender's awareness of the harm that has been done and to help the person come to grips with the crime while giving the victim the opportunity to see the criminal as a person. The reconciliation program offers the offender a chance to express remorse and helps the victim deal with the experience of the crime.[105]

THE RESULTS OF MODERN CRIMINAL JUSTICE REFORMS

The new facilities, the program innovations, the revised laws, the enlightened correctional philosophy, and the ongoing study and concern that have characterized corrections in recent decades raise two questions. Have the problems that marked the criminal justice system for so long finally been resolved? Have the refinements, the therapy, and the host of new programs had any marked impact on rehabilitation or on the incidence of crime?

Even a cursory examination of the criminal justice system reveals many problems. As we have seen, a great deal of crime goes undetected. Consequently, many criminals commit multiple offences before they are apprehended, and in some cases are never caught. In recent years offenders who do get arrested benefit from delays in their cases going to trial, from liberal bail provisions, and from a number of other measures that delay justice. In the meantime they are back on the streets, free to continue with their lawbreaking. In some cases an arrest can serve as an incentive to engage in more crime. Thieves or drug dealers who are brought up on charges now incur the financial burden of having to hire a lawyer and pay bail fees. Thus, they need to continue with their activities in order to make more money. Since they are not usually placed under surveillance or supervision, they are as free to act as they were before their arrest. Sometimes this lack of any official contact with an accused can result in tragedy.

A not untypical example of what can happen is illustrated by an incident in Halifax in the summer of 1988. After a public event associated with the city's natal day celebrations, a large crowd was exiting into the adjoining streets. A drunk driver hit and killed a nine-year-old boy while the youngster was in a crosswalk with his mother. The driver had already lost his licence for impaired driving and was awaiting trial on a second charge. A month earlier he had refused to take a breathalizer test. Yet the man was at liberty after the second offence and subsequently killed a child. The driver was given a penalty of thirty months in jail, which meant that he would be eligible for day parole at the end of six months.[106]

The courts themselves can sometimes contribute to the miscarriage of justice. One of the worst examples of the failure of the process was the case of Donald Marshall, a Nova Scotia Micmac Indian who spent eleven years in prison for a crime he did not commit. On May 28, 1971, sixteen-year-old Sandy Seale was stabbed in a park in Sydney and died the next day. Donald Marshall, seventeen at the time, was with Seale in the park and was subsequently accused, tried, and convicted of the murder. Part of the evidence that helped to convict Marshall came from testimony of witnesses claiming to have seen the proceedings on the night of the murder. In November of 1971 the RCMP conducted another cursory investigation when someone came forward and identified an elderly eccentric by the name of Roy Ebsary as the person who stabbed Sandy Seale. The police concurred with the earlier decision. In February, 1982, the RCMP reopened the case on the basis of new evidence that Marshall might be innocent.

By July the investigation was rewarded when three of the original witnesses filed affidavits claiming they had lied because of police pressure. On May 10, 1983, the appeals division of the Supreme Court of Nova Scotia set aside Marshall's conviction, and on January 17, 1985, Roy Ebsary, the man accused of Seale's murder back in 1971, was convicted of the killing. The Marshall affair caused such a storm of criticism against the Nova Scotia justice system and the provincial government that the government, in October, 1986, appointed a Royal Commission to examine the details of Marshall's conviction and the way the entire judicial apparatus functioned.

The hearings lasted until 1989 and became embroiled in controversy over the issue of whether or not the appeal court judges, who in their decision had suggested that Marshall was partly to blame for his troubles, could be required to testify. The Royal Commission report was finally released in January, 1990, and gave an extremely critical account of all of the proceedings associated with the Marshall case. It told a tragic story of incompetence at all levels, including the police, the court, and prosecution and defence lawyers, of a reluctance to co-operate with investigations, of lying, and of considerable judicial bungling. The Commission claimed, among other things, that Marshall was the victim of racial prejudice and that the entire justice system had failed him from the time of his arrest through to and even beyond the appeal court's acquittal.[107]

Court proceedings can be influenced by a variety of factors, not the least of which are the lawyers representing the crown and the defendant. Too often a trial comes down to a battle of wits between defence counsel and the crown prosecutor. The outcome hangs not on the law, or the guilt or innocence of the accused, but on the cunning and skill of the legal adversaries. Sometimes that skill is honed by some questionable ethics, by subterfuges, and by posturing. Some will go to great lengths to create a favourable climate of opinion for their clients. Others will try to minimize the nature of the offence. A case in point was the description of a crime given to the press by one of Canada's most prominent criminal lawyers. Three armed robbers who broke into a private home were caught and ultimately convicted. The lawyer was representing one of the trio and at the time of his client's arrest was quoted in the press as describing the armed robbery as a "minor break-in."

Another example of trivializing serious crime comes out of an appeal involving parole. The lawyer's client was a twenty-year-old man who had pleaded guilty to second-degree murder. He had been interrupted breaking into an automobile in the underground parking lot of an apartment building. The victim was a fifty-three-year-old woman who lived alone and was the sole support of an invalid husband confined in a nursing home. The young man stabbed the woman five times with a nine-inch knife because she caught him breaking into her car. The judge sentenced the killer to life imprisonment with eligibility for parole in twenty years. His lawyer described the parole provision as "harsh and excessive" and launched an appeal to have the time reduced. The arguments that he advanced on behalf of his client were that the man had not planned the killing and that the act was of short duration.[108]

In an effort to combat the drug trade more effectively the Canadian government made provisions to freeze temporarily the assets of people suspected of trafficking. The legislation allows a court appeal to have freeze orders rescinded and, in addition, provides for the payment of legal and other expenses from frozen funds. Although the measure is a considerable asset to the police in fighting serious crime, a number of lawyers have publicly attacked the legislation, one asking, "why get so moralistic about the drug trafficker?"[109]

The crisis in ethics is highlighted constantly by the number of lawyers being charged in court or taken before disciplinary committees. Even the legal profession's efforts at self-regulation leave something to be desired, as the following incident involving the Law Society of Upper Canada illustrates. The Society disbarred one of its members for false billing. On the surface it would seem that appropriate action was taken and that the public interest was protected. During the hearing, however, it was revealed that this was the lawyer's third time before the disciplinary board. Previously he had been found guilty of cheating on his bar admission exams and of lying to a judge. Yet it wasn't until his third offence that the Society judged the man unfit to practise law.[110]

While disreputable people are to be found in every profession, higher standards are expected of lawyers just as they are of police and judges. The ethics that guide them in their practice, their tactics, their professional conduct, and their public pronouncements all affect the ability of society to deal with the problem of crime and criminals. Lawyers influence their clients, public attitudes, and the courts, and since lawyers are given the responsibility to monitor and modify legal codes, they influence the law itself.

The next and most important component of the judicial system is the courts. As we have seen, many magistrates in an earlier day were unqualified amateurs. With the passage of time practically everyone appointed to the bench had legal qualifications. However, the mere fact of legal training has not solved the many problems that have plagued and continue to characterize the courts of Canada. Appointments still reflect political loyalties. This does not necessarily mean that those who get the job are not well qualified, but some are not. Sentence decisions are still lacking in uniformity across the country and sometimes in the same courts. Judges have reputations for being hard or lenient, of being learned or otherwise, of being stable or eccentric. Lawyers are well aware of the differences and make every effort to have their cases tried by the "right" judges.

Sentencing practices did not improve in spite of many changes and reforms elsewhere in the correctional system. By the mid-eighties magistrates' judgements were still the target of considerable criticism. For example, Mr. Justice Allen Linden, president of the Law Reform Commission of Canada, in 1985 characterized sentencing principles and practices as complex, inconsistent, outdated, and often unfair.[111] Additional confirmation of inconsistencies came out of a survey of judges published in 1988. Of 414 respondents to the Department of Justice survey, 12 per cent said there was too much variation in sentencing and 62 per cent said there was a fair amount of variation.[112]

While judges function within a certain legal framework they have sufficient flexibility to put their own stamp on the process. Thus, their personalities, their values, their political ideology, their ability, and even their personal problems colour their decisions. The 1986 Report of the Canadian Sentencing Commission pointed out that "In Canada over 1,000 independent decision-makers are handing down sentences for over three hundred different offences."[113] The report went on to say that "it would be almost impossible to expect no variation in the severity of sentences from judge to judge."[114] While anecdotes do not quantify the problem they do serve to illustrate the nature of it, and there are many examples of judicial idiosyncrasies. Sentences perceived by the public to be too lenient can be a particular problem because they taint the image of judges and open to question the justice of the courts. A case in point was a sentence handed out by a Vancouver judge to a drunk driver who killed a man in an automobile accident. The driver was fined $500 and had his licence suspended for six months.[115] The point is that the penalty satisfied none of the objectives of the correctional system. It had little, if any, punitive or deterrent value and no reformative dimension. Another drunk driver in Winnipeg was given a thirty-month prison sentence for criminal negligence. He ran a red light at a high speed and smashed into a car, killing three of the occupants and injuring the fourth. The man had a record of twenty driving convictions and had never had a driver's licence.[116]

Another Winnipeg judge handed out a sentence of twenty-three months in jail to a man who killed an acquaintance with a butcher knife during a fight. The judge let it be known that he was not in favour of incarceration and was quoted as saying, "It's unfortunate that a sentence of imprisonment must almost inevitably follow."[117] The dead man's mother was angry with the judge over the lenient sentence and equally disturbed with his comments. He told the woman that her son would not have died in vain if the killer was rehabilitated. The mother said she could not understand the judge's thinking, and in reference to the killer remarked, "If this man has a problem, he shouldn't have to go around killing people to get rehabilitation."[118]

The example illustrates problems with the court, ranging from insensitivity to poor judgement. Cases exhibiting these unfortunate traits on the part of judges are all too common. An Ontario judge, in separate incidents, ordered two spectators to be taken into custody because they started to leave the courtroom. The incident was investigated by the Judicial Council of Ontario and the judge was suspended. The Council concluded that the man was "unable to perform his judicial duties by reason of illness arising from a stress-related anxiety and depression disorder."[119] In one of the incidents witnesses reported that the young woman involved had attempted to leave the room quietly without disturbing the proceedings. Yet she was seized, taken to a cell, strip searched, and held for about an hour and a half.

A different Ontario judge ordered a female assault victim to be placed in handcuffs. She was not accused of any crime but had angered the judge by refusing to co-sign with her husband an agreement to keep the peace. Although she was the one who had been assaulted, the judge berated her and said she was to blame for all the problems in the marriage.[120] A case that caused one of the strongest public reactions in recent years involved a Vancouver judge in November, 1989. Following the trial of a thirty-three-year-old male accused of sexually fondling a three-year-old girl, the judge gave the man a suspended sentence. Many people criticized the judgement as too lenient but were even more disturbed by the judge's comments. In rationalizing the behaviour of the accused, he described the little girl as being sexually aggressive.[121]

Sometimes magistrates can be arbitrary and more concerned with their own egos than with dispensing justice and protecting the public. A case in point came out of the efforts of Halifax County Court judges to get trials started on time. They warned lawyers and prosecutors to be on time or face disciplinary measures. In one particular incident everyone was present before the proceedings were scheduled to begin at 9:30. The crown prosecutor left the room to meet with witnesses, telling the clerk that he would return within a few minutes. The judge arrived in court at 9:34, noted that the crown attorney was not there, and granted a motion for dismissal from the defence "for want of prosecution." "Court starts at 9:30, and the crown has been advised repeatedly," said the Judge. He added that the court "will not stand for this." He left the room at 9:37. To make his point he had summarily dismissed two men charged with robbery with violence.[122]

In light of the power and prestige enjoyed by judges, the public has every right to expect high standards of competence and performance. The agencies responsible for monitoring their conduct have been accused of protecting some whose actions warranted discipline, and there seems to be merit to the charges. In 1989, out of ninety-one outstanding complaints, seventy-seven had been processed by the Canadian Judicial Council at the end of the year. However, not one judge was penalized.[123] The Council deals with district, superior, and appeal court judges. One of the problems is that the sanctions available for disciplining judges fall into two extremes – they can either be dismissed or exonerated. This promotes a closing of ranks, which in turn can lead to a cavalier attitude. As the editor of the Criminal Lawyers Association newsletter pointed out, "Some of them become megalomaniacs with an aggrandized view of their importance."[124]

Besides the personal shortcomings of certain judges the courts have other troubles. A shortage of judges exists in some areas and there is a dearth of support staff. The court system has suffered from poor planning, poor administration, politics, and underfunding. Mr. Justice Thomas Zuber of the Ontario Court of Appeal completed a study of the province's courts in early 1989. He described the Ontario system as "a ramshackle and outmoded conglomerate," as well as "a fractured mosaic of individual fiefdoms."[125] The impact of harried courts is that justice is sometimes neither swift nor certain. This is borne out by Chief Justice William Howland of Ontario, who pointed out in January of 1989 that people were waiting twelve to fourteen months for a trial date to be set. The delays led to hundreds of accused criminals having their cases dismissed because too long a time had elapsed before they could be brought to trial.[126] In one six-day period in October, 1990, judges threw out 462 cases because of trial delays.[127]

For many of those who are tried and convicted, the next stage in the process is incarceration. As we have seen, contemporary facilities, programs, and much else are far superior to what they were even a few decades ago. There are still instances of cruelty, a lack of programs and facilities, overcrowding, and strict discipline, but the main problem is prison life itself. A culture pervades penitentiaries that can be repressive for inmates and can seriously undermine the effect of rehabilitation programs. The deprivation of freedom creates a resentful and unco-operative attitude that from the very outset works against rehabilitation, and prison populations include some very hardened, belligerent, and violent people. Their anger and aggression continue to be expressed inside penitentiary walls with the result that assaults, beatings, and intimidation are common occurrences. Gang associations develop and certain inmates emerge as authority figures and are able to exercise considerable control over other prisoners. The inmates who are victimized by this prison culture live in fear. Between 1983 and 1988, forty-two inmates were murdered in federal penitentiaries, 2,157 assaults on prisoners by other inmates were reported, 664 assaults were made on staff, and twenty-seven hostage-takings occurred.[128]

The hostile nature of a prison environment is further compounded by the large number of inmates who suffer from psychological problems. A recent study done by Correctional Services Canada concluded that three out of four prisoners had anti-social personalities. The study also revealed there were about 500 schizophrenics in the inmate population and as many as 300 others suffered from organic brain damage. The study also suggested that as many as 72 per cent were alcohol abusers and about 52 per cent used drugs.[129]

Penitentiaries are supposed to be rehabilitative institutions, yet another dimension of their internal problems is that they are crime-ridden. Along with the assaults, intimidation, and forced sex, theft, drug dealing, and a number of other illegal activities pose a constant problem. In 1982, for example, a full-scale counterfeiting operation was uncovered in the print plant at Drumheller Penitentiary in Alberta. Prisoners were making false United States $10 and $20 bills, American Express travellers' cheques, and Saskatchewan birth certificates.[130] In 1983 an organized crime figure, serving a life sentence, was convicted of arranging the murder of a Toronto mobster.[131] In some respects the modern penal institution is not only a school for crime but also a place to get practical experience.

Some of the crime inside prison is related to the need for money. The institution provides bed and board free of charge but extras, such as toiletries, soft drinks, cigarettes, snacks, and writing supplies, must be paid for by the inmates. In 1989 the standard earnings were in the vicinity of $31 per week. Some inmates claim that this is insufficient to meet their needs and therefore people borrow money and get into debt or steal. Unpaid debts can be a source of friction, as can theft. The chairman of the inmates' committee at Collins Bay claimed in a 1989 interview that these things generate violence. Prisoners who steal or renege on debts can "get their heads caved in with a bar or they get knifed," he said.[132]

One of the more serious prison crimes is drug trafficking. It is incongruous that people in federal prison can buy and sell drugs. Ironically, the privileges so many criminals now enjoy contribute to this and other forms of illegal activity. Many prisoners on day parole are in and out of the institution on a regular basis. Also, some offenders are allowed to serve their sentences on weekends in county jails. These people are put under a great deal of pressure to smuggle drugs into the facilities. If they refuse they are intimidated and sometimes beaten. While prisoners coming in from outside are carefully searched, it is still possible to smuggle drugs. A common way of avoiding detection is to put the contraband in a condom and swallow it.[133] In other cases drugs are taken in by visitors, and there is also suspicion that some guards have been involved in trafficking. With so many people in prison for drug abuse and related offences, the availability of drugs within the institutions is a serious handicap to their reformation.

The highly touted rehabilitation and therapy programs that were launched with such enthusiasm in the sixties and seventies have also fallen on hard times. Underfunding and the growth in the penitentiary population has put a great deal of stress on programs and facilities. There is a shortage of trained staff and program capacity to deal with the requirements of the system. The Brentwood program, started at Collins Bay, is an example. It caters to drug addicts, alcoholics, and hard-core criminals. It attempts to break the cycle of crime and substance addiction by strengthening the prisoners' internal resources and giving them the fortitude and confidence to resist temptation. The success rate of the program is estimated to be about 50 per cent. Counsellors claim that the ten-week session would be more successful if it was longer and could accommodate more people. However, there is such a long waiting list that they must turn over participants fairly rapidly.

In some cases the problem is a complete dearth of programs. Testifying before an inquest into a murder by a mentally disturbed parolee, two Correctional Services employees claimed that very minimal resources were provided for treatment and that therapy was limited.[134] This was reiterated by a psychologist at Toronto's Clarke Institute of Psychiatry, who maintained that therapy programs in the federal system "tend to be not very well organized, not very well funded or not very well researched."[135]

The situation outside the federal institutions is even worse. Programs are minimal or non-existent, and except for general counselling there is not much in-depth therapy. Just how bad things can be is illustrated by events at Oakalla jail in British Columbia in January of 1988. Thirteen prisoners escaped from the seventy-six-year-old building. The public scrutiny that the escapes brought to bear on the institution revealed that it suffered from old age, overcrowding, and inadequate financing. Guards were underpaid and overworked, and many were on sick leave due to stress. Some cells were still using buckets for toilets and a number of trades courses had been discontinued for lack of funding. To keep inmates occupied they were put to work simply digging holes in the ground for a dollar a day.[136]

In spite of a tendency by the courts to make more use of non-incarceral sentences, a significant increase in the jail populations continues in many places, leading to overcrowding and other problems. For example, in Quebec the numbers of accused kept in jail while awaiting trial or sentencing increased by 33.5 per cent between 1987-88, when 19,241 were jailed while waiting to be tried or sentenced, and 1988-89 when 25,691 people were thus jailed. The Parthenais Centre in Montreal, in the fall of 1988, had 525 prisoners in a facility built to accommodate 400. Inmates were sleeping in the infirmary, the recreation room, and on the floor. At least part of the problem in big cities like Montreal is due to the increased drug activity and the number of strung-out addicts who are picked up on drug and other offences. The increase in arrests and detentions also results in crowded court dockets, delays in trials, more plea bargaining, and rushed justice.[137]

A different type of problem related to jailings that has caused growing concern is the disproportionate number of Indians and Métis being incarcerated in the western provinces. For example, only 4 per cent of Alberta's population is Indian and Métis, yet they make up 30 per cent of the province's prisoners. Some attribute the discrepancy to the normal workings of the justice system and claim the natives are simply more prone to get into trouble because of higher levels of unemployment and alcoholism. Others argue that the natives are victims of prejudice and discrimination and are more liable to be arrested and put in jail than white people. The situation is yet another malady that marks the contemporary justice system.[138]

Throughout the 1980s overcrowding, tension, and demonstrations have troubled the Canadian correctional system. Some claimed that insensitivity and a lack of concern on the part of certain administrators contributed to the problem. Native prisoners have been especially critical. One man at Manitoba's Stony Mountain Penitentiary was refused permission to visit his dying father in the hospital. He was allowed out to attend the funeral but was shackled for a nine-hour period. Natives have the freedom to practise their sacred ceremonies in prison but they maintain that they are treated with derision. They charge that their ceremonial pipes and eagle feathers are sometimes mishandled by guards searching their cells. Finally, they claim that upon release they are sent away without money and left to fend for themselves.[139]

The continued use of solitary confinement is another source of irritation. The cells are sparsely furnished with sleeping accommodations in some institutions consisting of a mattress on a concrete slab on the floor. Inmates are confined for as much as twenty-three hours a day. Limited reading material, confinement, and inactivity add to the psychological pain of isolation.

A report of the prison ombudsman released in late March, 1989, accused a former head of the federal Correctional Service, Réal LeBlanc, of ignoring or delaying action on inmates' complaints. LeBlanc had left the service in March of 1988 to take a position with the Alberta government. During his tenure of office, it was claimed, prisoners in solitary confinement needing medical attention were ignored, prisoners were arbitrarily transferred from one institution to another, and there was double bunking in segregated areas. In the 1986-87 reporting year, 12,000 inmates in federal institutions made 2,329 official complaints.[140] In 1989 approximately 13,237 federal prisoners filed 14,911 grievances.[141]

Thus, the shortcomings have not been worked out of the criminal justice system, or, if old ones have been remedied, new ones seem to have taken their place. There are problems at all levels – from the police, to the lawyers, to the courts, to the judges, to the jails and penitentiaries. Not only are there problems, but they are so deeply rooted and so widespread as to debilitate the entire system, and they substantially diminish society's ability to deter crime and to treat criminals. Justice is not certain, or swift, or uniform. It does not always suit the crime or the person, and often it is not an effective deterrent, nor will it necessarily have any rehabilitative effect.

What is the impact of all of this? Many, especially among those who consult and work in the system, claim that rehabilitation programs work and that there is a high success rate in terms of offenders who stay out of criminal activity. In contrast, others argue that for all the time, effort, and money spent on the crime problem and on criminals, very little is being accomplished. Certainly the public perception is that whatever is being done is not sufficient to curtail the rate of crime and to provide the society with an appropriate level of security.

In the late 1960s a research team in the United States, led by Robert Martinson, did a major study on rehabilitation for the New York State Governor's Special Committee on Criminal Offenders. The final report was submitted in 1971. The researchers examined English-language publications for the period 1945-67 and chose 231 of these for an in-depth analysis. On the basis of the study they concluded that "With few and isolated exceptions, the rehabilitative efforts that have been reported so far have had no appreciable effect on recidivism."[142]

Martinson's conclusions were buttressed by another study on the effects of sentencing. Stephen Brody, a British researcher, did a detailed analysis on some seventy studies on sentencing from many countries. His evaluations and conclusions were published in *The Effectiveness of Sentencing* (1976). His study revealed that:

> Reviews of research into the effectiveness of different sentences . . . have unanimously agreed that the results have so far offered little hope that a reliable and simple remedy for recidivism can be easily found. . . . It has seemed, therefore, that longer sentences are no more effective than short ones, that different types of institutions work about equally as well, that probationers on the whole do no better than if they were sent to prison,

and that rehabilitative programs – whether involving psychiatric treatment, counselling, casework or intensive contact and special attention, in custodial or non-custodial settings – have no predictably beneficial effects.[143]

Both Martinson's and Brody's conclusions have been attacked in many quarters. However, critics have usually based their opposition on the limited results of highly specialized programs. Overall there is no convincing evidence that they were wrong. This is further illustrated in the 1986 Report of the Canadian Sentencing Commission. The Commission extracted excerpts from official reports from 1831 to 1983 to make the point that the judicial system has consistently failed to meet the objective of rehabilitation.[144] Typical of the judgements that have been made is the conclusion reached in 1977 by the Sub-Committee on the Penitentiary System in Canada, which stated unequivocally: "This Sub-Committee has found that the old system has failed."[145]

It may be argued that in more recent years considerable changes and improvements make these earlier assessments irrelevant. The fact is, however, that not that much has actually changed by way of treatment and there are no signs of any improvement in results. The comments and assessments of a few years ago are still being made today, and no evidence suggests that they are not just as valid. The Daubney Report on sentencing, released in 1988, observed that "It is now generally recognized that imprisonment has not been effective in rehabilitating or reforming offenders, has not been shown to be a strong deterrent, and has achieved only temporary public protection and uneven retribution...."[146] The judicial system is still engaged in planning overhauls and continues to revise the Criminal Code, and the Correctional Service is trying to move in a new direction, all of which suggest that what is currently in place is not doing the job. Indeed, certain programs considered to be key elements in the reform process have been the subject of considerable debate.

Among the most controversial rehabilitation programs have been parole and mandatory supervision. Proponents argue that these allow for the gradual re-integration of inmates to outside society. Also, it is asserted, they afford protection to the public because offenders are initially released under supervision rather than simply being turned loose upon completion of sentence. Both parole and mandatory supervision are considered integral parts of the rehabilitation program that starts in prison and continues after release. Supporters claim that the programs have a success rate of about 85 per cent. By that they mean that of the inmates on some form of release prior to the actual termination of sentences only about 15 per cent break the conditions of their early release.[147]

Parole and mandatory supervision have attracted considerable public attention and criticism because of a number of very serious crimes committed by inmates on these programs. A part of the public unease is explained by the results of a study done by the National Parole Board. The report, released in 1987, revealed that in the previous twelve years 130 people were killed by inmates on early release.[148] Three cases in particular have caused public uproar in recent years. In 1981 Clifford Olson killed eleven young people while out of prison on early release and under mandatory supervision. In another case a twenty-one-year-old university student was raped and stabbed to death in 1985 while working in a halfway house. The young woman was working an overnight shift and there was no security on duty in the house. An investigation revealed the murderer should never have been let out and that his disorders had been misdiagnosed by prison psychiatrists.[149]

Another violent killing in early 1988 brought to light a number of problems with early release. A young woman was slashed to death in her apartment by a resident of a halfway house who had a long history of violence and psychiatric problems. Born in 1956, he became involved in lawbreaking at twelve years of age. By 1970 he had a record of at least forty-six arrests for a variety of crimes, including theft and drug use. His first rape victim was a sixty-two-year-old woman and he also assaulted her husband when the man attempted to come to his wife's rescue. Following a stint in a mental institution, from which he escaped thirteen times, he killed his fourteen-year-old girlfriend on his last escape and was sentenced to six years for manslaughter. In spite of repeated pessimistic assessments by psychiatrists, he was allowed out on day parole in 1978. While out he committed a rape and six years were added to his sentence. In 1979 he escaped and committed another rape, this time on a woman who was five months pregnant. He was given an eight-year sentence for that crime. Although his sentence added up by that point to twenty-four years, with a release date in 1998, under the remission provisions he could be released in 1989. Consequently, in 1987 his supervisors began experimenting with a pre-release program during which on one occasion he made a threat with a knife. He continued to show problem behaviour, including a threat to commit suicide. Repeated psychiatric evaluations were so bad that one psychiatrist concluded that nothing more could be done for him in prison. Finally everyone, it seems, including the parole board, decided to take a gamble and released him to a halfway house. That gamble resulted in a young woman losing her life. The investigation that followed revealed a comedy of errors that included officials, the parole board, and the practices of the halfway house.[150]

Proponents of early release argue that incidents like these are not representative and should not be used to judge the program. Comprehensive statistics are not available on the success rate of people on parole or mandatory supervision, but one study of inmates granted full parole or released on mandatory supervision between 1979-80 and 1983-84 revealed that approximately 12.4 per cent of those on parole had their freedom revoked for technical violations and 13 per cent for committing new offences. Of those on mandatory supervision, 25.5 per cent committed a technical violation while 20 per cent had their remission revoked for new offences. In the reporting year 1988-89, of 1,785 who violated parole or mandatory supervision 24.7 per cent were readmitted for new offences.[151] Depending on one's point of view, this may be seen as a poor performance or a high success rate. Perhaps it is not very meaningful to talk about parole or mandatory supervision in terms of success. Released prisoners in both categories are still under sentence and therefore under pressure to behave or face losing their freedom. It is a little like measuring the success rate of imprisonment by the numbers who do not commit crimes while incarcerated.

A study done by Canadian bankers in 1988 suggested a less positive analysis than parole officials present. Between January 1, 1987, and June 30, 1988, 124 people were arrested in the greater Montreal area for armed robbery of financial institutions. Of that group, eighty-one, or about 65 per cent, were still under sentence for a previous crime. Of these, forty-five were on full parole, day parole, temporary absence, or mandatory supervision; twenty-three were on probation; and thirteen were escapees. A similar examination of bank robberies in Toronto over a twenty-six-month period between January 1, 1986, and March 1, 1988, revealed that of 133 people arrested, approximately 50 per cent were still under sentence and 92 per cent had previous records. Individual profiles reinforce the negative impression. A Winnipeg man charged with seven bank robberies and two failed attempts was given a five-year prison term on February 26, 1986. Ten months later he was paroled to a halfway house. A man in Vancouver was charged with seven counts of armed robbery in February, 1986, and was sentenced to four years in penitentiary on each charge, with the terms to run concurrently. In spite of an already lengthy criminal record and a four-year sentence, he was out on day parole by October, having served eight months of his sentence. Two months later he was arrested for another bank holdup.[152]

The real test of whether or not an offender is rehabilitated is if he or she returns to crime when the sentence is completed. Statistics for 1977-82 show that five years after their release on parole 35.6 per cent of former inmates were back in a federal institution and 39.4 per cent of those originally let out on mandatory supervision were re-incarcerated.[153] To get a complete picture it would also be necessary to know how many had been convicted of additional crimes or sent to local jails. Whatever the success or failure rate, there obviously are problems. Among them is the shortage of parole officers relative to the number of people under supervision. One study reported in February, 1990, that there was a need for 634 more community officers and 407 case workers inside the penitentiaries.[154] It also seems that the Parole Board itself needs some attention. In May of 1990 William Outerbridge, a former Parole Board chairman, claimed that a succession of governments appointed inexperienced people to the Board and that it was used as a political pork barrel. He also claimed that during his term in office he was constantly pressured by government to let more inmates out on parole, in part to relieve prison overcrowding. He pointed out that the whole situation was frustrating because there were inadequate programs, services, and parole officers to do a proper job and that poor leadership from a succession of solicitors general had left the bureaucracy confused and demoralized.[155]

There has never been any degree of certainty about the treatment of criminals. Warden Lavell of Kingston Penitentiary, speaking at a session of the National Prison Association back in 1888, remarked that "after nearly twenty years' experience of prison life, I have very little faith in the genuine reformation of criminals of that higher class."[156] He was referring to those sentenced to prison as opposed to terms in jails. A century later nine members of a Royal Commission headed by Judge Omer Archambault of Saskatchewan challenged the idea that people are sent to prison to be rehabilitated and recommended that criminals be required to serve most if not all of their sentence. The Commission also recommended the virtual abolition of the current parole system.[157] Much of the pessimism stems from the fact that at no time has the criminal justice system been successful in significantly lowering crime rates or in appreciably reducing recidivism.

The plethora of treatment strategies and programs seem to have little impact. Officials maintain that sex offenders are largely incurable, that drug and alcohol addicts can only be kept from substance abuse by daily doses of other drugs, and that hardened criminals will continue to commit crime until they eventually tire and burn out. Many who have worked with released prisoners report that the only remorse they show is for having been caught. Jacques Larente, serving a life sentence at the super maximum security unit at Ste. Anne des Plaines in Quebec summed it up in a 1989 interview with the *Montreal Gazette*: "Most of the guys don't believe in rehabilitation. If a guy is rehabilitated, it's because he's fed up with doing time. He does it on his own. Sure they had psychologists, and cultural programs, and chapel and Alcoholics Anonymous but it's always up to the guys."[158] The statement is reminiscent of a conclusion reached by the Saskatchewan Penal Commission in 1946, which observed that "Society can provide excellent equipment in its penal institutions and excellent programs looking to the rehabilitation of the prisoner but, unless it is able to awaken in him the desire to participate in his own reformation, the facilities and training offered may be relatively ineffective."[159]

Thus, the refinements and programs introduced into the correctional system in recent decades have had little apparent positive effect on rehabilitation or on the incidence of crime. Officials at all levels of the judicial system continue to struggle with many of the same problems that their predecessors faced for over 300 years in Canada. The fundamental objective is still to find ways of decreasing crime levels and reforming offenders. At no time in our history have so much money and effort been spent in pursuance of this elusive goal. The system and programs in place today are much more than nineteenth-century reformers ever thought possible. One army of people works at carrying out existing programs while another contingent plans new strategies and devises new laws. Whether the current generation has any more success than those who have gone before remains to be seen.

SUMMARY

The treatment of criminals since Confederation has been influenced by a growing conviction that, along with punishment and deterrence, a primary objective of the penal system should be the reform of the offender. For almost a century after Confederation that philosophy was honoured more in the breach than in the observance. While paying lip service to the concept of reform, many, both inside and outside the system, looked upon incarceration as serving primarily the dual purposes of punishment and deterrence. Personal attitudes on either side of the debate counted for little since circumstances dictated the reality: a lack of money and will power left the penal system to struggle along with poorly trained staff, administrators who were frequently ill-qualified political appointees, inadequate facilities, and insufficient programs. The result was a discontented and unco-operative prison population. The institutions were preoccupied with custodial functions and maintaining discipline. The ordered existence that was meant to be a part of the reform process became an end in itself as prisoners were subjected to numerous rules and regulations, harsh punishments, and a host of petty annoyances and restrictions. The conditions developed an attitude of resentment and rebellion among inmates rather than a receptiveness to reform.

All elements of the judicial system suffered similar maladies. Police were generally lacking in any form of professional training, judges were often appointed more for their political connections than for their competence, justice was subjective and uneven, and jails were frequently unfit for human habitation. Nothing about any part of the system was meaningful in reducing the incidence of crime or in assisting offenders to become law-abiding, responsible citizens. Study after study documented the shortcomings but to no avail. About the only signs of progress were sporadic changes in the laws and the occasional new or upgraded facility, which in some cases reduced punishments, discontinued the more barbaric penal practices, or introduced more liberal measures for the treatment of criminals. However, since so much of this was piecemeal and done within the framework of a custodial-oriented process, little progress was made.

Throughout, reformers pressed for the adoption of a detailed agenda of progressive and enlightened policies and programs, but they had minimal success. It wasn't until the post-World War Two period that prospects became bright for meaningful and deep-seated changes. The rehabilitative philosophy took on new life and saw concrete expression in the construction of maximum, medium, and minimum security institutions, in the introduction of a variety of rehabilitation and therapy programs, and in the granting of more privileges to prisoners. Over the last two decades these trends have continued with ongoing study and experimentation.

Since the war, penitentiaries have evolved from being places that were seen primarily as custodial institutions for punishment and deterrence to environments in which the preponderant focus was on rehabilitation. That change in emphasis did not achieve the anticipated results so the latest trend is to downplay prisons as appropriate environments for rehabilitation. Much greater use is being made of sanctions other than incarceration and of treatment programs in the community as opposed to the penitentiary. Consistent with this new direction is the tendency to move out people who are interned as quickly as possible. Correction officials, their staffs, and consultants continue to devise new approaches, modify objectives and philosophy, and revise the Criminal Code, as they have for many years, but all the experimentation has been unable to devise an efficient or effective approach to corrections. Currently the entire system that deals with crime and criminals is uncertain, chaotic, and largely unproductive. As Peter McMurty, a Toronto probation officer with thirty years' experience, put it, "It is hard to be caught, harder to be convicted and hardest still to go to jail."[160]

CHAPTER 9

▼

The Treatment of Juvenile Delinquents

Children were prized in pioneer Canada because they provided extra hands for the hard work of economic survival. They were also appreciated and loved in their own right, but for most their existence was coloured by the conditions of a primitive society. Life for some was one of being cared for and nurtured in a close-knit family. As we saw in New France, some children were allowed considerable freedom and exercised a good deal of independence at a young age. For many, however, life was hard. Children for the most part were expected to share the burden and frequently were subjected to adult standards. People were rough and uneducated; many were heavy drinkers; disease and death were common. In such an environment it is not surprising that children were apprenticed out to service, that some were sent into the streets by their parents to beg, steal, or prostitute themselves, and that others were exploited in the mines and emerging industrial enterprises.

Children were considered to be adults in training. That attitude was reinforced by society at large and the churches. Children were expected to contribute according to their age and capabilities. A hard life bred a hard people and therefore little distinction was made between standards of work and behaviour for adults and children. Demands undoubtedly varied from family to family, but children generally were expected to carry their share of the business of economic survival. The entire society of the day expected young people to be hard-working and responsible.

The churches set an equally high standard for young people, not of work but of moral behaviour. In English Canada the behavioural guidelines were rooted in a puritan ethic based on a literal interpretation of the Bible. Just as many of the laws reflected religious teachings, so did the standards set for the personal behaviour of adults and children. In both French and English Canada the churches were influential and clergy paid particular attention to the spiritual nurturing of the young.

The puritan tradition that was so strong in British North America was particularly strict, as is illustrated in a 1648 code of laws in Massachusetts – stubbornness or rebelliousness on the part of a son could be punished by death. With the passage of time such severity was substantially tempered, but the spirit if not the letter of early Puritan teachings continued to be influential in directing the treatment of the young as well as the morals of their parents. Church precepts were often broken, but most transgressions were not done in the spirit of challenging the basic teachings. Community standards were dictated by the churches and people paid great deference to religion and the clergy. Churches were everywhere, Lord's Day Acts kept shops and taverns closed on Sundays, and even governments admonished people to "apply themselves to duties of religion and piety" on the Sabbath.

The combined expectations of society and the church go far in explaining the treatment of juvenile delinquents in early Canada. Since standards of work and behaviour differed little for children and adults, the laws of the land were applied equally to both. The same harsh punishments prescribed for adult criminals could also be used to discipline young offenders. Misconduct on the part of children was especially disconcerting because it reflected poorly on basic values pertaining to the upbringing of the young and was seen as a harbinger of worse problems. Juvenile delinquents could easily grow into adult criminals. Therefore, a tough-minded, moralistic society did not hesitate to deal harshly with juvenile lawbreakers.

PIONEER PUNISHMENTS

All ranges of punishments were applied to juveniles. Samuel de Champlain executed a young girl for theft, at the very outset of colonization. With the growth of settlement young people were sentenced to hang from time to time but frequently benefited from the tendency of authorities to remit such penalties. More commonly, juveniles in New France were whipped when they were caught committing serious offences that could be punished by death. On rare occasions misbehaving girls would be put in detention under the supervision of nuns. For example, a thirteen-year-old girl was confined to the General Hospital in Quebec for three months and a fourteen-year-old was held for a six-year period.[1]

Although harsh penalties were prescribed for many crimes, the authorities were sometimes reluctant to apply them. This was especially true for young offenders. In early settlements in English Canada there was also sometimes confusion over just how severe the punishments could be. When Isaac Provender, a boy of ten or eleven years, set fire to his master's house and burned it to the ground in 1737, the authorities in Annapolis were faced with a number of problems. There was no jail in the community and officials were not even sure they could punish him because of his age.[2]

Whipping of delinquents was also the common practice in English Canada, especially in communities without jails. Once the Bridewells were built, young offenders were either whipped or incarcerated, or sometimes both. When jailed, they were mixed indiscriminately with adults and shared the same cells as drunks, prostitutes, hardened criminals, the aged, the sick, the indigent, and the mentally ill. As was the case with adults, justice was uneven. A kindly police officer might dismiss a delinquent with a warning or a humanitarian magistrate might prescribe a light punishment. But a child might feel the full weight of the law. In 1813, for example, a thirteen-year-old boy was hanged in Montreal for stealing a cow.[3]

In contrast, in 1818 in York, thirteen-year-old Jacob Pier was tried for burning down his master's barn. He was convicted of arson and sentenced to death. Instead of the punishment being carried out, however, the boy was put in jail. After two years of incarceration he petitioned for a pardon but was refused. Instead, his sentence was respited annually but not remitted. The judge in the case refused a pardon because he believed that if young children were pardoned for their offences they might be used by adults to commit crimes.[4]

Many children who were troublesome were arbitrarily apprenticed out by authorities or placed in indentured servitude. Apprenticeship offered the chance to learn a trade, depending on the will of the master, who was expected as well to guide and discipline the child. Those indentured were simply put to work. In either case they were legally bound to their employers, frequently until they were twenty-one years old. Sometimes children disposed of in this manner committed no crime but were simply uncared for or orphaned. Also, the natural precociousness and mischievousness of children, especially those lacking parental supervision, was sometimes interpreted as sign of delinquent tendencies. These had to be nipped in the bud before they flowered and so authorities did not hesitate to take such youngsters into custody.

As the population grew and more jails were built, children continued to be incarcerated with regularity. No special provisions were made and even when Upper Canada opened its first prison at Kingston in 1835 authorities did not hesitate to commit the young. The attitude toward delinquents is illustrated not only by the fact that very young children were put in prison but also by the discipline they were subjected to while there. The 1849 Report on Kingston Prison documented a number of examples of extreme cruelty. A ten-year-old boy, committed on May 4, 1845, for a seven-year term, was publicly lashed fifty-seven times in the space of eight and a half months. His offences were staring and laughing, which, although they might have broken prison rules, were normal behaviour for a boy of that age. An eight-year-old child, admitted on November 7, 1845, for a three-year term, received the lash within the first week of his arrival. Over a nine-month period he was similarly punished forty-seven times. An eleven-year-old French-Canadian boy, on Christmas Eve of 1844, was given twelve lashes for speaking French.[5]

Just as young boys were put in with the adult male prisoners, young girls were incarcerated in the female quarters. They, too, were flogged with regularity at Kingston. The records show that one fourteen-year-old was whipped seven times in four months while a twelve-year-old was similarly punished five times over another four-month period.[6] Both boys and girls were sentenced to terms the same as adults for the various crimes, and in prison they were subject to the same rules and conditions. At the time of the Brown Commission investigation, three children under twelve, including one eight-year-old, and twelve under sixteen were incarcerated at Kingston Prison.[7]

The children put in jails across the country continued to endure whippings and as well had to put up with the foul conditions typical of those institutions. As the population increased more jails were built and increasing numbers of children were put in them. It soon became apparent that the punishment was accomplishing very little. Many juveniles were corrupted by older offenders and instead of being turned away from crime they were schooled in the latest lawbreaking techniques. After being incarcerated, many young people went on to more serious offences and all too often ended up back in jail.

THE REFORM IMPULSE

Through the first half of the nineteenth century, concern grew over juvenile recidivism and the practice of putting young people in detention. On the one hand were those who were upset that the sanctions in use were not having the desired effect and so they called for harsher penalties. Others, however, were primarily concerned about the plight of incarcerated young people. They argued that it was morally detrimental to children to put them in such facilities and that they shouldn't be imprisoned under any circumstances for minor offences.

Criminal justice officials displayed the same ambivalence as the general public. Some were little concerned and thought that delinquents had to be punished like any other offender. Others thought it inappropriate to jail young people and regularly petitioned for the building of separate facilities so they could at least be segregated from adults. Officials also faced a dilemma in dealing with children in trouble. Since there were no social or welfare services available, they had to put them in jail, return them to often bad home situations, or turn them loose to fend for themselves. Communities were reluctant to spend funds for separate facilities for the young. For example, politicians and officials in New Brunswick expressed concern over the treatment of juveniles as early as 1845. There were periodic discussions in the House of Assembly on such matters as schooling, segregation, and separate facilities. However, it wasn't until 1895 that the province opened its first industrial home. Governments were equally reluctant to build social service institutions, so in most communities the lockup served both a welfare and a punitive function. Consequently, children continued to be put in jail even though this was distasteful to many. Between 1846 and 1857 over 300 youngsters under eighteen years of age were sentenced to the New Brunswick prison.[8]

For advocates of reform in the treatment of juvenile delinquents one of the first signs of encouragement came from the work of the Brown Commission and its recommendations. The commissioners devoted a section of their report to the treatment of juveniles, observing that "In waging war with crime, there is no department so satisfactory, so encouraging, as the rescue and reformation of the young; and there it is the battle should be fought with utmost warmth."[9] In this spirit they recommended the construction of Houses of Refuge for young offenders, suggesting that one be established at either Montreal or Quebec and another at Toronto or Hamilton. The refuges, according to the commissioners, should be divided into two departments, one to accommodate neglected or undisciplined children, the other to house those convicted for a crime. They further recommended that the centres be put under the control of the penitentiary inspectors and that a Board of Managers be appointed to carry out weekly visits, look after the apprenticing of the children, and see to "the general carrying out of the philanthropic objects of the Institution." The young people would be offered educational and vocational instruction and could be apprenticed out for trades training. They envisioned a system that would be "a combination of education, labor, and healthful exercise." The children apprenticed out would remain under the authority of the Board of Managers and could be taken back to the House of Refuge *if* they misbehaved.[10]

The recommendations of the Brown Commission helped to focus attention on the unsatisfactory practices governing the treatment of young delinquents and offered a concrete remedy. In particular, commissioners gave strong support for the need to separate the young from adult offenders. The report lent further credence to the contention that the young merited distinct treatment and underscored the importance of seeing them more as misbehaving children in need of guidance than criminals in need of punishment.

Through the 1850s the debate continued over whether or not separate facilities were desirable. For example, the Roman Catholic chaplain at Kingston argued in 1852 that "by too precipitate a legislation, we would become instrumental in endowing this country with such nurseries of crime."[11] On the other hand, Andrew Dickson, one of the prison inspectors, was strong in his support for separate institutions for juveniles and recommended that they be modelled on American institutions he had visited. In his report for 1852 he suggested that farms be attached to the proposed centres because young people with farm training would be more attractive to farmers seeking apprentices. He also passed the opinion that this would be better than placing them as apprentices in cities and towns because the temptations wouldn't be so great. He envisioned an institution in which the most effective agent for reform would be the keepers, who would be kind but firm in their supervision. The main objective, according to Dickson, would be "to give them habits of industry and reform, and make them useful members of society."[12]

INSTITUTIONALIZATION OF JUVENILES

As the nineteenth century progressed and the country became more civilized, the prevailing attitude toward children changed significantly. Society gradually turned from treating children as little adults to seeing them in their own context. Many people emphasized the importance of loving care in the upbringing of children and recognized their special needs. The former stern attitudes began to soften in many quarters, and the churches, benevolent and charitable societies, reformers, school officials, and others reflected and encouraged this change. The more humane attitude and reform advocacy set the stage for some notable developments in the treatment of juvenile delinquents. The first important breakthrough came in the form of special institutions for the incarceration of juveniles. Their establishment signalled a recognition of the needs that reformers had been urging for some time. Among the earliest of these new reformatories were Isle aux Noix on the Richelieu River and Penetanguishene on Georgian Bay, the former to serve Canada East and the latter Canada West.

Isle aux Noix, an old army barracks dating from the War of 1812, opened in October, 1858, with Andrew Dickson, the former prison inspector, as the first warden. Its main purpose was to provide a better environment for the detention of youthful offenders. Although the intentions were good the institution was a classic example of the lack of foresight and proper planning that characterized governments' approach to penal facilities. There were problems from the outset at Isle aux Noix. The location was less than ideal, there was dissension among the staff, and the age spread among the detainees was too great. Of the eighty young people incarcerated there in 1859, thirty were between nineteen and twenty-four. This latter group of adults included some with lengthy criminal records. Mixing very young people with much older criminals to some extent undercut the very purpose of the institution.[13]

In the first year of its operation nineteen escaped, though seventeen were recaptured. An additional cause of concern for the authorities was that a number of girls were also incarcerated there. Officials worried about the moral implications even though the girls were separated from the boys. The inspectors expressed the opinion that mixing the sexes would "present a permanent obstacle in the way of real reformation."[14] Other problems at Isle aux Noix included inefficient administration and discipline that was too severe. When the Board of Inspectors began its duties in 1860 it faced a major job of dealing with problems at the centre.[15]

Penetanguishene opened in August, 1859, in a converted army barracks and got off to a more satisfactory start than its sister institution. Because of the experience at Isle aux Noix, girls were not sent to Penetanguishene. Rather, the inspectors recommended that the government pay for their keep at any privately run institutions that would take them in and provide appropriate care and training.[16] The inmate population included a high percentage of older boys. Out of forty in custody at the end of the first year, twenty-one ranged in age from seventeen to twenty-one. A strong emphasis was placed on work, and almost immediately the boys were busy building roads and improving the grounds.[17] Trades training programs were gradually introduced at both institutions; at Penetanguishene the detainees were put to work at quarrying, farming, lumbering, brickmaking, tailoring, and cabinetmaking. Neither centre put any great effort into education or reform and they remained for quite some time primarily institutions of work and punishment rather than rehabilitation.[18]

The new detention centres fell short of expectations, but reformers were not discouraged and took solace from developments elsewhere. Many segments of society were becoming more concerned with child welfare and were active in agitating for reforms and protective legislation. This helped to create a climate of opinion favourable to improvements in dealing with juvenile delinquents. When it came to advancing specific proposals some of the most articulate and persistent were people within the correctional system itself. In the forefront was J.M. Langmuir, who was appointed in 1867 as Ontario's first Inspector of Prisons, Asylums and Public Charities.

From the outset of his tenure Langmuir made it clear that he did not like the way delinquents were handled at Penetanguishene. He complained that the place was too much like a prison, that the facilities were poor, that the boys' education was neglected, that the discipline was too harsh, and that the youth were worked too hard. In his 1874 report he expressed his displeasure in no uncertain terms, saying: "the Provincial Reformatory is unfit for the work it should perform, and is wrong in principle and faulty in practice."[19] In trying to effect improvement he ran into a stone wall in the person of the warden, William Moore Kelly, who did not share Langmuir's benign philosophy. Kelly was closely associated with the program in place at Penetanguishene and was naturally defensive. Also, he argued that his regimen worked and pointed to low rates of recidivism to support his claim.[20]

In 1879 Kelly retired and Langmuir seized the opportunity to press for his long-sought improvements that would shift the emphasis of incarceration from punishment to reform. His proposals reflect the significant change in the philosophy of dealing with young delinquents then current. Langmuir called for the complete reorganization of the operation of Penetanguishene, including its discipline, economy, and structure. He wanted to turn it from being primarily a penal establishment into a genuine reformatory school. As he described it, the emphasis would be on reform "in the most liberal sense of the term." It would become a school "for education, industrial training and moral reclamation of juvenile delinquents." He wanted all the prison terminology dropped. The "inmates" would become boys, in the classrooms scholars, and at their trades shoemakers, coopers, etc. The warden would be known as the superintendent and the guards as overseers or instructors. He wanted the care of the boys to equate with that "which obtains in a well regulated Christian family."[21]

Langmuir finally won the day. In 1880 the government issued a new charter and appointed a new superintendent. The designation of the institution was changed from a "reformatory prison" to "reformatory for boys." Another major change was the introduction of a remission system, which, in return for diligence and good conduct, allowed a boy to earn a reduction in his term of detention.[22] Thomas McCrossan, the new head of the centre, was much more co-operative than his predecessor and over the next few years improvements were made at Penetanguishene.

While the Penetanguishene saga was unfolding through the 1860s and 1870s there were other significant developments in the treatment of delinquent children. For example, in Nova Scotia legislation was passed to limit the imprisonment of juveniles to ninety days. There was also strong support for building a separate reformatory for young people. The mayor of Halifax in his 1862 annual report pointed out that delinquents were being put in the city prison because there was no alternative accommodation and that it was "impossible to separate them from a crowd of old and hardened offenders."[23] He said he felt compelled to call attention "to the crying necessity for the establishment of a Juvenile Reformatory in this city."[24] Reformers complained that too many children who simply needed help were being punished in prisons and jails because there were no appropriate reformatories for the young.

This was a common theme heard in many parts of Canada. For example, E.A. Meredith, a member of the Board of Inspectors of Asylums and Prisons for the Province of Canada, submitted a report in 1862 calling for alternate institutions. He argued that "imprisonment in jail tends to complete the ruin of the unfortunate child," and that the jails were "nurseries of vice and hotbeds of crime." He acknowledged that the reformatories at Isle aux Noix and Penetanguishene were a step in the right direction but pointed out that a boy had to be convicted of a crime before being sent to either one and that they were "remedial not preventative." What was needed, he maintained, were homes, industrial farms, refuges, or reformatories that would take not only children convicted of an offence but "destitute and neglected pauper children" and others who were at risk of becoming delinquents. Meredith reasoned that such children could be given proper care, educated, taught a trade, and thus prepared to earn an honest living if they could be taken from their miserable and vicious surroundings and put in a state home. His emphasis was prevention of crime, which he suggested was a better course "because it is more agreeable, more hopeful, more economical, more humane, and more Christian."[25]

In response to this type of advocacy, reformatories began to appear in a number of jurisdictions. One of the first was the Halifax Protestant Industrial School, opened in 1864. It provided an alternative to prison for convicted juveniles and a refuge for neglected children and those guilty of minor offences. It was open to Protestant boys – in 1867 thirty-nine boys were in residence, ranging in age from ten to twenty years. Some were transferred from the city prison, others had been picked up off the streets. The school provided training in the trades of shoemaking, cabinetmaking, and tailoring. Small boys were put to work splitting wood and making kindling. The residents lived in dormitories and were responsible for making their own beds and for the general housekeeping of the home. The boys were given academic schooling in the evenings and provided with regular church services and religious instruction.[26] In 1865 St. Patrick's Industrial School for Roman Catholic boys was opened in Halifax. Strict discipline, work, education, and a liberal dose of religious instruction made up the program.

The task these new juvenile institutions faced was formidable. In a relatively short period of time they aimed at reversing the results of years of neglect, maltreatment, and delinquency. Many of the children when they first arrived were undernourished, sickly, and diseased. The first task was to nurse them back to health. Most could neither read nor write and they ranged in intelligence from dull to talented. They were a mixture of emotions and personalities and many, although young, were well schooled in vice. As the 1867 report of the Halifax Protestant Industrial School explained it: "Think of the problem before us. Here are some lads whose education has been on the streets, the wharves, the Police Station, Rockhead (prison), the rumshop, the brothel. Here are boys young in years, but old in the ways of deceit and depravity."[27]

In succeeding years institutions that went by such designations as industrial schools, ragged schools, or refuges sprang up across the country. In contrast to centres like Isle aux Noix and Penetanguishene, which for a long time seemed to concentrate on custody and strict discipline, the industrial schools sought to create a family-like atmosphere and to prepare their young charges to be useful citizens. To create such an environment some established a cottage system, with each small living unit presided over by a matron and a guard who acted somewhat like foster parents. The youngsters did housekeeping chores, went to day school and Sunday school, and learned job-related skills. They were also allowed to participate in sports and other leisure activities. The regimen was considered to be the most advanced and enlightened form of institutional training for problem children. The first industrial school in Ontario, the Victoria Industrial School for Boys, was opened in Toronto in 1887. In 1892 the Alexandra Industrial School for Girls was established in Toronto and a number of others followed. By 1894 almost 200 children were housed in Ontario industrial schools. In 1893 a boys' industrial home opened in Saint John, New Brunswick, and in 1896 the Reformatory of the Good Shepherd for girls was incorporated. All such institutions emphasized reform through character development, moral and academic education, and vocational training. Most of the residents of these schools were committed by the courts.[28]

Among the more prominent detention centres for juveniles in Ontario was the Mercer Refuge for Girls. J.W. Langmuir was the moving force behind the construction of this refuge and it reflected his strong belief in the value of separate institutions for females. Partly in response to Langmuir's recommendations the Ontario government in 1879 approved the establishment of the Andrew Mercer Reformatory for Women. It also provided that part of the reformatory be used as a refuge for girls under fourteen.

The facility was open to girls convicted of offences but also to the neglected or vagrants who could be committed by a magistrate. The emphasis was placed on teaching skills that would enable the girls to live useful, self-supporting lives upon release. The mix at Mercer illustrated another dimension in the treatment of juvenile delinquents in institutions. Some of the young people were sent to these centres for care and in the context of crime prevention rather than rehabilitation. This was a common practice among many institutions of the time. Children perceived to be at risk because of parental neglect or other reasons were sometimes committed as a means of keeping them out of trouble and preparing them to live honest, law-abiding lives. They were given care and training that was otherwise not available to them.

In 1881-82 the Mercer Refuge admitted thirteen residents, one of whom was four years old. The others ranged in age from nine to sixteen. Two were sentenced to one year, two to twenty-three months, four to five years, and five for indefinite periods. The girls benefited from a kindly staff and an enlightened philosophy. The superintendent, M.J. O'Reilly, reported that "We surround them as far as possible with home comforts – keeping in mind the fact that these poor children are here because of the faults of their parents."[29] O'Reilly also summed up the approach that was common to many of the industrial schools and refuges: "Our discipline is the discipline of the family; we try to rule by kindly admonition, and by appeals to their better nature, rather than by terror of punishment."[30]

The number of residents in the refuge increased from thirty-three in 1881-82 to forty-nine in October of 1889. The commissioners who carried out the 1891 inquiry into the prison and reformatory system of Ontario visited the Mercer Refuge for Girls and reported, "This institution . . . appears to have thus far worked very satisfactorily."[31] The girls were kept busy and offered a varied routine. Most started their day at 6:50 a.m. Except for the young children, they began their work assignments at 7:30 and continued until 8:40 a.m., when they were taken to prayer services and also given catechism instruction. They then went to school until noon, with a short recess at 10:30. After lunch the girls had a recreation period and then returned to classes from 1:40 p.m. to 3:00. Their next stop was the sewing room, where they knitted and repaired clothes. After supper at 5:00, the time from 5:30 to 7:00 p.m. was devoted to recreation and study. Overall the girls were made to feel that they were not in a penal institution. Doors of offices and rooms, together with the main door of the refuge, were unlocked during the day and residents were sometimes sent out on errands. Girls who misbehaved inside the institution were usually punished by having leisure activities and other privileges taken away. Those who set a particularly good example were encouraged with such rewards as special Saturday outings.[32]

Some of the best-run industrial schools for boys were in Quebec. In the late 1880s seven reformatories, to which youth could be sentenced for periods not less than two years and not more than ten, were operating in the province. Officials had the power to apprentice or hire out the boys and girls with such working time deducted from their sentences. Many Quebec refuges were run by religious orders, such as the one in Montreal operated by the Brothers of Charity. The Brothers placed a strong emphasis on trades training so that the boys would be equipped to find good jobs upon release. The home taught shoemaking, tailoring, printing, carpentry and joining, upholstering, blacksmithing, baking, carriage and sleigh-making, gardening, and farming. All of the residents who were strong enough to work were required to take a vocational course. In addition, all the boys went to school for one hour a day while those who were sickly or too young to work attended school six hours per day. The daily routine was completed with two and a half hours for recreation and compulsory chapel attendance in the morning and in the evening. As an incentive to diligence and good behaviour the Brothers instituted a system of good conduct marks that could be used to reduce sentences. They were also generous in recommending pardons for boys who merited release. The number of such rewards averaged about twenty-five per year, and as many as fifty – out of an average annual population of 250 – were pardoned some years. During their period of detention one-fourth of their earnings was set aside and then given to them when they were let out. They were also given a set of clothes and passage to their homes.[33]

The Montreal reformatory seemed to be particularly well run. The Brothers interacted constantly with the residents as counsellors, instructors, and spiritual guides, so they were not seen as mere custodians. The system of rewards and the extensive vocational and academic educational programs motivated the boys and gave them a good preparation to earn an honest living if they so chose. The dormitories were well kept and decorated and the accommodations were described as being "bright and cheerful." Although the reformatory was not enclosed with prison walls, few attempts at escape were made. Some follow-up was made on the progress of the boys after release, and according to these reports most managed to stay out of trouble.[34] Unfortunately, there was little if any provision for aftercare for young people released from detention across the country, nor was there supervision for those put on probation. This remained a major gap in the reformatory program.

Another problem with the reformatories, industrial schools, and refuges was the great lack of uniformity. Hardly any two institutions were the same, nor did they follow a prescribed program. Some were better located and equipped than others, some offered a wider range of courses and more thorough instruction, and much depended on the attitude and calibre of the administration and staff. For example, in contrast to the organization run by the Brothers of Charity in Montreal, the industrial school at Mimico, Ontario, offered a limited range of trades courses and employed many at housekeeping and laundry work. The superintendent acknowledged that "We really don't teach them anything but tailoring well."[35] His aspiration for the boys who came under his care was that they should all go west and take up farming. He believed they should be taught to cook and sew and look after themselves. "My idea," he said, "is that they should go on farms, . . . to Manitoba for example, and perhaps keep bachelor's hall there."[36] His entire philosophy of institutional training was "to make them useful on a farm." In spite of the differences, however, such facilities were becoming more numerous and were taking the treatment of delinquents in a new direction.

Notwithstanding some improvements in the treatment of young offenders and more benign attitudes that made the changes possible, much remained the same. The harsh treatment and economic exploitation that many children endured in pre-industrial Canada continued and took on new forms with industrial growth. Child factory workers were exploited and maltreated. Children generally continued to be abused in many quarters, even in the face of legislation intended to protect them. Within the criminal justice system the same mix of attitudes and conditions prevailed. On the one hand, many changes had taken place; on the other, conditions and penal philosophy had remained constant in many quarters.

Among the more callous and inhumane acts to which young people were subjected was their incarceration in industrial homes due to lying parents. Such incidents were occasioned by the desire of some parents to get rid of troublesome or inconvenient children. One example was that of a mother who charged her eleven-year-old son with being bad, disobedient, and with having beaten her on a number of occasions. In reality, the mother was planning to remarry and one of the conditions set down by the husband-to-be was that she get rid of her son. Another example was that of a boy sentenced to a reformatory for five years. The boy's father had him arrested on a vagrancy charge. It seems that the father had remarried and the stepmother did not want the youngster around.[37]

While some officials, such as J.W. Langmuir, fought for humane improvements, others both inside and outside the criminal justice system opposed new directions in the treatment of distressed young people. During the 1891 commission hearings in Ontario, organized labour took a very negative stance against the industrial schools. One spokesperson stated that "Our labor bodies are unanimously opposed to manual training in the schools."[38] He maintained that the instruction was not up to trade standards and that employers were therefore able to hire the products of the industrial schools for lower pay. This, it was said, had the effect of depressing wages. Elsewhere, magistrates in many jurisdictions continued to hand down harsh sentences – children could be found in jails and prisons throughout the country, frequently being punished for very minor offences. In addition, some reformatories lost sight of their lofty aims and reverted to austere practices and severe discipline. All this caused reformers to maintain their efforts and continually brought new recruits into the battle. Bit by bit they made progress. Two of the most significant advances in the treatment of delinquent children came in the form of young offender legislation and the establishment of children's courts.

REFORMS IN THE TREATMENT OF JUVENILE DELINQUENTS

These new developments came against a background of widespread reform agitation. For example, the Prisoners' Aid Association, although primarily concerned with adults, had developed a detailed set of proposals for the treatment of juveniles by 1890. The organization was campaigning for special courts to deal with young offenders, limited use of detention for those under fourteen, and qualified staff for reformatories and industrial schools. The Association also called for an end to using industrial schools and reformatories as places of punishment. Rather, it argued that they should be primarily places for the reformation of character. The Prisoners' Aid Association also called for the use of indefinite detention. Members argued that it was not the term that was important but the rehabilitation;

thus, the period of detention should depend on the time it took to bring about a meaningful change in attitude.

Another impetus to reform came from the *Report* of the 1891 Ontario inquiry into the prison and reformatory system. During its deliberations the Commission examined a cross-section of the latest theories in penology, visited a number of institutions in the United States, interviewed a host of jail and prison officials, and listened to a wide variety of testimony from individuals. The Commission had much to say about juvenile delinquency. Of its forty-eight recommendations, sixteen touched directly on the subject.

The *Report* advocated measures to prevent delinquency and changes in the treatment of young offenders. Among the former were suggestions for strict enforcement of school attendance laws, municipal curfews to keep young people off the streets at night, inspection and regulation of second-hand stores and pawn shops, and assistance for child welfare agencies. In the area of improved treatment the Commission recommended:

- there should be one or more industrial schools in every city and large town;
- children under fourteen should not be publicly arrested and detained;
- when it is necessary to hold them they should not be detained in a common jail but in a place entirely away from the police station;
- all children under fourteen should be tried in special courts;
- convicted children under fourteen should never be incarcerated in a common jail, and should be sent to a reformatory or refuge only as a last resort;
- more use should be made of suspended sentences;
- a probation system should be introduced;
- earned remission for good conduct should be offered;
- a parole system should be adopted, as well as apprenticeship programs and boarding out;
- an association should be formed in every region of the province for aftercare of released juveniles;
- changes in the law should give more power to provincial officials over such things as pardon, parole, and the general supervision of delinquent children.

Though the *Report* dealt with Ontario, because of its nature it had a national impact. It heightened public awareness and focused attention on the juvenile reform campaign.[39]

Ontario also took the lead in something known as the child-saving movement. This was a band of people concerned about the plight of neglected children and determined to implement a program of child welfare measures. Among the most dedicated of this group was J.J. Kelso. He started his career as a reporter, and his contact with the poverty and child neglect in the streets of Toronto motivated him to try and remedy the distress. He played a major role in the organization of the Humane Society of Toronto, founded in 1887, and also in the establishment of the Toronto Children's Aid Society in 1891. The Ontario government recognized his dedication and ability by appointing him the first Superintendent of Neglected and Dependent Children for the province in 1893.[40]

Kelso devoted much of his adult life to helping needy children. A glance at his career reveals innumerable instances of personal intervention on behalf of young people in need of a helping hand. He was strongly opposed to the institutionalization of juveniles in trouble or need, instead advocating foster homes and loving care for reform therapy, an approach widely favoured by reformers of the day. When Penetanguishene reformatory was closed in 1904 some 100 boys had to be relocated and the intent was to place them in industrial schools. Rather than see the boys re-incarcerated, Kelso arranged for his office to assume responsibility for them. He personally took charge of placements and succeeded in finding homes with foster parents, family, or friends in various parts of the province. His success brought him a similar task in 1905 when he was asked to close out the Mercer Industrial Refuge for Girls. Once again, instead of transferring the girls to another institution, he found placements in homes for every one of them.[41]

Kelso had been intervening on behalf of delinquents for some time. Throughout the 1890s he carried on a scheme with the warden of the Central Prison in Toronto to redirect convicted juveniles and keep them out of institutions. When magistrates from various parts of the province sentenced young people to the reformatory or an industrial school, some would first be sent to the Central Prison in Toronto. The warden would inform Kelso of incoming boys and he would then try to find placements for them in foster homes. The diversion, of course, was a contravention of regulations, but both officials conspired in the practice for a number of years.[42]

J.J. Kelso and people like him in many parts of the country were able to use their influence and powers of persuasion to bring about a wide variety of humanitarian developments at both the provincial and federal levels. In response to such advocacy, Parliament passed the first piece of federal legislation pertaining to juvenile delinquents, the Youthful Offenders Act, on July 23, 1894. This legislation was the culmination of a series of enactments touching on the treatment of juveniles that dated back to 1857. In that year the Legislative Assembly of Canada passed an act providing the more speedy trial and punishment of juvenile offenders. In 1875 the federal government made a significant amendment to the Act respecting Procedure in Criminal Cases that permitted ordinary courts to send sixteen-year-olds to reformatory instead of prison for terms of not less than two years and not more than five. Sentences longer than five years still had to be served in penitentiary.[43]

In 1892 Parliament passed the Criminal Code and included a short section pertaining to juvenile delinquents, "Trial of Juvenile Offenders for Indictable Offences," which dealt mainly with the trial process.[44] A number of other sections also touched on young offenders. Section 9 provided that no one under the age of seven years could be convicted of an offence. Section 10 restricted convictions of children under fourteen to cases where the offender "was competent to know the nature and consequences of his conduct, and to appreciate that it was wrong."[45] At least on paper this was a significant limitation for reformers who had been struggling for years to have children treated more benignly before the courts. Finally, Section 550 provided that where appropriate and practical, trials of persons under sixteen be held apart from adult offenders and without publicity.[46]

Although such pieces of legislation were steps in the right direction, they fell far short of the comprehensive provisions that reformers wanted. Thus the Youthful Offenders Act of 1894 was a particularly significant development. Respecting arrest, trial, and imprisonment, the Act provided "for the separation of youthful offenders from contact with older offenders and habitual criminals during their arrest and trial," and for "better provision than now exists for their commitment to places where they may be reformed and trained to useful lives, instead of their being imprisoned." That "the trials of young persons apparently under the age of sixteen years, shall take place without publicity and separately and apart from the trials of other accused persons," that young persons "shall be kept in custody separate from older persons charged with criminal offences and separate from all persons undergoing sentences of imprisonment, and shall not be confined in the lock-ups or police stations with older persons charged with criminal offences or with ordinary criminals."[47]

The Act included special arrangements for Ontario that recognized the new role to be played by the Children's Aid Societies. It provided that instead of imprisonment, children could be placed by the courts in the care of homes for neglected or destitute children or in charge of the Children's Aid Society. Also, when any boy under twelve or girl under thirteen was charged with an offence the court was to notify an officer of the society for the purpose of conducting an investigation and offering advice. After such consultation the court could then use a variety of options for sentencing, which included placing the child in foster care, levelling a fine, suspending the sentence, or sending the child to the reformatory or to an industrial school.

The 1894 Act encompassed many of the changes that reformers had sought since at least the early part of the century. Children would now be kept away from the contaminating influence of adult criminals, afforded more privacy, and processed separately by the courts. The essence of the legislation was that delinquents would be treated not as criminals in need of punishment but as young people requiring help and understanding. Instead of their being sentenced strictly on the basis of their offence, background information would be provided to enable magistrates to channel delinquents in a direction that would be appropriate to their needs. Agencies outside the correctional system could now intervene and bring a different philosophy and perspective to the treatment of young people in trouble with the law.

Closely related to the reforms in the Youthful Offenders Act of 1894 was the movement for a children's court. Once again J.J. Kelso was one of the leaders in the campaign. Advocates believed that delinquent children should not be dealt with in the same manner as adult criminals. They maintained that children were not culpable for their offences and that instead of being punished they should be loved and cared for. As Kelso maintained, "It is not law, but only love and religion that can save or reclaim."[48] Consequently, reformers wanted juveniles not only to be treated differently but to be dealt with in an environment completely away from the adult judicial system. That entailed separate courts, special procedures, appropriately qualified officials, and an emphasis on reform rather than punishment. The entire atmosphere would be that found in a concerned family. Proponents of a children's court envisaged it functioning almost as a social welfare agency that would go well beyond trial and judgement in dealing with a young offender. They hoped that from the outset the court would be an integral part of the reform process.[49]

Some magistrates, in sympathy with these views, attempted to conduct proceedings with children in a less formal manner without waiting for government action. For example, George Denison, a magistrate in the Toronto Police Court, in 1892 began holding hearings in a basement room furnished with a table and chairs. He wanted to protect children from the experiences of a formal trial in a public court.[50] The mounting pressure finally persuaded the Ontario legislature in 1893 to pass legislation providing for a children's court; the following year the first such court in Canada was established in Toronto.

Advocates elsewhere were not as successful and the Toronto experiment was not duplicated. It wasn't until the passage of the Juvenile Delinquents Act in 1908 that further progress was made. This Act gave considerable impetus to the children's court movement. With few exceptions, it invested juvenile courts with "exclusive jurisdiction in cases of delinquency." It also provided for separate detention centres, probation officers, informal procedures, and a volunteer juvenile court committee. The latter would work with probation officers and recommend to the court the most advisable way of dealing with an offender.[51] Over the next few years children's courts of one kind or another were set up in a number of cities across the country. One was started in Winnipeg in 1909, and by 1911 courts were operating in Halifax, Montreal, Charlottetown, Victoria, Ottawa, Toronto, and

Vancouver. By the early 1920s over twenty courts were functioning in every province except New Brunswick. This was slow progress, however, and outside the cities most jurisdictions in Canada still did not have juvenile courts.

The delay in establishing children's courts was due in part to a lack of funding and to ongoing disagreements over the best strategy of dealing with young offenders. Many governments were reluctant to spend the required money. Even in jurisdictions where officials were sympathetic, the funds could not always be found. In addition, there was sometimes strong opposition to moving in the direction that reformers wanted to go with the treatment of delinquents.

The juvenile court movement and the campaign for a new delinquents act to provide for such facilities afford a good example of the dichotomy that still existed over the question of reform. The campaign was led and orchestrated by W.L. Scott, president of the Ottawa Children's Aid Society. He mounted a lobby in support of changes to the Juvenile Delinquents Act that would provide for the establishment of children's courts. He ran into some stiff opposition from a number of quarters, including the Toronto police department, the St. Vincent de Paul Children's Aid Society of Toronto, and R.E. Kingsford, a magistrate of the Toronto Police Court. The argument was made that Scott's proposal would reduce the role of the police in dealing with delinquents, which would be self-defeating. Opponents maintained that current procedures were effective and less costly and that police, because of their strict demeanour, had a better deterrent effect on misbehaving young people than others would. Some, such as Inspector David Archibald of the Toronto police, expressed their opposition in strong terms. Archibald dismissed reformers like Scott as "superficial and sentimental faddists." He complained that he did not want to be placed in a position in which he would have "to kiss and coddle a class of perverts and delinquents who require the most rigid disciplinary and corrective methods to ensure the possibility of their reformation."[52]

Scott spoke at public meetings, lobbied, and carried on a prodigious correspondence in an effort to win support. He even tried to placate people like Kingsford, but with disappointing results. In response to a letter from Scott the magistrate announced that he still retained his opinion "that the present courts are sufficient to administer the law with regard to juveniles, as well as of adults."[53] As the issue heated up a progressively more diverse group of people became involved, and Scott and his supporters were subjected to widespread attacks. Another illustration of the divergent opinion on the treatment of juveniles that still prevailed was an editorial in *Saturday Night* magazine in 1906.

The article complained that "the State carries on what may almost be called the continuous business of producing criminals," arguing that when a young offender was separated from family and put in detention the experience launched a life of crime. The associations, bad influences, and bravado a youngster encountered in such places were more likely to confirm a delinquent in anti-social behaviour than bring about reform. Instead of putting young lawbreakers in an institution the editorial proposed that they be given a good whipping and sent home. The writer reasoned that fear of corporal punishment was more of a deterrent than the coddling and immoral companions of reformatories.[54]

In spite of opposition and differing opinions over the best way to deal with delinquents, Scott was able to muster considerable support. The campaign afforded a good example of the powerful lobby that had coalesced across the country in pursuit of reform. Publicity campaigns were mounted, public meetings organized, and petitions gathered in support of the proposed legislation. Assistance came from such diverse sources as the National Council of Women and Premier Rutherford of Alberta. In the end Scott and his fellow reformers prevailed and in 1908 Parliament passed a new Juvenile Delinquents Act, which included provisions for juvenile courts.

Where the courts were established they not only effected a more humane treatment of delinquents but promoted a better attitude toward young offenders. Many officials saw the courts primarily as reform rather than punitive institutions and hoped that early intervention would prevent future lawbreaking. One judge expressed the opinion that the purpose of the court was to discover the causes of delinquency and to supply preventive measures. In this spirit many magistrates added sympathetic staff and sought out non-threatening court facilities and good detention centres. In 1921 the Toronto court had five probation officers and a full-time psychiatrist on its staff.

The welfare of the delinquent was clearly the primary concern of most courts, and magistrates looked to family-centred care either at home or in a foster home as the first resort in the response to delinquency. Consequently, most courts had high release and probation levels. Children's Aid Societies, probation officers, and citizens' committees often intervened to do pre-sentence assessments. Frequently the problem was settled without a formal court hearing. The overall benefits to the juvenile offender were interaction with a group of concerned, caring people, more attention to individual needs and circumstances, professional assessment, more sentencing alternatives, and a tendency to be dealt with in the least punitive manner.[55]

Although the juvenile court system offered many improvements, these courts were not without problems. Judges, staff, and facilities sometimes fell far short of the ideal. Contrary to the stated objective, some courts shared the same facility as was used for the trial of adult criminals, which could be intimidating for young offenders. Often the juvenile court judges also tried adult cases and had no special training in dealing with children. Court personnel, such as probation officers, frequently had inappropriate qualifications. For example, the first probation officer appointed by the Montreal juvenile court was a nurse by profession and for some time all the Montreal probation officers were English-speaking. Services and personnel frequently were inadequate, facilities were minimum, and some courts lacked proper pre-hearing detention centres.

The Montreal juvenile court in the early 1930s illustrates some of the problems. The facility was located in a converted house that was entirely inadequate as a detention centre or for the work of the court, and it was understaffed. Parents did not fully understand its role, and observers were convinced that the court did not win the confidence of the young people who came before it.[56] Police were sometimes unhappy with the lenient way the court dealt with offenders because they felt it interfered with their work. Similar problems were associated with a number of other courts as they were organized across the country.

In the meantime, the ranks of people interested in child welfare continued to grow and more individuals with high public profiles were giving leadership in the juvenile reform movement. Prominent among this group were W.L. Scott, British Columbia Juvenile Court Judge Helen Gregory MacGill, Judge Emily Murphy from Alberta, and Dr. Helen MacMurchy, chief of the Division of Child Welfare in the Department of Health in Ottawa from 1920 to 1924. In every province were to be found organizations wholly or partly concerned with reforms beneficial to children. They continually pressed for protective legislation, for welfare programs, and for better approaches to dealing with young offenders. Even the Imperial Order of Daughters of the Empire joined the campaign for the establishment of juvenile courts. In September of 1922 a national conference on child welfare was held in Toronto. In attendance were representatives of the National Council on Child Welfare, the Canadian Association of Child Protection Officers, and the Mothers' Allowance commissioners of the provinces. Among the subjects prominent on the agenda were delinquency and juvenile courts.[57]

The intervention of auxiliary organizations had been developing for some time, with their work ranging from crime prevention to legal aid for young people in trouble with the law. Another example was the Big Sisters' Association, founded in 1913, which enlisted volunteers to work with young girls in need of adult support outside the family. The objective was to encourage the girls to stay out of trouble by offering them friendship, guidance, and leisure-time activities, and also to lend assistance to those charged with criminal offences. By 1923 there were branches in Toronto, Hamilton, Montreal, Ottawa, and Edmonton.[58]

As a result of this widespread interest, a steady volume of legislation and ongoing developments had an influence on the way juvenile delinquents were treated. The number of juvenile courts was increasing, as were refuges, industrial schools, and homes for delinquents. Provinces were passing child welfare legislation and setting up government departments for its implementation. For example, in 1922 Manitoba passed a Child Welfare Act, established a Ministry of Public Welfare, and appointed a child welfare director. Included in the jurisdiction of the new department was responsibility for juvenile delinquents. At the federal level the government continued to respond with improvements in the delinquency legislation. Amendments to the new Juvenile Delinquents Act were made in 1912, 1914, 1921, 1924, and 1927. In 1929 the government made another major revision in the form of a new Act.

The Juvenile Delinquents Act of 1908 set out the guidelines for juvenile courts as well as making a clear statement of treatment philosophy. According to the 1908 Act "every juvenile delinquent shall be treated, not as a criminal, but as a misdirected and misguided child." In keeping with this, more sentencing options were defined and a restriction was placed on the punishment of young children. The Act stated that children under twelve were to be institutionalized only as a last resort. Jurisdiction over juveniles was extended to the provinces under certain terms and a clause was included providing that adults who contributed to juvenile delinquency could be held criminally responsible. Privacy protection was accorded both accused and parents or guardians. In general, the Act enlarged the powers of the court, and both the spirit and the letter were more paternalistic.[59]

The 1908 Juvenile Delinquents Act was a significant piece of legislation and set the tone for the justice system's approach to the problem of delinquency for some time. It was the revised Act of 1929, however, that guided the treatment of juvenile delinquents until the 1980s. The government action was another example of the influence of reformers and humanitarians within the criminal justice system. The moving forces behind the changes were the Canadian Council on Child Welfare and the Canadian Association of Child Protection Officers. They combined their efforts in pressing for modifications and asked for a conference to discuss their proposals. Their requests were well received by a sympathetic Minister of Justice, Ernest R. Lapointe.[60] The heart of the 1908 Act was left in place but its provisions were expanded and more clearly defined. The philosophy that was the cornerstone of the 1908 Act was restated in equally benevolent terms. A child was not to be treated as "an offender, but as one in a condition of delinquency and therefore requiring help and guidance and proper supervision." The new Act offered a more specific elaboration of the powers of judges and probation officers, and the range of treatment options was enlarged to include parole. The overall approach continued to be paternalistic and to allow for broad intervention and control by the state. Once a child was caught up in the juvenile justice system he or she could be juggled around by authorities until the age of twenty-one. About the only concession to due process was a provision that allowed for appeals of juvenile court decisions. However, an appeal would only be filed with the permission of a provincial Supreme Court judge.[61]

The paternalism that was designed to provide special care and treatment of juveniles also set the stage for some serious problems. Officials and institutions had so much control over young offenders that their power could be either well used or abused. The treatment of delinquents throughout the pre-World War Two period was characterized by a lack of uniformity in courts, sentencing, personnel, placements, facilities, and programs. Even the age limit for defining a juvenile varied across the country. In some provinces the limit was sixteen while in others it was eighteen.

The judicial process for an apprehended juvenile started with the arrest. At this point it was a personal judgement call on the part of the police. Some juveniles were given a scolding and let go; others ended up in court for the same offences. Juveniles awaiting trial were sometimes placed in detention homes, sometimes in jail, and sometimes in the custody of parents, relatives, or foster homes. Many jurisdictions had no juvenile courts while others used the same facilities in which adults were tried, but at different times. Juvenile court judges and magistrates frequently were unqualified and had little or no special training in dealing with child offenders, and in some provinces adult court judges also tried juvenile cases.

A few of the more advanced courts could call on psychiatric reports and advice from a community board, but most could not, and there were situations where judges made little use of citizen boards even when they were constituted. The personnel associated with the courts, such as probation officers, were not required to have any special training or qualifications. In many places, whether juvenile courts existed or not, the facilities were inadequate and improper for handling juveniles. Too often they emphasized the penal aspect of the process rather than the "help and guidance" philosophy of the Juvenile Delinquents Act.

Treatment options provided in the Act ranged from probation to fines to detention. The choice to some extent reflected the seriousness of the offence, but frequently the whim, fancy, and personal philosophy of the judge came into play. Some incarcerated juveniles were still ending up in local jails because of the absence of industrial schools. Some were sent to detention homes for the same offences for which others were given probation. There were complaints that certain judges were too lenient and that some juveniles were up on charges many times before receiving a sentence to a reformatory. On the other hand, a significant number of young people were still being sent to prison. In 1923, eighteen sixteen-year-olds and sixty-three seventeen-year-olds were in Kingston Penitentiary. In 1938, eighteen boys sixteen and under were sentenced to prison in Canada.

Foster homes were preferred to institutionalization in most provinces. This reflected the belief in many quarters that the best environment for reform was a home-like setting. Some foster homes were good but others were exploitative. The problems included harsh discipline, indifferent care, and a primary interest in the money rather than the children. Yet, inadequate payment interfered with the quality and quantity of foster homes available.

A large network of refuges and industrial schools was available for the detention and reformation of young people. By 1927 there were twenty-four institutions for juveniles across Canada. Quebec had nine, Ontario, five, Nova Scotia, four, British Columbia and Manitoba, two each, and Saskatchewan and New Brunswick each had one. The only provinces without juvenile centres were Alberta and Prince Edward Island.[62] Some were publicly operated and came under various government departments, but some provinces had a mix of private and government institutions. In Quebec all centres were privately run, mostly by religious organizations. The officials attempted to model their operation on the family. In some cases even the facility itself was designed to create a home-like atmosphere by providing cottages as living accommodations.

The regimen was a mixture of discipline, education, work, character development, and religious instruction. Detainees were usually placed for indefinite terms and were under the complete control of the administration. They could be kept at the institutions or apprenticed out, released early, or kept until they were twenty-one years old. Many of these centres were benevolent and well run, and most claimed to have a good record in effecting reform. Practically all could provide a dossier of letters from their former boarders attesting to the benefits of the program, which suggests that even the worst of them attracted some caring people to their staffs.

Most catered to a varied clientele. While some of the children were convicted delinquents, others were problem children committed by the courts, sometimes at the request of parents. Still others were simply neglected, abused, or homeless children sent by the courts, Children's Aid Societies, or certain officials for care and protection. Some housed only males or females while a few accepted both but in totally segregated facilities and programs.[63]

The best institutions were run by caring, dedicated staff who spared no effort to help troubled young people. The Industrial Training School at Portage la Prairie, Manitoba, is an example. F.W. McKinnon, the principal, constantly petitioned for better equipment and programs, encouraged and facilitated parental visits, and rewarded progress with special privileges. Education was stressed and the boys were provided with academic instruction by qualified teachers for half of the day. In addition, trades training in tailoring, shoemaking, and farming was provided.[64]

The training school at Portage la Prairie was also used by the province of Alberta. In 1908 the Alberta Legislative Assembly provided for the establishment of industrial schools and the appointment of a superintendent.

The legislation was indicative of the concern over the handling of juvenile delinquents. However, after a careful study the new superintendent, R.B. Chadwick, concluded that the cost of establishing a network of industrial schools was too high and he recommended that Alberta delinquents who had to be placed in detention be sent to Manitoba. The decision might have made economic sense, but it was hardly in the interests of youth who would have to serve their time far removed from home and family.[65]

In the East the Maritime Home for Girls in Truro, Nova Scotia, was another well-run reformatory. It opened in September, 1914, sponsored by the Presbyterian and Methodist churches to serve the three Maritime provinces. The first building was a large house and the girls lived in dormitories. As more accommodation was constructed the Home functioned on the cottage system. The institution accepted girls between the ages of seven and sixteen, some convicted offenders but many simply neglected, abandoned, or troublesome who were sent to the home for care and protection. Girls were placed for indeterminate periods and were under the supervision of the authorities until age twenty-one. They could be paroled from the home on probation and placed out to work under service contracts. The girls' situation was carefully monitored and employers were required to submit monthly reports.[66]

The stated objective of the Maritime Home for Girls was to make its residents "useful, independent members of society." To achieve this the Home followed a program that mixed school, vocational training, discipline, recreation, and moral education. The work day began at 6:30 a.m. and ended at 8:00 p.m. in the winter months and 9:00 p.m. in the summer. During the school year six hours were spent in class and the remainder of the day was filled with chores, study, Bible reading and prayer, recreation, and vocational instruction. The girls were prepared for life as homemakers and taught a variety of domestic skills such as cooking, sewing, housekeeping, etc. They shared in institutional chores and did some gardening and dairying and raised chickens. An honour system of merits and demerits was used to encourage diligence and good behaviour, with the rewards consisting of more privileges and outings in the town. The Home also had a system of student government, which allowed the girls to participate in the supervision and operation of the institution.

Upon entrance each girl was examined by the physician and quarantined for up to two weeks. The period of isolation was to give the girl a chance to adjust to the new environment and to prevent the spread of any contagious diseases. The only formal restrictions on admission pertained to girls who had worked as prostitutes, who would not be accepted but who could be sent to another church-run residence, in Sydney. Generally the facilities, program, care, and follow-up supervision provided by the Maritime Home were very good, according to the standards of the time.[67]

Institution officials were often caring, concerned, dedicated people, although some could be cruel, austere disciplinarians who did not spare the rod. Judged by their fundamental reform objectives, however, a common fault was that too many of these institutions were inadequately equipped and offered a narrow range of programs. The deficiencies interfered with proper classification and their ability to respond to special needs. There was no provision for training and care of the mentally handicapped, nor were there trained counsellors or therapy programs. A final glaring weakness in the treatment of juveniles was lack of aftercare and supervision of released offenders.

The shortcomings were not the fault of juvenile justice officials, however, since many continually pressed for improvements. Usually the problem was money. Provinces and municipalities were uniformly parsimonious when it came to funding penal facilities, even for the young, and some in positions of power still believed the surest way to deterrence and reformation was discipline and punishment. Critics attacked the reformatories for their emphasis on family-style care. Officials constantly had to contend with such people and defend their philosophy and approach to the treatment of problem children. For example, the superintendent of the Maritime Home for Girls, in her 1918 report, made a point of responding to those who said "that we are condoning wrong doing and providing a home for the rearing for a number of bad girls."[68] She rejected this type of characterization of young people and pointed out the good work the Home was doing and the positive results being realized.

The Boys' Industrial Home in East Saint John, New Brunswick, was a good example of how many of the reformatories were operating in the 1920s. The Home was under the control of a nine-member board – two representatives of the provincial government, two representatives of women's organizations, four businessmen, and the mayor of Saint John. Two board members were appointed monthly, on a rotating basis, to visit the Home, and a three-member placement committee, one woman and two men, was in charge of admissions and recommending boys for release or apprenticeship training. The day-to-day operation was handled by the superintendent and staff.

Boys between nine and sixteen years of age could be committed for undefined terms not exceeding five years. Convicted delinquents could be sent by the courts but the institution also took in dependent and neglected children. A report on child welfare services in New Brunswick released in 1929 by the Canadian Council on Child Welfare pointed out a number of undesirable aspects that illustrate the problems with some such institutions at that point in time. The accommodation was not suitable to meet the standards of care in vogue by the late twenties. Toilet facilities were singled out as being inadequate and the congregate system was still in use rather than the preferred cottage arrangement. All residents were under the same rules even though some were convicted delinquents and others were not.

The committee that evaluated the Industrial Home pointed out that "The whole purpose of the commitment of the delinquent to the care of an Industrial Home is the substitution of training and development of his moral and material well being, as opposed to straight penal incarceration."[69] In light of this the report maintained that a comprehensive study should be provided on each boy to determine his needs and his interests, and that as much as possible should be done to treat him while he was incarcerated. The authors concluded that the facilities did not accommodate such objectives and recommended that the home relocate to a smaller, farming operation far from the city. They also suggested that greater use be made of placements and probation.[70] In New Brunswick this work was sponsored by the Central Welfare Council of Saint John and the Kiwanis Club, a recently founded organization that had taken the promotion of child welfare as its main project. The Canadian Council on Child Welfare had done a similar study in British Columbia, also encouraging local organizations to become active.

The reformers of the 1920s and 1930s continued to press for improvements and prior to World War Two had defined a set of objectives that represented an awareness of existing shortcomings and a blueprint for the future. These reform ideas were summed up in the recommendations of the Archambault Commission in 1938. For serious cases a more structured procedure was needed before convicting juveniles, and this would include a formal charge and evidence presented under oath in the presence of the accused with the latter entitled to counsel. Cases of minor offences, the Archambault Commission said, should be dealt with by the courts in a "social clinic" context. They called for less formality, such as dispensing with judicial robes. Presiding officers should be called children's magistrates or, in French, magistrats des enfants.

The commissioners called for properly educated magistrates and probation officers and the widespread use of psychiatrists and pre-trial reports. They favoured the expansion of children's courts and increased use of foster homes rather than putting youngsters in reformatories. The report recommended that training schools should be located in the country and that their programs should include ample recreation and competitive games. The mainstay of the rehabilitation treatment would consist of "rigid discipline, efficient education, and ample healthful physical work." The commissioners also called for a good classification system and the segregation of the mentally deficient. In keeping with their desire to create treatment programs that were more therapeutic, the Commission recommended the establishment of boards of commissioners for each training school. Members would help out with the program and visit the children. The report also underlined the importance of crime prevention and called on the public, the churches, and social service agencies to co-operate in preventing juvenile crime.[71]

Most of these ideas had been around for some time, as had the opposition to some of them. The interest in having reformatories located in rural areas, for example, dates back to the previous century. Opponents then argued that it was of little use to take urban youths, locate them in the country, train them in farming skills, and then ultimately send them back to live and work in large towns and cities. More significant and perhaps less controversial by the late thirties was the concept of creating a social clinic environment with better therapeutic programs. The recommendations in this area identified a need and pointed a direction for future development.

The first half of the twentieth century witnessed some major advances in the treatment of problem children. The actual improvements did not always keep pace with the aspirations of reformers, but their caring philosophy succeeded in becoming the guiding force of the entire system. Young people, although sometimes dealt with in a harsh manner, generally benefited from a lenient judicial system. Table 40 shows the disposition of delinquents convicted of major offences between 1922 and 1945 and illustrates the variety and nature of sanctions applied to young offenders.

As the table shows, the majority of convicted delinquents were dealt with in some way other than by putting them in detention. In 1922 only 8.5 per cent of those convicted were put in industrial schools, 11.5 per cent in 1932, and 13.1 per cent in 1945. Over the twenty-four-year period the average annual percentage of those convicted of major offences put in industrial school was 11.1. In addition, an annual average of approximately 1.7 per cent were kept in detention for terms varying in length from a few days to a month. They were usually under observation or awaiting a hearing. The distribution of penalties fluctuated, with a tendency toward more incarcerations in the late 1930s. The use of fines dropped during the depression years, reflecting the reluctance of magistrates to impose a monetary penalty in difficult economic times when people were less able to pay. Probation was consistently the preferred sanction. Those so sentenced included youngsters placed in foster homes and those put in the care of agencies such as Big Brother and Big Sister associations. The lenient penalties suggested that most magistrates shared the philosophy of the Juvenile Delinquents Act and chose to treat delinquents as young people in need of help rather than punishment.

Table 41 shows the disposition of delinquents convicted of minor offences for the years 1922 to 1945. As was the case with those who were convicted of major offences, the tendency was in the direction of light punishment and limited use of incarceration. According to the statistics, until the late 1930s a very small percentage of those convicted of minor crimes were placed in detention. Between 1922 and 1937 an annual average of approximately 6.5 per cent of those convicted were sent to training schools. Most offenders in this category were either simply reprimanded or given a suspended sentence. There was, however, a substantial fluctuation

Table 40
Disposition of Delinquents Convicted of Major Offences, 1922–45

Year	Reprimanded		Probation of Court		Protection of Parents		Fined or Made Restitution		Detained Indefinitely		Sent to Industrial School		Sentence Suspended		Corporal Punishment	
1922	225	6.3%	1,631	40.1%	142	3.5%	582	14.3%	125	3.1%	345	8.5%	984	24.2%	1	–
1923	233	5.6	1,752	42.1	220	5.3	564	13.5	91	2.2	339	8.1	955	22.9	11	0.3
1924	437	9.4	1,633	35.1	321	6.9	984	21.1	108	2.3	453	9.7	680	14.7	39	0.8
1925	589	11.6	1,980	38.9	84	1.7	710	13.9	96	1.9	516	10.2	1,076	21.2	29	0.6
1926	543	10.7	1,199	23.5	130	2.5	957	18.8	243	4.8	466	9.2	1,508	29.6	44	0.9
1927	825	16.0	1,058	20.5	158	3.0	763	14.8	276	5.3	458	8.9	1,509	29.2	109	2.1
1928	1,093	21.6	1,097	21.7	137	2.7	716	14.1	153	3.0	510	10.1	1,293	25.5	64	1.3
1929	652	12.8	1,408	27.6	196	3.8	1,119	21.9	104	2.0	592	9.8	1,087	21.3	38	0.8
1930	758	13.4	2,165	38.3	59	1.0	795	14.1	53	0.9	524	9.3	1,278	22.6	22	0.4
1931	902	17.0	2,161	49.7	62	1.2	578	10.9	31	0.6	452	8.5	1,101	20.7	24	0.4
1932	845	16.6	1,956	38.4	81	1.6	352	6.9	13	0.2	584	11.5	1,233	24.2	32	0.6
1933	902	17.5	2,123	41.4	27	0.5	304	5.9	14	0.2	510	9.9	1,238	24.1	26	0.5
1934	821	15.3	2,433	45.5	30	0.6	253	4.7	22	0.4	488	9.1	1,273	23.8	33	0.6
1935	482	8.7	2,843	51.6	61	1.1	283	5.1	15	0.3	540	9.8	1,159	21.0	131	2.4
1936	470	9.5	2,419	48.6	36	0.7	317	6.4	25	0.5	559	11.3	1,087	21.9	57	1.1
1937	474	9.1	2,510	48.1	37	0.7	346	6.6	39	0.8	568	10.8	1,201	23.0	49	0.9
1938	383	7.6	1,949	38.6	38	0.8	301	6.0	36	0.7	614	21.1	1,686	33.3	48	0.9
1939	404	8.0	1,631	32.5	28	0.6	228	4.5	119	2.4	639	12.7	1,941	38.7	28	0.6
1940	296	5.6	2,108	39.8	33	0.6	281	5.3	111	2.1	785	14.8	1,643	31.0	41	0.8
1941	422	6.8	2,836	45.7	130	2.1	411	6.7	108	1.7	820	13.2	1,442	23.2	35	0.6
1942	432	6.2	1,984	28.7	83	1.2	854	12.3	96	1.5	847	12.2	2,573	37.2	51	0.7
1943	464	7.1	1,798	27.7	140	2.2	1,001	15.4	92	1.4	906	14.0	2,041	31.4	52	0.8
1944	395	6.0	1,745	26.7	112	1.7	1,545	23.7	83	1.3	838	12.8	1,747	26.8	64	1.0
1945	352	6.1	1,581	27.5	109	1.9	1,514	26.3	54	0.9	753	13.1	1,372	23.8	23	0.4

SOURCE: *Canada Year Book*, 1947.

Table 41
Disposition of Delinquents Convicted of Minor Offences, 1922-45

Year	Reprimanded and Allowed to Go Under Supervision		Detained Indefinitely		Sent to Training School		Fined or Paid Damage		Sentence Suspended	
1922	1,325	59.3%	44	2.0%	85	3.8%	504	22.6%	275	12.3%
1923	1,475	61.3	74	3.1	87	3.6	396	16.5	374	15.5
1924	1,940	62.5	79	2.5	189	6.1	468	15.1	428	13.8
1925	1,611	57.4	49	1.7	147	5.2	488	17.4	512	18.3
1926	1,438	52.5	41	1.5	84	3.1	814	29.7	364	13.2
1927	1,501	49.6	70	2.3	211	7.0	876	28.9	371	12.2
1928	1,601	60.7	47	1.8	121	4.6	611	23.2	256	9.7
1929	1,593	58.6	22	0.8	158	5.8	716	26.3	231	8.5
1930	1,357	49.0	17	0.6	195	7.0	473	17.1	730	26.3
1931	1,582	64.4	1	–	177	7.2	360	14.7	337	13.7
1932	1,338	59.2	1	–	196	8.6	192	8.4	539	23.8
1933	1,469	63.6	1	–	156	6.7	122	5.3	561	24.2
1934	1,495	61.0	–	–	182	7.4	84	3.4	692	28.2
1935	1,187	54.8	2	0.1	203	9.4	227	10.5	546	25.2
1936	1,241	55.4	3	0.1	220	9.8	211	9.4	566	25.3
1937	1,352	54.2	9	0.4	206	8.3	262	10.5	663	26.6
1938	756	38.2	9	0.4	233	11.8	171	8.6	811	41.0
1939	631	24.3	37	1.4	345	13.3	380	14.6	1,202	46.4
1940	1,340	42.8	52	1.7	409	13.0	542	17.3	790	25.2
1941	2,188	53.3	31	0.8	512	12.5	986	24.0	389	9.4
1942	1,085	22.4	22	0.5	607	12.6	1,448	29.9	1,676	34.6
1943	1,056	27.8	9	0.2	495	13.0	961	25.3	1,281	33.7
1944	1,035	30.5	9	0.3	538	15.9	1,002	29.6	804	23.7
1945	1,117	35.4	11	0.4	595	18.9	853	27.1	575	18.2

SOURCE: *Canada Year Book, 1947.*

in the use of the various penalties. Suspended sentences went from a low of 8.5 per cent of all sentences in 1929 to a high of 46.4 per cent in 1939. In 1938 the percentage of those put in training schools jumped and then continued higher through to 1945. The considerable variation in sentencing again illustrates the lack of uniformity in penal practices. More offenders were incarcerated in 1945 for minor offences than for major offences, for example. The saving feature was that the vast majority of sentences handed out to those convicted of both major and minor offences were uniformly light and did not involve incarceration, so the variations did not represent any great inequity.

Although the magistrates were apparently co-operating and trying to reform delinquents outside of institutions, and although there were progressively more children's courts, foster home placements, auxiliary agencies, and better programs, little headway seemingly was made. As we saw in another chapter, delinquency levels rose in a steady progression and recidivism rates remained high. Young offenders continued to grow up to be adult criminals. In spite of the poor results, few questioned the efficacy of the prevailing penal sanctions or the strong belief in the use of foster care for problem children. Most reformers sought even more reliance on the existing approach and called for increased foster home placements, more child-saving agencies, and expanded programs in institutions.

POST-WORLD WAR TWO DEVELOPMENTS

The post-war period saw more official attention paid to the treatment of juvenile delinquents, an ongoing building program, and the replacement of private care with government-run facilities. The more supportive attitudes reflected a greater social conscience that developed in the post-war years. Social legislation, welfare programs, and more concern for the unfortunate were the order of the day. Family problems, including juvenile delinquency, benefited from broad public interest. The new institutions springing up across the country were placing more emphasis on counselling, guidance, and education programs. Some set up their own full-time schools, employed more professionally trained staff, including case workers and counsellors, and offered up-to-date recreational facilities and leisure-time activities.

These developments were given an impetus by what many saw as the continued failure of the system to achieve objectives. British Columbia was a case in point. The increase in delinquency in that province in the 1950s prompted the government to set up a Board of Inquiry composed of twelve members of the legislature who undertook an examination of the problem. The Board reported in 1958 that juvenile delinquency was increasing in B.C. at a rate faster than for the nation as a whole and pointed out that in 1951 the province accounted for 12 per cent of court appearances in Canada while in 1956 it accounted for 14 per cent. It also revealed that juvenile delinquency in the province was increasing at a more rapid rate than the population in that age group.[72] In spite of the perceived urgency, little progress was made in subsequent years. In 1965 a study of youth services in metropolitan Vancouver and Victoria discovered that crime among juveniles was still escalating and that more young people were being put in detention. The report noted confusion among local agencies as well as a lack of effective communication and a lack of co-ordination and overall planning for youth services. The study pointed out that no agency in Vancouver had prevention of juvenile delinquency as its major aim. The same observation could be made of most communities in the country at the time. The shortcomings were generally recognized and so people were motivated to keep on working for improvements.[73]

One result was that more juvenile courts were established. For example, between 1962 and 1966 the number of children's courts in Nova Scotia increased from nine to twenty-one. When magistrates had to sentence offenders to detention there was a wider choice of institutions. Ontario again led the way by providing separate establishments for younger and older offenders, schools that specialized in academic or vocational training, and minimum or maximum security facilities. In most places the emphasis was on family-style living and community integration for both males and females. The schools ranged from ones with fairly close supervision to others that allowed a great deal of freedom and self-regulation. In Quebec, at least one school emphasized a close interaction between the detainees and the staff and provided a group therapy program. In many centres across the country much more attention was being given to the development of life skills. Staff worked with the young people to improve their communication ability, personal hygiene, and general behaviour and to promote more co-operative attitudes. In some places young people were permitted to attend local community schools if they reached a grade level not offered in the detention centre. In general, much more emphasis was placed on education, counselling, and preparation for re-integration into the community.

Although much attention was focused on reformatories and their programs, detention continued to be a little preferred sentence option during the 1960s. As we saw in Table 40, from 1922 to 1945 the average commitment to industrial schools of convicted juveniles was about 11 per cent. In 1963 the figure for detention of juveniles in training schools was 11.6 per cent. Half of those convicted, 49.8 per cent, were released on probation while 14 per cent were punished with a fine or restitution, and 18.1 per cent had their sentences suspended or adjourned. Overall, the courts dealt leniently with juvenile offenders.[74]

In spite of the ongoing concern, changes, and improvements, widespread discontent with the treatment of juvenile delinquents continued. Too many young people were recidivists and graduated into adult crime. Many reformatories still lacked proper programs, personnel, and therapy services. Liberalization in some cases resulted in a lack of discipline in the institutions and too much idleness. The Juvenile Delinquents Act still did not apply in some jurisdictions, including the entire province of Newfoundland. Age limits had not yet been standardized. In Saskatchewan, Ontario, New Brunswick, Nova Scotia, and P.E.I. the age limit was sixteen. In B.C., Manitoba, and Quebec it was eighteen. In Newfoundland the age limit, set by provincial legislation, was seventeen.

On another level, the issue of legal rights was beginning to touch on the juvenile offender. For much of our history juvenile offenders did not share the same rights before the law as adults. In earlier years they were dealt with summarily and later with a large degree of paternalism. In either case they were denied due process. The interest in human rights, the rights of the accused, and prisoners' rights, described elsewhere, also found an expression in the area of the rights of young people, especially those who got caught up in the criminal justice system. Law reformers and a number of corrections officials were challenging the continued paternalistic treatment of young people within the correctional system and arguing that they should be accorded the same legal rights as adults.[75]

The concern over judicial treatment of young people was not new. As far back as the debate over the 1908 Juvenile Delinquents Act critics raised the issue of the rights of children before the courts. The broad level of discretionary powers given to court officials, the lack of representation by counsel, and no trial by jury were among the points at issue. At the time, these complaints gained little support because reformers were primarily concerned with the welfare aspect of the process as opposed to the judicial. To some extent the attitude prevailed that the end more than justified the means. The spirit of the 1960s, however, no longer supported the denial of individual rights, even in pursuance of high-minded objectives. In addition, concern mounted over the ongoing increase in the levels of delinquency. Officials called attention to the growing population of young people and to the probability of more crime and advised that action be taken in the area of prevention. They recommended that more study be devoted to the problem and pointed out that although the existing Juvenile Delinquents Act had been in place since 1929, no in-depth evaluation of its effectiveness or shortcomings had ever been done. The result was a formidable demand from many quarters for significant changes in the treatment of juvenile delinquency.

That demand was given considerable impetus by the recommendations of the Department of Justice Committee on Juvenile Delinquency. The concern with the growth in adult crime, coupled with the belief that the problem started with juvenile delinquents, had prompted the Department of Justice to sponsor an inquiry. The Committee, appointed in November, 1961, was authorized to "inquire into and report upon the nature and extent of the problem of juvenile delinquency in Canada." Its findings and recommendations were published in 1965.

The report, titled *Juvenile Delinquency in Canada*, focused attention on the many shortcomings of the system that dealt with juvenile delinquents, pointing out the lack of "uniformity across Canada in terms of types or sizes of institutions, the number and qualifications of staff or the policies to be administered in the operation of training schools."[76] Committee members also noted that within the provinces seldom did any one government department have charge of children's services, and that many centres had inadequate facilities and some were poorly located. As well, the shortage of professional staff meant that children committed to training schools were not properly assessed.

The report made sweeping proposals for changes in the treatment of juvenile offenders. It placed even more emphasis than the Juvenile Delinquents Act on the non-judicial treatment of delinquents, called for stricter limitations on the exercise of court powers, and recommended the use of more disposal and sentencing options. The Committee suggested that the minimum age be raised to ten years and the maximum age be made uniform across the country at seventeen, that the term "juvenile delinquent" be replaced with "child offender" and "young offender," and that reformatory sentences be limited to a maximum term of three years.

The Committee called for more standardization of services and programs, equal application of the Juvenile Delinquents Act across Canada, better training for judges and other court officials, and mandatory pre-sentence reports. In the area of individual rights and due process, the report recommended that the court be obliged to inform the accused of his or her rights to retain counsel, that provision be made for more formal procedures and protection of the rights of the accused, and that broader rights of appeal be instituted. The Committee also called for more options for the disposition of cases and sentencing, including community-based sanctions and limited use of detention. The 100 specific recommendations touched on various aspects of juvenile delinquency, ranging from courts to research. The report became the focal point for discussion and debate for the next two decades.[77]

Meaningful progress on reform was delayed by the same considerations that had prevailed in the past. Some were reluctant to make the system too lenient; some supported certain reforms while opposing others. A main concern of the provinces was the additional costs that major changes in the system would necessitate. Also, the dichotomy over federal versus provincial jurisdiction continued to be a problem. In the meantime, minor changes in the treatment of juvenile offenders were being made. Better-trained and professional personnel were introduced into various reformatories, and there was some experimentation with treatment programs such as clinics and group homes. New facilities were constructed and improvements were made in existing ones.

By 1973 over forty training schools were operating across Canada, about 40 per cent of them for females.[78] They went by such names as the Boys' Home and Training School in Newfoundland, the Girls' Cottage School and the Centre Berthelet for boys in Quebec, the Pine Ridge School for boys and the Grand View School for girls in Ontario, and the Saskatchewan Boys' School in Saskatchewan. The nomenclature itself suggests the emphasis of these institutions on education and reform. Institutionalization was the least preferred sanction and only a small number of juvenile offenders ended up in detention. Among the main trends in disposition was the more frequent use of diversion programs, that is, the use of community resources and programs to deal with young people in trouble rather than processing them through the court system and putting them in detention. One study done in 1975 estimated that "70% of all rehabilitative efforts were community-based."[79]

Meetings, studies, and debate continued over the issue of how to deal with young offenders. In 1970 draft legislation, Bill C-192, was introduced in Parliament but failed to reach third reading. It was difficult to get agreement between the two levels of government over what changes should be introduced, and as usual the provinces were particularly concerned about the monetary implications of any new proposals. Finally, almost two decades after the publication of *Juvenile Delinquency in Canada*, the federal government produced a comprehensive proposal for a new Young Offenders Act. The legislation was given royal assent on July 7, 1982, and the Act became operative in all provinces and territories on April 2, 1984.

In the meantime, improved facilities and treatment programs had gradually been introduced, but these had effected little if any improvement in recidivism rates and failed to stem the increase in juvenile crime levels. There were problems with all aspects of the juvenile justice system. The lenient treatment and caring philosophy seemed to have little impact on offenders and did not serve as a deterrent. Foster care was riddled with unsatisfactory homes and foster parents, unhappy and rebellious young people, insufficient placements, and too little compensation. Experiments with group homes faced neighbourhood opposition, inadequate funding, supervisory problems, and unco-operative housemates. Agencies were understaffed, overworked, and underfunded. The detention centres lacked skilled staff, adequate professional counsellors, and sufficient programs. Many detainees were able to serve their time in idleness and came out no better prepared to live honest and useful lives than when they went in.

The entire atmosphere in some institutions worked against normal social development. One former employee of a girls' training school in Ontario reported that the residents developed strong emotional attachments to each other much in the manner of a boy and girl going steady. When such relationships broke up, the girls became considerably upset and distraught. In the same institution, girls who physically marked themselves achieved a certain status among their peers. Consequently, a number of them resorted to cutting themselves or getting tattooed. The staff insisted on being addressed by their proper titles, but the girls used insulting nicknames for them behind their backs. The situation was unhealthy and hardly conducive to reform.[80] Indicative of the poor results typical of many reformatories was a survey done among inmates at Millhaven Penitentiary, a federal maximum security prison. Over 50 per cent of the inmates had spent time in an Ontario juvenile training centre. In 1972 a study done by the Ministry of Correctional Services of Ontario revealed that 34 per cent of young people who were sentenced to a training school were convicted of an offence within eighteen months of release from their first detention.[81]

When offenders were released from custody there was still inadequate aftercare or follow-up. Even the various agencies working with delinquents and troubled families had difficulty co-ordinating their efforts and co-operating. There was more interest in preventive programs, but efforts generally were sporadic and not co-ordinated. Hence, juvenile delinquency continued to escalate, and discontent with the results of the existing system that dealt with young offenders grew among corrections officials and the general public.

THE YOUNG OFFENDERS ACT

The Young Offenders Act was designed to remedy many of the shortcomings in the treatment of juvenile delinquents; in particular, it addressed the issue of offenders' rights. The Act continued to make a distinction between youth and adult crime and to provide for a substantially different and much more benign approach to dealing with youth. At the same time it attempted to make young people more accountable for their actions. The Declaration of Principles expressed the new philosophy: "Young persons who commit offences should nonetheless bear responsibility for their contraventions." The legislation ended the paternalistic handling of delinquents by providing the same basic rights and freedoms before the law as those enjoyed by adults and as provided for in the Charter of Rights and Freedoms. It also set out a new range of penalties that included the options of financial restitution or compensatory work for the victim. One of the more significant changes, in keeping with the Act's benevolent thrust, was the provision raising the minimum age for prosecution to twelve years and setting a new Canada-wide maximum age at under eighteen.[82]

The Young Offenders Act guarantees an accused the right to legal counsel and the right to appeal a conviction. Detention cannot exceed two years, except where the crime would ordinarily incur a life sentence, in which case the maximum period of commitment may not exceed three years. The new law, in keeping with the principle of responsibility, allows for the transfer of more serious cases, such as sexual assault, armed robbery, and murder, to adult court under certain circumstances and providing the accused is fourteen or over. The intent of the Act, however, clearly is for most cases to be tried in youth court.

The new legislation also provides for a much wider choice of dispositions. They include: absolute discharge; a fine not exceeding $1,000; compensation for loss or damage to property; restitution; compensation in kind; community service; detention for treatment; probation; fine option; open custody in a community residential centre, group home, child-care institution, or forest or wilderness camp; secure custody; temporary absence or day release. At no time before, during, or after legal procedures is the identity of the young person allowed to be published. Subsequent to the completion of the sentence and no later than when the young offender reaches adulthood, the records must be destroyed.[83]

Among the sentence options it is clearly the intention of the Act to use incarceration only as a last resort. In actuality, the courts have been exercising other options for quite some time and in practice some of the dispositions under the new Act have been utilized at about the same rate as that under the old Act. For example, in 1983 only 11.2 per cent of convicted juveniles were put in detention. The vast majority, 42.2 per cent, were released on probation, and 21.4 per cent were either fined or required to make restitution. The final disposition for 13.7 per cent was suspension or adjournment.[84] In comparison, statistics for 1989-90 show that 11 per cent were sentenced to secure custody, 10 per cent were sentenced to open custody, 14 per cent were fined, 7 per cent were given a community service order, and 7 per cent were given an absolute discharge or other disposition. Half of the convicted young offenders were placed on probation.[85]

While the Young Offenders Act was greeted with enthusiasm in many quarters and is still seen as enlightened legislation, it has not been without its critics and its problems. From the outset the provinces complained about the cost of building the new facilities that the Act necessitated.[86] More serious, however, have been other aspects of the new legislation. Because the changed age limit provides no sanctions for lawbreakers under twelve, many young children are committing offences with impunity. In some cases they are being schooled in lawbreaking techniques and used by older children and adults to carry out a wide range of illegal activities from theft to the delivery of drugs. If they get caught nothing can be done to them.[87]

The generally light sentences, especially the two- and three-year limitations, combined with the new, well-appointed facilities in which the detainees are housed, are another dimension of the problem. The more sophisticated delinquents see the penalties as almost inconsequential. The prospect of spending a relatively short period of time in comfortable surroundings, provided with the most up-to-date facilities and recreation equipment, is not one that fills them with apprehension.[88] The application of adult rights to these young people further complicates the situation. They are now free to decide if they will participate in such activities as counselling and therapy programs. Thus it is possible to have a youth, with emotional or psychological problems that contribute to his or her delinquency, doing time in a detention centre but refusing any kind of treatment. The staff is also handicapped by the expanded rights of young offenders since they have fewer options for disciplining unruly and unco-operative residents.

The very moderate penalties, especially the three-year ceiling on detention, have generated a great deal of public criticism. Putting a juvenile in a reformatory for three years or less for a crime such as murder is seen as having no punitive or deterrent value and appears to some to be a most inappropriate way to deal with offenders who commit major crimes. Another practice that offends the public's sense of justice is the provision that wipes the record of young offenders clean once they pass the age limit. This means that the next crime committed as an adult is dealt with as a first offence and the perpetrator benefits from more lenient treatment.[89] Many youthful lawbreakers record a string of offences, sometimes very serious ones, before they become adults.

The widespread criticism has resulted in calls for changes and has caused the government to consider stiffening the penalties. At a meeting in Vancouver in June, 1989, the mayors of Canada's largest cities issued a common call for tougher penalties for juveniles who commit serious crimes.[90] In response to public concern the Minister of Justice has proposed amendments to the Young Offenders Act that would provide for longer sentences for youth convicted of violent crimes and broader provisions for transferring young offenders to adult courts.[91]

Generally, the Young Offenders Act is yet another example of an attempt to solve a problem where the solution seems to have created more difficulties. The current program has not succeeded in lowering crime levels, nor has it achieved much by way of reform and rehabilitation. It does not punish wrongdoers, it does not protect the public, it does not deter crime, and it does not seem to motivate problem youngsters to change their ways. Consequently, except for the more humane treatment of youthful offenders, many of the problems relating to children and crime that go back to the last century remain unsolved. A similar judgement may be made on prevention programs. Aside from anti-drug campaigns, inadequate attention has been given to juvenile crime prevention programs and so the delinquency dilemma continues with little prospect for improvement.

SUMMARY

In the early days of our history little distinction was made between standards of behaviour for adults and for children. Society placed great importance on the disciplined nurturing of children because they were in training as the future custodians of what was hoped would be a stable, law-abiding, God-fearing, civilized community. Misbehaving children were a signal that development practices had broken down and were, as well, a harbinger of future problems. Therefore, in the eyes of many, it was even more important that young delinquents be put on the right path than adults. Discipline and punishment were two generally accepted correctional procedures of the time and few questioned that child lawbreakers should be subjected to the same punishments. Thus the penalties prescribed for various crimes operated for all offenders without regard to age, sex, or physical or mental condition.

The punishments for young lawbreakers included whipping, incarceration, fines, and death. Children who were jailed shared the accommodation with hardened criminals, the sick, the indigent, and the mentally ill. Frequently the experience turned them out worse than when they entered. Fortunately, the kindly attitudes of police, magistrates, and jailors ameliorated the harsh penalties and young people frequently got off with lighter punishments than those prescribed by law. Both severe penalties and benign treatment occasioned public concern – some argued that little was being done to lower crime and recidivism rates; others complained that children should not be treated like adults if they were to be diverted from a life of crime.

The proponents of less severity eventually won the day, at least at the philosophical level. From the first half of the nineteenth century, reformist ideas began to replace the emphasis on punishment and deterrence. Throughout the century there was progressively more acceptance of the idea that child offenders should be treated as youngsters more in need of help than punishment. The 1894 Youthful Offenders Act represented a substantial victory for reformers and an official imprimatur of their agenda. In subsequent years many improvements in the treatment of delinquents were realized, such as the introduction of children's courts, the separation of young offenders from adults, and the opening of new facilities.

In spite of improvements the correctional system for delinquents always fell short of objectives and aspirations. It suffered from inadequate funding, untrained staff, poor facilities, and a number of other problems. And little progress was made in stemming the rise in crime or in reducing recidivism rates. Because of shortcomings and failures, reformers and judicial officials maintained a steady advocacy for changes and improvements. Nearly a century of studies, law amendments, and general concern culminated in 1984 with the Young Offenders Act. Its authors hoped it would remedy some of the worst deficiencies in the treatment of juveniles and result in a better track record for rehabilitation.

The treatment of juvenile delinquents since pioneer days has evolved from being the same as that accorded to adult criminals to a completely separate and distinct system of sanctions. This has now been refined to allow young people due process while almost eliminating the punitive component of procedures. Over the same period incarceration facilities have moved from jails and prisons, to refuges and reformatories, and now to detention centres that rival the accommodations of private schools. Throughout the period one consistent aspect of treatment has been the comparatively limited use of incarceration. The vast majority of youth who got caught up in the judicial system were disciplined by warnings, probation, and fines. Today, restitution and community service have been added to the list of frequently used sentence options.

Over the years many ideas, philosophies, and theories have been put forward in regard to juvenile delinquency. At one time there was strong support for a regimen of strict discipline and religious and character development education. At the end of the nineteenth century the child savers put great store in the importance of keeping troubled children in a family setting and they encouraged the use of foster homes. Throughout most of this century the emphasis has been on caring and kindly treatment and less and less on punishment. This has been encouraged by a theory which holds that juveniles are not really responsible for their crimes but are the victims of a poor environment. Thus the belief that if problem children are treated better and given the benefits of proper care, a stable environment, and adequate programs, they can be converted into responsible citizens.

Since the very early days of our history, justice officials and others have consistently blamed the home for producing delinquent children. The 1958 *Report of the Juvenile Delinquency Inquiry Board* in British Columbia summed up over two centuries of such observations:

> Delinquency seems to develop in those youngsters whose home life is lacking in many respects. Although this is not universally valid, it is believed that serious deficiencies in parental control and training are responsible. . . .
>
> Board members felt that the parents must accept the major responsibility for the delinquency of their children. Whether it be the lack of supervision or direct control over activities, lack of interest in friends and play habits, rejection or lack of love by either or both parents, or a break-up of the home, there is an abundance of unsatisfactory home conditions in the backgrounds of most delinquents.[92]

A few years later the Report of the Department of Justice Committee on Juvenile Delinquency noted that "The factor most frequently mentioned to us throughout the country is the importance of the role of the family in preventing delinquent behaviour."[93]

In spite of the various explanations for delinquency advanced over the years, and changing approaches to treatment that have reflected those theories, little has been accomplished. Crime levels remain unacceptably high, recidivism is still a problem, and the incidence of violent offences continues to cause concern. More attention is still paid to dealing with offenders than to preventing the offences in the first place. The record has been disappointing and suggests that the whole problem of delinquency among the young needs to be re-examined from a different perspective with a view to designing new approaches.

CHAPTER 10

▼

Treatment of the Female Offender

Throughout most of our history the role of women was defined in very narrow terms. Society and the church expected a woman to be a wife and mother, a guardian of family morals, and a virtuous role model. Single women were considered to be wives in training and so they were taught domestic skills at home or hired out as servants. During their terms in service they practised those tasks that would prepare them to be good housekeepers and cooks when they married and took charge of their own households. Whether at home or in service they were held to a high moral standard and were expected to guard their virginity and set an example by living a life that was virtuous in all respects.

The reality did not always conform to the ideal, especially in a pioneer society. Women shared the burden of homesteading alongside their husbands, and as settlement progressed the more well-to-do women in centres like Quebec and Montreal sometimes indulged themselves in dress and behaviour. Clergy in New France complained of lax morals and denounced the young women who chose to live with their boyfriends out of wedlock. Nevertheless, in the face of pioneer coarseness and a variety of immorality, the standard was not challenged and certainly never abandoned.

As Canadian society became progressively more established, as fledgling communities matured, and as manners refined, the standards of behaviour for women became more entrenched. By the Victorian era the ideal woman was pure, kind, gentle, serene, sober, prudent, and, if single, a virgin. Women were expected to be both the models and the guardians of all that was proper and virtuous in society. They were the protectors of home and hearth. In contrast, men were thought to have a much baser nature than women and consequently could not be expected to adhere to the same standards of conduct. Thus, for men there was a definition of desired behaviour but a greater tolerance for those who fell short of the mark. For women, who were saddled with much greater expectations, no deviance from the ideal was tolerated. A man who drank and caroused was sowing his wild oats but a female who did likewise was a fallen women, a disgrace to her sex.

Against this background it is easy to understand why society held female lawbreakers in such low regard, especially when their offences were so frequently transgressions of moral precepts. At the same time, however, there was an ambivalence toward the female offender. On the one hand, a woman who transgressed was quickly denounced and sometimes punished severely. Not only had she sinned but she had also betrayed her sex and threatened the moral order of her community.[1] On the other hand, women were pure, genteel, the weaker sex, and above all wives and mothers. Consequently, many men who presided over the criminal justice system found it difficult to deal with female offenders. Women were to be looked after and protected, not whipped, jailed, or hanged. The dilemma worked to the benefit of females and in many instances resulted in different and more lenient treatment before the courts. However, as we have already seen, consistency was not a high priority with magistrates and officials and neither was it in the treatment of the female offender.

THE PUNISHMENT OF FEMALE OFFENDERS IN PIONEER DAYS

During the early days of settlement the harsh punishments provided by law were sometimes meted out to women without hesitation. They included hanging, being placed in the yoke, public whippings, and incarceration. One of the earliest incidents of female punishment took place during the abortive attempt at colonization by the Sieur de Roberval and his party. Over the winter of 1542-43 various members of his company indulged in criminal activity and Roberval had both males and females whipped and placed in irons for their offences.[2] With permanent settlement, a number of cases in New France illustrate the range of punishments meted out to female offenders. In 1649 a woman was hanged for theft and thereby became one of the early victims to be dispatched by the colony's first official hangman.[3] In 1671 a Montreal woman, Françoise du Verger, was convicted of multiple abortions, infanticide, and complicity in the murder of her first husband. She was sent to Quebec to be put to the *question extraordinaire*, a practice rarely used for female offenders. The records indicate that only four women were thus tortured to extract confessions during the entire French regime. The earlier verdict was confirmed by the Supreme Council in Quebec and Françoise du Verger was sentenced to be hanged. The woman claimed to be pregnant and the Council agreed to postpone the punishment until after the birth of the baby. However, on examination by a doctor and a midwife, it was determined that she was not expecting and the sentence was carried out.[4] In 1672 Gilette Baune and her husband were convicted of murdering their son-in-law and both were hanged for their crime.[5]

The elaborate ritual that sometimes accompanied punishments for grave offences in New France was seldom prescribed for women, but in 1734 a black slave girl named Angélique was sentenced to the full ceremony. She had set fire to her mistress's house and then fled with her boyfriend. The fire spread and burned down forty-six houses in Montreal before it was finally extinguished. Angélique was condemned to:

> make amends, naked under a shirt, a rope around her neck, holding in her hands a burning torch weighing two pounds, in front of the main door and entrance of the parish church in Montreal, where she will be brought by the executioner of the High Justice, in a typcart used for garbage, with a sign 'Arsonist' on the front and back of the cart, and there, bareheaded, kneeling, declare that she maliciously set fire and caused the arson of which she was repenting and ask forgiveness from God, the King and justice, after which, to have her hand cut off, placed on a post and planted in front of the said church, after which she will be brought by the Executioner in the same typcart to the public square to be tied to a post with an iron chain and burned alive, her body reduced to cinders and the cinders scattered in the wind.[6]

The burning was doubly significant because it meant that she would be deprived of a Christian burial. In the eyes of the Church this was in itself a serious condemnation.

Angélique appealed her sentence to the Supreme Council, which tended to be less severe with its penalties. The Council upheld the decision but did tone down slightly the grisly sentence. The penalty was modified so that the woman's hand was not to be cut off and she would be put to death and then her body burned. Before her execution she was tortured in the hope of getting her to confess and repent for her crime. She eventually gave in but did not implicate anyone else. Having satisfied the need of the authorities to have guilt acknowledged, her death sentence was carried out.[7]

While severe punishments were occasionally meted out to female criminals, justice was also tempered with mercy. The Supreme Council frequently reduced death sentences given by a lower court. For example, in 1708 a woman was sentenced to hang for concealing her pregnancy and killing the baby at birth. She appealed to the Council and was given a much lighter sentence. Instead of losing her life she was placed in the yoke for public humiliation and banished from Quebec for a period of three years.[8] In 1747 another woman, Marie-Madeleine Boin, was caught trying to hide her pregnancy. She was married to a baker who was out of the country so naturally did not want it known that she had been cheating on her husband. She was condemned to hang in Quebec, but on appeal the Supreme Council sentenced her to be whipped and also branded on the shoulder with an impression of the fleur-de-lis.[9]

One of the most novel means of escaping supreme punishment was a custom that allowed the death penalty to be set aside if the condemned woman married the executioner. In 1751 Françoise Laurent was in jail awaiting execution for having stolen clothes from the people who employed her as a maid. While incarcerated she made the acquaintance of Jean Corollaire, the occupant of an adjoining cell, who was being punished for duelling. Corollaire fell in love with Françoise and applied for the job of executioner. Two days later he married the woman and thereby saved her from the gallows.[10]

Although women were sometimes put to death or branded in New France, the relatively small number of convicted female offenders over the years were more often whipped, subjected to public humiliation, fined, or placed in confinement. Unless awaiting trial or punishment few women were kept in detention, and those who were incarcerated for any length of time were put in the Hôpital Général. A small section of the building was set aside for female offenders and fallen women who were put in the care of the Ursulines, the religious order that operated the hospital. For example, in 1696 a woman found guilty of theft was sent there for a six-month term, at the end of which she was to be flogged and then set free. In 1733 Genevieve Millit was found guilty of adultery and sentenced to three years' seclusion at the Hôpital Général, along with the usual corporal punishment.[11]

Female offenders in New France frequently got off with lighter sentences than their male counterparts. This was true even when women were involved in the same crime with male partners. In 1675 Marie Pacault and two male companions were convicted of theft. The woman was punished by being beaten with rods and having a sign placed on her forehead which read "Maquerelle," literally, madam of a brothel; in contrast, one of her partners was hanged for his part in the crime.[12] In 1735 a man convicted of theft and a companion convicted of possessing stolen goods were both put to the *question extraordinaire* and then hanged. Two female accomplices, however, were sentenced to be stripped to the waist, beaten with rods at a number of places throughout the town, and jailed for three years in the Hôpital Général.[13] While far from a lenient sentence, the women got off much easier than their male friends. Aside from a death sentence the penalty most feared by men was galley service. This was one punishment women were spared because they were considered too weak physically.

Patterns of punishment established in the early days of settlement continued in New France through to the Conquest. In English Canada the penalty options were similar but with a few variations, one being the ducking stool. This apparatus consisted of a chair fixed to the end of a long post. The offender was secured in the stool and ducked in the water. There is little evidence that the punishment was ever prescribed except for one recorded incident in Annapolis, Nova Scotia, in 1734. Jeanne Picot was convicted of scandal for falsely accusing Mary Davis of murdering two children. The council sentenced Jeanne Picot to be ducked "at high water." Mary Davis took pity on her detractor and asked that the sentence be set aside and instead that Picot be allowed to make a public apology on the following Sunday at the door of the church. The council obliged and Mrs. Picot was spared a ducking.[14] Another variation in English punishment practices was one allowing female offenders to plead "benefit of clergy."[15] While this offered women an opportunity to reduce the severity of punishment, it appears that they seldom took advantage of the provision. One of the few recorded cases involved a petty thief who was tried in Halifax in 1755. The woman stole two saucepans, a copper pot, two pewter pots, and two brass candlesticks. She was sentenced to hang but when she pleaded "benefit of clergy" her death sentence was set aside and she was branded with the letter "T" and put in jail for two months.[16]

There were women who, on occasion, would certainly have welcomed a mitigation of punishment. Females were sometimes dealt with severely, even for petty crimes. In the early days of Halifax a servant girl was put to death because some household silver was missing. The following spring, when the snow thawed, the cutlery was found in the yard where the girl had lain it on the ground. She obviously had taken the silver outside to clean it and then had forgotten it.[17]

Women were put to death in public, as were men, but because a female hanging was a rarer event the crowds that attended were larger and more agitated than usual. In 1790 when a woman was hanged for murder in Halifax, officials were careful to choose a site for the gallows that would offer a good view to the anticipated crowd. She was taken from the jail in an open wagon, which the horses pulled directly under the rope. The noose was placed around the woman's neck and the wagon driven out from under her.[18]

Although a few were hanged, the more common punishments for female offenders were whipping, the yoke, and incarceration. The English were partial to the whip and, unlike their counterparts in New France, made much more use of detention as punishment for women. The growing reluctance to use extreme penalties for minor crimes prompted the government in Nova Scotia to build a combined jail and workhouse – a Bridewell – which was to be used for both the destitute and the criminals. The thirty-by forty-foot edifice housed men, women, children, the sick, the mentally ill, and the aged. Female offenders sentenced to the workhouse as punishment were first whipped, put in the stocks on the market wharf, and then taken to jail. The common period of incarceration was three months and at the end of their term they would be given ten more lashes with the whip and then released. Mary McDaniel, for her crime of armed robbery in 1781, was branded with a "T" and sentenced to hard labour in the workhouse for twelve months.[19] At that, she got off with a light sentence because the usual punishment for her crime was hanging.

Along with the poorhouse, or Bridewell, Halifax also constructed a county jail. Such places in early times were poorly ventilated, damp, and inadequately heated in the winter. Women sentenced to jail were treated no differently than male criminals, and like the opposite sex they suffered from vermin, disease, lack of sufficient food and adequate clothing, scanty bedding, and the foul air that came from poor sanitation. In 1759 Alice Wallice was charged with stealing a gold watch from a man who was lying dead drunk in the street and was sent to jail to await trial. Finally, after six months, she asked the court to hold her trial on the grounds that, "she being so low, is not able to live a winter in this miserable place."[20] The woman's petition is a comment on both the jail conditions and the speed of the justice system at the time.

The English, like the French, frequently applied a more lenient standard to women than men. Hanging for serious crimes was a punishment used less frequently, whippings were less severe, and jail sentences shorter. One example of such leniency came out of an incidence of piracy. This crime was considered to be among the most serious that could be committed and almost automatically incurred the death penalty. The piracy took place in October, 1809, and the details of the affair have been given elsewhere. The woman involved, the wife of Edward Jordan, the chief conspirator, played a full part in the whole venture. At one point she even attacked the already wounded captain with a boat hook. A special commission for the trial of piracies on the high seas conducted the hearing and Jordan was found guilty, hanged, and his body placed on a gibbet for public display. His wife, however, was acquitted. A fund-raising appeal was held and the woman was sent home to Ireland.[21]

The English approach to punishment also became the norm in Quebec after the Conquest. The first woman to be put to death under the English was Marie Josephe Corriveau for the murder of her husband. The woman was tried during the period of military government and before English criminal law was introduced. Marie was hanged in Quebec, near the Plains of Abraham, and her body was put in an iron cage. The contraption was made in the shape of a human body with sections for the arms, legs, and head. The cage was displayed on a stake at Point Levis and left hanging for sometime before the remains were finally buried.[22] As elsewhere, when the English prescribed punishment in French Canada they did not shy from using the whip on women, and a number were flogged in the early years of English rule. In 1764 Elinor March, her husband, and another man were convicted of theft. She was sentenced to have her back bared, to be tied to the tail of a cart along with her husband, conducted through the streets, and whipped at various intervals for a total of fifty stripes. The same court also convicted Elizabeth Upton for theft. She was sentenced to be flogged twenty-five times in prison and then released.[23]

The use of the whip in an exceedingly cruel manner continued for many years. In 1768 Anne Lyneford was convicted of larceny in Montreal and although she pleaded for mercy she was sentenced

> to be tied to a cart's tail and conducted, naked to the waist, to Quebec Gate, where she is to receive 5 lashes, and also 5 lashes at the Old Chapelle, 5 lashes at the Chateau, 5 lashes at Landruve's corner, 10 lashes at the Market Place, 5 lashes at the corner of the Court House, and she is then to be discharged on paying her fees.[24]

The following year another woman, convicted of felony, was also stripped to the waist, tied to a cart, conducted along the identical route, and given the same number of lashes.

During the last quarter of the eighteenth century most female offenders in eastern Canada were punished with fines and incarceration. As more communities built jails they became the preferred sanctions used by the magistrates, especially for the many prostitutes, drunks, and female indigents. The spread of the humanitarian penal philosophy inclined more courts to use harsh penalties less frequently, especially against women. For example, in 1792 Mary Campbell was convicted in Montreal of petty larceny and put in the pillory for half an hour.[25] Earlier she would have been punished more severely. One of the more unusual penal practices on record for the period involved eighteen-year-old Marie Gendron. In 1795 she was charged with theft and her accuser asked that she submit herself to the "Judgement of God," to which she agreed. She was blindfolded and placed before the barrel of a loaded gun into which she blew with all her might. The theory was that if she was guilty the weapon would discharge and kill her, if she was innocent it would not fire. The gun did not go off and she was declared innocent. Her father then demanded, and was paid, £1 in compensation as a gesture to restore his daughter's honour.[26]

By the first decades of the nineteenth century the Enlightenment penal philosophy was accepted to the point that overly severe or unjust sentences, especially in the case of women, frequently raised a wave of public condemnation. In 1809 the whipping of a female offender in Montreal provoked a storm of criticism. The usual penalty by that point in time was incarceration.[27] For example, in July, 1809, the court committed Maria Nelson and Margaret Morgan to six months at hard labour in the House of Correction for "being idle, loose and disorderly women." The hard labour part of the penalty meant little since there was a scarcity of work even for the men who were so sentenced. Maria Nelson let the court know what she thought of the judgement and for her contempt a whipping was added to her punishment.[28]

Jail sentences for women were undoubtedly preferable to whippings and public humiliation, but the conditions were such that they were by no means a light punishment, especially if the incarceration was for any length of time. As we have seen, the old jails offered uniformly poor conditions and women were treated no better than men. For example, convicted females in Montreal in 1783 were put in a jail located in a converted house. Four small rooms served the prisoners and there were no provisions for segregation or even for effective separation of males and females. A report on the facility called for its replacement, claiming conditions were so bad that the suffering of the inmates was heightened, passersby in the warm season were offended by the stench, and it was a nuisance to the neighbourhood because it didn't even have provisions for waste disposal.[29]

Nevertheless, incarceration was a concrete expression of the tendency to move away from corporal punishment. Other advances also benefited women, and a number of changes specifically applied to females. For example, although many women who concealed their pregnancies escaped punishment, the penalty was severe and women could be put to death. In 1810 New Brunswick lowered the penalty for concealment to a maximum of two years' imprisonment. Lower Canada followed suit in 1812 and Nova Scotia in 1813.

The pattern of treatment of the female offender that prevailed in the older parts of the country by the turn of the eighteenth century was repeated in Upper Canada as settlement spread to that region. Women were subject to the severe penalties prescribed by law but in practice were punished by fines or short jail sentences. Even whipping was slightly ameliorated for women by an 1800 legislature provision that they could be flogged only in the presence of other females. The death penalty for females who concealed their pregnancies and killed their newborn was retained in Upper Canada for some time but those convicted were usually given a much lighter penalty. For example, Angelique Pilotte was convicted in the Niagara district court in September, 1817, of concealment and sentenced to be hanged. The twenty-year-old Indian woman was a servant who had gotten caught up in an unfortunate love affair and was left on her own to deal with her pregnancy. In addition, she was ignorant of the law and its penalties. Consequently, her conviction aroused a wave of sympathy, public protests, and petitions for mercy. As a result her punishment was remitted to one year in jail. In 1823 another woman, Mary Thompson, was convicted at York for concealing a birth and was also sentenced to be hanged. Her execution, however, was delayed and her case re-examined although not re-tried. She was given a full pardon with no penalty. In 1831 Upper Canada also adopted legislation that set the maximum penalty for concealment at two years. Prince Edward Island followed in 1836, making the penalty uniform in all provinces.[30]

The women committed to jail in Upper Canada found pretty much the same situation that their sisters in other parts of the country experienced. Although the buildings were newer they quickly deteriorated to a loathsome condition. The problem, however, was one suffered overwhelmingly by urban dwellers. In the 1830s, for example, many district jails in Upper Canada went for an entire year without a female inmate.[31] When women were jailed, the same makeshift facilities used for the incarceration of males also housed females. Practically all jails provided a separate section or cells for women, but since jails were small they were immediately adjacent to the men's quarters. Jail regulations provided no distinctions for the treatment of males and females. Women received the same food allowances, frequently bread and water, and the same bedding, and if the jail did not provide clothing then no exceptions were made for females. The only ameliorating factor would be the personal disposition of the jailor. Some were inclined to be kinder to women, who otherwise endured the same unsanitary and uncomfortable conditions that men did. Aside from the repugnant circumstances, women were not subject to a harsh regimen, as jail reports for this period suggest disciplinary punishments were infrequent.

A concession to incarcerated females that was well intentioned but turned out sometimes to be an additional burden was the practice of allowing them to take their children to jail if there was no one to care for them. The problem was that in some jurisdictions there was no provision made for the children, not even a food allowance. For example, in 1835 in Toronto, one forty-eight-year-old woman took two children to jail with her and another thirty-eight-year-old female, who was put in custody awaiting trial, took one child with her.[32] The food allowance at the time was limited to bread and water for prisoners, so officially no food allowance or anything else was provided for children.[33] In cases like this the family was totally dependent on the good will of the jail keeper, other prisoners, or outside charity.

Women not only suffered through the same miserable jail sentences as men but were also subjected to similar indignities in other ways, including when they were given the death penalty for their crimes. They were hung on the same gallows and were the focus of the same public spectacles. On December 14, 1837, a twenty-one-year-old servant by the name of Julia Murdoch was hanged in Toronto for the murder of her employer, Mrs. Harriet Henry. An estimated 4,000 people turned out for the show, including a good representation of women and children. A contingent of troops was on hand to keep the crowd from pressing too close to the scaffold.[34] Although Julia Murdoch suffered the extreme penalty for her crime she was the first woman to be hanged in Toronto. Females were rarely condemned to death.

Female crime was mostly an urban problem and, as was the case in Halifax, most of the women who ran afoul of the law were prostitutes, vagrants, petty thieves, and drunkards. They were incarcerated in many instances as much for their own protection as anybody else's. They were a nuisance to judicial officials and many believed that they would be better served in hospitals, asylums, and poorhouses, while some officials held that females should not be put in jail at all. Another concern reflected the moral standards of the day. There was fear that the mixing of females and males in the same facility, even if not in the same cells, would somehow promote immorality among the inmates.

THE REFORM IMPULSE AND THE RESULTS

As we have seen, there was considerable philosophizing and theorizing on the treatment of male criminals in the first half of the nineteenth century; female criminals, however, were almost an afterthought. Their problem was attributed primarily to dissolute living and the males who controlled the judicial process could not get exercised over the philosophy of punishing such uniformly minor offenders. Also, they were embarrassed over having to deal with women in circumstances that were so out of character and so far removed from accepted concepts of the day. Wives, mothers, and genteel females generally were not a part of the criminal world, so males found it disconcerting and awkward when they had to deal with women in this context. Consequently, many women were treated leniently by the authorities because they found it difficult to prescribe harsh penalties.

A host of male penal reformers, men like Beccaria, Howard, Bentham, and Rush, campaigned on the national and international scene, but the ranks of prominent female reformers were much thinner. The woman who attracted the most attention and wielded the greatest influence was an Englishwoman, Elizabeth Fry. Born in Norwich in 1780, she came from a wealthy background. Her father was a merchant and banker. In August, 1800, she married Joseph Fry, a London merchant, and together they brought up a large family. She was a dedicated member of the Society of Friends, or Quakers, and early developed a concern for the poor and distressed. She also showed an interest in prisoners and even as a young girl had visited the house of correction at Norwich. The most notorious prison of the day was Newgate, and as the young Elizabeth began to learn more about the place she turned her attention to helping the women incarcerated there. At the time there were about 300 women, some with children, crowded into two wards and two cells. The tried and the untried, the hardened criminals and the first offenders were thrown together. They lacked proper bedding, clothing, and sanitation facilities.[35]

Elizabeth Fry mounted a campaign to improve the treatment of women at Newgate and to reclaim them to a useful life. She soon won widespread acclaim for her work and accomplishments and became an influential voice for penal reform at home and abroad. Fry's agenda pretty much constituted the penal reform program for women in most developed countries, including Canada, through the early decades of the nineteenth century. She called for the complete separation of the sexes, classification of criminals, supervision of female inmates by women, and provision of useful employment and adequate religious and secular instruction. In Canada the limited population, the parsimony of local governments, and the small number of female offenders meant that reforms such as those advocated by Elizabeth Fry would be a long time in coming.

The new prison at Kingston presented one of the earliest opportunities to introduce more advanced measures for female offenders, especially since the original plans called for a separate prison and prison yard for females. Although it was to be located on the same general site as the male prison, it was to be a completely independent building. However, when Kingston opened in 1835 there were no facilities specifically for women. Consequently, Warden Smith was caught by surprise when three female prisoners arrived on September 4. He knew women were to be incarcerated at Kingston but did not expect them so soon after opening. Since there were no female accommodations the women were temporarily kept in the prison hospital. This inauspicious beginning was a harbinger of the way women were to be treated in prisons across the country for at least the next century. The first group of females at Kingston were so closely confined in their makeshift quarters that they could not be subjected to the regular rules and discipline until they were eventually moved out.[36]

One concession to the more advanced ideas of the day was the hiring of a woman to supervise the female prisoners. The inspectors instructed the warden to hire a matron on the grounds that "it is impossible to employ the female convicts, with any advantage to the institution under the direction of keepers."[37] One was engaged in October, 1835, and under her direction the female convicts were immediately put to work mending the prisoners' clothing and bedding. The hiring of a female supervisor was about the only acknowledgement of the presence of females and their special needs for some time. Even the Duncombe report of 1836 on the subject of prisons and penitentiaries made no specific recommendations for the treatment of female offenders.[38] Canada was not alone in its neglect of incarcerated women. The first separate prison for women in the United States did not appear until 1839 when one was opened at Sing Sing in the state of New York. The staff were female but the institution was administered by men.

During the early years of Kingston's operation, very few women were incarcerated. Their numbers fluctuated from six in 1838 to fourteen in 1845 and eight in 1847. Between September 30, 1835, and September 30, 1847, a total of 106 women were sent to the prison. Notwithstanding their small numbers, they were subjected to many of the indignities, punishments, and abuses suffered by the male prisoners. The practice of allowing visitors to come and gawk at the inmates, like animals in a zoo, was particularly humiliating for women. The prison chaplain denounced the custom and described the impact on females as "beyond measure injurious."[39] Partly as a result of his intervention visitors were stopped from touring the women's quarters in 1845. The prison chaplain was particularly sensitive to the needs of the female prisoners and in his 1845 report he advocated a raise in the status of the female superintendent to a position of equality with the warden. He argued that it would make her more effective in the decision-making process and allow her to be consulted on important decisions. He maintained that her authority should be such that she would be looked up to by the inmates and thereby "command obedience by moral influence rather than physical force."[40]

The chaplain's recommendation was ignored and the matron's position was not made equal to that of the warden, who continued to maintain overall responsibility for both male and female inmates. As a consequence, aspects of the treatment of women in Kingston suffered because of the limitation of the matron's authority. Some of the shortcomings were made public in 1849 in the report on Kingston by the Brown Commission. One of the revelations was that the entire female prison population had suffered for some years from an infestation of bugs in their quarters. The women were housed in small, makeshift, pine cells, with little ventilation, ideal breeding places for vermin, and at times the bugs were so numerous they could be swept up in piles. The female inmates were severely bitten and sometimes their blisters bled from scratching, yet the frequent requests by the matron to do something were ignored by the warden. On occasion when the situation was virtually intolerable the matron would ask permission to allow the women to sleep in the day-room under her supervision, but the warden always refused. The Commission charged him with "great neglect" in the matter and observed that he should have requested approval for the construction of new cells for the women. The female inmates were also the victims of a number of other of Warden Smith's failings. There were charges made that the warden's son was seen in the women's quarters on at least two occasions when he should not have been there. There was also a complaint made that the prison doctor was too familiar with one of his patients. Mostly, however, the problems the women encountered were similar to those of the male prisoners. There was no provision for educational instruction, no library, no chapel, and the discipline was severe in the extreme.[41]

Women who broke the rules at Kingston were flogged, put on diets of bread and water, locked in the box, or placed in solitary confinement. Whippings usually averaged six strokes of the lash but there were exceptions. For example, Mary Glennon, on February 4, 1841, was lashed eighteen times with a rawhide whip. Men were stripped to the waist but women were permitted to leave their clothes on; in addition, a cotton handkerchief was placed over the back of the neck. Females were neither whipped nor confined in the box with the same frequency as men, probably because they were not as prone to breaking rules and their keepers were less inclined to use severe punishment than were the male guards. The commissioners, as we have seen, were very critical of disciplinary practices at Kingston and in particular commented "that the practice of flogging women is utterly indefensible."[42]

Had they begun their investigation earlier they might have spared one unfortunate female considerable pain. Charlotte Reveille was an especially troublesome inmate. She was also very sickly and, according to many of the staff, suffered from bouts of insanity. For her defiance she was punished at least fifty times over a fourteen-month period. She was given six lashes on one occasion and put in the box on bread and water sixteen times. After one such session she had to be carried back to her cell because she couldn't walk. The remainder of her punishments were mostly confinement in a dark cell and a few bread-and-water days.[43] The only consideration shown to the woman came at the expiration of her sentence on February 14, 1849. In view of her bodily and mental condition the authorities "felt it their duty not to discharge her from the establishment at this inclement season."[44]

At that point in the history of Kingston Prison the women were considered mostly an inconvenience by the warden. They were literally warehoused with no thought given to rehabilitation. Even the Brown Commission devoted little space to the female offender in its recommendations. Its Report called for dismissal of the current matron, maintaining the positions of matron and assistant matron with no change in their duties or authority, and the construction of a separate building for women. The commissioners noted that a new facility would enable the women to be better occupied in a manner that would partially offset the cost of supporting them. They also expressed the belief that more gainful employment would help in maintaining discipline.[45] In spite of the Commission's recommendations there was no new construction to accommodate female prisoners. Women continued to be sent to Kingston, but in consistently small numbers. Consequently, they were destined to be housed in makeshift accommodations until well into the next century.

A similar situation prevailed in the district and local jails across the country. In most places authorities could hardly afford to build any accommodations for criminals, let alone special or separate quarters for women. Consequently, they were subjected to the same circumstances under which men were incarcerated. Even the females who ended up in detention were usually guilty of very minor offences. Therefore they were locked up for periods of time too short to make it worthwhile to mount vocational or reform programs, even if the authorities were so inclined, which they were not. For example, in the month of June, 1864, some twenty women were jailed in Halifax for periods of ten to ninety days. Over half were in for sixty days or less.[46]

The first self-contained women's prison administered and run by females in Canada was the Fullum Street Female Prison, built in Montreal in 1874-75. The building was constructed within the city limits on twelve acres of land donated by the Montreal Seminary. A religious order of women, the Community of the Good Shepherd, was put in charge of the institution. There was some initial opposition to this from the Protestant community but the matter was resolved when it was agreed that a separate section under a matron would be provided for Protestant inmates. Interestingly, just such an idea had been proposed years earlier by Dr. W. Nelson, an inspector of Kingston Penitentiary. He thought it was inappropriate to keep women in prison and that they would be better placed in a non-penal institution under the supervision of nuns.

As usual, the motivation for building the separate jail for women was not wholly a concern for their welfare. The men's jail was overcrowded so it was not possible to segregate various categories of prisoners. Also, men continually had to be moved around to other jails because of the lack of room. Both problems would be solved if the women could be removed from their quarters and the space made available for male offenders. A number of prominent persons took the lead in persuading the Quebec government to approve the new building, including the prison inspectors, city aldermen, the mayor of Montreal, and the jail chaplains, Rev. Father Huberdeau and Rev. J.D. Borthwick. The inspectors believed the complete separation of the men and women would speed up the moral reform of both. One of the most persistent advocates and the leading spokesperson for a women's prison was Charles Alexander, a legislative representative from Montreal.[47]

In the old jail, although the women were housed in a separate section, it was possible for them to communicate with the men and the arrangement made no contribution to reform. Borthwick, the Protestant chaplain, said that the situation was so bad that he "would not dare to write what obscenities and blasphemous conversations were carried on in those days."[48] The new building and the work of the nuns had a much more salutary effect on the female inmates. The religious were devoted to their work and saw it not as a means of earning a living but as being in the service of God. Therefore, they did not function merely as custodians but mixed continually with the residents as counsellors, guides, and friends. One observer noted that the nuns exercised an influence that could only be explained by their charitable nature. They emphasized moral reform and tried to improve and refine the women who came under their care. They apparently met with some degree of success, for Rev. Borthwick reported that "abandoned women, who used to be the terror of the ward, have either been sent away quite changed creatures or are still in prison, quietly and patiently obeying the rules and behaving themselves as one would wish."[49]

The second separate women's prison in Canada was the Andrew Mercer Ontario Reformatory for Females, which opened in Toronto in 1880. This reformatory was the culmination of years of lobbying by J.W. Langmuir, the Ontario prison inspector. Except for women sentenced to Kingston, all female offenders in the province were detained in common jails. While the number of females incarcerated was not increasing significantly, by the late 1880s the commitments had reached 2,000 annually, a large enough number to be cause for concern. Langmuir was particularly disturbed by the situation facing females in the common jails. The lack of proper facilities and the indiscriminate mixing of all classes of offenders made them "training schools in vice and crime."[50]

Year after year, in his annual reports, he pressed for a female reformatory. He called for the most up-to-date facilities and programs for the reformation of female offenders, and his ideas represented the advanced thinking of penologists and reformers of his day. He recommended a completely separate facility that would not be located anywhere near a male institution. Langmuir saw great moral benefits in such a separation, and, in his view, not only should the facility be separate, but all aspects of its operation, from design to discipline, should be different from men's prisons. In order to benefit from such an institution, inmates should be carefully selected, Langmuir suggested. The courts, he anticipated, would sentence only those women who could clearly benefit from incarceration in such an establishment. He wanted to create a home-like environment and a mother-daughter relationship between staff and inmates, a reformatory that would be completely staffed by women and run with humaneness, but also with discipline. In addition, he stipulated that it be located in or near a city so that the various industries he considered necessary for an effective reform program would be viable. One of the main problems with the jails was that women spent their time in idleness, which was detrimental to reform. Another advantage in the reformatory being built in a city, according to Langmuir, was that it would be easier to transport offenders from other parts of the province.[51] For some time finances were the main stumbling block to Langmuir's proposal, but this impediment was removed when a large sum of money came into the provincial coffers from the estate of Andrew Mercer of Toronto, who died in 1871 without legal heirs. The government decided to use the funds to build welfare institutions and invited Langmuir to submit proposals. He naturally seized the opportunity to make a case for a women's reformatory.

Although Mercer was opened with good intentions and great expectations, the reality fell far short of the goal as problems developed early in the life of the institution. The first superintendent, Mrs. James O'Reilly, a widow from Kingston, was a well-intentioned, compassionate women. However, her only qualifications for the job were her political connections. Her training consisted of visits to two women's prisons in the United States prior to taking up her duties at Mercer.[52] Most of the staff were equally unqualified since there was no special training or experience required for the job. Women were sent to Mercer from many different jurisdictions and from a variety of backgrounds so the great diversity made effective classification almost impossible. Also, the women were sentenced for short terms, the average period of incarceration being eight to nine months. Mercer officials argued that sentences were too short to allow any reform program to take effect since many of the women were habitual offenders whose attitude and lifestyle could hardly be changed by a short-term program. The administration supported Langmuir's recommendation that the period of detention be not less than one year and for repeat offenders the maximum sentence allowed by law.[53]

In spite of the supposed uniqueness of Mercer much of the regimen was commonplace. The program was limited in design and scope and reflected the prevailing attitudes about women's work and role in society. Women were employed at cooking, sewing, knitting, laundry, and domestic work, and the only educational opportunity was limited to a night school. All this was designed to turn them from their wayward life and prepare them for careers as wives and mothers. In keeping with this, a strong emphasis was placed on religious services and instruction. Since the staff were expected to bring out the more gentle nature of the women the discipline at Mercer was not as severe as it was in male prisons. There was no elaborate set of rules such as male and female inmates were subject to at Kingston. Mrs. O'Reilly took pride in the fact that she governed the women by her own law. Since most of the inmates could not read, she reasoned that it would be pointless to publish a set of regulations. The punishments for misbehaviour consisted of confinement in a cell on bread and water and, on rare occasions, detention in a dark cell. Even a nursery was provided so women could take their young children with them or keep their babies born in the reformatory. Authorities believed this would have a softening effect on the women and assist with their reformation.[54]

Unfortunately for all concerned, the courts failed to co-operate with Mercer's aspirations. Instead of sending only those women who might benefit from such an environment, they sentenced anyone – from first offenders to the most hardened women. Many had long histories of alcoholism and debauchery and had no interest in learning domestic skills, nor were they inclined to work. Consequently, Langmuir's great hopes were not realized. Measured by its objectives, Mercer over its first two decades had little positive impact; even the administration admitted defeat. The superintendent, in testimony before the Commission of Enquiry into the Prison and Reformatory System of Ontario in 1890, said that if she were constructing a female institution she would not adopt the Mercer model. She stated that a reformatory would be better built away from the city and along the cottage system. Cottages, she argued, would facilitate better classification, which she maintained should be based on age, character, and the nature of the offence.[55] Lucy Coad, the assistant superintendent, when asked by a commissioner if the reformatory actually reformed, replied, "No, it is simply a place of detention."[56]

The commissioners recommended that the girls' refuge be entirely separated from Mercer and that the vacated space be used to change the arrangements for the female inmates. They suggested that with more room, a perfect classification of the women would be possible and this in turn would assist with reformation. They also recommended that repeat offenders and those imprisoned for serious crimes should be given indeterminate sentences or be committed for long terms. They called for more useful work for the women so as to keep them fully employed, but failed to specify what that work might be.[57] Once again, the female offender merited slight consideration – more space in the report was devoted to the subject of drunkards than to the Mercer Reformatory for Women. The recommendations, such as they were, had little impact. In the 1890s Mercer continued to be a catch-all, mixing some elderly women charged with vagrancy, the insane, the feeble-minded, first offenders, hardened recidivists, and the children of inmates. In 1893 ten children came in with their mothers and seven were born to incarcerated women.

Throughout the latter half of the nineteenth century the treatment of female offenders continued to be influenced by economics, public attitudes, and the crime patterns of the females themselves. Older jails were being replaced and new ones were being built in developing communities, but they still left much to be desired. There were practically no work or rehabilitation programs, only rudimentary provisions for recreation and exercise, and quarters were cramped and frequently overcrowded. The mentally ill, the sick, and the aged were still to be found in jails across the country. The vast majority of incarcerated women served their time in district jails where they continued to benefit from lighter sentences and possibly more benign treatment. Their time, however, was served in circumstances that paid little attention to their special needs. They were segregated in the jails but in most other respects put up with the same conditions as the male prisoners.

Small numbers of women continued to be sent to Kingston. Officials periodically expressed their concern, for example arguing that a female prison should be completely separate from a male facility, but their entreaties were of little avail. The government persisted in keeping the female inmates in makeshift or inadequate quarters within the walls of Kingston Prison. Inspector James G. Moylan in 1889 complained that the women's quarter was "unfit for the use that was made of it."[58] Some years later he observed that the cells and other facilities provided for women were still makeshift – they were below ground, and he described them as "gloomy and dismal."[59] Ironically, the relatively low incidence of incarceration worked against the female prisoners because, in spite of repeated calls by the inspectors and officials for the construction of a separate woman's facility, governments were still not inclined to make large expenditures for such a small group.

Although little progress was evident in the treatment of female offenders, the ranks of reformers seeking improvements expanded significantly during the latter part of the nineteenth century. One of the more influential spokespersons on the international scene was an Englishwoman, Mary Carpenter. Born in 1807, she was well educated in a private school for boys run by her father. In 1835 she turned her considerable talents to the cause of educating poor children and adults and in subsequent years she operated a reformatory school and became an advocate for juvenile delinquents. Her study, *Juvenile Delinquents, Their Condition and Treatment*, published in 1852, was influential in the passage in England of the Juvenile Offenders Act in 1854. She was also an influential voice in the penal reform movement for women and her work and ideas were well known among reformers in many countries, including Canada. In 1872 Carpenter presented a paper on "Women's Work in the Reformation of Women Convicts" at the meeting of the international prison congress and she campaigned for reform in India and Europe and, in 1873, visited the United States.[60] In Canada the problem of the female offender and her treatment was taken up by church societies, by groups such as the Woman's Christian Temperance Union, and by individual reformers. Women were knowledgeable about the latest ideas and trends. They were well aware of, and influenced by, the work of people like Mary Carpenter. They participated in international penal conferences, maintained contacts with their American counterparts, and campaigned at all levels with governments for penal reform.

Not all of the ideas about female offenders circulating in the latter part of the nineteenth century worked for positive change. For example, in 1895 the famous Italian criminologist Cesare Lombroso published *The Female Delinquent*, in which he applied his theories of biology and atavism to female criminals. Earlier he had claimed to have conducted scientific observations proving that criminals had different physical and mental characteristics than the non-criminal population and that they were a throwback to an early stage of evolution, standing somewhere between the lunatic and the savage. In applying his theories to women he acknowledged that they were not as inclined to criminality as men but those who were born criminals were more perverse than their male counterparts. His views supported those who believed that a fallen woman was a lower species than a male criminal and therefore was less likely to respond to reform attempts. The ideas of Lombroso and his followers made little impression on most advocates of reforms for females in Canada and they continued to press for improvements.[61]

THE REFORM AGENDA AT THE END OF THE NINETEENTH CENTURY

By the turn of the century, reformers concerned with the treatment of women in the justice system had compiled a set of objectives that served as the focal point for the next quarter-century. The agenda was predicated on a belief that the female offender was substantially different from the male criminal in her makeup, personality, and needs. Therefore, she should be dealt with differently at all stages of the criminal justice process. Most women were tried and sentenced in police courts, and magistrates in these courts frequently dealt out swift and arbitrary justice in a sometimes raucous atmosphere. It was argued that this was especially disconcerting for women and that it took from them their last shred of self-respect and dignity. To remedy this, reformers recommended that women's cases be heard in private, apart from the general court sessions and apart from men. They also called for fairer penalties and more equitable treatment in sentencing. Women were frequently fined with the option of a jail sentence for non-payment; however, many indigent women ended up in jail because they couldn't pay the fine. Other women who committed the same or even more serious offences escaped jail because they could afford the fine. Also, sentences were inconsistent. First offenders might be sentenced to a year or more and yet receive six months on a second offence. Women were given substantially different sentences for similar crimes, sometimes by the same judges.[62]

The Inspector of Prisons for Ontario, in his 1893 report, complained about such discrepancies. He pointed out that courts in such cities as Ottawa, Kingston, Hamilton, and London were giving women sentences of up to twenty-three months for crimes that in Toronto were punished with maximum sentences of six months. He maintained that the situation was so well known that hard-core offenders, upon release, would stay in Toronto knowing that if they got caught for their next crime, the sentence would be shorter than what they would receive in their home communities. A particular sore point related to the many prostitution cases that came before the courts. Inmates of a bawdy house might be sent to jail while the keeper was given a fine and the male customers were either acquitted or let off very lightly.[63]

Another area of concern in handling women's cases was the publicity. Newspapers followed court proceedings with relish. Convicted women were sometimes held up to ridicule in the press or subjected to flippant personal comments, so critics maintained that court proceedings involving women should be less publicized. They argued that the entire experience was humiliating enough without also being held up to public ridicule. In addition, they pointed out that press coverage meant embarrassment for the women's relatives and children.[64]

Once a woman was incarcerated, reformers maintained that she should be under the exclusive care of other females. Jails housing women should have female keepers on their staff, and reformatories should have all-female administration and staff. Further, there was still a strong advocacy for separate prisons for women, completely away from any male facility. Proximity to males, it was argued, was unsettling. It interfered with good discipline and reformation.

The system favoured for women was based on what many considered a scientific approach to reformation. Institutionalization was seen as the most efficient and effective means to achieve a cure, much in the same way that the sick were put in hospitals and those with mental problems were put in asylums to be treated. To facilitate this it was argued that sentences should be reasonably long or indeterminate. Short sentences militated against reformation because the inmate was not in the institution long enough to benefit from the treatment. The core of the program was moral reformation and character development. Church services and religious instruction were considered to be the cornerstone of reform, aided by a daily institutional routine that would teach discipline, good work habits, honesty, dignified behaviour, and self-respect. All this would be abetted by the promotion of good physical health, recreational activities, and pleasant surroundings, a prerequisite for women's positive mental attitude. A related plank in the reform platform called for the establishment of prison farms for women. This would get them into the great outdoors, doing healthful and useful work that, by its nature, would be conducive to reform.

Finally, reform advocates pointed out the need for aftercare agencies. Some argued that women should be discharged only on parole and under mandatory supervision. This would afford the released prisoner ongoing help and guidance. Women, it was argued, suffered special hardships from the ostracization they were subjected to on release. In addition, their job opportunities were extremely limited, domestic service being almost the only employment open to them. Therefore, they needed help in readjusting, finding employment, and avoiding a return to their former ways. Parole supervision or prisoners' aid organizations could serve as a source of support and assistance for women trying to make a better life.[65]

The realization of all these aspirations was a long time in coming. The police courts continued with crowded dockets and speedy justice. The female drunks, prostitutes, and petty thieves that passed through them were not liable to elicit the kind of sympathy and concern that would promote individual consideration or more dignified treatment. The often hardened, rowdy, and streetwise women would be the first to reject the suggestion that they needed more genteel surroundings or special procedures. The district jails of Canada hadn't the money, staff, or facilities with which to carry on any kind of reform program. In many jurisdictions very few women passed through the jail doors, so there was little reason to be concerned about female accommodations. In the urban jails that did house significant numbers of women the sentences were too short to warrant the bother involved in recognizing any distinct needs. The female offender thus posed a special dilemma. Without longer sentences there was little point in providing the kind of surroundings and programs called for by reformers. Yet the petty offences committed by the vast majority of women did not justify more severe punishment.

Even improvements in the application of the law were of little benefit to women since so few of them were incarcerated for long periods. For example, the 1899 Ticket of Leave Act, discussed elsewhere, was a considerable advance in the treatment of criminals. The provision applied to women and although male grantees of a ticket of leave had to report to the police at regular intervals women were exempted from the requirement. But because so few females drew long sentences a significant reform in penal justice had little impact on the treatment of women.

By the early decades of the twentieth century the brightest lights in women's institutions were still the Fullum Street Prison in Montreal and the Mercer Reformatory in Toronto. The number of Protestant inmates in Fullum was small so it wasn't feasible to run a varied program. Their activities were limited to sewing and knitting, chiefly for their own needs. The much larger Roman Catholic population occupied more spacious quarters and had a greater variety of work opportunities. The women were housed in dormitories with the few single cells in the building used for disciplinary purposes. Among a variety of activities that taught them skills and kept them occupied was the operation of a successful commercial laundry. The most significant aspect of this reformatory continued to be the care and understanding given by the nuns, reflected throughout the institution in the relationship they developed with the women under their supervision and in its order, discipline, and good management.[66]

The Mercer Reformatory in Toronto, by the end of the first decade of this century, was still operating with an informal set of rules, but in the context of encouraging dignity and self-respect. Work time was limited to eight hours daily but the work was still restricted – sewing, laundry, housework, and interior painting being the chief occupations. Discipline was not unreasonable and no corporal punishment was permitted. The main sanction used for especially troublesome inmates was a short period of solitary confinement. Two cells at Mercer were used for this purpose, and these were so insulated that if a woman wanted to scream and yell to cause a disturbance she could not be heard. The bread-and-water punishment was used very rarely, partly because building up the health of the women as an aid to overall reformation was emphasized. In keeping with this trend there was also more recreation time – an hour permitted at midday and an hour in the evening in the fine weather. As long as the women behaved they were allowed to have visitors, to pursue their own interests in their spare time, and to participate in the activities of an informal club that functioned at Mercer. It was another example of the great stress placed on moral reform since the purpose of the society was to promote clean speech. The only requirement for membership was to promise not to use indecent language.

By 1908 Mercer was also providing educational opportunities for its residents. The Prisoners' Aid Association conducted classes in literacy for one hour four evenings a week. A library helped to encourage education, and religious activities were facilitated by Protestant and Catholic chapels. While all this was a considerable improvement over what women experienced in the jails of the province, never more than a handful of women were sent to Mercer. In Ontario in 1907, approximately 1,228 females passed through the various district jails, but of that number only 109 were sent to the Mercer Reformatory. They were usually the ones with the longest criminal records and the worst ingrained habits of criminality. Offenders had to be sentenced to six months or more to be sent to Mercer, a period of incarceration still too short to effect any real change in most of the prisoners.[67]

At the federal level there were some slight improvements for women sent to Kingston Prison. New quarters for females were finally constructed after ten years of complaints, and inmates occupied the new Northwest Cell Block in February, 1913. While this was progress it still fell far short of what was being advocated by reformers and prison officials, who had been campaigning for a completely separate facility for women staffed and administered by women. Even the members of the Royal Commission on Penitentiaries concurred with this thinking. In fact, they carried it a step further, suggesting in 1914 that it would be better for female offenders to remain in their home provinces and be under the jurisdiction of provincial authorities.[68]

For a time female prisoners were scattered around the country in a number of federal prisons. Women were kept at various times in British Columbia, Alberta, Saskatchewan, and Dorchester in New Brunswick. This was not done as a result of any regionalization policy, however, and was only a temporary arrangement. The last female ward was closed out at Dorchester in 1923 and the remaining inmates and two matrons were transferred to Kingston. Along with the other changes, the discipline at Kingston was less harsh than in an earlier day. Whipping was no longer permitted, although a milder form of punishment, called strapping, was not officially abolished until 1972. Recreation opportunities had also improved somewhat, with the inmates being permitted to keep a small vegetable garden and flower beds in the prison yard.

While some improvements were realized, much remained the same. Through the 1920s and 1930s women continued to be employed at and trained in a very narrow range of occupations. Table 42 illustrates the work and productivity at the women's prison in Kingston. The women made a substantial contribution to the laundry, clothing, and maintenance needs of the institutions for which they worked.

THE NEW PRISON FOR WOMEN

After a century of complaints and recommendations a major breakthrough came on January 24, 1934, when the female inmates moved into the new prison for women, which became known as P4W. However, the rejoicing was somewhat tempered by the fact that little else changed. In spite of many recommendations to the contrary, the new building was constructed adjacent to Kingston Penitentiary and the female administration and staff remained under the ultimate authority of the male warden. The bulk of the inmates' time was still spent on sewing and making clothing for prisoners. The small number of incarcerated women continued to serve as an excuse not to expand vocational and treatment programs. The new prison had accommodations for 100 but the average daily population throughout the 1930s was less than half that number.

Among the many regrettable aspects of the P4W, one of a comic nature stood out. For a facility with an average annual population for the previous seven years of forty-one and inmates that did not exactly fall into the dangerous category, the prison provided maximum security. It was surrounded by a wall sixteen feet high topped by ten feet of wire mesh fence, topped again by six strands of barbed wire. (As recently as 1921 a report prepared by W.F. Nickle on the female prison recommended that any new facility built for women not be enclosed by walls.) In case that was not enough protection, the entire exterior was illuminated with electric lights placed at 100-foot intervals. The excuse given for all this, and for the expenditure of nearly $85,000, was that there were no guard towers built into the walls. The cells for the women contained no outside windows, and as a final precautionary measure the inmates' letters were censored twice, first in their own prison and again by the censor in the men's prison. Amenities such as landscaping, trees, grass, and flowers were non-existent and no outside recreation space was provided. The new prison had no school or teachers for the inmates, and the library of about 100 volumes could be accommodated in a small bookcase. However, the internal accommodations were good and the women apparently responded well to the new surroundings, since few discipline problems were reported.[69]

PIERS ISLAND PENITENTIARY

Besides Kingston, the only federal facility housing women was located at Piers Island in British Columbia. It was under the jurisdiction of the warden of British Columbia Penitentiary and was opened in 1932 for the express purpose of housing Doukhobours who had been jailed for parading

Table 42
Work Performed by Female Convicts,
April 1, 1932 – March 31, 1933

Work	Pieces
Laundry for custodial officers' mess	4,711
Repairs to linen	255
Officers' shirts	396
Convicts' shirts	2,014
Indian Department shirts	13
Discharge clothing shirts	568
Pajama pants	1,209
Pajama coats	625
Bed sheets hemmed	557
Pillow slips	628
Towels	463
Hospital dressings	1,505 dozen
Half sleeves	710
Repairs to Union Jacks	6
Matrons' uniforms	3
Female convict uniforms	55
Female convict aprons	22
Convict clothing mended	1,520
Cell curtain	1
Female discharge clothing	18
Hooked rugs	24
Household sewing	4
Collars	94
Infants' clothing	17
Caps for Sunday service	1
	Days
Office labour	310
Lawns and garden	441
Painting and decorating	174
Laundry, matrons' uniforms	104
Cooking and cleaning	2,399
For Piers Island Penitentiary	
	Pieces
Female convict uniforms	400
Female convict drawers	400
Female convict nightgowns	400
Bed sheets	255
Pillow slips	146
For Collins Bay Penitentiary	
Convicts' gala tea shirts	125
Pajama pants	100
Pajama coats	100
Altar linen	10
Department of National Defence	
Blue jeans collars	305

SOURCE: Adapted from Annual Report of the Superintendent of
Penitentiaries, 1933.

in the nude. The Doukhobours are a religious sect that originated in Czarist Russia. They were dissenters who rejected the beliefs and jurisdiction of the Russian Orthodox Church and so were persecuted by the Church and the government. Many fled Russia in pursuit of religious freedom and at the turn of the nineteenth century a large group immigrated to Canada, where they established their own communities in the West. Their beliefs and lifestyle rejected dogma in religion and government control in society. They only acknowledged the authority of the leader of their sect. Within the Doukhobour community a group emerged, known as the Sons of Freedom, who carried individualism to the extreme and as a result of their refusal to recognize and abide by Canadian laws and customs they came into conflict with government authorities. Some 6,000 Doukhobours moved to British Columbia in 1908, hoping to find less government interference in that province. Their hopes were not totally fulfilled, however, and when they wished to express their displeasure with government attempts to make them conform, they would strip and parade nude. As their conflicts escalated, both with authorities and with less extreme members of their own communities, the militants resorted to violence. They burned down the houses of their opponents and blew up railroads. Between 1932 and 1950 over 1,200 were put in prison.

In 1932 the government passed a provision that made nude protesting punishable by three years in prison, and because of the numbers arrested a special facility had to be opened for them. In 1932 some 370 Doukhobours were incarcerated at Piers Island for three-year terms. Of that number, 278 were women. The females were housed in four dormitories in a compound surrounded by barbed wire. They ranged in age from under twenty to over seventy, with eighteen in the latter category. They were vegetarians, extremely unco-operative, and frequently they refused to do work or carry out the instructions of administrators, claiming to recognize no authority other than God. It is not surprising that the twelve matrons in charge found them difficult to supervise. With the passage of time the women became more co-operative and willing to work. They knitted mitts and socks for the male inmates and also made the dresses they would need upon release. They made repairs on the uniforms of officials and also made discharge suits for their male counterparts. Most completed their sentences by 1935 and on March 28 of that year the discharge and transfer of prisoners was completed and the prison closed. During the final year of its existence there were no punishments recorded against women at Piers Island Prison.[70]

LOCAL JAIL CONDITIONS

The vast majority of incarcerated female offenders across the country spent their terms, ranging from a few days to a few months, in district, municipal, and county lockups in conditions far different from those at Mercer and

Kingston. The jails had changed little over the years. Women were segregated and sometimes treated with more consideration, but the conditions in many were horrible. There were some whose waste facility consisted of a bucket. Cells were cramped, poorly lighted and ventilated, and vermin-infested, and the stench permeated entire buildings. Mattresses and blankets were stained and worn and in some cases the bed kits were placed on the floor. Where such amenities as toilets and basins were provided, they were frequently caked with dirt and excrement. There were no work programs and many places did not provide recreation or exercise facilities. A study of Nova Scotia jails, completed in 1933, revealed that there were jails where prisoners had to use a communal towel. In one jail the male inmates had to pass through the female quarters about six times a day on their way to meals and other activities. Women were under the jurisdiction of an all-male staff in most jails and often experienced overcrowded conditions, with no segregation among young and old, first offender and hardened criminal. All were mixed together.[71]

The Montreal Protestant Gaol for Women was described as being in "a very verminous state" in 1932. There were no training facilities and the only work available to the inmates was kitchen duty and cleaning floors. The government refused to provide anything for activities, such as art supplies or games. The matron reported that the impact of idleness on the women was demoralizing and they became apathetic and anti-social. She also revealed that women with mental problems were left as long as three months in the jail before being transferred to a mental hospital and they received no treatment while awaiting hospitalization. Upon their discharge from the mental hospital they were first returned to jail before they could be released. There was no possibility for segregation in the Montreal Gaol since there were no cells. Women were housed in a ward. There were no rehabilitation programs and few activities so the inmates simply idled away their time until they were turned back out in the streets.[72]

The jail accommodations for women were not uniformly bad and from time to time governments did attempt to improve those that were. The Archambault Commission took note of a recently built jail for women in Quebec that provided accommodation for twenty-five inmates. It was described as a clean, comfortable institution "modern in every respect." In keeping with the conventions of the day the female prisoners were employed in the laundry and doing sewing and knitting.[73] Such institutions, however, were more the exception than the rule, and cramped quarters, old buildings, and a dearth of work and recreation programs were the common lot of the female inmate.

Governments at all levels were reluctant to spend money on the judicial system. Not only were facilities across the country poorly maintained but many were understaffed, keepers' pay was low, and no training was required or provided. It was not that women were singled out for neglect but rather that they were victimized, as were males, by the general situation. Women were, however, disadvantaged when it came to the consideration that they did merit. Their small numbers constantly mitigated against their special needs ever being seriously examined. Many studies and commissions over the years investigated and made recommendations pertaining to male criminals, but not one focused exclusively on the female offender. To be sure, many commission findings and recommendations were gender neutral and would apply to women as well as men, but by and large women were a tangential consideration. Their numbers were too small to contemplate special facilities or programs at a time when little was being done for the much larger population of male criminals. Consequently, the reform program that had been clearly defined by 1900 was largely unrealized a half-century later.

Many voices still called for separate facilities for females completely away from male prisons and staffed exclusively by women. Some people contended that any form of incarceration was inappropriate, but these and other proposals continued to receive little attention. Even the Archambault Commission, in its 1938 report, hardly mentioned the female offender except to suggest that women should not be put in prison but in reformatories. Out of some eight-eight recommendations, only one dealt exclusively with women and even that simply reiterated a suggestion that had been in the air for some time. The commissioners proposed that the provinces assume responsibility for the care of all convicted females.[74]

LACK OF SPECIAL PROGRAMS

The overall neglect encountered by women was intensified by the lack of treatment programs, a problem they shared with their male counterparts. Many women who ended up incarcerated had drinking problems. Some were arrested and jailed for being drunk while others were picked up for crimes that were sometimes liquor-related, such as assault, vagrancy, and petty theft. Yet no programs were in place to treat female alcoholism. It was simply assumed that the time spent in jail or prison would dry them out and that nothing more needed to be done.

Another crime-related dependency involved drugs. Through the 1920s and 1930s a growing number of women coming in and out of jails and prisons were drug users. In at least one province, Manitoba, the problem was so serious that the Attorney-General submitted a brief on the topic to the Archambault Commission. Women with a drug habit were usually convicted for another crime, such as theft or prostitution, and then their dependency would be discovered. In Manitoba all female addicts were sent to the jail for women at Portage la Prairie. The Attorney-General's brief documented the close relationship between drug use and other crimes. He pointed out that many of these women were arrested repeatedly, given short sentences and never cured of their habit. The ultimate fate of such women, said the Attorney-General, was death. The brief called for indeterminate sentences, separate institutions for addicts, and treatment programs.[75] The Commission showed little concern for the problem, commenting that "the geographical distribution of the population of Canada renders it impossible to provide a separate institution for prisoners addicted to drugs."[76] The Report recommended the establishment of separate institutions for habitual offenders and incorrigibles so the commissioners argued that if their recommendations were implemented drug addicts could be sent to these prisons. They obviously assumed that the addicts fell into one or the other of these categories. They did not mention any treatment programs, yet they assumed that the problem would be taken care of by warehousing addicts for long periods of time in these special prisons.[77]

Up to the outbreak of the Second World War, except for improvements in facilities and food and clothing, there were few significant changes in the treatment of female criminals for almost a century. The criminal justice system arrested women, warehoused them for various periods, and then turned them loose on their own resources. There was little effort at rehabilitating or helping them, and not much was done by way of assisting women to stay out of trouble. The saving feature for Canadian society, and ironically a contributing factor to the lack of concern, was that women did not break the law in large numbers, or if they did they managed to escape being caught. Those who were caught and incarcerated found little that would help them with their troubles.

World War Two focused the attention of governments and society at large on the war effort, so jails, prisons, criminals, and penal practices were given little attention. Nevertheless, reformers still endeavoured to get improvements. One example of such sustained efforts was the work of the Junior League of Montreal. In 1944 the League held a "Delinquency Week" to heighten public awareness about the changes needed in the criminal justice system. Members culminated their activities by sending a delegation to meet with Louis St. Laurent, the Minister of Justice and future Prime Minister. They presented four briefs with proposals for improvements in the penal system and urged the implementation of the recommendations made by the Archambault Commission, but were told that a war was on and that nothing could be done until it was over.[78]

One of the few examples of progress during the war was Oakalla Prison in British Columbia. In 1942 a woman's section was opened with accommodations for forty-five inmates. The building had a well-equipped infirmary, a library, rooms without bars, and a large number of the staff were trained nurses. While there was the usual instruction in sewing and knitting, there were also special courses, singing lessons, and entertainment, including concerts.[79] In contrast, on the other side of the country, was the city jail in Saint John, New Brunswick, which in 1942 was almost a century old.

Women were housed in a corner of the men's jail, sharing one large room in which they ate and slept. Entrance was through a long, dark corridor. Food was handed through an opening in the door, to be eaten at a common table in the middle of the room. Women did not have access to outdoor exercise and there were no activities. A bathroom had been installed in 1940 but prior to that the only amenity provided in the female quarter was a wash basin. If a woman was arrested at night she was left in a holding room. It had a cement floor and a board bench, with no outside light and no bed or mattress.[80]

TREATMENT OF THE FEMALE OFFENDER SINCE WORLD WAR TWO

During the early post-war years, as Canada struggled with readjustment problems, the judicial system gradually became the beneficiary of the more humane attitude that prevailed. The growing concern for the social needs of the population carried over to the subject of the care and treatment of criminals. The increase in criminal activity also helped to focus more public attention on the crime problem in general. Much of the pre-war reform program was dusted off as criminal justice officials and reformers renewed their efforts to improve the system. They called for:

- separate facilities for women, completely apart from male institutions;
- all female administrators and staff;
- new structures that would facilitate more effective classification;
- the introduction of the cottage system;
- more and better programs for women in the areas of education, job training, and recreation;
- rehabilitation programs such as alcohol and drug treatment and better counselling services;
- less use of incarceration;
- a wider variety of sentencing options;
- the closing of Kingston Prison for Women;
- the treatment of female offenders in or near their home communities;
- prisoners' aid societies;
- the provision of aftercare services.

As the social conscience of Canadian society continued to be raised through the sixties and seventies, the penal reform program for women became better and more forcefully articulated, and the agenda expanded and refined. The process was aided by an increasing number of service agencies, more women working in the correctional system, greater concern among the public and governments generated by the increased incidence of female crime, and the women's movement. The long-standing agenda was still in place but the emphasis was shifting. More reformers were stressing the need for vocational programs and life skills training. They argued that economic need was at the base of much female crime and pointed out that many women who broke the law lived below the poverty line, were under-educated, and lacked job skills. They noted also that the economic diffi-culty of some female offenders was made worse by the fact that they were single mothers and suggested that these women needed programs to teach them the vocational skills necessary to qualify for good-paying jobs. As well, they needed life skills training in such things as budgeting, prudent purchasing of goods and services, nutrition, personal care and hygiene, communication, and parenting.

Reformers contended that since the vast majority of female offenders did not commit crimes of violence, they did not need to be incarcerated. They called for alternative sanctions, such as community service, restitution, and victim-offender reconciliation programs. Many women who served time in community jails did so simply because they couldn't pay their fines. Up to 40 per cent of women in jail in some jurisdictions were in for non-payment of fines. This situation was condemned as a grave inequity and reformers argued that impoverished offenders should either be given more time to pay their fines or else a non-monetary penalty such as community service. One of the most forceful interventions was made on the issue of geography. Reform advocates became more militant over the standing concern about the special hardships experienced by women jailed a long distance from their homes. Throughout the century it had been pointed out that women removed from contact with their children, families, and friends suffered an additional punishment. Also, it interfered with rehabilitation and made readjustment upon completion of sentence more difficult. These consider-ations by themselves, it was argued, more than justified the need for regional facilities for women and for the greater use of non-jail sentences. Among the many manifestations of problems experienced by incarcerated women were attempted suicides, mental and emotional breakdown, and a total subservience of individuality to inmate relationships. The latter included cases of women coming under the control of other inmates and developing deep emotional attachments through correspondence with male convicts they had never actually seen.

This phenomenon seems to be more of a problem for incarcerated females than male convicts and dates well back in prison history. One of the reasons that correctional officials and reformers wanted to have male and female prisoners completely separated was because of the extraordinary lengths that they went to in attempts to communicate with each other. In jails where the sexes were in close proximity the language and immoral conversations presented a problem for the keepers, who claimed that it created an atmosphere hardly conducive to reform. Moral laxity was blamed for many of their problems in the first place and jails were places to get their baser instincts under control. The communication and emotional dependency problem has always been a concern at Kingston Penitentiary, where males and females have served their time in proximity to each other. As far back as the 1880s officials discovered that letters were being smuggled between the male and female prisoners. Many intricate schemes were devised over the years to carry on the clandestine communication. For example, in the 1960s female inmates were putting messages in waterproofed cigarette packs and flushing them down the toilet. They would later be retrieved from the sewage outlets at the lake by the male prison plumbing crew.[81]

Progress in the treatment of the female offender lagged well behind the articulation of the reform agenda. The centuries-old problems of public and government attitudes, priorities, money, the nature of female crime, and small numbers of female offenders continued to be stumbling blocks to reform. In the early post-war period the attitudes toward the treatment of women remained very traditional in many quarters, with the emphasis still on rehabilitation within an institutional environment. In those places in which women were incarcerated for longer periods of time, useful work was still considered to be the healthiest sign of a good reformatory. In 1866 the annual report of the warden of Kingston Prison, while offering little other comment on the women's section, noted that the female department was particularly important. "All the shirts for the Male Convicts are made by them, as also the drawers, and indeed, all the necessary sewing for the requirements of the Institution."[82] Almost a century later, in 1950, a report on the state of the jails in British Columbia remarked, in a tone of admiration, on the work of the Mercer Reformatory in Toronto. "The Andrew Mercer Reformatory for Women has a full constructive programme of work for the inmates, consisting of sewing and making uniforms for hospitals and other Provincial Institutions, and a large laundry where the laundry work for other Provincial institutions is done."[83]

Rehabilitation programs for women were still seen primarily in the context of good discipline, orderly habits, and traditional women's work. The local jails, where the vast majority of incarcerated females continued to be housed, for the most part paid little attention to rehabilitation programs. Physical facilities in many communities across the country gradually improved but little else changed. In some instances the new accommodations for women still left much to be desired. For example, in 1974 a special female unit was opened in the provincial jail in Saint John, New Brunswick; however, the motivation was not improvement but necessity. The Coverdale facility for women had been closed at a time when more females were being incarcerated. The government did not want to incur the costs of sending women outside the province to serve their jail terms so it provided a lockup in Saint John. But the building had been constructed in 1834 so at best the new female quarters had to be makeshift. Three large cells were built with a maximum capacity of twelve beds. The extra space allotted for recreation and any other activities was a small day room, and there were no provisions for outdoor exercise or facilities for visitors. No segregation was possible so women on remand were mixed in with others who had been convicted and sentenced.[84]

Even at Kingston Prison, changes for women lagged far behind developments in the male facilities. The treatment of male convicts and the facilities provided for them have undergone major changes in the past three decades. In 1956 there were eight federal prison facilities in Canada, thirty-seven in 1969, and by 1985 there were sixty-two. In 1956 there was one federal penitentiary for women, Kingston Prison, and in 1989 there was still one federal penitentiary for women, Kingston Prison. As had been the case for over a century, criminal justice officials and reformers continued to call for its closure. In the 1970s Kingston Prison for Women was being criticized for its poor physical facilities, inadequate programs and poorly trained staff, and rampant abuses of discipline evidenced by drug usage, intimidation, and lesbianism. The inmate sub-culture seemed to have taken over the prison, with the hard-core criminal being able to exert more influence over some of the inmates than the staff. A lack of proper segregation still resulted in a general mixing of all categories of offenders.[85]

The problems and discontent with the treatment of the female offender were analysed and summarized in detail by the Royal Commission on the Status of Women, which released its report in 1970. The commissioners looked at all aspects of female involvement with the law and the judicial system. The report called for sweeping changes:

- modifications to the Criminal Code in areas that dealt with offences such as prostitution and vagrancy;
- the establishment of halfway houses and hostels for women;
- equal penalties and equal judicial treatment for men and women;
- assignment of female officers to deal with women when they are taken into custody;
- more humane and dignified treatment;
- appropriate sentences, with incarceration used as a last resort;
- the provision of more and better vocational and educational programs and counselling services;
- treatment programs for alcoholics;
- an end to discrimination on the basis of sex or religion;
- special programs and facilities designed specifically for female offenders, such as small cottage-like institutions and open living arrangements;
- better arrangements for assistance at time of release and for after-care.[86]

Small beginnings were already under way in some of these areas, and in general the recommendations became the reform agenda through the 1970s and into the 1980s.

While some of the neglect outlined by the Commission was attitudinal, part of the problem was related to the nature of female crime, numbers, money, and priorities. As we have seen, much of female crime to the present day continues to be non-violent and minor. Consequently, the majority of women sentenced to detention are jailed for short periods. In 1956 the Minister of Justice, in the face of strong pressure to close Kingston, asked each province for an opinion on the feasibility of establishing provincial centres for federal female prisoners. Most pointed out that new facilities and programs would be a problem, especially in view of the small numbers.[87] This reluctance persisted and was especially pronounced in the smaller provinces. In 1977 a task force report on the female offender in Nova Scotia and New Brunswick recommended against the establishment of a federal regional secure facility. Because of the small numbers involved, the report suggested it would be better to send the women outside the area.[88] Such a decision, of course, would perpetuate the very problem that the proposal for replacing Kingston Prison for Women with regional facilities was meant to address.

Notwithstanding the many obstacles in the way of reform, the treatment of female offenders has gradually improved. Specialized facilities for females were opened in most provinces, designed specifically for the longer-serving offenders. Among the earliest and most innovative of the new generation of female accommodations was Twin Maples Correctional Centre for Women opened in British Columbia in 1960. Located on 320 acres of rural farmland between Mission and Maple Ridge, it started as a minimum security prison farm for the treatment of alcoholics. Twin Maples expanded out of the original farmhouse and in the mid-sixties new buildings were opened, including a dormitory. The latter was constructed by a female carpentry crew from Oakalla Women's Centre, another indication of the changes taking place in the treatment and training of offenders in some institutions.

Over the years programs at Twin Maples expanded and new approaches were experimented with. A thriving farming operation evolved that included the raising of laying hens, broiler chicks, cows, and hogs. In addition to farm work, Twin Maples also offered its residents educational opportunities and training in tailoring and ceramics. In 1971 the Centre branched out and accepted inmates who did not come primarily for treatment of alcoholism. A few years later, in 1974, an inmate gave birth and was allowed to keep her baby with her at the farm. This started a practice that was unique among detention centres at the time, and in subsequent years inmates at Twin Maples were permitted to have their children under two years of age live at the farm. In 1975 an expansion of the farm program made it necessary to house male prisoners to assist with the work. A twelve-man work gang moved to the facility, thus making it a co-ed operation. In 1980 a provincially licensed day care was opened, which further expanded work and training opportunities for the residents, as well as offering a service to the local community. Rounding out the regimen at Twin Maples are life skills, self-help, religious, and recreation programs. Overall the centre has provided an open, friendly, productive, and caring experience for its inmates that appears to have worked extremely well.[89] Nevertheless, the facility has been earmarked for closure with the opening of the new prison for women in Burnaby.

The campaign for completely separate jails for women has made considerable progress. In the 1950s new facilities were opened in Montreal and Quebec City and since then in many other parts of the country. Many jails added female staff and over the years more programs have been introduced. In 1956 a narcotic treatment program for women and men was started at Oakalla in British Columbia. During the 1960s and since, many drug abuse and alcohol treatment facilities have been opened. Some are associated with reformatories, others are in community centres open to female inmates. In Ontario the Andrew Mercer Reformatory was closed in 1969 and replaced with the Vanier Centre for Women. A grand jury report on Mercer in 1964 concluded "that the rehabilitation of girls and women from the Mercer Reformatory is practically non-existent."[90] The change mirrored a new direction in penal philosophy that was taking place. As the minister responsible for the Department of Correctional Services expressed it: "There must be socialization between inmates and the community, constructive work programs, academic upgrading, and so on."[91] Gradually, programs have been introduced across the country that provide a full range of services to female offenders: personal and group counselling, educational upgrading, vocational and trades training, and life skills instruction.[92]

The entire criminal justice system has gradually become more sensitive to the special needs of women. At the time of arrest women are processed in many jurisdictions by female officers or in the presence of a female and they are provided with legal aid, paid for by the province. Before passing sentence, magistrates are given extensive background information and they now have a greater variety of sentencing options open to them. They are more liable to consider the personal circumstances of the accused and to tailor the sentence accordingly. When jailed, women are allowed more freedom and greater attention is paid to their personal needs. They are permitted an individual choice in clothing, greater privacy, and liberal recreation and visiting privileges. Much more entertainment is provided in-house, and women are allowed escorted day excursions for a variety of purposes in many communities. Better-trained and more sensitive staff are continually experimenting with innovative ways to improve the morale and assist with the rehabilitation of the inmates. Some institutions have adopted a system that calls for total interaction between staff and prisoners. The inmates are allowed to participate in decision-making and open communication is encouraged. In one county correctional centre housing both males and females an experiment was tried that flew in the face of the preoccupation with keeping the sexes apart. One afternoon a week the female inmates put on a social and were allowed to invite a number of male prisoners into the female section for coffee and a lunch. The matron wanted to create as civilized an environment as possible and she hoped that the experiment would also encourage the women to look after themselves and help them to be more at ease in social situations.[93]

Notwithstanding the ongoing criticism of Kingston Prison for Women, even that institution has witnessed substantial changes over the years. Beginning in the 1950s women were given progressively more privileges and provided with a wider range of activities and programs. Crafts and arts were introduced, women joined the staff of the prison paper, *Telescope*, a poultry house was built, and gardening activities were provided. Corporal punishment was eliminated completely, better educational opportunities were offered, including day parole for university attendance and expanded vocational course offerings. In 1985 women were permitted to wear their own clothing. Counselling and rehabilitation programs were expanded and training standards for staff were upgraded. In addition, women have benefited from the prisoners' rights movement that flourished in the 1960s and 1970s.

Much more attention has also been given to the problems faced by women upon release from jail or prison. Along with the growth in the federal parole system, with its various forms of assistance, there has been a significant increase in the number of private agencies and groups who work with female offenders. The largest organization working exclusively with female offenders is the Elizabeth Fry Society. Modelled on the work of the famous English reformer, one of the earliest branches in Canada was organized in 1939 in Vancouver. Other branches were opened in 1949 in Kingston, in 1951 in Ottawa, and in 1952 in Toronto. By the mid-1980s there were approximately seventeen branches in cities and towns across the country. The societies are volunteer organizations that work with women and girls who have come into conflict with the law. They provide services to the offender, both while incarcerated and upon release, are involved in advocacy for the improvement of conditions for the female offender, prepare briefs on legal issues pertaining to women for government, and carry on educational programs to heighten public awareness. They also provide counselling services, halfway houses, and drop-in centres to help reintegrate released prisoners into the community, as well as advice in such areas as education and employment. The Elizabeth Fry work is complemented by a host of other organizations, such as the Salvation Army, the John Howard Society, and various church and private groups that either work exclusively with females or extend their services to women. The work of these organizations includes legal aid, drug and alcohol treatment, prison visiting, provision of recreation programs for inmates, educational and vocational training, counselling, halfway houses, and aftercare.[94]

Among the more recent developments in the treatment of the female offender have been special programs for native women in conflict with the law. At the national level the Correctional Service of Canada operates a Native Liaison Program that provides counselling and assistance to incarcerated natives, both male and female. The program, with agencies in British Columbia, Alberta, Manitoba, Ontario, Quebec, and Nova Scotia, is administered mainly by native organizations and the services are also provided after release. Other programs include alternative placements for native women, friendship centres that offer a range of services, from legal advice to counselling, and addiction centres. A group called Native Sisterhood offers a special program for native women serving time in the Kingston Prison for Women. It organizes social, cultural, and spiritual activities, including crafts, sweat lodges, pow-wows, and pipe ceremonies. The work of the Sisterhood encourages native women to take pride in their culture and in themselves and helps them to develop and retain their native customs and traditions.

Another benefit that at least some women have enjoyed is preferred treatment in deference to their sex. It is referred to as the "chivalry factor." While there is no way statistically to document the phenomenon, victim surveys and interviews with police leave little doubt that it exists. Some people, when they discover that the perpetrator of a crime was a woman, will drop the charges. Police are sometimes reluctant to arrest a woman and will let her go with a warning rather than charge her. Judges are quicker to dismiss a case against a woman than a man and prosecutors are more willing to settle out of court or go with a reduced charge when a woman is involved. Sentences seem to be lighter and even female recidivists get off easier. Of course, there is no way of determining just how many offenders benefit from the above practices because the bias is more subtle than open.[95]

By the end of the 1980s the programs available to the female offender were complemented by a range of social services that, while not directly concerned with the lawbreaker, nevertheless offered benefits and programs to support women in difficulty. Many who are convicted of illegality are poor, unemployed, and already clients of one or more social agencies. Nevertheless, there are still many gaps in programs for convicted women and consequently continued pressure for reform. Critics point out that the existing system is accomplishing little. They call no more for equal treatment for women in the criminal justice system but rather for distinct treatment. They argue that women need different facilities, programs, and services than men. They dismiss the long-standing excuses of small numbers and costs, and maintain that everything from special facilities to programs should be provided regardless of the cost. Many point out that the treatment of male offenders has not resulted in any significant diminution of the crime problem so why simply extend the same treatment to women? Reformers suggest that the relatively small number of female offenders is an advantage in that experimental programs could be designed and tried on a more personal level.

The plight of native women in the correctional system is another area of growing concern to reformers. The problem has existed for some time but in more recent years is attracting greater attention. For example, in 1970-71 over 87 per cent of admissions to the Pine Grove Correctional Centre for Women in Saskatchewan were indigenous women, yet natives accounted for only 6 per cent of the provincial population. In Manitoba, where native females made up 6 per cent of the total female population, over 91 per cent of the inmates at the Women's Prison at The Pas in 1971 were native. In 1976, although native women accounted for about 2.5 per cent of the female population of Canada, they made up 21.7 per cent of the prisoners at the Kingston P4W. In 1984 over 20 per cent of females incarcerated in Alberta and British Columbia and more than 70 per cent of female prisoners in Saskatchewan, Manitoba, Yukon, and the Northwest Territories were native women. A high percentage of indigenous females that get caught up in the judicial system have alcohol or drug problems. When they are put in detention they have a particularly difficult time because, along with losing their freedom, they are also isolated from their cultural communities and frequently are far from family and friends. Within a five-month period in late 1989 and early 1990 two native women at Kingston committed suicide. Reformers have called for more study to determine the cause of the disproportionate numbers of detentions and to determine if natives are being discriminated against.[96]

One of the latest in a growing collection of studies on the female offender was commissioned by Correctional Service Canada and the report was released in April, 1990. Once again the closing of P4W was called for and a recommendation made for the construction of five regional prisons in its place. The report suggested that they be located on several acres of property and that they be designed with cottage-like facilities, each of which would house six to ten inmates. The building of a healing lodge in western Canada was proposed for native women. The task force that prepared the report also recommended that a wide variety of treatment programs be provided and that the proposed new centres be capable of housing children of the female offenders. They pointed out that treatment should be a primary concern for female inmates in light of their finding that 80 per cent of 170 women interviewed, among 203 federally sentenced women, had been physically or sexually abused at some time in their lives.[97] The initial response to the recommendation was that the task force proposals would have to be costed to determine how feasible it would be to implement them. Ole Ingstrup, Correctional Service commissioner, observed: "That is obviously a very expensive recommendation."[98]

The Report of the Task Force on Federally Sentenced Women is a wide-ranging document that will probably set the agenda for the treatment of the female offender through the 1990s. It is a thorough analysis of the needs of federally incarcerated women as well as a detailed outline of the shortcomings of the present system. The Correctional Service has indicated support for the thrust of the recommendations and has already implemented a number of them. The intention of proceeding with the establishment of the regional centres has also been announced.

At the beginning of the last decade of the century much progress has been made in the treatment of the female offender but much still remains to be done. While more long-term inmates are serving their time in provincial institutions, Kingston Prison for Women continues to operate and to house women from across the country. Even inmates serving their time in provincial reformatories can be far removed from family and friends. The jails across the country continue to be short-term holding places. Some are overcrowded, poorly staffed, and have inadequate facilities and no programs. Women are still being sent to jail for non-payment of fines. In many communities there are few or no facilities such as supervised houses in which women could serve their sentences or halfway houses to help them readjust to civilian life. Another ongoing problem is the lack of consistency. Women are still treated differently in various jurisdictions and there is no uniformity in sentencing practices, incarceration facilities, programs, or aftercare across Canada.

One of the worst shortcomings in the entire criminal justice system continues to be the lack of prevention programs. No headway is being made in reducing female crime in such areas as shoplifting, petty theft, and substance abuse, which are main categories of offences for women. Although progressively more attention in recent years has been focused on convicted females, especially those who end up incarcerated, little emphasis has been placed on reducing the incidence of crime. To date not much has been achieved by way of either prevention or reformation and the prospects for any change in the short term are not promising.

SUMMARY

The treatment of the female offender throughout our history has been characterized by a good deal of ambivalence, uncertainty, and a lack of uniformity. A male-dominated correctional system, in light of prevailing attitudes toward women, found it awkward to treat females as criminals. Yet in the eyes of many they deserved even harsher punishment for their crimes than men because they had betrayed their sex and violated a sacred trust. Consequently, some women felt the full wrath of the law while others escaped altogether or were punished very lightly. Much depended on the outlook of the magistrate or official making the decision. Those who were incarcerated shared the same inadequate accommodations and odious conditions as their male counterparts. They occupied makeshift quarters in facilities designed for male criminals. Always their small numbers and short sentences made governments at all levels reluctant to spend money on special facilities and programs for women. The problem goes back to pioneer days. Only in the past few decades have any significant improvements been realized, and even now there are many deficiencies.

There was a long-standing belief that females were not criminal by nature and that when they did break the law it was due more to a moral failing or character defect than anything else. Since the vast majority of females who passed through the jails in earlier years were drunks, prostitutes, or "loose women," this view seemed to have considerable credibility. Therefore, many were convinced that the way to reclaim these fallen women was to put them in an ordered, disciplined environment for a period of time, give them religious education, remove the rough edge by restoring their femininity, teach them to cook, sew, and clean, and instil good work habits. This rehabilitative formula was seldom tested because the circumstances in which most women were incarcerated offered little chance to implement such a program.

By the late nineteenth century, reformers were applying environmental explanations to poverty and distress and early into the twentieth century such theories became paramount. Reformers saw the remedy for social problems in slum clearance programs, employment, and the stabilization of family life among the lower classes. The latter was to be achieved by encouraging habits of sobriety, honesty, thrift, hard work, and self-discipline. A stable and caring family was considered the best remedy for social distress as well as the surest guarantee of an orderly society. These principles were applied to the treatment of the female offender and in large measure resulted in a continuation of the ideal that had existed for some time. The difference was that there were a few more institutions in which the agenda at least might be tried. An orderly structured environment was still considered the key to the development of desired character traits. A combination of appropriate example, enforcement of rules and regulations, and religious instruction would promote the objective. An important corollary to all of this continued to be instruction in domestic skills such as sewing, housekeeping, cooking, and laundering. The ultimate aim was to restore the woman to her appropriate role in society, that of a good wife and mother.

What is important to understand is that in the context of the times this philosophy did not represent the neglect of women or a conspiracy to put them down. Rather, this resolution was consistent with the approach of female reformers and women's organizations to a range of social problems. The family was a central concern and the mother was the cornerstone of the family unit. Preservation of the moral and social influence of the home was the main objective and the campaign hinged on the central role of the mother as the homemaker. Consequently, the cultivation of domestic skills made sense in two ways. It prepared the inmate to be a more self-confident and effective homemaker and it taught skills for one of the major employments of women, domestic service. Judged by today's standards this was inadequate, but for that time it made economic sense and was compatible with the prevailing value system. The treatment of women in well-run penal institutions was a microcosm of the approach to social problems that prevailed in society at large.

Some have sought to explain the historical neglect of the female criminal as being due to a lack of concern for, or even a tendency to write off or abandon, such lawbreakers. There is little evidence to support the contention that women have been discriminated against because society held little regard or hope for the fallen woman. In fact, those closest to the female offender, the jail and prison officials, have been the most vociferous in calling for less use of detention, better facilities, and reforms of all kinds. Among generations of middle- and upper-class female reform advocates the same holds true. If the fallen woman was to be abandoned, surely it would be her more proper and prosperous sisters who would be the first to shut the door. Yet from the ranks of such women came the reform advocates who lobbied governments and carried on public awareness campaigns. From the pockets of the "proper elements in society" the money has come to support the work of the Elizabeth Fry Societies, the churches, the Junior Leagues, and other such organizations. The hindrance to change came more often than not from a government strapped for funds and directing what was available to those projects that would return the largest number of votes.

At the jail level, the problems to be found were visited on both male and female convicts for pretty much the same reasons. However, within a very unsatisfactory system there are innumerable examples of special care and consideration being extended to women. Time and again keepers expressed their opinion that women should not be put in jail, and many lobbied for female staff. Women in some jurisdictions were given special privileges, disciplined more leniently, and provided with slightly better accommodations. Police frequently arrested street women more to protect than punish them. In jail there were practically no programs for women and this has been attributed to the fact that women generally commit minor crimes and therefore are given short sentences. Consequently, they are not incarcerated long enough to warrant the introduction of rehabilitation programs. Critics have attacked such arguments as mere rationalization and have cited the situation as another example of the dismissal and neglect of the female offender. However, rather than a mere excuse for inaction, this is in fact a genuine problem and always has been.

Rehabilitation, education, and vocation programs are only effective over time. Participation for a few weeks or months, as has long since been shown, accomplishes very little. In recognition of this, institutional officials, going back to the nineteenth century, have called for indeterminate sentences that would require inmates to remain incarcerated long enough for rehabilitation programs to have some chance for success. Indeterminate sentencing would also serve as a rationale for the introduction of a greater variety of programs. Once again, however, the minor nature of female crime could never justify the widespread use of indeterminate sentences and so the dilemma remained.

In spite of the good intentions being expressed recently the problem will still not be easy to resolve. Even at the federal level, although the numbers are small, female inmates are far from homogeneous. They differ in educational levels, talent, character, background, and personality. Also, along with those who have committed non-violent crimes are women who have tortured children and committed armed robbery, violent assaults, and murder. There are tough, street-wise, unprincipled females, and some disturbed psychopaths, among the female prison population. To establish satisfactory accommodations and treatment programs for such diverse needs will be difficult.

Finally, the problem of the female offender is not merely an issue of how to treat those women who end up in prison. An even more important consideration is how to persuade the vastly larger population of less serious offenders to desist and how to discourage young people from becoming adult criminals. At present much of the concern is devoted to a very small number of female offenders who end up in prison. Without neglecting that segment, much more time, effort, study, and money need to be put into preventative programs. The reality is that we have had very little success in over three centuries in persuading females who break the law to reform. Yet we have, over the same period, substantially neglected programs that might help to prevent the problem in the first place.

EPILOGUE

Since the early days of settlement men and women, boys and girls, people in all walks of life, from the social outcasts of seaport slums to the highest officials in government, have committed crimes. Murder, rape, assault, burglary, treason, smuggling, fraud, duels, theft, and a host of other offences were common fare throughout colonial history. Friends assaulted and murdered each other at neighbourhood work bees, gentlemen fought duels, and an entire underclass of chronic offenders who frequented the taverns and brothels of seaports and larger towns stole, fought, and prostituted. A high percentage of this illegal activity was lubricated with generous amounts of liquor.

Men broke the law much more frequently than women, and urban dwellers were more crime-prone than their rural counterparts. The alcoholics, the poor, the idle, the prostitutes, and the slum dwellers disproportionately found their way into the criminal records while the middle- and upper-class lawbreakers, the white-collar criminals, and the juvenile delinquents from the "better homes" were shielded from the law through position, influence, and status.

To control crime in the colonies the early settlers were provided with the legal codes and judicial apparatus that prevailed in the mother countries. They also inherited a set of harsh and cruel penalties that prescribed hanging for some 200 offences and that included branding, whipping, and time in the stocks. Fortunately, for many felons in pioneer days the severe punishments were mitigated by lenient officials and courts, incompetent and unqualified magistrates, friends failing to testify, juries unwilling to convict, and if all else failed, the plea of benefit of clergy.

Concern over crime motivated many communities to build jails. At first they were meant to be temporary holding places, but with the passage of time they evolved into a punishment option as the reluctance to hand down the more severe penalties became more pronounced. The influence of the Enlightenment reformers and changing attitudes eventually brought about a shift to using incarceration and fines as preferred sanctions over corporal punishment. Jails proliferated and in many communities became handy social welfare institutions to house the sick, indigent, aged, and insane. Not only did the jails become catch-alls for society's social problems, they also quickly deteriorated to run-down, vermin-infested, stench-ridden blots on community landscapes.

The lack of segregation, the growth in crime, and the rates of recidivism were all causes of concern, and a groundswell of criticism was levelled at the jails as schools of crime and at the failure of the more benign treatment of criminals to have any positive effect. Some called for a return to harsher treatment, others argued for better-appointed facilities that would allow for a more disciplined regimen. The latter talked of institutionalizing criminals much in the way sick people would be put in a hospital for treatment. They proposed an ordered, scientific approach to replace the haphazard system that was failing in so many ways.

Reflecting a variety of considerations, Upper Canadian officials opened Kingston Prison as a gesture to the new penology and as a hoped-for remedy to some long-standing problems. The aspirations of the supporters of Kingston were never realized and the new institution simply became another part of the malaise. The discipline that was supposed to put order into disordered lives, the work that was meant to break idle habits, and the religious education that would help offenders see the error of their ways either floundered at the start or laid the foundation for a custodial emphasis that undermined any possibility of a positive influence. Generally, harsh punishments, reform philosophies, new institutions, and scientific methods failed to reduce crime or to reform criminals. The saving features for most communities during the pre-Confederation period were that crime levels were apparently low and the bulk of offences were minor in nature. The actual incidence of crime in an earlier day is difficult to gauge because of a lack of policing, an inefficient judicial system, and poor reporting. As is the case today, there was probably much more crime than ever got recorded but not so much or of a nature that the average citizen needed to worry about his or her personal security or worldly goods.

Whatever the actual level of crime, the recorded lawbreaking continued to go up and the nature of offences expanded with national developments – Confederation, population increase, railroad-building, business expansion, and the growth of industries. Throughout the first half of the nineteenth century, reformers devised a comprehensive program of rehabilitation that included advocacy for paid, useful prison work, the indeterminate sentence, remission and leave, education and vocational training, better facilities, more humane treatment, and aftercare.

Although many correctional officials supported the reform agenda the system remained bogged in government neglect, public apathy, underfunding, untrained staff, a lack of consensus on treatment strategies, and the dominance of a custodial mentality inside the prisons. Some progress was made toward more humane treatment and fewer punishments, and governments in various jurisdictions undertook studies and made recommendations. However, these positive signs bore few results either inside jails and prisons or outside. Crime rates rose, offenders repeated in large numbers, and people incarcerated in the country's penitentiaries rioted.

The post-World War Two period ushered in an era of change. An outpouring of new construction, innovative treatment programs, government studies and investigations, trained staff, new laws, aftercare agencies, changing philosophies and objectives virtually inundated the judicial system. That trend continues to this day. Practically every measure the early reformers ever dreamed of has been put in place. To date, however, the results have been very disappointing. The 1960s and 1970s witnessed an unprecedented increase in crime that has overburdened the justice system almost to the point of inertia. Police cannot effectively cope with criminals, courts are hard-pressed to keep up with cases, jails and prisons are overcrowded, and the latter still have poor rehabilitation records.

Lawbreaking remains at unprecedented levels, still fuelled as in the past with liquor and the modern substance of choice, drugs. The latter is now a factor in a high percentage of street crime in larger urban centres and is a presence in everything from partner abuse to murder. Also, in recent decades there has been a trend toward more violent offences, increased organized crime activity, more white-collar lawbreaking, and increasingly sophisticated and serious endeavours on the part of the young.

The failure of the new programs and theories about crime and its treatment is itself empirical evidence that their underlying assumptions need to be re-examined. A long-standing dicohotomy has existed between theorists who weaved solutions that called for environmental engineering, innovative treatment strategies, or changing the political and economic system and others on the front line of corrections. Among the latter there has been an oft-stated belief, dating back to pioneer days, that the likelihood of being caught and the certainty of being punished are the most effective deterrents to crime. Samuel Lawrence Bedson, the first warden of Manitoba Penitentiary in 1876, observed that "knowing that the swiftness and certainty of the punishment of crime, and not the severity of it, is the strongest deterrent."[1] In 1938 the Archambault Commission concluded "that the fear of being swiftly caught and surely punished has prevented and will prevent, the commission of crime by those who would be, or are tempted to become criminals."[2] In 1965 the report on *Juvenile Delinquency in Canada* stated that "Most law enforcement officers hold the belief – shared by many criminologists – that sure detection, swift prosecution and a rational disposition by the court are still the best deterrents to unlawful behaviour."[3]

There has also been substantial disagreement among reformers over the years as to the best methods of dealing with crime and criminals. At one point the dominant belief held that education in religion and character development was the key to rehabilitation. That gave way to an emphasis on education and vocational training programs. Eventually, psychological counselling and behaviour modification programs became the preferred approach. The solution now being pressed is rehabilitation within a community setting and a concomitant trend to use a prison sentence as a last resort, and even then to get inmates out as fast as possible. In the midst of all this are the new mission statements, the law amendments, and ongoing experimentation.

Modern treatment strategies have been based on a number of assumptions, including the following:

- Rehabilitation can be achieved in a prison environment.
- Fixed sentences are compatible with the objective of reform.
- The majority of people in prison are reformable.
- Rehabilitation is possible within a group setting.
- Inmates are basically good people who will respond to decent treatment.
- Criminals are victims of circumstances beyond their control.
- Early release is an effective rehabilitative tool.
- It is better to keep offenders out of jails and prisons than to put them in.

Most of these assumptions have been and still are subjects of debate both inside and outside the criminal justice system.

Regardless of the similarities and differences among criminal justice personnel, advisers, consultants, researchers, theorists, and the general public, the bulk of attention has consistently focused on the individual after a crime has been committed. Prevention programs have been largely neglected throughout our history. Another common denominator that has characterized the approach to crime and criminals for most of this century is that environmental causes and solutions have been pursued almost to the exclusion of considerations such as values, attitudes, and character.

The complex nature of crime suggests that there is no one cause and no monolithic solution. The increased knowledge about white-collar crime, gangs such as the Mafia, revelations of victim surveys and self-reporting studies all challenge some long-standing assumptions about the nature of crime and criminals and appropriate treatment programs. It is even possible that there is no solution to the problem and that the most that can be accomplished is to keep lawbreaking within tolerable boundaries. In any event, the results of contemporary strategies, theories, and programs suggest that some long-standing assumptions need to be reconsidered.

NOTES

1.   CRIME IN PIONEER CANADA

1. Catharine Parr Traill, *The Canadian Settler's Guide* (Toronto: McClelland and Stewart, reprint, 1969), p. 44.
2. Marcel Trudel, *The Beginnings of New France 1524-1663*, trans. Patricia Claxton (Toronto: McClelland and Stewart, 1973), pp. 47-50.
3. *Ibid.*, pp. 63-64.
4. H.P. Biggar, ed., *The Works of Samuel de Champlain* (Toronto: University of Toronto Press, reprint, 1971), vol. 2, pp. 25-34.
5. Quoted in William Bennett Munro, *Crusaders of New France* (New Haven: Yale University Press, 1918), p. 162.
6. Quoted in Dale Miquelon, *New France 1701-1744* (Toronto: McClelland and Stewart, 1987), p. 154.
7. Quoted in A. Leblond De Brumath, *Bishop Laval* (Toronto: Morang & Co., 1910), p. 36.
8. *Ibid.*, p. 37.
9. See, for example, *ibid.*, *passim.*
10. *Ibid.*, p. 113.
11. Richard C. Harris, *The Seigneurial System in Early Canada* (Québec: Les Presses de l'Université Laval, 1966), p. 163; De Brumath, *Bishop Laval*, p. 36; P.F.X. De Charlevoix, *History and General Description of New France*, trans. J.G. Shea (Chicago: Loyola University Press, 1962), vol. 2, p. 242.
12. Munro, *Crusaders of New France*, p. 162.
13. Adam Shortt and Arthur G. Doughty, eds., *Canada and Its Provinces* (Toronto: Glasgow, Brook & Company, 1914), vol. 2, *New France*, pp. 472-73.
14. Munro, *Crusaders of New France*, pp. 167-71.
15. Raymond Boyer, *Les Crimes et Les Châtiments Au Canada Français Du XVIIᵉ Au XXᵉ Siècle* (Montréal: Le Cercle Du Livre De France, 1966), p. 88.
16. André Vachon, ed., *Taking Root: Canada From 1700 to 1760* (Ottawa: Public Archives of Canada, 1985), p. 47.
17. *Ibid.*, p. 100.
18. De Brumath, *Bishop Laval*, p. 113.
19. Vachon, *Taking Root*, pp. 47, 59.
20. *Ibid.*, pp. 13, 237.

21. Jean Bruchési, *A History of Canada*, trans. R.W.W. Robertson (Toronto: Clarke, Irwin, Co., 1950), p. 97.

22. André Lachance, "La Criminalité à Québec Sous Le Régime Français Étude Statistique," *Revue d'Histoire de l'Amérique Français*, 20 (December, 1966), pp. 410-13.

23. André Lachance, "Women and Crime in Canada in the Early Eighteenth Century, 1712-1759," in Louis A. Knafla, ed., *Crime and Criminal Justice in Europe and Canada* (Waterloo: Wilfrid Laurier University Press, 1981), pp. 158, 171; André Morel, "Réflexions Sur La Justice Criminelle Canadienne, Au 18ᵉ Siècle," *Revue d'Histoire de l'Amérique Français*, 29 (September, 1975), p. 244.

24. Harris, *The Seigneurial System in Early Canada*, p. 167.

25. Letter of Bishop of Quebec, October 4, 1725, in S.D. Clark, *The Social Development of Canada* (Toronto: University of Toronto Press, 1942), p. 61.

26. Letter from Governor General de Beauharnois and Hocquart to the Minister, October 15, 1730, in Vachon, *Taking Root*, p. 115.

27. Letter of Beauharnois and Hocquart to the Minister, October 15, 1730, in Clark, *The Social Development of Canada*, p. 61.

28. Thomas Chapais, *The Great Intendant* (Toronto: Glasgow, Brook & Company, 1914), p. 105.

29. For an historical examination of duels in pioneer Canada, see Aegiduis Fauteux, *Le Duel Au Canada*, Collection du Zodiaque, no. 35 (Montréal: Deom, 1934).

30. Archibald M. MacMechan, ed., *Original Minutes of His Majesty's Council at Annapolis Royal 1720-1739* (Halifax: McAlpine Publishing Co., 1908), *passim*; Charles Bruce Ferguson, ed., *Minutes of His Majesty's Council at Annapolis Royal 1736-1749* (Halifax: Public Archives of Nova Scotia, 1967), *passim*.

31. MacMechan, *Original Minutes of His Majesty's Council*, p. 302.

32. R.E. Kroll, "Confines, Wards and Dungeons," *Nova Scotia Historical Society Collections* (Kentville: Kentville Publishing Co., 1980), vol. 40, pp. 93-94; Thomas H. Raddall, *Halifax: Warden of the North* (Toronto: McClelland and Stewart, 1984), p. 32.

33. Raddall, *Halifax: Warden of the North*, *passim*.

34. T.B. Akins, *History of Halifax City* (Belleville, Ontario: Mika Publishing, reprint, 1973), p. 160.

35. *Ibid*., p. 81. The impressment of fishermen was illegal unless done through due process of law, which was a complicated procedure. The legal requirement was ultimately extended as a preliminary requisite to all impressment on land. For a brief discussion on impressment, see G.A. Rawlyk, ed., *Historical Essays on the Atlantic Provinces* (Toronto: McClelland and Stewart, 1967), pp. 7-16.

36. H.F. Pullen, "The Attempted Mutiny Onboard H.M. Sloop Colum-

bine on 1 August 1809," *Nova Scotia Historical Quarterly*, 8 (December, 1978), p. 310.

37. Akins, *History of Halifax City*, p. 138.

38. *Ibid.*, p. 127.

39. Cornwallis to Lords of Trade, July 24, 1749, RG 1, vol. 35, no. 2, Public Archives of Nova Scotia (hereafter PANS).

40. Raddall, *Halifax: Warden of the North*, pp. 101-05. For a description of the temper and manners of the gentry of the period, see R.E. Kroll, *Intimate Fragments, An Irreverent Chronicle of Early Halifax* (Halifax: Nimbus Publishing, 1985). The work is historical fiction but the events, people, and conditions described are based on extensive archival research and, according to the author, the description is factually accurate.

41. *Acadian Recorder*, 24 July 1819, p. 3.

42. Clark, *Social Development of Canada*, pp. 148-49.

43. Beamish Murdoch, *A History of Nova Scotia* (Halifax: James Barnes, 1867), vol. 3, p. 41.

44. *Nova Scotia Royal Gazette*, 10 October 1809, p. 3; Akins, *History of Halifax City*, pp. 144-45.

45. James Bowes, ed., *Trial of Jones, Hazelton, Anderson and Trevaskiss, alias Johnson for Piracy and Murder On Board Barque Saladin* (Halifax: Petheric Press, reprint, 1967).

46. Clark, *Social Development of Canada*, pp. 124-25.

47. *Ibid.*, p. 160.

48. Halifax City Annual Report, 1858, p. 18, PANS.

49. Report of Committee of City Prison, October 1, 1861, to October 25, 1862, p. 42, PANS.

50. Rainer Baehre, "Pauper Emigration to Upper Canada in the 1830s," *Social History*, XIV (November, 1981), pp. 339-67.

51. M.T. Campbell, *A Century of Crime* (Toronto: McClelland and Stewart, 1970), p. 2.

52. E.C. Kyte, ed., *Old Toronto* (Toronto: Macmillan of Canada, 1972), p. 169.

53. John K. Elliott, "Crime and Punishment in Early Upper Canada," Ontario Historical Society, *Papers and Records*, 27 (1931), p. 2.

54. C.K. Talbot, *Justice in Early Ontario 1791-1840* (Ottawa: Crimcare, 1983), pp. 145-53.

55. Warden's Report, Provincial Penitentiary, Province of Canada Sessional Papers, 25 to 58, vol. XVII, no. 4, 1860.

56. Annual Report of the Warden of the Provincial Penitentiary for 1864 (Quebec: Hunter Rose & Co., 1865), p. 11.

57. Michael D. Whittingham, "Criminality and Correctional Reformism in Ontario 1831-1954" (Ph.D. thesis, York University, 1988), p. 90.

58. Edith G. Firth, ed., *The Town of York 1793-1815* (Toronto: University

of Toronto Press, 1962); W.R. Riddell, *Old Province Tales Upper Canada* (Toronto: Glasgow, Brook & Co., 1920), pp. 96-116.

59. Paul Craven, "Law and Ideology: The Toronto Police Court 1850-80," in David H. Flaherty, ed., *Essays in the History of Canadian Law* (Toronto: The Osgoode Society and the University of Toronto Press, 1983), vol. 2, p. 263.

60. J. Douglas Borthwick, *A History of the Montreal Prison From A.D. 1784 to A.D. 1886* (Montreal: A. Periard, 1886), p. 268.

61. Donald Smith, "The Mississauga and David Ramsay," *The Beaver*, 306 (Spring, 1975), pp. 4-8.

62. John Hale, ed., *Settlers* (London: Faber & Faber, 1950), p. 23.

63. *Ibid.*, pp. 33-34.

64. Murdoch, *History of Nova Scotia* (1865), vol. 1, pp. 73-80.

65. Biggar, *The Works of Samuel de Champlain*, p. 63.

66. Paul Surette *et al.*, *Memramkouke, Petcoudiac et La Reconstruction de L'Acadie* (Memramcook: la Société historique de la vallée de Memramcook, 1981), pp. 43-48.

67. Murdoch, *History of Nova Scotia*, vol. 1, pp. 584-86.

68. Raddall, *Halifax: Warden of the North*, p. 71.

69. W.R. Riddell, "Criminal Law in Upper Canada a Century Ago," *Journal of the American Institute of Criminal Law and Criminology*, 10 (1920), p. 529.

70. For a detailed account of the rebellion, see Joseph Schull, *Rebellion: The Rising in French Canada 1837* (Toronto: Macmillan of Canada, 1971).

71. See Colin Read and Ronald J. Stagg, eds., *The Rebellion of 1837 in Upper Canada. A Collection of Documents* (Toronto: The Champlain Society, 1985).

72. Bruce Wilson, "The Struggle for Wealth and Power at Fort Niagara 1775-1783," *Ontario History*, LXVII (September, 1976), pp. 137-53.

73. N. Bosworth, *Hochelaga Depicta: The Early History and Present State of the City and Island of Montreal* (Toronto: Coles, reprint, 1974), p. 234.

74. A.R. Hassard, *Famous Canadian Trials* (Toronto: Carswell, 1924), pp. 194-219.

75. Martin Robin, *The Bad and the Lonely* (Toronto: James Lorimer, 1976), p. 98; also see Orlo Miller, *The Donnellys Must Die* (Toronto: Macmillan of Canada, 1962), pp. IX-61.

76. Robin, *The Bad and the Lonely*; Miller, *The Donnellys Must Die*.

77. Paul Romney, "The Ordeal of William Higgins," *Ontario History*, 67 (1975), pp. 74-75.

78. Report of the Commissioners appointed to investigate certain proceedings at Toronto, connected with the Election for that City, August 3, 1841, *Journals of the Legislative Assembly of Canada*, Appendix 1,

Vol. 1, 1841, appendix S.; Bruce West, *Toronto* (Toronto: Doubleday Canada, 1967), pp. 143-45.

79. Dean Jobb, "Cases From the Past," *Halifax Mail-Star*, 7 January 1989, pp. 4N-5N.

80. S.W. See, "The Orange Order and Social Violence in Mid-Nineteenth Century Saint John," in P.M. Toner, ed., *New Ireland Remembered* (Fredericton: New Ireland Press, 1988), pp. 71-89. Also see Cecil J. Houston and William J. Smyth, *The Sash Canada Wore: A Historical Geography of the Orange Order in Canada* (Toronto: University of Toronto Press, 1980); and Gregory S. Kealey, "The Orange Order in Toronto: Religious Riot and the Working Class," in G.S. Kealey and Peter Warrian, eds., *Essays in Canadian Working Class History* (Toronto: McClelland and Stewart, 1979), pp. 13-34.

81. Kathleen Jenkins, *Montreal* (New York: Doubleday, 1966), pp. 328-29.

82. Michael S. Cross, "'The Laws Are Like Cobwebs': Popular Resistance to Authority in Mid-Nineteenth Century British North America," in P. Waite, S. Oxner, and T. Barnes, eds., *Law in a Colonial Society: The Nova Scotia Experience* (Toronto: Carswell, 1984), p. 103.

83. Jenkins, *Montreal*, pp. 349-50.

84. "The Gold Rush Society of British Columbia and the Yukon," in S.D. Clark, *The Developing Canadian Community* (Toronto: University of Toronto Press, 1962), pp. 81-98.

85. Quoted in Clark, *The Social Development of Canada*, p. 341; also see "Crime and the Moral Order," pp. 335-44.

86. Clark, *The Developing Canadian Community*, p. 94.

87. Province of Nova Scotia, *Report on the Mines 1927* (Halifax: Department of Public Works & Mines, 1928), part II, p. 729.

88. John Hartlen, *Gold* (Hantsport, N.S.: Lancelot Press, 1988), pp. 52-53.

89. Michael S. Cross, "The Shiners' War: Social Violence in the Ottawa Valley in the 1830s," *Canadian Historical Review*, 54 (March, 1973), p. 3.

90. *Brockville Recorder*, October 23, 1835, in Talbot, *Justice in Early Ontario 1791-1840*, p. 165.

91. Cross, "The Shiners' War," pp. 15-23.

92. Denonville to the Minister, September 13, 1865, in Clark, *The Social Development of Canada*, p. 60.

93. *Ibid.*

94. Letter of Bishop of Quebec, October 4, 1725, *ibid.*, p. 61.

95. *Ibid.*, p. 228.

96. Quoted in W.J. Eccles, *Canadian Society During the French Regime* (Montreal: Harvard House, 1968), p. 63.

97. *Ibid.*

98. Akins, *History of Halifax City*, pp. 16-17, 221; Raddall, *Halifax: Warden of the North*, pp. 37-38, 65, 83.
99. Raddall, *Halifax: Warden of the North*, pp. 52-53.
100. Quoted in Clark, *The Social Development of Canada*, p. 144.
101. Harold A. Innis, ed., *The Diary of Simeon Perkins 1766-1780* (Toronto: The Champlain Society, reprint, 1948), p. 29.
102. Clark, *The Social Development of Canada*, p. 149.
103. Quoted in M.A. Garland and J.J. Talman, "Pioneer Drinking Habits and the Rise of the Temperance Agitation in Upper Canada Prior to 1840," *Ontario Historical Society Papers and Records*, XXVIII (1931), p. 345.
104. For a good account of work bees and the liquor problem, see Edwin C. Guillet, *Early Life in Upper Canada* (Toronto: University of Toronto Press, 1967), pp. 273-94.
105. Garland and Talman, "Pioneer Drinking Habits," p. 342.
106. Talbot, *Justice in Early Ontario 1791-1840*, p. 162.
107. Garland and Talman, "Pioneer Drinking Habits," pp. 341-42.
108. Quoted in J. Jerald Bellomo, "Upper Canadian Attitudes Towards Crime and Punishment (1832-1851)," *Ontario History*, 64 (1972), p. 14.
109. *Ibid.*
110. *Ibid.*
111. *Ibid.*
112. Helen Boritch and John Hagan, "Crime and the Changing Forms of Class Control: Policing Public Order in 'Toronto the Good,' 1859-1955," *Social Forces*, 66 (December, 1978), p. 322.
113. Elliott, "Crime and Punishment in Early Upper Canada," p. 7.
114. M.T. Campbell, *A Century of Crime* (Toronto: McClelland and Stewart, 1970), p. 3.

2. CRIME SINCE CONFEDERATION

1. Journaux de Assemblée Legislative de la province de Québec, vol. I, 1867-1868, appendice No. 10, 1868.
2. L'assemblée Legislative de la province de Québec, Documents De La Session 1 à 31, vol. II, 1877-1878, p. 21.
3. Pierre Berton, *The National Dream/The Last Spike* (Toronto: McClelland and Stewart, 1974), p. 301.
4. *Ibid.*, p. 177.
5. *Ibid.*, pp. 177-78.
6. *Ibid.*, pp. 278-82.
7. T. Thorner and N. Watson, "Patterns of Prairie Crime: Calgary, 1875-1939," in Louis A. Knafla, ed., *Crime and Criminal Justice in Europe and Canada* (Waterloo, Ont.: Wilfrid Laurier University Press, 1981), pp. 220-21.
8. James G. MacGregor, *A History of Alberta* (Edmonton, 1972), pp.

93-96; Paul F. Sharp, *Whoop-up Country* (Norman: University of Oklahoma Press, 1973), pp. 48-106.

9. *Settlers and Rebels*, Official Reports, Royal North-West Mounted Police, 1882-1885 (Toronto: Coles, reprint, 1973), Report of the Commissioners of the RNWMP, pp. 8-9.

10. Edgar McInnis, *Canada* (Toronto: Holt, Rinehart and Winston, 1969), pp. 362-66.

11. *Ibid.*, pp. 397-98.

12. *Settlers and Rebels*, RNWMP Report, 1885, p. 43.

13. Harold Fryer, *Frog Lake Massacre* (Aldergrove, B.C.: Frontier Publishing, 1975).

14. S.D. Clark, *The Social Development of Canada* (Toronto: University of Toronto Press, 1942), p. 406.

15. Report of Superintendent S.B. Steele, Commanding North-West Mounted Police, Yukon Territory, January 10, 1899, in Clark, *The Social Development of Canada*, p. 355.

16. See *ibid.*, pp. 308-59, for a good summary; also see Pierre Berton, *Klondike* (Toronto: McClelland and Stewart, 1978).

17. James H. Gray, *The Roar of the Twenties* (Toronto: Macmillan of Canada, 1975), p. 156.

18. *Report of the Commissioners Appointed to Enquire into the Prison and Reformatory System of Ontario 1891* (Toronto: Warwick and Sons, 1891), p. 25.

19. *Ibid.*, p. 24.

20. *Ibid.*, p. 111.

21. E.C. Kyte, ed., *Old Toronto* (Toronto: Macmillan of Canada, 1954), pp. 193-94.

22. *Report of the Commissioners Appointed to Inquire into the Prison and Reformatory System of Ontario 1891*, p. 104.

23. James H. Gray, *Booze* (Toronto: Macmillan of Canada, 1972), p. 10.

24. Harold Horwood and Ed Butts, *Pirates and Outlaws of Canada* (Toronto: Dell, 1984), p. 220.

25. Frank W. Anderson, *Bill Miner Stagecoach and Train Robberies* (British Columbia: Frontier Books, 1982).

26. Toronto *Globe*, 17 August 1887.

27. J.S. Moir, ed., *Character and Circumstance* (Toronto: Macmillan of Canada, 1970), p. 80; C. Heron and B.D. Palmer, "Through the Prism of the Strike: Industrial Conflict in Southern Ontario 1901-1914," *Canadian Historical Review*, LVII (December, 1977), pp. 423-58.

28. Terry Copp, *The Anatomy of Poverty: The Condition of the Working Class in Montreal 1897-1929* (Toronto: McClelland and Stewart, 1974), p. 133.

29. Judy M. Torrance, *Public Violence in Canada, 1867-1982* (Kingston and Montreal: McGill-Queen's University Press, 1988), pp. 26-27.

30. *Report of the Royal Commission to Inquire Into Industrial Unrest Among the Steel Workers at Sydney, Nova Scotia,* February 9, 1924.
31. J.E. Rea, ed., *The Winnipeg General Strike* (Toronto: Holt, Rinehart and Winston, 1973).
32. Torrance, *Public Violence,* p. 22.
33. *Ibid.,* pp. 30-32.
34. For a comprehensive study of the treatment of Asians in British Columbia, see W. Peter Ward, *White Canada Forever* (Kingston and Montreal: McGill-Queen's University Press, 1978).
35. Michael Bliss, "Pure Books on Avoided Subjects: Pre-Freudian Sexual Ideas in Canada," Canadian Historical Association, *Historical Papers,* 1970, pp. 89-108.
36. M.C. Urquhart, ed., *Historical Statistics of Canada* (Toronto: Macmillan, 1965), Series D, pp. 107-22; Angus McLaren, "Birth Control and Abortion in Canada, 1870-1920," *Canadian Historical Review,* LIX (1978), p. 320.
37. S.M. Trofimenkoff and A. Prentice, eds., *The Neglected Majority* (Toronto: McClelland and Stewart, 1977), p. 180.
38. See, for example "The Winnipeg Conference on Moral Education," *Queen's Quarterly,* XXVII (January, 1920), pp. 317-19; *Canadian Annual Review,* 1922, p. 405; Trofimenkoff and Prentice, eds., *The Neglected Majority,* p. 123; *Canadian Annual Review,* 1923, p. 460.
39. W.L. Mackenzie King, *Report on the Need for the Suppression of the Opium Traffic in Canada* (Ottawa: S.E. Dawson, 1908).
40. *Maclean's,* 15 April 1920, p. 11.
41. *Canadian Annual Review,* 1922, pp. 420-21.
42. *Ibid.,* pp. 423-24.
43. Gray, *Roar of the Twenties,* pp. 170-71.
44. *Canadian Annual Review,* 1922, p. 424; *ibid.,* 1933, p. 92.
45. Gray, *Booze,* p. 92.
46. James H. Gray, *The Winter Years* (Toronto: Macmillan, 1966), pp. 147-60.
47. Thomas H. Raddall, *Halifax: Warden of the North* (Toronto: McClelland and Stewart, 1984), pp. 298-99.
48. *Ibid.,* pp. 299-305.
49. See, for example, S.D. Clark, "Movements of Protest in Post-war Canadian Society," Royal Society of Canada, *Proceedings and Transactions,* VIII, 4th series (Ottawa, 1970), pp. 223-37; John Miseck, "Campus Revolt 1968," *Dalhousie Review,* 48 (1968-69), pp. 299-311; Muriel Le Bel, "La révolution sur le campus," Royal Society of Canada, *Proceedings and Transactions,* IX, 4th series (Ottawa, 1971), pp. 155-70; Murray G. Ross, "A Decade of Upheaval," *Education Canada,* 10 (June, 1970), pp. 18-22.

50. Alden Nowlan, *Double Exposure* (Fredericton, N.B.: Brunswick Press, 1978), p. 86.

51. For a statistical overview of the drug traffic and trends, see *National Drug Intelligence Estimates* (Ottawa: Royal Canadian Mounted Police, published yearly since 1981).

52. *Halifax Mail-Star*, 22 March 1990, p. A1.

53. *Globe and Mail*, 27 March 1989, p. A8.

54. *Halifax Mail-Star*, 21 March 1990, p. C3.

55. "Coin Swindlers," *Canadian Business* (January, 1965), p. 49.

56. Cyril Greenland, *Child Abuse in Ontario* (Toronto: Ministry of Community and Social Services, 1973), p. 3.

57. *Nova Scotia Child Abuse Register*, Statistical Information for the Calendar Years 1983-1987, Halifax, Nova Scotia.

58. *Globe and Mail*, 14 November 1987, p. D1.

59. "Pornography and Prostitution in Canada," *Globe and Mail*, 6 February 1984, p. 8.

60. *Globe and Mail*, 7 March 1990, p. A10.

61. Donald G. Dutton, *The Criminal Justice System Response to Wife Assault* (Ottawa: Solicitor General Canada, 1984), User Report No. 1984-26, p. 7.

62. *Globe and Mail*, 25 June 1988, p. D5.

63. *Globe and Mail*, 8 October 1990, p. A5.

64. *Ibid*.

65. Statistics Canada, *Homicides in Canada*, 1987, Catalogue 85-209.

66. *Globe and Mail*, 8 December 1989, p. A4.

67. *Globe and Mail*, 16 December 1989, p. A4

68. *Globe and Mail*, 8 December 1989, p. A1.

69. *Globe and Mail*, 23 March 1990, p. A8.

70. Frank J. Porporino and J.P. Marton, *Strategies to Reduce Prison Violence* (Ottawa: Solicitor General Canada, 1984), Programs Branch User Report No. 1984-14, p. 1.

71. *Globe and Mail*, 28 November 1989, p. A18.

72. *Globe and Mail*, 19 December 1989, p. A10.

73. Torrance, *Public Violence in Canada*, pp. 35-39.

74. *Halifax Mail-Star*, 28 August 1982, p. 1; 13 March 1985, p. 1.

75. *Montreal Gazette*, 17 January 1987, p. A3.

76. *Halifax Mail-Star*, 21 March 1990, p. A10.

77. *Globe and Mail*, 13 January 1990, p. A7.

78. Ottawa/Hull *Info*, October, 1989, p. 1.

79. *Halifax Mail-Star*, 6 April 1990, p. C1; 7 April 1990, p. A1.

80. *Halifax Mail-Star*, 7 December 1989, p. A16.

81. *Canadian Urban Victimization Survey* (Ottawa: Solicitor General Canada, 1983), Bulletin No. 1, p. 3.

82. *Ibid.*

83. *Ibid.*, pp. 3-6; Bulletin 4, 1985, pp. 1-6.

84. Irwin Waller, *Canadian Crime and Justice in Comparative Perspective* (Ottawa: University of Ottawa, 1982), Table 3.

3. WHITE-COLLAR CRIME

1. W.J. Eccles, *Canada Under Louis XIV 1663-1701* (Toronto: McClelland and Stewart, 1964), pp. 82-85.

2. Gustavus Myers, *A History of Canadian Wealth* (Toronto: James Lewis & Samuel, 1972), pp. 7, 9; Adam Shortt and A.G. Doughty, eds., *Canada and Its Provinces* (Toronto: Glasgow, Brook & Company, 1914), vol. 2, *New France*, pp. 486-87.

3. Michael Bliss, *Northern Enterprise* (Toronto: McClelland and Stewart, 1987), p. 47.

4. Myers, *History of Canadian Wealth*, p. 6.

5. Shortt and Doughty, *New France*, p. 487.

6. Eccles, *Canada Under Louis XIV*, p. 140; Dale Miquelon, *New France 1701-1744* (Toronto: McClelland and Stewart, 1987), p. 248.

7. Thomas Chapais, *The Great Intendant* (Toronto: Glasgow, Brook & Company, 1914), pp. 64-66.

8. J.S. McLennan, *Louisbourg* (Sydney, N.S.: Fortress Press, 1957), pp. 75-78, 100-01.

9. Bliss, *Northern Enterprise*, p. 44.

10. Peter C. Newman, *Caesars of the Wilderness* (Markham, Ont.: Penguin Books, 1988), vol. 2, pp. 221-75.

11. Myers, *History of Canadian Wealth*, p. 45.

12. Beamish Murdoch, *A History of Nova Scotia or Acadie* (Halifax: James Barnes, 1866), vol. 2, p. 207.

13. T.B. Akins, *History of Halifax City* (Belleville, Ont.: Mika Publishing, reprint, 1973), p. 94.

14. Report of the Commissioners Appointed to Inquire Into and Report Upon the Conduct, Economy, Discipline and Management, of the Provincial Penitentiary, *Journals of the Legislative Assembly of Canada*, 1849, Appendix B.B.B.B.B.

15. Lower Canada House of Assembly, *Journals*, and Appendix III to vol. 45, 1835-6, Appendice v.v., 16 January 1836.

16. *Ibid.*

17. Quoted in Michael S. Cross, "The Shiners' War: Social Violence in the Ottawa Valley in the 1830s," *Canadian Historical Review*, LIV (March, 1973), p. 9.

18. Toronto *Daily Globe*, 27 February 1855.

19. Myers, *History of Canadian Wealth*, pp. 168-95; for a detailed account of the corruption associated with railroad building, see pp. 150-243.

20. Report of the Royal Commision to Inquire Into a Certain Resolution Moved by the Honourable Mr. Huntington, in Parliament, On April 2nd, 1873, Relating to the Canadian Pacific Railroad. *Journals of the House of Commons*, vol. 7, 1873, Appendix no. 6.
21. Paul-André Linteau *et al.*, *Quebec, A History: 1867-1929*, trans. Robert Chodos (Toronto: James Lorimer, 1983), pp. 82-83, 251-52.
22. *House of Commons Debates*, Session 1886, vol. 11, pp. 998-1000.
23. *House of Commons Debates*, Session 1890, vol. 1, pp. 571-72, 1717-18, 1735-38.
24. Michael Bliss, "The Protective Impulse: An Approach to the Social History of Oliver Mowat's Ontario," in Donald Swainson, ed., *Oliver Mowat's Ontario* (Toronto: Macmillan of Canada, 1972), p. 176.
25. John Hartlen, *Gold* (Hantsport, N.S.: Lancelot Press, 1988), p. 82.
26. J. Douglas Borthwick, *From Darkness to Light* (Montreal, 1907), p. 99.
27. David R. Morrison, *The Politics of the Yukon Territory, 1898-1909* (Toronto: University of Toronto Press, 1968), p. 13.
28. *Monetary Times*, 17 August 1900, p. 204.
29. Quoted in *Canadian Annual Review*, 1910, p. 225.
30. *Ibid.*, p. 224.
31. *Globe*, 21 April 1910, p. 6.
32. Dean Jobb, "Barnum and the Bank Robbers," *Halifax Mail-Star*, 19 November 1988, p. 2N.
33. R.T. Naylor, *The History of Canadian Business, 1867-1914*, vol. 1 (Toronto: James Lorimer, 1975), pp. 135-38.
34. *Ibid.*, pp. 138-39.
35. *Ibid.*, p. 215.
36. *Monetary Times*, 15 September 1899, p. 331.
37. *Monetary Times*, 12 January 1900, p. 916.
38. James H. Gray, *The Roar of the Twenties* (Toronto: Macmillan of Canada, 1975), pp. 293-303.
39. *Canadian Annual Review*, 1922, p. 423.
40. *Canadian Annual Review*, 1930-31, pp. 544-45.
41. *Ibid.*, p. 545.
42. *Report of the Royal Commission on the Relations of Labor and Capital* (Ottawa, 1889), pp. 38, 63.
43. *Ibid.*, Appendix E, p. 36.
44. David Spector, "The 1884 Financial Scandals and Establishment of Business Government in Winnipeg," *Prairie Forum*, 2 (1977), pp. 167-71.
45. John C. Weaver, "The Meaning of Municipal Reform: Toronto, 1895," *Ontario History*, 66 (1974), pp. 89-100.
46. H.V. Nelles, *The Politics of Development: Forests, Mines, and Hydro Electric Power in Ontario 1849-1941* (Toronto: Macmillan of Canada, 1974), pp. 376-86.

47. *Ibid.*, p. 280.
48. Royal Commission on Customs and Excise, Interim Report No. 1, Ottawa, 1926, pp. 3-4.
49. Royal Commission on Customs and Excise, Interim Report No. 10, Ottawa, 1927, pp. 52-55.
50. *Ibid.*, pp. 58-59.
51. James Dubro, *Mob Rule* (Toronto: Totem Publishing, 1985), p. 282.
52. *Canadian Annual Review*, 1922, p. 421.
53. Barry Broadfoot, *Six War Years* (Toronto: Doubleday Canada, 1974), pp. 190-95, 278-79.
54. Anne Fromer, "Where Will Our Child Labor Problems Lead Us?" *Saturday Night*, 23 January 1943, p. 5.
55. *Ibid.*
56. Robert Bothwell and William Kilbourn, *C.D. Howe* (Toronto: McClelland and Stewart, 1980).
57. E.N. Larsen, "Lobbying the Canadian Way: An Analysis of Corporate Crime in Canada," *Canadian Criminology Forum*, 4 (Fall, 1981), pp. 26-27.
58. Christina McCall-Newman, *Grits* (Toronto: Macmillan of Canada, 1982), pp. 18-19.
59. *Halifax Mail-Star*, 13 January 1989, p. 29.
60. *Globe and Mail*, 7 February 1989, p. A1.
61. *Ibid.*, 24 May 1989, p. A1.
62. *Ibid.*, 4 April 1990, p. A10.
63. *Third Findings Report on Organized Crime in British Columbia* (British Columbia: Ministry of the Attorney General, 1979), p. 36.
64. Carol LaPrairie, "The Development of Sanctions For Stock Market Manipulations in Ontario" (M.A. thesis, University of Toronto, 1975), p. 8.
65. *Globe and Mail*, 21 December 1989, p. B6.
66. *Ibid.*
67. *Globe and Mail,* 15 July 1987, p. B2; 9 December 1988, p. B1.
68. *Globe and Mail*, 10 January 1987, p. B4.
69. *Initial Report on Organized Crime in British Columbia* (British Columbia: Department of the Attorney General, 1974), p. 26.
70. Joe Queenan, "Scam Capital of the World," *Forbes*, 29 May 1989, pp. 132-40.
71. John Stackhouse "The Great Grain Robbery," *Report on Business Magazine* (March, 1990), pp. 66-69.
72. See Organized Crime in British Columbia, Second Findings Report, 1975, p. 11; Initial Report on Organized Crime, 1974, p. 35.
73. *Halifax Chronicle-Herald*, 1 April 1983, p. 4.
74. S.E. Varette *et al.*, *Research on White Collar Crime: Exploring the*

Issues (Ottawa: Ministry of the Solicitor General of Canada, 1985), Programs Branch User Report No. 1985-07, p. 36.

75. *Globe and Mail*, 21 May 1984, p. A1; 31 August 1984, p. M1.
76. *Maclean's*, 9 April 1979, p. 42.
77. *Globe and Mail*, 29 April 1985, pp. B1, B11; 29 May 1985, pp. M1, M5.
78. *Globe and Mail*, 8 December 1990, p. A1.
79. *Globe and Mail*, 6 February 1987, p. A1.
80. *The Financial Post*, 23 April 1966, p. 25.
81. *Globe and Mail*, 3 November 1987, p. A2.
82. *Ibid.*
83. *Globe and Mail*, 3 April 1990, p. A3.
84. *Globe and Mail*, 18 April 1990, p. 37.
85. *Globe and Mail*, 2 January 1988, p. A3.
86. *Globe and Mail*, 22 December 1989, p. A9.
87. *Globe and Mail*, 4 November 1989, p. A2.
88. *Canadian News Facts*, 15 November 1980, p. 2376.
89. *Globe and Mail*, 10 February 1990, p. A1.
90. *Third Findings Report on Organized Crime in British Columbia*, p. 41.
91. *Ibid.*, p. 45.
92. *Calgary Herald*, 3 April 1976.
93. *Calgary Herald*, 10 June 1976, p. 12.
94. *Halifax Mail-Star*, 10 September 1985, p. 1; 30 November 1985, p. 3; *Halifax Chronicle-Herald*, 22 February 1986, p. 23; 20 February 1987, p. 3.
95. *Third Findings Report on Organized Crime in British Columbia*, p. 32.
96. Quoted in Bruce Barnes, "The Problem of Internal Theft," *Canadian Business* (December, 1966), p. 50.
97. *Ibid.*
98. *Monetary Times* (May, 1970), p. 39.
99. A.W. Despard, "Defalcations – the Increasing Trend," *Canadian Chartered Accountant* (November, 1969), pp. 338-39.
100. *Halifax Chronicle-Herald*, 24 May 1982, p. 9.
101. *Globe and Mail*, 8 October 1988, p. B3.
102. *Halifax Mail-Star,* 13 January 1990, p. A4.
103. Gary Ross, "The Gambler and the Heiress," *Report on Business Magazine* (November, 1987), pp. 62-71. Molony's full story is told in Gary Ross, *Stung: The Incredible Obsession of Brian Molony* (Toronto: Stoddart Publishing, 1987).
104. *Globe and Mail*, 19 November 1988, p. A1.
105. *Globe and Mail*, 19 January 1989, p. A11.
106. *Globe and Mail*, 25 January 1989, p. A9.
107. *Globe and Mail,* 10 October 1988, p. A4.
108. *Globe and Mail*, 10 January 1990, p. A1.

109. *Calgary Herald*, 18 August 1985, p. 3; Dianne Francis, *Contrepreneur* (Toronto: Macmillan of Canada, 1988), pp. 287-94.
110. *Globe and Mail*, 16 November 1989, p. A3.
111. Quoted in *Globe and Mail*, 10 January 1990, p. A1.
112. Quoted in *Globe and Mail*, 26 January 1990, p. B7.
113. *Halifax Mail-Star*, 30 September 1989, p. A28.
114. *Ibid.*, p. D1.
115. *Globe and Mail*, 24 March 1990, p. A7.
116. *Halifax Mail-Star*, 13 January 1989, p. 29.
117. *Halifax Mail-Star*, 1 October 1988, p. 26.
118. *Montreal Gazette*, 3 June 1989, p. 1.
119. *Globe and Mail*, 10 January 1990, p. A11.
120. *Globe and Mail*, 13 December 1990, p. A3.
121. *Globe and Mail*, 11 January 1991, p. B3.
122. *Globe and Mail*, 23 June 1990, p. A3.
123. *Globe and Mail*, 14 July 1990, p. B1.
124. *Halifax Mail-Star*, 5 April 1990, p. B1.
125. Royal Canadian Mounted Police, *National Drug Intelligence Estimate 1987/88* (Ottawa: Drug Enforcement Directorate, 1988), p. 99.
126. *Ibid.*, pp. 99-103.
127. *Globe and Mail*, 1 February 1989, p. B3.
128. *Globe and Mail*, 23 September 1989, p. B1.

4. ORGANIZED CRIME

1. Harold Horwood and Ed Butts, *Pirates and Outlaws of Canada* (Toronto: Dell, 1984), pp. 132-34.
2. Adam Shortt and Arthur G. Doughty, eds., *Canada and Its Provinces* (Toronto: Glasgow, Brook & Company, 1914), vol. 2, *New France*, pp. 524-27.
3. Raymond Boyer, *Les Crimes et Les Châtiments au Canada Français Du XVIIe Au XXe Siècle* (Montréal: Le Cercle du Livre de France, 1966), p. 88.
4. J.M. Beattie, *Attitudes Towards Crime and Punishment in Canada, 1830-1850: A Documentary Study* (Toronto: Centre of Criminology, University of Toronto, 1977), pp. 45-50.
5. Albert R. Hassard, *Famous Canadian Trials* (Toronto: Carswell, 1924), pp. 6-18.
6. D.C. Masters, *The Rise of Toronto 1850-1890* (Toronto: University of Toronto Press, 1947), p. 79.
7. Michael S. Cross, "The Shiners' War: Social Violence in the Ottawa Valley in the 1830s," *Canadian Historical Review*, LIV (March, 1973), pp. 3, 4, 13, 22.
8. Hamar Foster, "The Kamloops Outlaws and Commissions of Assize in Nineteenth-Century British Columbia," in David H. Flaherty, ed.,

Essays in the History of Canadian Law (Toronto: The Osgoode Society and University of Toronto Press, 1983), vol. 2, pp. 308-64.

9. Dean Jobb, "Barnum and the Bank Robbers," *Halifax Mail-Star*, 19 November 1988, pp. 1N-6N.

10. Horwood and Butts, *Pirates and Outlaws of Canada*, pp. 195-206.

11. For an account of the prohibition movement in Canada, see R.E. Spence, *Prohibition in Canada* (Toronto: Ontario Branch of the Dominion Alliance, 1919).

12. *The Fight Against Organized Crime in Quebec*, Report of the Commission of Inquiry on Organized Crime and Recommendations (Quebec: Quebec Official Publisher, 1977), pp. 17-23; also see *The Kefauver Committee Report on Organized Crime* (New York: Didier, 1952), pp. 128-29.

13. See *Kefauver Report*.

14. James Dubro, *Mob Rule* (Toronto: Totem Publishing, 1985), pp. 31-42.

15. For a full account of Perri's career, see James Dubro and F. Rowland, *King of the Mob* (Toronto: Viking, 1987).

16. See, for example, Frederick Lewis Allen, *Only Yesterday* (New York: Harper & Row, 1964), pp. 204-24.

17. *Kefauver Report*, p. 239.

18. Jean-Pierre Charbonneau, *The Canadian Connection* (Ottawa: Optimum Publishing, 1976), p. 80.

19. W.E. Mann and L.G. Hanley, "The Mafia in Canada," in W.E. Mann, ed., *Deviant Behaviour in Canada* (Toronto: Social Science Publishers, 1968), p. 143.

20. Alan Phillips, "The Mafia in Canada," *Maclean's*, 24 August 1963, p. 11.

21. Charbonneau, *The Canadian Connection, passim.*

22. *Ibid.*, pp. 82-83.

23. *Ibid.*

24. *Globe and Mail*, 21 September 1984, p. 3.

25. *The Fight Against Organized Crime in Quebec*, pp. 29-38.

26. Charbonneau, *The Canadian Connection*, p. 83.

27. *Ibid.*, pp. 70-75.

28. *Ibid.*, pp. 222-47.

29. Marjorie Lamb and Barry Pearson, *The Boyd Gang* (Toronto: Peter Martin Associates, 1976), p. 29.

30. *Time* Canada, 15 December 1975; also see Lorne Tepperman, *Crime Control* (Toronto: McGraw-Hill Ryerson, 1977), pp. 142-51.

31. Jill McIntyre and A.G. Henderson, *The Business of Crime: An Evaluation of the American R.I.C.O. Statute from a Canadian Perspective* (Victoria, B.C.: Ministry of the Attorney General, 1980), pp. 8-9.

32. *Canadian Police Chief*, 69 (October, 1980), p. 54.

33. *Ibid.*

34. *Report of the Royal Commission into Certain Sectors of the Construction Industry* (Toronto: Government of Ontario, 1974).
35. *The Fight Against Organized Crime in Quebec*, pp. 327-31.
36. *Globe and Mail*, 27 August 1988, p. 1; also see Réal Simard, *The Nephew: The Making of a Mafia Hitman* (Scarborough, Ont.: Prentice-Hall Canada, 1988).
37. Alan Phillips, "Organized Crime's Grip on Ontario," *Maclean's*, 21 September 1963, pp. 15-17, 55-64.
38. *Ibid.* p. 61.
39. Peter Moon, "The Mob Part 2," *Canadian Magazine*, 21 November 1970, p. 3.
40. Peter Moon, "The Mob Part 1," *Canadian Magazine*, 14 November 1970, p. 4.
41. *Ibid.*
42. *Third Findings Report on Organized Crime in British Columbia* (Victoria, B.C.: Ministry of the Attorney General, April, 1979), pp. 27-35; also see *Initial Report on Organized Crime*, 1974, and *Second Findings Report*, 1975.
43. *Globe and Mail*, 21 October 1984, p. 17.
44. *Globe and Mail*, 7 December 1988, p. A22.
45. For a more detailed account of the Commisso family's criminal activities, see Cecil Kirby and Thomas C. Renner, *Mafia Assassin* (Toronto: Methuen, 1986).
46. *Globe and Mail*, 21 March 1988, p. 1.
47. L. Lamothe and R. Lamberti, "Mob Boss: A Profile of Rocco Zito," *Toronto Sunday Sun*, 22 May 1988, pp. 52-53.
48. "The Dubois Brothers Gang," *The Fight Against Organized Crime in Quebec*, pp. 102-59.
49. Maritime Crime Index Section, *Hostile Motorcycle Gangs*, 1971, p. 2.
50. *Ibid.*, p. 11.
51. *Scotian Journalist*, 1, 18 (1971), p. 7; *R.C.M.P. Gazette*, 49, 5 (1987), p. 36.
52. *R.C.M.P. Gazette*, 42, 10 (1980), p. 29.
53. "Outlaw Motorcycle Gangs," *Canadian Police Chief*, 69 (October, 1980), pp. 50-51.
54. McIntyre and Henderson, *The Business of Crime*, p. 25.
55. *Ottawa Citizen*, 21 September 1981, p. 41.
56. Yves Lavigne, *Hell's Angels* (Toronto: Deneau & Wayne, 1987), pp. 219-339.
57. *Halifax Chronicle-Herald*, 2 December 1986, p. 40.
58. *Ibid.*; *Globe and Mail*, 31 August 1984, p. 1; *Halifax Mail-Star*, 26 November 1987, p. 3.
59. *Canadian Police Chief*, pp. 51-53.
60. *Halifax Mail-Star*, 16 December 1986, p. 1.

61. *Globe and Mail,* 22 May 1989, p. A1.
62. Paper prepared by A.P. Lee, Asian Investigative Unit, Metropolitan Toronto Police, February, 1991.
63. *Globe and Mail,* 24 September 1988, p. D1; 13 June 1990, p. A6.
64. *Globe and Mail,* 12 June 1990, p. A6.
65. *Globe and Mail,* 19 March 1987, p. 1.
66. CTV television program *W5,* January 3, 1989.
67. *Globe and Mail,* 4 January 1988, p. 1.
68. *Globe and Mail,* 8 August 1990, p. A1.
69. *Canadian Police Chief,* p. 55.
70. Kirby and Penner, *Mafia Assassin.*
71. *Ibid.,* pp. 157-69.
72. *Halifax Mail-Star,* 12 November 1981, p. 3.
73. *Montreal Gazette,* 17 January 1987, p. A3.
74. *Ibid.*
75. *Globe and Mail,* 3 May 1988, p. 1.
76. *Globe and Mail,* 3 December 1988, p. D2.
77. *Globe and Mail,* 23 August 1989, p. A8.
78. See RCMP, *National Drug Intelligence Estimate 1987/88* (Ottawa: Drug Enforcement Directorate, 1988).
79. *The Financial Post,* 29 March 1975, p. 23.
80. H. Jensen *et al.,* "Hiding the Drug Money," *Maclean's,* 23 October 1989, pp. 42-55.

5.   JUVENILE DELINQUENCY

1. Raymond Boyer, *Les Crimes et Les Châtiments au Canada Français du XVIIe Au XXe Siècle* (Montréal: Le Cercle du Livre de France, 1966), p. 131.
2. J. Herbert Cranston, *Étienne Brûlé, Immortal Scoundrel* (Toronto: Ryerson Press, 1969), pp. 7-17.
3. Quoted in W.J. Eccles, *Canada Under Louis XIV, 1663-1701* (Toronto: McClelland and Stewart, 1964), p. 141.
4. Memoir of de Meulles to the Minister, Quebec, November 12, 1684, and Beauharnois to the Minister, Quebec, October 15, 1738, in S.D. Clark, *The Social Development of Canada* (Toronto: University of Toronto Press, 1942), pp. 45-46.
5. Boyer, *Les Crimes et Les Châtiments,* pp. 106-07.
6. Dale Miquelon, *New France 1701-1744* (Toronto: McClelland and Stewart, 1987), p. 155.
7. John Hale, ed., *Settlers* (London: Faber & Faber, 1950), p. 23.
8. Miquelon, *New France,* p. 156.
9. Denonville to the Minister, September 13, 1685, in Clark, *The Social Development of Canada,* pp. 57-58.

10. Beamish Murdoch, *History of Nova Scotia* (Halifax: James Barnes, 1865), vol. 1, p. 522.
11. *Acadian Recorder*, 10 October 1818.
12. Patricia T. Rooke and R.L. Schnell, eds., *Studies in Childhood History: A Canadian Perspective* (Calgary: Detselig, 1982), p. 89.
13. *Globe*, 26 February 1848.
14. K.R. Williams, "Social Conditions in Nova Scotia 1749-1783" (M.A. thesis, McGill University, 1936), pp. 206-11.
15. Rainer Baehre, "Pauper Emigration to Upper Canada in the 1830s," *Social History*, XIV (November, 1981), pp. 345-55.
16. *Ibid.*, p. 350.
17. Kathleen Jenkins, *Montreal* (New York: Doubleday, 1966), p. 325
18. Baehre, "Pauper Emigration," p. 356.
19. Report of Commissioners on the Subject of Prisons, Penitentiaries, *Journal of Assembly of Upper Canada*, 2nd sess., 12 Parl., 1836, No. 71, p. 4.
20. Wesley Turner, "80 Stout and Healthy Looking Girls," *Canada*, 3 (December, 1975), pp. 37-49.
21. Rooke and Schnell, *Studies in Childhood History*, p. 85; Isle aux Noix Report for 1860, *Province of Canada Sessional Papers*, 25 to 58, 1860.
22. George N. Gordon, *Halifax Its Sins and Its Sorrows...* (Halifax: Conference Job Printing Office, 1862).
23. Judith Fingard, "Jailbirds in Mid-Victorian Halifax," in P. Waite, S. Oxner, and T. Barnes, eds., *Law in a Colonial Society: The Nova Scotia Experience* (Toronto: Carswell, 1984), pp. 89-90, 93-94.
24. Kenneth Bagnell, *The Little Immigrants* (Toronto: Macmillan of Canada, 1980).
25. *Report of the Commissioners Appointed to Enquire Into the Prison and Reformatory System of Ontario 1891* (Toronto: Warwick & Sons, 1891), p. 215.
26. Bagnell, *The Little Immigrants*, p. 72.
27. *Report of the Commissioners of Ontario 1891*, p. 125.
28. Bagnell, *The Little Immigrants*, pp. 88-89.
29. *Ibid.*, p. 89.
30. Provincial Penitentiary Warden's Report, Province of Canada, Journals of the Legislative Assembly, Appendix No. 2, vol. 10, 1851, Appendix W.
31. *Report of the Commissioners of Ontario 1891*.
32. *Ibid.*, pp. 89-90.
33. *Ibid.*, p. 25.
34. Quoted in W. Gordon West, *Young Offenders and the State: A Canadian Perspective on Delinquency* (Toronto: Butterworths, 1984), pp. 24-25.
35. *Report of the Commissioners of Ontario 1891*, pp. 689-90.

36. "Memorandum on the Draft of a Bill For the Further Promotion of Education in the Cities and Towns of Upper Canada, in Regard to Vagrant and Neglected Children. By the Reverend Doctor Ryerson," *Documentary History of Education in Upper Canada,* XVII, 1861-1863 (Toronto, 1907), p. 177.

37. Principal Millar, Dartmouth High School, "A Provincial Reformatory for Incorrigible Pupils," in Alison L. Prentice and Susan E. Houston, eds., *Family, School and Society in Nineteenth Century Canada* (Toronto: Oxford University Press, 1975), pp. 280-81.

38. *Report of the Commissioners of Ontario 1891*, p. 133.

39. Prentice and Houston, eds., *Family, School and Society*, p. 282.

40. Albert R. Hassard, *Famous Canadian Trials* (Toronto: Carswell, 1924), pp. 173-93.

41. Twenty-Sixth Annual Report Upon the Common Gaols, Prisons and Reformatories of Ontario, 1893, p. 92.

42. Elisabeth Wallace, "The Origins of the Social Welfare State in Canada, 1867-1900," *Canadian Journal of Economics and Political Science*, XVI (August, 1950), p. 387.

43. Constance B. Backhouse, "Nineteenth-Century Canadian Prostitution Law Reflection of a Discriminatory Society," *Social History*, XVIII (November, 1985), p. 397.

44. *Province of Canada Sessional Papers* 25 to 58, XVIII, 4 (1860), Paper No. 32, p. 18.

45. Terry Copp, *The Anatomy of Poverty: The Condition of the Working Class in Montreal 1897-1929* (Toronto: McClelland and Stewart, 1974), p. 113.

46. Neil Sutherland, *Children in English-Canadian Society: Framing the Twentieth-Century Consensus* (Toronto: University of Toronto Press, 1978), p. 103.

47. Report of the Superintendent, Twenty-Sixth Annual Report Upon the Common Gaols, Prisons and Reformatories of Ontario, 1893, p. 118.

48. *Canada Year Book*, various years, author's calculations.

49. *Ibid.*

50. James Dubro, *Mob Rule*, pp. 19-21; Catherine Wismer, *Sweethearts* (Toronto: James Lorimer, 1980), pp. 3-13.

51. Rooke and Schnell, eds., *Studies in Childhood History*, p. 177.

52. Annual Report, Maritime Home for Girls, 1918, pp. 17, 21.

53. *The Canadian Annual Review 1922*, p. 406; Emily F. Murphy, *The Black Candle* (Toronto: Coles, reprint, 1973), p. 129 and *passim*.

54. Murphy, *The Black Candle*, p. 286.

55. *Ibid.*, p. 65.

56. *Canadian Annual Review 1922*, p. 407.

57. Frank Sharpe, *Youth in Revolt* (Ottawa: Canadian Council on Child Welfare, 1930), pp. 2-3.

58. *Ibid.*, pp. 7-8.
59. *Canada Year Book*, 1947, p. 256.
60. *Ibid.*, Table 9, p. 258.
61. R.G. Smart, "Drug Use in Canada," from a speech delivered to the Annual Meeting of the John Howard Society of Kingston, February 23, 1970, pp. 4-5.
62. *Juvenile Delinquency in Canada*, The Report of the Department of Justice Committee on Juvenile Delinquency (Ottawa: Queen's Printer, 1965), pp. 7-9.
63. *Ibid.*, p. 5.
64. Data taken or calculated from Statistics Canada Catalogues 85-201, 85-202, 85-205, various years.
65. *Globe and Mail*, 17 March 1989, p. A5; 8 April 1989, p. A1.
66. *Halifax Mail-Star*, 6 January 1989, p. 47.
67. *Globe and Mail*, 9 February 1989, p. A12.
68. *Globe and Mail*, 22 November 1989, p. A1.
69. *Globe and Mail*, 30 January 1989, p. A1.
70. *Halifax Mail-Star*, 27 February 1990, p. A4.
71. *Halifax Mail-Star*, 2 October 1989, p. A4.
72. *Halifax Mail-Star*, 17 April 1989, p. 14.
73. *Halifax Mail-Star*, 1 June 1988, p. 13.
74. *Halifax Mail-Star*, 5 December 1989, p. A3; 12 December 1989, p. A8.
75. See Kenneth H. Rogers, *Street Gangs in Toronto* (Toronto: Ryerson Press, 1945).
76. *Ibid.*, p. 81.
77. For an overview of juvenile gang activity in Toronto, see *Toronto Star*, 12 March 1989, pp. A1, A4.
78. *Globe and Mail*, 30 January 1989, p. A1.
79. *Toronto Star*, 12 March 1989, p. A1.
80. *Ibid.*
81. *Globe and Mail*, 23 May 1990, p. A1.
82. *Globe and Mail*, 29 March 1989, p. A3.
83. *Halifax Mail-Star*, 28 March 1989, p. 4.
84. "With the Bankers," *Canadian Police Chief*, 69 (October, 1980), p. 52.
85. *Globe and Mail*, 29 March 1989, p. A3.
86. Quoted in *Globe and Mail*, 29 October 1990, p. A5.
87. "Chinese Organized Crime in Canada," *Canadian Police Chief*, 69 (October, 1980), pp. 51-52.
88. *Globe and Mail*, 3 January 1989, p. A3.
89. *Ibid.*
90. *Globe and Mail*, 6 January 1989, p. A8.
91. Vivian Bercovici, "Confronting Canada's Asian Gangs," *Globe and Mail*, 24 September 1988, p. D1.
92. *Globe and Mail*, 30 October 1987, p. A3.

93. *Halifax Mail-Star*, 8 November 1989, p. C7; *Globe and Mail*, 8 March 1990, p. A1.
94. *Globe and Mail*, 4 August 1988, p. A3.
95. *Halifax Mail-Star*, 3 February 1982, p. 3.
96. *Halifax Mail-Star*, 12 June 1989, p. 10.
97. *Globe and Mail*, 25 November 1989, p. A12.
98. Calculations by author from Statistics Canada publications, catalogues 85-205, 85-202.
99. See Dean Jones, "School Vandalism: A Survey Report," *R.C.M.P. Gazette*, 42, 4 (1980), pp. 8-13; Province of Ontario, *Vandalism*, Provincial Secretariat for Justice, n.d., pp. 1-13; *Halifax Chronicle-Herald*, 11 May 1977, p. 5.
100. Louise Biron and Danielle Gauvreau, *Portrait of Youth Crime* (Ottawa: Secretary of State, 1984), p. 32.
101. *Globe and Mail*, 24 September 1988, p. D1.
102. Biron and Gauvreau, *Portrait of Youth Crime*, p. 14.
103. Wismer, *Sweethearts*, pp. 6-8.

6. THE FEMALE OFFENDER

1. F.X. De Charlevoix, *Histoire de la Nouvelle-France* (Ottawa: Éditions Élysée, reprint, 1976), Tome III, p. 173.
2. André Vachon, ed., *Taking Root: Canada from 1700 to 1760* (Ottawa: Public Archives Canada, 1985), p. 206.
3. Charlevoix, *Histoire*, Tome I, p. 360.
4. Thomas Chapais, *The Great Intendant* (Toronto: Glasgow, Brook & Company, 1914), p. 70.
5. Raymond Boyer, *Les Crimes et Les Châtiments, Au Canada Français du XVIIᵉ au XXᵉ Siècle* (Montréal: Le Circle du Livre de France, 1966), p. 127.
6. *Ibid.*, p. 106.
7. *Ibid.*, p. 131.
8. W.J. Eccles, *Canada Under Louis XIV 1663-1701* (Toronto: McClelland and Stewart, 1964), p. 142.
9. Memoir of Denonville to Seignelay, Quebec, August 10, 1688, in S.D. Clark, *The Social Development of Canada* (Toronto: University of Toronto Press, 1942), p. 60.
10. André Lachance, "Women and Crime in Canada in the Early Eighteenth Century, 1712-1759," in Louis A. Knafla, ed., *Crime and Criminal Justice in Europe and Canada* (Waterloo, Ont.: Wilfrid Laurier University Press, 1981), pp. 158, 167, 170-71.
11. See, for example, Hocquart to the Minister, Quebec, October 3, 1733, in Clark, *The Social Development of Canada*, p. 68.
12. Lachance, "Women and Crime in Canada," p. 160.

13. Boyer, *Les Crimes et Les Châtiments*, p. 132.
14. W.R. Riddell, "The First British Courts in Canada," *Yale Law Journal*, XXXIII (April, 1924), pp. 578-79.
15. Harold Horwood and Ed Butts, *Pirates and Outlaws of Canada* (Toronto: Dell, 1984), pp. 101-04.
16. R.E. Kroll, "Confines, Wards, and Dungeons," *Nova Scotia Historical Society Collections*, 40 (1980), p. 93.
17. George N. Gordon, *Halifax Its Sins and Its Sorrows...* (Halifax: Conference Job Printing Office, 1862), p. 24.
18. Kroll, "Confines, Wards, and Dungeons," p. 100.
19. Thomas H. Raddall, *Halifax: Warden of the North* (Toronto: McClelland and Stewart, 1984), p. 96.
20. Judith Fingard, *Jack in Port* (Toronto: University of Toronto Press, 1982), p. 134.
21. Mary Ellen Wright, "Unnatural Mothers: Infanticide in Halifax 1850-1875," *Nova Scotia Historical Review*, 7 (1987), p. 17.
22. Kroll, "Confines, Wards, and Dungeons," p. 95.
23. T.B. Akins, *History of Halifax City* (Belleville, Ont.: Mika Publishing, reprint, 1973), pp. 144-45.
24. City Prison Registry of Prisoners, RG 35-102, Series 18B, VB2, Public Archives of Nova Scotia.
25. *Ibid*.
26. York, Canadian Freeman, May 26, 1831, in E.G. Firth, ed., *The Town of York 1793-1815* (Toronto: University of Toronto Press, 1962), pp. 285-86.
27. "Report of the High Bailiff," Toronto *Globe*, 26 February 1848.
28. *Province of Canada Sessional Papers* 25-58, XVIII, 4 (1860), Paper No. 32, p. 11.
29. "Report of High Bailiff," *Globe*, 26 February 1848.
30. Constance B. Backhouse, "Desperate Women and Compassionate Courts: Infanticide in Nineteenth-Century Canada," *University of Toronto Law Journal*, 34 (Winter, 1984), p. 456.
31. *Ibid*.
32. "Warden's Report Provincial Penitentiary," *Sessional Paper* No. 32, pp. 73-77.
33. *Report of the Commissioners Appointed to Enquire Into the Prison and Reformatory System of Ontario 1891* (Toronto: Warwick & Sons, 1891), pp. 730-31.
34. *The Statistical Year Book of Canada 1899* (Ottawa: Department of Agriculture, 1900), pp. 586-87, 590. Averages and percentages calculated by author.
35. Alan Hustak, *They Were Hanged* (Toronto: James Lorimer, 1987), pp. 43-44.

36. *Ibid.*
37. Harold Horwood and Ed Butts, *Bandits and Privateers* (Halifax: Formac Publishing, 1988), pp. 109-21.
38. Kenneth Bagnell, *The Little Immigrants* (Toronto: Macmillan of Canada, 1980), pp. 63-68.
39. Wesley Turner, "80 Stout and Healthy Looking Girls," *Canada*, 3 (December, 1975), pp. 37-49.
40. "Annual Report of the Halifax, Nova Scotia Immigration Agent," *Canada Sessional Papers*, No. 12, 1887, p. 61.
41. "Report of the Halifax Agent, July 1, 1902, *Canada Sessional Papers*, No. 25, 1903, p. 45.
42. James H. Gray, *Red Lights on the Prairies* (Scarborough, Ont.: New American Library of Canada, 1973), pp. 15-41.
43. *Ibid.*, p. 28.
44. James H. Gray, *The Roar of the Twenties* (Toronto: Macmillan of Canada, 1975), p. 99.
45. Gray, *Red Lights on the Prairies*, pp. 30-34.
46. Raddall, *Halifax: Warden of the North*, p. 245.
47. *The Canadian Annual Review 1922*, p. 423.
48. *The Canadian Annual Review 1929-30*, p. 58.
49. Emily Murphy, "The Underground System," *Maclean's*, 15 March 1920, p. 12.
50. See, for example, T.L. Chapman, "The Anti-Drug Crusade in Western Canada, 1885-1925," in D.J. Bercuson and L.A. Knafla, eds., *Law and Society in Canada in Historical Perspective* (Calgary: University of Calgary Press, 1979), pp. 89-115; Emily F. Murphy, *The Black Candle* (Toronto: Coles, reprint, 1973).
51. Royal Commission on Customs and Excise Interim Report, no. 10, 1927, p. 56.
52. James Dubro, *Mob Rule* (Toronto: Totem Publishing, 1985), pp. 265-76.
53. *Ibid.*, pp. 277-86.
54. *The Canadian Annual Review 1934*, p. 173.
55. Alison Prentice *et al.*, *Canadian Women: A History* (Toronto: Harcourt Brace Jovanovich, 1988), pp. 295-303.
56. Raddall, *Halifax: Warden of the North*, p. 299.
57. Prentice *et al.*, *Canadian Women*, pp. 304-05, 311-12.
58. Marjorie F. Campbell, *Torso* (Toronto: Macmillan, 1974).
59. Hustak, *They Were Hanged*, p. 43.
60. Diane Francis, *Contrepreneurs* (Toronto: Macmillan of Canada, 1988), p. 134.
61. A.W. Despard, "Defalcations – the increasing trend," *Canadian Chartered Accountant* (November, 1969), p. 336.

62. *Canada Year Book*, 1947, p. 240.
63. See, for example, Kate Dunn, "The Cocaine Babies," *Montreal Gazette*, 17 February 1990, p. A1.
64. *Halifax Mail-Star,* 9 June 1989, p. 1.
65. *Globe and Mail*, 24 November 1989, p. A12.
66. *Globe and Mail,* 11 September 1989, p. A2.
67. *Globe and Mail,* 13 August 1988, p. C7.
68. *Globe and Mail*, 20 April 1989, p. A1.
69. *Halifax Mail-Star*, 26 May 1989, p. 9.
70. *Globe and Mail*, 14 April 1989, p. A5.
71. *Globe and Mail*, 27 May 1989.
72. *Vancouver Sun*, 24 February 1988, p. D16.
73. *Halifax Chronicle-Herald*, 3 November 1987, p. 17.
74. *Report of the Committee on Sexual Offenses Against Children and Youths* (Ottawa: Ministry of Supply and Services, 1984), vol. 2, p. 997.
75. *Halifax Chronicle-Herald*, 6 April 1983, p. 3; 7 April 1983, p. 3; 8 April 1983, p. 3; 9 April 1983, p. 3; 12 April 1983, p. 3; 14 April 1983, p. 1.

7.   THE EUROPEAN LEGACY AND PIONEER PUNISHMENTS

1. Quoted in Michel Foucault, *Discipline and Punish* (Middlesex, England: Penguin Books, 1986), p. 3.
2. For a detailed description of English punishments, see William Andrews, *Old-Time Punishments* (Toronto: Coles Publishing, 1980).
3. *Ibid.*, p. 155.
4. T.G. Barnes, " 'As Near As May Be Agreeable to the Laws of This Kingdom': Legal Birthright and Legal Baggage at Chebucto, 1749," in P.B. Waite, Sandra Oxner, and Thomas Barnes, *Law in a Colonial Society: The Nova Scotia Experience* (Toronto: Carswell, 1987), p. 20.
5. André Morel, "La Justice Criminelle En Nouvelle-France," *Cité libre* (January, 1963), p. 28.
6. *Ibid.*, p. 27.
7. *Ibid.*, p. 28.
8. Raymond Boyer, *Les Crimes et les Châtiments au Canada Français du XVIIᵉ au XXᵉ Siècle* (Montréal: Le Circle du Livre de France, 1966), p. 106.
9. W.J. Eccles, *The Government of New France* (Ottawa: The Canadian Historical Association, 1971), pp. 16-17.
10. George Gale, *Historic Tales of Old Quebec* (Quebec: Telegraph Printing Co., 1920), pp. 186-87.
11. André Lachance, "Les Prisons Au Canada Sous le Régime Française," *Revue d'Histoire de l'Amérique Français*, XIX (1966), p. 563.
12. Boyer, *Les Crimes et les Châtiments*, pp. 161-64.

13. Thomas Chapais, *The Great Intendant* (Toronto: Glasgow, Brook & Company, 1914), p. 71.
14. Boyer, *Les Crimes et les Châtiments*, p. 131.
15. General Regulations of the Superior Council of Quebec for the Police, May 11, 1676, in S.D. Clark, *The Social Development of Canada* (Toronto: University of Toronto Press, 1942), p. 47.
16. Boyer, *Les Crimes et les Châtiments*, pp. 107, 113.
17. *Ibid.*, p. 129.
18. Adam Shortt and Arthur G. Doughty, eds., *Canada and Its Provinces* (Toronto: Glasgow, Brook & Company, 1914), vol. 2, *New France*, pp. 571-77.
19. Eccles, *The Government of New France*, pp. 3-14.
20. Boyer, *Les Crimes et les Châtiments*, p. 88.
21. *Ibid.*, p. 232.
22. *Ibid.*, p. 255.
23. Eccles, *The Government of New France*, pp. 14-17.
24. Shortt and Doughty, *New France*, p. 575.
25. A.J.B. Johnston, "The Men of the Garrison: Soldier's Punishments at Louisburg, 1751-53," paper read at the French Colonial Historical Society Conference, Indiana University, May, 1987, pp. 6, 9, 10, 14, 19.
26. Boyer, *Les Crimes et les Châtiments*, pp. 114-15.
27. A.M. MacMechan, ed., *Nova Scotia Archives III,* Original Minutes of His Majesty's Council at Annapolis Royal 1720-1739 (Halifax: McAlpine Publishing Co., 1908), p. 301.
28. T.B. Akins, *History of Halifax City* (Belleville, Ont.: Mika Publishing, reprint, 1973), p. 30.
29. Thomas H. Raddall, *Halifax: Warden of the North* (Toronto: McClelland and Stewart, 1984), p. 51.
30. *Ibid.*, pp. 65, 79.
31. Akins, *History of Halifax City*, p. 51.
32. John W. Regan, *Sketches and Traditions of the Northwest Arm* (Willowdale, Ont.: Hounslow Press, reprint, 1978), pp. 18-21.
33. Raddall, *Halifax: Warden of the North*, p. 41.
34. Regan, *Sketches and Traditions*, pp. 114-16.
35. Beamish Murdoch, *Epitome of the Laws of Nova Scotia* (Holmes Beach, Florida: Wm. W. Gaunt & Sons, reprint, 1971), vol. 4, pp. 198-99.
36. H.A. Innis, ed., *The Diary of Simeon Perkins 1766-1780* (Toronto: The Champlain Society, 1948), p. 29.
37. Quoted in Clark, *The Social Development of Canada*, p. 148.
38. L.N. Cowie, "Bridewell," *History Today*, 23 (1973), pp. 350-58.
39. R.E. Kroll, "Confines, Wards, and Dungeons," *Nova Scotia Historical Society Collections*, 40 (1980), p. 94.

40. K.R. Williams, "Social Conditions in Nova Scotia 1749-1783" (M.A. thesis, McGill University, 1936), pp. 204-05.
41. Kroll, "Confines, Wards, and Dungeons," pp. 96-98.
42. Quoted in Williams, "Social Conditions in Nova Scotia," p. 164.
43. Sandra Oxner, "The Evolution of the Lower Court of Nova Scotia," in Waite, Oxner, and Barnes, *Law in a Colonial Society*, pp. 63-64, 68.
44. Beamish Murdoch, *History of Nova Scotia* (Halifax: James Barnes, 1865), vol. 3, p. 506.
45. Quoted *ibid.*, p. 507.
46. *Ibid.*, p. 508.
47. Quoted *ibid.*, p. 512.
48. *Ibid.*, p. 507.
49. Lorne Callbeck, *The Cradle of Confederation* (Fredericton, N.B.: Brunswick Press, 1964), pp. 103-04.
50. Luc Gusselin, *Prisons in Canada* (Montreal: Black Rose Books, 1982), p. 72.
51. J.D. Borthwick, *From Darkness to Light* (Montreal: n.p., 1907), pp. 20-21.
52. *Ibid.*, p. 30.
53. J.D. Borthwick, *History of the Montreal Prison From A.D. 1874 to A.D. 1886* (Montreal: A. Periard, 1886), pp. 3-4.
54. Borthwick, *From Darkness to Light*, p. 39.
55. *Ibid.*, p. 35.
56. *Ibid.*
57. *Ibid.*, p. 39.
58. *Ibid.*, pp. 39-49.
59. Report of the Special Committee, *Lower Canada House of Assembly Journals* and Appendix III to Vol. 45, 1835-36, Appendix ww, p. I (author's pagination).
60. *Ibid.*, pp. 2-3.
61. *Ibid.*, pp. 3, 5-6.
62. Osgoode to John Graves Simcoe, May 23, 1795, in W. Colgate, "Letters from the Honourable Chief Justice William Osgoode," *Ontario History*, XLVI (Spring, 1954), p. 94.
63. C.K. Talbot, *Justice in Early Ontario 1791-1840* (Ottawa: Crimcare, 1983), p. 150.
64. Adam Shortt, ed., *Early Records of Ontario Being Extracts From the Records of the Court of Quarter Sessions for the District of Mecklenburgh* (Kingston: Daily News, 1900), p. 11.
65. Talbot, *Justice in Early Ontario*, pp. 246, 254, 256, 261, 263.
66. "Report on the Petition of the Prisoners in York Gaol," in Edith Firth, ed., *The Town of York 1815-1834* (Toronto: University of Toronto Press, 1966), pp. 281-82.

67. Gaol Reports, Upper Canada Appendix to Journal of Assembly, 2nd sess., 12th Parliament, vol. 3, 1836, p. 5.
68. Talbot, *Justice in Early Ontario*, p. 176.
69. *Ibid.*, pp. 283-86.
70. J.K. Elliott, "Crime and Punishment in Early Upper Canada," 2, reprint from the *Ontario Historical Society Papers and Records*, XXVII (1931).
71. La Rochefoucault, "Tour Through Upper Canada, June 1795," in *Thirteenth Report of the Bureau of Archives for the Province of Ontario*, 1916, p. 40.
72. Bruce West, *Toronto* (Toronto: Doubleday Canada, 1967), p. 43.
73. W.R. Riddell, "The First Legal Execution For Crime in Upper Canada," *Ontario Historical Society Papers and Records*, XXVIII (1931), p. 515.
74. Talbot, *Justice in Early Ontario*, p. 167.
75. J.M. Beattie, *Attitudes Towards Crime and Punishment in Upper Canada, 1830-1850: A Documentary Study* (Toronto: Centre of Criminology, University of Toronto, 1977), pp. 57-58.
76. West, *Toronto*, pp. 136, 139.
77. Marcello T. Maestro, *Voltaire and Beccaria as Reformers of Criminal Law* (New York: Columbia University Press, 1942), pp. 51-63.
78. L. Stephen and S. Lee, eds., *Dictionary of National Biography* (Oxford: Oxford University Press, 1950), vol. II, pp. 268-80.
79. *Dictionary of National Biography*, vol. XLIX, p. 188.
80. *Dictionary of National Biography*, vol. X, pp. 44-48.
81. Dumas Malone, ed., *Dictionary of American Biography* (New York: Charles Scribner's Sons, 1963), vol. VIII, pp. 227-31.
82. Blake McKelvey, *American Prisons: A History of Good Intentions* (Montclair, N.J.: Patterson Smith, 1977), pp. 6-19.
83. Orlando F. Lewis, *The Development of American Prisons and Prison Customs, 1776-1845* (Montclair, N.J.: Patterson Smith, 1967), pp. 77-106.
84. McKelvey, *American Prisons,* p. 5.
85. Report of the Royal Commission on Penitentiaries, Canada Sessional Paper No. 252, 1914, p. 28.
86. Kroll, "Confines, Wards, and Dungeons," p. 99.
87. *The British Colonist*, January 23, 1829, in Clark, *The Social Development of Canada*, p. 160.
88. Borthwick, *From Darkness to Light*, pp. 48-49.
89. Frank W. Anderson, "Prisons and Prison Reforms in the Old Canadian West," *Canadian Journal of Corrections*, 2 (1960), pp. 209-10.
90. J.T.L. James, "Gaols and Their Goals in Manitoba 1870-1970," *Canadian Journal of Criminology*, XX (January, 1978), p. 35.
91. Talbot, *Justice in Early Ontario,* p. 14.

92. Kroll, "Confines, Wards, and Dungeons," p. 101.
93. Report of Commissioners on the Subject of Prisons, Penitentiaries, *Journal of Assembly of Upper Canada*, 2nd Session, 12th Parliament, 1836, no. 71, p. 2.
94. *Ibid.*, p. 3.
95. *Ibid.*, p. 4.
96. *Ibid.*, p. 5.
97. Quoted in Lewis, *The Development of American Prisons*, p. 81.
98. *Ibid.*
99. Richard B. Splane, *Social Welfare in Ontario 1791-1893* (Toronto: University of Toronto Press, 1965), pp. 128-32.
100. Quoted in Jennifer McKendry, "The Early History of The Provincial Penitentiary, Kingston, Ontario," *Society for the Study of Architecture in Canada Bulletin*, 14 (December, 1989), p. 93.
101. Talbot, *Justice in Early Ontario*, p. 300.
102. Rules and Regulations made by the Inspectors of the Provincial Penitentiary, in Beattie, *Attitudes Towards Crime and Punishment*, p. 121.
103. *Ibid.*, p. 118.
104. *Ibid.*, pp. 128-29, 122-23.
105. *Ibid.*, pp. 128-29.
106. First Report of the Commissioners Appointed to Inquire Into And Report Upon the Conduct, Economy, Discipline and Management, of the Provincial Penitentiary, *Journal of the Legislative Assembly*, 1849, appendix B.B.B.B.B. (Brown Report), not paginated; author's pagination, p. 189.
107. Second Report of the Brown Commission, *Journals of the Legislative Assembly*, 1849, appendix B.B.B.B.B., p. 281.
108. Quoted in Beattie, *Attitudes Towards Crime and Punishment*, p. 131.
109. Warden's Report, Provincial Penitentiary, Preliminary Report of the Board of Inspectors of Asylums, Prisons, etc., 1860, *Province of Canada Sessional Papers* 25 to 58, vol. XVIII, no. 4, 1860, Paper No. 32, pp. 69-78.
110. *Ibid.*, p. 9.
111. *Ibid.*
112. Quoted in Paul Craven, "Law and Ideology: The Toronto Police Court 1850-80," in D. Flaherty, ed., *Essays in the History of Canadian Law* (Toronto: The Osgoode Society and University of Toronto Press, 1983), vol. 2, p. 265.
113. *Ibid.*; Oxner, "The Evolution of the Lower Court of Nova Scotia," pp. 76-78.
114. Cravin, "Law and Ideology," p. 277.
115. Albert R. Hassard, *Famous Canadian Trials* (Toronto: Carswell, 1924), pp. 13-14; Craven, "Law and Ideology," pp. 268-72.
116. Rainer Baehre, *The Prison in Atlantic Canada Before 1880* (Ottawa:

Solicitor General of Canada, 1985), Programs Branch User Report No. 1985-25, pp. 15-19, 27.
117. *Ibid.*, pp. 30-33.
118. *Ibid.*, p. 19.
119. *Ibid.*, pp. 23, 30.
120. Quoted *ibid.*, p. 32.
121. E.A. Meredith, *Glance at the Present State of the Common Gaols of Canada.* A paper read before the Literary and Historical Society of Quebec, April 6, 1864 (Quebec: Hunter Rose & Co., 1864), pp. 4-17

8. THE TREATMENT OF CRIMINALS SINCE CONFEDERATION

1. Quoted in *Sentencing Reform, A Canadian Approach* (Ottawa: Minister of Supply and Services, 1986), p. 30.
2. *Ibid.*, p. 32.
3. John Vincent Barry, *Alexander Maconochie of Norfolk Island* (London: Oxford University Press, 1958).
4. *Correctional Philosophy*, Correctional Law Review Working Paper No. 1 (Ottawa: Solicitor General Canada, 1986), p. 8.
5. E.C. Wines and T.W. Dwight, *Report on the Prisons and Reformatories of the United States and Canada* (New York: AMS Press, reprint, 1973).
6. Corinne Bacon, comp., *Prison Reform* (New York: AMS Press, 1974), pp. 35-42.
7. Frank W. Anderson, "The Therapeutic Use of Prisons," *Canadian Welfare*, XXXIV (May, 1958), p. 5.
8. *Ibid.*
9. Report of Inspector James G. Moylan, *Canada Sessional Papers*, No. 12 (Ottawa, 1878), p. 13.
10. Sir John A. Macdonald to John Creighton, Ottawa, October 31, 1871, in J. Alex Edimison, "Some Aspects of Nineteenth-Century Canadian Prisons," in W.T. McGrath, ed., *Crime and Its Treatment in Canada* (Toronto: Macmillan, 1976), pp. 366-67.
11. J.D. Scott, *Four Walls in the West* (British Columbia: Federal Prison Officers Association, 1984), p. 4.
12. *Ibid.*, pp. 3-8.
13. *Ibid.*, p. 9.
14. *Ibid.*, p. 23.
15. *Ibid.*, pp. 13-14, 23-31.
16. *Ibid.*, p. 21.
17. J.T.L. James, "Gaols and Their Goals in Manitoba 1870-1970," *Canadian Journal of Criminology*, 20-21 (1978-79), pp. 38-39.
18. *Ibid.*, pp. 40-41.
19. W.A. Calder, "Convict Life in Canadian Federal Penitentiaries, 1867-1900," in L.A. Knafla, ed., *Crime and Criminal Justice in*

Europe and Canada (Waterloo, Ont.: Wilfrid Laurier University Press, 1981), pp. 305, 311-12.

20. *Report of the Commissioners Appointed to Enquire Into the Prison and Reformatory System of the Province of Ontario* (Toronto: Warwick and Sons, 1891), pp. 147-48.
21. *Ibid.*, p. 121.
22. *Ibid.*, p. 147.
23. *Ibid.*, p. 148.
24. *Ibid.*, pp. 145-46.
25. *Ibid.*, p. 145.
26. *Ibid.*, pp. 219-20.
27. Quoted in Donald G. Wetherell, "To Discipline and Train: Adult Rehabilitation Programmes in Ontario Prisons, 1874-1900," *Social History*, XII (May, 1979), p. 152.
28. *Report of the Royal Commission on the Relations of Labor and Capital* (Ottawa: Queen's Printer, 1889), Appendix N, pp. 70-71.
29. *Ibid*.
30. Quoted in Wetherell, "To Discipline and Train," p. 153.
31. Colonel George T. Denison, *Recollections of a Police Magistrate* (Toronto: Musson, 1920), p. 10.
32. Paul Craven, "Law and Ideology: The Toronto Police Court 1850-80," in D. Flaherty, ed., *Essays in the History of Canadian Law* (Toronto: The Osgoode Society and the University of Toronto Press, 1983), vol. 2, pp. 286-92.
33. *Settlers and Rebels, Reports to Parliament of the R.N.W.M.P. 1882-1885* (Toronto: Coles, facsimile edition, 1973), p. 20.
34. An Act to provide for the Conditional Liberation of Penitentiary Convicts, 1899, *Statutes of Canada 1899*, 62-63 Victoria, Chapter 49, pp. 271-75.
35. Quoted in Wetherell, "To Discipline and Train," p. 165.
36. *Proceedings of the Annual Congress, National Prison Association, 1904*, pp. 200-201, 216.
37. R.G. Moyles, *The Blood and Fire in Canada* (Toronto: Peter Martin Associates, 1977), pp. 5-7, 61-72.
38. W.P. Archibald, "The Parole System – An Historical Review," *Canadian Law Review*, 6 (1907), p. 227.
39. *Ibid.*, pp. 226-29.
40. W.P. Archibald, "Annual Report of the Prison Gate Movement," *Proceedings of the Annual Congress, National Prison Association, 1904*, pp. 20-21.
41. Archibald, "The Parole System," p. 227.
42. Archibald, "Annual Report of the Prison Gate Movement," p. 222.
43. *Saturday Night*, 15 December 1906, p. 1.

44. Report of the Royal Commission on Penitentiaries, *Canada Sessional Papers*, 1914, Paper No. 252, p. 1.
45. *Ibid.*, p. 9.
46. *Ibid.*, p. 13.
47. *Ibid.*, p. 32
48. *Canadian Annual Review 1922*, pp. 421-22.
49. *Report of the Royal Commission Concerning Jails, Province of Nova Scotia* (Halifax: King's Printer, 1933), p. 33.
50. *Ibid.*, p. 40.
51. *Ibid.*, p. 42.
52. *Proceedings of the 59th Annual Congress of the American Prison Association*, Toronto, Sept. 20-26, 1929, pp. 246-47, 313.
53. *Ibid.*, pp. 319-20.
54. *Ibid.*, pp. 321-23.
55. *Ibid.*, pp. 320-24.
56. *Ibid.*, p. 327.
57. *Ibid.*, pp. 326-27.
58. *House of Commons Debates*, 12th Parliament, 3rd Session, 1914, vol. 1, 4, pp. 482-89; vol. 5, pp. 4514-21; 5th Session, 1915, vol. 1, pp. 42-43, 127-40, 264-84; 7th Session, 1917, vol. 1, pp. 1012, 1016-18.
59. Margaret Stewart and Doris French, *Ask No Quarter* (Toronto: Longmans, Green, and Co., 1959), *passim*.
60. John Kidman, "Work Among and on Behalf of Delinquents," *Social Welfare* (November, 1927), p. 29.
61. "Beating Back," *Maclean's*, 15 May 1933, pp. 21, 22, 40; Austin Campbell, "House of Hate," *Maclean's*, 1 August 1933, pp. 10-11, 41-43.
62. Campbell, "House of Hate," part II, *Maclean's*, 15 August 1933, p. 25.
63. "Beating Back," *Maclean's*, 15 May 1933, pp. 21-22, 40.
64. "House of Hate," *Maclean's*, 15 October 1933, pp. 31-32.
65. *Report of the Royal Commission to Investigate the Penal System of Canada* (Ottawa: J.O. Patenaude, 1938), pp. 28-31, 54. (Hereafter Archambault Report.)
66. Scott, *Four Walls in the West*, p. 61.
67. *Ibid.*, p. 62.
68. *Report of the Superintendent of Penitentiaries Re Kingston Penitentiary Disturbances 1932* (Ottawa: F.A. Acland, 1933), p. 28.
69. Archambault Report, p. 277.
70. *Ibid.*, pp. 81-97.
71. *Ibid.*, p. 54.
72. *Ibid.*, pp. 354-61.
73. S.K. Jaffary, *Sentencing of Adults in Canada* (Toronto: University of Toronto Press, 1963), p. 86.
74. *Report of General R.B. Gibson Regarding the Penitentiary System of Canada* (Ottawa: King's Printer, 1947), pp. 4-5.

75. Jaffary, *Sentencing of Adults in Canada*, pp. 86-87.
76. J.C. McRuer, "Sentences," *Canadian Bar Review*, XXVII (November, 1949), p. 1009.
77. A.J. MacLeod, "Corrections in Canada – 1947 and Today," *Proceedings of the Canadian Congress of Corrections, Montreal, May 26-29, 1957*, p. 29.
78. J.A. McLaughlan, "Using Existing Prison Facilities For Training Purposes, and Adapting the Training to the Type of Institution," *Proceedings of the 83rd Annual Congress of Correction of the American Prison Association, Toronto, October 11-16, 1953,* p. 114.
79. R.E. March, "The Classification Program in Canadian Federal Penitentiaries," *Proceedings of the 83rd Annual Congress of Correction*, pp. 47-54.
80. Cecilia Blanchfield, *Crime and Punishment*, 15 July 1985, pp. 4, 7.
81. R.B. Gibson, "Treatment in Federal Institutions," *Canadian Bar Review*, XXVII (November, 1949), p. 1051.
82. Dominion Bureau of Statistics, *Statistics of Criminal and Other Offenses 1955* (Ottawa, 1957), Catalogue 85-201, percentages calculated by author.
83. *Report of a Committee Appointed to Inquire Into the Principles and Procedures Followed in the Remission Service of the Department of Justice of Canada* (Ottawa, 1956), p. 5. (Fauteux Report.)
84. *Ibid., passim.*
85. *Report of the Canadian Committee on Corrections: Towards Unity* (Ottawa: Queen's Printer, 1969).
86. Herbert Gamberg and Anthony Thomson, *The Illusion of Prison Reform: Corrections in Canada* (New York: Peter Lang, 1984), pp. 51-70.
87. An Act to provide for the Conditional Liberation of Persons Undergoing Sentences of Imprisonment, 1958, *Statutes of Canada*, 7 Elizabeth 11, vol. 1, 1958.
88. A.M. Kirkpatrick, "Prisoners' Aid Societies in Canada," *American Journal of Corrections* (January-February, 1959), pp. 12, 14, 25.
89. Canada, *Report to Parliament by the Sub-Committee on the Penitentiary System in Canada* (Ottawa: Supply and Services, 1977), p. 5.
90. Department of the Solicitor General, *Annual Report for the Fiscal Year April 1, 1971 to March 31, 1972* (Ottawa, 1972), p. 43.
91. *Globe and Mail*, 7 November 1989, p. A1.
92. Blanchfield, *Crime and Punishment*, p. 6.
93. Cecilia Blanchfield, *Crime and Punishment*, 15 September 1985, p. 2; *Report of the Task Force on Community-Based Residential Centres* (Ottawa: Solicitor General Canada, 1973).
94. *Directory of Community-Based Residential Centres in Canada, 1987-1988* (Ottawa: Correctional Service of Canada, 1988).

95. *Globe and Mail*, 24 April 1990, p. A1.

96. C.H.S. Jayewardene, "The Canadian Movement Against the Death Penalty," *Canadian Journal of Criminology and Corrections*, 14-15 (1972-73), pp. 367-82.

97. Robert Miller, "Hanging," *Maclean's*, 8 October 1984, pp. 48-58.

98. *Standards for Adult Corrections in Canada* (Ottawa: Canadian Criminal Justice Association, 1985).

99. *Mission of the Correctional Service of Canada* (Ottawa: Correctional Service of Canada, 1989), p. 12.

100. *Ibid.*, p. 13.

101. *Globe and Mail*, 31 March 1989, p. A1.

102. *Globe and Mail*, 12 March 1990, p. A4.

103. *Globe and Mail*, 23 March 1990, p. A1.

104. *Globe and Mail*, 2 May 1990, p. A3.

105. *Victims and Corrections* (Ottawa: Solicitor General Canada, 1987), pp. 2-3, 23-25.

106. *Halifax Mail-Star*, 1 September 1989, p. 29.

107. *Royal Commission on the Donald Marshall, Jr. Prosecution, Commissioners' Report* (Halifax: Province of Nova Scotia, 1989), vol. 1.

108. *Halifax Mail-Star*, 20 September 1989, p. C3.

109. *Globe and Mail*, 23 August 1989, p. A4.

110. *Globe and Mail*, 9 November 1989, p. A1.

111. *Globe and Mail*, 18 October 1985, p. A1.

112. *Views of Sentencing: A Survey of Judges in Canada* (Ottawa: Department of Justice, 1988), p. 7.

113. *Sentencing Reform, A Canadian Approach* (Ottawa, Minister of Supply and Services, 1986), p. 62.

114. *Ibid.*

115. *Halifax Chronicle-Herald*, 15 July 1982, p. 18.

116. *Halifax Mail-Star*, 4 February 1982, p. 5.

117. *Globe and Mail*, 14 October 1985, p. A8.

118. *Ibid.*

119. *Globe and Mail*, 26 August 1989, p. A6.

120. *Ibid.*

121. *Globe and Mail*, 28 November 1989, p. A11.

122. *Halifax Mail-Star*, 3 March 1990, p. A1.

123. *Globe and Mail*, 17 August 1990.

124. *Globe and Mail*, 4 March 1989, p. A7.

125. *Ibid.*

126. *Globe and Mail*, 7 January 1989, p. A1.

127. *Globe and Mail*, 1 November 1990, p. A3.

128. *Solicitor General of Canada, Annual Report 1987-1988*, Appendix 8, p. 74.

129. *Globe and Mail*, 23 November 1989, p. A1.

130. *Halifax Chronicle-Herald*, 2 October 1982, p. 13.
131. *Globe and Mail*, 21 March 1988, p. 1.
132. *Globe and Mail*, 17 April 1989, p. A3.
133. *Halifax Mail-Star*, 8 February 1990, p. B2.
134. *Globe and Mail*, 19 April 1989, p. A10.
135. *Globe and Mail*, 23 November 1989, p. A1.
136. *Globe and Mail*, 7 January 1988, p. A5.
137. *Globe and Mail*, 22 December 1989, p. A9.
138. *Globe and Mail*, 13 January 1990, p. A9.
139. *Globe and Mail*, 13 April 1989, p. A4.
140. *Globe and Mail*, 1 April 1989, p. A8.
141. *Basic Facts About Corrections in Canada 1990* (Ottawa: Correctional Service Canada, 1990), p. 11.
142. Robert Martinson, "What Works? – questions and answers about prison reform," *The Public Interest* (Spring, 1974), p. 25.
143. S.R. Brody, *The Effectiveness of Sentencing* (London: Her Majesty's Stationery Office, 1976).
144. *Sentencing Reform, A Canadian Approach* (Ottawa, 1986), pp. 40-44.
145. Report of the Standing Committee on Justice and Legal Affairs, *House of Commons Journals*, June 7, 1977, p. 929.
146. *Taking Responsibility*, Report of the Standing Committee on Justice and Solicitor General on its Review of Sentencing, Conditional Release and Related Aspects of Corrections (Ottawa: Queen's Printer, 1988), p. 75. (Daubney Report.)
147. *Globe and Mail*, 22 August 1988, p. A1.
148. *Globe and Mail*, 15 September 1987, p. A4.
149. *Globe and Mail*, 17 April 1987, p. A8; *Halifax Mail-Star*, 1 September 1989, p. 28.
150. *Globe and Mail*, 4 October 1988, p. A1.
151. *Basic Facts About Corrections in Canada 1990*, p. 13.
152. *Halifax Mail-Star*, 2 December 1988, p. 7.
153. *Basic Facts About Corrections in Canada 1988* (Ottawa: Correctional Service Canada, 1988), p. 21.
154. *Globe and Mail*, 27 February 1990, p. A1.
155. *Globe and Mail*, 10 May 1990, p. A4.
156. *Proceedings of the Annual Congress of the National Prison Association, Boston 1888.*
157. *Halifax Mail-Star*, 28 March 1987, p. 4.
158. *Montreal Gazette*, 4 June 1989, p. A5.
159. *Report of the Saskatchewan Penal Commission 1946* (Regina: T.H. McConica, King's Printer, 1949), p. 19.
160. *Toronto Star*, 25 June 1989, p. B4.

9. THE TREATMENT OF JUVENILE DELINQUENTS

1. André Lachance, "Women and Crime in Canada in the Early Eighteenth Century, 1712-1759," in Louis A. Knafla, ed., *Crime and Criminal Justice in Europe and Canada* (Waterloo, Ont.: Wilfrid Laurier University Press, 1981), p. 165.

2. Beamish Murdoch, *History of Nova Scotia* (Halifax: James Barnes, 1865), vol. 1, p. 522.

3. J. Douglas Borthwick, *From Darkness to Light* (Montreal: n.p., 1907), p. 43.

4. Edith G. Firth, ed., *The Town of York 1815-1834* (Toronto: University of Toronto Press, 1966), pp. 263-64.

5. First Report of the Commissioners Appointed to Investigate into the Conduct, Discipline and Management of the Provincial Penitentiary, *Journal of the Legislative Assembly*, 12 Victoria, 1849, Appendix B.B.B.B.B., pp. 10, 190, 192. (Brown Report, author's pagination.)

6. *Ibid.*, p. 190.

7. *Ibid.*, p. 10.

8. Patricia T. Rooke and R.L. Schnell, "Guttersnipes and Charity Children: Nineteenth Century Child Rescue in the Atlantic Provinces," in P.T. Rooke and R.L. Schnell, eds., *Studies in Childhood History: A Canadian Perspective* (Calgary: Detselig, 1982), pp. 89-90.

9. Second Report of the Brown Commission, *Journal of the Legislative Assembly*, 1849, Appendix B.B.B.B.B., p. 283. (Author's continuous pagination with first report.)

10. *Ibid.*, pp. 287-88.

11. Quoted in Sydney Shoom, "The Upper Canada Reformatory, Penetanguishene: The Dawn of Prison Reform in Canada," *Canadian Journal of Criminology and Corrections*, 14-15 (1972-73), pp. 262-63.

12. Report of the Inspector of Gaols for Canada West, *Journals of the Legislative Assembly of the Province of Canada*, 1852, Appendix AA-JJ, vol. 11, no. 4.

13. Report of the Reformatory Prison, Canada East, Province of Canada *Sessional Papers 25 to 58*, vol. XVIII, no. 4, 1860, *Sessional Paper* No. 32, pp. 23-40.

14. Report of the Inspectors of Asylums and Prisons, Province of Canada *Sessional Papers 25 to 58*, Paper No. 32, p. 18.

15. Richard B. Splane, *Social Welfare in Ontario 1791-1893* (Toronto: University of Toronto Press, 1965), pp. 148-49.

16. Preliminary Report of the Board of Inspectors of Asylums, Prisons, etc., Province of Canada *Sessional Papers 25 to 58*, vol. XVIII, no. 4, 1860, Paper no. 32, p. 20.

17. *Ibid.*, pp. 40-44.

18. Splane, *Social Welfare in Ontario*, p. 151.

19. Quoted *ibid.*, p. 173.
20. *Ontario Sessional Papers*, 1878, Paper No. 4, pp. 88-89; Splane, *Social Welfare in Ontario*, pp. 172-74.
21. *Ontario Sessional Papers*, 1880, Paper No. 8, pp. pp. 176-80.
22. Splane, *Social Welfare in Ontario*, p. 175.
23. *Mayor's Report*, September 22, 1862, pp. 14-15.
24. *Ibid.*
25. Separate Report of E.A. Meredith, Annual Report of the Board of Inspectors of Asylums, Prisons, etc., Province of Canada, *Sessional Papers*, No. 19, 1862, in Alison L. Prentice and Susan E. Houston, eds., *Family, School and Society in Nineteenth Century Canada* (Toronto: Oxford University Press, 1975), pp. 270-71.
26. "Report of the Halifax Protestant Industrial School, 1867," in Prentice and Houston, eds., *Family, School and Society*, pp. 272-76.
27. *Ibid.*, p. 273.
28. James M. Whalen, "Social Welfare in New Brunswick 1784-1900," *Acadiensis*, 2 (1973), pp. 62-63.
29. Report of the Superintendent, Province of Ontario, *Sessional Papers*, Paper No. 8, 1883, p. 111.
30. *Ibid.*
31. *Report of the Commissioners Appointed to Enquire Into the Prison and Reformatory System of Ontario 1891* (Toronto: Warwick & Sons, 1891), p. 96.
32. *Ibid.*, pp. 96-97.
33. *Ibid.*, pp. 94-95.
34. *Ibid.*
35. *Ibid.*, p. 486.
36. *Ibid.*
37. Prentice and Houston, eds., *Family, School and Society*, p. 288.
38. *Report of the Commissioners 1891*, p. 739.
39. *Ibid.*, pp. 214-18.
40. A. Jones and L. Rutman, *In the Children's Aid: J.J. Kelso and Child Welfare in Ontario* (Toronto: University of Toronto Press, 1981).
41. *Ibid.*, pp. 107-11.
42. *Ibid.*, p. 106.
43. Danièle Gagnon, *History of the Law for Juvenile Delinquents* (Ottawa: Solicitor General of Canada, 1984), Programs Branch User Report No. 1984-56, pp. 21-26.
44. *The Criminal Code 1892* (Ottawa: Edward Dawson Law Printer, 1892), pp. 259-67.
45. *Ibid.*, p. 143.
46. *Ibid.*, p. 551.
47. An Act Respecting Arrest, Trial and Imprisonment of Youthful Offenders, *Statutes of Canada*, 1894.

48. J.J. Kelso, *The Children's Court*, pamphlet (Toronto: n.p., n.d), p. 8.
49. *Ibid.*, pp. 1-15.
50. G.T. Denison, *Recollections of a Police Magistrate* (Toronto: Musson, 1920), p. 254.
51. An Act Respecting Juvenile Delinquents, *Statutes of Canada 1908*.
52. W.L. Scott, *The Genesis of the Juvenile Delinquents Act* (Ottawa: Canadian Welfare Council, 1969), p. 46.
53. *Ibid.*, p. 45.
54. *Saturday Night*, 15 December 1906, p. 1.
55. For a succinct overview of juvenile courts, see Neil Sutherland, *Children in English-Canadian Society: Framing the Twentieth-Century Consensus* (Toronto: University of Toronto Press, 1978), pp. 124-51.
56. L.E. Mendelsohn and S. Ronald, "History of the Montreal Juvenile Court" (M.S.W. thesis, McGill University, 1969), pp. 26-32.
57. *Canadian Annual Review 1922*, p. 404.
58. *Canadian Annual Review 1923*, p. 508.
59. An Act Respecting Juvenile Delinquents, 1908.
60. W.L. Scott, *The Juvenile Court in Law and the Juvenile Court in Action* (Ottawa: Canadian Council on Child Welfare, 1930), pp. 7-8.
61. An Act Respecting Juvenile Delinquents, *Statutes of Canada, 1929*.
62. C.W. Topping, *Canadian Penal Institutions* (Chicago: University of Chicago Press, 1930), p. 20.
63. *Proceedings of the Annual Congress of the National Prison Association of the United States, Toronto, September 10-15, 1887* (Chicago: Knight & Leonard Co., 1889), pp. 167-69.
64. Sutherland, *Children in English-Canadian Society*, pp. 136-37.
65. Rebecca Coulter, " 'Not to Punish But to Reform': Juvenile Delinquency and Children's Protection Act in Alberta, 1909-1929," in Rooke and Schnell, eds., *Studies in Childhood History*, p. 168.
66. *Annual Report Maritime Home for Girls 1915*, pp. 8-14.
67. *Ibid., 1915; 1916; 1917; 1918*.
68. *Ibid., 1918*, p. 17.
69. *Report of the New Brunswick Child Welfare Survey* (Saint John: Canadian Council on Child Welfare, 1929), p. 176.
70. *Ibid.*, pp. 174-77.
71. *Report of the Royal Commission to Investigate the Penal System of Canada* (Ottawa: J.O. Patenaude, 1938), pp. 186-94, 175-76.
72. *Report of the Juvenile Delinquency Inquiry Board*, Province of British Columbia, 1958, p. 5.
73. C.W. Gorby, *A Report and Recommendations on Co-ordination of Youth Services in Greater Vancouver and Greater Victoria* (Victoria, B.C.: Queen's Printer, 1965).
74. Dominion Bureau of Statistics, *Juvenile Delinquents 1963*, 14, Catalogue 85-202.

75. See, for example, H. Berkeley *et al.*, eds., *Childrens Rights: Legal and Educational Issues* (Toronto: Ontario Institute for Studies in Education, 1978).
76. *Juvenile Delinquency in Canada* (Ottawa: Queen's Printer, 1969), p. 179.
77. *Ibid.*, pp. 283-98 *passim*.
78. Statistics Canada, *Training Schools, 1973* (Ottawa: Information Canada, 1973), pp. 35-38.
79. K. Ruphalvis, "An Assessment of Rehabilitation in Correctional Services: The Case of Juvenile Diversion Programmes," *Canadian Criminology Forum*, 1-3 (Spring, 1975), p. 33.
80. Dennis Conly, "A Critique of the Institutional Responses to Juvenile Delinquency in Ontario," in Berkeley *et al.*, eds., *Children's Rights*, p. 80.
81. *Ibid.*, p. 81.
82. The Young Offenders Act, *Statutes of Canada, 1980-81-82-83*, 29-30-31 Elizabeth 11, C110.
83. *Ibid.*, *passim*.
84. Statistics Canada, *Juvenile Delinquents 1983,* pp. 16-17. Catalogue 85-x-202, author's calculations.
85. Statistics Canada, *Juristat*, 10 (September, 1990), p. 1. Catalogue 85-002.
86. See, for example, *Globe and Mail*, 30 November 1984, p. N8.
87. *Halifax Mail-Star*, 6 November 1985.
88. *Reviews of the Young Offenders Act: A Bibliography* (Ottawa: Solicitor General Canada, 1987), Programs Branch User Report No. 1987-17, p. 73.
89. *Globe and Mail*, 30 January 1989, p. A1.
90. *Halifax Mail-Star*, 12 June 1989, p. 4.
91. *Globe and Mail*, 21 December 1989, p. A1.
92. *Report of the Juvenile Delinquency Inquiry Board* (Victoria, B.C.: Province of British Columbia, 1958), p. 7.
93. *Juvenile Delinquency in Canada*, p. 16.

10.   TREATMENT OF THE FEMALE OFFENDER

1. See, for example, André Lachance, "Women and Crime in Canada in the Early Eighteenth Century, 1712-1759," in Louis A Knafla, ed., *Crime and Criminal Justice in Europe and Canada* (Waterloo, Ont.: Wilfrid Laurier University Press, 1981), p. 168.
2. Marcel Trudel, *The Beginnings of New France 1524-1663* (Toronto: McClelland and Stewart, 1973), p. 50.
3. George Gale, *Historic Tales of Old Quebec* (Quebec: The Telegraph Printing Co., 1920), p. 86.

4. Raymond Boyer, *Les Crimes et Les Châtiments au Canada Français du XVIIe au XXe Siècle* (Montréal: Le Cercle du Livre de France, 1966), p. 127.
5. *Ibid.*, pp. 106-07.
6. *Ibid.*, p. 132.
7. *Ibid.*
8. *Ibid.*, pp. 128-29.
9. *Ibid.*, p. 167.
10. André Lachance, "Les prisons au Canada sous le Régime Français," *Revue d'Histoire de l'Amérique Française*, XIX (1966), pp. 563-65.
11. Boyer, *Les Crimes et Les Châtiments,* pp. 339-40.
12. *Ibid.*, pp. 130-31.
13. *Ibid.*, pp. 132-33.
14. Beamish Murdoch, *History of Nova Scotia or Acadie* (Halifax: James Barnes, 1865), vol. 1, p. 500.
15. Beamish Murdoch, *Epitome of the Laws of Nova Scotia* (Holmes Beach, Florida: N.N. Gaunt and Sons, reprint, 1971), Vol. IV, p. 199.
16. K.R. Williams, "Social Conditions in Nova Scotia, 1749-1783" (Master's thesis, McGill University, 1936), p. 132.
17. John W. Regan, *Sketches and Traditions of the Northwest Arm* (Ontario: Hounslow Press, reprint, 1978), p. 110.
18. Thomas H. Raddall, *Halifax: Warden of the North* (Toronto: McClelland and Stewart, 1984), p. 107.
19. R.E. Kroll, "Confines, Wards, and Dungeons," *Nova Scotia Historical Society Collections,* 40 (1980), pp. 94-95.
20. *Ibid.*, p. 97.
21. T.B. Akins, *History of Halifax City* (Belleville, Ont.: Mika Publishing, 1973), pp. 144-45.
22. W.R. Riddell, "The First British Courts in Canada," *Yale Law Journal,* XXXIII (April, 1924), pp. 578-79.
23. J. Douglas Borthwick, *From Darkness to Light* (Montreal: n.p. 1907), pp. 20-21.
24. *Ibid.*, p. 22.
25. *Ibid.*, p. 32.
26. Boyer, *Les Crimes et Les Châtiments*, p. 265.
27. *Ibid.*, p. 42.
28. Borthwick, *From Darkness to Light,* p. 42.
29. *Ibid.*, p. 131.
30. Constance B. Backhouse, "Desperate Women and Compassionate Courts: Infanticide in Nineteenth-Century Canada," *University of Toronto Law Journal*, 34 (1984), pp. 450-54.
31. See, for example, Gaol Reports, Upper Canada Appendix to *Journal of Assembly*, 2nd Session, 12th Parliament, vol. 3, 1836, No. 117.
32. *Ibid.*, No. 44.

33. *Ibid.*, p. 12.
34. E.C. Kyte, ed., *Old Toronto* (Toronto: Macmillan, 1972), pp. 172-74.
35. Leslie Stephen, ed., *Dictionary of National Biography* (London: Smith, Elder & Co., 1889), vol. XX, pp. 294-95.
36. Report of the Inspectors of the Provincial Penitentiary 1835, in J.M. Beattie, *Attitudes Towards Crime and Punishment in Upper Canada, 1830-1850* (Toronto: Centre of Criminology, University of Toronto, 1977), p. 106.
37. Warden's Report to the Inspectors of the Provincial Penitentiary Oct. 15, 1836, in Beattie, *Attitudes Towards Crime and Punishment,* p. 116.
38. Report of Commissioners on the Subject of Prisons and Penitentiaries, *Journal of Assembly of Upper Canada*, 2nd Session, 12th Parliament, 1836, no. 71.
39. First Report of the Commissioners Appointed to Investigate into the Conduct, Discipline and Management of the Provincial Penitentiary, *Journal of the Legislative Assembly*, 12 Victoria, 1849, Appendix B.B.B.B.B., p. 10. (Brown Report, authors' pagination.)
40. *Ibid.*
41. *Ibid.*, pp. 33, 94, 136.
42. *Ibid.*, p. 190.
43. *Ibid.*, pp. 203-04.
44. *Ibid.*, p. 204.
45. Second Report of the Brown Commission, *Journal of the Legislative Assembly*, 1849, Appendix B.B.B.B.B., p. 292 (continuous pagination with first report).
46. City Prison Registry of Prisoners, RG 35-102, Public Archives of Nova Scotia.
47. Borthwick, *From Darkness to Light,* pp. 113-16.
48. *Ibid.*, p. 117.
49. *Ibid.*, p. 114.
50. Ontario, *Sessional Papers,* 1879, no. 8, p. 105.
51. *Ibid.*, p. 107.
52. Carolyn Strange, "The Criminal and Fallen of Their Sex: The Establishment of Canada's First Women's Prison, 1874-1901," *Canadian Journal of Women and the Law*, 1 (1985), p. 86.
53. Ontario, *Sessional Papers,* 1883, no. 8, p. 104.
54. *Ibid.*, pp. 109-12.
55. *Report of the Commissioners Appointed to Enquire Into the Prison and Reformatory System of Ontario 1891* (Toronto: Warwick & Sons, 1891), p. 732.
56. *Ibid.*, p. 745.
57. *Ibid.*, p. 218.
58. D. Curtis and A. Graham, *Kingston Penitentiary: The First Hundred*

and Fifty Years, 1835-1985 (Ottawa: Ministry of Supply and Services, 1985), p. 87.

59. *Ibid.*
60. L. Stephen and S. Lee, eds., *The Dictionary of National Biography* (London: Oxford University Press, 1950), vol. 3, pp. 1068-70.
61. For a succinct outline of Lombroso's ideas, see G. Vold and T.J. Bernard, *Theoretical Criminology* (Oxford: Oxford University Press, 1986), chs. 3 and 4.
62. *Report of the Ontario Commissioners 1891,* p. 732.
63. *Proceedings of the Annual Congress of the National Prison Association 1907,* p. 238.
64. *Ibid.*, pp. 236-37.
65. *Ibid.*, p. 239.
66. *Proceedings of the Annual Congress of the American Prison Association 1908*, p. 247.
67. *Ibid.*, pp. 246, 248-49.
68. Report of the Royal Commission on Penitentiaries, *Canada Sessional Paper* no. 252, 1914, p. 9.
69. *Report of the Royal Commission to Investigate the Penal System of Canada* (Ottawa: J.O. Patenaude, 1938), pp. 312-15. (Archambault Report.)
70. J.D. Scott, *Four Walls in the West* (British Columbia: Federal Prison Officers' Association of British Columbia, 1984), pp. 69-71.
71. *Report of the Royal Commission Concerning Jails, Province of Nova Scotia* (Halifax: King's Printer, 1933), *passim.*
72. Florence E. Orr, "The Problem and Treatment of the Woman Offender," *Proceedings of the Fourth Canadian Penal Congress, Windsor, Ontario, Oct. 7-8, 1946.* p. 21.
73. Archambault Report, p. 19.
74. *Ibid.*, p. 358.
75. *Ibid.*, pp. 159-61.
76. *Ibid.*
77. *Ibid.*
78. *Proceedings of the Fourth Canadian Penal Congress*, 8 October 1946, p. 3.
79. *Ibid.*, p. 2.
80. *Ibid.*, p. 3.
81. Curtis and Graham, *Kingston Penitentiary,* p. 90.
82. Annual Report of the Warden of the Provincial Penitentiary for 1866, p. 14.
83. *Report of the Commission Appointed to Inquire into the State and Management of the Gaols of British Columbia 1950,* p. 14.
84. *The Female Offender Nova Scotia and New Brunswick* (Provinces of

Nova Scotia and New Brunswick: Correctional Services, 1977), pp. 58-59.

85. Rona Tietolman, "A Study of the Female Offender in Quebec and Ontario Prison and Community Facilities," unpublished, 1972, Ottawa, Library, Ministry of the Solicitor General.

86. *Report of the Royal Commission on the Status of Women in Canada* (Ottawa, 1970), pp. 365-85.

87. S. Lloyd, "A Chronology of Events Pertaining to Female Inmates in Pre-Confederation Canada and in the Federal Penitentiary System: from the 1790's to 1979," unpublished paper prepared for Director of Research, Correctional Service Canada, 1979.

88. *The Female Offender Nova Scotia and New Brunswick,* pp. 67, 73.

89. S.J. McKay, "A Brief History of Twin Maples Correctional Centre," unpublished manuscript, Twin Maples Correctional Centre, 1989, pp. 1-13. (The author is a parole co-ordinator at the Centre.)

90. Quoted in Margaret Benson, "Admissions to the Provincial Correctional Centre for Women in Ontario," working paper no. 5, unpublished, Centre for Criminology, University of Toronto, 1971, p. 5.

91. Quoted *ibid.*, p. 10.

92. *A Canadian Directory of Programs and Services for Women in Conflict with the Law* (Ottawa: Ministry of the Solicitor General of Canada, 1985), Programs Branch User Report No. 1985-10.

93. Interview with Matron, Sackville Correctional Centre, Sackville, Nova Scotia, October 16, 1981.

94. *A Canadian Directory of Programs and Services for Women, passim.*

95. Canadian Corrections Association, *Brief on the Woman Offender* (Ottawa, 1967), pp. 28-30; *Report of the Royal Commission on the Status of Women in Canada,* (Ottawa, 1970), p. 375.

96. Claire Culhane, "Women and Prisons," *Resources for Feminist Research* (1982), p. 32; *Halifax Mail-Star,* 23 April 1990, p. D2.

97. *Creating Choices, The Report of the Task Force on Federally Sentenced Women* (Ottawa: Correctional Service Canada, 1990), pp. 135, 136, 51.

98. *Globe and Mail,* 21 April 1990, p. A7.

10. EPILOGUE

1. Quoted in J.T.L. James, "Gaols and their Goals in Manitoba, 1870-1970," *Canadian Journal of Criminology,* 20-21 (1978-79), p. 38.

2. *Report of the Royal Commission to Investigate the Penal System of Canada* (Ottawa: J.O. Patenaude, 1938), p. 8.

3. *Juvenile Delinquency in Canada* (Ottawa: Queen's Printer, 1969), p. 109.

SELECT BIBLIOGRAPHY

BIBLIOGRAPHIES

Bibliography of Canadian Criminal Justice History. Ottawa: Ministry of the Solicitor General of Canada, 1984.

Hardisty, Pamela. *Publications of the Canadian Parliament.* A Detailed Guide to the Dual-Media Edition of Canadian Parliamentary Proceedings and Sessional Papers, 1841-1970. Washington: The United States Historical Documents Institute, 1974.

Henderson, G.F. *Federal Royal Commissions in Canada 1867-1966: A Checklist.* Toronto: University of Toronto Press, 1967.

Smandych, Russel C., Catherine J. Matthews, and Sandra J. Cox. *Canadian Criminal Justice History.* Toronto: University of Toronto Press, 1987.

BOOKS

Akins, T.B. *History of Halifax City.* Belleville, Ont.: Mika Publishing, 1973.

Allen, Richard. *The Social Passion: Religion and Social Reform in Canada, 1914-1928.* Toronto, 1965.

Anderson, Frank W. *Bill Miner . . . Stagecoach and Train Robberies.* British Columbia: Frontier Books, 1982.

Andrews, William. *Old-Time Punishments.* Toronto: Coles Publishing Company, 1980.

Bagnell, Kenneth. *The Little Immigrants.* Toronto: Macmillan of Canada, 1980.

Baldwin, Ged. *Frontier Justice.* Edmonton: University of Alberta Press, 1987.

Ball, John. *Canadian Anti-Trust Legislation.* Baltimore: Williams and Williams Co., 1924.

Beattie, J.M. *Attitudes Towards Crime and Punishment in Canada, 1830-1850: A Documentary Study.* Toronto: Centre of Criminology, University of Toronto, 1977.

Bercuson, David J., ed. *Canadian Labour History.* Toronto: Copp Clark Pitman, 1987.

Bercuson, D.J., and L.A. Knafla, eds. *Law and Society in Canada in Historical Perspective.* Calgary: The University of Calgary, 1979.

Berton, Pierre. *The National Dream – The Last Spike.* Toronto: McClelland and Stewart, 1974.

Biggar, H.P., ed. *The Works of Samuel de Champlain*. Toronto: University of Toronto Press, 1971.

Bizier, Hélène-Andrée. *Crimes et châtiments: La petite histoire du crime au Québec*. Montréal: Libre Expression, 1983.

Blakeley, Phyllis. *Glimpses of Halifax from 1867-1900*. Belleville, Ont.: Mika Publishing, 1973.

Blyth, Jack A. *The Canadian Social Inheritance*. Toronto: Copp Clark, 1972.

Borthwick, J. Douglas. *A History of the Montreal Prison From A.D. 1784 to A.D. 1886*. Montreal: A. Periard, 1886.

Borthwick, J.D. *From Darkness to Light. History of the Eight Prisons ... Montreal, from A.D. 1760 to A.D. 1907*. Montreal: n.p., 1907.

Bosworth, N. *Hochelaga Depicta: The Early History and Present State of the City and Island of Montreal*. Toronto: Coles, 1974.

Boyer, Raymond. *Les Crimes et Les Châtiments au Canada Français du XVIIᵉ au XXᵉ Siècle*. Montréal: Le Circle du Livre de France, 1966.

Boydell, Craig, *et al.*, eds. *Deviant Behaviour and Societal Reaction*. Toronto: Holt, Rinehart and Winston of Canada, 1972.

Broadfoot, Barry. *Six War Years, 1939-1945*. Toronto: Doubleday, 1974.

Brown, R.C., and Ramsay Cook. *Canada 1896-1921: A Nation Transformed*. Toronto: McClelland and Stewart, 1974.

Burt, A.L. *The Old Province of Quebec*. Toronto: University of Toronto Press, 1933.

Campbell, M.F. *A Century of Crime*. Toronto: McClelland and Stewart, 1970.

Chandler, David B. *Capital Punishment in Canada*. Toronto: McClelland and Stewart, 1976.

Chapais, Thomas. *The Great Intendant*. Toronto: Glasgow, Brook & Company, 1914.

Charbonneau, Jean-Pierre. *The Canadian Connection*. Ottawa: Optimum Publishing Company, 1976.

Clark, S.D. *Canadian Society in Historical Perspective*. Toronto: McGraw-Hill Ryerson, 1976.

Clark, S.D. *The Developing Canadian Community*. Toronto: University of Toronto Press, 1968.

Clark, S.D. *The Social Development of Canada*. Toronto: University of Toronto Press, 1942.

Clement, Wallace. *The Canadian Corporate Elite*. Toronto: McClelland and Stewart, 1975.

Copp, Terry. *The Anatomy of Poverty: The Condition of the Working Class in Montreal 1897-1929*. Toronto: McClelland and Stewart, 1974.

Cranston, J. Herbert. *Étienne Brûlé, Immortal Scoundrel*. Toronto: The Ryerson Press, 1969.

Curtis, D., and A. Graham. *Kingston Penitentiary: The First Hundred and Fifty Years, 1835-1985.* Ottawa: Ministry of Supply and Services, 1985.

De Brumath, A. Leblond. *Bishop Laval.* Toronto: Morang & Co., 1910.

De Charlevoix, F.X. *History and General Description of New France.* Translated by J.G. Shea. Chicago: Loyola University Press, 1962.

Denison, Colonel George T. *Recollections of a Police Magistrate.* Toronto: The Musson Book Company, 1920.

Dubro, James. *Mob Rule.* Toronto: Totem Publishing, 1985.

Eccles, W.J. *Canada Under Louis XIV 1663-1701.* Toronto: McClelland and Stewart, 1964.

Ekstedt, John W., and Curt T. Griffiths. *Corrections in Canada: Policy and Practice.* Toronto: Butterworths, 1984.

Edwards, John, L.L.J. *Perspectives in Criminal Law.* Aurora, Ont.: Canada Law Books, 1985.

Fauteux, Aegidius. *Le Duel au Canada.* Collection du Zodiaque, no. 35. Montréal: Déom, 1934.

Firth, Edith, ed. *The Town of York, 1793-1815.* Toronto: University of Toronto Press, 1962.

Firth, Edith, ed. *The Town of York, 1815-1834.* Toronto: University of Toronto Press, 1966.

Flaherty, David H., ed. *Essays in the History of Canadian Law.* Toronto: The Osgoode Society and the University of Toronto Press, 1983.

Francis, Diane. *Contrepreneurs.* Toronto: Macmillan of Canada, 1988.

Gagnon, Daniele. *History of the Law for Juvenile Delinquents.* Ottawa: Solicitor General of Canada, 1984.

Gale, George. *Historic Tales of Old Quebec.* Quebec: The Telegraph Printing Co., 1920.

Gamberg, Herbert, and Anthony Thompson. *The Illusion of Prison Reform Corrections in Canada.* New York: Peter Lang, 1984.

Goff, Colin H., and Charles E. Reasons. *Corporate Crime in Canada.* Scarborough, Ont.: Prentice-Hall of Canada, 1978.

Gordon, George W. *Halifax, Its Sins and Its Sorrows* . . . Halifax: Conference Job Printing Office, 1862.

Gormely, Sheila. *Drugs and the Canadian Scene.* Toronto: Pagurian Press, 1970.

Gray, James H. *Booze.* Toronto: Macmillan of Canada, 1972.

Gray, James H. *The Roar of the Twenties.* Toronto: Macmillan of Canada, 1975.

Greenland, Cyril. *Child Abuse in Ontario.* Toronto: Ministry of Community and Social Services, 1973.

Griffiths, Curt T., John F. Klein, and Simon N. Verdun-Jones. *Criminal Justice in Canada.* Toronto: Butterworths, 1980.

Gusselin, Luc. *Prisons in Canada.* Montreal: Black Rose Books, 1982.

Hagan, John. *Disreputable Pleasures: Crime and Deviance in Canada.* Toronto: McGraw-Hill Ryerson, 1977.

Hale, John, ed. *Settlers.* London: Faber & Faber, 1950.

Hassard, A.R. *Famous Canadian Trials.* Toronto: Carswell, 1924.

Hennigar, Ted R. *The Rum Running Years.* Hantsport, Nova Scotia: Lancelot Press, 1981.

Horwood, Harold, and Ed Butts. *Bandits and Privateers.* Halifax: Formac Publishing Company, 1988.

Horwood, Harold, and Ed Butts. *Pirates and Outlaws of Canada.* Toronto: Dell Distributing, 1984.

Hustak, Alan. *They Were Hanged.* Toronto: James Lorimer, 1987.

Jaffary, Stuart King. *Sentencing of Adults in Canada.* Toronto: University of Toronto Press, 1963.

Jenkins, Kathleen. *Montreal.* New York: Doubleday, 1966.

Jobb, Dean. *Shades of Justice.* Halifax: Nimbus Publishing, 1988.

Jones, A., and L. Rutman. *In the Children's Aid: J.J. Kelso and Child Welfare in Ontario.* Toronto: University of Toronto Press, 1981.

Jones, James Edmund. *Pioneer Crimes and Punishments.* Toronto: George N. Morang, 1924.

Katz, Gertrude. *The Time Gatherers.* Montreal: Harvest House, 1970.

Kelso, J.J. *Early History of the Humane and Children's Aid Movement in Ontario, 1886-1893.* Ontario: King's Printer, 1911.

Kidman, John. *The Canadian Prison.* Toronto: The Ryerson Press, 1947.

Kirby, Cecil, and Thomas C. Renner. *Mafia Assassin.* Agincourt, Ont.: Methuen, 1986.

Knafla, Louis A., ed. *Crime and Criminal Justice in Europe and Canada.* Waterloo, Ont.: Wilfrid Laurier University Press, 1981.

Kyte, E.C., ed. *Old Toronto.* Toronto: Macmillan of Canada, 1972.

Lavell, A.E. *The Convicted Criminal and His Re-establishment as a Citizen.* Toronto: The Ryerson Press, 1926.

Lavigne, Yves. *Hell's Angels – Taking Care of Business.* Toronto: Deneau and Wayne, 1987.

Lewis, Orlando F. *The Development of American Prisons and Prison Customs, 1776-1845.* Montclair, N.J.: Patterson Smith Reprint Series, 1967.

Lowe, Mick. *Conspiracy of Brothers.* Toronto: Macmillan of Canada, 1988.

MacDonald, Neil, and Alf Chaiton, eds. *Egerton Ryerson and His Times.* Toronto: Macmillan, 1978.

Maestro, Marcello T. *Voltaire and Beccaria as Reformers of Criminal Law.* New York: Columbia University Press, 1942.

Manderson, Cynthia. *The Female Offender in Nova Scotia: Community Programs and Services.* Ottawa: Solicitor General, 1985.

Mann, W.E., ed. *Deviant Behavior in Canada.* Toronto: Social Science Publishers, 1968.

Mann, W.E., ed. *Social Deviance in Canada.* Toronto: Copp Clark, 1971.

Mann, W.E. *Society Behind Bars.* Toronto: Social Science Publishers, 1967.

Mann, W.E., ed. *The Underside of Toronto.* Toronto: McClelland and Stewart, 1970.

Masters, D.C. *The Rise of Toronto 1850-1890.* Toronto: University of Toronto Press, 1947.

McGrath, W.T., ed. *Crime and its Treatment in Canada.* Toronto: Macmillan of Canada, 1965.

Miller, Orlo. *The Donnellys Must Die.* Toronto: Macmillan, 1962.

Miquelon, Dale. *New France 1701-1744.* Toronto: McClelland and Stewart, 1987.

Morton, W.L., ed. *Shield of Achilles.* Toronto: McClelland and Stewart, 1970.

Murdoch, Beamish. *A History of Nova Scotia or Acadie.* Halifax: James Barnes, 1866, 3 vols.

Murphy, Emily F. *The Black Candle.* Toronto: Thomas Allen, 1922.

Myers, Gustavus. *A History of Canadian Wealth.* Toronto: James Lewis & Samuel, 1972.

Naylor, R.T. *The History of Canadian Business.* 2 vols. Toronto: James Lorimer, 1975.

Newman, Peter C. *Caesars of the Wilderness.* Markham, Ont.: Penguin Books, 1987.

Porter, Glenn, and Robert D. Cuff, eds. *Enterprise and National Development.* Toronto: Halabert, 1973.

Prentice, Alison, *et al. Canadian Women: A History.* Toronto: Harcourt Brace Jovanovich, 1988.

Raddall, Thomas H. *Halifax: Warden of the North.* Toronto: McClelland and Stewart, 1984.

Reynolds, L. *The Control of Competition in Canada.* Cambridge, Mass.: Harvard University Press, 1940.

Robin, Martin. *The Bad and the Lonely.* Toronto: James Lorimer, 1976.

Rogers, K. *Streetgangs of Toronto.* Toronto: The Ryerson Press, 1945.

Rooke, Patricia T., and R.L. Schnell, eds. *Studies in Childhood History.* Calgary: Detselig Enterprises, 1982.

Royal North-West Mounted Police Official Reports. *Settlers and Rebels 1882-1885.* Toronto: Coles Publishing Company, 1973.

Scott, W.L. *The Genesis of the Juvenile Delinquents Act.* Ottawa: Canadian Welfare Council, 1969.

Scott, W.L. *The Juvenile Court in Law and the Juvenile Court in Action.* Ottawa: Canadian Council on Child Welfare, 1930.

Sharp, Paul F. *Whoop-Up Country.* Norman: University of Oklahoma Press, 1973.

Sharpe, Frank T. *Youth in Revolt: A Study of Youthful Offenders in Cana-*

dian Penitentiaries. Toronto: Canadian Council on Child and Family Welfare, 1931.

Shortt, Adam, and Arthur G. Doughty, eds. *Canada and Its Provinces.* Vol.2, *New France.* Toronto: Glasgow, Brook & Company, 1914.

Shortt, Adam, ed. *Early Records of Ontario Being Extracts From the Records of the Court of Quarter Sessions for the District of Mecklenburg.* Kingston, Ont.: Daily News, 1900.

Silverman, Robert A., and James J. Teevan. *Crime in Canadian Society.* Toronto: Butterworths, 1980.

Skinner, Shirley, Otto Driedger, and Brian Grainger. *Corrections – An Historical Perspective of the Saskatchewan Experience.* Regina, Sask.: Canadian Plains Research Centre, 1981.

Splane, Richard B. *Social Welfare in Ontario 1791-1893.* Toronto: University of Toronto Press, 1965.

Stewart, Margaret, and Doris French. *Ask No Quarter.* Toronto: Longmans, Green & Co., 1959.

Sutherland, Neil. *Children in English-Canadian Society: Framing the Twentieth-Century Consensus.* Toronto: University of Toronto Press, 1976.

Talbot, C.K. *Justice in Early Ontario 1791-1840.* Ottawa: Crimcare Inc., 1983.

Tepperman, Lorne. *Crime Control.* Toronto: McGraw-Hill Ryerson, 1977.

Tones, P.M., ed. *New Ireland Remembered.* Fredericton, N.B.: New Ireland Press, 1988.

Topping, C.W. *Blood on the Snow.* Vancouver: College Printers and Publishers, 1980.

Topping, C.W. *Canadian Penal Institutions.* Chicago: University of Chicago Press, 1930.

Torrance, Judy M. *Public Violence in Canada 1867-1982.* Kingston and Montreal: McGill-Queen's University Press, 1986.

Trudel, Marcel. *The Beginnings of New France 1524-1663.* Translated by Patricia Claxton. Toronto: McClelland and Stewart, 1973.

Vachon, André, ed. *Taking Root: Canada From 1700 to 1760.* Ottawa: Public Archives of Canada, 1985.

Vaz, Edmund W., and A.Q. Lodhi, eds. *Crime and Delinquency in Canada.* Scarborough, Ont.: Prentice-Hall of Canada, 1979.

Waite, P., S. Oxner, and T. Barnes, eds. *Law in a Colonial Society: The Nova Scotia Experience.* Toronto: Carswell, 1984.

Wallace, W. Stewart. *Murders and Mysteries, A Canadian Series.* Toronto: Macmillan, 1931.

Waller, Irvin, and Norman Okihiro. *Burglary: The Victim and the Public.* Toronto: University of Toronto Press, 1978.

West, Bruce. *Toronto.* Toronto: Doubleday Canada, 1967.

West, Gordon W. *Young Offenders and the State: A Canadian Perspective on Delinquency.* Toronto: Butterworths, 1984.

Wines, E.C., and T.W. Dwight. *Report on the Prisons and Reformatories of the United States and Canada.* Albany: Van Benthuysen and Sons Steam Printing House, 1867.

Wismer, Catherine. *Sweethearts.* Toronto: James Lorimer, 1980.

Withrow, Oswald C.S. *Shackling the Transgressor.* Toronto: Thomas Nelson and Sons, 1933.

Zubrycki, Richard M. *The Establishment of Canada's Penitentiary System: Federal Correctional Policy 1867-1900.* University of Toronto, Faculty of Social Work, May, 1980.

ARTICLES IN JOURNALS AND MAGAZINES

Alberts, Laurie. "Petticoats and Pickaxes," *Alaska Journal,* 7 (1977), pp. 146-59.

Alexander, Julian P. "The Philosophy of Punishment," *Journal of Criminal Law and Criminology,* XIII (Aug., 1922).

Allen, Richard. "The Social Gospel and the Reform Tradition in Canada, 1890-1928," *Canadian Historical Review,* XLIX (Dec., 1968), pp. 381-99.

Anderson, Frank W. "Prisons and Prison Reforms in the Old Canadian West," *Canadian Journal of Corrections,* 2 (April, 1960), pp. 209-15.

Anderson, Frank W. "The Therapeutic Use of Prisons," *Canadian Welfare,* XXXIV (May 1, 1958), pp. 4-9.

Arbuckle, D., and L. Litwick. "A Study of Recidivism among Juvenile Delinquents," *Federal Probation,* XXIV (Dec., 1960), pp. 45-48.

Backhouse, Constance B. "Desperate Women and Compassionate Courts: Infanticide in Nineteenth Century Canada," *University of Toronto Law Journal,* 34 (Fall, 1984), pp. 447-78.

Baehre, Rainer. "Origins of the Penitentiary System in Upper Canada," *Ontario History,* 69 (1977), pp. 185-207.

Baehre, Rainer. "Pauper Emigration to Upper Canada in the 1830's," *Social History,* XIV (November, 1981), pp. 339-67.

Bensley, M. "They Kill for Cash," *National Home Monthly,* 47 (Nov., 1947), pp. 17, 36.

Benson, Margaret. "Special Problems Related to the Adult Female Offender," *Canadian Journal of Corrections,* 10 (1968), pp. 206-16.

Berkeley, H., C. Gaffield, and W.G. West, eds. "Children's Rights in the Canadian Context," *Ontario Institute for Studies in Education* (1978), pp. 3-14.

Berzins, Lorraine, and Renée Collette-Carrière. "La Femme en Prison. Un Inconvenient Social," *Santé Mentale au Québec,* IV (Nov., 1979), pp. 87-93.

Berzins, Lorraine, and Sheelagh Cooper. "The Political Economy of Correctional Planning for Women: The Case of the Bankrupt Bureaucracy," *Canadian Journal of Criminology,* 24 (Oct., 1982), pp. 399-416.

Blois, Judge E.H. "Delinquency: Some Causes and Remedies," *Social Welfare,* XI (Sept., 1929), pp. 281-86.

Boyer, Raymond. "The Question: Judicial Torture in New France," *Canadian Journal of Criminology and Corrections,* 5 (1963), pp. 284-91.

Canadian Corrections Association, "Brief on the Woman Offender," *Canadian Journal of Corrections,* 11 (1969), pp. 26-60.

Cousineau, D.F., and J.E. Veevers. "Incarceration as a Response to Crime: The Utilization of Canadian Prisons," *Canadian Journal of Criminology and Corrections,* 14-15 (1972-73), pp. 10-31.

Cowie, L.W. "Bridewell," *History Today,* 23 (1973), pp. 350-58.

Cross, Michael S. "The Shiners' War: Social Violence in the Ottawa Valley in the 1830s," *Canadian Historical Review,* LIV (March, 1973), pp. 1-26.

DeVilliers-Westfall, William E. "The Dominion of the Lord: An Introduction to the Cultural History of Protestant Ontario in the Victorian Period," *Queen's Quarterly,* 83 (1976), pp. 47-70.

Doob, Anthony N., and Janet B.L. Chan. "Factors Affecting Police Decisions to Take Juveniles to Court," *Canadian Journal of Criminology,* 24 (1982), pp. 25-37.

Edmison, J.A., and W. Turner. "Canada's Prison Shame," *National Home Monthly,* 40 (Sept., 1939), pp. 5-7.

Elliot, A.J. "Our Juvenile Delinquency," *Echoes* (March, 1941), pp. 6, 41.

Elliott, John K. "Crime and Punishment in Early Upper Canada," Ontario Historical Society, *Papers and Records,* 27 (1931), pp. 335-40.

Fattah, Ezzat A. "Making the Punishment Fit the Crime: The Case of Imprisonment. The Problems Inherent in the Use of Imprisonment as a Retributive Sanction," *Canadian Journal of Criminology,* 24 (1982), pp. 1-12.

Flint, Maurice. "An Experiment in the Rehabilitation of Women Offenders," *Canadian Journal of Corrections,* 2 (1960), pp. 240-54.

Fox, John. "Changing Social Roles and Female Crime in Canada: A Time Series Analysis," *Canadian Review of Sociology and Anthropology,* 16 (1979), pp. 96-104.

Geoghegan, J. Herbert. "Practicing the New Penology," *Sociology and Social Research,* XXI (1936-37), pp. 327-32.

Gibson, James G. "Political Prisoners: Transportation for Life, and Responsible Government in Canada," *Ontario Historical Review,* 67 (1975), pp. 185-98.

Graff, Harvey J. "Pauperism, Misery, and Vice: Illiteracy and Criminality in the Nineteenth Century," *Journal of Social History,* 11 (1977), pp. 245-68.

Greenland, Cyril. "Dangerous Sexual Offenders in Canada," *Canadian Journal of Corrections,* 14-15 (1972-73), pp. 44-54.

Hagan, John. "Criminal Justice in Rural and Urban Communities: A Study of the Bureaucratization of Justice," *Social Forces,* 55 (1977), pp. 597-612.

Hartlen, John. "When Waverly Wished for Gold," *Nova Scotia Historical Quarterly,* 7 (1977), pp. 338-50.

Haslam, Phyllis. "The Female Prisoner," *Canadian Journal of Corrections,* 6 (1964), pp. 463-66.

Houston, Susan E. "Victorian Origins of Juvenile Delinquency: A Canadian Experience," *History of Education Quarterly,* 12 (1972), pp. 254-80.

James, J.T.L. "Gaols and their Goals in Manitoba, 1870-1970," *Canadian Journal of Criminology,* 20-21 (1978-79), pp. 34-42.

Jayewardene, C.H.S. "The Canadian Movement Against the Death Penalty," *Canadian Journal of Criminology and Corrections,* 14-15 (1972-3), pp. 366-89.

Jobb, Dean. "A Motley Crew and Mutiny Aboard the Zero," *Nova Scotia Historical Quarterly,* 8 (June, 1978), pp. 6-7.

Johnson, Elmer H. "Work Release: Conflicting Goals Within a Promising Innovation," *Canadian Journal of Corrections,* 12 (1970), pp. 67-77.

Johnson, Walter S. "Jeremy Bentham and the Law, 1748-1832," *Canadian Bar Review,* XXVII (Dec., 1949), pp. 1200-08.

Johnstone, W.F., and B.W. Henheffer. "History of Treatment in Canadian Penitentiaries," *Canadian Welfare* (Sept., 1953), pp. 5-9.

Jones, Andrew. "Closing Penetanguishene Reformatory: An Attempt to Deinstitutionalize Treatment of Juvenile Offenders in Early Twentieth Century Ontario," *Ontario History,* LXX (December, 1978), pp. 227-44.

Kellough, W.S., S.L. Brickley, and W.K. Greenaway. "The Politics of Incarceration: Manitoba, 1918-1939," *Canadian Journal of Sociology,* 5 (1980), pp. 253-71.

Kirchwey, George W. "The Prison's Place in the Penal System," *Annals of the American Academy of Political and Social Science,* 157 (Sept., 1931), pp. 13-15.

Kirkpatrick, A.M. "Jails in Historical Perspective," *Canadian Journal of Corrections,* 6 (Oct., 1964), pp. 405-15.

Kirkpatrick, A.M. "The Birth of Prison Reform," *Canadian Welfare* (May 1, 1957), pp. 3-11.

Kroll, R.E. "Confines, Wards, and Dungeons," *Nova Scotia Historical Society Collections,* 40 (1980), pp. 93-107.

Lachance, André. "La Criminalité à Québec Sous Le Régime Français Étude Statistique," *Revue d'Histoire de l'Amérique Français,* 20 (December, 1966), pp. 409-14.

Larsen, E.N. "Lobbying the Canadian Way: An Analysis of Corporate Crime in Canada," *Canadian Criminology Forum,* 4 (Fall, 1981), pp. 23-29.

Le Bourdais, D.M. "Our Barbaric Penal System," *Canadian Magazine,* 90 (Sept., 1938), pp. 16-17, 38.

Leon, Jeffrey S. "New and Old Themes in Canadian Juvenile Justice: The Origins of Delinquency Legislation and the Prospects for Recognition of Children's Rights," *Interchange,* 92 (1977-78), pp. 151-75.

MacDonald, Bruce C. "Criminality and the Canadian Anti-Combines Laws," *Alberta Law Review,* 9 (1965), p. 69.

MacDonald, Lynn. "Crime and Punishment in Canada: A Statistical Test of the 'Conventional Wisdom'," *Canadian Review of Sociology and Anthropology,* VI (Nov., 1969), pp. 212-36.

Macphail, A.C. "Report on Penal Reform," *Canadian Forum,* 26 (Dec., 1946), pp. 206-08.

Martinson, Robert. "What Works? – Questions and Answers about Prison Reform," *The Public Interest,* no. 35 (Spring, 1974), pp. 22-54.

Mathieu, Jacques. "Les causes devant la prévôté de Québec en 1667," *Social History,* 3 (April, 1969), pp. 101-11.

McLaren, Angus. "Birth Control and Abortion in Canada, 1870-1920," *Canadian Historical Review,* 59 (1978), pp. 319-40.

Morel, André. "La Justice Criminelle en Nouvelle-France," *Cité libre* (Jan., 1963), pp. 26-30.

Morel, André. "Reflexions sur la Justice Criminelle Canadienne, au 18e siècle," *Revue d'histoire de l'Amérique française,* XXIX (September, 1975), pp. 241-53.

Morrison, W.R. "Their Proper Sphere: Feminism, The Family and Child-Centered Social Reform in Ontario, 1875-1900," *Ontario History,* LXVIII (June, 1976), pp. 65-79.

Mullins, H. "Prison Library in 1857," *Ontario Library Review,* 31 (Aug., 1947), pp. 307-08.

Needham, H.G. "Historical Perspectives on the Federal-Provincial Split in Jurisdiction in Corrections," *Canadian Journal of Criminology,* 22 (July, 1980), pp. 298-307.

Nicholls, A.G. "Canada and the Traffic in Narcotic Drugs," *Canadian Medical Association Journal* (September, 1934), pp. 308-09.

Normandeau, André. "Organized Crime in Canada and Quebec," *International Criminal Police Review* (Oct., 1971), pp. 204-09.

O'Brien, Patricia. "Crime and Punishment as an Historical Problem," *Journal of Social History,* 11 (June, 1978), pp. 508-20.

Phillips, L.H. "Preventative Detention in Canada," *Canadian Forum,* 26 (June, 1946), pp. 56-57.

Plummer, H.C. "How Business Protects Itself," *Canadian Business,* 19 (Oct., 1946), pp. 25-27, 86.

Purdy, J.D. "John Strachan's Educational Policies," *Ontario History,* 64 (1942), pp. 45-64.

Rhodes, J. "New Life for a Tired System – The Prison Library," *Canadian Library Journal,* 30 (1973), pp. 246-49.

Rico, José M. "La criminalité d'affaires au Québec: Bilan d'une recherche exploratoire," *Canadian Journal of Criminology,* 24 (1982), pp. 191-205.

Riddell, W.R. "Administration of Criminal Law in the Far North of Canada," *Journal of the American Institute of Criminal Law and Criminology,* 20 (Aug., 1929), pp. 294-302.

Riddell, W.R. "Bygone Phases of Canadian Criminal Law," *Journal of Criminal Law and Criminology,* 23 (May, 1932), pp. 51-66.

Riddell, W.R. "Criminal Courts and Law in Early Upper Canada," *Journal of the American Institute of Criminal Law and Criminology,* 9 (Aug., 1918), pp. 173-86.

Riddell, W.R. "Criminal Circuit in Upper Canada a Century Ago," *Journal of the American Institute of Criminal Law and Criminology,* 12 (May, 1921), pp. 91-104.

Riddell, W.R. "Day in Court in Old Niagara, 1792," *Royal Society of Canada, Proceedings and Transactions,* 3, serial 2, section 22 (1928), pp. 125-30.

Roberts, Julian. "Early Release From Prison: What Do the Canadian Public Really Think?" *Canadian Journal of Criminology,* 30 (July, 1988), pp. 231-49.

Rupkalvis, Kristina. "An Assessment of Rehabilitation in Correctional Services: The Case of Juvenile Diversion Programmes," *Canadian Criminology Forum,* 1-3 (1979-81), pp. 32-38.

Scott, W.L. "The Juvenile Delinquents Act," *Canadian Law Times and Review,* 28 (1908), pp. 892-904.

Sharpe, Frank T. "Do Reformatories Reform? The Recidivist Group," *Social Welfare,* X (November, 1927), pp. 25-27.

Shoom, Sydney. "The Upper Canada Reformatory Penetanguishene: The Dawn of Prison Reform in Canada," *Canadian Journal of Criminology and Corrections,* 14-15 (1972-73), pp. 260-67.

Siren, Amy. "An Analysis of Correctional Services for Adults in Ontario," *Canadian Journal of Criminology and Corrections,* 14-15 (1972-73), pp. 268-81.

Stephenson, P. Susan. "Myths About Juvenile Delinquency," *Canadian Journal of Criminology and Corrections,* 14-15 (1972-73).

Spector, David. "The 1884 Financial Scandals and Establishment of Business Government in Winnipeg," *Prairie Forum,* 2 (1977), pp. 167-78.

Strange, Carolyn. "The Criminal and Fallen of their Sex: The Establishment of Canada's First Women's Prison, 1874-1901," *Canadian Journal of Women and the Law,* 1 (1985), pp. 79-92.

Topping, C.W. "The Engineering Approach to the Delinquent and the Criminal," *Sociology and Social Research,* XXI (March-April, 1937), pp. 346-50.

Torrance, Judy. "The Response of Canadian Governments to Violence," *Canadian Journal of Political Science,* 10 (1977), pp. 473-96.

Turner, Wesley. "80 Stout and Healthy Looking Girls," *Canada,* 3 (1975), pp. 36-49.

Urwick, E.J. "Penal Commissions Report," *Queen's Quarterly,* 46 (Aug., 1939), pp. 320-23.

Ward, W. Peter. "Unwed Motherhood in Nineteenth-Century English Canada," Canadian Historical Association, *Historical Papers* (1981), pp. 34-56.

Watts, R.E. "The Trend of Crime in Canada," *Queen's Quarterly,* 39 (Aug., 1932), pp. 402-13.

Weaver, John C. "The Meaning of Municipal Reform: Toronto, 1895," *Ontario History,* 66 (1974), pp. 89-100.

Wright, Mary Ellen. "Unnatural Mothers: Infanticide in Halifax, 1850-1875," *Nova Scotia Historical Review,* 7 (1987), pp. 13-29.

Wynn, Graeme. "Notes on Society and Environment in Old Ontario," *Journal of Social History,* 13 (1979-1980), pp. 49-65.

INDEX

Crime and
Punishment
in Canada,
A History

D. Owen Carrigan

M&S

Canadian Cataloguing in Publication Data
Carrigan, D. Owen
  Crime and punishment in Canada, a history

Includes bibliographical references and index.
ISBN 0–7710–1892–4

1. Crime – Canada - History.   2. Punishment – Canada – History.   3. Criminal justice, Administration of – Canada – History.   I. Title.

HV6803.C37 1991   364.971   C91-093320-0

McClelland & Stewart Inc.
The Canadian Publishers
481 University Avenue
Toronto, Ontario
M5G 2E9

Printed and bound in Canada

CONTENTS